Agriculture and Economic Growth

Agriculture and Economic Growth

Theory and Measurement

Yair Mundlak

Harvard University Press
Cambridge, Massachusetts
London, England
2000

Printed in the United States of America

Library of Congress Cataloging-in-Publication Data

Mundlak, Yair, 1927–
Agriculture and economic growth : theory and measurement / Yair Mundlak.
p. cm.
Includes bibliographical references and index.
ISBN 0-674-00228-8 (alk. paper)
1. Agriculture–Economic aspects. 2. Economic development. 3. Agriculture and state–United States. 4. United States–Economic policy. I. Title.

HD1433.M863 2000
338.1–dc21 99-089905

To Yaffa

Contents

	Preface	*ix*
	Acknowledgments	*xv*
1	*Issues, Evidence, and Attributes*	*1*

Part One • Agriculture as a Sector

2	*The Economy under Constant Resources and Technology*	*25*
3	*An Evaluation of Policy Measures*	*57*
4	*The Consequences of Resource Changes*	*93*
5	*The Consequences of Technical Change*	*130*
6	*Heterogeneous Technology*	*167*

Part Two • Factor Growth and Allocation

7	*Growth Models: An Overview*	*201*
8	*Dynamics and Distortion in Factor Markets*	*227*
9	*The Dynamics of Resource Allocation: Labor*	*247*
10	*The Dynamics of Resource Allocation: Capital*	*284*

Part Three • Technology

11	*Agricultural Production Functions: An Overview*	*319*
12	*Empirical Production Functions: Statistical Aspects*	*331*
13	*Agricultural Productivity*	*353*

Part Four • Static and Dynamic Behavior

14 *The Agricultural Supply* 393
15 *Growth and the Economic Environment* 419

Notes 441
References 453
Author Index 473
Subject Index 477

Preface

In writing a book on such a broad subject the author tests his ability to understand the world as well as his ability to communicate his own thinking and work to his readers. To a large degree, this volume is a progress report on the way I have organized and tried to verify my thinking about agricultural growth. It is intended to provide a framework to assess and quantify the impact of important policy measures affecting agriculture. At the same time, its purpose is to serve as a guide for organizing research to pursue further questions and to examine some of the common wisdom that is often recited but which can still benefit from additional analysis.

In pursuing these goals, this book reflects the range of my interests, and therefore its chapters accommodate theory, econometrics, and also empirical analysis. The reason is not coincidental or idiosyncratic. Maxim Gorki wrote in *My Universities,* "Very seldom have I found in books ideas that I have not already encountered in real life."[1] This can be taken as a strong support for empiricism. There is, however, a great deal of difference in how various disciplines bring reality into one's work and thinking. Unlike in literature, in economics our reliance on evidence requires a formal discipline; empirical and formal approaches thus serve as complements and must be used simultaneously. It can be argued that at several important junctions the profession took a wrong turn as the result of inappropriate empirical analysis. One such example is the view of increasing returns to scale in agriculture as derived from aggregate production functions. This view of agriculture is obviously inconsistent with the fact that in every country agriculture consists of numerous farmers. Other examples include the notion that domestic prices, particularly in developing countries, are not affected by world prices or that agricultural output is not responsive to price variations. These results are based on erroneous measurements, at best, or, worse, on no measurements at all but rather on preconceived dogmas. This route leads to inappropriate policy recommendations.

These are just a few examples of the dilemma of how to study and understand the process of economic growth. To compound the problem, there is an underlying current in the recent literature that can be described as an attempt to find the single right lever for lifting the subject. The most popular password is human capital. This concept is not new, and its importance has long been recognized by policymakers, as can be seen in a statement made by President Calvin Coolidge in the early 1920s: "Wealth is the product of industry, ambition, character and untiring effort. In all experience, the accumulation of wealth means the multiplication of schools, the increase of knowledge, the dissemination of intelligence, the encouragement of science, the broadening of outlook, the expansion of liberty, the widening of culture."[2] The voluminous economic research on the various aspects of the role of human capital, however, has indicated that the empirical application of this concept is not as simple as it may appear. There are issues of measurement, of identifying the pertinent components of human capital, and of sorting out their net impact on income and growth. Progress in this area requires the continuous confrontation of theory with evidence. My indulgence in measurement issues is mostly restricted to conceptual questions, the answers to which should help to enlighten the understanding of growth.

Is this a text or a reference book? The book has elements of both. It is a text in the sense that it provides a systematic presentation of the subject. However, it does so in a way that intends to bring the reader to areas of current research. In empirical analysis in economics, it is impossible to present an innocuous text that can be studied mechanically with ingenuity applied more to the formal properties of the model and less to its relevance. If we want to think about actual economic problems, we must become acquainted with efforts to confront models with the data.

The book contains exercises for Chapters 2–7, which constitute the "textbook" component. The exercises supplement the discussion and offer an opportunity to apply some of the results. The remaining chapters are more research oriented, and the natural exercises there would require more proficiency in a variety of subjects. The instructor can compose exercises for these chapters that are suited to the background of the class. Such exercises can emphasize theoretical or econometric aspects of the discussion.

The plan of the book is as follows. Chapter 1 provides the empirical background for the discussion. It presents a picture of the cross-country variability and time trends of the main economic variables related to agriculture

Part I displays the comparative static model for analyzing agriculture within a static general-equilibrium framework. Chapter 2 displays a two-sector model where the economy consists of agriculture and nonagriculture. The supply side of the economy is well known and discussed in the trade literature within the framework of the small open economy. In the present discussion, the demand side is general and accommodates the case of a closed economy. It is shown that this framework is general enough and contains, with appropriate interpretation, the inclusion of land as a factor of production in agriculture. It also takes account of the fact that most of the agricultural product is sold to the consumer in the form of food, where the agricultural component is combined with nonagricultural components to form the final product.

Before the construction of the model is continued, the framework of Chapter 2 is used in Chapter 3 to introduce the major types of policy measures that affect agriculture either directly or indirectly. These include subsidies, tariffs, quotas, food aid, taxing factors of production, and macro policies. It is shown that domestic agricultural prices are strongly affected by world prices, and as such global developments dictate to a large extent the welfare of agriculture in individual countries. The relevant framework for discussing global developments is that of a closed economy, and the chapter therefore treats both the closed and the open economy.

Chapter 4 discusses the impact of resource endowment on the equilibrium position of the economy. Initially, in the tradition of much of the discussion of trade, the changes in the endowment are introduced exogenously. This is followed by allowing the resource supply to be price responsive. The last part of the chapter endogenizes the size of the cultivated area and its quality in a Ricardian-type model where the extensive and intensive margins are determined internally within the economic system.

The response of the economy to technical change is examined in Chapter 5. The discussion is conducted within the traditional framework where the scope for the producer's decision is limited to resource allocation between the two sectors and the technology is predetermined. The discussion deals with Hicks-neutral and factor-augmenting forms of technical change. Chapter 6 takes a sharp turn in the discussion of technical change by introducing heterogeneous technology. Within this framework, there is a distinction between available and implemented technology. The scope for producers' decisions is extended to include the choice of the technology to be implemented in addition to the decision on resource allocation. Accordingly, the rate of technical change is largely affected by the economic environment. This framework constitutes an important element in the discussion of subsequent sections, particularly in the last two parts of the book.

Part II deals with factor accumulation and intersectoral allocation and introduces the implications of intertemporal decisions. Capital accumulation as a component of the growth process is discussed in Chapter 7. The discussion begins with the neoclassical one-sector growth model with exogenous technology, and continues with the examination of leading models where the technology is endogenized. These models do not differentiate between the available technology and its implementation. Some of the important conceptual problems of the growth literature are reviewed in such a way that they can be visited empirically in subsequent discussion.

Chapters 2–7 seek to provide a conceptual framework for thinking about the more important issues of agricultural growth. As such, they provide propositions that can be tested empirically. If these propositions are not validated, the analysis is challenged to unveil the reasons for the invalidation and to extend the model to make it more helpful in the interpretation of the data. The discussion in Chapters 2–7 assumes competitive conditions and full employment. These are stringent conditions when it comes to reality, and it is the reality that generates the data. The latter part of the book extends the model to accommodate some important elements of reality.

For a variety of reasons, countries do not generally operate on their efficiency frontier, and the model is modified to take this fact into account. Chapter 8 examines the effect of deviations from the static-competitive assumptions on the performance of the sectoral economy and on the propositions developed in Chapters 2–5. The elimination of distortions in the factor markets constitutes an important source of growth. The intersectoral resource allocation along the path of convergence to the frontier differs from that associated with the movement along the frontier or movements of the frontier itself.

What seems to be distortion in the factor market in the comparative static sense may arise due to differences between dynamic and static equilibria. The behavior of the economy in such cases is examined in Chapters 9 and 10. Chapter 9 considers the intersectoral allocation of labor that has led to continuous migration of labor from agriculture to the rest of the economy. The theory is substantiated by empirical results. Chapter 10 introduces explicitly the dynamic framework for analyzing the demand for capital. This framework serves as a basis for the derivation of the empirical investment function and the intersectoral allocation of investment.

Technology along with the competitive conditions constitutes the core of the supply side of the economy. Hence the empirical analysis of technology and its changes is of cardinal importance. Part III deals with various aspects of the analysis of production. We begin in Chapter 11 with an overview of the empirical analyses of production that bear on the main parameters of interest and address important methodological issues pertinent to the interpretation of empirical studies and to future research. Issues related to estimation are discussed in Chapter 12. There have been two fundamental approaches to estimate production functions: direct and indirect, using duality. In Chapter 12,

I argue that indirect estimation of the production structure is inferior to direct estimation and propose an estimator that uses all of the available information most efficiently. The discussion brings up the role played by various error components in the identification of the production function.

Most of the literature is based on the assumption that there exists a unique production function to be estimated, but many of the empirical results are inconsistent with this naive assumption. In Chapter 13 I extend the analysis by following the discussion in Chapter 6 and allowing the technology to consist of more than one technique. The choice of the implemented technique is an economic decision, and the analysis is modified accordingly. The empirical analysis provides insight into the importance of the economic environment as a determinant of the level and growth of productivity.

Part IV focuses on the behavior of the economy in response to changes in the economic environment. The long-standing analysis of agricultural supply is discussed in Chapter 14. The key question is the role of prices in production decisions. The issues discussed in these chapters are also related to the empirical discussions in Chapters 9 and 10. The dynamic model of capital demand is replaced with the dual-dynamic model, and its performance is evaluated in light of the results reported in the literature.

Chapter 15 examines empirically the important role that the economic environment plays in influencing economic growth. This is done by bringing together the various components of the model. Even though our ultimate interest is agriculture, the economy is examined as a whole. The theme of this volume is that agriculture does not operate in isolation; its fortunes are related to what happens in the rest of the economy. The converse is also true, unless agriculture is of negligible importance. The analysis takes explicit account of the dependence of agriculture on the economic environment, namely the available technology, world prices, domestic policies, political instability, and the like. It does this by analyzing the competition among sectors in the factor market, tracing the impact of shocks that affect resource accumulation in the economy and the real exchange rate, and examining the impact of political instability on the main sectors of the economy.

In conclusion, I note that the model and its various components are supported by evidence that comes from studies over several decades and various geographical regions. It is hoped that this demonstrates the staying power of the theory.

Acknowledgments

This volume, which evolved from my lecture notes at the University of Chicago, integrates research conducted over a long period. Some of the early work was written as joint papers with former students at the Department of Agricultural Economics of the Hebrew University: Yigal Danin, Ron Mosenson, Zvi Tropp, and Zvi Volcani. The empirical work was conducted jointly with Rita Butzer, Juan Eduardo Coeymans, Domingo Cavallo, Roberto Domenech, Donald F. Larson, Anya McGuirk, and John Strauss. Through our investigations I have learned to appreciate the positive externalities generated by a collaboration in empirical research. I note in particular my work with Domingo Cavallo, with whom I developed and applied our analytic framework in studying the sectoral growth in Argentina over a seventy-year period. When in doubt on technical issues, I benefited from talking to Jose Scheinkman. I also benefited from the reading Victor Ginsburgh gave to Chapter 2. Finally, I was fortunate to have the comments made by Rita Butzer while she was editing the final draft before its submission to the press. I thank them all.

Agriculture and Economic Growth

1

Issues, Evidence, and Attributes

Many roads lead to an interest in agricultural development, and it is only natural that we find differences among economists in their analyses and more so in their perspectives, emphases, and conclusions about the process and its outcome.[1] To provide a perspective for our discussion, it is useful to list the central issues related to agricultural growth:

- Agriculture as a supplier of food
- The welfare of farmers and, more generally, the rural population
- The role of agriculture in economic development
- The impact of government intervention on the performance of the agricultural sector as a subject of political economy

Traditionally agriculture has been studied for the purpose of checking the validity of general economic propositions, and this also applies to the study of various aspects of growth. With this diversity of interests in mind, it is instructive to conduct the discussion against a background of the evidence. To do so, this chapter presents an overview based on a comprehensive examination of a data base of a large number of countries for the period 1960–1990 or thereabouts.[2] The presentation highlights important empirical propositions—mostly known but often ignored—and provides a quantitative dimension of the cross-country variability of levels and rates of change over time. This overview is supplemented with additional evidence presented in subsequent chapters.

The Evidence

Supply and Demand

The Global Food Experience: An Overview

There is a keen interest in future market developments related to the food supply. This interest is more intense than in other sectors, because of the unique

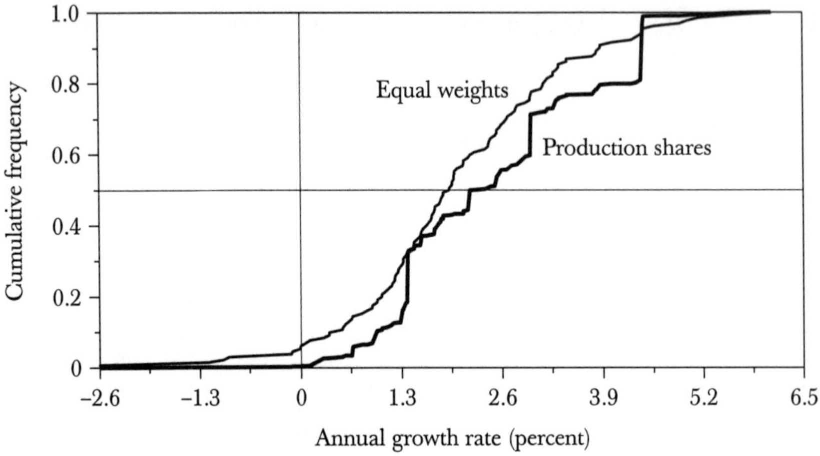

Figure 1.1 Agricultural production, 1967–1992: 130 countries. (From Mundlak, Larson, and Crego, 1998, fig. 8.1.)

role of food and the nature of its demand. Much of the concern with the food supply can be explained by the fear of supply shortages and hunger at some point in the near or remote future. In the dialogue on this issue, reference is sometimes made to the experience of countries that have suffered food shortages for extended periods of time or to episodes of hunger in affluent economies. Although traumatic, such episodes do not generalize to give an accurate global picture. It is here that the empirical perspective is essential.

A summary of the growth experience is given in Figure 1.1, which presents a frequency distribution of total agricultural production growth rates for the period 1967–1992 for 130 countries.[3] The curve to the left is drawn with equal weight for each country. At any point on the graph, the reading on the vertical axis shows the proportion of countries whose growth rate did not exceed the corresponding value on the horizontal axis. There is a large spread in country performances, but most countries had positive growth, and the median rate is 1.92 percent per year. Because some of the low-growth countries are small in terms of their agricultural production, this curve does not provide a good view of the changes in global supply. A better view is obtained when the relative size of the country is taken into account. This is done in the curve to the right, where the countries are weighted by their relative importance in world agricultural production. A comparison of the two curves shows that the countries with negative growth rates carry very little weight in terms of their contribution to overall food production. The median growth rate of the weighted distribution is

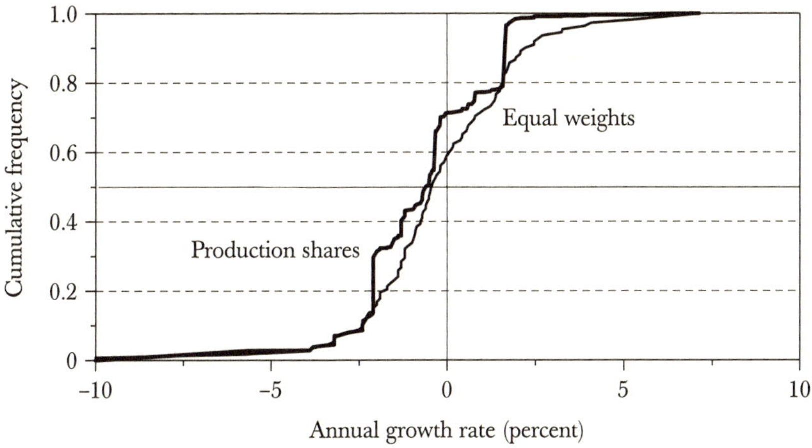

Figure 1.2 Agricultural prices, 1967–1992: 112 countries. (From Mundlak, Larson, and Crego, 1998, fig. 8.2.)

2.25 percent. This means that 50 percent of the food production was produced in countries whose growth rates exceeded 2.25 percent, and the remaining was produced by countries with lower, but usually positive, growth rates. Put another way, growth rates have been somewhat higher in countries with large agricultural production.

Has supply lagged demand? If this were the case, agricultural prices would have risen, but this has not happened. This is seen in Figure 1.2, which presents the distribution of the rates of change of agricultural prices over the same time period.[4] Domestic farm prices are deflated by domestic consumer price indices. The median of the unweighted distribution is −0.45 percent per year. When we weight the countries by their importance in world production, the median changes to −0.61 percent per year. Note that the vertical line at zero growth rate cuts the graph of the weighted distribution at 0.71, indicating that 71 percent of world production in the period 1967–1992 was produced in countries where real prices fell.

Because the prices in Figure 1.2 are of aggregate output, their rates of change tend to be biased upward. As income increases, there is a shift in consumption and production to higher-value products, and this change in composition causes the aggregate price to increase. Thus the fact that we observe a decline in prices despite an upward bias suggests that supply grew faster than demand. This result is consistent with the downward trend in the world real prices of important agricultural commodities reviewed in Chapter 5.

This evidence indicates that the world's recent experience, which generalizes well to the entire postwar period, is one of faster growth of supply compared with demand.

Demand and Agricultural Growth

What are the sources of the spread in growth rates? This is of course the main question in the study of growth in general and of agricultural growth in particular. The search for answers naturally focuses on the supply side. Before examining factors related to supply, however, it is instructive to examine the role of demand.

On the whole, agricultural products are tradable, and therefore there is no need for each country to increase its production to meet domestic demand changes. Some countries can benefit from comparative advantage and reduce their production in an environment of growth and of reduction of trade restrictions. Such behavior may explain some of the observed spread in growth rates. For instance, Singapore's agricultural production more than doubled between 1967 and 1979, but declined thereafter to such an extent that 1992 production was below that of 1967. Other countries do not fully utilize their potential in agricultural production in order to protect farm income and are engaged in policies that involve a reduction of their domestic production and restrictions on imports. This is indicative of excess supply or of demand restricting the expansion of production in exporting countries as potentially importing countries attempt to use their own markets for the development of their farm sector.

An indirect view of the role of demand can be obtained by comparing the distribution of growth rates of *per capita* output, presented in Figure 1.3, with *total* output in Figure 1.1. The median rate of change of per capita production of the equal weight distribution is −0.03 percent. Taking into account the production weights, the median growth rate is 0.7 percent, and output growth exceeded population growth in countries that accounted for 81 percent of world production. Such a pronounced difference between the two distributions underlines the importance of distinguishing between country problems and global problems and the pitfall of generalizing from country performance to world performance.

Note also that the graphs in Figure 1.3 are steeper than the corresponding graphs in Figure 1.1.[5] This implies a higher concentration of countries around the median growth rate, that is, the variance of *total* growth rates is larger than that of *per capita* rates. This concentration in the center indicates that many countries met a large part of their growth in demand through home

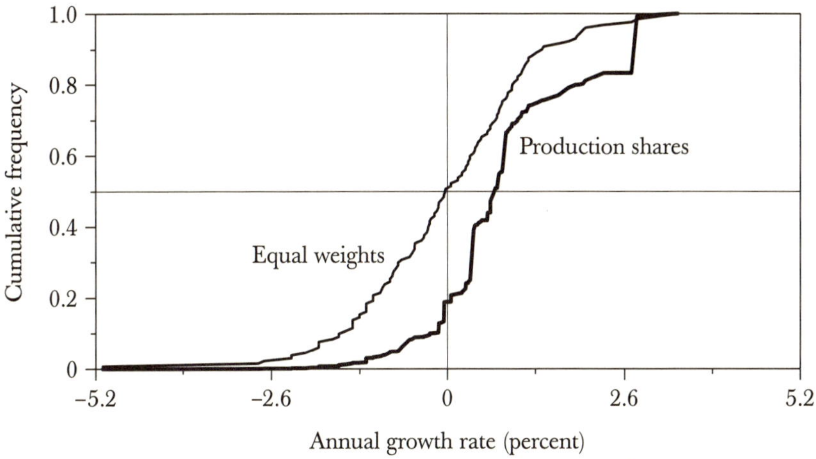

Figure 1.3 Per capita agricultural production, 1967–1992: 130 countries. (From Mundlak, Larson, and Crego, 1998, fig. 8.3.)

production. In fact, on the whole, production growth exceeded population growth somewhat, because of the increase in demand due to the rise in income as well as the decline in prices. This development is consistent with demand-derived production growth.

A more direct view of the role of demand is obtained by comparing the rate of growth of agricultural per capita output with that of per capita total output, taken as a measure of income. Ignoring trade for a moment, note that for the closed economy under constant prices this ratio is roughly the income elasticity for food. We say "roughly" because agriculture is not identical with food, and it includes industrial crops whose demand is not the same as that of food. In most countries, however, food dominates agricultural production.

Figure 1.4 presents the distribution of such a ratio for growth in real *value* for 91 countries during 1960–1992.[6] The median values are 0.82 and 0.86 for the weighted and unweighted distributions respectively. Since prices were not constant but rather declined, this result serves as an upper bound for the income elasticity. The spread of the distribution is smaller than that of Figure 1.3, which implies that countries with a low growth rate in agriculture also suffered from a low growth rate in nonagriculture. This means that the factors that contributed to poor performance were not necessarily agriculture specific, and therefore the search for a remedy to poor performance should take us beyond issues specific to agriculture, a theme to be developed in this book.

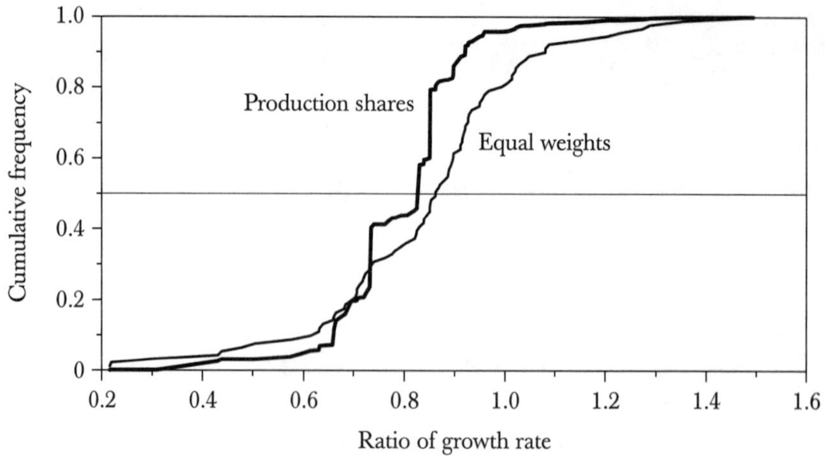

Figure 1.4 Per capita GDP growth, ratio of agriculture to total, 1960–1992: 91 countries. (From Mundlak, Larson, and Crego, 1998, fig. 8.4.)

The role of demand needs emphasis because most discussions of economic growth examine a single-good economy where there are no prices, except for the discount rate. The single-good economy is an aggregate of many sectors, however, and therefore the discussion of growth at the sectoral level adds a dimension missing from aggregate models. Indeed, when it comes to agriculture, it is demand that has an enormous impact on the dynamics of the sector.

Trade

Agriculture produces a tradable product, but the foregoing review indicates a tendency toward self-sufficiency. This is reflected in the fact that trade accounts for only 10–12 percent of total world production. Countries' tendency toward self-sufficiency is in part due to policy, as indicated above, but is also due to objective market conditions. The margins between import and export prices may be wide: distribution costs within the country, both for the exporter and the importer, can be high, especially in countries with inadequate infrastructure. The distribution cost is due to the fact that agriculture is spread geographically throughout the country. Inadequate infrastructure and noncompetitive distribution systems aggravate the problem.

Inputs and Productivity Changes

On the supply side, the joint event of output growth and declining prices indicates that productivity growth more than offsets the effect of declining

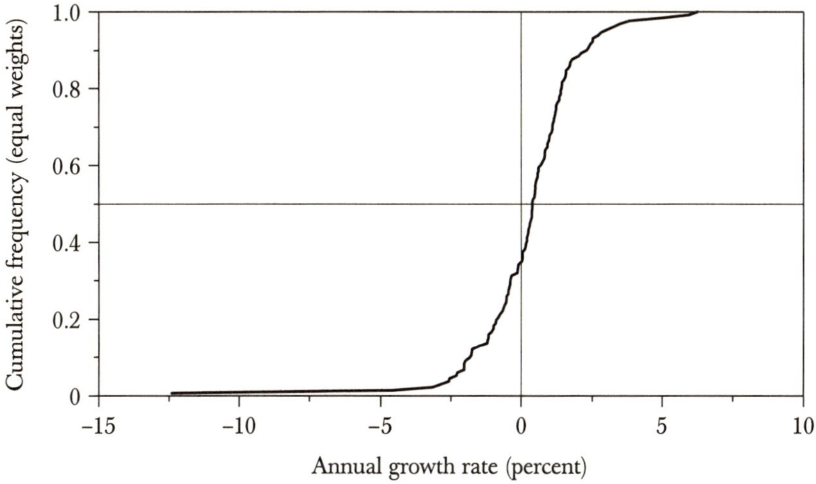

Figure 1.5 Harvested land, 1967–1992: 131 countries. (From Mundlak, Larson, and Crego, 1998, fig. 8.5.)

prices on profitability. To evaluate the sources of growth let us examine changes in land and labor, the two inputs that together account for the major proportion of output.

Land

It is often thought that agricultural land is a fixed quantity. This view is true for countries' total physical area. However, cultivated land, from here on referred to simply as "land," is an economic quantity, and as seen in Figure 1.5, its quantity has been subject to change. In 65 percent of the countries the cultivated area increased during 1967–1992, with a median annual growth rate of 0.4 percent. For the world as a whole, the annual growth rate was 0.58 percent, which amounts to about 15.7 percent growth for the period as a whole. Land growth was faster in tree crops, 1.48 percent per year, than in annual crops, 0.52. Thus, in spite of the lower prices for agriculture, it was still profitable to expand the area of agricultural land.

The growth rate of land is much smaller than that of output, and this indicates an increase in land productivity. Figure 1.6 presents the distribution of growth rates in average land productivity for 87 countries. In 11 countries (13 percent of the countries) the average productivity declined, but these countries carry small production weights (less than 2 percent of total production), and the weighted distribution shows a concentration in positive growth rates. Thus the

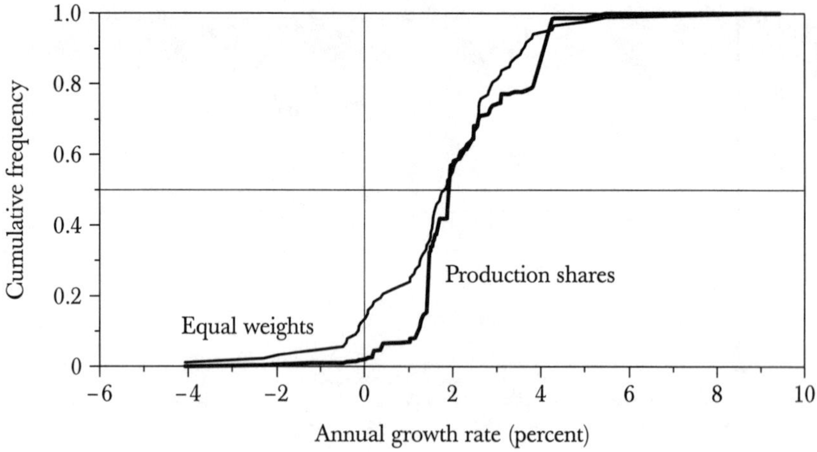

Figure 1.6 Land productivity, 1960–1992: 87 countries. (From Mundlak, Larson, and Crego, 1998, fig. 8.6.)

bulk of world production was obtained with an increase in land productivity. The median growth rates are 1.8 and 1.92 percent for the unweighted and weighted distributions respectively.

Labor

Changes in the agricultural labor force have followed a somewhat different pattern. In 40 percent of countries, *total* agricultural labor declined. Figure 1.7 presents the distribution of changes in the labor force for 148 countries from 1950 to 1990. The median growth rate was 0.56 percent; while this rate is similar to that of harvested land, there is a substantial spread across countries.

Several technological factors affect labor demand. In part, the labor requirement, particularly harvest labor, is increasing with the level of output and as such increases with yields. Similarly, when the composition of output changes from cereals to fruits and vegetables, labor requirements increase as well. An increase in livestock production also frequently increases requirements for agricultural labor. Finally, the increase in cultivated land adds to the labor demand. On the other hand, the mechanization of agriculture reduces the labor requirements. These are all components of labor demand, but the data report a different variable, the labor force in agriculture. This measure includes workers not fully employed in agriculture, many of whom eventually leave agriculture. The timing and degree of such migration depends on the

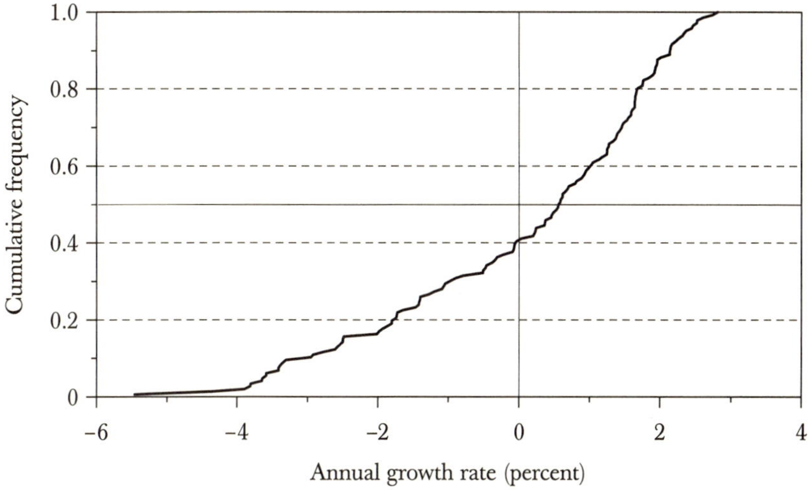

Figure 1.7 Agricultural labor, 1950–1990: 148 countries. (From Mundlak, Larson, and Crego, 1998, fig. 8.7.)

off-farm work and income opportunities and as such reflect conditions outside agriculture.

With all these qualifications, the net effect of mechanization on agricultural labor input is detected by the labor-to-land ratios, which are presented in Figure 1.8. In about half of the countries this ratio declined, and the rate of decline was stronger than the rate of increase in the other half of the countries. This uneven effect is attributed to the dependence of the degree of mechanization on the economic environment that determines the profitability of mechanization. It is the poorer countries, with lower wage-rental ratios, that rely more heavily on labor than on machines. In those countries, the off-farm migration was not sufficient to yield a decline in the actual labor input in agriculture.

When output per unit of land increases while the labor per unit of land is constant, there is an increase in labor productivity. The distribution of the growth rates of average labor productivity in 87 countries is drawn in Figure 1.9. The growth rates of average labor productivity are somewhat higher than those of average land productivity. The median rates are 2.0 and 2.6 percent for the unweighted and weighted distributions respectively. A comparison of the weighted distributions of average labor and land productivity for 87 countries is presented in Figure 1.10.[7]

Changes in these partial-productivity measures reflect changes in the agricultural labor force, cultivated land, other inputs, and technology. The major

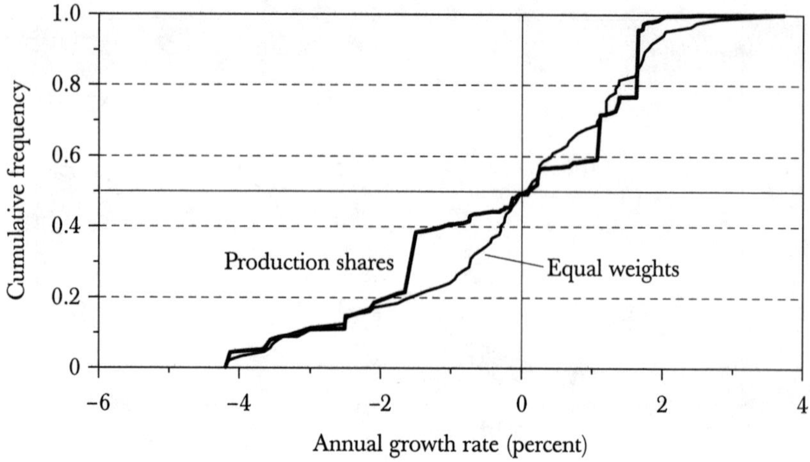

Figure 1.8 Labor to land ratio, 1960–1992: 87 countries. (From Mundlak, Larson, and Crego, 1998, fig. 8.8.)

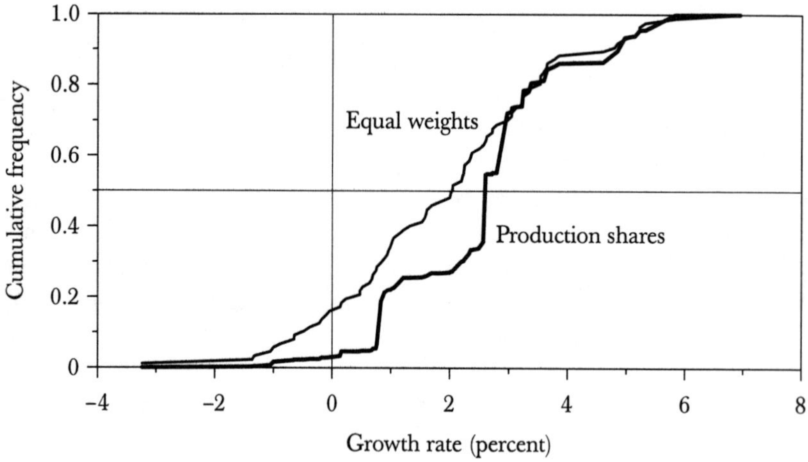

Figure 1.9 Average labor productivity, 1960–1992: 87 countries. (From Mundlak, Larson, and Crego, 1998, fig. 8.9.)

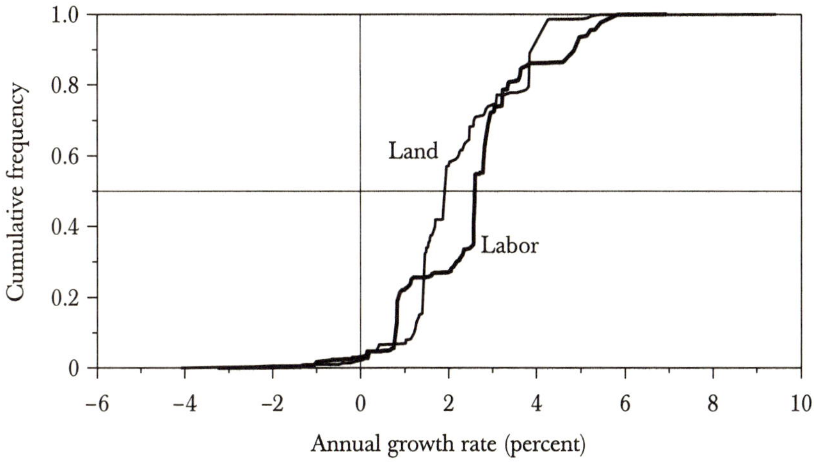

Figure 1.10 Labor and land productivity, 1960–1992: 87 countries. (From Mundlak, Larson, and Crego, 1998, fig. 8.10.)

input that is missing from the discussion so far, as well as from most of the writings on the subject, is capital. This omission can be attributed to the fact that data on this variable are limited, and little work has been done to document the importance of capital in agricultural production, particularly in cross-country comparisons. A recent effort to alleviate this deficiency resulted in a series of capital stock in agriculture for 58 countries (Crego et al., 1998). The discussion of this subject requires some detail and is therefore deferred to Chapter 10. In any case, it is important to emphasize that perceived productivity changes are the outcomes of joint decisions on inputs and implemented technology. These decisions are endogenous and have to be studied in conjunction with, and as a part of, the productivity analysis. We will return to this subject below.

How does the productivity performance in agriculture compare with that in nonagriculture? Figure 1.11 presents the distribution of the differences in the growth rates of average labor productivity in nonagriculture and agriculture. The median values are −1.58 and −1.1 for the unweighted and weighted distributions respectively, which imply a higher growth rate in average labor productivity in agriculture. It is striking that in about 80 percent of the countries labor productivity grew faster in agriculture than in the rest of the economy.

Summary

What is demonstrated from this description is the existence of a large spread in input and output changes across countries. The important question here

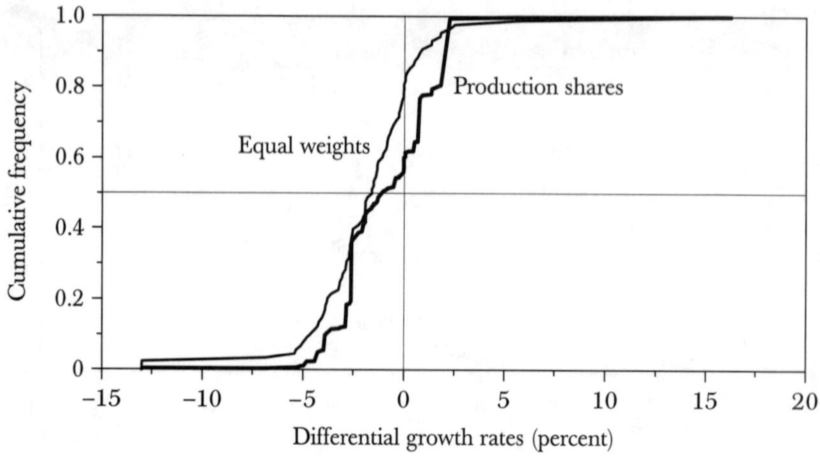

Figure 1.11 Growth rate of labor productivity, nonagriculture minus agriculture, 1960–1992: 88 countries. (From Mundlak, Larson, and Crego, 1998, fig. 8.11.)

is what factors account for the spread and, specifically, to what extent does the economic environment contribute to this spread? The term "economic environment" is used here to represent the set of all the variables that affect the production decisions made by firms. These include prices, interest rates, price uncertainty, availability of inputs, the competitiveness of the input markets, availability and quality of infrastructure, access to new information, the legal and organizational infrastructure needed to conduct business activity, the stability of the economic variables, tax structure, and the like. Not all of these variables change to a degree that affects production in a given country in any given period, and the strategy of research is to concentrate on isolating the effects of the important variables that did change. The list of pertinent variables may vary from country to country, and the purpose of a country analysis is to identify them and thereby supplement the results obtained in a cross-country analysis.

Agriculture and Farmers

In evaluating the impact of technical change on agriculture it is important to differentiate between agriculture as an economic activity, or a sector, and farmers. The welfare of the sector is measured by the returns to land, which is the factor specific to agriculture. The main welfare issue related to farmers is their income level and, to a lesser extent, its stability. Farm operators benefit from increases in land rent and labor income. In this discussion, income from other forms of capital is ignored without affecting the main conclusions of the discussion.

As economic theory and the empirical literature tell us, the returns to land are reflected in land prices. Thus if the agricultural sector benefits from technical change, land prices would be expected to increase, and it is therefore of interest to observe the changes in land prices over time. Unfortunately, there is no readily available comprehensive data set with time series of land prices for various countries. We can, however, review data assembled for Canada, Japan, South Africa, and the United States.[8]

A cross-country comparison of land prices is a difficult task because of quality differences, notwithstanding the difficulty of quantifying the importance of the economic environment that affects such prices. Nevertheless, the time path of land prices in the various countries is telling. There are two ways, pertinent to our discussion, to look at land prices. The first is to deflate land prices by the price of the agricultural product, and the second is to deflate them by the price of the consumption good as measured by the consumer price index (CPI). The first, referred to as the output measure, provides the price of land reflecting its productivity, whereas the second, referred to as the consumption measure, indicates the value of land in terms of its purchasing power of an aggregate consumption good whose price is measured by the CPI.

Figure 1.12 shows the pattern of real agricultural land prices for the four countries for which we have longer time series, reported as indices with 1986 = 1. The upper panel shows the output measure of land prices; the lower panel shows their consumption measure. By both measures, land prices declined in the prewar period. They were gradually increasing in the immediate postwar period. This rise gained impetus during the inflationary period of the 1970s and came to an end in the early 1980s when the economies started to deflate.

Comparing land prices at the beginning and end of the period of each series, we see that by the output measure prices are considerably higher, but according to the consumption measure there is little change. In the United States, the index of the consumption measure of land prices was 0.84 in 1992 compared with 0.73 in 1910. For Canada the values for 1990 and 1914 are 0.87 and 0.76 respectively. The series for South Africa begins in 1940 at a level of 0.88, whereas the 1993 value is 0.65. Data for other countries show the same trend. On the whole, prices in the 1990s are historically relatively low, and it is remarkable that land prices today are not much different from those at the beginning of the century. Moreover, land prices reflect subsidies to agriculture.

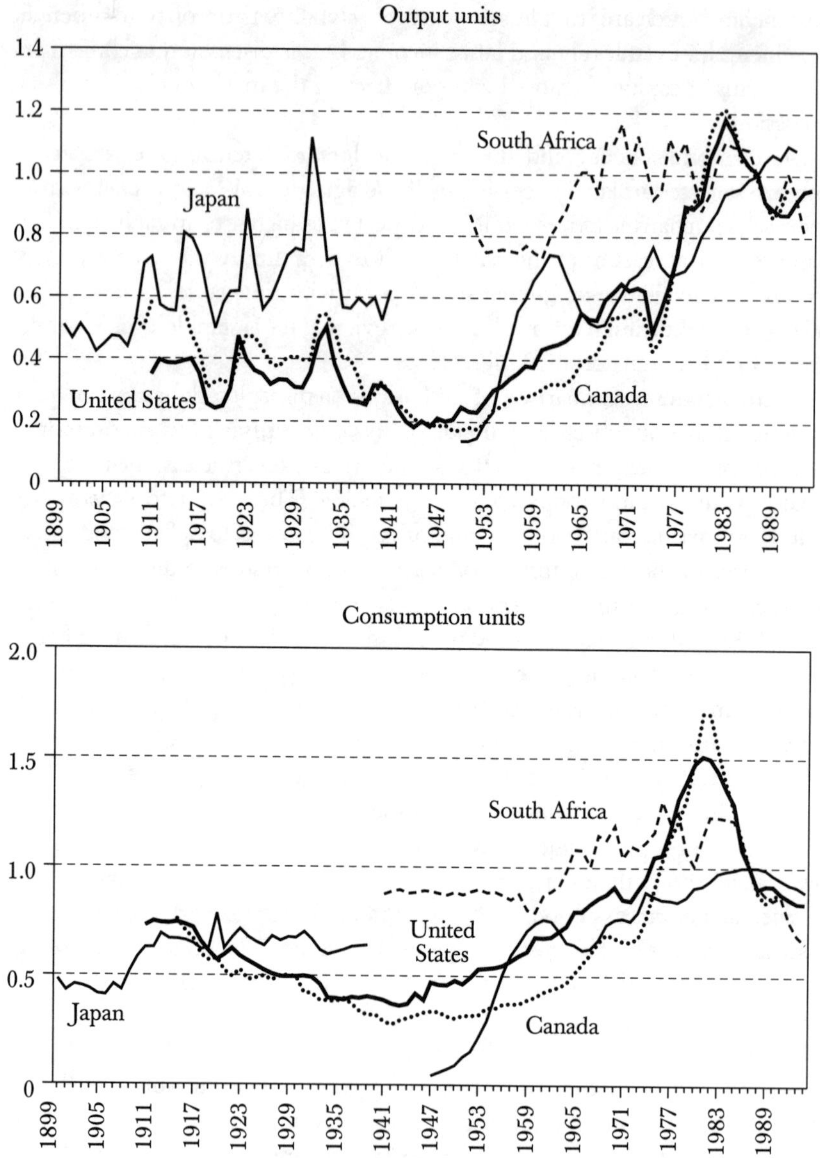

Figure 1.12 Real land prices. (From Mundlak, Larson, and Crego, 1998, fig. 8.12.)

If subsidies (which are relatively new) were taken into account, then land prices would exhibit even less growth over their historic level.

Another striking observation is the high correlation between the price movements for the four countries plotted in Figure 1.12, as well as for most countries. The correlation is stronger for the output measure than for the consumption measure. This correlation indicates that much of the impact of the dramatic changes in agricultural technology was transmitted to the various countries (or at least to those observed here). The benefits were not captured by agriculture, however, and eventually were distributed to the consumers. This occurred through a decline in agricultural prices relative to the prices of the other consumption goods.

The changes in the welfare of people in agriculture is a different and more complex story. The income of farmers is the return to their labor and factors in their possession. Aside from the returns to land discussed above, which applies mainly to land owners, labor income is the main income source for farm operators and primarily the only source for landless labor.[9] Data on returns to labor are deficient. Therefore, we will examine changes in the structural composition of the labor force and infer from them the impact of the changes in technology on labor.

Even though in most countries there was an increase in the agricultural labor force (Figure 1.7), this increase lagged behind the increase in the total labor force *generated in* agriculture. The difference constitutes the migration of labor out of agriculture. This is seen by comparing the growth rates of agricultural labor with that of the population. Under the assumption of equal fertility rates in agriculture and nonagriculture, the growth rate of agricultural labor less that of the population gives the rate of labor migration from agriculture to nonagriculture, expressed as a percentage of the agricultural labor force.[10] The distribution of this difference in growth rates for 148 countries is plotted in Figure 1.13, which shows that such migration took place in practically all countries. The median annual migration rate for the period 1950 to 1990 is 1.97 percent. That is, at the median, migration drained about 2 percent of the agricultural labor force.

In interpreting this result it should be noted that off-farm migration is determined not only by changes in agricultural profitability, but also by changes in labor demand in nonagriculture as well as by sectoral differences in the level of the standard of living. This subject is discussed in Chapter 9. Naturally, when labor income in agriculture is low, people will migrate to other sectors. Thus off-farm migration is probably the most important single process that contributes to the alleviation of rural poverty. This result should be kept in mind in judging not only economic processes but also institutional and legal

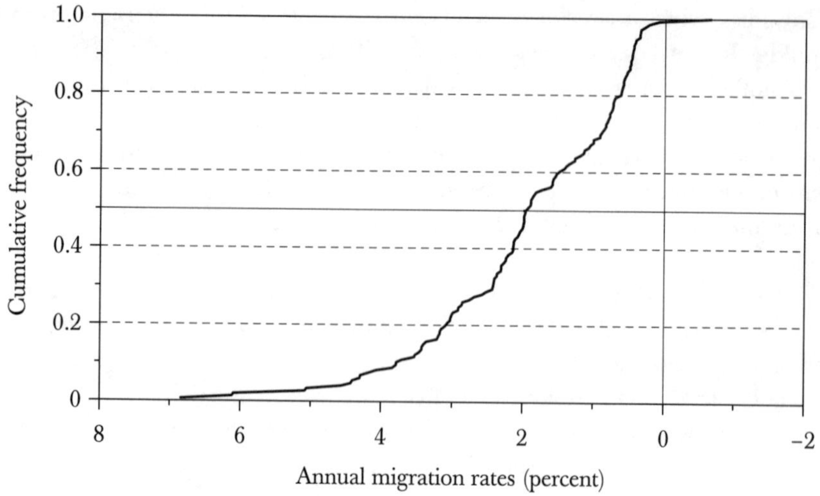

Figure 1.13 Off-farm migration rates, 1959–1990: 148 countries. (From Mundlak, Larson, and Crego, 1998, fig. 8.13.)

reforms. There is nothing more effective in improving people's welfare than allowing them to choose freely among opportunities and thus escape areas of hardship. The traditional exploitation of agricultural labor may have taken place because migration opportunities for such labor were restricted by institutional arrangement, lack of infrastructure, or lack of opportunities outside of agriculture. For migration to take place, opportunities in nonagriculture are required. This is where economic growth comes in as a factor in the alleviation of agricultural-based poverty.

Agriculture and Development

The technological change in agriculture had two important effects on the economy as a whole. First, it improved the overall food supply while prices declined and thus improved consumer welfare. Second, it made it possible to produce more output with relatively less labor and thus facilitated the development of nonagriculture. As a result of the migration, the share of agriculture in the total labor force has declined. This is seen in Figure 1.14, in which the share is plotted for 148 countries for the years 1950 and 1990. The share varies considerably among countries, being high in less developed economies and declining with the level of development. Even so, an inspection of the data (not reported here) indicates that it has declined in all countries.

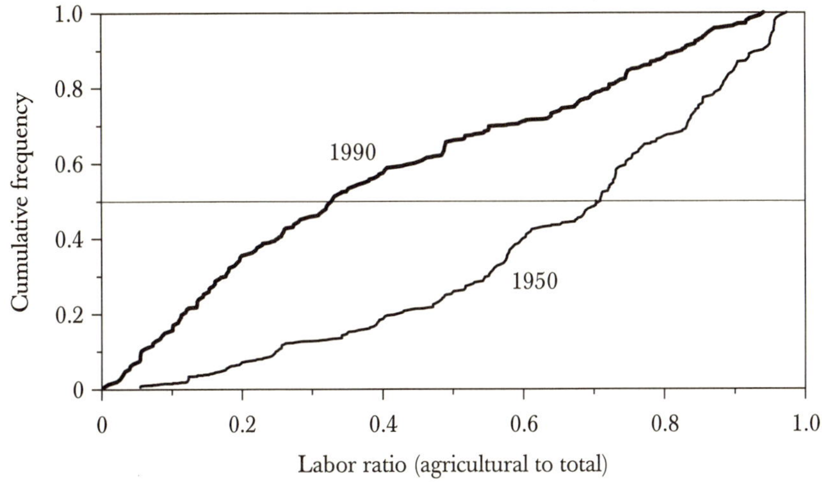

Figure 1.14 Share of agriculture in labor force, 1950, 1990: 148 countries. (From Mundlak, Larson, and Crego, 1998, fig. 8.14.)

The median share was 70 percent in 1950, but only 33 percent in 1990. The proportion of countries with a share below 10 percent increased from 1.3 percent in 1950 to 15 percent in 1990. There is hardly any single indicator that better illustrates the story of the role of agriculture in economic development. The freeing of labor is a necessary condition for development. Therefore understanding the process of off-farm migration and the determinants of its rate contributes to our understanding of the process of development.

The net outcome of the processes reviewed above is a decline in the relative importance of agriculture in total output. The change in the distribution of this share in the 40-year period between 1950 and 1990, as seen from Figure 1.15, is indeed noteworthy; the median for this group of 67 countries declined from 30 percent to 8 percent over this period.[11]

In summary, the technological change in agriculture serves the rest of the economy by increasing supplies at lower prices and contributing labor to the development of nonagriculture. At the same time, in the longer run, none of the benefits is captured in agriculture. Who would stand to benefit from further increases in agricultural productivity in the future? There is no reason to think that the future will be any different from the past.

This welfare conclusion has an important policy implication for the financing of agricultural research. Historically, much agricultural research was publicly financed because the fruits of the research cannot be captured by the

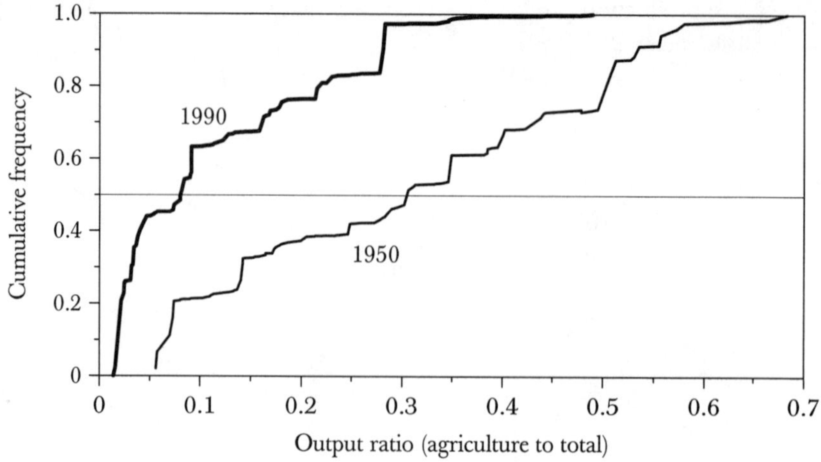

Figure 1.15 Share of agriculture in GDP, 1950, 1990: 67 countries. (From Mundlak, Larson, and Crego, 1998, fig. 8.15.)

researcher. The foregoing discussion indicates that it is indeed in the interest of the public at large to promote research that will produce technological change in agriculture. The burden of this research should therefore be carried by the public at large and not by agriculture, which does not seem to capture and maintain the benefit from it. Furthermore, as the fruits of the research are eventually spread to all countries, there is a strong case to be made for financing research internationally. But countries can take a lead in advancing technology and benefit from it until the new technology spreads to other countries. For countries to take advantage of global developments, they must have an ongoing active research program. Thus there is a strong case for a country to finance its own research as well.

Attributes of Agriculture

Environment

Agricultural production is a biological process that involves land and is affected by weather and climate. Climate is the permanent component of the weather, and it varies geographically. Geographic differences also exist in other environmental factors that affect production, such as land quality and water availability. The variations in performance over time are affected by weather, which is the transitory component and constitutes the main source of uncertainty. The production process depends on calendar time and has a distinct seasonal character.

Production Organization

The periodic nature of production makes it impossible to break down the process into components that can be performed on an assembly line. There is thus a limit to the division of labor in agricultural production that makes it costly to monitor labor. This is one of the reasons that farming is mostly a family operation in which the managerial, or human capital, component is of prime importance.

Market Organization

Because production requires land, it is stretched out geographically. Much of the cultivated area is remotely located from the markets, which makes production strongly dependent on infrastructure. Being far from the market helps to create local monopolies, decreases the competitive process in the industries serving agriculture, and increases the cost of the services. The weak market connection encourages production for self-sufficiency. Such production is expected to be less susceptible to market conditions.

Rural communities are isolated and have to solve their economic problems, such as risk sharing, within their local settings. How they do so is an interesting area of research. Part of this research is related to explaining variations in the cross-section rather than over time, which is the motto of growth.

Demand

Agriculture is not subject to demand shocks as other sectors are and therefore is less susceptible to the effects of business cycles in nonagriculture. Food is an essential commodity in that its marginal utility goes to infinity as consumption goes to zero. Hence, it is consumed and produced in all economies. It is not a durable commodity; therefore it is impossible to shut down, or reduce drastically, the production of food for a length of time, as is the case with some manufactured goods, in the course of the business cycles.

Agriculture is, however, subject to supply shocks caused by weather. Because the primary agricultural products are storable, supply shocks may generate price cycles.[12] By the nature of demand, food constitutes a large proportion of total expenditure for low-income families and thus low-income countries. Consequently a spell of high prices may have a serious effect on such countries.

Farmers

In general, agricultural households have larger families and a higher concentration of poverty. The larger family and the distance from the market encourage the pooling of family resources, the division of labor, and intrafamily insurance.

The Agrarian Problem

Traditionally, low mobility of labor out of agriculture due to weak linkage with the rest of the economy made it possible to exploit farmers, particularly landless labor. The process of "modernization" opens up agriculture to the rest of the economy, brings education to rural areas, and improves the quality of education, thereby reducing the scope for such exploitation. Labor can improve its prospects of escaping poverty by moving out of agriculture.

The Macro Environment

Agricultural products are tradable; therefore the producer's price is determined by the world price, the real exchange rate, tariffs, and other trade interventions. The real exchange rate depends on general macro policies that are sector-neutral but nevertheless affect agriculture more than nonagriculture. On the whole, the macro environment often has a stronger impact on agriculture than policies directed at agriculture.

Political Power of Agriculture

In most countries there is some intervention in the market forces related to agriculture. It is commonly stated as a generalization that low-income countries tax agriculture and high-income countries subsidize it. There is an extended literature that tries to understand the forces that lead to a particular policy, but the matter is largely unresolved. I want to suggest here the following observations on this process. First, the geographical spread of agriculture gives it political power in democratic systems where the source of power, at least in part, is geographically based. A good example is the U.S. Senate, where agriculture can translate its power into economic gains. When the source of power is based in the cities, agriculture is likely to be taxed. Second, in the high-income or industrial countries, farmers constitute a small fraction of the population. Democratic governments based on coalitions often need a minority party to stay in power, and agriculture is a convenient partner because its demands are largely orthogonal to the main issues that split the competing blocs.

Policy Orientation

The issues of interest discussed at the outset–food supply, food prices, welfare of the rural population and the role of agriculture in economic development–are also the central policy issues. As such, this volume is policy oriented even though that may not be immediately obvious.

Finally, assuming that we know more today about growth and the consequences of policies, will past mistakes be avoided in the future? They may be reduced but will not necessarily disappear. Knowledge does not necessarily prevent wrongdoing, as is well demonstrated by the consumption of drugs. In the case of policy, the difficulty is rooted in the fact that governments, as pure as they may be, are not social planners of the kind that a theory often assumes. They differ in one fundamental respect from the community that they are supposed to serve; the difference is in the relevant time horizon. It is not productive to ignore political survival as a major driving force in government decisions. One does not have to be predator to want to survive. In this sense, there is less scope for overlapping generations and altruism in government utility functions, and this may lead to decisions that are inconsistent with what we might think is conducive to long-term growth.[13]

PART ONE

Agriculture as a Sector

2

The Economy under Constant Resources and Technology

This chapter lays out the basic analytic framework for evaluating the relationships between agriculture and the rest of the economy. The model is based on strong assumptions that are removed as the discussion progresses, but nevertheless it captures some of the important features for understanding the main issues associated with agricultural growth.

It is assumed that the economy consists of two sectors, agriculture and nonagriculture. Each sector uses two factors of production, labor and capital, whose supply is fixed. In addition, agricultural production uses land. Each sector is characterized by competitive conditions and full employment. Technology does not change. The demand specification is general; in particular, the underlying utility function is not restricted to be homothetic.

This simple framework introduces concepts and results that are important for the subsequent discussion: the sectoral supply function, the relationship between the product and factor markets, the shadow price of the fixed factors of production, and the presentation of the equilibrium solution in a form that highlights the interdependence of these results. The link between factor and product markets depends on factor intensity; thus a discussion of the measurement of factor intensity is essential. At the end of the chapter, two other aspects related to the application of this model to agriculture are discussed: the introduction of land as a factor of production and a differentiation between food and agriculture. It is shown that with appropriate interpretation, the framework developed here accommodates these extensions.

Supply

Assumptions

The economy consists of agriculture (sector 1) and nonagriculture (sector 2), and two factors, capital (K) and labor (L).

Admissible allocation: The total sectoral use of the two factors does not exceed their total supply.

$$K \geq K_1 + K_2. \tag{2.1}$$

$$L \geq L_1 + L_2. \tag{2.2}$$

Technology: The technology is represented by concave, twice differentiable, constant returns to scale (CRS) production functions:[1]

$$Y_i = F_i(K_i, L_i), \quad i = 1, 2, \tag{2.3}$$

where Y_i is the output of sector i.

Competition: Perfect competition exists among firms and consumers within each sector and between sectors. Consequently, the value marginal productivities are equal to their respective factor prices. Let p_i, w, and r be the accounting price of product i, the wage, and the rental rates, respectively, then

$$r = p_i \frac{\partial F_i}{\partial K_i} \tag{2.4}$$

$$w = p_i \frac{\partial F_i}{\partial L_i}. \tag{2.5}$$

The micro underpinnings of the model will not be discussed in detail until later. The assumptions of perfect competition and of CRS, however, raise the question of how the size of the firm is determined. This question can be answered in various ways, including uncertainty and cost of adjustment. These, however, require an extension of the framework that will complicate the discussion. Instead, it is assumed, for now, that the sectoral output is determined by the exit and entry of firms. For this purpose it is assumed that the production function of each firm contains a variable representing the entrepreneurial or managerial capacity of the firm. The production function is linear homogeneous in all the inputs including entrepreneurial capacity, which at this stage is assumed to be fixed for the firm. It is assumed that the supply of entrepreneurs is perfectly elastic, which results in zero profits.

The Structure of Supply

The eight relations in (2.1)–(2.5) summarize the supply conditions under constant technology and fixed factor supply. The endogenous variables in the economy are L_i, K_i, Y_i, w, r, and p_i. The system has no money, and therefore it determines only the product price ratio $p = p_1/p_2$. With equations

(2.1)–(2.5), the supply side can be summarized by solving the system in terms of one of the endogenous variables.

For convenience, the system is written in more compact form. In this, we assume full employment conditions so that (2.1) and (2.2) are combined to yield

$$k = \ell_1 k_1 + \ell_2 k_2 \tag{2.6}$$

$$1 = \ell_1 + \ell_2, \tag{2.7}$$

where $k = K/L$ is the overall capital-labor ratio, $k_i = K_i/L_i$ is the sectoral capital-labor ratio, and $\ell_i = L_i/L$ is the share of sector i in the total labor force, so that $1 \geq \ell_i \geq 0$.

Using the assumption of CRS, the sectoral marginal and average productivities are uniquely determined by the sectoral capital-labor ratios. Label the average sectoral labor productivity, $Y_i/L_i = f_i(k_i)$, the first derivative of f, $f'(k)$, and per capita sectoral output, $Y_i/L = y_i$. Then per capita sectoral output is

$$y_i = \ell_i f_i(k_i), \tag{2.8}$$

and the competitive conditions are

$$r = p_i f_i'(k_i) \tag{2.9}$$

$$w = p_i[f_i(k_i) - k_i f_i'(k_i)]. \tag{2.10}$$

We solve the system in terms of the wage-rental ratio. Under the competitive assumptions, the wage-rental ratio is equal to the ratio of marginal productivities of labor and capital, labeled ω. The basic relations are shown in Figure 2.1 where, ignoring sectoral notations, the average labor productivity is drawn as a function of the capital-labor ratio. For the value of k given by OD, the value of $f(k)$ is DA, $f'(k) = \tan\alpha$, $F_L = f(k) - kf'(k) = OB$, and using the triangle similarities, $\omega = OC$. It is now simple to see that ω is monotonically increasing in k. This monotonicity can also be established analytically:

$$\omega(k) = \frac{f(k)}{f'(k)} - k \quad \text{and} \quad \omega'(k) = -\frac{f(k)f''(k)}{(f'(k))^2} > 0. \tag{2.11}$$

By definition, ω is well defined for all k, and everywhere, $\omega'(k) > 0$.

The competitive condition implies the same ω for all sectors. The restriction of admissible allocation imposes restrictions on the value of ω. Some allocations that maintain the competitive conditions may require more resources than are actually available.

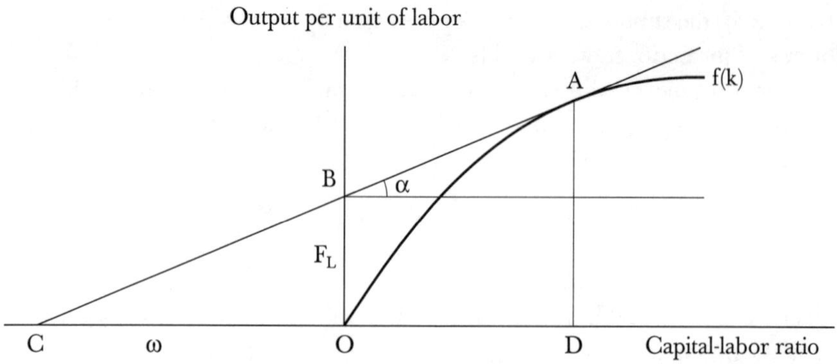

Figure 2.1 The production function

DEFINITION Wage-rental ratios that are consistent with admissible allocations are referred to as *admissible.*

To characterize an admissible allocation we note that $\omega_i(k_i)$ is strictly monotonic so the inverse function, $k_i(\omega_i)$, exists. Let $\underline{k}(\omega) = \min[k_1(\omega), k_2(\omega)]$ and $\overline{k}(\omega) = \max[k_1(\omega), k_2(\omega)]$. Then ω is admissible if

$$\underline{k}(\omega) \leq k \leq \overline{k}(\omega). \tag{2.12}$$

The determination of the set of admissible wage-rental ratios is illustrated graphically in Figure 2.2. The intersection of the two functions $\omega_i(k_i)$ with the vertical line at k determines the boundaries of the admissible values of ω in the economy: $\underline{\omega}(k) = \min[\omega_1(k), \omega_2(k)]$ and $\overline{\omega}(k) = \max[\omega_1(k), \omega_2(k)]$. In what follows we deal only with $\omega \in [\underline{\omega}(k), \overline{\omega}(k)]$. By construction, an allocation is admissible if it is determined by an admissible ω.

The properties to be derived are related to the sectoral factor intensities. Without a loss in generality sector 2 is assumed to be capital intensive.

DEFINITION (factor intensity) Sector 2 is capital intensive if, for any admissible ω, $k_2(\omega) > k_1(\omega)$.

Figure 2.2 is drawn in accordance with this assumption. Another definition is given below, and equivalent definitions are derived in the exercises. Each of these definitions is useful in certain contexts.

The solution of the supply side in terms of ω is now easily determined. Let ℓ be the fraction of the labor force in the labor-intensive sector, sector 1 in our

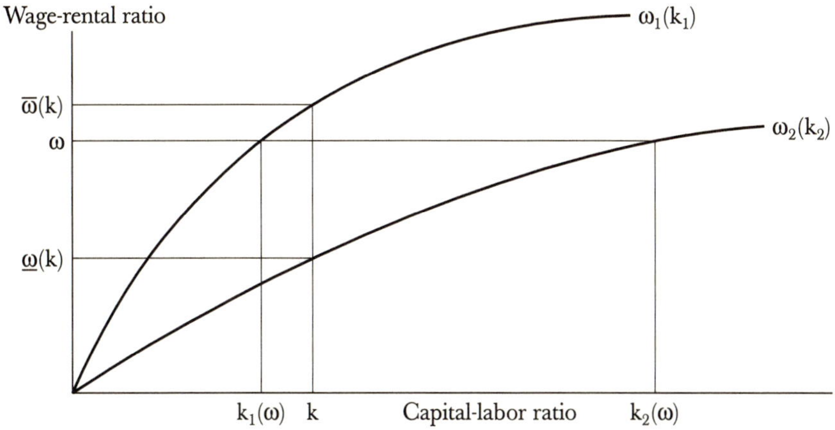

Figure 2.2 Factor ratio and factor-price ratio

case, and use equations (2.6) and (2.7) to obtain ℓ as a function of ω and k:

$$\ell(\omega, k) = \frac{k_2(\omega) - k}{k_2(\omega) - k_1(\omega)}. \tag{2.13}$$

Combine (2.13) and (2.8):

$$\begin{aligned} y_1(\omega, k) &= \frac{k_2(\omega) - k}{k_2(\omega) - k_1(\omega)} f_1[k_1(\omega)], \\ y_2(\omega, k) &= \frac{k - k_1(\omega)}{k_2(\omega) - k_1(\omega)} f_2[k_2(\omega)]. \end{aligned} \tag{2.14}$$

The dependence of ℓ and y_i on k is indicated here for later reference. In the present discussion k is assumed to be constant, and therefore ω is the only pertinent determinant. Having determined $k_i(\omega)$, the marginal productivities are determined. Using the competitive conditions, real factor prices are determined by conditions (2.9) and (2.10), and the product price ratio is given by

$$p(\omega) = \frac{f_2[k_2(\omega)]}{f_1[k_1(\omega)]}. \tag{2.15}$$

Note that p, r, and w are functions of ω only and are independent of k. We refer to $p(\omega)$ as the price function. As shown in equation (2.16) below, $p(\omega)$ is monotone in ω. Thus the system can be solved in terms of any one of the endogenous variables and, in particular, in terms of p using equation (2.15).

The Response to Price Variations

The dependence of the system on prices is monotonic. To see this, use equation (2.13) to write

$$\frac{\ell(\omega, k)}{1 - \ell(\omega, k)} = \frac{k_2(\omega) - k}{k - k_1(\omega)}.$$

Because $k_i(\omega)$ is monotonically increasing in ω, the numerator increases and the denominator shrinks as ω increases. Hence, for $\omega^* > \omega$, $\ell(\omega^*, k) \geq \ell(\omega, k)$. This result follows from the full employment conditions in (2.13): $k_i(\omega)$ can increase with ω if and only if the labor-intensive sector expands and the capital-intensive sector shrinks. The simultaneous increase of $k_i(\omega)$ and $\ell(\omega, k)$ with ω implies a shift of resources to the labor-intensive sector. That is, L_1 and K_1 increase and L_2 and K_2 decline with ω. Consequently, Y_1 increases and Y_2 declines with ω. The discussion is now summarized:

PROPERTY 2.1 (resource allocation) An increase in the wage-rental ratio is associated with an increase in the employment of labor and capital by the labor-intensive sector and a corresponding decline in resource employment by the capital-intensive sector. Consequently, the output of the labor-intensive sector increases and that of the capital-intensive sector declines.

Since $k_i'(\omega) > 0$, we also have

PROPERTY 2.2 (factor prices) An increase in the wage-rental ratio is associated with an increase in the wage rate (w) and a decline in the rental rate (r).

Solving the system for all the admissible values of ω generates all the attainable combinations of y_1 and y_2 which, when plotted, generate the transformation curve. The transformation curve is the set of admissible production plans which are efficient in the sense that it is impossible to reallocate resources to increase the output of one product without decreasing the output of the other product. The concavity of the transformation curve follows from the concavity of the production functions (see the appendix to this chapter for a proof).

There is a monotone relationship between the product price ratio p and the factor price ratio ω. By the strong concavity of the transformation curve, the derivative dy_2/dy_1 increases in absolute value as y_1 increases. This derivative represents the marginal real cost of producing y_1 and given the competitive conditions, it is equal to p. But as $y_1(\omega)$ is monotone in ω, it is also monotone in p. This relationship between the product price ratio and the factor price ratio is the essence of the factor-price equalization theorem (Samuelson, 1948, 1949).

PROPERTY 2.3 (product-factor prices) The wage-rental ratio is monotonically increasing with the price of the labor-intensive product relative to that of the capital-intensive product.

Factor Intensity and the Price Equation

At this point it is appropriate to indicate that there are two distinct measures of factor intensity. The two measures are equivalent under the competitive conditions but, as shown in Chapter 8, when the competitive conditions are violated the two measures may diverge. The measure introduced now is related to the cost function, defined below, and it is expressed in terms of the factor shares. The share of capital in total output of sector i is $S_{iK} = rK_i/p_iY_i$ and that of labor is $1 - S_{iK} = S_{iL}$. Hence, $k_i(\omega)/\omega = rK_i/wL_i = S_{iK}/1 - S_{iK}$ and $k_2(\omega) > k_1(\omega)$ if and only if $S_{2K}(\omega) > S_{1K}(\omega)$. We introduce this result as a definition:

DEFINITION (factor-cost intensity) Sector 1 is *labor-cost intensive* if for any admissible ω, $I(\omega) \equiv S_{1L}(\omega) - S_{2L}(\omega) > 0$.

The price function depends on the cost intensity definition, as can be seen by deriving $p(\omega)$ using the cost function and the competitive condition. The cost function gives the lowest cost for producing output y for given factor prices:

$$C_i(w, r, Y_i) = \min_{K_i, L_i} [wL_i + rK_i; Y_i = F_i(K_i, L_i)].$$

As such, it is a function of the factor prices and output. The cost function takes on a simpler form when the production function is homogeneous of degree $\mu > 0$:

$$C_i(w, r, Y_i) = Y_i^{1/\mu} c_i(w, r).$$

Hence under CRS, $\mu = 1$, and $c_i(w, r)$ is the average cost. In competition, free entry and exit forces profits to zero, and therefore $c_i = p_i$. By definition, the cost function is homogeneous of degree 1 in w and r, which allows us to write $p_i = r\phi_i(\omega)$. Since $p = p_1/p_2$, we have the price function: $p = p(\omega)$. It follows from the envelope theorem (or Shephard's lemma) that $\partial c_i/\partial w = L_i(w, r, Y_i)/Y_i$ or $\partial \ln c_i/\partial \ln w = S_{iL}$ and $\partial \ln c_i/\partial \ln r = S_{iK}$. Write the total differential of p_i in its logarithmic form, using $\hat{x} \equiv dx/x$, to obtain

$$\hat{p}_i(w, r) = S_{iL}\hat{w} + (1 - S_{iL})\hat{r} = \hat{r} + S_{iL}\hat{\omega}.$$

Hence

$$\hat{p}(\omega) = \hat{p}_1 - \hat{p}_2 = (S_{1L} - S_{2L})\hat{\omega} \equiv I(\omega)\hat{\omega}. \quad (2.16)$$

Consequently, sign $\hat{p}(\omega)/\hat{\omega} = \text{sign } I(\omega)$. $I(\omega)$ is positive when sector 1 is labor-cost intensive; thus in this case $p(\omega)$ is monotone increasing in ω.

This presentation has an important economic insight. When the wage rate increases proportionately more than the rental rate, the cost of production will increase more in the sector that pays a larger share of its product to labor. Note that the admissible values of p are bounded by $\underline{p} = \min[p(\underline{\omega}(k)), p(\overline{\omega}(k))]$ and $\overline{p} = \max[p(\underline{\omega}(k)), p(\overline{\omega}(k))]$.

When trading countries use the same technologies, they will have identical price functions. Trade between them leads to equality of p and therefore to equality of ω. But since the technologies are the same, factor prices will be the same. This is the meaning of the factor-price equalization theorem.

Since $-1 < I(\omega) < 1$, we have $|\hat{p}| < |\hat{\omega}|$; an increase in p will affect ω more than proportionately. Jones (1965) refers to this as the magnification effect and uses it to place boundaries on price changes.

Graphical Presentation of the Supply Side

The supply structure is summarized in Figure 2.3, which consists of four panels. The resource allocation is illustrated in panel I. Starting with an arbitrary wage-rental ratio ω_A, $k_{iA} \equiv k_i(\omega_A)$ are determined, and given a capital-labor ratio k, the resource allocation is determined, resulting in a production plan A marked on the transformation curve in panel IV. The supply price is determined by the slope of the transformation curve. It can also be determined directly by utilizing the price function presented in panel II. Thus, given ω_A, the price p_A is read directly from $p(\omega)$. Finally, panel III presents the supply function for sector 1, $y_1(p)$. It is obtained from $y_1(p) = y_1(\omega(p))$. As sector 1 is the labor-intensive sector and p is its relative price, the slope of the supply function is positive, $y_1'(p) \geq 0$. Knowing p_A, y_{1A} is determined. This corresponds to point A on the transformation curve.

It is now clear that the system can be solved in terms of variables other than ω. For instance, knowing y_1 or p makes it possible to solve for all the remaining variables. Similarly, the system can be solved in terms of per capita income, $y = py_1 + y_2$, measured in terms of nonagriculture. In Figure 2.3, given income level y_A, a tangent line is drawn from y_A to the transformation

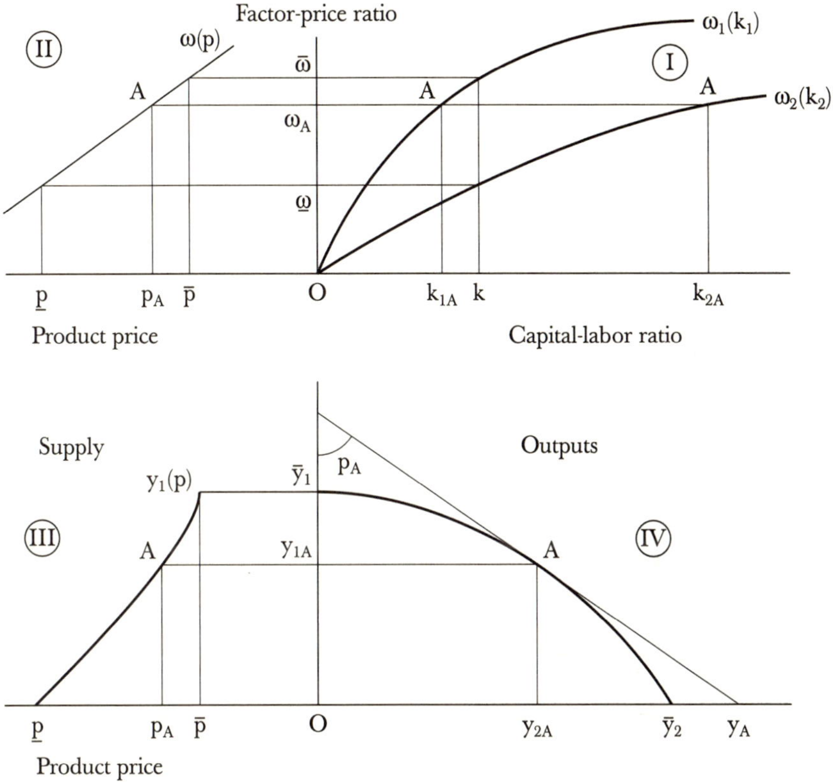

Figure 2.3 The supply side

curve and thus p_A, y_{1A}, and y_{2A} are derived. If both y and p are given, it is possible that a tangent line does not exist, implying that the chosen y, given p, is inadmissible. In this case the economy specializes in one of the two sectors, depending on p.

This is a strong result which says that knowing y and p allows us to determine the output composition. However, the result has to be qualified by emphasizing that it is obtained conditional on technology and resources. Thus, its empirical validity is limited only to situations where these conditions are met.

Small Open Economy

The solution of the system in terms of p is of particular interest in that it describes the situation of a small open economy that trades in both products. In the absence of interventions, the country takes the international prices as given. It is useful to repeat the foregoing results for such an economy by summarizing the response of the economy to an increase in the relative price of the labor-intensive product. Such an increase in p leads to an increase in the wage-rental ratio, in the sectoral capital-labor ratios, and in the real wage, to a decline in the real rental rate, to a shift of both resources away from the capital-intensive to the labor-intensive sector, and therefore to an increase in the output of the labor-intensive sector and a decline in the output of the capital-intensive sector.

Alternatively, the consequences of a change in price can be evaluated by starting with the supply response. An increase in p leads to an increase in y_1 and a decline in y_2. Because p is the price of the labor-cost-intensive product, its rise causes a rise in ω and hence an increase in $k_i(\omega)$ in both sectors. All this can be inferred from Figure 2.3. We can now summarize the supply conditions.

Summary of Supply

Admissible prices:

$$\omega \in [\underline{\omega}(k), \overline{\omega}(k)], \underline{\omega}'(k) > 0, \ \overline{\omega}'(k) > 0.$$

Let p be the relative price of the labor-cost-intensive sector then,

$$p(\omega) > 0; p'(\omega) > 0$$

$$p \in [\underline{p}(k), \overline{p}(k)], \underline{p}'(k) > 0, \overline{p}'(k) > 0.$$

Resource allocation:

$$k_i(\omega) > 0; k_i'(\omega) > 0, \qquad i = 1, 2.$$

Let ℓ be the proportion of the labor-intensive sector (sector 1) in total employment then,

$$1 \geq \ell(\omega, k) \geq 0; \quad \partial\ell(\omega, k)/\partial\omega > 0.^2$$

Outputs:

$$\frac{\partial y_i(\omega, k)}{\partial \omega} \begin{matrix} > 0 & \text{for the labor-intensive sector} \\ < 0 & \text{for the capital-intensive sector} \end{matrix}$$

but always:

$$\partial y_1(p, k)/\partial p > 0$$

$$\partial y_2(p, k)/\partial p < 0.$$

Demand

It is assumed that the preferences of consumers in the economy can be summarized by a well-behaved utility function. Under such an assumption, the equilibrium position in a closed economy is determined by a tangency of the indifference and the transformation curves. Such a solution is shown by point A in Figure 2.4 where $u(A)$ is the indifference curve with the utility level associated with the product bundle at A. Changes in supply conditions which lead to changes in the transformation curve will result in a new equilibrium point, to be determined in a way similar to the determination of A. This result is too general, and as such it is not sufficiently informative. Specifically, it does not use our empirical knowledge about the demand for agricultural output. Considerable insight can be gained by conducting the analysis in terms of demand. The assumptions of a well-behaved utility function and rational choice yield demand functions which are homogeneous of degree 0 in nominal income and prices. Using this property, we can write the demand in real terms, normalizing by one of the prices, say p_2:

$$x_1 = D_1(\underset{-}{p}, \underset{+}{y}), \quad x_2 = D_2(\underset{+}{p}, \underset{+}{y}), \tag{2.17}$$

where x_i is the per capita demand of the ith product and the underlying signs are those of the partial derivatives. We assume that the two products are normal (positive income coefficients), desirable and unsatiated so that the demand functions are asymptotic to the price-quantity axes. The assumption

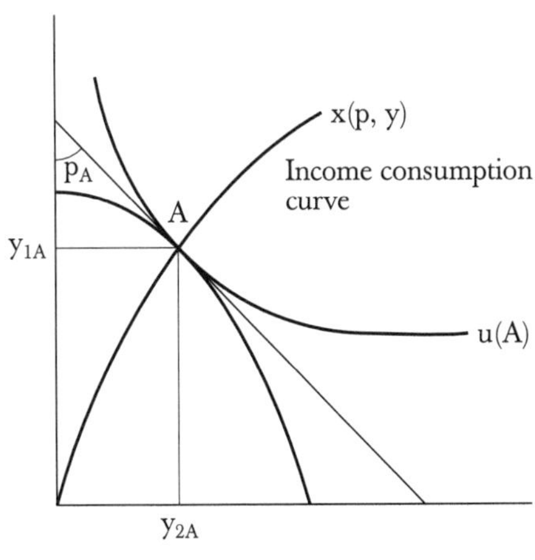

Figure 2.4 Demand

is justifiable when the commodities are broadly defined and it leads to[3]

$$\lim_{p\to\infty} D_1(p, y) = 0; \quad \lim_{p\to 0} D_1(p, y) = \infty$$

$$\lim_{p\to\infty} D_2(p, y) = \infty; \quad \lim_{p\to 0} D_2(p, y) = 0$$

In the graphical illustration we repeatedly use the income-expansion curve, which is the locus of $x_i = D_i(p, y)$ with p held constant.[4] It is labeled $x(p, y)$ in Figure 2.4. Since the two products are assumed to be normal, it is possible to combine the two equations in (2.17) to

$$\begin{aligned} &x_1 = D(\underset{-}{p}, \underset{+}{x_2}); \quad D(p, 0) = 0 \\ &\lim_{p\to\infty} D(p, x_2) = 0; \ \lim_{p\to 0} D(p, x_2) = \infty. \end{aligned} \tag{2.18}$$

Wherever convenient, the compact notation $x_1(p, x_2) = D(p, x_2)$ is used.

We make frequent use of the demand price, p^d, which is the price that corresponds to a given consumption bundle. Using the monotonicity of x_1 in p (see equation 2.18), the function can be inverted to yield

$$p^d = p(\underset{-}{x_1}, \underset{+}{x_2}). \tag{2.19}$$

Equilibrium

The structure of the model meets the conditions of a well-behaved competitive economy, and consequently general results imply the existence of a competitive equilibrium. It is instructive to take advantage of the simple structure of the present model and to show graphically the determination of equilibrium. We will use this construction repeatedly in discussing the response of the system to various changes.

In a closed economy, equilibrium is characterized by a price p that equates supply and demand. For the small open economy the price is given, and trade is used to close the difference between the domestic supply and demand. Consequently, the analysis of equilibrium determination depends on whether the economy is open or closed. Although most economies trade in agricultural products and are largely price takers, we are still concerned with the analysis of a closed economy for two reasons. First, every economy has a nontradable sector which cannot be ignored in discussing the relationship between agriculture and nonagriculture. In a related way, not all of the agricultural product is traded. This subject is introduced in Chapter 3, and its implications will be examined in the subsequent discussion. Second, many of the agricultural

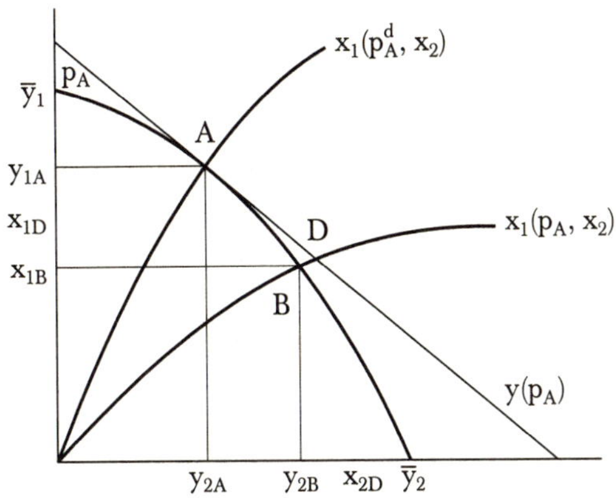

Figure 2.5 Equilibrium in a small open economy

problems are global and should be addressed as such. For that purpose, the closed economy framework is the relevant one.

Open Economy

The equilibrium characterization of a small open economy is as follows. Given the world price p, outputs $y_i(p)$ are determined, which in turn determine income $y(p)$. At this point, there is no domestic saving, so (per capita) consumption, $c(p)$, is equal to income plus net import, defined as the excess of import over export or trade deficit. To simplify, assume balanced trade so that $c(p) = y(p)$. The consumption of the ith product is determined by the demand function, $x_i[p, y(p)]$, or simply $x_i(p)$, and the sectoral identities are

$$y_i = x_i^c + x_i^e,$$

where $x_i^c = x_i(p)$ is per capita consumption and x_i^e is per capita net export. Since $y(p) = c(p)$, we have $px_1^e + x_2^e = 0$.

The solution is illustrated in Figure 2.5, where the world price is p_A. The optimal production is given by A, and the corresponding income is $y(p_A)$. The demand curve corresponding to this price, $x_1(p_A, x_2)$, intersects the income line at D, yielding the optimal consumption. Because $y_{1A} > x_{1D}$, the country is an exporter of the agricultural product and an importer of the nonagricultural product, with export $y_{1A} - x_{1D}$ and import $x_{2D} - y_{2A}$.

Closed Economy

We begin the analysis with an arbitrary supply price, $p_A^s = p_A$, in Figure 2.5. The corresponding supply is at point A, and the demand is at B, not at D as for the open economy because now the consumption possibilities are bounded by the transformation curve and not by the market line. Thus at p_A there is an excess supply of agriculture, $x_1(p_A) - y_1(p_A) < 0$, implying that p_A is too high for the market to clear. A decline in the price will move the production point to the right and the consumption point to the left. Eventually, a market-clearing price is achieved.

More formally, to search for an equilibrium price, examine the demand price that will induce the consumption of the output at A. This is obtained by using equation (2.19): $p_A^d = p(x_{1A}, x_{2A} \mid x_{iA} = y_{iA})$. Because $y_{1A} > x_1(p_A)$, we have $p_A^d < p_A$. Can instead p_A^d be an equilibrium price? The answer is no because as p declines from p_A to p_A^d, the output $y_1(p)$ declines, and the optimal output at p_A^d is below and to the right of A, resulting in an excess demand for agriculture, $x_1(p_A^d) - y_1(p_A^d) > 0$. Therefore p_A^d is too low for the market to clear. We have thus established boundaries on the equilibrium price and by the continuity of the demand and supply functions, there exists an equilibrium price p_E, such that $p_A^d < p_E < p_A^s$, and $x_1(p_E) = y_1(p_E)$. By construction, this price also clears the nonagricultural market.

The Restricted Demand

The analysis can also be illustrated in terms of the supply and demand equations familiar from partial equilibrium analysis. In so doing, we should keep in mind that in our framework the supply and demand are obtained subject to the economywide constraints and as such are not partial equilibrium functions. To find the equilibrium price we have to search for p such that $x_i(p) = y_i(p)$. To do so, we replace x_2 in (2.18) with the value of y_2 on the transformation curve that corresponds to the price p, $x_2 = y_2(p)$, to obtain

$$x_1 = D[p, x_2 \mid x_2 = y_2(p)] = x_1(p). \tag{2.20}$$

We refer to (2.20) as the restricted demand.

DEFINITION (restricted demand) The *restricted demand* is obtained by restricting the demand $x_1(p, x_2)$ to the domain $x_2 = y_2(p)$.

The concept is illustrated in Figure 2.6. Starting with $\underline{p}$, draw $x_1(\underline{p}, x_2)$ in the right panel and continue it to point A where $x_2 = y_2(\underline{p}) \equiv \overline{y}_2$. Thus point A meets the condition of the restricted demand, and it is marked in the left

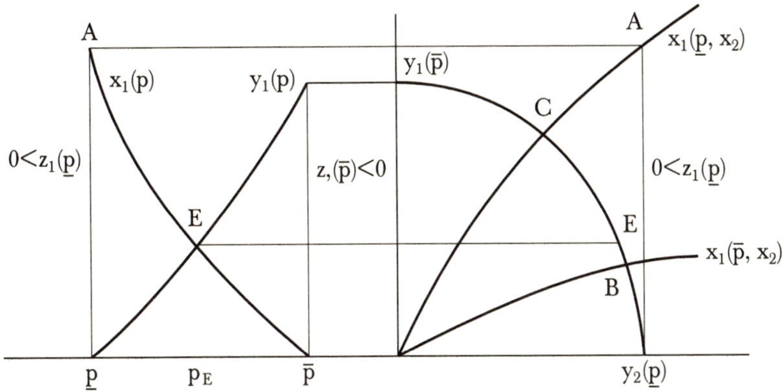

Figure 2.6 Restricted demand: Closed economy

panel as a point on the function $x_1(p)$. Turning to the other extreme, at $\overline{p}$, $y_2(\overline{p}) = 0$, and hence $x_1(\overline{p}, 0) = 0$. This procedure can be repeated for other prices. The restricted demand is continuous, and it is drawn in the left panel joining the points illustrated above. The supply $y_1(p)$ is obtained as before, and the intersection of supply and demand gives the equilibrium point E.

The difference between the restricted demand and the supply is the excess demand:

$$z_1(p) = x_1(p) - y_1(p).$$

Note that $z_1(p)$ is everywhere declining since $x_1'(p) < 0$ and $y_1'(p) > 0$. The graphical derivation of the restricted demand also generates the excess demand. In terms of the left-hand panel, it is the vertical distance between $x_1(p)$ and $y_1(p)$. Thus, at $\underline{p}$, the excess demand is simply $x_1(\underline{p})$, since $y_1(\underline{p}) = 0$. Similarly, at $\overline{p}$, $x_1(\overline{p}) = 0$. The reason is that at this point there is no production of y_2 and therefore no consumption of this product. By the assumptions on demand, zero consumption of a product can only take place when there is no consumption at all. In this case, $z_1(\overline{p}) = -\overline{y}_1$.

The analysis shows that for low p, $z_1(p) > 0$, for high p, $z_1(p) < 0$, and there is a price, p_E, such that $z_1(p_E) = 0$. Convergence to equilibrium is achieved when a positive excess demand generates an increase in p:

$$z_1(p)dp \geq 0.$$

The equality is achieved when both $z_1(p)$ and dp are equal to zero.

The same analysis can also be carried out for an open economy. However, in this case, the values of the excess demand are different in that for any p the

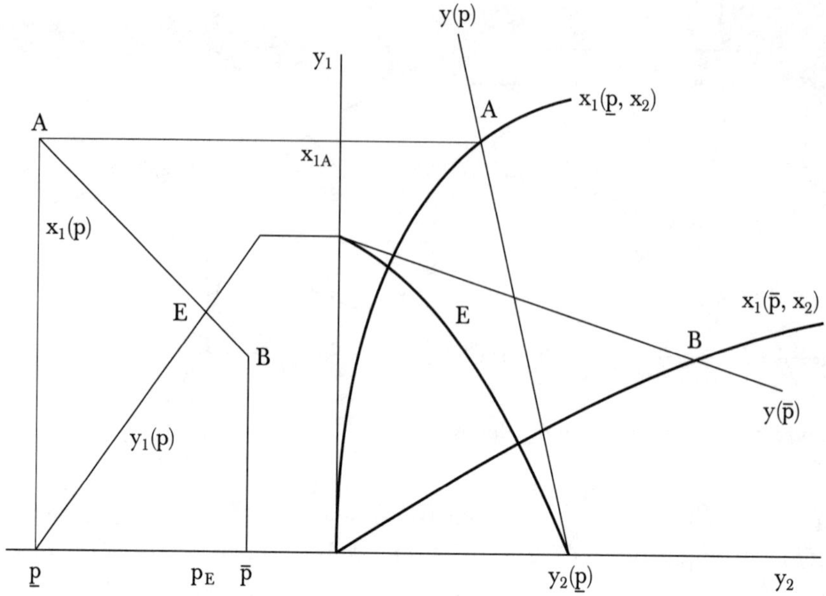

Figure 2.7 Restricted demand: Open economy

consumption possibilities are represented by the market line rather than the transformation curve. It is therefore more meaningful for the presentation of an open economy to restrict the consumption of x_2 to values of $y_2(p)$ that are attainable at value output $y(p) : x_1(p) = D[p, x_2(p, y(p))]$, where $y(p)$ is the income corresponding to price p.

The derivation of the restricted demand for an open economy is portrayed in Figure 2.7. When the world price is $\underline{p}$, the economy specializes in sector 2. The generated income, $y(\underline{p})$, represents the budget constraint. It intersects the income expansion curve $x_1(\underline{p}, x_2)$ at A in the right panel. Point A marked on the restricted demand in the left panel has coordinates $\underline{p}$ and $x_{1A} = x_1(\underline{p})$. Similarly, point B corresponds to $\overline{p}$. At E supply and demand intersect, and there is no trade. Therefore E is also a point on the restricted demand of a closed economy (not shown in the figure).

Equal Factor Intensities

The foregoing discussion does not properly cover the case of equal factor intensities, where $k_1(\omega) = k_2(\omega)$. Such equality may hold locally where $k_i(\omega) = k$,

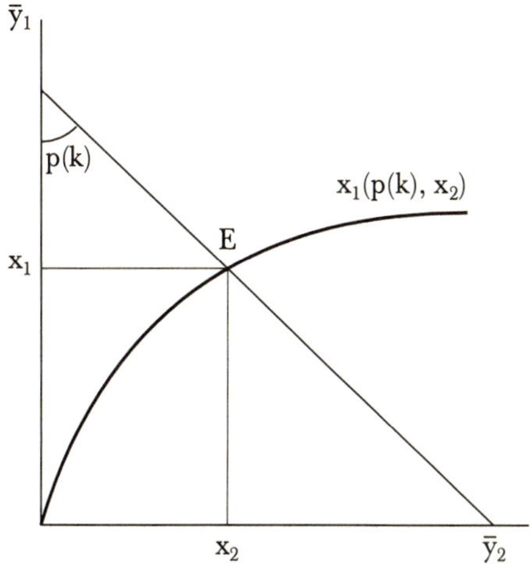

Figure 2.8 Equilibrium: Equal factor intensities

or in the large, in which case the $k_i(\omega)$ functions in the two sectors are identical. In either case equation (2.6) cannot be used to determine ℓ, and the subsequent discussion based on this equation has to be modified. Still, the economy does have an equilibrium point, and its determination is rather simple.

Under equal factor intensities the transformation curve is a straight line. Since by assumption $k_1(\omega) = k_2(\omega) = k$, we have $\omega = \underline{\omega}(k) = \overline{\omega}(k)$. That is, the admissible value of ω for the economy is unique, and it is a function of k, $\omega(k)$. Since p is uniquely determined by $p(\omega)$, it has a constant value determined by $p(\omega(k)) = p(k)$.

Utilizing (2.8), the intercepts of the transformation curve are $\overline{y}_i = f_i(k)$. Utilizing the competitive conditions, $p = f_2'(k)/f_1'(k)$, and since k is constant, so is p. In other words, the transformation curve represents the combination of outputs $\ell f_1(k)$ and $(1 - \ell) f_2(k)$. Consequently,

$$dy_2/dy_1 = \frac{f_2(k)}{f_1(k)} \frac{d(1-\ell)}{d\ell} = -\frac{f_2(k)}{f_1(k)} = -\frac{\overline{y}_2}{\overline{y}_1}.$$

All this is shown in Figure 2.8, where we read $p(k)$ directly from the transformation curve. The equilibrium, E, is determined graphically by drawing the demand curve corresponding to $p(k)$, resulting in consumption (x_1, x_2).

Income Distribution

Differences in income among individuals arise due to differences in the attributes that generate and affect income. Growth changes the supply and demand of these attributes, their market values, and therefore the income distribution. The most basic attributes are the ownership of factors of production, and the starting point for any discussion is to trace the effect of growth on the returns to factors of production. At this stage of static analysis some preliminary concepts are presented that are related to the more general discussion below.

Income generated by production is distributed as wages to labor and rental to the owners of the capital good. Variations in factor prices affect the income distribution between labor and capital. When the demand depends only on the level of income and not on its source, the income distribution is determined by the equilibrium position but does not affect it. A change in factor prices may increase or decrease the share of labor in total income (labor share) depending on the ease of factor substitution to be measured by the elasticity of substitution (ES).

For the case of a two-factor production function, the ES is defined by

$$\sigma = d \ln k / d \ln \omega. \tag{2.21}$$

The functional distribution of income can be measured by the ratio of the labor share to that of capital:

$$\theta_i \equiv S_{iL}/(1 - S_{iL}) = wL_i/rK_i = \omega/k_i.$$

Thus, sign $\partial S_{iL}/\partial\omega = \text{sign } \partial\theta_i/\partial\omega = \text{sign}(1 - \sigma_i)$. Consequently, the share of labor in the total income of sector i increases (decreases) with the wage-rental ratio when $\sigma_i < 1 (\sigma_i > 1)$. It is unaffected by the wage-rental ratio when $\sigma_i = 1$. If everywhere $\sigma_i = 1$, the production function is Cobb-Douglas.

The relationship between σ_i and the concavity of $\omega_i(k_i)$ is illustrated in Figure 2.9.[5] As ω increases, θ decreases for sector 1 ($\sigma_1 > 1$) and increases for sector 2 ($\sigma_2 < 1$). An elasticity of substitution larger than 1 describes a situation where an increase in ω causes more than a proportional substitution of capital for labor.

It is clear from the foregoing discussion that a given change in ω may affect the labor shares in the two sectors in different directions when $(\sigma_1 - 1)(\sigma_2 - 1) < 0$. In this case, the net effect of such a change on the labor share in the economy at large depends on the relative importance of the sectors and the change in the sectoral composition called for by the change in ω.

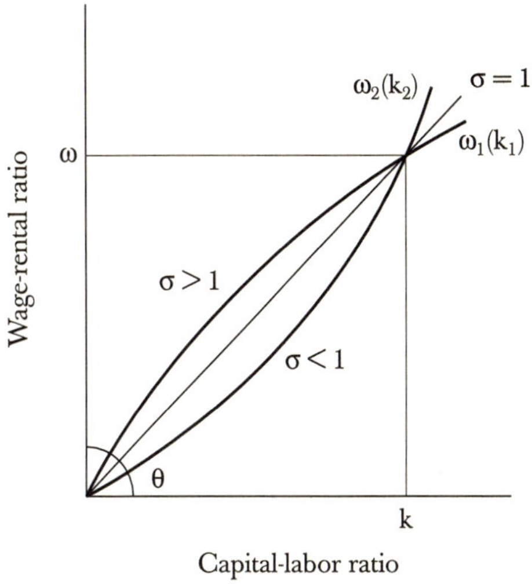

Figure 2.9 Factor intensities and factor price-ratio

Much of the discussion on agricultural policy deals with a comparison of income in agriculture with that in nonagriculture. This is related to another dimension of income distribution. Let $S_1 = py_1/y$ be the proportion of agriculture in total value output. In terms of Figure 2.3, it is the ratio $(y_A - y_{2A})/y_A$. Clearly, this ratio increases monotonically with y_1. Thus under the conditions of the model, changes leading to an increase in y_1 increase the share of agriculture in total output.

The Introduction of Land

Agricultural production requires land; therefore it must be introduced into the analysis. As a first step, we turn now to show how the foregoing results should be interpreted when land is included under the assumption that land is of homogeneous quality. This assumption is removed in a more detailed discussion of land in Chapter 4 and thereafter.

We write the agricultural production function with land (A) included and with population held constant, and therefore ignored, as

$$Y_1 = A^{1-\mu}[F_1(K_1, L_1)]^{\mu}, \tag{2.22}$$

where F_1 is concave, twice differentiable, linear homogeneous, and $0 < \mu < 1$. The degree of the function, μ, can be a function of various variables, including land. However, locally it is considered to be constant. Consequently, by a simple transformation we can write

$$Y_1^* = (Y_1)^{1/\mu} = A^{\epsilon} F_1(K_1, L_1),$$

where $\epsilon = (1 - \mu)/\mu$. Let $y_1^* = Y_1^*/L$, and write

$$y_1^* = A^{\epsilon} \ell f_1(k_1). \tag{2.23}$$

Thus instead of dealing with per capita agricultural output, y_1, we deal with a monotonic transformation of it, y_1^*. To derive the actual output from y_1^*, simply reverse the transformation: $y_1 = y_1^{*\mu}$.

Under this specification, land is weakly separable from the other inputs in that the marginal rate of substitution of capital and labor is independent of the size of land. Consequently $\omega_1(k_1)$ remains unchanged, as does the solution for the resource allocation, ω and $\ell_i(\omega)$. Figure 2.10 illustrates the transformation curves between y_2 and y_1^* as well as y_1. Without loss in generality, we assume now that land is held constant.

The supply price of the transformed output, labeled p^*, reflects the fact that its production function is linear homogeneous. However, the production function of actual output displays decreasing returns to scale in capital and labor. Therefore the price of the actual output will be higher than that of the transformed output, except for small outputs. In deriving the supply price it is assumed that there is no alternative use for land, and therefore the return to land is rent. Thus the cost function that corresponds to (is dual to) actual output is written as $C = y^{1/\mu}\phi(w, r)$, and the average cost is $c = y^{\epsilon}\phi(w, r)$. Applying this to sector 1, we have $p_1 = C_1/y_1 = y_1^{\epsilon}\phi(w, r)$. The transformed variable is linear homogeneous, and we can attach to it an average cost, $p_1^* = \phi(w, r)$. Thus

$$p = \frac{p_1}{p_2} = y_1^{\epsilon}\frac{\phi(w, r)}{p_2} = y_1^{\epsilon}\frac{p_1^*}{p_2} = y_1^{\epsilon} p^*. \tag{2.24}$$

The price functions $p^*(\omega)$ and $p(\omega, y_1)$ are drawn in panel II of Figure 2.10, and the supply functions $y_1(p)$ and $y_1^*(p)$ are drawn in panel III.[6]

To obtain the equilibrium solution, demand must be expressed in the same units as supply. The quantity demanded is then transformed by $x_1^* = x_1^{1/\mu}$, and as such it can be expressed as a function of p and x_2:

$$x_1^* = [D(p, x_2)]^{1/\mu}. \tag{2.25}$$

The foregoing analysis conducted by ignoring land applies immediately to the transformed variable y_1^*. To obtain the results in terms of the original

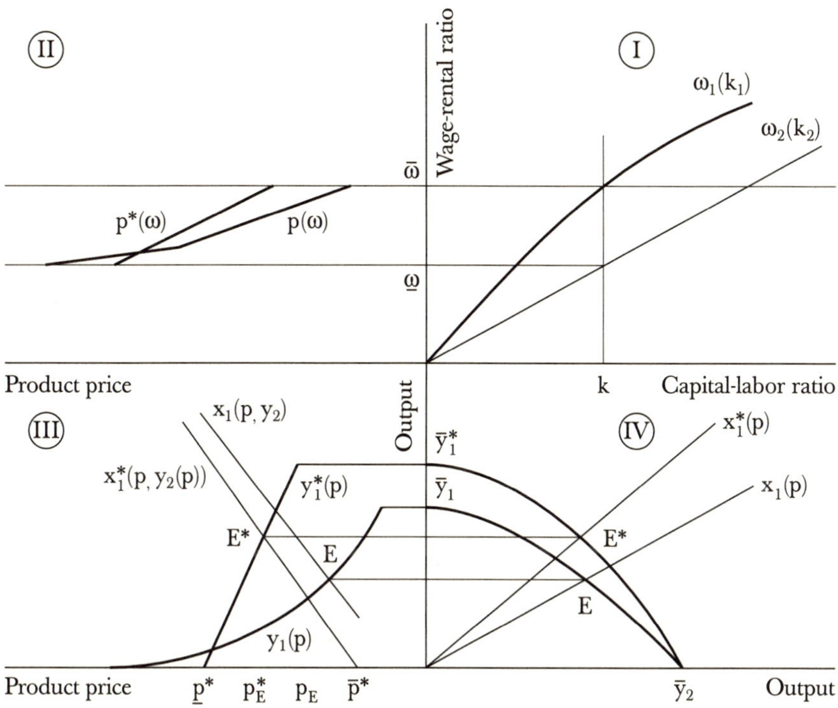

Figure 2.10 The economy with land

variables, we transform y_1^* and x_1^* to y_1 and x_1 respectively. The model is illustrated in Figure 2.10 in terms of the two systems. Qualitatively, the supply price of agricultural output increases more sharply with y_1 than with y_1^*. This is shown in panel III of Figure 2.10 as a downward shift of the supply function for y_1. In this sense, much of the qualitative analysis can be conducted by ignoring land. Land becomes important when dealing with specific issues related to land itself such as: (1) identifying the determinants of the returns to land, (2) land as a source of farm income, (3) the determinants of the size of the arable land, and (4) the effect of land scarcity on the composition of the implemented technology in agriculture. These and related issues are addressed in subsequent discussion in later chapters.

Under the present specification, using the Euler condition for a CRS production function, $1 - \mu$ is the factor share of land. Denote the rent on land, measured in terms of y_2, by R, and the population by L, then

$$R = (1 - \mu) p y_1 L / A. \tag{2.26}$$

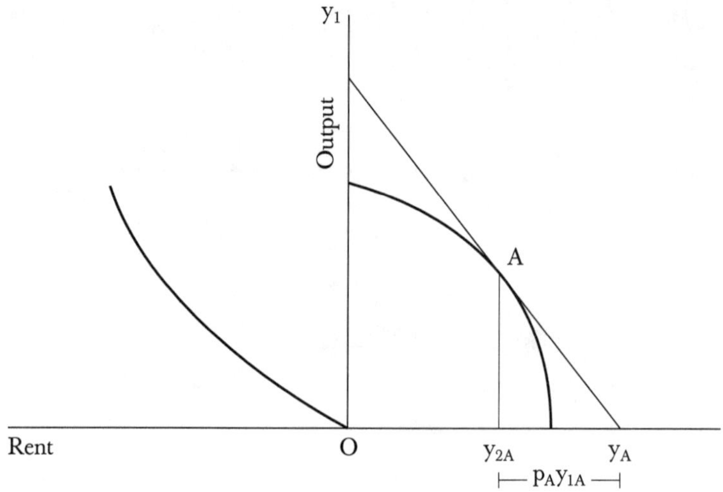

Figure 2.11 Rent and the level of activity

With A and $(1 - \mu)$ held constant, the rent increases monotonically with the value of the agricultural output, py_1. But in view of the supply function, R is monotone increasing with either y_1 or p.

The rent can be shown graphically as in Figure 2.11 by drawing a tangent to point A with an intercept $y_A = p_A y_{1A} + y_{2A}$ and $p_A y_{1A}$ is given by the segment $y_A - y_{2A}$. Note that rent varies from 0, when the economy specializes in nonagriculture, to $(1 - \mu)L\overline{p}\,\overline{y}_1/A$. Clearly, an increase in the ratio of population to land increases the rent.

Food and Agriculture

In much of the public discussion and economic analysis, food is assumed to be identical with agriculture, and this is the approach taken here. However, for some purposes this assumption is too restrictive in that it does not allow for the fact that food contains other inputs originating in nonagriculture such as processing, packaging, and transportation, as well as food consumed in restaurants. The quantity of the nonagricultural inputs and their prices affect the consumer price of food. This raises two questions: first, what effect should it have on our analysis and second, what is the empirical implication. This topic is discussed in Mundlak (1986), and what follows summarizes results pertinent to our discussion.

Let the utility function of a representative consumer be written as

$$u = U[F(A, Q), N]. \tag{2.27}$$

The function is weakly separable in food, F, and nonfood, N. Food has an agricultural component, A, and a nonagricultural component, Q. The ratio $q = Q/A$ can serve as a measure of quality of food.[7] Since the price of Q and N is the same, we can view $Q + N = \overline{N}$ as a composite good, and write the utility function as $U(A, \overline{N})$, resulting in demand functions unambiguously signed:

$$A(p, u), \quad \overline{N}(p, u). \tag{2.28}$$

To analyze the short-run equilibrium we utilize (2.28) to derive the demand function

$$x_1 = D(\underset{-}{p}, \underset{+}{x_2}), \tag{2.29}$$

where x_1 is per capita demand of A, and x_2 is per capita demand of $\overline{N}$. The function has the properties assumed for (2.18). Consequently, it can be shown that a unique stable short-run equilibrium is established which determines p, A, and $\overline{N}$ (Mundlak, 1986).

Empirical Evidence

The focus here is on demand alone, because supply is discussed at length in Chapter 14.

Demand

Demand plays a crucial role in the determination of the dynamics of agriculture. Particularly, sectoral growth depends on income elasticities. The role of demand is related to Engel's law, which states that the proportion of the consumer's budget spent on food declines with income. In other words, the utility function is not homothetic, and the income elasticity for food is less than one. In fact, it is much lower than one. Empirical work has been conducted with aggregate time-series data, and with household data. In general, price elasticities can be obtained more reliably from time-series data, where there are more fluctuations in prices. However, such analysis is complicated by other factors, so it will not be reviewed here except to indicate that the price elasticities of demand for the aggregate product are low, well below one (in absolute value).

On the other hand, income elasticities can be obtained by analyzing micro data where there exists a big spread in income between individuals. In general, the message from such studies is quite robust. Early empirical estimates of income elasticities are reviewed by Houthakker (1957), who concludes the analysis by stating that "[i]f no data on the expenditure patterns of a country are available at all, one would not be very far astray by putting the partial elasticity with respect to total expenditure at .6 for food, 1.2 for clothing, .8 for housing, and 1.6 for all other items combined and the partial elasticity with respect to family size at .3 for food, zero for housing and clothing, and −.4 for miscellaneous expenditures" (p. 550). More recent results obtained with more advanced estimation methods further confirm the earlier results. As indicated above, the income elasticities for food expenditures are likely to exaggerate the income elasticities of demand for the agricultural product when the income elasticity for quality exceeds that for agriculture. A positive relationship between food quality and income in consumer budget analysis was reported by Prais and Houthakker (1955, 1971) and by subsequent studies.

Above we interpreted the increased quality with a relative decline of the agricultural component in food. This is reflected in the cost composition of food at the retail level. The share of agriculture in the retail cost of food in the United States declined from a level of 50 percent in the mid-1940s to 33 percent in 1983 (Dunham, 1984). More specifically, over the period 1946–1982, this share declined at an average annual compounded rate of 0.35 percent. Over the same period, the terms of trade, p, declined by an average annual rate of 1.16 percent, whereas per capita income and the quality measure, as defined in the previous section, increased by 2.1 and 0.3 percent respectively. Additional empirical evidence for other countries is reviewed in Mundlak (1986).

Discussions of the demand of low-income individuals focus on the nutrient content of food, which does not reflect nonagricultural inputs. Strauss and Thomas (1998) examined the literature dealing with the extent to which wealth affects nutrition and the methodologies used in these studies. They report a positive caloric response to income up to a given level of income, and thereafter the response is weak. Orders of magnitude for income elasticities of caloric intake of low-income individuals are 0.35–0.55. The income elasticity for aggregate agricultural demand reflects the demand of all income groups and therefore is likely to be below these values, particularly in the more developed countries.

Factor Intensity and Agriculture

Because many of the results depend on factor intensity, it is important to examine whether agriculture is labor or capital intensive. We now know that there are two different concepts of factor intensity, one related to factor ratios and one related to factor shares. The first one affects the response of factor allocation to change in factor prices, and the second determines the relationship between factor and product prices. It is of interest to compare the two measures, but this is not a simple matter because of limitations on data on sectoral capital stock. We return to this in Chapter 10. At this point we look instead at some indirect measures that can be confronted with data more readily available. Let $\rho = K_1/K$ be the share of agriculture in the capital stock, and note that

$$[k_1(\omega) - k_2(\omega)][\rho(\omega) - \ell(\omega)] \geq 0.$$

The equality holds when the two terms are simultaneously equal to zero. This is, however, of little help when ρ is unknown. A more useful observation is that the share of agriculture in total output, $S_1 \equiv pY_1/Y$, can be expressed as a weighted average of the shares of agriculture in resources,

$$S_1 = \frac{wL_1 + rK_1 + RA}{Y} = S_L\ell + S_k\rho + S_AS_1,$$

where $S_L = wL/Y$, $S_K = rK/Y$, and $S_A = RA/pY_1$. We will concentrate on the relation between S_1 and ℓ. For this purpose we can aggregate physical capital and land and rewrite $S_1 = S_L\ell + (1 - S_L)\rho_T$, where ρ_T is the share of agriculture in capital, including land. If agriculture is labor intensive, we should observe $\ell > S_1$. The data on S_1 and ℓ are presented in Figures 1.14 and 1.15 and are summarized in Figure 2.12, which reports the distribution of the ratio S_1/ℓ for 68 countries in 1950 and 1990. On the whole, this ratio is well below one.

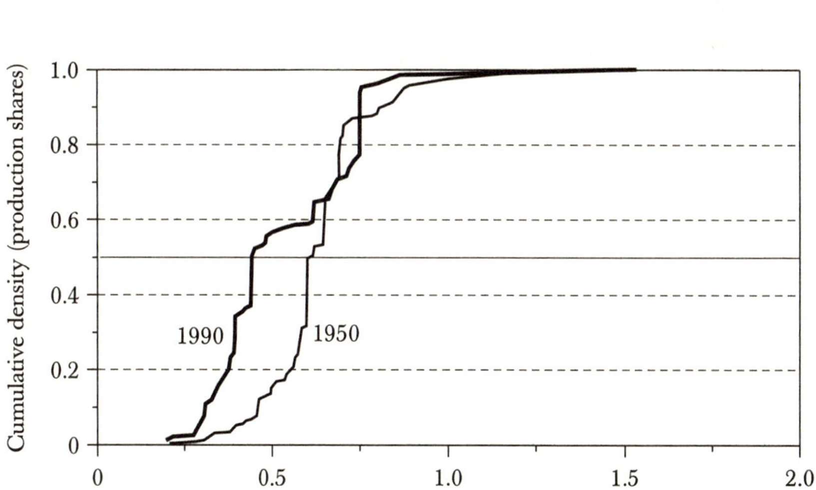

Figure 2.12 Agriculture: Ratio of share in GDP to share in labor force, 68 countries. (Based on database of Mundlak, Larson, and Crego, 1998.)

Turning to the measure of cost-factor intensity, we may compare the sectoral factor share of labor. Such a comparison is also restricted by data problems. In general, however, the labor share in agriculture is smaller than that in nonagriculture, indicating that agriculture is cost-capital intensive. Thus there seems to be a contradiction between the two measures of factor intensity. Two possible explanations come to mind. First, when we take land into consideration, a low value for the factor share of labor may be due to the factor share of land and not to a high value for the factor share of capital. In this case, there is no contradiction with the direct measure, but the implications seem nevertheless to indicate a contradiction. An increase in the wage rate will affect the cost of production in nonagriculture more than in agriculture. Second, it is possible that the assumption of equal factor prices across sectors, on which the equivalence of the two measures is based, is violated. This conclusion is consistent with the notion that the wage rate in agriculture is lower than in nonagriculture. We return to this subject in Chapters 8 and 9 (see also exercises 2.8–2.10).

Appendix 2A

1. Bibliographic note.

   The basic structure of supply in a two-sector economy can be found in Stolper and Samuelson (1941) and Samuelson (1948, 1949). It was adopted for growth analysis by Uzawa (1961, 1963). A uniform exposition is given by Jones (1965), following a somewhat different route from that used here. Although Jones's main analysis is for the small open economy, he also allows for product substitution on the demand side. Growth considerations require allowance for income effect on demand. This is introduced in Mundlak (1965) and further extended by Mundlak and Mosenson (1967, 1970). An early empirical formulation of the relationship between agriculture and the rest of the economy appears in Tolley and Smidt (1964).

2. The set of all admissible allocations is convex.

   Proof: Consider two admissible allocations:

$$\lambda' k_1' + (1 - \lambda')k_2' \leq k$$
$$\lambda'' k_1'' + (1 - \lambda'')k_2'' \leq k.$$

   What we want to show is that any convex combination of admissible allocations is also admissible. To form a convex combination of such

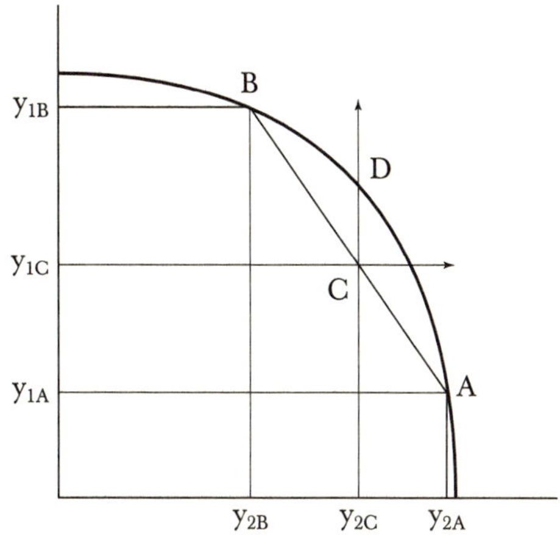

Figure 2A.1 Concavity of the transformation curve

admissible allocations, let $0 \leq a \leq 1$, multiply the first inequality by a and the second by $(1 - a)$, and add them up:

$$a\lambda' k_1' + a(1 - \lambda')k_2' + (1 - a)\lambda'' k_1'' + (1 - a)(1 - \lambda'')k_2'' \leq k.$$

This can be written in the form:

$$\tau \bar{k}_1 + (1 - \tau)\bar{k}_2 \leq k ,$$

where $\tau = a\lambda' + (1 - a)\lambda''$; $0 \leq \tau \leq 1$ and $\bar{k}_1 = [a\lambda' k_1' + (1 - a)\lambda'' k_1'']/\tau$ and a similar expression for the other components. ■

3. The concavity of the transformation curve.

We show that the concavity of the transformation curve follows from the concavity of the production functions. Let ω_A and ω_B be two admissible values of ω, and y_{iA} and y_{iB} be the corresponding outputs. To simplify the discussion, normalize the labor force to $L = 1$. For any $0 \leq \lambda \leq 1$, define point C with outputs: $\bar{y}_i = \lambda y_{iA} + (1 - \lambda) y_{iB}$. Points A, B, and C are shown in Figure 2A.1. To prove concavity it is necessary to show that there exists a feasible production plan, say D, such that $y_{iD} \geq \bar{y}_i$.

Consider the allocation $\bar{k}_i$, $i = 1, 2$: $\bar{k}_i = \lambda k_{iA} + (1 - \lambda)k_{iB}$, which is admissible because it is a convex combination of admissible allocations. Let $\bar{y}_i \equiv \lambda \ell_{iA} f_i(k_{iA}) + (1 - \lambda)\ell_{iB} f_i(k_{iB})$, label $\bar{\ell}_i = \lambda \ell_{iA} + (1 - \lambda)\ell_{iB}$, and $y(\bar{k}_i) \equiv \bar{\ell}_i f_i(\bar{k}_i)$, then due to the concavity of the production functions, $y_i(\bar{k}_i) > \bar{y}_i$. Consequently, if $\bar{\ell}$ represents an optimal allocation, the proof is completed; otherwise, there exists an optimal allocation with a larger output. Thus for any initial points A, B and for any $\lambda \in [0, 1]$ there exists an admissible allocation that dominates point C.

4. The unit profit.

In some instances it is useful to deal with a somewhat different convergence rule which states that whenever the cost of production is below the demand price, output will increase. Define $\pi_1(y_1) = p^d(y_1) - p^s(y_1)$ as the unit profit in sector 1. Equilibrium is achieved by finding y_1 such that $\pi_1 = 0$. The demand price, defined in (2.19), is evaluated here only for quantities on the transformation curve:

$$p^d(\underset{-}{x_1}, \underset{+}{x_2} \mid x_i = y_i; \underset{-}{y_2(y_1)}) = \underset{-}{p^d(y_1)}.$$

In terms of Figure 2.6, the demand price at C is obtained from $p^d(y_{1C}, y_{2C}) = p^d(y_{1C}) = \underline{p}$. Similarly, at B, $p^d(y_{1B}) = \overline{p}$.

The supply is drawn as before except that now it is expressed as $p^s(y_1)$. Equilibrium is established at E, where $p^d(y_{1E}) = p^s(y_{1E})$. For outputs $y_1 > y_{1E}$ the profit is negative. Thus, $\pi(y_1)$ alternates sign at E, and it is monotone declining in y_1:

$$\frac{d\pi(y_1)}{dy_1} = \frac{dp^d(y_1)}{dy_1} - \frac{dp^s(y_1)}{dy_1} < 0.$$

The convergence rule is $\pi_1(y_1)dy_1 \geq 0$, with equality achieved only when the two terms are identically zero. Note that the convergence rule is maintained if and only if the system is stable.

5. Results using duality.

The discussion in this volume is primarily related to resource allocation and technology choice. This has dictated the form of the analysis. Some results can be made more compact, however, by using duality theory. This has already been demonstrated above in the use made of the cost function and will also be used in subsequent chapters. Some of the discussion is therefore repeated here, in particular the characterization of the equilibrium conditions using duality.

Revenue functions In the discussion of the restricted demand in an open economy, a reference was made to $y(p)$, the value of output obtained as a result of the optimization on the supply side. This is in fact the value of the revenue function defined as

$$R(p, k, T) = \max_y (py; (y, k) \in T).$$

This definition introduces some new notation. The term py is the inner product $p_1 y_1 + p_2 y_2$, and recall that in the present discussion $p_1 = p$ and $p_2 = 1$. The expression $(y, k) \in T$ implies that we only consider vectors $y = (y_1, y_2)$ that can be produced with inputs k and technology T. Thus $R(p, k, T)$ indicates the maximum revenue attainable with (p, k, T).

In the present discussion outputs are expressed on a per capita basis, and the resources are summarized by the capital-labor ratio k. The definition of R is general in that k can be a vector of J inputs and y can be a vector of I outputs.

The revenue function is nondecreasing, convex, and linear homogeneous in p. By Hotelling's lemma, the partial derivatives are equal to the supply functions $R_p(p, k, T) = y(p, k, T)$. When it is understood that the technology is constant, there is no need to mention T explicitly in the argument of R. Similarly, when resources are fixed ("short run"), there is no need to include k in the argument. This has been the case in the foregoing discussion of supply. Nevertheless, at this point, where the properties of R are summarized, it is also useful to summarize its behavior in the inputs, and therefore k is mentioned here explicitly. Specifically, $R(p, k)$ behaves in k like a production function where R is a measure of output, known as a Hicks composite good. It is obtained by aggregating the outputs for a given price. R is nondecreasing and concave in k. The partial derivatives of R with respect to k give the factor (shadow) price: $R_k(p, k) = w$, where w here is the vector of the prices of the elements of k. In our particular case, k is the capital-labor ratio, and hence its price is $r/w = 1/\omega$. Note that we do not differentiate in the notation between vectors and scalars.

Demand Let $u(x)$ be a well-defined utility function of x. The uncompensated demand functions, written in vector notation, $x(p, y)$, are obtained from the solution to

$$\max_x [u(x); y \geq px].$$

Substituting $x(p, y)$ for x in $u(x)$ gives the indirect utility function, which indicates the maximum level of utility that can be attained at (p, y):

$$v(p, y) = u[x(p, y)].$$

The compensated demand function, $h(p, u)$, is obtained as a solution to

$$\min_x [px; u(x) \geq u].$$

Substituting $h(p, u)$ in the budget constraint gives the expenditure function, indicating the minimum cost that has to be paid for achieving u at price p:

$$e(p, u) = ph(p, u).$$

The expenditure function is nondecreasing in p, linear homogeneous in p, concave in p, continuous in p with all prices strictly positive and

$$e_p(p, u) = h(p, u).$$

Since $e(p, u)$ is linear homogeneous in p, $h(p, u)$ is homogeneous of degree 0 in p, implying

$$ph_p(p, u) = 0.$$

The equivalence of the maximum and minimum optimization setups produces the following identities:

$$x(p, y) = h[p, v(p, y)]$$

$$h(p, u) = x[p, e(p, u)].$$

Differentiation of the latter gives the Slutsky equation

$$\frac{\partial h_i}{\partial p_j} = \frac{\partial x_i}{\partial p_j} + x_j \frac{\partial x_i}{\partial y},$$

which can be written in terms of elasticities:

$$e_{ij} = E_{ij} + \pi_j E_{ic},$$

where

$$e_{ij} = \partial \ln h_i / \partial \ln p_j,\ E_{ij} = \partial \ln x_i / \partial \ln p_j,\ e_{iy} = \partial \ln x_i / \partial \ln y,$$

$$\text{and } \pi_j = p_j x_j / y.$$

Equilibrium We can now restate the equilibrium conditions. The equality of income and consumption can be expressed as the equality of the values of the revenue and expenditure functions.

$$R(p, k) = e(p, u).$$

This equality yields the solution u^o conditional on k and p. In the closed economy p is determined by

$$R_p(p, k) = e_p(p, u).$$

Given the solution, p^o and u^o, $e_p(p^o, u^o)$ and $R_p(p^o, k)$ indicate the equilibrium values of consumption (x_i^o) and production (y_i^o) respectively. By construction, $y_i^o = x_i^o$. In the small open economy, p^o is given, and $R_p(p^o, k) - e_p(p, u^o)$ is the vector of net exports.

Exercises

2.1 Draw the four-panel production diagram for the case where agriculture (sector 1) is capital intensive. Mark the limiting values for ω, p, and y_i wherever applicable. Summarize in words the qualitative changes that occur in each of the panels due to the change in factor intensity of agriculture from labor to capital intensive.

2.2 Draw a modified panel III where the vertical axis is the ratio y_1/y_2. Do it for the two possibilities of factor intensities.

2.3 Draw another modified panel III where now the horizontal axis is the wage-rental ratio (ω). Do it for the two possibilities of factor intensities. How does it compare with the previous results?

2.4 Draw a two-panel diagram with ω on the common vertical axis. The horizontal axis of the right panel is w, and that of the left panel is r. Show all the boundary points. Is this diagram affected by the factor intensity assumption?

2.5 Draw a four-panel production diagram where the excess demand replaces the supply and the restricted demand in panel III.

2.6 Add to 2.5 another panel (V) underneath panel IV, with the vertical axis denoting the unit profit, $\pi = (p^d - p^s)$. Draw the unit profit against y_2. Indicate the equilibrium point.

2.7 Derive graphically the restricted demand curve for an open economy when the world price is allowed to be outside the range of admissible domestic prices, that is, $\overline{p} < p^*$, or $p^* < p$.

2.8 Show that the factor measure of factor intensity, $k_1(\omega) < k_2(\omega)$ is equivalent to $\rho < \ell$ where $\rho = K_1/K$ and $\ell = L_1/L$.

2.9 Show that under the assumptions of the model the share of agriculture in total output (S_1) is bounded by its share in the labor force and in the capital stock $\rho < S_1 < \ell$. (Meaning: when agriculture is labor intensive, its share in the labor force is larger than its share in total output.)

2.10 To examine the relationship between factor intensity and factor-cost intensity, we aggregate land and capital in the sense that all nonwage income is considered as capital income. Show that when factor prices are not equal across sectors,

$$S_1 = \delta_w S_L \ell + \delta_r (1 - S_L)\rho, \quad \text{where} \quad \delta_w = w_1/w \quad \text{and} \quad \delta_r = r_1/r.$$

2.11 Assume the following utility function:

$$u(x_1, x_2) = \frac{1}{\gamma}([\frac{1}{\alpha_1}(x_1^{\alpha_1} - 1) + a\frac{1}{\alpha_2}(x_2^{\alpha_2} - 1)]^{\gamma} - 1).$$

Solve the following problem: maximize $u(\cdot)$ subject to $p_1 x_1 + p_1 x_2 = c$. Use the first-order condition to derive the demand function

$$x_1 = \theta p^{-\sigma_D} x_2^{\eta}$$

and express the parameters in the demand in terms of the parameters of the utility function.

2.12 Use the revenue function to show how the supply side of the economy can be solved parametrically in terms of per capita value output.

3

An Evaluation of Policy Measures

Most countries implement agricultural policies. The motives behind them are not fully understood and probably are not unique. Moreover, economic policies are carried out toward other sectors as well, and as such the motives should be somewhat general. The actual policies are likely to reflect the political power of agriculture, which, as indicated in Chapter 1, may have something to do with the geographical spread of agriculture and the prevailing electoral system. Whatever the motives behind them, the policies cause distortions and have a welfare cost. This has been documented in various studies (Johnson, 1973, 1991; Cavallo and Mundlak, 1982; Binswanger and Scandizzo, 1983; Krueger, 1992; Schiff and Valdès, 1992; Tyers and Anderson, 1992; Bautista and Valdès, 1993; Hag Elamin and El Mak, 1995; among others). In general, it appears that countries tax the sector in which they have the comparative advantage. A related observation is that the protection of agriculture takes place largely in the more affluent countries, whereas the poorer countries tax agriculture. However, agriculture is affected not only by policies directed toward the sector, or sector-specific policies, but also by sector-neutral policies, such as macro policies. In fact, often the effect of such neutral policies on agriculture is stronger than that of the sector-specific policies.

In this chapter we take the first step toward evaluating the impact of economic policies. Policies are generally designed to affect prices or quantities directly; they thereby modify the equilibrium position of the economy and, as such, may affect the growth path of the economy. It is therefore instructive, even at this stage, to start discussing the impact of some typical policies.

A direct intervention in the pricing of agricultural products involves the introduction of a wedge between consumer and producer prices. In an open economy, taxes are also used to introduce a wedge between domestic and world prices and thereby affect agricultural prices indirectly. The results for closed and open economies may therefore be different. Specifically, a policy of maintaining low food prices favors agriculture in a closed economy. On the other hand, when an export tax is used to achieve low food prices in an open economy, agriculture is taxed. Another common set of policies affects the sectoral quantity balances directly. As an example, we examine here the effect of food aid. The two sets of policies, taxes and aid, are then used to take the first step in evaluating the effect of macro policy on agriculture through the analysis of the real rate of exchange.

The evaluation is greatly simplified by using a comparative statics analysis in which we are not concerned with expectations with respect to future changes in the tax rates and in which we hold resources and technology constant. This restriction is somewhat artificial. The discussion focuses on evaluating the effect of policies on resource allocation. As we shall see in subsequent discussion, changes in resource *allocation* require time. But, with time, the *quantity* of resources and the technology also change, and in part their change may be a response to the policies. In reality, therefore, we do not observe the kind of controlled experiment discussed here. Nevertheless, the gradual addition of new elements to the model is analytically convenient. Having said this, we shall see that the present model, as simple as it is, provides useful insight into the impact of commonly applied policies.

Two questions can be raised in this connection. First, to what extent does the analysis depend on an overly simplistic view of the world? Second, the discussion shows that the policies cause income loss, and as such they affect the income level; the question is whether they also affect growth. Later discussions in this volume will consider these questions.

Taxes and Subsidies

The simple economy discussed here does not include a government as an economic entity; some important policies can be analyzed within this framework by assuming that there is a costless mechanism to manage payment transfers between sectors or factors. This mechanism can be the design of the government. The important assumption made at this stage is that the government uses no resources for its activities and as such has no life of its own. It deals strictly with transfer programs. A direct consequence of this is that the income of the private sector is identical to total income, and when there are no savings, it is equal to its expenditure.

Food Subsidies: Closed Economy

Often agricultural policies emphasize low food prices. Here, we therefore use the terms *food* and *agriculture* interchangeably. Product subsidies generate discrepancies between demand and supply prices. The model is now modified to allow for such a wedge between the two prices:

$$p_i^d = p_i^s T_i; \quad T_i \equiv (1 + t_i). \tag{3.1}$$

A negative value for t_i implies a subsidy. In a closed economy a product can be subsidized only from the income generated in the economy, and therefore the subsidy is financed by some form of tax. Assume that the tax is collected on the sales of the unsubsidized product and let p represent the supply price. Then the income-expenditure identity, in per capita terms, becomes[1]

$$p_1 y_1 + p_2 y_2 \equiv p_1 T_1 x_1 + p_2 T_2 x_2. \tag{3.2}$$

This identity reflects the fact that government has no life of its own, that the economy is closed, and that domestic production is the only source of supply and domestic private consumption is the only utilization. In what follows, it is important to keep in mind that demand, x_i, is a function of p^d, whereas supply is determined by p^s. Consequently, the economy reaches an equilibrium, subject to (3.1), when

$$y_i(p^s) = x_i(p^d). \tag{3.3}$$

Imposing the equilibrium condition on the identity in (3.2) reduces to $p_1 t_1 x_1 + p_2 t_2 x_2 \equiv 0$, which implies that the product $t_1 t_2$ is either negative or both terms are identically zero. This means that the subsidy to agriculture is financed by a tax on nonagriculture. To examine the effect of the subsidy on the equilibrium position, write

$$p^d = \frac{p_1 T_1}{p_2 T_2} = p^s T, \quad T \equiv \frac{(1 + t_1)}{(1 + t_2)} \equiv 1 + t. \tag{3.4}$$

Note that the product tt_1 is nonnegative, and is zero only if both terms are zero.[2]

For any p, under the rule of convergence, $(x_1(Tp) - y_1(p))dp \geq 0$, with equality holding only in equilibrium. When not in equilibrium and $T < 1$, the price increases to reach an equilibrium price, p_E, bounded by $p < p_E < p/T$. The proof of the upper bound is left for the reader. More generally, $(T - 1)dp \leq 0$. Once the change in p is determined, the change in the rest of the system is determined accordingly.

We now study the changes in the system graphically. The equilibrium solution is shown in the right panel of Figure 3.1. Point A is the initial equilibrium with $t = 0$. Introducing a subsidy to agriculture implies that T is

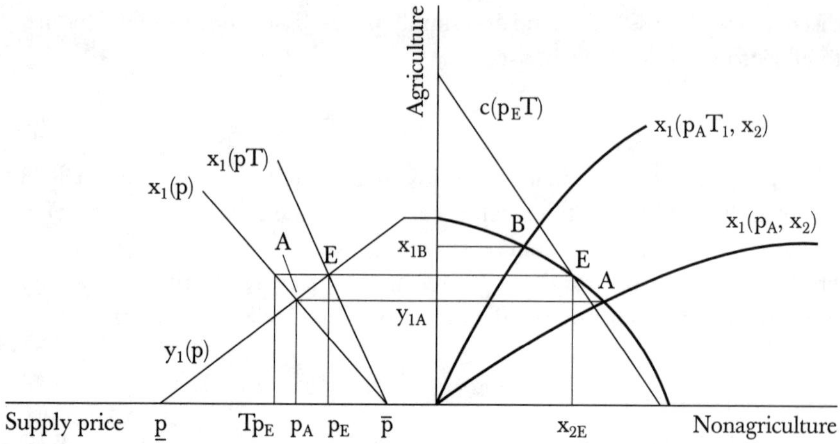

Figure 3.1 Food subsidy: Closed economy

less than 1, and the demand for agriculture $x_1(p_A T, x_2)$ rotates and intersects the transformation curve at B. Hence, at p_A there is an excess demand: $x_{1B} - y_{1A}$, and an equilibrium is reached at E, located between A and B, where $x_1(p_E T, x_{2E}) = y_1(p_E)$.

The effect of the subsidy on consumption consists of substitution and income components. The substitution effect favors the consumption of the subsidized product at the expense of the taxed product. The income effect calls for a reduction in the consumption of both products. The net effect is a reduction in the consumption, and therefore the production, of the taxed product. Because the economy is producing on the efficiency frontier, this implies an expansion of the subsidized product. The solution is also illustrated in the left panel of Figure 3.1, where the horizontal axis represents the *supply* price. When the *demand* is plotted against the *supply* price, as is the case for the restricted demand in Figure 3.1, the change is represented by a rotation of the demand curve with the point of specialization in agriculture remaining unchanged.

PROPERTY 3.1 (product market) In a closed economy, a subsidy to agriculture increases agricultural output and its supply price and decreases its demand price and the output of nonagriculture.

The tax scheme does not affect full employment or the competitive condition, and therefore the price and resource allocation functions are unaffected by it. Because consumers are utility maximizers, the new equilibrium point is on the production efficiency frontier. However, the wedge between the demand and the supply prices causes a welfare loss. To illustrate this point, let $x_i(pT)$ be the value of the restricted demand, and evaluate the expenditure in terms of consumer prices:

$$c(pT) = x_1(pT)pT + x_2(pT). \tag{3.5}$$

The line $c(pT)$ drawn in the x_1, x_2 plane has a slope pT, and it therefore intersects the transformation curve at the point $y_i(p)$ where the slope is equal to p_E.

PROPERTY 3.2 (welfare loss) The gap between the demand and supply prices generates a welfare loss.

Welfare evaluation of taxes is broadly discussed (see Harberger, 1971). A simple evaluation of the loss is given below for the small open economy, which can be further generalized to the closed economy.

The demand price is the price producers obtain directly from the consumers. It declines due to the subsidy because part of the supply price is paid by the consumers indirectly, through the tax scheme. The rise in the supply price reflects the increase in the cost needed to attract resources to agriculture in order to produce the rise in food consumption induced by the subsidy. This rise in supply price is transferred to factor prices. The direction of the changes in factor prices depends on the factor-cost intensity. When agriculture is the labor-cost-intensive sector, this shift leads to an increase in the wage-rental ratio, in the sectoral capital-labor ratios, and therefore in the wage rate and to a decline in the return to capital. The wage rate measured in terms of food, referred to as food wage, w/p, increases as well. Nonagriculture being the taxed sector, its supply price $(1/p)$ and its output decline. If agriculture were capital-cost intensive, then the increase in p would result in a decrease in the wage-rental ratio and in the sectoral capital-labor ratios, which in turn would cause the real wage to decline and the real rental rate to increase.

An alternative way to view the changes in the factor markets is to note that the subsidy also affects the factor demands and thereby their prices. Specifically, the subsidy increases the output of the subsidized sector and thereby increases the demand for the factor that is used intensively in this sector. Similarly, it decreases the output of the taxed sector and thereby the demand for the factor used intensively in that sector. Consequently, the price of the factor in which the subsidized product is cost intensive increases and that of the other factor declines. For instance, when agriculture is labor-cost intensive, the subsidy to agriculture increases the wage rate and decreases the rental rate.

PROPERTY 3.3 (factor market) A subsidy to agriculture raises the price of the factor that is used more intensively by agriculture.

The strength of the tax effects depends on the demand and supply elasticities. In terms of Figure 3.1, the degree of the rotation of the demand curve in the left panel depends on the demand elasticity. When the elasticity is small, the rotation will be small, and point B will be close to point A. This implies that there is little response to the subsidy by the quantity demanded. The net effect also depends on the supply elasticity.

The problem can be stated in a form familiar from partial equilibrium analysis. Differentiating (3.3) logarithmically with respect to T, subject to (3.4), yields[3]

$$\hat{p}/\hat{T} = \epsilon_{ld}/(\epsilon_{ls} - \epsilon_{ld}), \tag{3.6}$$

where ϵ_{ld} is the price elasticity of the restricted demand and ϵ_{ls} is the supply elasticity of $y_1(p)$. Since $\epsilon_{ld} < 0$, $\epsilon_{ls} > 0$, the expression is negative. The absolute value of (3.6) is less than 1, indicating that only part of the subsidy is transmitted to the supply price. Hence, $-1 < \hat{p}/\hat{T} < 0$. This result can be shown in terms of the left panel of Figure 3.1, where the new equilibrium supply price is p_E, the corresponding demand price is Tp_E, and the initial equilibrium price, p_A, is in the interval (Tp_E, p_E), whose length is determined by the size of the subsidy. The exact location of p_A in this interval depends on the values of the supply and demand elasticities. When the demand elasticity is nil, the supply price will not change, and the subsidy will be absorbed by the consumers of agriculture. On the other hand, when the supply elasticity is small relative to the demand elasticity, the subsidy benefits mostly the producers of food.

Who gains from the subsidy? This is not a trivial question. In the present framework, by assumption, demand is identical for all consumers, and therefore differences in consumption reflect only differences in income. Because the income elasticity for agriculture is low, the low-income consumers spend a larger proportion of their budget on food, and therefore their benefit from the subsidy is larger than their share in the tax needed to finance the subsidy plus their share in the total decline in income due to the distortion. The situation is reversed for high-income consumers.[4]

The subsidy increases the supply price and the agricultural output; this is achieved by a resource shift into agriculture. Therefore there is a change in the set of agents that make up agriculture. Consequently, the gains of agriculture are shared with individuals who were previously in nonagriculture. In order to have a clear indication of sectoral gain, it is necessary to have a sector-specific factor. In the case of agriculture, this role is served by land. Following the discussion in Chapter 2, an increase in agricultural revenue will increase the rent on land. Under the assumptions made in Chapter 2, the rent is given by $R = (1 - \mu)py_1L/A$. Then, using (3.6) and the assumption of constant population and land, the elasticity of the rent with respect to T is

$$\begin{aligned}\hat{R}/\hat{T} &= \hat{p}/\hat{T} + \hat{y}_1/\hat{T} = (1 + \epsilon_{ls})\hat{p}/\hat{T} \\ &= \epsilon_{ld}(1 + \epsilon_{ls})/(\epsilon_{ls} - \epsilon_{ld}) \leq 0.\end{aligned} \tag{3.7}$$

PROPERTY 3.4 (agricultural gain) A subsidy to agriculture increases the rent on land and, as such, benefits the land owners.

The impact of the tax on rent depends on the supply and demand elasticities. The magnitude of the demand elasticity depends on whether or not the product is traded internationally. The magnitude of the supply elasticity, as we will see later on, depends on the length of the run. Therefore, it is instructive to evaluate the sensitivity of the impact to the magnitude of the elasticities. This is assigned as an exercise.

Food Subsidies: Small Open Economy

The open economy has two outlets for its product, domestic consumption and export, and two sources of supply, domestic production and import. Thus, in addition to the effect of the tax on domestic production and consumption, it also affects the trade pattern. Let x_i^c, x_i^e, and x_i^m be the per capita quantities of the ith product demanded, exported, and imported respectively. In the present discussion, we assume agriculture to be the exporting sector, and write the sectoral resource identities:

$$y_1 \equiv x_1^c + x_1^e, \quad y_2 \equiv x_2^c - x_2^m. \tag{3.8}$$

Let p^* be the world price, then trade is balanced when

$$p^* x_1^e - x_2^m = 0. \tag{3.9}$$

The analysis can be conducted conditional on any exogenously given level of trade deficit. The nature of the analysis is unaffected, but the results will depend on the level of the deficit. With zero trade deficit, the subsidy is financed domestically, and as for the closed economy, this leads to a price wedge: $p^d = Tp^s$, $T = (1 + t)$, with supply and demand given by $y_i(p^s)$ and $x_i(p^d)$

respectively. Equilibrium is achieved by imposing the zero deficit constraint as given in (3.9) above:

$$p^*[y_1(p^s) - x_1(p^d)] = [x_2(p^d) - y_2(p^s)]. \tag{3.10}$$

Rearrange (3.10) to obtain

$$p^*y_1(p^s) + y_2(p^s) = p^*x_1(p^d) + x_2(p^d) \tag{3.11}$$

or, more compactly, $y(p^*, p^s) = c(p^*, p^d)$, where $y(p^*, p^s)$ is the income generated by the production plan associated with p^s and evaluated in world prices, and similarly, $c(p^*, p^d)$ is the expenditure on the consumption plan corresponding to p^d and the budget constraint evaluated in world prices. By this definition, $y(p^*, p^*)$ is the value of the revenue function indicating the maximum attainable income evaluated in world prices under the given resources and technology. Therefore, when $p^s \neq p^*$ the tax generates a welfare loss. The reason for the loss is that producers optimize their production under domestic prices, whereas the value of their output is determined by world prices. Similarly, $c(p^d, p^d)$ is the value of the expenditure function indicating the least cost of purchasing utility level $u(x_i(p^d))$, and therefore when $p^d \neq p^*$, $c(p^d, p^d) \leq c(p^*, p^d)$.

The welfare loss has two sources: first, as for the closed economy, the inequality of domestic supply and demand prices, and second, the inequality of domestic and world prices, resulting in the budget constraint's being evaluated in terms of world prices while the consumers respond to domestic prices. The first is covered by Property 3.2, and the second will be discussed in the next section.

As an illustration, exercise 3.2 examines the case of $p^s \geq p^* \geq p^d$ and compares it with the alternative of no tax, so that domestic prices are equal to world prices. The outcome of this divergence from world prices is an increase in the supply and consumption of food and a decline in the consumption and production of nonfood.

Tariffs: Small Open Economy

Tariffs introduce a wedge between domestic and foreign prices. Countries impose tariffs for a variety of reasons; often they are used for maintaining domestic food prices below world prices. This is achieved by taxing agriculture rather than by subsidizing it, as in the case discussed above. A policy of low food prices has also been followed by developing countries in order to transfer resources from agriculture and thereby to promote industrial development.

In contrast, developed countries such as the United States or the European Community follow an opposite policy of protecting agriculture at the expense of nonagriculture.

We examine here the case of a tax on exports and a tariff on imports, at rates t_1 and t_2 respectively. The competitive forces will drive domestic prices to

$$p_i = T_i p_i^*, T_1 \equiv (1 - t_1), T_2 \equiv (1 + t_2) \quad \text{and} \quad p = Tp^*, T = T_1/T_2. \tag{3.12}$$

Producers and consumers respond to domestic rather than to world prices, and therefore the supply and the restricted demands are given by $y_i = y_i(p)$ and $x_i^c = x_i(p)$ respectively. That means that the effect of the tariff on resource allocation depends on T and not on the individual rates, T_i. This has an important consequence:

PROPERTY 3.5 (indirect taxation) Agriculture can be taxed either directly, $T_1 < 1$, or indirectly by protection of nonagriculture, $T_2 > 1$.

The income and consumption evaluated at world prices are

$$\begin{aligned} y(p^*, T) &\equiv p^* y_1(p) + y_2(p) \\ c(p^*, T) &\equiv p^* x_1^c(p) + x_2^c(p). \end{aligned} \tag{3.13}$$

Using the balanced trade constraint, we obtain $c(p^*, T) \equiv y(p^*, T)$, which is a special case of (3.11). Thus the level of consumption is determined by the income evaluated at world prices. This case is illustrated in Figure 3.2, where, given world prices, the production is at A and the consumption is at A^*. The taxation of agriculture causes production to change to B and consumption to C located on the income line $y(p^*, T)$ determined by the optimal production plan B. Obviously, the consumption possibilities represented by B are lower than those at A. The discussion is now summarized:

PROPERTY 3.6 (welfare loss) A wedge between world and domestic prices reduces the consumption possibilities of the economy.

The income loss due to the tax is given by

$$L(p^*, T) \equiv y(p^*, 1) - y(p^*, T). \tag{3.14}$$

The loss can be represented in terms of Figure 3.2 as the distance between the market lines that go through A and B. Because income is measured in terms of nonagriculture, the distance is measured horizontally, along the x-axis. We note that as T declines or, more generally, as the rate of distortion increases, the loss increases. Similarly, for $T > 1$, the loss increases with T. Thus the loss increases with the absolute value of the tax rate, $T - 1$ (see the appendix to this

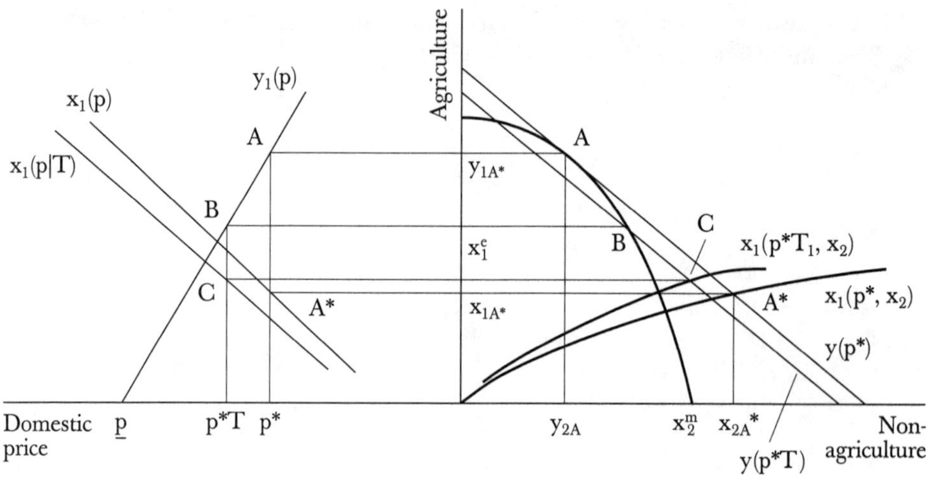

Figure 3.2 Export tax

chapter for details). Moreover, as can be seen in Figure 3.2, the loss increases at an increasing rate with the absolute value of $T - 1$. The proof is given in the appendix.

PROPERTY 3.7 (convexity of the welfare loss) The loss is a convex function of the distortion rate as given by the absolute value of $T - 1$.

We turn now to examine the effect of an export tax on trade when agriculture is the exporting sector, so that $T < 1$. In terms of Figure 3.2, $x_1(p^*T, x_2)$ rotates upward, and consumption is obtained at point C, where the demand intersects the budget line $y(p^*, T)$. The price effect of the tax is to increase agricultural consumption, whereas the income effect is in the opposite direction. For nonagriculture, or the protected sector, the price and income effects both cause consumption to decline while output increases; therefore imports decline. In order to maintain the zero trade deficit, the decline in imports implies a corresponding decline in exports.

The ratio of exports to output or, alternatively, of imports to consumption can serve as a measure of the openness of the economy. Consequently, we have

PROPERTY 3.8 (trade effect) A tax on exports reduces trade and leads to a closure of the economy.

It is also instructive to illustrate the tax effect in terms of the restricted demand curve, as shown in the left panel of Figure 3.2. Since we deal with an open economy, the restricted demand declines as a result of the welfare loss caused by the tax.

In conclusion, the effect of this scheme is to shift production in the direction of the protected industry, to reduce exports of the product in which the country has a comparative advantage, and to reduce overall consumption. Clearly, this has a cost. The justification for such programs is given in terms of favorable long-run effects on the protected industry. This argument cannot be supported either on preliminary considerations or by empirical findings. In fact, when we examine the dynamics that such programs generate, we find that they have a cumulative deteriorating effect (see Mundlak, Cavallo, and Domenech, 1989).

The foregoing analysis can of course be reversed to evaluate the consequences of trade liberalization, where the country reduces the absolute value of $(T - 1)$ and as such moves closer to world prices. In this case income and consumption, both evaluated in world prices, increase. Food consumption may increase or decrease depending on the strength of the income and substitution effects, whereas the consumption of nonagriculture will increase. Agricultural production will increase at the expense of nonagriculture, and consequently trade will increase.

Trade Restrictions

Countries often impose import restrictions in order to protect agriculture as well as other sectors. Such restrictions reduce trade and increase the output of the protected sector at the expense of the other sector. In Figure 3.2, the free trade production and consumption are given by A and A^* respectively. Assume that the imposed import restriction causes production to move to point B and consumption to C, the same points that were generated by the tax scheme discussed in the previous section. In this case, we can refer to the tax rate as the shadow price of the production or import quota. When nonagriculture is the protected industry, this scheme is equivalent to a direct taxation of agriculture. The consequences for resource allocation are therefore the same as discussed in the previous section.

The two schemes differ in their benefits. Tariffs are collected by the government and therefore can be distributed to the population. The benefits from quotas go only to the holders of the quotas. In theory, the quota can be auctioned by the government, but this is seldom practiced. There is another important reason for preferring tariffs to quotas; the tax rate is known, whereas the total damage of import restriction is not transparent and therefore does not obtain the appropriate consideration.

Taxing Factors of Production

We have seen that taxing products affects factor prices. Similarly, taxing factors of production affects product prices. Taxes on factors of production are applied for a variety of reasons. Taxation may have to do with the desire to affect income distribution directly through a tax on capital and a subsidy to labor. Conversely, it may be motivated by a desire to improve returns to capital in order to attract investment, in which case capital is subsidized at the expense of labor. It may also be motivated by the efficiency of collection. For instance, it may be easier to collect taxes on wages than on profits. In this section we consider schemes that apply uniform tax rates across sectors. Nonuniform rates generate intersectoral differences in factor prices, a case considered in Chapter 8.

Let t_w and t_r be the tax ($t > 0$) or subsidy ($t < 0$) rates on the wage and on the rental rate respectively. Labor and capital receive the observed market prices w and r respectively. The prices firms face, to be referred to as factor-cost prices, are wT_w and rT_r, where $T_w = 1 + t_w$ and $T_r = 1 + t_r$. The taxes affect the cost of production, and therefore in order to restore zero profits, the initial product prices have to change. To determine the implied change in p, write the cost functions, recalling that they are linear homogeneous in prices:

$$c_i(T_w w, T_r r) = T_r r\, c_i(\tau\omega), \quad \tau \equiv T_w/T_r.$$

We impose the zero profit restriction to obtain: $p(\tau\omega) = c_1(\tau\omega)/c_2(\tau\omega)$. The price function with factor tax included, $p(\tau\omega)$, is a generalization of $p(\omega)$. The value of $p(\tau\omega)$ is the supply price when the market-factor price ratio is ω and the tax rate is τ. The price function is differentiable, and with p being the price of the labor-cost-intensive sector, $p'(\tau\omega) > 0$. Hence, $\partial p(\tau\omega)/\partial\tau > 0$. Specifically, as τ increases, p increases accordingly. For any pair τ, ω we can find $T(\tau)$ such that

$$p(\tau\omega) \equiv T(\tau)p(\omega). \tag{3.15}$$

The function $T(\tau)$ is the (relative) product-tax equivalent of the (relative) factor tax rate τ. Under the factor-cost-intensity assumption, $T'(\tau) > 0$, and $T(1) = 1$. Hence, we derive

$$(\tau - 1)(T - 1) \geq 0, \tag{3.16}$$

with equality holding if and only if $T = \tau = 1$. For instance, a subsidy to labor will result in $\tau < 1$; therefore, by (3.16), $T < 1$, which means that such a subsidy reduces the supply price of the labor-intensive product.

PROPERTY 3.9 (product-factor tax equivalence) The supply price of the labor-cost-intensive product increases (decreases) with a relative tax (subsidy) on labor. Under equal factor intensities, the factor tax does not affect the product price.

This is the essence of the Stolper-Samuelson proposition. The relationship between the corresponding rates of change of T and τ can be derived by differentiating (3.15): $\hat{p}(\tau\omega) = \hat{T} + \hat{p}(\omega)$, or $\hat{T} = \hat{p}(\tau\omega) - \hat{p}(\omega)$, and using (2.16) to obtain

$$\hat{T} = I(\tau\omega)\hat{\tau} + [I(\tau\omega) - I(\omega)]\hat{\omega}, \tag{3.17}$$

where, recall, $I(\omega) \equiv S_{1L}(\omega) - S_{2L}(\omega)$. Thus the last term on the right is of second order of magnitude and can be neglected. The absolute value of $I(\omega)$ is less than 1, and hence the relative change of factor prices due to the tax is larger than the corresponding effect on product prices and conversely.

Once T is derived, the foregoing analysis of the product tax can be applied to determine the effect of a factor tax at a rate τ on the equilibrium position of the economy. With the introductoin of factor tax rate $\tau < 1$, the supply price of the labor-cost-intensive product declines so that this case is equivalent to that of a subsidy to the labor-cost-intensive sector illustrated in Figure 3.1. The outcome is an increase in the output and consumption of the labor-cost-intensive sector.

A detailed description of the effect of the factor tax on the economy is illustrated in Figure 3.3 for the case of $\tau < 1$. As a result of the factor tax, the supply price of the labor-cost-intensive sector declines, and when plotted against the market price, p, it is represented as a shift of supply from $p^s(y_1)$ to $Tp^s(y_1)$, as shown in panel III. Consequently, there is a new equilibrium at E where $y_{1E} > y_{1A}$ and $p_A > p_E$. Note that these are market, or demand, prices. The supply price, or the real price, of producing y_1, $|dy_2/dy_1|$, increases, since it is a positive monotone function of y_1.

Looking at the change in the labor market, we note that the initial allocation, $k_i(\omega)$, is not optimal under the new price with the tax, $\tau\omega$. Labor is now relatively cheaper, and firms will substitute labor for capital, but because the labor supply is fixed, there will be competition for the existing labor. As the labor-cost-intensive sector benefits more from the new prices, it is in a better position to bid away labor from the capital-cost-intensive sector. When labor

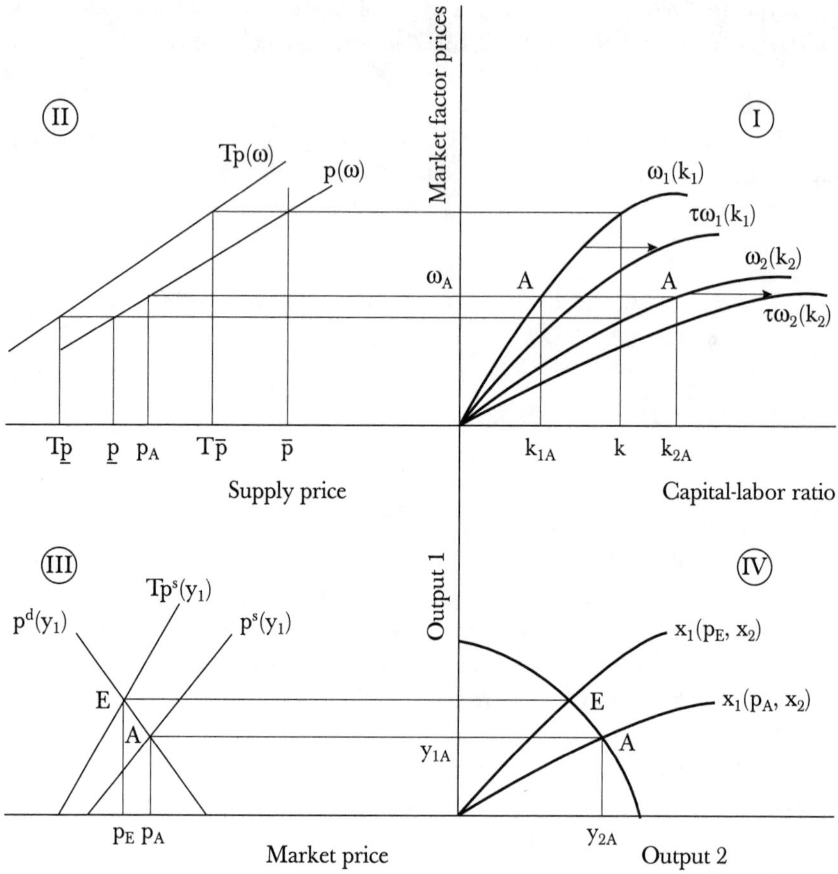

Figure 3.3 Factor tax: Closed economy

moves away from the capital-intensive sector, the capital-labor ratio in this sector increases rather than declines, as called for by the new price. To avoid it, this sector will also lose capital to the labor-intensive sector. This move is represented by a shift of the $k_i(\omega)$ functions, as shown in panel I. The corresponding shift in the price function in panel II reflects the fact that the market price of the labor-intensive product declines.

In a small open economy where the country is a price taker, $p(\tau\omega) = p^*$, where p^* is the world price; therefore $\tau\omega$ is constant, and the factor prices fully absorb the tax, $\hat{\tau} + \hat{\omega} = 0$. In this case, (3.17) yields exactly $\hat{T} = I(\omega)\hat{\tau}$. Thus the subsidy to labor will increase the supply of the labor-cost-intensive sector, and therefore its net export will increase. The final outcome of trade depends also on the demand, which declines due to the negative income effect of the tax.

The effect on rent is given above. In the case of the small open economy, the indirect tax on agriculture has its strongest effect on rent because the price does not change, and therefore it does not compensate in part for the change in supply.

Food Aid

One form of aid to developing countries is aid in food. Sometimes food is delivered as relief from a natural disaster such as drought. Often, however, the purpose is to help the development of the country, and yet food is treated as an entity by itself. For instance, public institutions calculate country needs for food aid. What is the criterion for such calculations and, more important, how does food aid differ from general aid, which provides the recipient country with resources without restricting their product composition? The answer is simple; there is no economic criterion for the calculation of country needs for food aid, and the attempt to present it as if there is does not contribute to the clarity of the public discussion on the merit of such aid. The restriction of the aid to food changes the supply of food in the recipient country and, thereby, causes a displacement in the initial equilibrium position. The resulting changes are different for closed and for open economies.

Closed Economy

Assume the food aid to be g units per capita and to have an equilibrium price, prior to the aid, of p_A. The aid generates an excess supply at the initial price, $y_1(p_A) + g - x_1(p_A) > 0$, and therefore the equilibrium price is forced to decline. It is worth emphasizing that in this framework, where the two goods are normal, it is impossible for p to increase. Normality implies that as income increases due to aid, the demand for both goods will increase and therefore part of the augmented income will be spent on nonfood. To finance this increase in the consumption of nonfood, it is necessary that some of the additional food be traded for nonfood, and this causes the price of food to decline.[5]

The decline in food price causes food production to decline, which in turn causes a shift of resources to nonfood and an increase in its output. On the other hand, the consumption of food increases, since its price is lower (substitution effect) and the consumption possibilities increase (income effect).

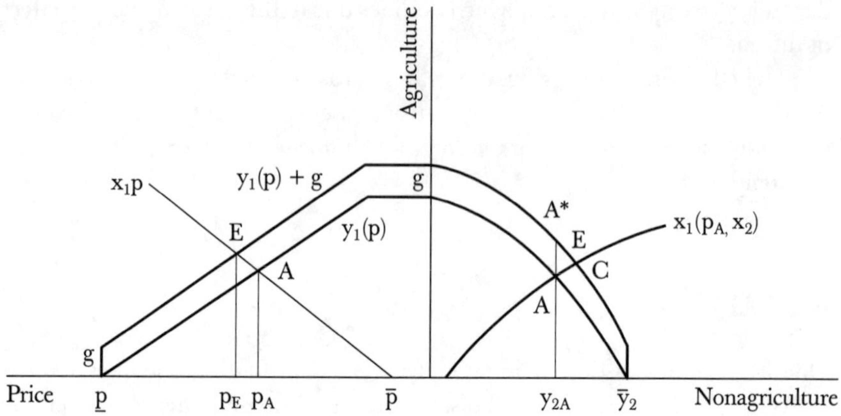

Figure 3.4 Food aid: Closed economy

This is illustrated in the right panel of Figure 3.4. Food aid generates a difference between the production and the consumption sets. The first is bounded by the transformation curve, whereas the second is bounded by the outer curve, which reflects the aid. Thus the difference between points A and A^* is g units of y_1, whereas the level of y_2 is the same at both points.

Because food aid does not affect the price equation, the output at price p_A is still given by point A, with $y_{iA} = y_i(p_A)$. At p_A the demand $x_1(p_A, x_2)$ is at C, and the supply is at A^*. Consequently, the equilibrium point E is obtained between A^* and C. The change in equilibrium is also illustrated in the left panel, where the restricted demand remains unchanged because $y_2(p)$ is unchanged. This is summarized:

PROPERTY 3.10 (food aid in a closed economy) Food aid increases the consumption of the two products and the production of nonfood. It induces a decline in food production and its price. As a result, the share of food income, py_1, in total income, $y = py_1 + y_2$, declines.

The effect on factor prices depends on factor-cost intensity. When food is labor-cost-intensive, a decline in p results in a decline in ω and a decline in k_i. Consequently the real wage rate declines, and the rate of return on capital increases. Thus, in this case, the food wage is expected to decline, contrary to statements often made that food aid increases the food wage.

The response of factor shares to the foregoing changes depends on the elasticities of substitution. It decreases (increases) the share of labor when the elasticities of substitution are smaller (larger) than one.

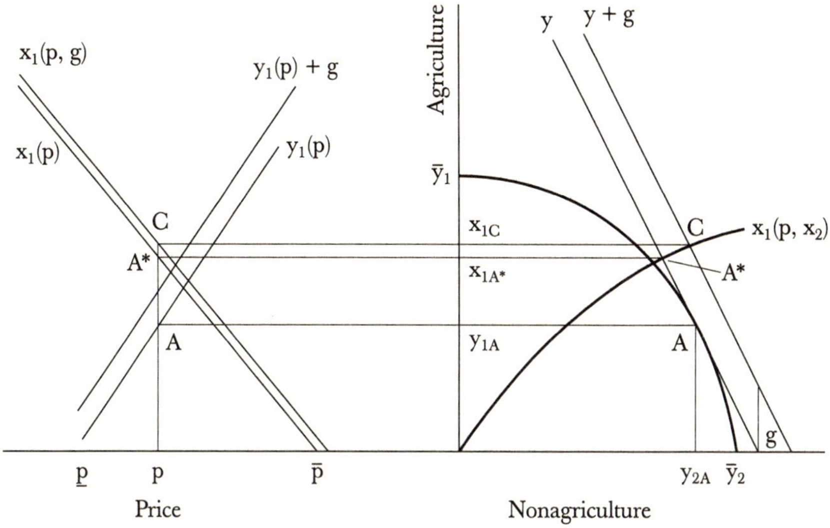

Figure 3.5 Food aid: Open economy

Small Open Economy

The country with a small open economy is a price taker, and it is assumed to be an importer of food at the going world prices. If the country is allowed to trade the aid in the world market, the aid becomes general aid, and the consumption possibilities are given by the market line with a constant price. In this case imports, net of aid, must decline.

This is shown in the right panel of Figure 3.5 where initially production is at A, consumption is at A^*, and food import is $x_{1A^*} - y_{1A}$. Under aid consumption moves to C, production is unchanged because p is constant, and the change in food consumption is $x_{1C} - x_{1A^*} < g$. Since the income elasticity of nonfood is greater than zero (actually greater than one), an increase in income by g units of food generates an increase in nonfood consumption. Consequently, the increase in the consumption of food is less than g. In fact, when the income elasticity of food is low, only a small fraction of g will constitute new consumption, and the remaining will result in a decline of imports.

The change caused by aid is also shown in the left panel of Figure 3.5, where the restricted demand function is shifted upward by the income effect of aid on the demand for food. This shift is smaller than the shift in the supply. Consequently, imports will decline.

To summarize, when prices are given, output is unaffected by the aid, and imports must decline. Under balanced trade such a decline in imports implies a decline in the export of nonfood. This is, of course, the mirror image of the increase of nonfood consumption while production remains constant. Thus we have:

PROPERTY 3.11 (food aid in a small open economy) Food aid to a food-importing country is likely to cause the country to substitute aid for trade.

Mixed Economy

Importing countries are not closed. Yet they are often not completely open; they may have various restrictions on trade. In general, such restrictions result in a lower domestic price for food compared with that in the world market. Therefore, the foregoing analysis needs to be generalized. The pertinent part of the system is

$$\begin{aligned} x_1^m(Tp^*, g) &= x_1^c(\underset{-}{Tp^*}, \underset{+}{y+g}) - [y_1(\underset{+}{Tp^*}) + g] \\ x_2^e(Tp^*, g) &= y_2(\underset{-}{Tp^*}) - x_2^c(\underset{+}{Tp^*}, \underset{+}{y+g}) \\ p^* x_1^m &= x_2^e, \end{aligned} \tag{3.18}$$

where y is per capita income, and T is the wedge between world and domestic price. In the closed economy the traded quantities are zero, whereas in the open economy, $T = 1$. In the mixed economy, before the aid, $g = 0$ and $T = 1$.

Food aid of g units per capita generates an income effect on demand and increases the supply of food, thereby affecting the traded quantities. The system reaches equilibrium with the aid by a combination of a decline in the domestic price ($T < 1$) and a decline of the nonaid import of food. In principle, maintaining lower food prices increases the excess demand for food and thereby increases the demand for imports. For a recipient country, this also increases the demand for aid, but it is unrealistic to assume that aid will fill growing gaps forever. The alternative is then to develop domestic production, but this possibility is not well served by low price levels. Thus, at some point, prices will have to be realigned with world prices.

The Donor Country

Donor countries of food must be surplus producers of food. Otherwise, the form of aid would not be restrictive. What is the particular advantage of giving aid in the form of food? From the perspective of the collective of all food donors, giving aid in terms of food, rather than general aid, is desirable if it increases the overall demand for food. This requires a decline in food prices in the recipient countries. Maintaining food prices below world prices requires imposing a tax on agriculture. This tax is explicit if the country maintains a free-trade policy, or implicit if the country imposes quantitative barriers to trade and as such is considered a closed economy. In both cases, this implies distortion, and thus the good intentions of aid impose some cost on the recipient countries. The efficiency, or rather the lack of it, of food aid from the point of view of the United States was initially discussed by Schultz (1960).

Sector-Neutral Policies and Agriculture

The programs discussed above are sector specific in that they affect the price or quantity of a sector directly and thus affect the income generated in the sector. However, sectoral income is also affected by sector-neutral programs, the most important of which are macro policies. The importance of macro policies for U.S. agriculture was recognized by Schuh (1974), who argued that the overvalued U.S. dollar depressed U.S. agricultural prices. The subject is also discussed by Chambers and Just (1981), Cavallo and Mundlak (1982), Longmire and Morey (1983), Rausser et al. (1986), Snape (1989), Mundlak, Cavallo, and Domenech (1990b), and in other studies cited below.

Macro policies affect domestic prices and thereby the opportunities facing producers. Commodities that are easily traded respond to this change in terms of quantities traded, whereas the others have to respond entirely in terms of domestic production and consumption. This phenomenon is related to the ability of a sector to adjust through trade and is not specific to agriculture. Because different sectors vary in this ability, they will be affected differently.

In what follows we examine the effect of the macro and trade environment on sectoral prices and quantities through their effect on the real exchange rate, a concept widely used. After the concept is introduced, we will analyze the dependence of the real exchange rate on supply and demand in the short run and its susceptibility to macro policies. The discussion of the real exchange rate continues in Chapters 4 and 5, where the impact of long-run changes is examined. Empirical aspects are introduced here and discussed in more detail in Chapter 15.

The Real Exchange Rate

Agriculture is a tradable commodity, and as such its price is affected by the rate of exchange. In order to examine such an effect we make, initially, the strong assumption that the domestic price of agriculture is $p_1 = p_1^* T_1 E$, where

p_1^* is the world price in dollars, T_1 is the tax, and E is the nominal rate of exchange which gives the price of one dollar (more generally, the price of foreign currency) in terms of domestic currency. The domestic product price ratio is $p = p_1^* T_1 E / p_2$. It is possible that nonagriculture is also tradable, and its price is $p_2^* E$. In this case, with no taxes, the domestic price ratio is the same as the world price, and a change in the exchange rate has no effect on the profitability of agriculture. In order for the exchange rate to matter, we have to assume that nonagriculture is not tradable. In this case this framework is not very meaningful, though, because if there are only two products and one is not traded, the second product will not be traded either. This is the only way to maintain balanced trade. Hence, in order to examine the impact of the exchange rate on agriculture, it is necessary to add at least one more sector into the analysis. Let the three sectors be named x, m, and h for the exporting, importing, and home (or nontradable) sectors respectively.

Even though we now have three sectors, we can still use the two-sector structure to analyze issues related to the competition between the tradable and nontradable sectors. Specifically, this allows us to discuss the impact of macro policies, and this is where we begin. This discussion will be followed by the explicit introduction of a third sector in order to discuss the impact of the world terms of trade and trade policies, which affect the competitive positions of the exportables and importables.

To force the discussion to the two-sector framework, we hold the world terms of trade, p_x^*/p_m^*, constant. This assumption allows us to treat the two traded sectors as a Hicks's composite sector and collapse the analysis to the two-sector framework.[6] The output of the tradable sector is the composite output of the importable and exportable sectors. A similar interpretation applies to demand. If p_T^* is the world price of the aggregated tradable product, and T the corresponding tax, then $p_T = p_T^* TE$ is the domestic price, and p_h the price of the home product. The domestic price ratio of the tradable to the home product is $p = p_T^* TE / p_h = p_T^* e$, where $e \equiv TE / p_h$ is the real exchange rate (RE). It measures the price of the tradable good in terms of the home good, after allowing for changes in world prices. Often, the term *real exchange rate* is applied to p rather than to e. From the point of view of the current analysis, either term is applicable because the adjustment from one to another is mechanical and does not affect the analysis. We will use both versions, and the context will identify which version is used.

Presumably, the definition shows how the nominal exchange rate, E, can affect the price of the tradable product. However, matters are not that simple in that a change in E affects both supply and demand, and consequently it affects p_h. It is for this reason that the analysis of exchange rate is conducted in terms of the real rate.

The problem has now been framed within the two-sector model, and the real exchange rate is viewed as the clearing price in the domestic market, where the tradable product is traded for the nontradable product. Thus, even though the economy is open, the supply of nontradable goods can only be produced domestically. In this sense, the economy behaves as if it were a closed economy, and the analysis of the real exchange rate can be carried out within our closed economy framework. In order to suppress at this point the effect of world prices, we set $p_T^* = 1$ so that $e = p$. Changes in the supply or demand of the two products will cause a change in e.

This model constitutes a major extension of our analysis because p_h is affected not only by E but by other macro policies as well, and this subject cannot be fully discussed within a static framework. This discussion will therefore allude heuristically to dynamic effects. The purpose of conducting the analysis in such an incomplete form is that it still allows us to capture some of the main effects of policies without extending the discussion. In so doing, it should be noted that in this analysis, the magnitude of the change in p depends on the difference in factor-cost intensity. In the limiting case when there is no difference in factor-cost intensity of the two sectors, the prices will remain unchanged.

Trade Account

A deviation from balanced trade affects the supply of the tradable product and thereby the equilibrium price. A deficit in the trade account implies an excess supply of the tradable good at the going price p, and therefore the price must decline in order for the market to clear. This case is analogous to the food aid discussed above, and we can use Figure 3.4 for illustration. We assume that there is a per capita net import of g units, and this causes a decline of RE from p_A to p_E.

The form of financing the deficit generates dynamic effects. If the deficit is generated by aid or other unilateral transfers, this is the end of the discussion. If, however, the deficit is financed by loans, it will eventually have to be repaid. Servicing the debt will reduce the supply of the tradable product in the future and thereby should eventually have an opposite effect to that of the deficit; namely, RE will have to increase. This discussion is very schematic and as such ignores various implications of such pending debts.

Government Expenditures

The analysis is extended by assuming that the government now becomes an entity with its own demand function for the two products. The effect of this extension on the economy depends on three important aspects: the product composition of government expenditures, the substitution in consumption of government and private expenditures, and finally, how the government finances its activity.

With government, the aggregate demand consists now of two components, private and government (or public). The composition of government demand is likely to differ from that of the private sector. In general governments use a lower proportion of the traded good compared with the private sector. Therefore increasing the share of government in total demand will increase the demand for the home good, increase its price, and lower RE.

The strength of this effect depends on the substitution between private and government expenditures. In part, the public good consists of services, such as education, health, or infrastructure, which are close substitutes to similar services that could be provided by the private sector. In this case, an increase in the expenditure of the public sector reduces the expenditure of the private sector. However, governments do not limit their activities to the production of public goods desired by the private sector. Often a large component of government expenditures generates services that do not substitute for private demand. Why would governments produce services that are not demanded by consumers? The answer is not unique, and it is related to the nature of the political process. This subject is beyond the scope of the present discussion, and therefore only a short comment is made on it below.

More formally, we now extend the utility function to include government expenditure of g units per capita. For simplicity, it is assumed that the utility function is weakly separable, so that the marginal rate of substitution of x_1 for x_2 is independent of g: $u = u(B(x_1, x_2), g)$. Consequently, the private demand, $x_1(p, x_2)$, is independent of g.

In order to analyze the effect of g on RE, assume that it is financed by a uniform tax that does not affect relative prices. Thus the new equilibrium position will depend on the composition of g. To simplify matters, assume that g consists exclusively of the nontradable product, and that the demand for the tradable product comes exclusively from the private sector. The sectoral balances can then be written as $x_1 \equiv y_1, x_2 + g \equiv y_2$. Consequently the demand for the tradable good is written as $x_1 = x_1(p, y_2 - g)$. An increase in g reduces the amount of the nontradable product available for households. Because of the positive relationship between x_1 and x_2, this causes a decrease in the demand for the tradable product, and therefore its price should decline. Thus,

$$\frac{\partial x_1}{\partial g} = \frac{\partial x_1}{\partial x_2} \frac{dx_2}{d(y_2 - g)} \frac{d(y_2 - g)}{dg} < 0.$$

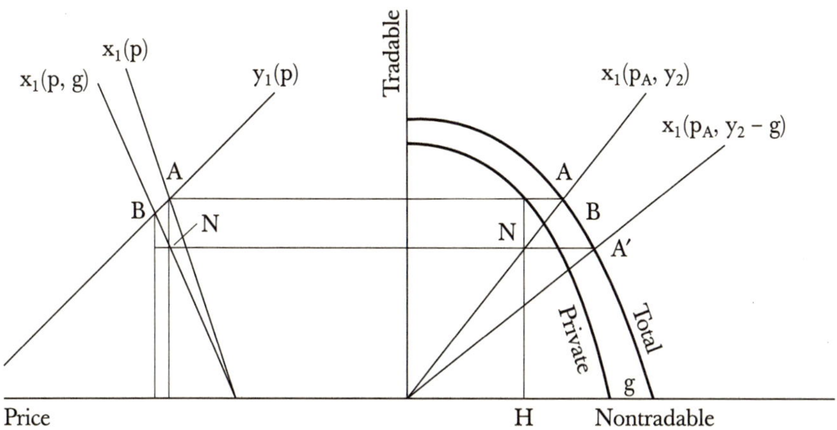

Figure 3.6 The real exchange rate

The effect of government is illustrated in Figure 3.6, where the appearance of government changes the demand in favor of the nontradable good. For any output of the nontradable good, y_2, the supply to the private sector is $y_2 - g$. For this supply to be absorbed at price p_A, the demand for the tradable good is $x_1(p_A, y_2 - g) < x_1(p_A, y_2)$. The demand now intersects the transformation curve at A' instead of at A, the initial equilibrium with $g = 0$. This rotation generates an excess supply of the tradable product, and a new equilibrium is achieved at B with $p_B < p_A$, indicating a lower real exchange rate.

The analysis can also be carried out in terms of the market for goods for the private sector. The diversion of g units of y_2 away from private consumption can be represented as a horizontal shift of the transformation curve. At p_A production is at A, but the quantity of the nontradable product available for private consumption is given by H. Consequently the quantity demanded of the tradable product is reduced to N, which constitutes a point on the restricted demand of the private sector. Thus there is an excess supply of the tradable good, and its price declines. The private demand curve $x_1(p, x_2)$ rotates to the left until a new equilibrium is reached. The output of the tradable good at the new equilibrium is above N. The total consumption of the nontradable good in the economy increases, but part of this consumption, g, is produced for the public sector, whereas the private production of the nontradable product declines.

The analysis in terms of the restricted demand is similar in nature. The restricted demand for the tradable product by the private sector is $x_1(p, g)$. Because some of the nontradable product is consumed by the public sector, it is taken away from the private sector, and this causes the function to rotate to the left. Since, by assumption, the government does not consume the tradable good, the supply to the private sector is given by the aggregate supply function $y_1(p)$, and as such is unaffected by g. Consequently reducing the demand for the tradable good, which is produced with a constant supply function, causes the price to decline.

To be sure, the outcome depends on the product composition of government demand. Hypothetically, if g consisted largely of the tradable product instead of the nontradable one, the real exchange rate would have risen with g. In general, the public sector uses mainly the nontradable good, and thereby, as shown above, it suppresses the real rate of exchange. This change is associated with lower production of the tradable good. Because agriculture is a component of the tradable sector, it suffers from such a change. The exact impact on the composition of the tradable sector requires more information, but this is not important for our present discussion.

Method of Finance

The outcome also depends on the method used by the government to finance its expenditures. If the government conducts a balanced budget, it must tax the private sector to the extent of its expenditure, and the foregoing analysis applies. The effect of a uniform tax was discussed above. The effect of a nonuniform tax can be analyzed by first considering a uniform tax and then applying a different tax scheme.

When the government runs a deficit, the method of financing the deficit also affects RE and the speed at which it changes. If the deficit is financed by borrowing from abroad, this leads to a deficit in the current account, and as we have seen, this has a suppressing effect on RE. In this case the government expenditure increases the demand for the nontradable good, whereas the finance of the expenditure increases the supply of the tradable good. Alternatively, the government can borrow domestically. Since, however, the economy is assumed to be open, borrowing domestically will cause interest rates to increase above the world level and thereby induce an inflow of foreign capital, which presses the interest rates back to their initial level. This method is therefore very similar to borrowing from abroad.

Thus far the discussion has dealt with a barter economy. To complete the discussion we also consider the use of money to finance the debt. We assume that prior to the formation of the debt, individuals had been holding the desired amount of money. The printing of money to finance the purchases of the government disturbs this equilibrium, and therefore individuals will exchange money for commodities in order to restore it. When the nominal exchange rate is fixed, the price of the tradable product is constant, and the expanded demand for the tradable good is met by an increase in net imports. On the other hand, an increase in supply of the nontradable good can be achieved only from domestic production, and this implies an increase in its price and consequently a decline in RE. The increase in net imports, or inflow of capital, generates a deficit in the current account and as such it is not sustainable. Thus, eventually, the country will have to take measures to control both the inflation and the trade deficit.

When the exchange rate is flexible, part of the response to the inflationary pressure generated by the monetization of the deficit will be to increase the nominal exchange rate. In this case the decline in RE should be smaller than under a fixed exchange rate regime. However, even if the exchange rate is completely free to vary, the real exchange rate will decline because the monetization facilitated a change in the composition of aggregate demand and in the equilibrium position of the economy.

The foregoing discussion abstracts from the effects that such changes in macro policies generate on expectations for inflation and future policies, which in turn affect the dynamics of the economy. This subject is beyond the scope of the present discussion. The main findings of the present discussion, however, prevail under a more complex environment. This assertion will be substantiated by empirical results to appear subsequently.

Factor Markets

The effect of the aforementioned measures on the product price is uniquely signed. On the other hand, the effect on factor prices depends on the factor-cost intensity. It is usually assumed that the home good is labor-cost intensive, in which case a decrease in the real exchange rate is associated with an increase in the wage-rental ratio.

Sometimes the real exchange rate declines by a reverse chain of events. Labor, and perhaps more specifically labor in the public sector, succeeds in increasing its wage rate without a corresponding change in productivity. This in turn increases the wage-rental ratio and causes a decline in RE.

Trade Policy

Trade policies here are defined as policies aimed at affecting trade directly through prices or through quantity restrictions. The full range of possibilities is covered by the discussion of the internal terms of trade below, whereas here we consider only a program that applies a uniform tax to the two tradable products. In this case, we can think of the real exchange rate as the supply price of the tradable good, and therefore the effect of the program on this rate is easily judged by its effect on the output composition. If the output of the tradable product increases, the real exchange rate increases accordingly. For instance, consider an incentive to the traded sector, to be financed by the nontradable sector. This will cause a shift of resources into the production of tradable goods and thereby an increase of the real exchange rate. This policy can be illustrated with the use of Figure 3.1, by identifying sectors 1 and 2 with the tradable and home sectors respectively. The demand price of the tradable product is $(1-t)p$, where p is the supply price. Consequently, the equilibrium p increases from p_A to p_E.

Internal Terms of Trade

We turn now to examine the internal terms of trade, for which we need to deal with the tradable sectors separately. The domestic price of a tradable product is $p_j = p_j^* T_j E$, $j = x, m$, where T is the tax. The domestic terms of trade are determined by the world terms of trade and by the trade policy: $p_x/p_m = (p_x^*/p_m^*)(T_x/T_m)$. Specifically, it is independent of the price of the home good. This is true only if the tradable sectors are homogeneous in the sense that they do not contain a component of the home good. Actually, this is not the case, but for now, it helps to sharpen the discussion to assume such homogeneity. On the other hand, a change in the terms of trade affects the domestic demand and supply of x and m. This causes a supply effect through the change in resource allocation and a demand effect through the substitution and income effects. Thus the terms of trade affect the price of the home good and thereby the real exchange rate, with the causality going one way.

To avoid sidetracking, we leave the details of the background analysis to Appendix 3A, where the excess demand function for the home good, $\Phi(p_x/p_h, p_m/p_h)$ is derived. We differentiate the excess demand at the equilibrium point, where its value is zero, and rearrange the terms to show the dependence of the real exchange rate on the terms of trade. The expression for the exportables is

$$d\ln(p_x/p_h) = \omega(d\ln p_x - d\ln p_m), \tag{3.19}$$

where here $\omega \equiv \Delta_m/(\Delta_m + \Delta_x)$, $\Delta_j \geq 0$ is the excess supply elasticity of the home good with respect to the price of the jth good. As such, ω measures the degree of substitution between the importables and the home good. Decompose the price to the two components, foreign terms of trade and the tax, assume ω to be locally constant, and integrate the equation to get

$$\ln(p_x/p_h) = a + \omega \ln(p_x^*/p_m^*) + \omega \ln T. \tag{3.20}$$

This is a measure of the real exchange rate in terms of exportables. A similar expression can be derived for importables:

$$\ln(p_m/p_h) = a - (1-\omega)\ln(p_x^*/p_m^*) - (1-\omega)\ln T. \tag{3.21}$$

Let $p_T \equiv (p_x)^b (p_m)^{1-b}$, and combine equations (3.20) and (3.21) to obtain the expression for the conventional measure, $p = p_T/p_h$, which can be thought of as an aggregate of the two measures:

$$\ln p = a - (1-b-\omega)\ln(P_x^*/P_m^*) + (1-b-\omega)\ln T_m - (1-b-\omega)\ln T_x. \tag{3.22}$$

When $b = 1$, the price of the tradables is the same as that of the exportables and p varies positively with the foreign terms of trade. The opposite is true when $b = 0$.

The message of equation (3.22) is that if foreign prices and trade policies are constant, then domestic prices will remain unchanged. This equation represents only the effect of the terms of trade on the real exchange rate. We also have to include the effect of the macro policies, which is additive, on the real exchange rate. Let s be the vector of the pertinent macro variables and ϵ be the vector of the corresponding elasticities, we can write the final form of the empirical equation:

$$\begin{aligned} \ln p = a - 1(1-b-\omega)\ln(P_x^*/P_m^*) + (1-b-\omega)\ln T_m \\ - (1-b-\omega)\ln T_x + \epsilon s. \end{aligned} \tag{3.23}$$

Tradability and Sectoral Prices

The tradable-nontradable dichotomy is a convenient analytic device, but its empirical application is not that simple. In a multi-product and multi-input economy with intermediate products, it is difficult to designate a sector which has no tradable inputs. In this case, a change in a given price, and specifically in the rate of exchange, affects all sectors. For instance, if housing requires imported inputs, then a change in import price affects the construction cost. On the other hand, tradable sectors have nontradable inputs. When buying

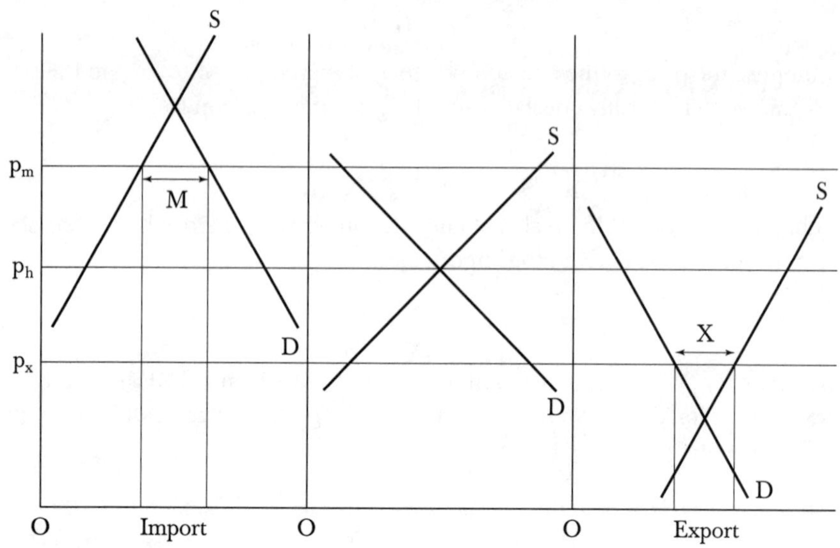

Figure 3.7 The product composition of agriculture: Trade orientation

a foreign car the consumer pays not only for the car but also for domestic services, such as the dealer's time and facilities.

Our interest in this model at this point is derived from our interest in the effect of policies on sectoral prices, where the sectoral definition depends on one's interest, and ours is the dichotomy of agriculture and nonagriculture. In reality, each of these sectors is an aggregate of many products, which can be grouped into importable, exportable, and home goods. This grouping is determined by the cost structure and demand as illustrated in Figure 3.7. A big spread between import and export prices creates a scope for the middle group of nontraded products. This spread reflects transportation costs, broadly defined, between countries as well as high distribution costs within the countries. The latter reflects the fact that agriculture is spread geographically throughout the country, and in many countries with poor infrastructure the costs are high. On top of this, taxes and similar programs affect the wedge between the border prices.

With such a decomposition, the aggregate sectoral price is determined by the prices of the individual components. We can think of this price as being the cost function of the aggregate product, so that the price of sector j is

$$P_j = \alpha_0 P_{xj}^{\alpha_1} P_{mj}^{\alpha_2} P_{hj}^{1-\alpha_1-\alpha_2},$$

where P_{xj}, P_{mj}, and P_{hj} are the domestic prices of the exportable, importable, and home goods respectively. Rearranging,

$$\frac{P_j}{P_{hj}} = \alpha_0 \left(\frac{P_{xj}}{P_{hj}}\right)^{\alpha_1} \left(\frac{P_{mj}}{P_{hj}}\right)^{\alpha_2}. \tag{3.24}$$

The ratio of the sectoral price to the price of the home good is expressed as a geometric-weighted average of the real exchange rate of exportable and importable goods respectively. The effect of the real exchange rate depends on the sum of the exponents, which provides us with a measure of the degree of tradability of the sector. Different sectors can be ranked according to their degree of tradability. The price of the more tradable sectors is more responsive to changes in the real exchange rate.

In principle, the sectoral price equation can be estimated. Countries publish data on the prices of exported and imported goods. The problem is with the nontraded good, because such a good does not exist in the form that it appears in the theory. Therefore, empirical analysis requires the use of substitutes. Empirical applications are discussed in Chapter 15.

On Openness and Agriculture

As we have seen, the response of an economy to changes in the economic environment depends on whether the economy is closed or open. Also, we have noted that even an open economy is closed to some extent in that not all products can be imported. When it comes to agriculture, Chapter 1 mentioned that for the world as a whole, only 10–12 percent of world production is traded internationally and that countries tend to meet changes in demand by local production. On the surface, it seems that by doing so, countries do not fully utilize their comparative advantage. To gain better insight into this issue, we need more structure, which requires a detour from the main course of the current discussion.

Most countries import some agricultural products, export others, while the bulk of products are not traded at all. The structure is described in Figure 3.7. As indicated above, the spread between import and export prices reflects the fact that agriculture is distributed geographically throughout the country, and in many countries with poor infrastructure, the costs are high. Taxes and similar programs affect the wedge between the border prices and as such contribute to the spread. On the face of it, all these considerations complicate the relationships between world and domestic prices. Indeed, as

Johnson (1973, 1991) observed, there are considerable differences among countries in the prices of agricultural commodities, which he took as a sign that world agriculture is in disarray. The fact of the matter is that there are considerable differences in the prices of other commodities as well. The relative difference in the prices of shirts between the streets of Bangkok and those in Europe or the United States is probably bigger than the relative difference between the price of Thai and Japanese rice. One can then extend Johnson's observation to other sectors. Thus agricultural policies or, more generally, trade policies are not the only culprit, and sometimes not the main one. Some of the cross-country differences can be traced to differences in factor prices.

All this has an important implication for our thinking about the dynamics of world agriculture. Under free trade, we can think of the world as being a closed economy, so that producers face a downward-sloping demand function that constrains production growth. The trend in world prices is determined by the relative growth in world demand and supply. But as indicated above, the bulk of agricultural production is consumed domestically and is not traded in the world market. Therefore, the question is to what extent are domestic prices influenced by world prices. This is of course an empirical question, and this is the way it should be answered.

The Law of One Price

The relationship between domestic and world prices is an old and well-investigated subject under the title of the *law of one price*. The idea is that, abstracting from the cost of transportation and taxes, trade should equate commodity prices across countries. As stated above, there are large price differences across countries which indicate that the law does not hold in practice. This is the static situation, but there is a dynamic aspect as well, which is related to the question of what happens to domestic prices if the world price changes. This turns our attention to price changes, and to avoid problems of units of measurement, we should examine *relative* price changes.

The subject is analyzed by Mundlak and Larson (1992) in reference to the (relative) law of one price, where the domestic price, P, is expressed as a product of the world price, P^*, the nominal exchange rate, E, and the tax policy $S = (1 + t)$. This formulation assumes that the product is homogeneous, so that the world and domestic prices refer to the same product, and that marketing margins and other nontradable inputs are ignored. This is an unrealistic assumption, and therefore a stochastic disturbance U is added. The domestic price of product i in year t is $P_{it} = P^*_{it}E_tS_{it}U_{it}$. If we rewrite it, with lowercase letters indicating logs, we have

$$p_{it} = p^*_{it} + e_t + s_{it} + u_{it}. \tag{3.25}$$

$$u \sim IID(\mu, \sigma^2); \quad E(eu) = E(su) = E(p^*u) = 0.$$

When the disturbance represents nontransitory shocks, its mean, μ, is not necessarily zero.

Two questions are of interest for our discussion. First, what proportion of the variations in world prices is transmitted to domestic prices? Second, what proportion of the variations in domestic prices can be attributed to variations in world prices? The answers to both questions are obtained, in principle, by estimating the following equation:

$$p_{it} = \alpha + \beta p^*_{it} + \gamma e_t + \epsilon_{it}. \tag{3.26}$$

The basic equation (3.25) can be expressed in terms of (3.26) subject to the restrictions $H_1 : \beta = 1$, $H_2 : \gamma = 1$. The coefficient β is the elasticity of the domestic price with respect to the world price, to be referred to as the elasticity of transmission. The value of this elasticity is the answer to the first question. A value of 1 implies that the variations in world prices are fully transmitted to the domestic prices, whereas a value of 0 implies no transmission at all. Why would this elasticity differ from unity? Several reasons can be offered. First, omitted variables, specifically s, are correlated with p^*. Second, there may be measurement errors in p^*. Such errors may reflect the fact that the world price used in a given study differs from the one pertinent for the particular country because prices relate to different qualities broadly interpreted. Third, if the economy is closed, the world price is irrelevant. Of course, very few countries are completely closed, but many countries are partially closed by means of trade policies, and this may affect the value of the estimate.

To answer the second question, note that the contribution of world prices, measured in domestic currencies, to the variations in p are given by the value of R^2 of the regression (3.26). A low value means that only a small proportion of the variations in domestic prices are accounted for by world prices and exchange rates, and the main sources of the variations are due to the other variables in question.

Various forms of equation (3.26) were estimated. By way of generalization, the deviation from unitary transmission elasticity is, on the whole, surprisingly small. Such deviation is in part due to policy measures and in part due to domestic inputs that are not necessarily synchronized with world agricultural prices. This does not imply that policies generated with respect to particular products are not important in affecting the prices of these products. They certainly affect the price levels, and whenever a country taxes agriculture, the domestic prices will differ from world prices. Consequently, there are cross-country variations of prices. However, such policies did not prevent domestic prices from moving along with world prices. Furthermore, the world price is the major contributor to variations in domestic prices.

What then is the role for domestic supply and demand? They determine the traded quantities of traded goods, and the prices of traded goods affect to a large extent the prices of the specific factors in agriculture and thereby the supply of nontraded goods. This is basically the mechanism of the factor-price equalization. For instance, depressed world prices affect land prices, agricultural wage rates through their effect on labor supply, and the price of quasi-fixed inputs. This spreads to all commodities.

To conclude, even though domestic policies affect prices, they cannot prevent the covariation of domestic prices with world prices in the long run and therefore do not change the direction of the developments called for by the fundamentals. There may be a simple reason for this. Price distortion is costly, and as we have seen, it increases at an increasing rate with the rate of taxation. Public resources, just like private resources, are finite, and therefore there is a limit to the intervention.

Appendix 3A

1. The loss function is increasing with the absolute value of the tax rate.

   We limit our interest here to efficient production plans (points on the transformation curve), in which case we can write y_2 as a function of y_1: $L(p^*, T) = y(p^*) - [p^* y_1(T) + y_2(y_1(T))]$. Then $dL/dT = -dy_1/dT[p^* + dy_2/dy_1]$. Recall that $-dy_2/dy_1 = p$, $p = Tp^*$, $dp/dT = p^*$. Then $(dy_1/dT) = p^* dy_1/dp$ and for $T \neq 1$ we have $dL/dT = (dy_1/dp)p^{*2}(T - 1)$, and sign $dL/dT = \text{sign}(T - 1)$.

2. The loss function is convex in the absolute value of the tax rate, $T - 1$.

   Label $y(T) = p^* y_1(T) + y_2(y_1(T))$ and note that p^* is held constant. Then we can suppress p^* and write $L(p^*, T) = y(1) - y(T)$. Note that $y(T)$ is a sum of concave functions in T. To see this, select $h = \lambda T + (1 - \lambda)$, $0 \leq \lambda \leq 1$, then following the proof in Chapter 2 of the concavity of the transformation curve, $y(h) \geq (1 - \lambda)y(1) + \lambda y(T)$ (see Appendix 2A). Thus, $y(T)$ is concave, and its negative is convex. As $y(1)$ is independent of T, $L(p^*, T)$ increases at an increasing rate as the absolute value of $T - 1$ increases.

3. The real exchange rate.

ASSUMPTIONS: We consider a small open economy, divided into three sectors, x, m, and h, with production functions $F_j(K_j, L_j)$. Assume that the nominal exchange rate is 1, then the world prices in local currency are p_x^* and p_m^*. The intensity assumption is $k_x(\omega) > k_m(\omega) > k_h(\omega)$, for any given ω.

Supply

Tradable

Prices: The wage-rental ratio is determined by price function $\omega^* = \omega(p_x^*/p_m^*)$.
Inputs: The capital-labor ratio is determined by $k_j^* = k_j(\omega^*)$. Let $L_T = L_x + L_m$; $\ell = L_x/L_T$. Let $k_T = \ell k_x^* + (1 - \ell)k_m^*$. Hence $k_x^* > k_T(\omega^*) > k_m^*$.
Factor prices: Determined at k_j^* from the production functions.
Output: $Y_x = L_T[\ell f_x(k_x^*)]$, $\quad Y_m = L_T[(1 - \ell) f_m(k_m^*)]$.
The output of the two tradable sectors is thus determined conditional on L_T.
Note that $p_x^* f_x(k_x^*) = w^* + r^*k_x^*$, and $p_m^* f_m(k_m^*) = w^* + r^*k_m^*$, Hence

$$p_T^* Y_T = L_T[w^* + r^* k_T^*] = w^* L_T + r^* K_T.$$

Nontradable

Given ω^*, the price ratio p_x^*/p_h^* is determined by the price function $\frac{p_x^*}{p_h^*} = \frac{p_x}{p_h}(\omega^*)$, but p_x^* is known, and thus p_h^* can be determined. The capital-labor ratio, $k_h^* = k_h(\omega^*)$, is constant, and value output is $p_h^* Y_h = L_h(w^* + r^* k_h^*)$. Because all the asterisked variables are determined by p_x^* and p_m^* we can summarize the supply side conditional on $L_h : Y_h(p_x^*, p_m^*, L_h)$.

Real exchange rate

Note that the supply of the T and h sectors is linear in their labor input. Consequently, the real exchange rate is constant. To see this, write the output differential:

$$p_T^* dY_T = w^* dL_T + r^* dK_T$$
$$p_h^* dY_h = w^* dL_h + r^* dK_h.$$

Under the resource constraints, $-dL_T = dL_h$ and $-dK_T = dK_h$, hence

$$p_h^* dY_h = -p_T^* dY_T,$$
$$-dY_h/dY_T = p_T^*/p_h^*.$$

This implies a constant real exchange rate, determined solely by the terms of trade, independently of demand. This is not a coincidence, because the supply does not reflect any attribute that distinguishes between the tradable and the nontradable sectors. To amend this, we have to introduce a specific factor to the production function of one or more of the sectors. But before that, we complete the discussion of this model by bringing in demand.

Demand

The composition of production is determined by the demand so as to meet the zero deficit condition. National income can be determined from the factor costs. The per capita output is

$$y^* = w^* + r^* k.$$

Sectoral per capita demand is given by $x_j(p_x^*/p_h^*, p_m^*/p_h^*, y^*, g) \equiv x_j^*$, where y^* is income (which reflects the technology and resources) and g is a parameter affecting the composition of demand, $\partial(x_h/x_T)/\partial g > 0$. Again, the asterisked values are determined by p_x^* and p_m^*. We can write for the total demand of nontradable,

$$X_h^* = X_h(p_x^*/p_h^*, p_m^*/p_h^*, Y^*, g).$$

Equilibrium

Let $(\cdot) \equiv (p_x^*/p_h^*, p_m^*/p_h^*, Y^*, g)$, then $\Phi(\cdot) = X_h(\cdot) - Y_h(p_x^*, p_m^*, L_h)$ is the excess demand for the home good. For equilibrium, set it equal to zero, solve for L_h, and with knowledge of L_h, the rest of the system is solved for. A change in g affects the composition of production but not the prices. The fulfillment of the budget constraint implies zero trade deficit.

Specific Factors

The introduction of a fixed factor makes the production function display decreasing returns to scale in K and L. Although any sector may have specific factors, the natural one for our discussion is the home-good sector because it is the specific factor that makes it nontradable.

To underline the importance of the specific factors, consider an increase in p_x^*. This causes a decline in ω^* (x is the capital-intensive sector), and consequently a rise in the real exchange rate. This change is consistent with the fact that resources will have to move to the exportable sector to facilitate the supply response there, and hence the relative price of x will increase. Now consider an extreme alternative, where the home good (h) is produced by only a specific factor, "land," whose supply is fixed, and the demand for h is a function of the income generated by the export sector. The rise in P_x^* will induce an increase in the demand for h and hence an increase in p_h, and thus a decline in the real exchange rate. This is in contrast to the above analysis. The time pattern of the response depends on the speed of the resource allocation, as dicussed subsequently.

Exercises

3.1 (Indirect taxation)
A subsidy to agriculture is financed by taxing sectoral income at the rate of $0 < t < 1$. The collected tax is distributed as a subsidy to agriculture. Show that this scheme amounts to taxing nonagriculture.

3.2 (Policy reform)
Assume a small two-sector open economy operating at world prices, p^*. Agriculture is the exporting sector.

(a) Write down the equations fully specifying the model describing this economy.
(b) Show graphically the initial position of the economy.

Under political pressure, the country is now subsidizing agriculture by setting $p^s > p^* > p^d$. The policy is financed by a lump sum tax of equal rate per capita.

(c) Using the specification in (a), where possible sign the effect of the policy on production, consumption, export, and income evaluated in terms of world prices.
(d) Illustrate graphically the changes examined in (c) above.

3.3 How does a subsidy to agriculture in a closed economy affect: (a) factor prices and (b) factor shares?

3.4 The response of rent to changes in the tax rate depends on the supply and demand elasticities. The magnitude of the demand elasticity depends on whether or not the product is traded internationally. The magnitude of the supply elasticity, as we will see later on, depends on the length of run. For this reason, it is of interest to evaluate the expression $\hat{R}/\hat{T}$ for the extreme values of the supply and demand elasticities. Do it for the following:

(a) Let $0 < \epsilon_{ls} < \infty$ and evaluate $\hat{R}/\hat{T}$ for $\epsilon_{ld} \to 0$ and for $\epsilon_{ld} \to -\infty$.

(b) Let $0 > \epsilon_{ld} > -\infty$ and evaluate $\hat{R}/\hat{T}$ for $\epsilon_{ls} \to 0$ and for $\epsilon_{ls} \to \infty$.

Interpret the results in terms of the impact on the price and output.

3.5 Modify the case discussed in Figure 3.2 to an import ban, so that the country is forced to change its output from A to a point of no trade. Evaluate:

(a) The effect on p and real factor prices.

(b) How does your answer to (a) depend on factor intensity?

(c) Indicate what tariff level would be required to achieve the same effect on the country.

3.6 Introduce land explicitly into the agricultural production function. How do the following policies affect the rent on land:

(a) Subsidy to agriculture in (1) a closed economy, (2) an open economy.

(b) Tax on wages in (1) a closed economy, (2) an open economy.

(c) Food aid in (1) a closed economy, (2) an open economy.

3.7 Suppose all the rent was taxed away and distributed as a lump sum. What effect would this tax have on the equilibrium position of the economy?

3.8 It has been argued that the elimination of protection of agriculture in the Common Market will improve world agricultural prices and thereby benefit less-developed countries (LDCs) that export food. Show how trade liberalization in a country that protects agriculture by imposing a tariff on imports will change the equilibrium position of this country and relate it to the foregoing argument.

3.9 If trade liberalization is to be accepted as a norm of behavior for all countries, exporting countries will be required to eliminate taxes on exports. What effect would this have on world agricultural prices?

4

The Consequences of Resource Changes

The output composition of the economy depends on resource endowment. Land-abundant countries are the main suppliers of cereals, and countries rich in labor and short on capital produce labor-intensive products. As such, differences in resource endowment explain cross-country differences in the composition of production. While the size of the country is fixed, its capital is not, and the growth process brings about changes in resources, thereby directly affecting the output composition. As we shall see in subsequent chapters, resources also affect the form and perhaps the pace of technical change, and thereby they affect the output composition indirectly.

Continuing the discussion of Chapter 2, note that the initial resource supply is represented by k alone. The question then is what effect does a change in k have on the economy. Because we are interested in growth, we concentrate on an increase in k, which we refer to as capital deepening. Of course, the consequences of a decline in k, or labor deepening, can be evaluated in a similar way. The direct consequence of a change in k is on supply, and this is taken up first. This is followed by the analysis of the long-run equilibrium, where the term "long run" in this context indicates that resources are allowed to change. Such a terminology serves as an analytic convenience of isolating effects rather than as a description of reality. It is artificial to isolate resource change from technological change. The analysis is subsequently extended to allow resources to change in response to changes in economic variables. Under such varying factor supply the transformation curve is modified. In the limiting case, when the supply of one of the factors is perfectly elastic, the transformation curve becomes a straight line, and the output composition is determined by demand. The size of the cultivated land is an economic variable. The supply of land in any country is given by the boundaries of the country. Yet not all the land is cultivated, and furthermore, there are variations in the area under cultivation over time. The last part of the chapter introduces a framework for analyzing the variations of the area under cultivation.

The Model

We rewrite some key equations developed in Chapter 2:

$$\ell(\omega, k) = \frac{k_2(\omega) - k}{k_2(\omega) - k_1(\omega)},$$

$$y_1(\omega, k) = \ell(\omega, k)[f_1(k_1(\omega))],$$

$$y_2(\omega, k) = (1 - \ell(\omega, k))[f_2(k_2(\omega))],$$

$$x_1 = D(p, x_2).$$

We then have equilibrium in a closed economy:

$$z_i(p) = x_i(p) - y_i(p) = 0,$$

and equilibrium in a small open economy:

$$px_1(p) + x_2(p) = py_1(p) + y_2(p).$$

Supply

Output Response

The main result here is due to Rybczynski (1955).

PROPERTY 4.1 (supply; expansion-pattern) An increase in the capital-labor ratio, holding p constant, increases the output of the capital-intensive sector and decreases the output of the labor-intensive sector.

This result follows immediately from equation (2.13). Under constant prices, $k_i(\omega)$ are also constant, and hence $\partial\ell(\omega, k)/\partial k < 0$. With constant k_i, a decline in ℓ implies a decline in $\rho = K_1/K$. With prices constant, the only way for the economy to absorb a larger capital-labor ratio is to increase the share of the capital-intensive sector in total resources. Consequently, the total employment of resources in the labor-intensive sector declines and so does its output. The opposite is true for the capital-intensive sector. This is all summarized by taking partial derivatives of (2.14) with respect to k. For sector 1 we have

$$\frac{\partial y_1(\omega, k)}{\partial k} = f_1[k_1(\omega)]\frac{\partial \ell(\omega, k)}{\partial k}.$$

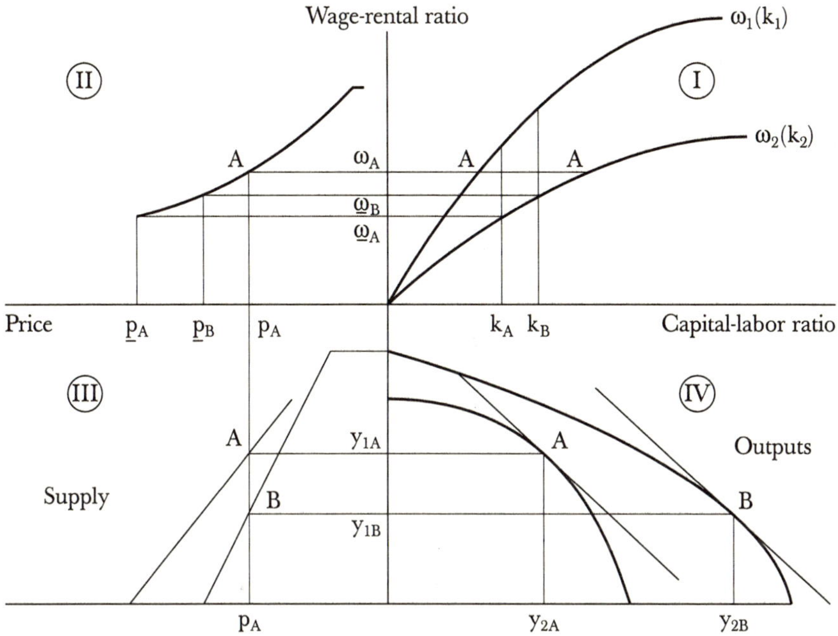

Figure 4.1 A supply shift due to a resource change

The last term is negative as ℓ is the labor share for the labor-intensive sector. A similar expression is obtained for sector 2 (the capital-intensive sector) with $(1 - \ell)$ replacing ℓ.

The changes just considered can be presented in terms of the shift of the transformation curve and the supply functions. In panel IV of Figure 4.1, the initial output corresponding to k_A and p_A is at A, and the output under $k_B > k_A$ and p_A is at B. The important thing to note is that B is in the southeast quadrant with respect to A. Panel III shows the corresponding shift in the supply from y_{1A} to y_{1B}. Thus, holding prices constant, the supply clearly depends on factor endowment.

Comparative Advantage: Hecksher-Ohlin

Basically, the foregoing discussion is a statement of the essence of the Hecksher-Ohlin theorem, which relates the trade pattern to the relative factor endowment. A "large" capital-labor ratio implies a "relatively large" production of the capital-intensive good and a "relatively small" production of the labor-intensive good. There are no absolute large or small quantities. The statement is comparative in nature, and it should be. The consequences for trade are drawn in reference to a simple world consisting of two countries that differ in relative resource endowment, employing the same technology. Trade results in a single world price faced by both countries. In this case the capital-abundant country exports the capital-intensive product and imports the labor-intensive product. Thus the capital-abundant country is said to have a comparative advantage in the production of the capital-intensive good. The orders of magnitude of the traded quantities depend of course on demand, but the discussion of demand can be postponed without affecting the nature of the argument. Originally, the concept of comparative advantage was developed by Ricardo to indicate differences in the costs of production due to differences in technology. We return to this below, but for now we note that the link between the two is related to the dependence of prices on resource endowment, which is taken up in the next section.

The dependence of supply on factor endowment can be applied to the evaluation of the growth pattern of a given country. As capital is accumulated, the country will increase the production of the output of the capital-intensive good. If the scope is broadened to include land, it is anticipated that land-abundant countries will tend to concentrate in the production of land-intensive products, such as grains. Indeed, countries with high land-labor ratios are big grain producers. Yet grain is also produced in countries with high labor-land ratios, such as India and China. India has turned from importing to self-sufficiency, even accumulating some surpluses. This achievement indicates that the foregoing considerations are not sufficient to guide us to the data. One of the reasons is that in this analysis it is assumed that the various countries use the same technology, but this need not be the case. The assumption of constant technology serves the purpose of isolating the effect of resource endowment on output composition and trade. However, it is always important to resist the temptation of identifying an assumption with evidence. Indeed, countries use different techniques in their production. In fact, we shall see later that the technology itself may depend on the resource endowment and that such a dependency affects the outcome.

Admissible Prices

Changes in resource endowment cause changes in the set of feasible prices. The nature of the shift is examined by observing the changes in the boundaries of the admissible prices. As a result of the monotonicity of the $\omega_i(k_i)$ functions and the full employment conditions, the boundaries of the admissible ω are monotonically increasing with k. If we assume that $\omega_i(k_i) \to \infty$ as $k_i \to \infty$, then for all $k > \bar{k}(\omega)$, ω is nonadmissible.[1] This means that under constant technology, capital deepening eventually forces any given wage-rental ratio to be too low to be admissible.

Capital deepening increases the wage relative to rental on capital, and consequently, the cost of production of the labor-intensive product increases relative to that of the capital-intensive product. Thus, in the process, any arbitrary price eventually becomes nonadmissible, and we have $\underline{p}(k) = p(\underline{\omega}(k))$, $\underline{p}'(k) > 0$.

PROPERTY 4.2 (admissible prices) Capital deepening raises the lower bound of the admissible wage-rental ratio and with it the lower bound of the admissible price of the labor-intensive product.

The dependence of prices on k is shown in panels I and II of Figure 4.1 for the change in the lower bound: $\underline{p}_B \equiv p[\underline{\omega}(k_B)] > \underline{p}_A \equiv p[\underline{\omega}(k_A)]$. Assume that initially the price is p_A, then there is a value of k, say $\bar{k}(p_A)$, such that for all $k > \bar{k}(p_A)$, p_A is inadmissible because $\underline{p}[k > \bar{k}(p_A)] > p_A$.

The price function $p(\omega)$ is invariant to changes in k that affect only its boundaries. To see this, recall that $d \ln p/d \ln \omega = S_{1L} - S_{2L}$, but $S_{iL}/1 - S_{iL} = \omega/k_i(\omega)$; hence S_{iL} is determined uniquely and independently of k. We can now relate the comparative advantage à la Hecksher-Ohlin with the cost of production by asking why the country moves to the Rybczynski point as k changes. Suppose that there is an increase in the capital-labor ratio, but the country tries, by inertia, to maintain a production pattern similar to the one prevailing prior to the change. The exact location of this point of inertia is purposely kept vague so that it can be applied to any point on the new transformation curve that lies in the northeast quadrant with respect to the initial point. All the points in the northeast quadrant are to the left of the Rybczynski point and therefore represent higher prices for the labor-intensive product compared with the initial ongoing world price. Thus even though this concept of comparative advantage is expressed in terms of resource endowment, it is rooted in the differences of costs of production. In the Hecksher-Ohlin framework, the cost of production associated with a given resource allocation changes because resources change.

As shown above, a change in k causes a change in output composition, a process that continues until $k = \bar{k}(p^*)$, at which point and beyond the country will specialize in the production of the capital-intensive good. This is the description of the product cycle that takes place in traded commodities when the price is determined in the world market. When a country is a price taker, as it accumulates capital, its production will shift from labor-intensive to capital-intensive products.

Summary

The summary of the supply conditions in Chapter 2 is now extended to cover the effect of resource change. For the labor-intensive sector we have

$$\underset{+\ -}{\ell(\omega, k)},\ \underset{+\ -}{\rho(\omega, k)},\ \underset{+\ -}{y_1(p, k)}.$$

The signs are permuted for the capital-intensive sector.

Accumulation and the Equilibrium Position

Small Open Economy

A change in resources produces a move from the initial equilibrium point to a new equilibrium point that we now try to characterize. From Property 4.1 it is clear that, under constant prices, an increase in k generates a decline in the production of the labor-intensive product. At the same time income goes up with k, resulting in an increased demand for the two products and generating an excess demand for the labor-intensive product. An open economy closes this gap through trade.

Figure 4.2 illustrates the changes for a price-taker country with an initial equilibrium at A where there is no trade. As k increases from k_A to k_B, the output, under p_A, changes to B. This causes a downward shift of the supply of the labor-intensive product, $y_1(p, k)$, as shown in panel III of Figure 4.1 by the movement of the schedule with A to that with B. The change in the equilibrium condition is shown in Figure 4.2. Initially A is on the demand curve $x_1^d(p_A, x_2)$, and there is no trade. With the change in k, the demand is at C, and the country becomes an importer of agriculture, with an import of $x_{1C} - y_{1B}$ and an export of nonagriculture of $y_{2B} - x_{2C}$. Other cases can be shown in a similar way. Try, for instance, to show the case where a country changes from exporting to importing nonagriculture. The change can also be shown in terms of the restricted demand function of a small open economy, and this is assigned as an exercise.

We now derive the result in terms of the excess demand:

$$z_i(p, k) = x_i[p, y(p, k)] - y_i(p, k)$$

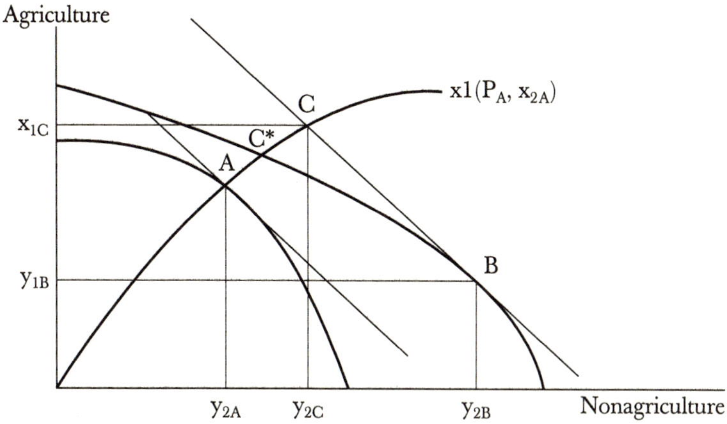

Figure 4.2 The impact of resource change: Small open economy

where $y(p, k)$ is income, evaluated at price p and resource level k. The sign of $\partial y_i/\partial k$ is determined by the factor intensity, but the response of total output, $\partial y/\partial k$, is always positive. The essence of this discussion is that the effect of a change in k on z_i is unambiguously signed for the labor-intensive sector, since for this sector

$$\frac{\partial z_i}{\partial k} = \frac{\partial x_i}{\partial y}\frac{\partial y}{\partial k} - \frac{\partial y_i}{\partial k} > 0.$$

In an open economy the excess demand is fulfilled by trade. Under balanced trade, the change in the value of import in one sector is equal to the change in the value of export of the other sector. Therefore the export of the capital-intensive sector increases with capital deepening. Hence

PROPERTY 4.3 (trade; expansion-pattern) The net import of the labor-(capital-)intensive product increases (decreases) with capital deepening.

A distinction should be made between a change in import and the corresponding change in the volume of trade. When the country is importing the labor-intensive product, an increase in net import implies an increase in the level of trade. On the other hand, if the country is exporting the labor-intensive product, capital deepening leads to a decline of trade.

The empirical validity of this discussion is straightforward but not simple to uncover without a detailed analysis, because time-series data reflect changes in resources, prices, and technology. This may be the reason for insupportable assertions that are sometimes made on the importance of increasing food import in generating overall economic growth. It is therefore useful to emphasize the partial result established here. Other things being equal, capital deepening will increase net import and decrease production of agriculture when it is labor intensive. Conversely, agricultural output will increase and net import will decline when agriculture is capital intensive. The implication of this for actual trade depends on whether the country is importing or exporting the labor-intensive product.

If we assume that all countries accumulate capital, it is inconceivable that all of them will increase the net export of the capital-intensive good. To set the world trade in equilibrium, the price of the capital-intensive good will have to decline. The situation is similar to that of a closed economy, to which we now turn.

In passing it is noted that under equal factor intensities, the Rybczynski proposition does not apply. If the country produces the two products, there is no trade. The change in demand associated with capital deepening will be determined solely by the income elasticities.

Closed Economy

The discussion of the closed economy is conducted with reference to Figure 4.3. The excess demand for agriculture at p_A generated by increasing k to k_B is given by the difference between the demand at C^* and the production at B. The gap is closed by increasing p, so that a new equilibrium point is found at E. We have thus established

PROPERTY 4.4 (price path; closed economy) Capital deepening raises the wage-rental ratio and the relative price of the labor-intensive product.

While the change in prices caused by accumulation is uniquely determined, this is not the case with respect to outputs and therefore resource allocation. Recall that $\ell(\omega, k)$ increases with ω and declines with k. Thus the resource allocation depends on the strength of the change in ω with respect to k, which in turn depends on the change in p, and this in turn depends on demand.

The increase in p called for by Property 4.4 generates a substitution effect in demand in favor of the capital-intensive product. Hence the income and substitution effects have the same sign for the capital-intensive product and contradicting signs for the labor-intensive product. Therefore the equilibrium consumption of the capital-intensive product increases unambiguously, whereas the change in the consumption of the labor-intensive product depends on the relative strength of the substitution and income effects. Thus the only restriction on point E in Figure 4.3 is that it is to the east of A, meaning that

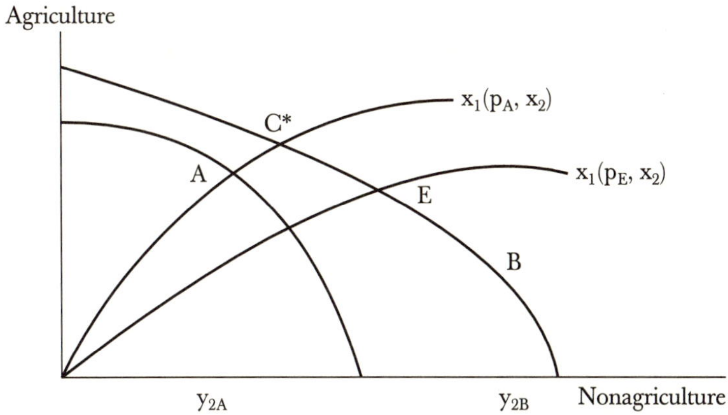

Figure 4.3 The impact of resource change: Closed economy

the labor-intensive product may increase or decrease. The discussion is now summarized:

PROPERTY 4.5 (output path; closed economy) Capital deepening raises the per capita output of the capital-intensive sector, whereas the direction of the change in the output of the labor-intensive sector is ambiguous. It depends on the relative strength of the income and substitution effects on the demand side and the change in product composition on the supply side.

The importance of the demand elasticities is illustrated in terms of Figure 4.3. The income elasticity is reflected in the position of C^* with respect to A; the lower the income elasticity is, the closer x_{1C^*} will be to x_{1A}. The price elasticity is reflected in the degree of the rotation of the demand curve caused by a given change in p. A low price elasticity will cause E to be close to C^*, and thus the income effect will dominate. Alternatively, a high price elasticity will bring E closer to B and possibly lead to a decline in agricultural consumption.

Empirical Implications

The importance of the foregoing result, particularly the dependence of sectoral growth on income elasticities, cannot be overemphasized. It is all related to Engel's law, which states that the proportion of the consumer's budget spent on food declines with income. In other words, the utility function is not homothetic, and the income elasticity for food is less than one. The effect of the income elasticity is observed in Figure 1.4, which shows that in most countries the rate of growth of agricultural output was lower than that of total output, in spite of the decline in the relative price of agriculture. With all the necessary refinements and caveats, it is clear that faster growth in agriculture is concomitant with faster growth in nonagriculture. This is simply the reflection of consumers' preferences.

Sectoral Inputs

We turn next to an examination of the changes in factor employment along the equilibrium path. For a small open economy the price, and hence the factor-price ratio, are given. The response of the economy to an increase in k occurs completely through changes in output composition. The capital-intensive sector increases its output, and its employment of both capital and labor will increase. The labor-intensive sector will lose both labor and capital. In the closed economy part of the adjustment is made through the price. The increase in the wage-rental ratio encourages the substitution of capital for labor. By assumption, however, all the available labor has to be employed. Therefore this substitution is restricted by the full employment condition as well as by the need to satisfy the demand for the final products. In what follows we examine employment under these conditions, trying to separate the induced changes to various effects.

The possibilities in the adjustments of sectoral inputs are illustrated in Figure 4.4. To simplify the presentation here, we omit the sectoral notation. Point A represents the initial equilibrium position, where Y_A is produced with

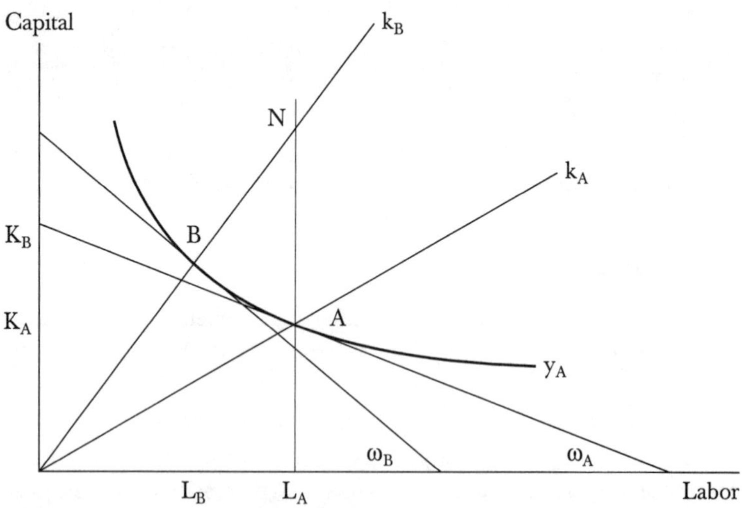

Figure 4.4 Intrasector resource allocation

L_A units of labor and K_A units of capital, yielding a capital-labor ratio of k_A and a wage-rental ratio ω_A. Point B is the least-cost input combination that produces the initial output Y_A under ω_B. We can refer to the decline in sectoral employment, $L_A - L_B$, as the factor substitution effect of employment. Similarly, $K_A - K_B$ represents the factor substitution effect of capital use.

The change in the actual sectoral employment depends on the strength of the expansion effect relative to the substitution effect. In terms of Figure 4.4, let N represent the point where the two effects are equal so that the initial labor input, L_A, is optimal under the new prices. The new equilibrium is on a ray through N. If it is below N, such as B, the sectoral labor input declines, and conversely, when it is above N, the sectoral labor input goes up. The situation is different with respect to capital, where the factor substitution effect supplements the expansion effect. We can then summarize the discussion by presenting the various effects along the equilibrium path generated by an increase in the capital-labor ratio:

Effect	Labor-intensive sector		Capital-intensive sector	
	Labor	Capital	Labor	Capital
Product expansion	+	+	+	+
Product substitution	−	−	+	+
Factor substitution	−	+	−	+

Of the four cases, only one is uniquely signed. The employment of capital in the capital-intensive sector increases with capital deepening. In all other cases, the final outcome depends on the relative strength of the various effects. It should, however, be noted that the capital-labor ratios increase in both sectors, that is, $(\hat{k}_i/\hat{k})\,|_{\text{eq}} > 0$, where eq stands for changes along the equilibrium path. This simply follows from the fact that $(\hat{\omega}/\hat{k})\,|_{\text{eq}} > 0$.

More can be said when we know the relative strength of the various effects. For instance, if the income elasticity of agriculture is negligible, then the product substitution effect exceeds the product expansion effect. In the limiting case of zero income elasticity for agriculture, there is no product expansion in agriculture. When agriculture is labor intensive, its labor will decline. If the product substitution effect is also negligible, then K_1 will increase.

Alternatively, if the product substitution effect is negligible and that of income is not, then the sectoral capital will definitely increase, whereas the change in labor depends on the relative strength of the income elasticity and the factor elasticity of substitution. Finally, when the factor elasticities of substitution are small, the changes in the final demand will determine the changes in factor employments. It is therefore evident that the final outcome depends on the relative magnitude of the demand elasticities and the elasticities of substitution and on factor intensities. The impact of capital deepening on factor use in agriculture can thus be summarized:

PROPERTY 4.6 (input path; closed economy) Capital deepening raises the capital-labor ratio in both sectors and the use of capital in the capital-intensive sector. When the demand elasticities for agriculture are small, the main changes in inputs are supply driven. Thus when agriculture is labor intensive, it is likely that its total use of capital will increase, whereas labor employment will decline.

Price-Responsive Factor Supply

The foregoing analysis assumed factor supply to be perfectly inelastic. This assumption is rather restrictive and can be relaxed by allowing factor supply to depend on their prices (Frenkel and Razin, 1975). The consequences of this generalization are examined below. Chapters 9 and 10 consider the determinants of factor supply.

Labor

We now introduce the assumption that labor supply responds positively to the wage rate, $L'(w) > 0$. In evaluating labor supply, it is important to distinguish between long-term effects and cyclical responses. The empirical literature on labor supply does not give a clear indication of the numerical value of the labor-supply elasticity. Some of the development literature assumes, at least implicitly, that labor supply is price responsive to the food wage, w/p. In the present framework, w (measured in terms of nonagriculture) and w/p (measured in terms of agriculture) move in the same direction, and therefore there is no particular advantage in dealing specifically with the food wage.

In what follows we differentiate between labor supply and population, N, which is taken to be exogenous. The supply side of the model is now modified by restating the full employment conditions:

$$L(w) = L_1 + L_2, \quad L'(w) > 0,$$
$$K = K_1 + K_2,$$
$$L(w) \leq N.$$

The labor supply also depends on the population and on other demographic variables, such as the age distribution, that are taken here to be exoge-

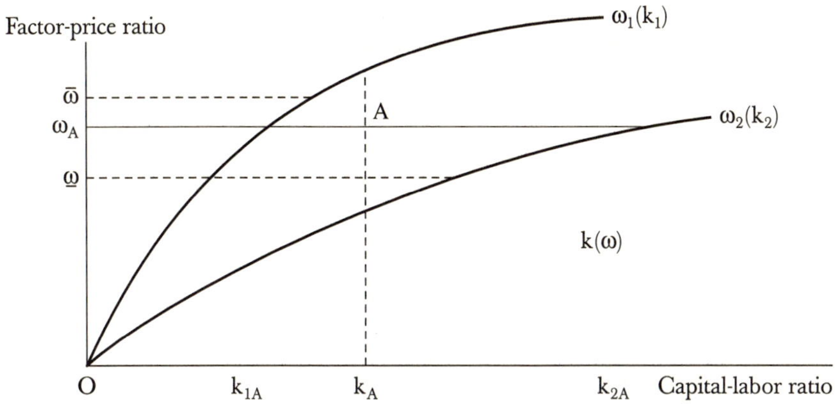

Figure 4.5 Admissible factor-price ratios

nous. These variables are assumed to be constant in the analysis and therefore are not included explicitly as arguments of $L(w)$.

The production functions (2.3) and the competitive conditions (2.4 and 2.5) remain unchanged. The overall capital-labor ratio is now a declining function of wage,

$$k(w, K) = K/L(w), \quad \frac{\partial k(w, K)}{\partial w} < 0.$$

This property can be expressed in terms of the wage-rental ratio. Recall that w/p_2 is monotonically increasing in k_2. When p_2 is the numeraire, $w/p_2 = w$, and therefore $w(k_2)$ is monotonically increasing in k_2. Combining this with the monotonicity of $k_2(\omega)$, we can write $k(\omega, K)$, $\partial k(\omega, K)/\partial\omega < 0$. Let $\ell = L_1/L(\omega)$, and write the full employment condition:

$$\ell(\omega, K) = \frac{k_2(\omega) - k(\omega, K)}{k_2(\omega) - k_1(\omega)}.$$

The determination of the resource allocation is shown in Figure 4.5 where k is now a declining function of ω. The admissible values of ω are bounded by $\underline{\omega} = \min(\cdot)$ and $\overline{\omega} = \max(\cdot)$, where $(\cdot) = [\omega_i(k(\omega_i, K)),\ i = 1, 2]$. For any admissible ω, k is determined by $k = k(\omega, K)$. Thus k_A is the capital-labor ratio corresponding to ω_A, and similarly $k_{iA} = k_i(\omega_A)$. Per capita outputs are obtained from

$$y_i = \frac{L(\omega)}{N}[\ell_i(\omega, K) f_i(k_i(\omega))]. \tag{4.1}$$

The correction factor for the participation rate in the labor force, $L(\omega)/N$, increases in ω. Given ω, factor prices and the product price ratio, p, are determined as before. This concludes the solution of the supply side for a given ω, where the equilibrium value is determined by introducing the demand function.

To analyze the behavior of the system in terms of ω, we first examine the labor allocation:

$$\frac{\ell(\omega, K)}{1-\ell(\omega, K)} = \frac{k_2(\omega) - k(\omega, K)}{k(\omega, K) - (k_1(\omega)}. \tag{4.2}$$

Since $k_i'(\omega) > 0$, $\partial k(\omega, K)/\partial\omega < 0$, and $k_1(\omega) \leq k(\omega, K) \leq k_2(\omega)$, the expression in (4.2) is monotonically increasing in ω. Consequently,

$$\partial\ell(\omega, K)/\partial\omega > 0. \tag{4.3}$$

As ω increases, k declines, whereas k_1 and k_2 increase and therefore ℓ increases. Consequently, $\partial[\ell(\omega, K)f_1(k_1(\omega))]/\partial\omega > 0$, and therefore,

$$\partial y_1(\omega, K)/\partial\omega > 0. \tag{4.4}$$

Using the definition of ℓ, it follows that L_1, the employment in the labor-intensive sector, increases with ω. Since also $k_1'(\omega) > 0$, it follows that $K_1(\omega)$ increases in ω, and because K is fixed, $K_2(\omega)$ must decrease with ω. But since $k_2'(\omega) > 0$, it follows that $L_2(\omega, K)$ declines in ω. Consequently the capital-intensive sector employs fewer resources, and its output declines. It is possible to view this change in two steps. First, an exogenous increase of wage increases labor supply. The second step is basically the Rybczynski effect, which favors the labor-intensive sector.

The analysis of the supply side can be summarized by the transformation curve. This curve is determined by $k(\omega, K)$ and is denoted as $T(k(\omega, K))$. As such it differs from the transformation curve obtained under fixed resources, $T(k)$. The relationship between the two transformation curves is discussed below.

Introducing a demand curve allows the determination of the equilibrium point for the economy in the same way as before. Note, however, that in the present case, the level of employment in the economy is determined jointly with the other dependent variables.

Price-Responsive Capital Supply

A similar analysis follows for the case where the supply of capital depends on the rate of return. This relation may represent the positive effect that the rate of return may have on saving. Alternatively, we can think of a country that borrows from abroad and is faced with an upward-sloping supply function of capital. Since the present analysis is timeless, we can express the capital stock (rather than investment) as dependent on r. Thus the full employment conditions will be

$$K(r) = K_1 + K_2, \quad K'(r) > 0,$$
$$L = L_1 + L_2.$$

The analysis is similar to the analysis with varying labor supply. Since r declines in k_2 and k_2 increases with ω, we have $r'(\omega) < 0$, and for fixed L, $k(\omega, L) = K[r(\omega)]/L$, $\partial k(\omega, L)/\partial\omega < 0$.

It is now possible to describe the present case in terms of Figure 4.5. To any feasible ω corresponds a rate of return $r(\omega)$ that determines the level of the capital stock, which in turn determines k for a fixed labor force. Resource allocation is determined conditional on ω, and this in turn determines outputs. Thus a parametric solution of the system conditional on ω generates the transformation curve. Again, as in the previous case, the introduction of demand makes it possible to determine the equilibrium point. In this case, the level of capital is determined jointly with the other dependent variables. The exogenous increase in the rental rate increases the capital stock and consequently causes an expansion of the capital-intensive sector and a shrinkage of the labor-intensive sector.

A Generalization

The analysis can now be generalized by combining the two cases discussed above where the overall capital-labor ratio is a function of ω alone: $k(\omega) = K(\omega)/L(\omega)$, $k'(\omega) < 0$. The foregoing analysis is immediately applicable to this more general case. Total employment and the level of the capital stock are now determined along with the other dependent variables.

We begin the analysis by comparing the production possibilities under fixed resources, $T(k)$, with those under varying factor supplies, $T(k(\omega))$. Since the labor force is not constant anymore, the outputs are measured in per capita, rather than per worker, terms. We return to this point below. In Figure 4.6, $T(k_A)$ is drawn for the capital-labor ratio k_A, which under varying factor supply corresponds to $k_A = k(\omega_A)$. Point A on this curve corresponds to ω_A, whereas point B corresponds to $\omega_B < \omega_A$. At B, the output of the labor-intensive sector is lower than at A.

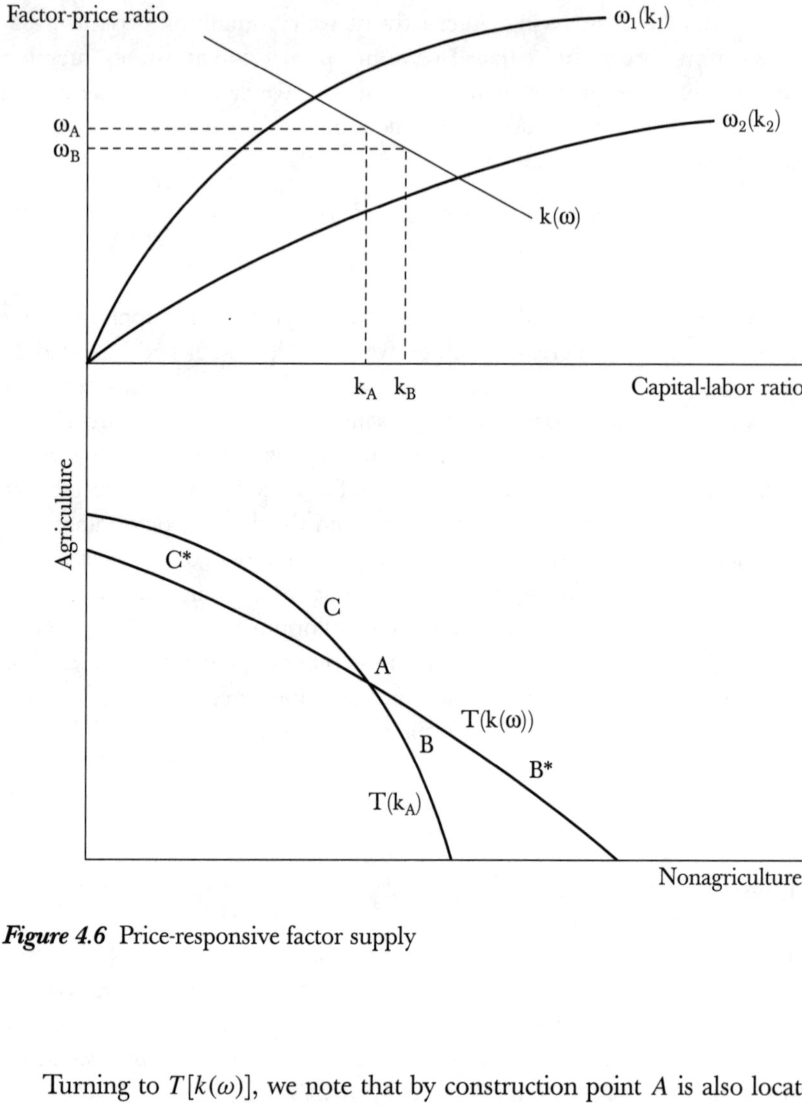

Figure 4.6 Price-responsive factor supply

Turning to $T[k(\omega)]$, we note that by construction point A is also located on this curve. However, a decline in ω increases k so that at $k_B = k(\omega_B) > k_A$ output is at B^* on $T(k_B)$. B^* is a Rybczynski point, located in the southeast quadrant with respect to B, reflecting an increase in the output of the capital-intensive sector and a decrease in the output of the labor-intensive sector. The question is whether B^* is outside or inside $T(k_A)$. The answer depends on the direction of the resource change. When only L changes, then with $\omega_B < \omega_A$, $L(\omega_B) < L(\omega_A)$, and B^* will be inside $T(k_A)$. When only K changes, then $k(\omega_B) > k(\omega_A)$, and therefore B^* is outside $T(k_A)$, as shown in Figure 4.6.

A similar analysis can be conducted for $k_C = k(\omega_C) < k_A$, $\omega_C > \omega_A$. The resulting point C^* on $T[k(\omega)]$ is in the northwest with respect to C on $T(k_A)$. Again, the location of C^* with respect to $T(k_A)$ depends on whether the change is in L or K. If only labor changes, $L(\omega_C) > L(\omega_A)$, and therefore C^* will be outside $T(k_A)$. The opposite is true when only K changes in response to a change in ω. In this case K declines and C^* is inside $T(k_A)$ as shown in Figure 4.6.

When the two factors are price responsive, a change in ω causes opposite effects on the quantities supplied of the two factors. For instance, an increase in ω causes a rise in the real wage and hence in the labor supply. At the same time the real rate of return declines and therefore K declines. The net effect on total output may be positive or negative depending on the supply elasticities and the productivity of the two inputs.

This framework makes it possible to prove that the product supply functions are more elastic the more elastic are the factor supply functions (Frenkel and Razin, 1975). This topic is discussed in some detail in Chapter 14. Initially, $T[k(\omega)]$ and $T(k_A)$ intersect at A. Let $\omega_B = \omega_{B^*} < \omega_A$, and $p(\omega)$ is the price of the labor-intensive product, y_1 in our case. Consequently, $p'(\omega) > 0$ and $p(\omega_B) = p(\omega_{B^*}) < p_A$. Since B^* is in the southeast quadrant with respect to B, we have shown that reducing p causes a stronger response of Y_i when the factor supplies are price responsive.

PROPERTY 4.7 (product and factor supply elasticities) The product supply elasticities monotonically increase with the factor supply elasticities.

One outcome of the present analysis not commonly appreciated is that the supply price is not equal to the slope of the tangent line to $T[k(\omega)]$.[2] This follows from the fact that any point on $T[k(\omega)]$, say A, is also located on some $T(k)$, in this case $T(k_A)$, which intersects $T[k(\omega)]$ at A. Since p_A can be derived as the slope of the tangent line to $T(k_A)$, the tangent line to $T[k(\omega)]$ must have a different slope. Under fixed factor supply we have $|\, dy_2/dy_1 \,| = p$. This represents the concept of real marginal cost, a trade-off between two outputs. Under varying factor supplies, the movement along a transformation curve implies a change in the factor quantities, and there is no pure trade-off.[3]

The equality of $|\, dy_2/dy_1 \,|$ and p is often used to derive the concavity of the transformation curve. The equality, however, does not hold for $T[k(\omega)]$. In any case, the concavity, or lack of it, is not of immediate relevance to the discussion. What matters here is that the supply function is positively sloped and that $Y_1(Y_2) = Y_1[Y_2 : (Y_1, Y_2) \in T(k(\omega))]$ is ever declining in Y_2. With these properties, the equilibrium is uniquely determined. To summarize the supply conditions, we note

PROPERTY 4.8 (supply determinants) The product supplies are functions of the product price ratio and the factor supply functions.

Given the factor supply functions, inputs and outputs can be written as functions of the price alone. Thus for the labor-intensive sector, we have $\partial \ell(\omega \mid \cdot)/\partial \omega > 0$, $\partial y_1(p \mid \cdot)/\partial p > 0$, where $\mid \cdot$ indicates holding factor supply *functions* (and of course technology) constant, and $p = p(\omega)$ is the price of the labor-intensive product. The signs for the capital-intensive sector are reversed. On the surface, this result is very strong in the sense that the product supply functions are not constrained by the available resources, because those can change subject to their supply functions. In an economy that behaves according to this model, including constant technology, the data should reveal a positive relationship between output and price, with no other variables added to the equation. However, this is only true as long as the factor supply functions remain constant. This restriction limits the usefulness of this result for empirical analysis using cross-country data because the factor supply functions are not the same in the various countries. Thus the model is merely useful as a reference and not as a final formulation.

Equilibrium Analysis

The outcome of the foregoing analysis is that the production structure that was used for fixed factor supply can be used also for varying supply, with a proper interpretation that takes into account the dependence of the transformation curve and the supply functions on the factor supply functions rather than on the factors themselves. The feasible prices are well defined as before. Hence, if the factor supply functions give finite quantities for finite prices, then the transformation curve represents finite outputs that constitute the efficiency frontier. The supply of each of the products varies positively with its own price. Consequently the equilibrium analysis can be conducted in the same way as in the fixed supply case and need not be repeated. The main point here is that an equilibrium output is well defined.

Perfectly Elastic Factor Supply

To complete the discussion of factor supply we now consider the limiting case of perfectly elastic factor supply, where the factor supply is neither price responsive nor exogenously given. This can be thought of as the case of a small open economy that can borrow at a constant rate. This assumption is often used in the discussion of the real exchange rate for a small open economy (Obstfeld and Rogoff, 1996, chap. 4).

Suppose that there is a perfectly elastic supply of capital at a rental rate r^0. The full employment condition now binds only the labor allocation, whereas capital can be used at any desirable level. Knowing r^0, the system is solved for k_i, ω, w, and p, all of which are now constants. Labor allocation, as given by $\ell = (k_2^0 - k)/(k_2^0 - k_1^0)$, is now a function of k alone, but k depends on K, which is undetermined without knowing the demand. Per capita sectoral output is $y_i = f_i(k_i^0)\ell_i(r^0, k)$. The transformation curve is generated by changing the value of ℓ from zero to one. It is a straight line with slope

$$\frac{dy_2}{dy_1} = \frac{f_2(k_2^0)}{f_1(k_1^0)} \frac{d(1-\ell)/dk}{d(\ell)/dk} = -\frac{f_2(k_2^0)}{f_1(k_1^0)}.$$

The slope of the transformation curve is not equal to the price. The cost of production associated with each worker in the ith sector is $w^0 + r^0 k_i^0 = \zeta_i^0$; $\zeta_i^0 = \zeta_i(r_i^0)$, and under zero profit it is equal to the average value output per worker, $p_i f_i(k_i^0)$. Hence

$$p^0 = \frac{p_1}{p_2} = \frac{\zeta_1^0/f_1}{\zeta_2^0/f_2} = -\frac{dy_2}{dy_1}\frac{\zeta_1^0}{\zeta_2^0}.$$

gain, the reason for the inequality of the functions p and dy_2/dy_1 is that K varies along the transformation curve, and as such the slope represents an expansion effect in addition to a trade-off.

When the price is constant, the supply is perfectly elastic for all feasible allocations, and the production is determined by demand. In the case of the small open economy, this implies specialization: if $p^* > p$, the economy will specialize in agriculture and conversely for $p^* < p$. In the case of equality, there is no unique determination of output composition. In the case of a closed economy, the equilibrium is determined by the intersection of the demand and the transformation curve. The equilibrium determines outputs, which in turn determines the resource allocation, which in turn determines k, which in turn determines K.

PROPERTY 4.9 (perfectly elastic factor supply) When the supply of one of the factors is perfectly elastic, the price is constant, and the product supplies are also perfectly elastic. In a closed economy the output composition is determined by demand.

How instructive is this model? Because we do not see wide fluctuations in the production of agriculture and nonagriculture, it appears that this model is not very realistic. There may be other reasons, however, for the lack of wide fluctuations in outputs. First, we note that this is a long-run model, and by the nature of things the response is slow, though not necessarily weak (see Chapter 14). Second, as countries borrow heavily, the risk of their default increases; therefore the cost of borrowing has to increase accordingly, which leads to the case of less than perfectly elastic capital supply. Third, to speak of a small open economy in this context overlooks the fact that some products are nontradable. This brings us to the dichotomy of tradable and nontradable sectors. In this case, the price is the real exchange rate. The output composition is determined by the domestic demand, and hence there is no tendency for specialization in production. Fluctuations in domestic demand will be absorbed by net import, and the real exchange rate is stabilized at a level determined by the cost of borrowing. An interesting message comes out of this discussion; elastic supply of capital helps to stabilize the real exchange rate in this artificial world.

Obviously, this framework is oversimplified, and specifically, it overlooks the dynamic aspect of the problem. The derived net import of capital is determined by the intersection of the demand curve with the transformation curve and by available domestic capital. If the gap is big, the country will be a big importer of capital. Such a situation may not be very stable, and therefore may not exist for a long time period. Changes in the supply of capital will cause changes in the real exchange rate.

We have concentrated on capital, but the stabilization comes also from a perfectly elastic supply of labor. Indeed, many affluent countries depend on migration to supplement the domestic labor supply. This international migration contributes to the stabilization of wages (or to slowing down their increase). In fact, labor migration may be more effective as a stabilizer than is capital inflow. When the economy turns sour, international capital often flies out at the speed of electronic transactions, whereas labor tends to stay in the country.

For the sake of completeness, we mention also the case where the supply of both factors is perfectly elastic. Consequently, the supply of each of the products is perfectly elastic, and the demand determines the level of production in each of the sectors. The important thing here is that the production side of each sector can be analyzed independently of the other sector. This case is applicable when one of the sectors is relatively small, and it can be considered as a price taker in all the pertinent factor markets.

Extensions

The Equilibrium Path under Tax

The question is what changes, if any, should be made in the characterization of the equilibrium path if the economy is operating under a tax-subsidy on products. To answer this we note that with p measuring the supply price, the supply function $y_1(p, k)$ is unaffected by the tax, and therefore the shift of $y_1(p, k)$ caused by k is independent of the tax. Introducing a restricted demand function under distortion, as in Figure 3.1, facilitates the determination of the equilibrium solution. Accordingly, capital accumulation decreases the supply of the labor-intensive good, and therefore its price increases. The case of an open economy is even simpler. It can thus be concluded that the qualitative behavior of the system in response to changes in k is the same as that observed under no tax.

Also, allowing for varying factor supply does not change the qualitative results. The response to price changes caused by the tax will be stronger, however, because the supply elasticity is larger than that obtained for fixed resources. For instance, subsidizing agriculture increases the agricultural prices, and therefore a stronger supply response is generated. As a consequence the equilibrium price will be lower and output higher as compared with fixed resources.

There are some additional aspects to the behavior of the real exchange rate as a result of resource change, but they bear similarity to the effect of productivity changes; therefore we defer the discussion on these to Chapter 5.

Aid and Resource Change

Capital deepening increases the net import of the labor-intensive product. If agriculture is labor intensive, and the country is an importer of food, its import will grow with capital deepening. Food aid to such a country can supply some of the augmented demand. Thus it is possible to have simultaneous growth in food aid and food import. This is consistent with the conclusions drawn in Chapter 3 that aid replaces commercial imports. It is a mistake, however, to attribute the increase in commercial import to food aid.

Although emphasis is placed on capital accumulation, we should pause to consider the case where labor grows faster than capital, generating population pressure on given resources. This is still the case in some low-income countries that, largely due to political conflict, are unable to divert sufficient resources to investment. In such countries, a decline in k leads to an increase in the *per capita* supply of agriculture and a decline in the *per capita* import. This is a direct outcome of the analysis. However, note that in this case *total* import, as well as total consumption, may rise. This will happen when the relative decline in per capita import is smaller than the rate of population growth. Thus it may happen that the country jointly increases its food consumption, production, and import. In this case, some food aid will reduce the commercial import but not to the extent of showing a decline in import.

In a closed economy, we find that the depressive effect of food aid on agriculture is stronger under varying factor supply, simply reflecting larger supply elasticities.

Price-Responsive Land Supply

As shown in Figure 1.5, the cultivated area varies over time with different rates across countries. We now extend the discussion in Chapter 2 by allowing the size of the agricultural land to be determined endogenously. To do so, we introduce two new elements into the discussion, land quality and land-specific cost.

Land is a factor specific to agriculture, and therefore the rent on land is the meaningful measure of the terms of trade of agriculture (Mundlak, 1969). When the expected rent is positive, investment will be made in land expansion, and when it is negative, land will go out of production. The expansion often requires investment in reclamation, bush clearing, roads, communications, or other infrastructure facilities. Such investments constitute set-up costs, and once made, they do not affect decisions on the intensity of land utilization. On the other hand, there are costs incurred as a result of holding or cultivating the land, and as such they affect the decisions of whether and to what extent the land is utilized. It is therefore important to differentiate between the expansion and contraction of cultivated area.

We turn to examine the effect of the various determinants of land size and the relationships between the size and the intensity at which land is cultivated. This brings us to a consideration of the Ricardian extensive and intensive margins. The main determinants to be examined are factors affecting the profitability of agriculture, the resource constraints, the role of infrastructure, and tax. Technical change is taken up in Chapter 5. The discussion abstracts from all the institutional factors affecting farmers' behavior with respect to land, particularly those emerging from differences between ownership and operation.

The model is developed in steps in order to evaluate the role played by the main pertinent variables. In each step the simplest version needed to make the point is presented. As indicated above, the cost of land may take different forms, affecting long-run and short-run decisions differently. We do not differentiate between them in the discussion, but the results can be interpreted according to the case of interest. To economize the discussion, cost will sometimes be referred to as tax, but this is a generic term to be interpreted according to the case at hand. The model assumes two factors of production, land and

Table 4.1 Summary results

Exogenous variables	$k(q)$	z	A	K	Y	R	r	p
	Agriculture is a price taker							
r/p	−	+	−	−	−	−	··	··
c/p	0	+	−	−	−	−	··	··
	Capital constraint							
K	+	−	+	··	+	+	−	··
c/p	+	+	−	··	−	−	−	··
	Output quota							
Y	+	−	+	+	··	+	··	+
r	−	−	+	−	··	+	··	+
c	+	+	−	+	··	−	··	+

Note: ·· Irrelevant.

capital. The first version assumes agriculture to be a price taker, the second model assumes a capital constraint, and the third model assumes an output constraint. These three versions provide the needed insight and background for the empirical analysis. The effect of technical change is taken up in Chapter 5.

The results of the analysis are summarized in Table 4.1, which can be studied without working through the details of the developments.

Initial Specification

The starting point is the model used by Lucas (1978) to analyze the distribution of firms. The quality of land, denoted by q, is assumed to be a continuous variable that takes on nonnegative values; the higher the value of q, the better the land. Let $A(q)$ be the available amount of land of quality q. To normalize the units of quality, we can refer to the distribution of land by quality, as illustrated in the upper panel of Figure 4.7.[4] The land used by agriculture, referred to as cultivated land, is all the land of quality $q \geq z$, where z is the marginal quality to be determined by the model. The area under cultivation is

$$A = \int_{z}^{\infty} A(q)dq. \tag{4.5}$$

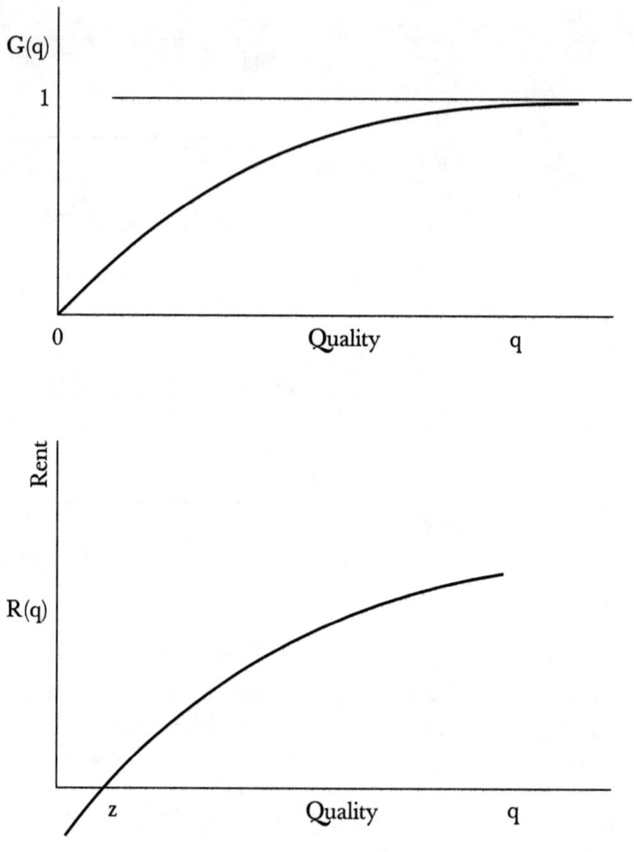

Figure 4.7 Distribution of land quality

The cultivated land, adjusted for quality is

$$Q = \int_{z}^{\infty} qA(q)dq. \tag{4.6}$$

To simplify the discussion, assume that there is only one factor of production in addition to land, labeled as capital.[5] $K(q)$ is the amount of capital allocated to quality q land, and $k(q)$ is the capital-land ratio, $k(q) = K(q)/A(q)$. Total capital used by agriculture is

$$K = \int_{z}^{\infty} k(q)A(q)dq. \tag{4.7}$$

To allow the marginal rate of factor substitution to depend on land quality, the production function is expressed in terms of land measured in quality units, $qA(q)$. Assuming CRS, the function for quality q land is

$$Y(q) = F[qA(q),\ K(q)] = A(q)qf[k(q)/q], \tag{4.8}$$

where $qf(k/q)$ is the output per unit of quality q land. By assumption, the function $f(\cdot)$ is twice differentiable, increasing, and strictly concave, $f(0) = 0$, $f'(0) = \infty$, $f(\infty) = \infty$, $f'(\infty) = 0$. Total output is

$$Y = \int_z^\infty Y(q)dq = \int_z^\infty qf(k(q)/q)A(q)dq. \tag{4.9}$$

The quantities A, K, and Y are functions of z and $k(q)$; these in turn are determined by the state variables, which vary with the specification of the model. Let the user price of capital (rental rate) be r, the product price be p, and c be the unit cost of using land, independent of its quality. The rent on quality q land is

$$R(q) = pqf[k(q)/q] - c - rk(q). \tag{4.10}$$

Differentiating $R(q)$ with respect to q, we obtain $R'(q) = [R(q) + c]/q > 0$, implying that the rent increases monotonically with q. The marginal quality z is determined by $R(z) = 0$. Hence for all $q > z$, $R(q) > 0$, whereas the rent of the low-quality land, defined by $q < z$, is negative, and therefore that land is not cultivated. This is illustrated in the lower panel of Figure 4.7. The cost, c, plays an important role here because it forces low-quality land out of production.[6] The economic problem is to determine what land to cultivate and at what level of intensity, measured by $k(q)$. The different models considered below will endogenize some of the prices in equation (4.10).

Agriculture as a Price Taker

In this model it is assumed that there is a perfectly elastic supply of capital at the rental rate r and a perfectly elastic product demand at price p, and the cost c is independent of the land quality. In this specification, the level of intensity is determined independently of the extensive margin, z, because there is no resource or output constraint. Nevertheless, we will employ a general formulation that will serve us in the other cases. The formal presentation of the present problem is

$$\max_{k(q),z} L(k(q), z) = \int_{z}^{\infty} [pqf(k(q)/q) - rk(q) - c]A(q)dq. \qquad (4.11)$$

The first-order conditions for an internal solution (FOC) are

$$L_1(\cdot) = pf'[k(q)/q] - r = 0, \qquad (4.12)$$

$$L_2(\cdot) = pzf[k(z)/z] - c - rk(z) = 0, \qquad (4.13)$$

where L_1 and L_2 are the partial derivatives with respect to $k(q)$ and z respectively. In this model, the solution is recursive; we first solve from (4.12) for $k(q)$. We insert the solution to equation (4.13), compute the rent for all q, and determine z according to the second condition. The order of the solution cannot be reversed because the value of z does not affect $k(q)$. If we keep this in mind, the solution for z can be illustrated by drawing the graphs of the FOC in the (k, q) plane. Starting with equation (4.12), $f'(k(q)/q)$ is a monotone function; its inverse exists and we can rewrite it as

$$k(q) = q\Phi(r/p), \qquad (4.14)$$

where $\Phi(r/p) = f'^{-1}(r/p)$, $\Phi'(r/p) < 0$. This function indicates the optimal intensity for all q, and is shown in Figure 4.8. Given r/p, $k(q)$ is a monotone increasing function of q, so that $k(q_A) < k(q_B)$ for $q_A < q_B$.

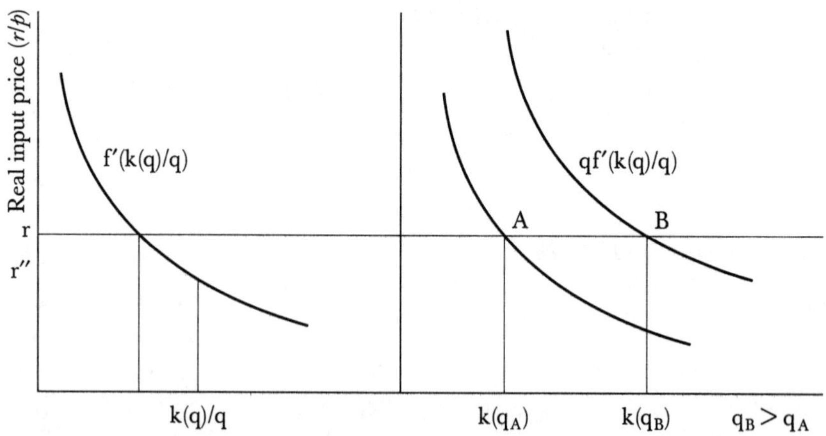

Figure 4.8 Input demand

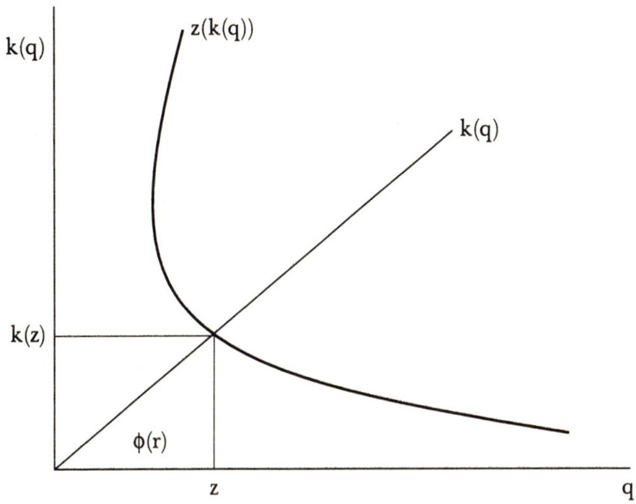

Figure 4.9 Intensive and extensive margins

To determine z, we obtain the graph $R(k, q) = 0$ which traces the combinations of k and q that result in zero rent. Using equation (4.13), we calculate the zero rent quality for any arbitrary k,

$$z(k) = \frac{rk}{pf(k/z)} + \frac{c}{pf(k/z)}. \tag{4.15}$$

This graph is drawn in Figure 4.9. As k increases the second term on the right-hand side of equation (4.15) declines, and the first term increases due to the concavity of $f(k)$, so that the cost of capital increases linearly at rate r, but its marginal productivity decreases; in the limit, $k \to \infty$ implies $z \to \infty$. On the other hand, as k declines, the first term on the right-hand side declines due to the concavity of $f(k)$, whereas the second term increases at a faster rate; in the limit, $k \to 0$ implies $z \to \infty$. This means that to stay in production the quality must increase in order to compensate for the decline in output resulting from the decline in intensity of cultivation. Because resources are costly, producers are limited in their choice of k, and the optimal choice is given by equation (4.14). Thus the intersection of the two functions, (4.14) and (4.15), provides the solution for z and $k(z)$.

The Margins

How do the margins respond to changes in the state variables r, p, and c? To answer this question, we differentiate the first-order conditions. Without a loss in generality we set $p = 1$ so that r and c are measured in product units. When it is desirable to emphasize the role of p, we will switch notation and rewrite the real factor prices as r/p and c/p. To simplify the notations when ambiguity does not arise, we use in what follows $f(q) \equiv f(k(q)/q)$ and $f'(q) \equiv df(k(q)/q)/dk(q)$.

We differentiate equation (4.12), using equation (4.14), $f''(q)dk(q) = qdr$ (note that $k(q)$ is independent of c), to obtain for $f''(q) \not\equiv 0$

$$\frac{1}{q}\frac{dk(q)}{dr} = \frac{1}{f''(q)} = \Phi'(r/p) < 0. \tag{4.16}$$

Thus equation (4.16) is simply the condition that the demand for an input declines with its real price. For any pair (y, x), we label the elasticity of y with respect to x as $E(y, x)$ and rewrite equation (4.16) as elasticity:[7]

$$E(k(q), r) = \frac{d \ln k(q)}{d \ln r} \equiv -\sigma < 0,$$

where $\sigma > 0$ is a measure of the degree of concavity of the production function. The stronger the diminishing returns are, the smaller σ is, and therefore the weaker the relative response of capital intensity to a given change in r will be.

Turning to the marginal quality, differentiate (4.13) and rearrange, using the FOC:[8]

$$c/z\ dz = k(z)\ dr + dc. \tag{4.17}$$

It then follows that $\partial z/\partial c = z/c > 0$ and $\partial z/\partial r = zk(z)/c > 0$. Writing the response as elasticities:

$$E(z, c) = 1, \tag{4.18}$$

$$E(z, r) = \frac{rk(z)}{c} = \frac{S(k; z)}{S(c; z)}, \tag{4.19}$$

where $S(k; q) = rk(q)/qf(q)$ and $S(c; q) = c/qf(q)$ are the factor shares of capital and tax in the output of quality q land. At the margin, where $q = z$, the two shares add up to 1.

Equations (4.18) and (4.19) indicate that the marginal quality increases with r and c and therefore declines with p. This is illustrated in Figure 4.10. A decline in c moves the graph of equation (4.15) downward from $R = 0$ to $\tilde{R} = 0$, and the solution moves from B to C with lower z and $k(z)$. However, as $\Phi(r)$ is unchanged, $k(q)$ remains constant for every q. On the other hand, a decline in r also moves the graph downward, but it also changes $\Phi(r)$ so that $k(q)$ increases for every q. Consequently, the solution moves from B to N with lower z and higher $k(q)$ for all admissible q.

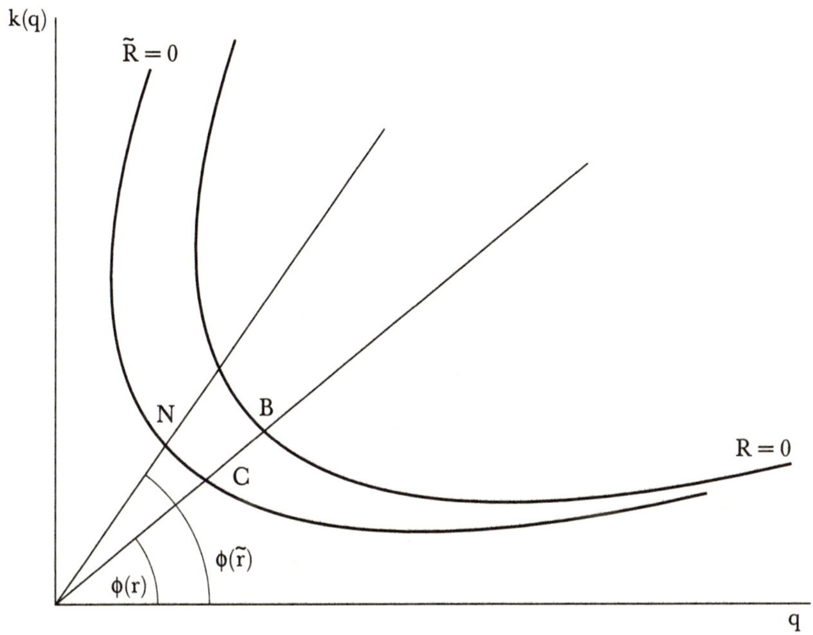

Figure 4.10 Margin displacement

PROPERTY 4.10 An increase in r/p causes an increase in the marginal quality of land and a decline in the capital intensity. An increase in c/p increases the marginal quality of land and does not affect the capital intensity.

This property is summarized in the first block of Table 4.1.

Total Agriculture

The size of cultivated land is determined by the marginal quality alone, and $\partial A/\partial z = -A(z) < 0$ or $E(A, z) = -zA(z)/A$. Combining this result with Property 4.10 we obtain the response function for cultivated land, $A(r/p, c/p)$. The total use of capital increases with $k(q)$, and unlike $k(q)$, it is also affected by z, $\partial K/\partial z = -K(z) < 0$. We combine this with Property 4.10 to obtain $K(r/p,\ c/p)$.[9] We can write an aggregate production function $Y = F(K, A)$, where Y is defined in (4.9). Using the results on the response of K and A, we summarize the supply function: $Y = F(r/p, c/p)$. These results are summarized in the first block of Table 4.1.

PROPERTY 4.11 Cultivated area, total capital use, and output all decline with r/p and c/p.

COROLLARY In this model, a change in the economic environment (r/p and c) affects land and capital in the same direction, and specifically, a land-augmenting shock is also land expanding.

The difference in the responses of the two margins lies in their magnitude. To compare the strength of the response with changes in r, we use (4.18) and write $E(A,c) = E(A,z)$. Also, $E(A,r) = E(A,z)E(z,r)$, using (4.19)

$$\frac{E(k(q),r)}{E(A,r)} = -\frac{\sigma}{E(A,z)}\frac{S(c;z)}{S(k;z)}.$$

The ratio is inversely related to the thickness of the land margin as given by $E(A,z)$ and to the share of capital in the output of the marginal land, $S(k;z)$. It is positively related to the demand elasticity of capital.

PROPERTY 4.12 When the demand elasticity of capital is "high," the change in capital, in response to a change in the rental rate, dominates that of land.

This is an extremely important result. Under the choice of technique framework to be introduced in Chapter 6, the demand elasticity for capital in agriculture, in the domain of the coexistence of techniques, is likely to be very high, and consequently most of the increase in output comes from capital deepening.

If we turn to rent, the total rent to agriculture, R, is

$$R = \int_z^\infty R(q)A(q)dq = Y - rK - cA.$$

Invoke the envelope theorem, $\partial R/\partial r = -K < 0$, $\partial R/\partial c = -A < 0$. We write the result in terms of elasticities:

$$\begin{aligned} E(R,r) &= -S(K)/S(R) \\ E(R,c) &= -S(c)/S(R), \end{aligned} \tag{4.20}$$

where $S(K) = rK/Y$, and $S(c) = cA/Y$ respectively. As $S(K) + S(c) + S(R) = 1$, we can write

$$E(R,r) + E(R,c) = [S(R) - 1]/S(R).$$

It then follows

PROPERTY 4.13 The larger the share of total rent in total output, the more robust the total rent is to changes in the economic environment, represented here by r, c, and p.

Resource Constraint

In this model we replace the assumption that agriculture is a price taker in the market for capital goods with the assumption that capital is fixed at K, and consequently the economic problem is to allocate it to lands of different quality. The allocation decision is described by

$$\max_{k(q),z,r} L(k(q), z, r) = \int_z^\infty [qf(k(q)/q) - c]A(q)dq - r[\int_z^\infty A(q)k(q)dq - K], \tag{4.21}$$

where r is the shadow price of capital, measured in units of output. The FOC are equations (4.12) and (4.13) with p set at 1 and the resource constraint

$$L_3(\cdot) = \int_z^\infty A(q)k(q)dq - K = 0. \tag{4.22}$$

The solution for $k(q)$ and z is similar to the first case. The difference is that now r is endogenous, and therefore we cannot solve for $k(q)$ independently from the solution for z and r. With this qualification, the solution can be illustrated in terms of Figure 4.10.

To obtain the response of resource allocation to the state variables K and c, we differentiate the first-order conditions. The derivative of the first of these conditions is given by equation (4.16) above, and that of the second is given by equation (4.17). Finally, to differentiate equation (4.22), we use equations (4.14) and (4.6) to rewrite it:

$$\Phi(r)Q = K. \tag{4.23}$$

Hence $\Phi(r)dQ + \Phi'(r)Qdr = dK$. Use equation (4.6) to write $dQ = -zA(z)dz$ and write the differential of equation (4.23) as

$$-\Phi(r)zA(z)dz + \Phi'(r)Qdr = dK. \tag{4.24}$$

Use equation (4.14) to write equations (4.17) and (4.24) in matrix notations:

$$\begin{bmatrix} c & -\Phi(r)z^2 \\ -\Phi(r)zA(z) & \Phi'(r)Q \end{bmatrix} \begin{bmatrix} dz \\ dr \end{bmatrix} = \begin{bmatrix} zdc \\ dK \end{bmatrix} \tag{4.25}$$

The system is solved for dr and dz in terms of dK and dc. Label the matrix M, and note that except for M_{11}, all elements of M are negative; therefore det M is negative as well. As $M_{11} = c$, we obtain

$$c(\det M)^{-1} = \partial r/\partial K < 0. \tag{4.26}$$

Equation (4.26) bridges the two models, and the qualitative results of the first model are preserved.

The Effect of Capital

An increase in K causes a reduction of r which in turn increases the level of intensity and the rent on all cultivated lands. Consequently, the rent on the marginal land becomes positive, and the marginal quality declines.[10]

PROPERTY 4.14 An increase in capital causes a decline in the marginal quality land and in the real rental rate, r/p, and an increase in capital intensity. As a result, cultivated land, output, and total rent on land increase.

The strength of the response of A to K is proportional to the abundance of marginal land, measured by $E(A, z)$, to the capital intensity of the technology as measured by the share of capital on the marginal land, and to the response of r to changes in K as determined by the degree of concavity of the production function.

The elasticity $E(z, r)$ in this model has the same appearance as that of equation (4.19), but it is important to note that in this model both z and r are endogenous, and as such they vary only in response to changes in K or c. Thus, in the present case, the elasticity is just a characterization of the changes in z and r along the path generated by a change in K with c held constant.

Effect of Tax

The main difference of this model from the first one is that under a resource constraint a change in the tax affects the level of intensity. A rise in the tax rate causes a decline in the rent, and thereby the marginal quality land is forced out of production. This frees capital to be distributed to the cultivated land and thus causes an increase in the intensity of capital and a decline in the rate of return. This can be seen by solving equation (4.25) to obtain $\partial z/\partial c > 0$, $\partial r/\partial c < 0$, and

$$E(k(q), c) = E(k(q), r)E(r, c) > 0. \tag{4.27}$$

Qualitatively, the response of the size of the cultivated land is similar to that obtained in the first model:

$$E(A, c) = E(A, z)E(z, c) < 0. \tag{4.28}$$

When a unit of marginal land goes out of production, output declines by $zf(z)$ and increases by reallocation of capital to the cultivated land by $rk(z)$, the difference between these two terms is c, which is the net decline of output due to the increase in the tax. The total loss of output depends on the size of the margin. This result can be obtained formally by differentiating (4.11) with respect to z, using the optimal quantities of $k(q)$.

PROPERTY 4.15 An increase in the land real tax rate, c/p, causes an increase in the marginal quality land, a decline in the shadow rental rate, and a rise in capital intensity. As a result, cultivated land, output, and total rent decline.

We thus see that taxing land is not costless, and a decrease in the tax increases output. Any cost specific to land will have a similar effect to that of a land tax. It is important to differentiate between a fixed set-up cost and ongoing or variable cost. The first will affect the pace of reclamation of new land; the latter will affect the size of the land actually cultivated in a given year.

The qualitative results of this model are summarized in the second block of Table 4.1.

Output Quota

In the foregoing discussion, product demand was taken to be perfectly elastic. We now analyze the other extreme case, where the demand is perfectly inelastic, and examine the changes in factor demand caused by a change in output. The analysis is related to a variety of subjects, of which the most important is the differentiation between the substitution and expansion effects of a change in the economic environment on the demand for land. The substitution effect is relevant for the evaluation of the consequences of support programs with production quotas.

When output is held fixed, the problem of optimal resource allocation is that of cost minimization:

$$\min_{k(q),z,p} L(k(q), z, p) = rK + cA - p(Y - Y^*), \tag{4.29}$$

where A, K, and Y are defined in equations (4.5), (4.7), and (4.9) respectively. The Lagrange multiplier, p, is the marginal cost of producing Y^*. The interpretation is that when the demand is perfectly inelastic, the price is determined by the supply function. The FOC are

$$L_1 \equiv \partial L(\cdot)/\partial k(q) = r - pf'(q) = 0, \tag{4.30}$$

$$L_2 \equiv \partial L(\cdot)/\partial z = pzf[k(z)/z] - c - rk(z) = 0, \tag{4.31}$$

$$L_3 \equiv Y^* - \int_z^\infty qf(k(q)/q)A(q)dq = 0. \tag{4.32}$$

Differentiation of the FOC yields

$$dr = pf''(q)/q\ dk(q) + f'(q)\ dp, \tag{4.33}$$

$$c/z\ dz + zf(\cdot)\ dp = k(z)\ dr + dc, \text{ [11]} \tag{4.34}$$

$$dY^* - (m/p)\ dr = -mr/p^2\ dp - Y(z)\ dz, \text{ [12]} \tag{4.35}$$

where $m \equiv Q\Phi'(r/p)(r/p) < 0$. The system (4.34) and (4.35) can be written in matrix notation:

$$\begin{bmatrix} -mr/p^2 & -Y(z) \\ zf(z) & c/z \end{bmatrix} \begin{bmatrix} dp \\ dz \end{bmatrix} = \begin{bmatrix} 1 & -m/p & 0 \\ 0 & k(z) & 1 \end{bmatrix} \begin{bmatrix} dY^* \\ dr \\ dc \end{bmatrix}. \tag{4.36}$$

$-Y(z)$ is the only negative term in the matrices in (4.36). We can therefore sign the partial derivatives as follows:

$$\underset{-\ -\ +}{z(Y, r, c)}, \quad \underset{+\ +\ +}{p(Y, r, c)}. \tag{4.37}$$

We solve for dp from equation (4.36) and use equation (4.33) to solve for $dk(q)$.

With these results we can now make inferences about the response of the rest of the system to a change in the economic environment. An increase in r causes an increase in p, but relatively less than the increase in r because capital is not the only input. Consequently, the ratio r/p rises, and $k(q)$ declines. To meet the output quota, land must expand, and therefore z must decline. The final outcome is also a decline in K, because of the increase in A while the level of output is unchanged. For z to decline in response to the rise in r, it is required that the rent on the marginal land increases; this is accomplished by the increase in p. If the rent increases on all quality land, the total rent to agriculture increases. This result reflects only the supply side, and it is unlikely that consumers would be willing to buy the initial quantity at higher prices. The actual implementation of such a scheme requires policy measures that would entail a welfare loss.

In contrast to the case of unrestricted output, summarized in Properties 4.11 and 4.12, under an output quota the demand for land and the demand for capital move in opposite directions. This movement represents the substitution effect, or a movement along an isoquant of the aggregate production function. The expansion effect is in the same direction for the two inputs. An increase in Y causes a decline in z, an increase in A, an increase in p, a decline in r/p, an increase in $k(q)$ for all q, and hence an increase in K. From this we infer that when output is unrestricted, the expansion effect, as in the case covered by Property 4.11, generated by a change in the factor prices, dominated the substitution effect. To obtain the point where the two effects on the demand for land are equal, we impose $dA = 0$ which implies $dz = 0$ and solve equation (4.36), allowing output to change. This is assigned as an exercise.

An increase in c causes an increase in z, a decline in A, and an increase in K. Also, p increases, hence r/p declines, and $k(q)$ increases for all q. The rent decreases due to the increase in the tax on agriculture. Here again, as in the case of capital constraint, a land tax affects resource allocation.

The results are summarized in Property 4.16 and in the third block of Table 4.1.

PROPERTY 4.16 Under an output quota, the quality of marginal land declines with r and increases with c. A change of either of these prices causes land and capital to move in opposite directions.

The Role of Prices and the Competitive Position of Agriculture

The foregoing analysis has repercussions for several attributes of cardinal importance for policy considerations. The nature and the strength of the response of agriculture to external or internal shocks is related to its competitive position, a concept we want to define explicitly.

DEFINITION The *competitive position* is measured by the factor share of land that makes up the agricultural-specific factor of production.

The higher the factor share of land, the less agriculture is susceptible to shocks. It is important to emphasize that the measure does not speak of the competitive position of farmers. Farmers who operate on the margin of their profitability because of low ability or because of past decisions affecting their balance sheets may be wiped out by unfavorable shocks. However, the land remains in agriculture and will be acquired by others. Unfavorable shocks will thus cause revaluation of assets, sometimes severely, but the effect on output and resource utilization will be much milder.

The effect of shocks on agriculture can then be viewed at two levels, the effect on land and the effect on output. The effect on land is related to the effect on the rent of the marginal land. When the rent becomes negative, land goes out of production. The effect on output is analyzed in Chapter 14.

Exercises

4.1 (Food import)
A small open country is exporting nonagriculture (NA) and importing agriculture (A). Under what conditions, if any, would capital deepening (increasing k) increase jointly food consumption, production, and import?

4.2 (Equilibrium path)
Use the restricted demand function to show the case where capital accumulation causes the country to change from exporting to importing nonagriculture.

4.3 (Equilibrium path under distortion)
Repeat the analysis of the equilibrium path of a closed economy generated by an increase in k for an economy that subsidizes agriculture. What is the similarity and the difference from that obtained for an economy free of intervention?

4.4 (Land economics)
Assume that the production function of quality q land is

$$Y(q) = qF[A(q), K(q)],$$

so that the quality does not affect the marginal rate of substitution of K and A. Examine the three models discussed in Chapter 4. What propositions, if any, are affected by this change of specification of the production function?

4.5 Assume that the "land tax" is an increasing function of quality: $dc(q)/dq > 0$. Examine the case of agriculture as a price taker, using the production function in the chapter, and to simplify set $p = 1$. Derive the condition for the marginal quality.

4.6 Assume that output is exogenous.

(a) There is a permanent decline in price (rental rate) of capital, r, whereas the tax on land, c, remains constant. Derive the change in the marginal cost and in the output under the condition that the extensive margin (z) is unchanged.

(b) Interpret the result.

Note: the point of departure is the equilibrium under an output quota.

5

The Consequences of Technical Change

The performance of the economy depends to a large extent on the nature of its implemented technology. The empirical determination of the role of technology, however, is not a simple matter, as can be seen from the voluminous work on the subject. Basically, the difficulty arises from the fact that technology is not an observed quantity but rather an abstract concept. The standard approach has been to identify technology with a production function; technological change has thus been associated with shifts in the production functions. The concept of a production function is borrowed from the sciences, where input-output relationships are generated by what are thought to be well-described processes. As such, the production functions describe some laws of nature. Empirical applications that are close in spirit to such a concept are given by agricultural production functions (see Heady and Dillon, 1961). Examples from agriculture had a general flavor in the early days of economic theory, when agriculture accounted for a large part of total output. This attribute has diminished with time, and it became desirable to have applications similar to nonbiological processes, leading to "engineering production functions" (Chenery, 1949). Thus, in the words of Solow (1967, p. 26), "The pure theory of production is fundamentally microeconomic in character: it deals with physically identifiable inputs and outputs. In the classroom one usually says that the economic theory of production takes for granted the 'engineering' relationships between inputs and outputs and goes on from there. By contrast, much (though not quite all) of the recent interest in the theory of production has been macroeconomic in character. Since the 'inputs' and 'outputs' are statistical aggregates like 'labor,' 'plant,' 'equipment,' 'durable manufactures,' there is no possibility of finding engineering relationships. Econometric methods have to do the duty instead. Still, it remains an intriguing idea to deduce economically useful production functions from raw technological information."

The role attributed to econometric analysis in this statement is rather narrow and basically an impossible one. For one thing, the aggregation of inputs and outputs depends on prices, and to do it right, it requires a knowledge of the production functions, exactly what one wants to estimate with the aggregated variables. But more important, micro "engineering functions" change with time and as such affect the relationships among the aggregates. Thus there is no pure engineering-type relationship that can be revealed by econometrics.

The work on production functions has progressed in several directions, determined largely by the objective of the study. The empirically oriented work has searched for algebraic relationships that make economic sense and at the same time can be fitted to the data. The economic sense is judged by requirements that are imposed on the micro functions. The estimation is conducted under the basic, but tacit, assumption that all the observations were generated from the same aggregate relationship, which by itself is allowed to change with time in one way or another. That work alone is very rich, and some aspects of it are reviewed in Chapter 11.

Alternatively, theoretical work on technical change has concentrated on formulations that can be conveniently analyzed. The outcome of such analysis is not the same as the outcome of the empirically oriented literature. The difference between the two approaches can be attributed to the complexity of the subject matter, and more work is needed to integrate the various approaches.

Our interest in the subject covers both aspects. We want to trace the effect of technical change on the behavior of the economy with the purpose, however, of being able to come up with empirically verifiable conclusions. In this we continue with the procedure we have followed thus far. The chapter begins by tracing the effect of technical change on the behavior of our simple economy. For that matter, the convenient conventional formulations of technical change are adopted. Later on, Chapter 6 will take up a somewhat different view of technology that is expected to be more realistic and therefore more pertinent empirically. Basically, that approach recognizes that at any time, the economy employs many techniques, each identified with a production function. Technology is thus identified with the collection of all techniques. This is in contrast to the standard approach, to be followed in this chapter, which assumes that the technology of each sector can be represented by a well-defined production function. The empirical aspects are discussed in Chapters 11 to 14.

A general formulation of technical change is to write the production function with an explicit representation of a technology shifter, t. For a single-output production function with two inputs, this is written as

$$Y = F(K, L, t), \quad \frac{\partial F}{\partial t} \geq 0. \tag{5.1}$$

The essence of technical change is that a given set of inputs gives a larger output, or alternatively, that the same output can be obtained with less inputs. The formulation in (5.1) is too general to allow specific results. A common simplification is that of factor-augmenting technical changes (FATC):

$$Y = F[A_L(t)L, A_K(t)K], \tag{5.2}$$

where $A_L(t)$ and $A_K(t)$ are positive functions of the technology index t. Because it is assumed that technology improves with time, we usually identify t with time. Actually, A_L and A_K can be functions of various variables. This possibility is further discussed in Chapters 6 and 13. For the present discussion, however, they are assumed to be determined uniquely by the technology, which in turn is monotonic increasing with time. As such, the identification of t with time is just a question of language. The essence of (5.2) is that the new technology expresses itself only as a result of an interaction with the inputs. Consequently, the products $A_L(t)L$ and $A_K(t)K$ are viewed as effective inputs measured in quality units, often referred to as efficiency units. The functions can be standardized so that for any arbitrary technology, designated as $t = 0$, we have $A_L(0) = A_K(0) = 1$. $A_L(t)$ and $A_K(t)$ are referred to here as labor- and capital-augmenting functions respectively.

A special case of this formulation is that of equal augmentation $A_L(t) = A_K(t) = A(t)$ for all t. Since F is homogeneous of degree 1, $A(t)$ can be factored out so that

$$Y = A(t)F(K, L). \tag{5.3}$$

In this case, technical change (TC) is referred to as Hicks neutral (NTC). The neutrality of this concept is related to the invariance of the marginal rate of factor substitution to technical change.

Other cases of interest occur when only one input is affected by the TC. The case of $A_L(t) > 1$ and $A_K(t) = 1$ is identical with what is known as Harrod-neutral TC (HNTC), whereas the opposite case of $A_L(t) = 1$ and $A_K(t) > 1$ is known as Solow-neutral TC (SNTC). These concepts of neutrality are discussed below.

There is analytic convenience, as well as economic insight, in dealing separately with NTC and factor augmentation. For that purpose (5.2) is rewritten by factoring out one of the A's. For instance

$$Y = A_L(t)F[a_k(t)K, L], \tag{5.4}$$

where $a_k(t) = A_K(t)/A_L(t)$.

Note that $a_k(t)$ can now be viewed as a capital-augmenting function, if $a_k(t)$ is larger than 1. If $a_k \leq 1$, then, holding K constant, the term $a_k(t)K$ will decline with time. In this case it is more meaningful to factor out A_K. Thus for $F(\cdot)$ to increase with t, the rule for factoring out should be: $\underline{A}(t) = \min(A_L(t), A_K(t))$. The factored function $A(t)$ is the common rate of augmentation of the two factors. This is the neutral component.

We now turn to the two-sector economy where we have two production functions. The TC in each sector is decomposed according to (5.4). The analysis of the effect of TC on the economy is first conducted by considering only NTC in the two sectors. This is followed by analyzing only one factor augmentation in each sector. The final outcome of course is obtained by combining the two cases.

Technical change affects the supply side of the economy and consequently the equilibrium position. In tracing the effect on the supply side, we differentiate among various possible effects: allocation, productivity, and cost, to be explained below.

Hicks-Neutral Technical Change

The presentation builds up gradually to cover the various possibilities with the aid of graphical presentation, followed by a summary. Some readers may prefer to start with the summary and supplement it with the graphical presentation.

General Results

In this section we examine the effect of NTC in the two sectors. Incorporating this assumption, we replace the production functions in (2.8) with

$$y_1 = \ell A_1(t) f_1(k_1) \tag{5.5}$$

$$y_2 = (1 - \ell) A_2(t) f_2(k_2). \tag{5.6}$$

The competitive conditions are modified accordingly:

$$r/p_i(\omega, t) = A_i(t) f_i'(k_i) \tag{5.7}$$

$$w/p_i(\omega, t) = A_i(t)[f_i(k_i) - k_i f_i'(k_i)]. \tag{5.8}$$

The supply system is now given by equations (5.5) to (5.8) and the full employment condition, (2.13).

The wage-rental ratios, $\omega_i(k_i)$, are unaffected by $A_i(t)$, and consequently the labor allocation is determined by (2.13). On the other hand, the price and the supply functions depend on the technology and are therefore labeled $p(\omega, t)$, and $y_i(p, k, t)$, or $y_i(p, t)$ when the dependence on k is suppressed.

To derive the price equation, we follow the procedure employed in Chapter 2 and evaluate the ratio of the sectoral cost functions. We utilize the fact that $k_i(\omega)$ is unaffected by the NTC. Consider an initial allocation (K_{i0}, L_{i0}) producing output Y_{i0} with technology $A_i(0) = 1$. The average cost is $c_i(w, r, 0)$. Given the *same* input allocation and the new technology $A_i(t)$, *total* cost remains the same, but *average* cost declines: $c_i(w, r, t) = c_i(w, r, 0)/A_i(t)$. Consequently, the price equation at t can be related to that of the base technology:

$$p(\omega, t) = \frac{A_2(t)}{A_1(t)} p(\omega, 0). \tag{5.9}$$

DEFINITION The sector with a larger rate of technical change is referred to as the *progressive sector.*

PROPERTY 5.1 (the price effect of NTC) The relative price of the progressive sector declines.

It is only in the special case of $A_2(t) = A_1(t)$ that $p(\omega, t) = p(\omega, 0)$.

Next we turn to examine the changes in the outputs corresponding to a given allocation. Resources are held constant, and therefore the dependence on k is suppressed in the notation.

Neutral Technical Change of Equal Rates

The assumption here is that $A_1(t) = A_2(t) = A(t)$. Because the $\omega_i(k_i)$ functions are unaffected by the NTC, there is no change in resource allocation for any given ω. The change in outputs corresponding to a given resource allocation is determined by $A(t)$. This is defined as the productivity effect.

DEFINITION The *productivity effect of technical change* is the increase in output derived from a constant bundle of resources.

By assumption, we deal here with the case where the productivity effect is the same for both sectors. This is illustrated in Figure 5.1 as a shift of the transformation curve. Point A is the initial point, and point B, located on a ray from the origin through A, represents the productivity effect. Equal rates of NTC leave the price function unchanged so that $p_B = p_A$, and the supply functions are augmented by the productivity effect, $y_i(p, t) = A_i(t)y_i(p, 0)$.

On the demand side, the technical change increases income, thereby increasing the consumption possibilities of the economy, and the demand increases accordingly. Let $y(p, t) = A(t)y(p, 0)$ represent the income attained at

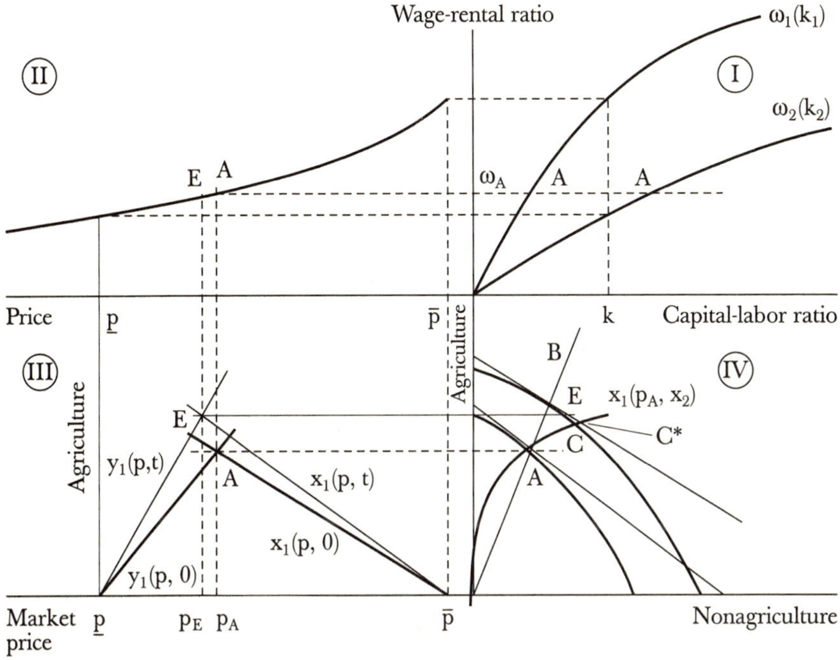

Figure 5.1 Hicks-neutral technical change: Equal rates

price p and technology t. The rate of change of income due to t is $\hat{A}$. This is also the rate of the shift of the supply functions of both products. Thus there is an upward shift in supply and demand, and consequently the outputs and the consumption of the two goods increase. The change in the excess demand depends on the relative rates of growth of supply and demand, the latter depending on the income elasticity. Because the income elasticity for agriculture is less than 1, the demand for agriculture shifts relatively less than the supply, and hence an excess supply of agriculture is likely to occur. As derived from equation (5.13) below, this is true only when the ratio of output to consumption in agriculture, y_1/x_1, is larger than the income elasticity E_{1c}, a condition that is generally met.

Small Open Economy

For the small open economy, an increase in excess supply implies an increase in the net export of agriculture. This can be shown in Figure 5.1 where the output changes from A to B. Consumption is at C^*, obtained at the intersection of the new budget line with the demand $x_1(p_A, x_2)$. Initially the country did not trade, and under the new technology it becomes an exporter of agriculture.

PROPERTY 5.2 (neutral technical change of equal rates; open economy) In general, neutral technical change of equal rates in the two sectors increases the net export of the income-inelastic product.

The statement is qualified by the term "in general" to account for the case where agricultural production is small relative to consumption, in which case the increase in demand is larger than the increase in production. The condition for this qualification is derived below (equation 5.12).

The foregoing analysis has important implications for possible changes in trade resulting from technical change. With equal rates of technical change, the changes in trade reflect the income elasticities and the position of the economy. When import does not constitute a major component of consumption, the technical change increases the excess supply of the income-inelastic product. As a consequence, if the country is initially self-sufficient, it will now become an exporter of agriculture. Alternatively, the country can change from importing to exporting food. This simple framework can explain a change such as the one that occurred in India, which switched from importing to exporting grain. This example emphasizes the crucial role played by the income elasticity. If the income elasticity of food were larger than 1, the situation would be reversed.

Closed Economy

In the case of a closed economy, output is equal to consumption in each sector. It is therefore sufficient that the income elasticity for food is less than 1 for the technical change to produce an excess supply of food and for the price of agriculture to decline. The change in the equilibrium position is illustrated in Figure 5.1, where the demand at the initial price, p_A, increases to C, not C^* as in the case of the open economy. The new equilibrium point E is located between B and C. It is also shown in panel III, where the initial point A is located on the initial supply function, labeled as $y_1(p, 0)$, whereas E is located on the new supply curve, labeled $y_1(p, t)$. The reader is invited to trace the new equilibrium values in the remaining panels of Figure 5.1 and to show that ω declines to ω_E as p declines from p_A to p_E, and k_i declines correspondingly. The corresponding change in resource allocation takes place under a constant k, and as follows from the discussion in Chapter 2, it requires a shift of resources to the capital-intensive sector. Since the productivity effect is the same in the two sectors, the change in resource allocation implies a larger relative increase in the output of sector 2, which is the capital-intensive and the high income elasticity sector.

The dependence of the solution on income elasticity is illustrated by the location of point C relative to B. In the special case when the demand is homothetic, C and B will coincide, and the price will remain unchanged. If the income elasticity of agriculture were larger than 1, point C, and therefore E, would be to the left of B, with $p_E \geq p_A$ and consequently $\omega_E \geq \omega_A$.

PROPERTY 5.3 (neutral technical change of equal rates; closed economy) A neutral technical change of equal rates produces equal productivity effects in the two sectors. As a result, outputs increase in the two sectors. The relative price of the product whose income elasticity is smaller than 1 declines. The wage-rental ratio decreases (increases) when the income-inelastic sector is labor (capital) intensive. Prices are unaffected when both income elasticities are unitary or when factor intensities are the same.

The discussion is pertinent to the understanding of the developments in the world market for basic agricultural products. For this purpose the world is considered as a closed economy. Initially, this market is postulated to be in equilibrium at A, as shown in Figure 5.1. Technical change moves it to E with a decline in world price. This is consistent with the evidence summarized in Figures 1.1 to 1.4. This discussion is illustrative and not exhaustive, of course, as there are other forms of technical change, considered below and in Chapter 6, which also affect the outcome. However, recall the discussion at the beginning of this chapter, where neutral technical change of equal rates was interpreted as the common rate to all sectors. As such this extracts a considerable portion of the technical change that has taken place.

Neutral Technical Change of Unequal Rates

Next we turn to unequal rates of NTC. In dealing with this case it suffices to consider TC in one sector only, because any NTC in the two sectors can be decomposed as follows: label $[\cdot] = [A_1(t), A_2(t)]$, and define $\underline{A}(t) = \min[\cdot]$, $\overline{A}(t) = \max[\cdot]$. The equal rate is given by $\underline{A}(t)$, and the differential rate is $\overline{A}(t) - \underline{A}(t)$.

In what follows we let agriculture be the progressive sector in that $A_1(t) > 1$ and $A_2(t) = 1$. Consequently, the productivity effect is limited to agriculture. It is shown in panel IV of Figure 5.2 as a movement from A to B. Both of these points are obtained with the resource allocation corresponding to the wage-rental ratio ω_A.

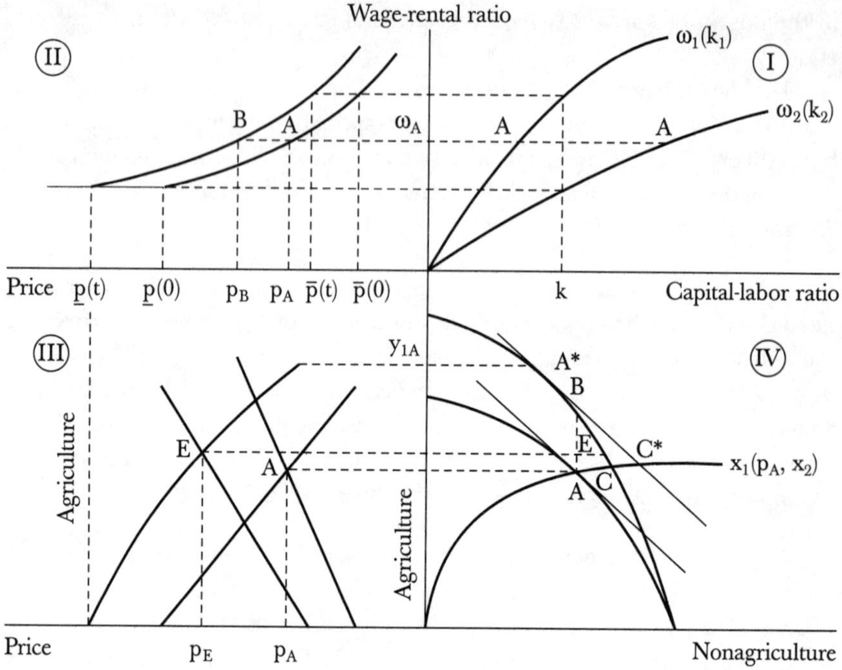

Figure 5.2 Hicks-neutral technical change in agriculture

Unequal rates of technical change affect the price equation, as can be seen from equation (5.9). This is shown in panel II of Figure 5.2, with $p_B < p_A$. The initial price, p_A, can be restored by shifting resources to the progressive sector, resulting in point A^* where $p_{A*} = p_A$. The movement from B to A^* is referred to as the cost effect. More formally, the cost effect is $y_i(p,t) - A_i(t)y_i(p,0), i = 1, 2$.

DEFINITION (cost effect) The *cost effect* of technical change is the shift of supply, over and above the productivity effect, necessary to maintain a constant price.

PROPERTY 5.4 (cost effect) The cost effect of technical change on output is positive for the progressive sector and negative for the passive sector.

Thus, in the progressive sector, the cost effect supplements the productivity effect. In the passive sector, the cost effect reduces output, whereas the productivity effect leaves the output of that sector unchanged. The shift of the supply function of the progressive sector is illustrated in panel III of Figure 5.2.

The technical change has a positive income effect on the demand of both products. Thus, for the passive product, the demand increases, whereas the supply declines; therefore its excess demand increases. For the progressive sector both demand and supply increase, but demand increases less than supply. With the two products being normal, the increase in income is distributed between the two products, and therefore the increase in demand for either product is smaller than the increase in income. The increase in income is equal to the productivity effect, which is smaller than the increase in supply, which also includes the cost effect. Consequently, the excess supply of the progressive sector increases. The open economy case is illustrated in Figure 5.2 where output changes from A to A^* and demand moves to C^*.

PROPERTY 5.5 (technical change in one sector; open economy) A neutral technical change in one sector increases the net export of the progressive sector.

In the closed economy, the increase in the excess supply of the progressive sector results in a decline of its price and an increase in its equilibrium output. If this increase in output is smaller than the productivity effect, resources are released from the progressive sector to increase production in the passive sector. The actual outcome depends on the demand elasticity, as is shown below. Another way of viewing the change is to indicate that in the progressive sector the income and price effects supplement each other, and the equilibrium quantity will increase. For the passive sector the two effects contradict each other, and the direction of the change is ambiguous.

The discussion is illustrated in Figure 5.2, where the demand $x_1(p_A, x_2)$ intersects the new transformation curve at C. At p_A, the excess supply is given by $z_1(p_A, t) = y_{1A^*} - x_{1C} > 0$, and the equilibrium price will be lower than p_A. The output of the progressive sector will increase. The equilibrium output of the passive sector depends on the price elasticity of demand. To see this we obtain from (5.9) $\hat{p}(\omega)\mid_{\omega,A_2(t)} = -\hat{A}_1(t)$. That is, with ω and technology in nonagriculture held constant, the rate of change in p is equal to the rate of technical change (with sign reversed). Consequently, $p_B = p_A(1 - \hat{A}_1)$. On the other hand, $y_{1B} = y_{1A}(1 + \hat{A}_1)$. Thus B represents the same proportionate increase in y_1 and decline in p. Therefore the new demand curve will pass through B when the price elasticity of (2.18) is unitary. It will intersect to the left of B when the price elasticity is larger than 1 and to the right of B when the elasticity is smaller than 1.

To trace the implications of the shift in equilibrium for resource allocation, we note that because B represents the same resource allocation as A, $\omega_B = \omega_A$. Let the progressive sector be labor intensive, and p be its relative price. Then points on the transformation curve to the right of B correspond to values of

ω that are lower than ω_A and conversely for points to the left of B. In other words, points to the right of B imply a shift of resources to the passive sector, which in our case is capital intensive, whereas points to the left of B imply a shift of resources away from the passive sector. The discussion can now be summarized:

PROPERTY 5.6 (neutral technical change in one sector; closed economy) A neutral technical change in one sector leads to an increase in the output and a decline of the equilibrium price of the progressive sector. The equilibrium output of the passive sector declines, remains constant, or increases when the absolute value of the demand elasticity for the progressive product is larger, equal, or smaller than 1 respectively. Resources shift in the same direction as the output of the passive sector. The wage-rental ratio moves in the direction of the resource allocation to the labor-intensive sector.

Effect on Trade

The relationships among technical change, growth, and food import have attracted some attention. It has been observed that countries that have enjoyed a fast economic growth have also increased their food import. Such an association is sometimes erroneously interpreted to mean that food import is the source or the cause of growth. It is therefore useful to summarize the foregoing discussion by evaluating the effect of NTC on trade for the open economy and its further consequences on world food prices.

The output of the small open economy is determined by the world price. The technical change causes an increase in output and hence in income and thereby an income effect on demand. The excess demand for agriculture is then affected by the change in demand and supply. The net import in this case is equal to the excess demand. Let

$$z_1(p,t) = x_1[p, y(p,t)] - y_1(p,t). \tag{5.10}$$

Let E_{1c} be the income elasticity of x_1 with respect to y, $S_1 = py_1/y$, and differentiate $y(p,t)$ with respect to t:

$$\frac{\partial \ln y}{\partial t}\Big|_p = S_1\hat{A}_1 + (1 - S_1)\hat{A}_2 \equiv \hat{A}, \quad \text{then}$$

$$\partial z_{1t}/\partial t = x_1(E_{1c}\hat{A} - \frac{y_1}{x_1}\hat{A}_1), \quad \text{substituting for} \hat{A},$$

$$\partial z_{1t}/\partial t = x_1(\hat{A}_1(E_{1c}S_1 - \frac{y_1}{x_1}) + E_{1c}(1 - S_1)\hat{A}_2]. \tag{5.11}$$

Consider leading cases.

Equal rates. $\hat{A}_2 = \hat{A}_1$, then

$$\text{sign } \partial z_{1t}/\partial t = \text{sign}(E_{1c} - y_1/x_1). \tag{5.12}$$

For countries that do not import agriculture, $y_1/x_1 \geq 1$, and since $E_{1c} < 1$, $\partial z_{1t}/\partial t < 0$, implying an increase of agricultural export. With the exception of countries where domestic agricultural production covers only a small fraction of consumption, food-importing countries are likely to decrease their import. The exception requires that the fraction of domestic production in consumption should be smaller than the income elasticity. In this case, an increase in output at rate $\hat{A}$ in both sectors increases demand for agriculture by $\hat{A}E_{1c}x_1$, whereas supply increases by $\hat{A}y_1$. When y_1/x_1 is relatively small, excess demand increases. This case is not applicable to most countries.

Agricultural-based growth. In this case agriculture is the progressive sector, $\hat{A}_2 = 0$, then

$$\text{sign } \partial z_1/\partial t = \text{sign}(S_1 E_{1c} - y_1/x_1). \tag{5.13}$$

This expression is similar to (5.12), except that now E_{1c} is replaced by $S_1 E_{1c}$ because the increase in income originates only in agriculture. In this case the agricultural net export will increase.

Nonagricultural-based growth. Here technical change occurs only in nonagriculture, $\hat{A}_1 = 0$, and (5.11) reduces to

$$\partial z_1/\partial t = x_1 E_{1c}(1 - S_1)\hat{A}_2. \tag{5.14}$$

The income effect increases the demand, whereas the cost effect causes a decline of supply. Consequently, *net* agricultural import increases. This is a result of the fact that agriculture is the passive sector.

The effect on the volume of trade depends on whether the country is initially importing or exporting agriculture. In the first case, import increases, and under balanced trade export of nonagriculture increases as well. Thus the nonagricultural growth is the source of financing needed for the growth of agricultural imports. If the country exports agriculture, export declines, and with it, total trade declines.

To conclude, the *net* import of agriculture is positively related to technical change in nonagriculture and, with unimportant exceptions, negatively related to technical change in agriculture.

Closed Economy and the Global Effect

In the closed economy the changes in the excess demand cause price changes. In this case, it is convenient to express the excess demand in terms of a given resource allocation, which we identify by ω, because ω is unaffected by NTC. Thus the supply of the ith product conditional on resource allocation is written as $y_i(\omega, A_i)$. As total resources are held constant, k is suppressed. The excess demand for the closed economy is

$$z_1(\omega, t) = x_1(p(\omega), y_2(\omega, A_2)) - y_1(\omega, A_1), \tag{5.15}$$

where A_i are functions of the technology index t. Under NTC, $y_i(\omega, A_i) = A_i y_i(\omega)$. Differentiate $z_1(\omega, t)$ with respect to t and impose $x_2 = y_2(\omega, A_2)$,

$$\frac{\partial z_1}{\partial t}\Big|_\omega = \frac{\partial x_1}{\partial p}\frac{\partial p}{\partial t} + \frac{\partial x_1}{\partial x_2}\frac{\partial y_2}{\partial t} - \frac{\partial y_1}{\partial t}.$$

Write the expressions in terms of elasticities, using (5.9):

$$\begin{aligned}\frac{\partial z_1}{\partial t}\Big|_\omega &= x_1[\hat{A}_1(E^r_{1p} - 1) + \hat{A}_2(E^r_{1c} - E^r_{1p}].\\ &= x_1[\hat{A}_1(E^r_{1c} - 1) + (\hat{A}_2 - \hat{A}_1)(E^r_{1c} - E^r_{1p})]\end{aligned} \tag{5.16}$$

where E^r_{1c} and $-E^r_{1p}$ are the income and price elasticities for agriculture derived from the demand $x_1(p, x_2)$: $E^r_{1c} = \partial \ln x_1/\partial \ln x_2$, $-E^r_{1p} = \partial \ln x_1/\partial \ln p$.

If we assume that the economy is initially in equilibrium, then the change in price can be signed by utilizing the convergence assumption; for $z_1 \neq 0$, $z_1 dp > 0$. When the technical change generates a positive excess demand, the price will increase accordingly. More generally,

$$\text{sign}\ \frac{\partial p}{\partial t}\Big|_{\text{eq}} = \text{sign}\ \frac{\partial z_1}{\partial t}\Big|_\omega.$$

Under equal rates,

$$\hat{A}_1 = \hat{A}_2 = \hat{A},\ \text{sign}\ \partial z_1/\partial t = \text{sign}(E^r_{1c} - 1).$$

Agriculture, being income inelastic, will realize a net excess supply and a decline in p. In this case the rate of technical change is the same in both sectors; therefore the price equation remains unchanged, and the change in p is sufficient to determine the change of the other variables in the system. For instance, if agriculture is labor intensive, a decline in p causes a decline in ω and in $k_i(\omega)$ and a move of resources to nonagriculture.

For agricultural-based growth, $\hat{A}_1 > 0$ and $\hat{A}_2 = 0$, and therefore

$$\text{sign}\ \partial z_i/\partial t = \text{sign}(E^r_{1p} - 1).$$

Because the demand for agriculture is price inelastic, the technical change generates excess supply and therefore a decline in p.

To evaluate the effect on the rest of the system, note that in this case the price equation changes, and the change in p cannot characterize the changes in the other variables. Instead, such changes are better characterized in terms of the output of the passive sector.

For nonagricultural-based growth, $\hat{A}_2 > 0$ and $\hat{A}_1 = 0$, hence

$$\frac{\partial z_1}{\partial t} |_{\omega} = x_1 \hat{A}_2 (E^r_{1c} - E^r_{1p}).$$

The direction of the change in the excess demand is determined by the magnitudes of the income effect and the substitution effect in demand away from agriculture. When the income effect is dominating, the excess demand increases, as does the price of agriculture. When the income effect is relatively weak, the demand for agriculture declines because the price of nonagriculture declines due to the technical change, and therefore the production of the initial level of agriculture is now more costly.

Note that under unequal rates of NTC, the importance of the difference $\hat{A}_2 - \hat{A}_1$ depends on the relative strength of the income and price elasticities.

The Contribution of Agriculture to Economic Growth

This is a good place to return to the remark in Chapter 1 on the contribution of agriculture to economic growth, a subject often discussed in the literature. This subject makes sense only in an environment of changes, and the most important source for change is technology. In the case of nonagricultural-, or manufacturing-, based growth, the excess demand generated for food is met by agriculture, and the stronger the response of agriculture, the less food prices will increase. This is a straightforward, and perhaps natural, role one would expect of agriculture. In the other cases considered above, equal rates of change or a greater rate in agriculture, food prices decline, and resources move away from agriculture to nonagriculture. The contribution of agriculture is in lower food prices and in labor and possibly capital. Thus, regardless of the case, agriculture is contributing, but so is nonagriculture. This comment is intended to indicate that in an economy with active trade between sectors, the question of contribution has a limited meaning. It is more meaningful to evaluate the changes themselves.

Factor-Augmenting Technical Change

The specification of the technology in equation (5.2) does not indicate whether the augmentation is factor specific or sector specific. It is factor specific when quality factors are homogeneous, and it is immaterial in which sector the technical change takes place. For instance, if we assume $A_{2L} = 1$ and $A_{1L} > 1$, then moving a unit of labor from agriculture to nonagriculture implies moving A_{1L} quality units, and the labor force in nonagriculture after this move will be $L_2 + A_{1L}$. Think of A_{1L} as the years of schooling of agricultural labor, where the units are standardized so that A_{1L} has a value of 1 in a base year. The size of the quality-labor force is the total school years, and the factor augmentation increases the total factor supply measured in quality units. In this case the economy can be viewed as operating in terms of quality factors; factor augmentation increases the labor supply.[1]

When the augmentation is sector specific, the change in the factor productivity depends on the sector of employment. Given the above assumption on the augmentation, when a unit of labor moves from agriculture to nonagriculture, the quality-labor in nonagriculture will be $L_2 + 1$ rather than $L_2 + A_{1L}$ as in the previous case. In this case, it is simpler to think about the factor markets for physical rather than quality inputs. The full employment conditions are stated in terms of the physical inputs and are unaffected by the augmentation. Still, factor augmentation can be viewed as a change of factor supply.

Thinking about factor-augmenting technical change as a change in factor supply makes it possible to draw an analogy to the discussion in Chapter 4. However, there is one modification: the change in the augmentation function immediately disturbs the competitive conditions in that it affects the wage-rental ratio in the progressive sector. This is the new effect introduced here. The other two effects, productivity and cost, are similar in nature to those considered under NTC.

The discussion begins with the evaluation of the effect of FATC on resource allocation at a given wage-rental ratio. The sector-specific FATC is less obvious than that of the factor-specific, and therefore the discussion deals with this case. The required modification for analyzing factor-specific FATC is straightforward. The productivity and cost effects are then added to the allocation effect, and the change in the equilibrium position is evaluated.

The Response of the $\omega(k)$ Function

We begin by examining some general properties related to factor-augmenting technical change. For that purpose there is no need, at this point, to use sectoral notations. Consider the production function: $Y = F(K^e, L^e)$, where $K^e = A_K K$ and $L^e = A_L L$ are capital and labor measured in terms of quality units, respectively. $F(\cdot)$ is a CRS, concave, and twice differentiable function in K^e and L^e. We can thus write the average labor productivity for physical labor,

$y = Y/L$, $y = A_L f(k^e)$, where k^e is the quality capital-labor ratio, $k^e = ak$, $a = A_K/A_L$. As the function is defined in terms of quality units, the marginal productivities are also defined in terms of quality units, and those can be expressed in terms of quality prices:

$$F_{K^e} = f'(k^e) = r^e/p \tag{5.17}$$

$$F_{L^e} = f(k^e) - k^e f'(k^e) = w^e/p. \tag{5.18}$$

The quality price indicates the unit value of a quality input. But when the augmentation is sector specific, there is no economywide market for quality inputs and thus the quality prices are unobserved. We therefore turn to physical inputs. The marginal productivity of physical inputs are $F_K = F_{K^e}A_K$ and $F_L = F_{L^e}A_L$. The competitive conditions require that $r/p = F_K$ and $w/p = F_L$. Combining this with (5.17) and (5.18), we obtain the relationships among factor prices in physical and quality units:

$$r = A_K r^e; \quad w = A_L w^e, \tag{5.19}$$

and consequently,

$$\omega(k) = (1/a)\omega^e(ak). \tag{5.20}$$

The FATC affects differently the input ratios and their marginal productivities, which are functions of the input ratios. This implies a rotation of the isoquants for any value of k or equivalently, a change of the $\omega(k)$ function. To evaluate this change, we note that the production function is defined in terms of the quality factors, and therefore σ is the elasticity of substitution of that function. Consequently we can write $\sigma\, d \ln \omega^e = d \ln k^e$. But by definition, $d \ln \omega^e = d \ln \omega + d \ln a$ and $d \ln\ k^e = d \ln k + d \ln a$. Hence, using rates of change notation,

$$\sigma(\hat{\omega} + \hat{a}) = (\hat{k} + \hat{a}) \tag{5.21}$$

$$\frac{\partial \ln \omega}{\partial \ln a}\Big|_k = \frac{1}{\sigma} - 1, \quad \text{and} \quad \frac{\partial \ln k}{\partial \ln a}\Big|_\omega = \sigma - 1. \tag{5.22}$$

This change is illustrated graphically in Figure 5.3, where we derive $\omega(k)$ from $\omega^e(k^e)$. We begin with an arbitrary point k_0 and set $a(0) = 1$ for the initial technology. Thus $\omega(k_0 \mid a = 1) = \omega^e(k^e \mid a = 1)$, as represented by point C. Now introduce technical change, and without a loss in generality, let $a > 1$, so that the value of k_0 in terms of quality units becomes $k_1^e = ak_0$. Then, by (5.20), we have $\omega(k_0 \mid a) = (1/a)\omega^e(k_1^e \mid k_1^e = ak_0)$. We can add to the right-hand side of this equation the term $[1 - (1/a)]0$ and express $\omega[k_0 \mid a(t)]$ as a weighted average of $\omega^e(k_1^e)$ and the origin. Consequently, when $\omega^e(k^e)$ is

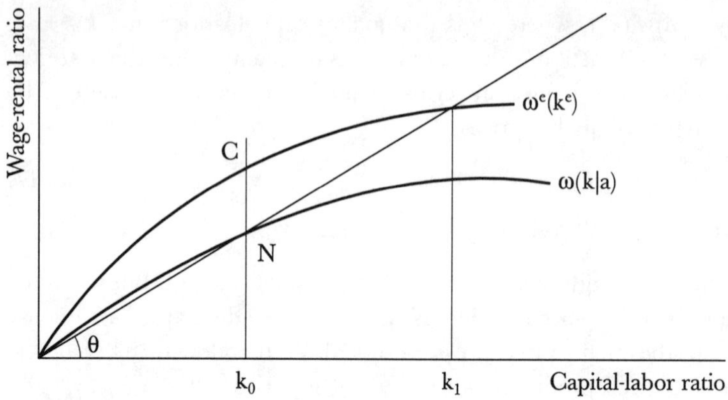

Figure 5.3 Factor-augmenting technical change

concave, $\omega(k_0 \mid a > 1)$ will be below point C, say at point N. We can now repeat the procedure for other initial values instead of k_0 and thereby generate the function $\omega(k \mid a > 1)$. The graph of this function will go through points like N and thus will be below and to the right of $\omega^e(k^e)$ when the function is strictly concave, above and to the left of $\omega^e(k^e)$ when the function is strictly convex, and identical with $\omega^e(k^e)$ when that function is a straight line through the origin. Those three possibilities correspond to σ larger, smaller, or equal to 1, respectively.

Having established the geometry, we can turn to the economic explanation. The question asked here is what price adjustment is needed to absorb an increase in the supply of quality inputs. To answer, assume capital-augmenting technical change, so that $a = A_K$, and the supply of quality capital increases. When σ is large, this increment is absorbed with little change in the marginal rate of substitution of the quality factors, namely ω^e. In the extreme case of $\sigma \to \infty$, ω^e remains unchanged. On the other hand, the rate of return to physical capital increases by a, and therefore $\omega = \omega^e/a$ declines. The situation is reversed when σ is small, in which case ω^e has to increase considerably in order to absorb the change in k. This change in ω^e is larger than the change in A_K, and therefore ω increases. The two effects are equal when $\sigma = 1$. The discussion is concluded with the following proposition.

PROPERTY 5.7 (factor intensity) Factor-augmenting technical change in favor of one factor increases (decreases) the intensity of that factor, under constant wage-rental ratio, if and only if σ is larger (smaller) than 1. When $\sigma = 1$, the intensity is constant.

A change in the function $\omega(k)$ leads to a change in the income distribution as measured by the ratio of the two factor shares, $wL/rK = \omega/k$. At any point we have $\omega/k = \omega^e/k^e$, but a change in a affects ω^e/k^e and therefore also affects ω/k. In terms of Figure 5.3 this ratio is equal to $\tan\theta$. Consequently, the movement from C to N reduces the labor share in output. This change in the factor shares is used as a measure of factor saving.

DEFINITION (factor saving) An exogenous change is said to be *factor saving* if it reduces the share of this factor in value output. The change is *factor using* if it increases the factor share in output.

In this discussion, the changes in the factor shares are evaluated for constant ω, and as such are sometimes referred to as factor saving in the Hicks sense (Binswanger, 1978). Returning to our example, note that the decline in the labor share is obtained by capital-augmenting technical change and elasticity of substitution larger than 1. The logic of it is clear; an increase in quality capital and the "ease" of its absorption results in a substitution of capital for labor to the extent that the share of labor in total output is reduced. It should be emphasized that the classification of a particular factor augmentation as a factor saver depends not only on the factor that is augmented but also on the elasticity of substitution. We can then state the following corollary to Property 5.7.

PROPERTY 5.8 (factor saving) The share of the augmented factor in total output, with the wage-rental ratio held constant, increases, remains constant, or declines if and only if σ is larger, equal, or smaller than 1, respectively.

Allocation and Productivity Effects

In a full employment economy, a change in factor intensity in one sector, with resources held constant, requires a change in resource allocation, otherwise the full employment conditions are violated. An increase in $k_i(\omega)$ in either sector, regardless of capital intensity, can take place only if the shares of the capital-intensive sector in the employment of both resources decline. This follows from the full employment condition as stated in equation (2.13), which is rewritten in the following form:

$$\frac{\ell(\omega, t)}{1 - \ell(\omega, t)} = \frac{k_2(\omega, t) - k}{k - k_1(\omega, t)}.$$

Thus $\ell(\omega, t)$, which in this case is interpreted as the share of the labor-intensive sector in total employment, is positively related to either $k_1(\omega, t)$ or $k_2(\omega, t)$. Since we deal here with a FATC in one sector only, $k_i(\omega)$ remains constant in the passive sector. For this ratio to remain constant in the passive sector, the change in the share of the passive sector in the total use of capital, $\rho(\omega, t)$, should follow the same pattern as that of labor, $\ell(\omega, t)$. We thus have

PROPERTY 5.9 (resource allocation) Labor(capital)-saving technical change in either sector increases the relative share in factor employment of the labor(capital)-intensive sector.

Note the similarity of this proposition to the Rybczynski proposition. Labor-saving technical change can be viewed as an increase in the supply of quality labor. The production function is defined in terms of quality labor. Thus, following the Rybczynski proposition, the technical change should increase the share of the labor-intensive sector in both resources. Holding ω constant implies k_i are constant, but since ℓ increases, so must ρ increase. This is the essence of Property 5.9.

The change in factor allocation that takes place at a constant ω causes a change in sectoral output not realized under NTC. We therefore give it a name.

DEFINITION (allocation effect) The change in outputs necessary to maintain a constant wage-rental ratio under FATC is defined as the *allocation effect.*

The analogy of the allocation effect to that of a change in resources provides an insight to Property 5.10.

PROPERTY 5.10 (allocation effect) The allocation effect is positive (negative) for the progressive sector when that sector is intensive (extensive) in the factor saved. The sign of the allocation effect of the passive sector is opposite to that of the progressive sector.

The allocation effect may supplement or contradict the productivity effect. The allocation and productivity effects of a capital-augmenting technical change in sector 1 are illustrated in Figure 5.4. Panel I shows the change in $\omega_1(k_1) : \omega_B = \omega_1(k_{1A}, t) \neq \omega_1(k_{1A}, 0) = \omega_2(k_{2A})$. Consequently, the initial allocation represented by (k_{1A}, k_{2A}) becomes inefficient under technology $t > 0$. With the new technology, the capital-labor ratio in the progressive sector evaluated at ω_A is $k_1(\omega_A, t) = k_{1C}$, and consequently, the share of the labor-intensive sector in total labor is $\ell(\omega_A, t) > \ell(\omega_A, 0)$. This is simply an illustration of Property 5.9 for the case where the technical change is labor saving. The implied impact of this change on outputs is given by point C on the transformation curve. This represents the combined productivity and allocation effects. The productivity effect alone is represented by B, which is not on the transformation curve under the new technology. It is dominated by points like B^* corresponding to $\omega_{B^*} < \omega_A$.

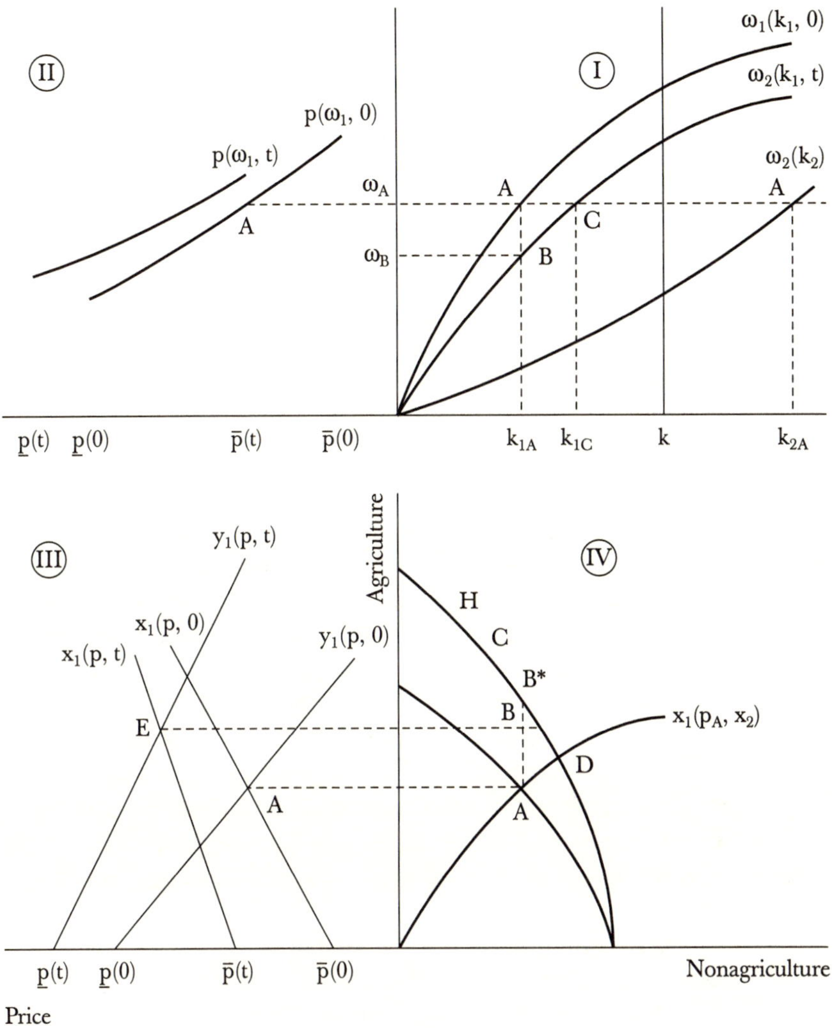

Figure 5.4 Factor-augmenting technical change in agriculture

The Cost Effect

To obtain the total shift of supply, we have to add the cost effect. For this we need the price equation. Since the production function is defined in terms of quality inputs, the dual cost functions are defined in terms of quality prices. Thus we have for the average cost function in sector i: $c_i(w^e, r^e) = c_i(w/A_{iL}, r/A_{iK})$, and consequently

$$p(\omega, t) = c_1(w^e, r^e)/c_2(w^e, r^e). \tag{5.23}$$

The cost function is increasing in factor prices; therefore, if technology in sector 2 is kept constant, any increase in A_{1L} or A_{1K} or both decreases the relative price of the output of sector 1.

PROPERTY 5.11 The supply price of the progressive sector declines.

Thus the change in price depends on the origin and the degree of augmentation and not on the direction of factor saving. Returning to the case under consideration, $p(\omega, t) < p(\omega, 0)$, and therefore, the change in output necessary to restore the original price calls for a shift of resources to the progressive sector. Thus the cost effect supplements the productivity effect. In terms of Figure 5.4, the cost effect is represented by the move from C to H.

Equilibrium

The qualitative difference in the dislocation of supply between FATC and NTC is in the allocation effect. Consequently when the allocation effect supplements the cost and productivity effects, the nature of the displacement caused by the FATC will be similar to that analyzed for NTC in one sector. In Figure 5.4, the supply at the initial price moves from A to H. The new equilibrium point of a closed economy will be located between the following two points: (1) The intersection of the demand curve, corresponding to the initial price, with the new transformation curve. That point gives the quantity demanded at the original price, and thereby it represents the income effect alone. It is represented by a movement from A to D in Figure 5.4. (2) The new product mix at the original price, H, also the equilibrium production of a small open economy.

When the allocation effect is contradicting the productivity and cost effects, it pulls the supply downward, and there is no a priori reason why the supply cannot decline so that H would be to the right of point B^*.

With the equilibrium price of the progressive sector declining, its output increases. The question is what happens to the output of the passive sector. Does it increase as well? The answer depends on the relative strength of the price and income effects generated by technical change and on the price and income elasticities.

The dependence of the solution on demand elasticities is intuitively clear. If the income and price elasticities for the product of the progressive sector were very high, then the increase in income and the decline in its price caused by technical change might cause a big shift of demand in the direction of the progressive sector and cause a decline in the output of the passive sector. It is indeed the case for perfectly elastic demand, as for the small open economy, that the output of the passive sector will shrink. In that case, H will represent the equilibrium output. The consumption will be determined by the intersection of demand functions with the income line corresponding to output H.

Factor-augmenting Technical Change in Two Sectors

The foregoing analysis was conducted for the special case where the FATC occurred in one sector. With two sectors and two factors, there are various possible scenarios. Those, however, can be reduced to the situations analyzed above plus an additional one to be outlined here, FATC in two sectors.

Our foregoing discussion dealt with four factor-augmenting functions: $\hat{A}_{1L}$, $\hat{A}_{1K}$, $\hat{A}_{2L}$, and $\hat{A}_{2K}$. For each sector this is reduced to $\hat{A}_i$, $\hat{a}_i$, where $\hat{A}_i = \min(\hat{A}_{iL}, \hat{A}_{iK})$, and $\hat{a}_i = \max(\hat{A}_{iL} - \hat{A}_i, \hat{A}_{iK} - \hat{A}_i)$. The case of $\hat{a}_i = 0$ for $i = 1, 2$ was dealt with under the NTC. The case of $\hat{a}_i \neq 0$ for one sector was dealt with above. To complete the discussion we thus have to consider the case of $\hat{a}_1 \hat{a}_2 \neq 0$.

Productivity Effects

By definition, the productivity effects in both sectors are positive. The strength of the effects depends on the values of a_i and on the factor shares of the augmented factors.

Allocation Effect

If the technical change in both sectors is saving the same factor, then the allocation effect is uniquely determined–it increases the output of the sector that is intensive in the saved factor. This situation, covered by Property 5.9, is of particular interest. As we will see in Chapter 6, there is a reason to expect technical change to be on the whole labor saving. Thus this process has the partial effect of transferring resources to the labor-intensive sector. The relative strength of this effect depends on the difference in factor intensity, on the rates of factor augmentation, and on the values of σ_i. Specifically, recall that if $\sigma_i = 1$ for $i = 1, 2$, there are no allocation effects.

Cost Effect

While the allocation effect depends on the factors that are saved, the cost effect depends on the factors that are *augmented* and on their shares in total output (factor shares). To concentrate on the case under consideration, assume $\hat{A}_{1K} > 0$, $\hat{A}_{2K} > 0$, $\hat{A}_{1L} = \hat{A}_{2L} = 0$. In the special case where the rate of factor augmentation is the same ($\hat{A}_{1K} = \hat{A}_{2K}$), we obtain

$$\hat{p}(\omega, t) \mid_{\omega} = (S_{1L} - S_{2L})\hat{A}_{iK}.$$

That is, capital-augmenting technical change of equal rates in both sectors reduces cost more in the capital-cost-intensive sector and thereby increases the price of the labor-cost-intensive product corresponding to any given wage-rental ratio.

Income Distribution

In general factor-augmenting technical change leads to changes in the factor distribution of income, as measured by the ratio of factor shares. Rearranging (5.21) we obtain

$$d\ln(\omega/k) = (\frac{1}{\sigma} - 1)d\ln(ka). \tag{5.24}$$

There are three conditions under which the factor shares are unaffected by technical change:

1. $\hat{a} = 0$. This is Hicks-neutral technical change, where ω/k is constant when k is constant.
2. $\sigma = 1$. This is equivalent to a Cobb-Douglas production function where the factor shares are constant everywhere.
3. $\hat{k} = -\hat{a}$. This implies that the quality-capital-labor ratio is constant and so is $f(ak)$. As a matter of definition,

$$Y/L^e = f(k^e). \tag{5.25}$$

When k^e is held constant, the factor prices in quality units are constant as well. Two cases have been widely discussed in the literature. First, Harrod-neutral technical change,[2] where the technology is labor augmenting; it is characterized by $A_K = 1$ and $a = A_L^{-1}$. Rewrite (5.25) and divide through by $k^e = K/A_L L$ to obtain

$$\frac{Y}{K} = \frac{f(ak)}{ak}, \quad \text{which is constant.} \tag{5.26}$$

Thus, with labor-augmenting technical change, the factor shares remain constant along expansion paths that maintain constant Y/K. In this case $r^e = r$, and because the quality prices are constant, r is constant as well.[3] While Y/K is constant, the average labor productivity, $Y/L = A_L f(ak)$ is an increasing function of A_L, and the wage rate is increasing accordingly: $w = w^e A_L$.

By a similar argument, we can examine the consequences of capital-augmenting technical change where $A_L = 1$ and $A_K > 1$. From the definition, $y = f(ak)$, and hence the factor shares are constant along expansion paths that maintain Y/L constant. This is Solow neutrality. Here the wage rate is constant along Y/L, whereas the rate of return is increasing with A_K.

These concepts of neutrality generate corresponding classifications of factor saving. For instance, technical change is labor saving in the Harrod sense if the labor share declines along a given output-capital ratio.

The Real Rate of Exchange: Long-Run Aspects

Discussions of the real exchange rate deal generally with short-term variations in external terms of trade and macro policies. However, the real exchange rate is also affected by long-run changes in supply and demand. Long-run changes on the supply side emerge from capital accumulation and technical change. If the nontradable product is labor intensive, its price increases along the equilibrium path generated by capital deepening, and therefore the real rate of exchange declines. This is true as long as the two products are normal. The degree of this effect depends on the difference in factor intensities and in income elasticities.

Less can be said on the supply effect that comes from technical change without knowing the nature of the change. It has been argued (Balassa, 1964; Samuelson, 1964) that technical change is faster in the production of commodities, which are largely tradable, than in nontradables. In this case, there is a downward trend in the real exchange rate. This is a very plausible argument; nevertheless, its underlying premise calls for a quantitative perspective. This qualifier is always true, but it is particularly important in this case. Much of the nontradable product is produced in the public sector, so the output is measured by the cost of production. Technical change is measured by comparing the changes in output with the changes in the cost of inputs; therefore when the measure of output is the same as that of the input, no technical change can be detected. This is also true for some services produced in the private sector whose output is measured by cost, for instance, medicine. The increase in life expectancy, as well as in the (physical) quality of life, is not captured in the measurement of output, and therefore we obtain a distorted view of the changes in productivity in the nontradable sector.

If we turn to the demand side, we note that capital deepening and technical change generate an increase in income that in turn generates an increase in demand. At the private level, beyond a certain income, the demand for services increases faster than the demand for commodities. Since commodities are largely tradable and services are largely nontradable, an increase in income results in an increase in the relative price of nontradables, or a decline in the real exchange rate. The public sector demand for nontradables may also have a strong positive income response; social and welfare programs are developed as the economy becomes more affluent. The net effect of such programs depends on two factors: first, the extent that they constitute a net addition to spending over and above what the private sector would have spent on these programs, and second, the form of finance. For instance, if the programs are financed by a progressive income tax that generates a more equal income distribution, and if the income elasticity of nontradables is larger than 1, then the net effect may be a decline in the demand for nontradables and therefore an increase in the real exchange rate. On the other hand, if the programs reduce the price of nontradables, such as health and education, then their demand will increase, and the real exchange rate will decline.

To conclude, this discussion indicates that as an economy develops, the real exchange rate is likely to decline. This is structural change that should not be attributed to short-run policy or other shocks. The quantitative effect of the various considerations discussed here is a subject for empirical analysis.

Empirical Implications

The discussion in this chapter is empirically oriented in that it derives the comparative static implications for growth paths of various forms of technical change. Clearly, the range of possible outcomes is wide. Still, some empirical generalizations applicable to agricultural growth can be made. Such generalizations are derived from the low income and price elasticities for agriculture, and as such they are fairly robust to the possible variations in the orders of magnitudes of the various forms of technical change.

We now turn to review trends in agricultural prices and in sectoral outputs. Such trends are determined, of course, by various other variables in addition to demand and technical change. Furthermore, they are generated under market conditions that violate our assumptions and which are introduced into the analysis as we go along. Nevertheless, with all these qualifications, it is instructive to refer to the data at this stage and to highlight some of the important processes.

Agricultural Prices

Changes in productivity lead to changes in excess demand and thereby affect agricultural prices. For countries that trade in agricultural products, such changes in excess demand are transmitted to the world market, where world supply and demand determine world prices. The world is then viewed as a closed economy. Countries that do not trade in agriculture are, by definition, also analyzed within a closed economy framework. Consequently, we can begin the discussion by referring to equation (5.16), which summarizes the effects of neutral technical change. Obviously, technical change of equal rates generates an excess supply for agriculture. Similarly, the excess supply increases when the technical change in agriculture exceeds that in nonagriculture. Can the excess supply decline? Yes, but for this to occur the technical change in nonagriculture must exceed *considerably* that in agriculture, and the income elasticity of agriculture must be larger than its price elasticity. As we saw even in the crude evidence presented in Chapter 1, however, technical change in agriculture, if anything, exceeded that of nonagriculture, and this accounts for the excess supply. Thus for the excess demand in agriculture to rise, technology in agriculture must stagnate. There is no empirical evidence that leads us to expect such an event in the foreseeable future.

An increase in excess supply leads to a decline in prices. Hence an efficient way to examine the importance of technical change is to examine the trends in world agricultural prices. The country story is presented in Figure 1.2. A view of the global situation is obtained from Table 5.1, which presents estimates of the average annual percentage change in prices of some primary agricultural commodities. The prices are deflated by the index of U.S. wholesale prices. These estimates were obtained from semilogarithmic trend regressions. Two facts immediately emerge. First, there has been a deterioration at an average annual rate of 0.5–0.7 percent in most of the relative prices of agriculture. This implies a deterioration by a factor of one-half over the period 1900–1983. Second, the degree of fit of the trend regressions, as measured by R^2, is relatively low. This reflects wide annual variations in supply and demand conditions over this period, which includes two world wars, energy crises, and other shocks. As such, the trend is a poor predictor for *short-term* price variations. Yet, considering the length of the period, these numbers are suggestive with regard to the long-term trend.

Over this period world population increased by a factor of 3, from 1.6 billion in 1900 to nearly 5 billion in 1984. Add to this the increase in per capita income, and we obtain an increase in food demand by a factor of 4 or more. The decline in world prices indicates that production increased more than demand. Since the supply function is positively sloped, it is clear, as is well known, that there were large changes in supply that made it profitable to expand production in spite of the decline in the relative price. If we take such a long-term view, changes in supply make it possible to identify the demand function empirically. That is, the deterioration in prices implies that the growth in supply could only be absorbed at some price decline. In turn, the decline in

Table 5.1 Time-trend of agricultural prices deflated by U.S. wholesale prices, 1900–1983

Commodity	Coefficient	t-ratio	R^2
Sugar	−0.7	(3.7)	0.14
Wheat	−0.7	(7.2)	0.39
Maize	−0.6	(7.1)	0.31
Rice	−0.6	(5.5)	0.27
Cotton	−0.5	(5.4)	0.26
Wool	−0.1	(8.9)	0.49

Source: Binswanger et al. (1985).

Note: The coefficients are obtained from the semilogarithmic regression: $\ln p_t = a + bt$. The slope, b, indicating the rate of growth, is multiplied by 100 to be expressed in percent. The numbers in parentheses are the ratios of the coefficients to their standard errors (t-ratios).

price had a depressing effect on the growth of output. This implies that demand has acted as one of the determinants of agricultural growth. Thus the results are in line with the predictions that can be drawn from equation (5.16).

How should equation (5.16) be modified if the technical change has a factor-augmenting component? As indicated, technical change on the whole tends to be labor saving, and as such it tends to increase the output of the labor-intensive sector. This then supplements the effect derived under neutral technical change. On the other hand, under the present framework where the technology is exogenous, capital accumulation tends to increase the price of the labor-intensive product. To the extent that such an effect prevailed, it was not sufficient to offset the effect of technical change.

On Sectoral Growth

Technical change and capital accumulation increase real income, and therefore, with prices held constant, consumption of the two products should increase. At the global level, consumption of each of the two products is nearly equal to output. The difference between consumption and production reflects a change in inventories that is a small fraction of production in any given year and more so when longer periods are considered. Thus, under constant prices, the relative change in production reflects income elasticities. Because agriculture is income inelastic, its growth is constrained by income elasticity. It is also constrained by the low price elasticity that contains the substitution effect on demand expansion in response to the price decline.

The foregoing discussion has dealt with a closed economy. In an open economy, output need not equal consumption, and therefore the growth pattern of output need not follow that of demand. Therefore, the patterns of sectoral growth in individual countries are expected to differ in accordance with their trade patterns. This is well illustrated in Figure 1.4, which shows the spread in the ratio of growth rates of agriculture to that of total output. In only 19 percent of the countries did the rate of growth of agriculture exceed that of total output, but these countries accounted for only 4 percent of world agricultural production.

At this point it is useful to go back and review the mechanism that determines sectoral growth. Consider the typical case where technical change creates an excess supply of agriculture. This presses agricultural prices down, and value output declines. Value output is distributed to labor and capital, and therefore there is now less to be distributed. Consequently labor and capital find their way to nonagriculture, where the remuneration is higher. This shift of resources contributes to output in nonagriculture.

To summarize, the determinants of the process of agricultural growth are low income elasticity for agriculture and the desire of individuals to increase, whenever possible, the returns for their services. The process moves on with less friction when competitive markets exist. However, as we shall see in subsequent discussion, the process takes place under less favorable conditions as well. All that is required is that individuals be able to improve their position by reallocating the resources at their command.

Technical Change and Land Expansion

We now continue the discussion in Chapter 4 of land expansion by considering three natural forms of technical change. We begin with the case where agriculture is a price taker and thereby obtain the supply response under constant prices. The nature of the results changes when a capital constraint is introduced. The investigation concentrates on agriculture and therefore avoids sectoral notations.

Neutral Technical Change

The production function is $\tau F[qA(q), K(q)] = \tau qA(q)f[k(q)/q]$. The role of the technology index τ is the same as the price p in the constant technology model of Chapter 4, and the results of this model are immediately applicable. Specifically, neutral technical change causes the two margins to expand.

Land-augmenting Technical Change

The production function is

$$F(\tau q A(q), K(tq)) = \tau q A(q) f(k(\tau q)/\tau q). \tag{5.27}$$

The optimization problem is

$$\max_{k(\tau q),z} L(k(\tau q), z)) = \int_{z}^{\infty} [\tau q f(k(\tau q)/\tau q) - rk(\tau q) - c] A(q) dq \tag{5.28}$$

The first-order conditions are

$$L_1 = f'[k(\tau q)/\tau q] - r = 0, \tag{5.29}$$

$$L_2 = \tau z f[k(\tau z)/\tau z] - rk(\tau z) - c = 0. \tag{5.30}$$

Differentiating equation (5.29) and rearranging to obtain

$$\frac{\partial k(\tau q)}{\partial \tau} \Big|_r = \frac{k(\tau q)}{\tau} > 0. \tag{5.31}$$

Differentiating equation (5.30) and rearranging to obtain

$$\frac{\partial z}{\partial \tau} \Big|_r = -\frac{z}{\tau} < 0, \tag{5.32}$$

or $E(z, \tau) = -1$. To interpret this result, differentiate the rent,

$$\frac{\partial R(\tau q)}{\partial \tau} = \frac{R(\tau q) + c}{\tau} > 0.$$

Hence, as τ increases, the rent increases for all q; therefore the margin is moved, and z declines.

PROPERTY 5.12 When agriculture is a price taker, land-augmenting technical change causes the expansion of land, the capital-land ratio, and total output.

Capital-augmenting Technical Change

The production function is

$$F(qA(q), \tau K(q)) = qA(q) f[\tau k(q)/q]. \tag{5.33}$$

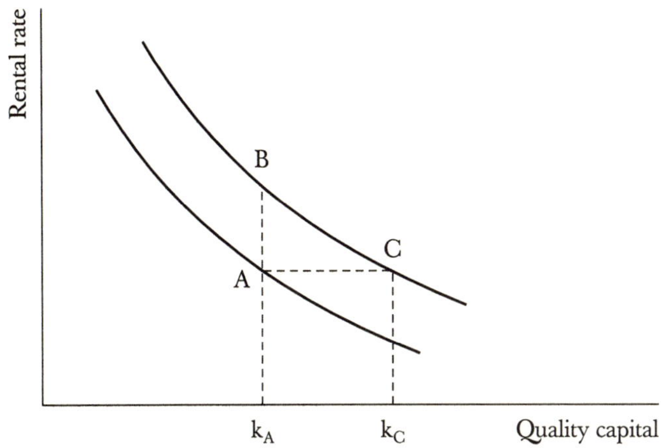

Figure 5.5 Demand for quality capital

The optimization problem is

$$\max_{k(q),z} L[k(q), z] = \int_{z}^{\infty} [qf(\tau k(q)/q) - rk(q) - c]A(q)dq \tag{5.34}$$

The first-order conditions are

$$L_1 = \tau f'[\tau k(q)/q] - r = 0, \tag{5.35}$$

$$L_2 = zf[\tau k(z)/z] - rk(z) - c = 0. \tag{5.36}$$

Differentiating $L_2(\cdot)$ to obtain

$$E(z, \tau) = -\frac{S(k; z)}{S(c; z)} < 0. \tag{5.37}$$

Next, differentiating L_1 and rearranging to obtain[4]

$$\frac{d \ln k(q)}{d \ln \tau} = \sigma - 1. \tag{5.38}$$

We can interpret this result with the aid of Figure 5.5. An examination of equation (5.38) shows that the technical change has two effects. First, it shifts the marginal productivity of capital so that the initial point A, with quality-capital k_A, shifts to B. This shift disturbs the first-order condition, and to restore it, the quality-capital increases to k_C that corresponds to point C. The proportional change in the marginal productivity between A and B is $\hat{\tau}$, and the movement from C to B is along the curve whose elasticity in absolute value is σ so that the relative change of quality-capital between A and C is $\sigma\hat{\tau}$. The larger the numerical value of this elasticity, the larger the relative difference between k_C and k_A. Second, to translate the rate of change in quality-capital to that of physical capital, we subtract $\hat{\tau}$. The new level of physical capital is the net outcome of these two effects as equation (5.38) indicates. When the demand for capital is inelastic, the retraction dominates, and the capital intensity declines. In this case, land augmentation and land saving move in opposite directions. But this is not an interesting case empirically because it calls for the expansion of land and a decline in the capital-land ratio.

The discussion is summarized by

PROPERTY 5.13 When agriculture is a price taker, capital-augmenting technical change reduces the marginal quality land and thereby increases the cultivated area. The corresponding change in capital intensity depends on the elasticity of capital demand; it increases (decreases) when the demand is elastic (inelastic).

Of the three cases of technical change analyzed here, this is the only case in which land expansion and augmentation can take different directions, but as indicated, it is not an interesting case from an empirical point of view. A different result is obtained when the supply of capital is not perfectly elastic. To deal with this case, we take up the extreme version of perfectly inelastic supply of capital, examined in Chapter 4, together with land-augmenting technical change.

Land-augmenting Technical Change and Capital Constraint

The production function is given by (5.27), and the optimization problem is

$$\max_{k(q),z,r} L(k(q),z,r) = \int_z^\infty [\tau q f(k(\tau q)/\tau q) - c]A(q)dq - r[\int_z^\infty A(q)k(\tau q)dq - K]. \tag{5.39}$$

The first-order conditions are

$$L_1 = f'[k(\tau q)/\tau q] - r = 0, \tag{5.40}$$

$$L_2 = \tau z f[k(\tau z)/\tau z] - rk(\tau z) - c = 0, \tag{5.41}$$

$$L_3(\cdot) = \int_z^\infty A(q)k(\tau q)dq - K = 0. \tag{5.42}$$

Differentiating L_1, we obtain[5]

$$1 - \sigma \frac{d \ln r}{d \ln \tau} = \frac{d \ln k(\cdot)}{d \ln \tau}. \tag{5.43}$$

When agriculture is a price taker, r does not change and equation (5.43) reduces to equation (5.31), which states that the relative increase in k is equal to the rate of the technical change. When the supply of capital is not perfectly elastic, the increase in r will reduce the relative increase in k by σ.

Differentiating L_2, simplifying and imposing $dc = 0$,

$$(\tau/c)k(\tau z)dr - \tau dz/z = d\tau. \tag{5.44}$$

To differentiate L_3 we modify (4.23),

$$\tau\Phi(r)Q = K. \tag{5.45}$$

Then,[6]

$$\tau z A(z)/Q\ dz + \tau\sigma/r\ dr = d\tau. \tag{5.46}$$

To solve for $dr/d\tau$ and $dz/d\tau$, write equations (5.44) and (5.46) in matrix notations:

$$\begin{bmatrix} -1 & rk(\cdot)c \\ z^2 A(z)/Q & \sigma \end{bmatrix} \begin{bmatrix} d \ln z \\ d \ln r \end{bmatrix} = \begin{bmatrix} 1 \\ 1 \end{bmatrix} d \ln \tau \tag{5.47}$$

Except for the element in the (1,1) position, all the elements are positive; hence the determinant (det) is negative. The solution is

$$d \ln z/d \ln \tau = (1/\det)[\sigma - rk(\cdot)/c] \quad \text{The sign is ambiguous.} \tag{5.48}$$

$$d \ln r/d \ln \tau = (1/\det)[-1 - z^2 A(z)/Q] > 0. \tag{5.49}$$

The technical change shifts to the right the demand for capital; therefore its shadow price rises, and the rent declines. On the other hand, the rent increases as a result of the technical change. The net effect of the technical change depends on the magnitude of these two effects. When the elasticity is large, the increase in r reduces k, and capital is freed to allow the expansion of cultivated land; consequently z declines. On the other hand, when the elasticity is small, the increase in r causes an increase in z, the area declines, and the capital freed by the reduction in the cultivated area is used to satisfy the increase in the demand for capital triggered by the technical change.

Empirical Analysis

To apply the foregoing analysis to the data, we have to differentiate between short-term fluctuations in land use and changes of a more permanent nature.

Because the necessary data for such an analysis are lacking, this is not an easy task. Alternatively, we can look at a situation where permanent expansion was dominating, such as Thailand. It was examined in Mundlak (1993), and some of the results of that analysis are summarized here.

Thailand's agricultural growth has been impressive. During the period 1961–1990, world agricultural production grew at an average annual rate of 2.3 percent, whereas that of Thailand grew at a 4 percent rate. If we reduce the output to three major components, crops, fruits (tree crops), and livestock, we find that Thailand excelled in all three. The growth in fruit production was faster than that of crops, and this indicates an intensification in the use of capital. Still, crops form the major subsector of agriculture, accounting for about three-quarters of total agricultural value added. Thailand's performance is even more impressive when viewed on a per capita basis: its output increased at an average annual rate of 1.6 percent compared with 0.6 percent for the world as a whole. Thailand could achieve such a performance by maintaining strong exports, which in the last four decades, on average, made up from 13 to 17 percent of agricultural output; at the same time, its imports fluctuated from 1.9 to 5.4 percent. Cultivated land increased from 8.3 million hectares in 1950 to 23.6 million in 1990. This new land was obtained by clearing forests. The annual average growth rate of land amounted to 2.84 percent, implying that the output-land ratio increased at an annual average rate of about 1.2 percent. Agricultural labor increased over the period from 1954 to 1990 from 9.0 million to 20.1 million, an average annual growth rate of 2.1 percent. Data for other inputs are available only for the period beginning in 1961, and therefore subsequent analysis covers only the years 1961–1990. During this period the average annual growth rates of inputs per hectare, in percent, are: agricultural labor, −0.42; fertilizers, 9.5; irrigation, 2.2; tractors, 14.8. These developments cannot be explained by attributing them to more favorable prices, because the price ratio of agriculture to that of nonagriculture trended downward over the period, particularly from the mid-1970s. It is clear that the drastic expansion in cultivated land was accompanied by a considerable intensification in the use of capital as measured by the increase in the application per hectare of fertilizers, tractors, and irrigation. The labor use per hectare declined but at a relatively slow rate.

The land expansion that took place in Thailand was largely an initiative of the private sector (Siamwalla, Setboonsarng, and Patamasiriwat, 1993). As for the future, analysts note: "Thai agriculture is now at a crossroads. The two factors that fueled its past growth–surplus land and buoyant foreign market–cannot sustain it in the future. . . . These developments . . . present a set of delicate problems for the government. First, the factor intensity of Thai agriculture will change. . . . At the same time, domestic demand will dictate that the more capital-intensive and technology-intensive horticultural sector must expand" (ibid., p. 116).

From these comments it is clear that past behavior was the outcome of farmers' decisions; the question what will happen in the future–and the role of government in it–is focused on issues related to the extensive-intensive margins. With this background, we turn to the analysis.

Our discussion suggests that land expansion can be explained by capital accumulation, the cost of reclamation, the terms of trade of agriculture, and technology. Land expansion is also expected to be positively correlated with land augmentation, measured by the increase of other inputs. Table 5.2 presents correlation coefficients between land and other variables. The correlation between land and the other agricultural inputs is obviously very high, and this is also the case on a per hectare basis. The third panel of the table shows the high positive correlation between land, length of roads, and the investment in road maintenance and the low negative values between land and cost of road construction. This cost is taken as a partial indicator of the cost of clearing land for agricultural production.

The relationships between the size of agricultural land and these variables are summarized by regressions presented in Table 5.3. The investment variable is for the economy as whole, and it represents a measure of resource availability. The table presents four empirical equations. The first and the third were obtained by ordinary least squares (OLS); the second and the fourth were obtained by instrumental variables. The last two equations were corrected for serial correlations. These regressions clearly indicate the strong positive relationships between land and capital accumulation, the terms of trade of agriculture, and roads and the negative or zero relationships with the cost of construction.

Can this model account for the main developments of Thai agriculture? The joint expansion of land and capital-land ratio required considerable resources. The question is, what induced this big expansion? The terms of trade of agriculture were deteriorating over time, and this should have discouraged expansion. The answer is capital accumulation, improvement in the infrastructure, and technical change in agriculture. However, the major technological event in this area was the green revolution, the introduction of modern cereal varieties. This began in Thailand only in the late 1960s, whereas land had been expanding rapidly even before then. The empirical analysis suggests that capital availability and the decline in the cost of reclamation were important factors in this expansion.

Table 5.2 Thailand: Correlation coefficients, 1961–1990

Total inputs

	Agricultural land	Irrigation	Fertilizer	Tractor	Investment
Agricultural land	1	0.95	0.92	0.89	0.89
Irrigation		1	0.95	0.98	0.9
Fertilizer			1	0.95	0.97
Tractor				1	0.89
Investment					1

Inputs per hectare

	Irrigation	Fertilizer	Tractor	Investment
Irrigation	1	0.88	0.96	0.79
Fertilizer		1	0.93	0.95
Tractor			1	0.86
Investment				1

Variables related to land regression

	Agric. land	State highways: length	Provincial roads: length	State highways: construction costs	State highways: maintenance costs	Provincial roads: total cost*
Agric. land	1	0.98	0.94	−0.084	0.83	−0.147
State highways: length		1	0.96			
Provincial roads: length			1			
State highways: construction costs				1	−0.042	0.56
State highways: maintenance costs					1	−0.22

Source: Mundlak (1993).
*Series is from 1975 to 1990 only.

Table 5.3 Thailand: Agricultural land expansion, regression analysis, 1961–1990

Regression	Constant	Capital	Price of agriculture	Cost of highways	Length of roads	*AR*(1)	R^2	D.W.	Obs.
1	5.198	0.107	0.275	−0.004	0.277		0.990	0.874	30
	(10.15)	(8.45)	(4.59)	(0.34)	(9.30)				
2	7.004	0.171	0.163	−0.038	0.159		0.991	1.115	29
	(7.18)	(5.57)	(2.12)	(1.74)	(2.74)				
3	6.531	0.189	0.213	−0.009	0.133	0.484	0.993	1.800	29
	(8.68)	(3.98)	(3.25)	(0.66)	(1.63)	(3.28)			
4	6.751	0.197	0.197	−0.011	0.118	0.497	0.992	1.770	28
	(7.22)	(3.65)	(2.62)	(0.46)	(1.26)	(3.19)			

Source: Mundlak (1993).

Note: Regressions 1 and 3 were estimated using ordinary least squares. Regressions 2 and 4 were estimated using two-stage least squares, using as instruments, price of agriculture, capital, PEAK, relative price of rice to fertilizer, and as inputs, agricultural labor lagged one year, tractors, fertilizer, and irrigation. *AR*(1)–auto regression of the first degree; D.W.–Durbin Watson statistics.

Exercises

5.1 In Chapter 4 we signed the changes in demand for sectoral inputs in response to resource change, taking into account the various effects. Do the same for technical change, where the change to be evaluated is between two equilibrium points ("original" and "new"). Do it systematically for the following cases:

(a) NTC of equal rates in both sectors.
(b) NTC in agriculture alone.
(c) Capital-augmenting TC in agriculture.
(d) Labor-augmenting technical change in agriculture.
(e) The introduction of a modern cereal variety in agriculture that is more productive and more capital intensive than the traditional variety.

Solve first for the small open economy and second for the closed economy.

Which of these cases (or what combinations of them) will yield results which are consistent with the data on agricultural capital summarized in Chapter 10? Do we do better if we combine these results with those on capital accumulation presented in Chapter 4?

Make the following assumptions:

Factor prices are equal across sectors.
Agriculture is the labor-intensive sector.
Demand elasticities of $x_1(p, x_2)$ and income elasticities, using class notations, are restricted by $\sigma_D < 1, \eta < 1$.
The elasticities of substitution in both sectors are smaller than 1.

6

Heterogeneous Technology

So far we have assumed that the technology in each sector consists of a single technique. When there is an improvement in technology, producers are expected to replace the old technique with the new one. Within this framework, there is no reason to use the old technique, and only the new, more productive technique should be employed. This conclusion, however, is inconsistent with the data, which show that the process of transition from old to new techniques takes time, often a long time, during which different techniques coexist. This observation is important for understanding the process of the implementation of new techniques, which is the main vehicle for economic growth. This chapter examines two issues related to this process. First, we consider the reasons for the coexistence of techniques with an emphasis on the relationships between resource constraints, specifically capital accumulation, and the implementation of new techniques. Second, we analyze the effect of the appearance of a new technique on the equilibrium position of the economy. This discussion is continued in subsequent chapters, particularly in Chapter 13, where we also take up the implications of this framework for the empirical analysis of productivity and growth.

This discussion draws on the experience of the introduction of modern cereal varieties, known as the green revolution, which began in the mid-1960s. An empirical study of food grain growth in India based on district data provides empirical evidence for some of the propositions developed here (Bhalla and Khan, 1979). In comparing production changes from the period 1962–1965 (pre–green revolution) to 1970–1973, a period when the new technology in Indian agriculture was well established, the study concludes that the introduction of modern varieties:

1. represents technical change in that yields are increased and the productivity of all inputs is increased, including that of labor, whose factor share declines,
2. has required capital inputs,

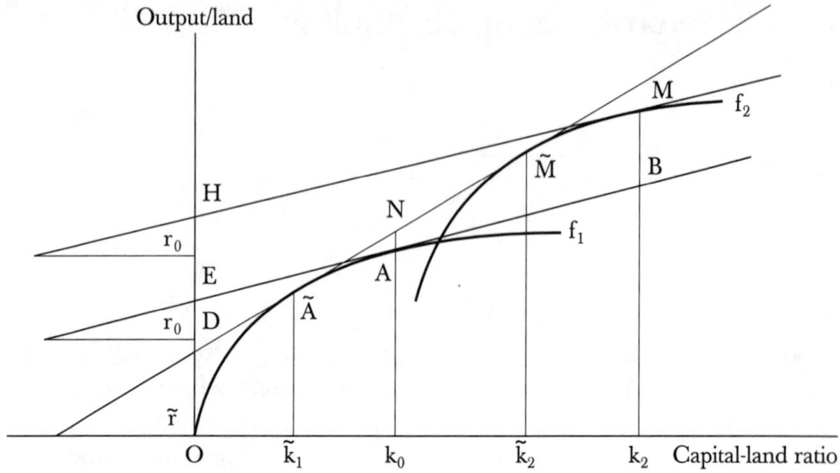

Figure 6.1 Resource constraint and the choice of technique

3. is capital intensive in the sense that it increases the share of capital inputs in total output, and
4. most important, has taken a long time to implement and after twenty years is far from being completed. The transition period is characterized by the coexistence of traditional and modern techniques.

Points 1–3 are consistent with the institution of labor-saving technical change generated by factor augmentation that, with given prices, results in higher capital-labor ratios. This is demonstrated in Figure 6.1, where f_1 and f_2 describe the production functions of the traditional and modern varieties respectively. Let k in this example be the ratio of capital to land, ignoring labor for the time being, and f_j be the output per unit of land of technique j. When the technology consists of the traditional variety alone, producers produce at point A, with capital-land ratio k_0 and a rate of return, or marginal productivity of capital, $r_0 = f_1'(k_0)$. The appearance of a modern technique, f_2, opens up new possibilities. With a perfectly elastic supply of capital at rental rate of capital r_0, producers move to point M, where $f_2'(k_2) = r_0$, and the return to land is higher than at A. In this case there is no scope for coexistence of the traditional and modern varieties, and the traditional variety should disappear.

The coexistence of techniques indicates that either the supply of capital is not perfectly elastic at the going rate or else that there are other reasons not taken into account in the analysis. Often the reason given for the coexistence is that producers have imperfect knowledge about the new technique. Although this explanation appears reasonable, it cannot by itself account for the length of time that it has required to introduce the modern varieties (MV) nor can it explain the geographical variability in the pattern of their use. The green revolution is considered here as an example, indeed a very important one. Another example is the mechanization of agriculture, which has also taken a long time to be implemented.

The explanation given here for the delayed response is the scarcity of capital needed for full implementation of the modern technique. We illustrate it in terms of Figure 6.1 where, by assumption, the initial capital-land ratio is k_0. With k_0 given, the traditional variety dominates the modern one because it produces a higher yield. Under the new technology, however, it is possible to obtain higher output by allocating the scarce resource to the two varieties. For such an allocation to be optimal, it should produce equal marginal productivity of capital for the two varieties; otherwise some producers could gain by reallocating the capital among the varieties. The optimal allocation is shown by the line tangent to the two production functions at the points $\tilde{A}$ and $\tilde{M}$ with a slope $\tilde{r} = f_j'(\tilde{k}_j)$, where $j = 1, 2$. The average yield with capital-land ratio k_0 is now given by point N, which dominates the yield at A.

To increase the share of land allocated to the MV it is necessary to increase the available capital-land ratio. The increase in capital is prompted by the appearance of the MV, which causes the rate of return to capital to increase from r_0 to $\tilde{r}$, thereby attracting capital. But this process takes time. It is in this sense that the pace of the transition is related to the scarcity of capital, which cannot be mobilized within a short period. All this is discussed in greater detail below.

The foregoing analysis is somewhat simplified in order to enable graphical illustration. Nevertheless it brings forward the important points for our subsequent discussion. We begin the discussion by reviewing empirical evidence that will help us to place the discussion within an appropriate perspective. This is then followed by constructing the choice of technique framework, which considers the choice to be endogenous within the economic system. The discussion generates a direct link between capital accumulation and technical change.

Underlying the choice of the implemented technology is the available technology, which changes with the appearance of new techniques. The new techniques are not entered into the economy exogenously. Some agents invest resources in the production of new techniques. Thus economic considerations must also have an effect on the flow of new techniques. Hence both the supply and the demand of new techniques are endogenous, and in this sense the technology is endogenous.

The Transformation of Punjab Agriculture

The application of this framework to Indian Punjab agriculture was studied by McGuirk and Mundlak (1991), and their results are pertinent for our discussion. The study seeks to determine the level and pace of the implementation of the modern wheat and rice varieties, as well as new varieties of cotton and maize, introduced in Punjab during 1960–1979. The implementation of these new varieties resulted in a dramatic growth in crop production. The techniques that are included in the analysis, described in Table 6.1, constitute the most important crops, accounting for about 67 to 80 percent of the sown area in the period under consideration. The analysis considers three levels of decisions–area allocation, yield determination, and finally, investment-type decisions (to be explained below)–and is based on district-level data.

We turn immediately to the results, providing only necessary details here and postponing the explicit formulation to subsequent discussion, particularly in Chapter 13. At each stage of the analysis the state variables, those variables that affect the decisions, are grouped into three categories: incentives, constraints, and environment. Our immediate interest is in the role of the constraints in the pacing of implementation of the new varieties. The degree of implementation is measured in terms of the area allocated to the MV. Table 6.2 reports results for the empirical equations that explain the *shares* of wheat and rice varieties, the most important crops, in total area. The constraints consist of

Table 6.1 Punjab: Cropping alternatives

	Rabi	Kharif
Irrigated	Modern variety wheat Traditional wheat	Modern variety rice Traditional rice
	Gram Other	Irrigated maize* Cotton (American and Desi) Other
Dry	Wheat Gram Other	Rice Maize Cotton Other

Source: McGuirk and Mundlak (1991).

Note: Rabi and Kharif are two different seasons. Gram is a well-known legume in Asia.

*The irrigated maize category includes both improved and traditional varieties.

areas irrigated from private sources, mainly tube wells, and from government sources, mainly canals, the quantity of fertilizers *expected* to be available for the planting season, and roads. The results show that an increase in irrigation (mainly private), fertilizers, and roads was associated with an increase in the share of the MV of wheat in the total area and at the same time in a decrease in the area of traditional irrigated wheat.

For rice, fertilizers and roads were associated with an increase in the share of the MV in total acreage, but irrigation was associated with a decline in their share. This is consistent with the view that the irrigation favored wheat, and that therefore the *share* of rice declined. Note, however, that the table reports shares and not total area. Total area sown in MV of rice increased. Without going into further detail at this stage, we can say that the results indicate that with prices (or more generally the level of incentives) held constant, the transition to the MV was associated with an increase in the level of these quasi-fixed, capital inputs.

The results for the equations that explain the yield variations are reported in Table 6.3. The dependent variable in this equation is the average crop yield, which can be written as $y = (1 - S)y_1 + Sy_2$, where S is the share of the modern variety in the total area. The incentives were empirically irrelevant and therefore are not included in the equations. What is interesting is that the fertilizer variable, which in this equation is the actual quantity applied rather than the expected quantity used in the area equation, is not significantly different from zero. Thus, the only variable that matters is the proportion of the MV in total area, or simply S. The coefficient of this variable indicates the yield difference of the traditional and modern varieties,

$$\frac{\partial y}{\partial S} = \frac{\partial[(1 - S)y_1 + Sy_2]}{\partial S} = y_2 - y_1.$$

The empirical results are consistent with Figure 6.1, which shows the effect of a change in the level of the constraint. The proportion of the MV in total area changes as the constraint, k, changes, whereas the input ratio of each technique is kept constant at a level that equates the shadow price of the constraint over all the implemented techniques.

The results indeed indicate that the pace and level of the transition to the MV were determined to a large degree by the availability of the quasi-fixed inputs. The expansion of their supply required resources that had to be taken from other productive uses. But resources, of course, are finite, and if the implementation of a new technique requires resources, it cannot move faster than the necessary change in the supply of such resources.[1]

Table 6.2 Estimates of area allocation equations

	Irrigated wheat				Irrigated rice		
Variables	MV	Trad.	Dry wheat	Variables	MV	Trad.	Dry rice
Incentives				*Incentives*			
MV wheat	0.00123	−0.00089		MV rice	0.00020	−0.00012	
	(6.15)	(−6.20)			(3.36)	(−2.80)	
IT wheat	−0.00089	0.00041		IT rice	−0.00012	0.00011	
	(−6.20)	(2.81)			(−2.80)	(1.64)	
I gram	−0.00005	−0.00008		I maize	−0.00004	0.00001	
	(−1.12)	(−1.59)			(−1.24)	(0.21)	
D wheat			−0.00077	I cotton	0.000085	−0.00002	
			(−3.04)		(3.35)	(−0.89)	
D gram			0.00009	D rice			0.00021
			(0.53)				(3.79)
				D maize			0.00003
							(0.97)
				D cotton			0.00004
							(2.05)

Constraints			
IRR priv.	0.74701	−0.73056	0.12686
	(6.24)	(−8.59)	(1.68)
IRR govt.	0.23259	−0.17860	0.88662
	(1.55)	(−1.63)	(7.28)
E fert.	0.00125	−0.00090	−0.00177
	(3.3)	(−3.08)	(−4.57)
Roads	0.02376	−0.00590	−0.00272
	(2.35)	(−0.75)	(−0.33)
Environment			
June–Sept.	0.00123	−0.00095	0.000749
	(3.16)	(−3.30)	(2.58)
R^2	0.949	0.8097	0.9261

Constraints			
IRR priv.	−0.17733	0.03924	0.04272
	(−3.06)	(0.91)	(1.68)
IRR govt.	−0.11958	−0.13078	−0.00294
	(−1.79)	(−2.69)	(−0.09)
E fert.	0.00053	0.00018	0.00010
	(3.55)	(1.49)	(0.96)
Roads	0.05195	−0.01477	−0.00097
	(11.16)	(−3.69)	(−0.45)
Environment			
May	−0.00083	0.00014	−0.00007
	(−1.00)	(0.23)	(−0.14)
June	−0.00051	0.00093	0.00067
	(−1.13)	(2.64)	(2.49)
R^2	0.9621	0.8759	0.9058

Source: Based on McGuirk and Mundlak (1991), table 7.

Note: The incentive variables are expected revenues per thousand hectares deflated by wage for the indicated variety. MV, IT, I, and D indicate whether the particular crop variety is modern, irrigated traditional, irrigated, or dry. IRR priv. and IRR govt. are net irrigated area by private and government sources deflated by net cropped area (in thousands of ha.). E fert. is expected fertilizer available (nutrient kgs. per 1,000 ha. of net cropped area available in previous year). Roads measures km. of roads in district/1,000 ha. June-September, May, and June are preplanting rainfall variables (.01 mm.). District intercept shifters and a pre–green revolution intercept shifter are included in the estimated equations but are not included in the table. The Kharif irrigated and dry area equations (including rice) are all adjusted to correct for positive first-order autocorrelation following Parks (1967). T-statistics are in parentheses.

Table 6.3 Punjab: Estimates of yield equations

	Dependent variable: Yield				
Explanatory variable	Wheat	Gram	Rice	Maize	Cotton
Technology					
MV wheat	1.19928 (12.12)				
Irrigated gram		0.2215 (0.64)			
MV rice			1.32789 (7.18)		
Irrigated maize				2.07472 (4.66)	
Irrigated cotton					0.41771 (3.15)
American cotton					0.11413 (4.49)
Constraints					
Fertilizer	0.00316 (1.30)	0.00141 (1.66)	0.00189 (1.00)	0.00201 (1.46)	0.00116 (2.2)
Fertilizer technology	−0.00301 (−1.27)	−0.00314 (−1.69)	0.00115 (0.59)	−0.00121 (−0.74)	−0.00135 (−2.45)
Environment					
Rain	−0.00955 (−2.12)	−0.00437 (−0.64)	0.00212 (0.94)	−0.00118 (−0.36)	0.002306 (1.58)
Rain technology	0.00342 (0.53)	0.00622 (0.35)	0.00183 (0.59)	−0.01200 (−2.82)	−0.002679 (−1.69)
R^2	0.831	0.172	0.833	0.539	0.716

Source: Based on McGuirk and Mundlak (1991), tables 15 and 16.

Note: The numbers in parentheses are *t*-statistics. The district effects are not reported here.

The technology variables are:

Irrigated cotton, gram, and maize–proportion of area irrigated.

MV rice and wheat–proportion of MV in rice and wheat areas respectively.

American cotton–proportion of American cotton in cotton area.

The rain variables are:

Cotton–district rainfall, June–September.

Maize and rice–district rainfall, July–September.

Wheat and gram–district rainfall, October–April.

By the very nature of the fact that k is a constraint, the introduction of the MV increases its marginal value productivity, referred to as its shadow price. This can be seen in Figure 6.1, where the rate of return changes due to the appearance of the new technique from r_0 to $\tilde{r}$. With time, this increase in the rate of return will attract more capital and thereby facilitate further implementation of the new techniques. This is indeed what actually happened: the Punjab experienced a dramatic increase in the supply of fertilizers, tube wells, electricity, and roads as well as other variables that provide the infrastructure conducive for the adaptation of the modern varieties. Some of these variables are plotted in Figure 6.2. The most dramatic change is in the use of fertilizers, which increased from 46 thousand tons in 1965 to 1,199 thousand tons in 1992, a 26-fold increase that amounts to an average annual growth rate of 13 percent. The rate was even higher, 17 percent, for the twenty-year period from 1965 to 1985. For most of the period, the total supply of fertilizers and its expansion was controlled by the Indian government, which gave priority to the development of domestic production and restricted imports. Thus the growth rate of fertilizer supply, and thereby the shift to the new varieties, largely reflects the pace at which resources were allocated to domestic production. With this background we turn to formulate the process just described.

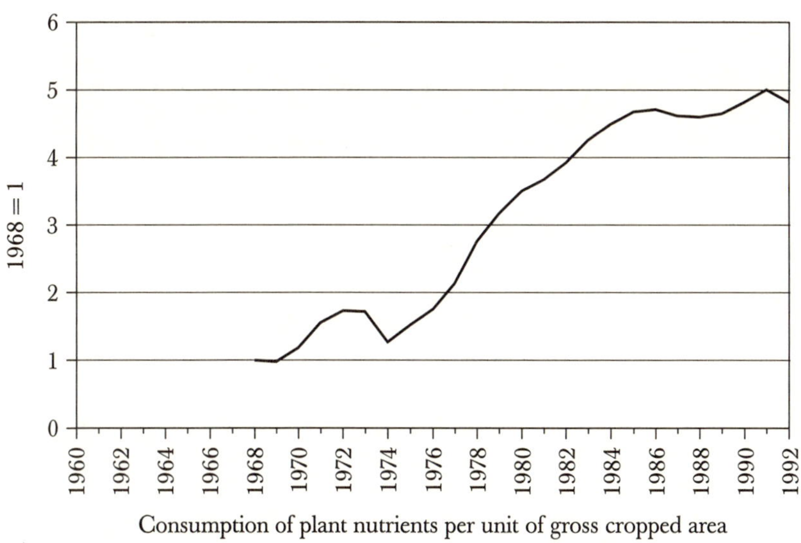

Figure 6.2 Punjab: Selected inputs. (From *Statistical Abstracts of Punjab,* Chandigarh: Economic and Statistical Organization, various years.)

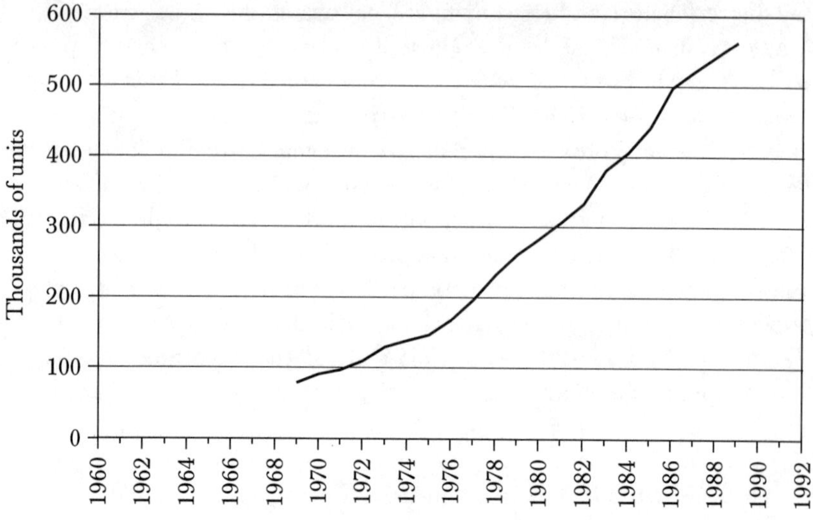

Number of electric tubewells and pumping sets

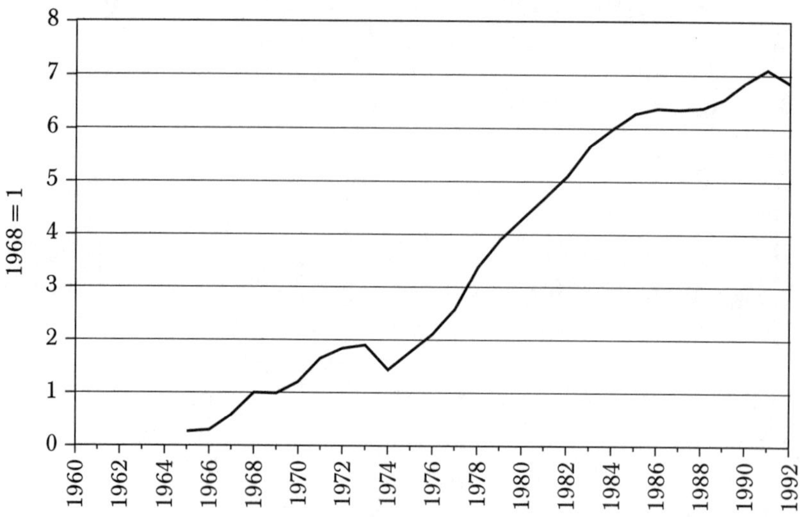

Use of fertilizers

Figure 6.2 *(continued)*

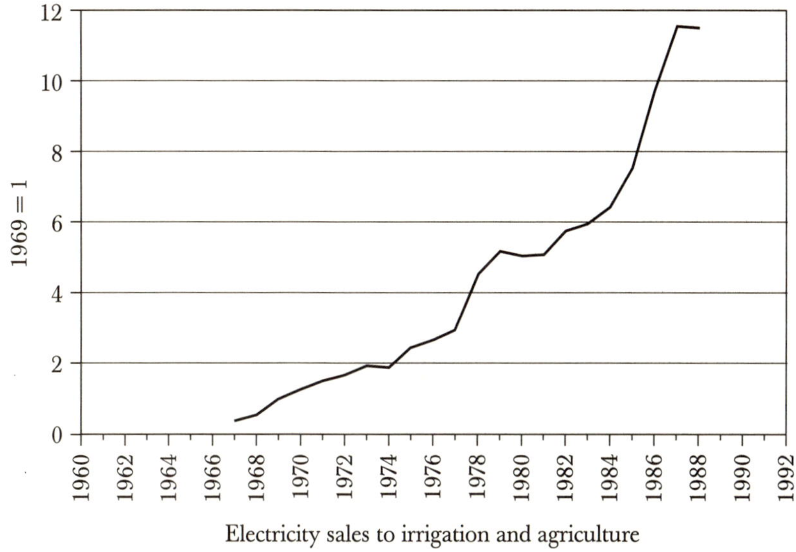

Figure 6.2 *(continued)*

The Production Structure

General

At this point it is helpful to broaden our discussion of the production structure.[2] For this we need the concept of the input requirement set.

DEFINITION The *input requirement set,* $V(Y)$, is the set of all inputs that can possibly produce a given output Y.

It is assumed that $V(Y)$ is nonempty, containing nonnegative inputs, closed, convex, and monotone in the sense that if $x \in V(Y)$, $x^* > x$, then $x^* \in V(Y)$ also. $V(Y)$ is bounded from below by the isoquant that also belongs to $V(Y)$. With this structure it is possible to derive the production function associated with $V(Y)$.[3]

The model is now extended to allow for more than one production function in each sector. We examine in detail the simplest case, two production functions in one sector, say in agriculture. Since a production function is associated with an input requirement set, there are now two such sets, as shown in Figure 6.3. Some input combinations belong only to one input requirement set; others are common to both. This suggests that we can now broaden the concept of technology to allow for more than one production function. For instance,

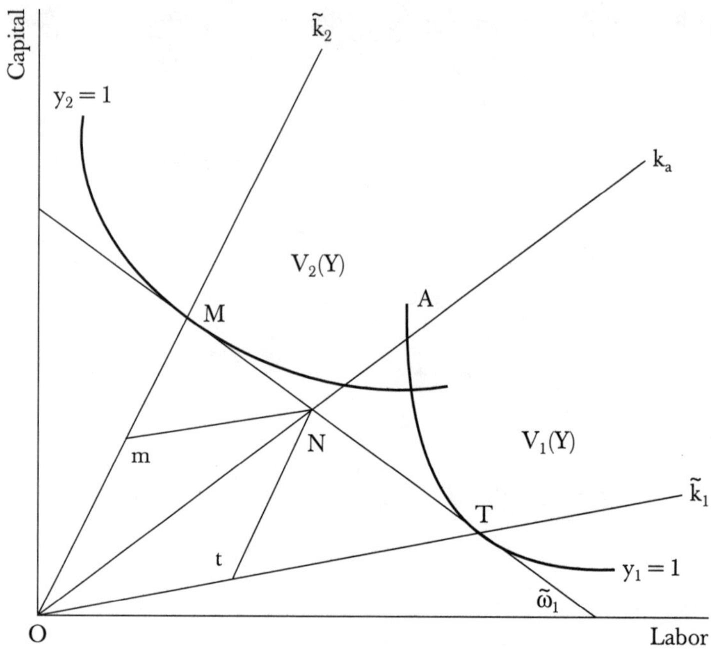

Figure 6.3 Input constraint and the composition of techniques

the first production function associated with $V_1(Y)$ is assumed to describe a traditional grain variety, whereas the second function, associated with $V_2(Y)$, is assumed to describe a modern grain variety. A technique is a method of production that can be described by a production function. It can be defined as narrow or as disaggregated, as desired. The basic assumption made here is that the technology is convex, so that it is possible to use the two techniques simultaneously. This means that some of the land can be used for the modern variety and some of the land can be used for the traditional variety. To assist the discussion, some terminology needs to be introduced.

DEFINITION The *available technology (AT)* is the collection of all available techniques.

Let $F_j(x)$ be the production function associated with the jth techniques; then the available technology is

$$T = \{F_j(x);\ j = 1, \ldots, J\}. \tag{6.1}$$

In our example, the technology, T, consists of the two varieties. Since each variety generates an input requirement set, so does their collection, $V(Y)$, which is the union of $V_1(Y)$ and $V_2(Y)$. Under the assumption that the technology is convex, it consists of all convex combinations of $V_1(Y)$ and $V_2(Y)$. The isoquant of $V(Y)$, or the efficiency frontier of $V(Y)$, is identical with that of the traditional variety for capital-labor ratios smaller or equal to $\tilde{k}_1$ that corresponds to point T in Figure 6.3. It is associated with the isoquant of the modern variety for capital-labor ratios larger than $\tilde{k}_2$ that corresponds to point M. For $\tilde{k}_1 \leq k \leq \tilde{k}_2$, the isoquant consists of the segment MT. The introduction of modern techniques opens up efficient production plans that were not feasible under the traditional variety. This motivates the definition of technical change.

DEFINITION *Technical change* is a change in the technology set T.

The appearance of the modern variety, or any new technique for that matter, implies technical change. This change is of *potential* consequence only if it changes the frontier of T. It is of *actual* relevance only if it is implemented. In terms of our illustration, the technical change occurs in the form of the appearance of the modern variety. The degree of its implementation depends on the available resources. If $k \leq \tilde{k}_1$, the economy does not have sufficient capital to implement the new technique. Consequently, the empirical observations will be of the traditional technique alone. It is therefore important to distinguish between available technology and implemented technology.

DEFINITION *Implemented technology (IT)* is a subset of the available technology containing all the techniques that are actually implemented.

The Composite Production Function

We turn now to specify the production structure in one sector, say agriculture, where the technology is made up of two techniques represented by production functions homogeneous of degree 1, twice differentiable, and concave. Let L_j and K_j be the labor and capital assigned to technique j, $j = 1, 2$, and L_a, K_a be the labor and capital available to agriculture. Define $\ell = L_1/L_a$ and $k_j = K_j/L_j$, then the technology and full employment conditions in agriculture are

$$\ell k_1 + (1 - \ell)k_2 = k_a \tag{6.2}$$

$$Y_1/L_a = \ell f_1(k_1) \tag{6.3}$$

$$Y_2/L_a = (1 - \ell) f_2(k_2) \tag{6.4}$$

$$k_2(\omega) > k_1(\omega) \quad \text{for all admissible } \omega.$$

If we add the competitive conditions, we get a system that describes a two-sector economy where the two sectors produce the same agricultural output with different techniques. Because the product is the same, the price ratio is 1, and the price function dictates a constant wage-rental ratio.

PROPERTY 6.1 (technique coexistence and factor prices) Factor prices are constant under the coexistence of techniques.

As the capital-labor ratio increases, the economy moves along the Rybczynski path in the direction of the capital-intensive technique until the labor-intensive technique disappears. Throughout the domain of coexistence of the two techniques, the wage-rental ratio is constant, and therefore the sectoral capital-labor ratios are also constant. These factor ratios are the threshold values. Figure 6.4 describes the relationship between the available resources in agriculture, k_a, and output and its composition by techniques. At point A, $k_a = \tilde{k}_1$ and only technique 1 is employed, therefore at this point $y_a = y_1$. At point B, $k_a = \tilde{k}_2$ and only technique 2 is employed, therefore at this point $y_a = y_2$. The pair $(\tilde{k}_1, \tilde{k}_2)$ makes up the threshold values.

DEFINITION (threshold values) The capital-labor ratios that define the domain of coexistence of the two techniques are referred to as *threshold values.*

PROPERTY 6.2 The threshold values of the capital-labor ratio are determined by the technology.

As k_a increases from $k_a = \tilde{k}_1$ to $k_a = \tilde{k}_2$, the Rybczynski path, connecting points A and B, is generated. Because the price is 1, the output level at any point on the path is the sum of the two coordinates of that point.

PROPERTY 6.3 (composition of techniques) Under coexistence of techniques, the relative importance of the labor-intensive technique declines with capital deepening.

When k_a is not bounded by the threshold values, only one technique is used. We have basically outlined the composite production function for agriculture. For future reference, we develop the results analytically. Agricultural output, Y_a, is the sum of outputs produced by the individual techniques: $Y_a = Y_1 + Y_2$. Using (6.2) and (6.3), the average labor productivity in agriculture is

$$Y_a/L_a \equiv f_a(k_a) = \ell f_1(k_1) + (1 - \ell) f_2(k_2). \tag{6.5}$$

The optimization problem is to maximize output under the resource constraint. This is the same as maximizing the output-labor ratio, Y_a/L_a:

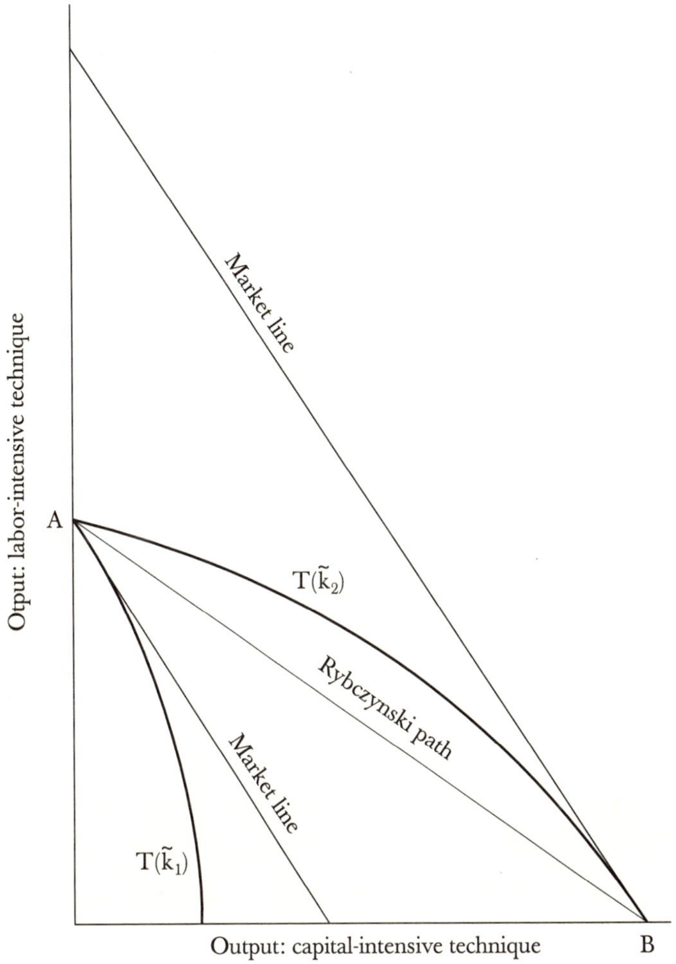

Figure 6.4 Construction of a composite production function

$$\max_{k_j \geq 0, \ell_j \geq 0} G(k_a, L_a) = \sum_j \ell_j f_j(k_j) + r(k_a - \sum_j \ell_j k_j) + w(1 - \sum_j \ell_j). \quad (6.6a)$$

The Kuhn-Tucker conditions require that

$$\begin{aligned} &[f_j'(k_j) - r]k_j = 0 \quad [f_j(k_j) - rk_j - w]\ell_j = 0 \\ &f_j'(k_j) - r \leq 0 \qquad f_j(k_j) - rk_j - w \leq 0. \end{aligned} \quad (6.6b)$$

A technique is implemented when the marginal productivity of each of the inputs is equal to its shadow price. Hence, for the two techniques to coexist, the marginal productivity of each factor should be the same across techniques. To derive the domain of coexistence, we solve for the threshold values:

$$f_1'(\tilde{k}_1) = f_2'(\tilde{k}_2) \tag{6.7}$$

$$f_1(\tilde{k}_1) - \tilde{k}_1 f_1'(\tilde{k}_1) = f_2(\tilde{k}_2) - \tilde{k}_2 f_2'(\tilde{k}_2). \tag{6.8}$$

The labor allocation among the techniques is determined by

$$\ell(\tilde{\omega}, k_a) = \frac{\tilde{k}_2 - k_a}{\tilde{k}_2 - \tilde{k}_1}. \tag{6.9}$$

The real factor prices, $\tilde{w}$ and $\tilde{r}$ are given by the marginal productivity of labor and capital derived from the composite function, $f_a(\cdot)$, respectively. Those can be obtained by differentiation and to do so, write $f_j(\tilde{k}_j) = \tilde{w} + \tilde{r}\tilde{k}_j$ and substitute it in (6.5) to obtain

$$f_a(k_a) = \tilde{w} + \tilde{r}k_a. \tag{6.10}$$

The marginal productivity of capital, $\tilde{r}$, is derived directly from (6.10). When k_a is outside the domain bounded by the threshold values, only one technique is used. This follows from the full employment condition. In this case the composite production function is identical to that of the active technique.

The discussion may be summarized by giving a complete description of the composite production function.

$$\text{For}\quad k_a \leq \tilde{k}_1,\quad \text{or}\quad k_a \geq \tilde{k}_2,\ f_a(k_a) = f_j(k_a),\quad j = 1, 2,\ \text{respectively.} \tag{6.11}$$

$$\text{For}\quad k_a \in [\tilde{k}_1, \tilde{k}_2],\quad f_a(\tilde{k}_a) = \tilde{w} + \tilde{r}k_a,\quad f_a'(k_a) = \tilde{r},\quad \omega_a(k_a) = \tilde{\omega}.$$

PROPERTY 6.4 (composite production function) The composite production function obtained under the coexistence of techniques, characterized by differentiable concave production functions, is also differentiable and concave.

The composite production function is illustrated in Figure 6.5. The upper panel shows the wage-rental ratio as a function of k_a where $k_j(\tilde{\omega})$ are fixed at $\tilde{k}_j$. The lower panel shows $f(k_a)$; it starts at the origin along f_1 until $\tilde{A}$, from there on it moves along the segment $\tilde{A}\tilde{M}$ and thereafter continues along f_2. Note that for any value of $k_a \in k_a(\tilde{\omega})$, the average productivity of labor, $f_a[k_a(\tilde{\omega})]$ and the marginal productivity of capital, $f_a'[k_a(\tilde{\omega})]$, are uniquely defined. For any

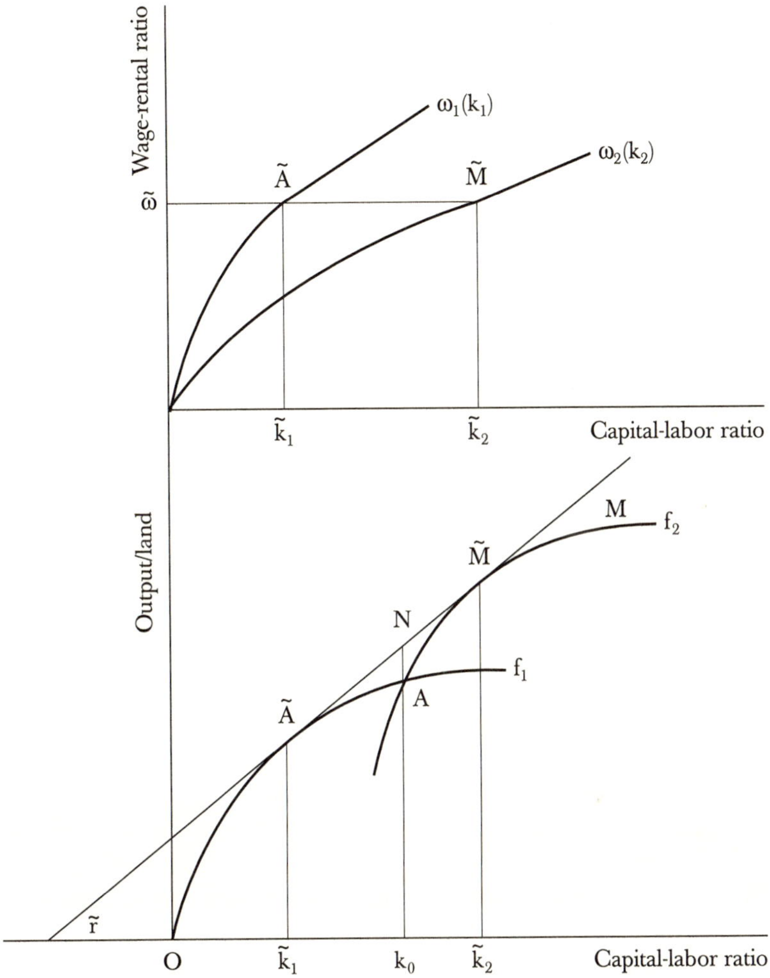

Figure 6.5 The composite production function

other value of k_a only one technique is used, and because $k_j(\omega)$ is monotonic in ω, the solution can again be expressed in terms of k_a.

The Economy

Having derived the production structure in agriculture, we turn to examine the effect of the introduction of the modern technique on the economy as a whole. This we do under the assumption that the technology in nonagriculture consists of a single technique. We rewrite the relevant part of the system with the obvious change of notation:

$$\ell_a k_a + (1 - \ell_a) k_n = k \tag{6.12}$$

$$Y_a / L = \ell_a f_a(k_a) \tag{6.13}$$

$$Y_n / L = (1 - \ell_a) f_n(k_n) \tag{6.14}$$

$$k_n(\omega) > k_a(\omega) \quad \text{for all admissible } \omega.$$

Because the agricultural production function maintains all the properties of the production function assumed in Chapter 2, the results of that chapter are immediately applicable. There is only one difference: the method of solving the system is modified to allow for the fact that k_a is not uniquely defined in terms of ω. As $\omega(k_a)$ is uniquely determined, however, so is $k_n(\omega)$. Hence the system can be solved in terms of k_a.

The solution is demonstrated in Figure 6.6. At levels of k_a below the threshold value of the traditional technique, $k_a \leq \tilde{k}_1$, only technique 1 is used, and the corresponding segment of the transformation curve displays an upward-sloping supply, which we write as $p'(y_a) > 0$. Similarly for $k_a \geq \tilde{k}_2$ only technique 2 is used, and again $p'(y_a) > 0$. In both cases, $\omega(k_a)$ is monotonically increasing. The new results are obtained for the case of coexistence, where ω is constant at $\tilde{\omega}$, as is $k_n(\tilde{\omega})$ as well as the marginal productivity in the two sectors. Consequently, p is constant and the corresponding segment of the transformation curve is a straight line.

PROPERTY 6.5 (technique coexistence and product price) When two techniques coexist, the product price is constant and is unaffected by capital deepening.

As k_a varies within the domain of coexistence, the resource allocation changes in order to maintain the full employment condition. Recall that in this domain $k_n(\omega)$ is constant, let $\ell_a = L_a/L$, and rewrite the full employment condition as

$$\frac{1 - \ell_a}{\ell_a} = \frac{k - k_a}{k_n(\omega) - k}. \tag{6.15}$$

Equation (6.15) is solved for varying values of k_a:

$$\text{sign} \frac{d\ell_a}{dk_a} |_{k_n} = \text{sign}[k_n(\omega) - k].$$

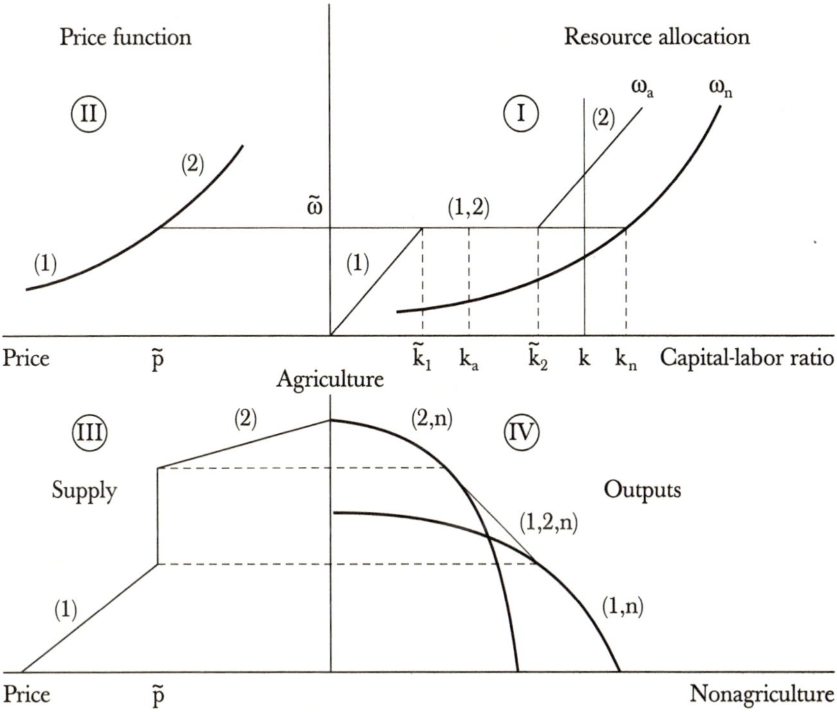

Figure 6.6 Coexistence of techniques: Supply side

This is simply a property discussed in Chapter 2 for the case where agriculture employs only one technique. This result applies independently of the factor intensity. To generalize the result, however, we may consider k_a to be the capital-labor ratio in the sector with the heterogeneous technology. We note that the relative importance of the labor-intensive sector grows with k_a. The importance of k_a is derived in Property 6.2, which highlights the fact that the degree of utilization of the new, more productive, and capital-intensive technique is through capital deepening. This can now be summarized.

PROPERTY 6.6 (resource allocation) The transition to a capital-intensive *technique* under fixed resources requires an increase in the share of the labor-intensive *sector* in resources and output. The result is independent of the sector in which the new technique is introduced.

It is important to note that in this discussion, it is the direct measure of factor intensity, rather than the factor-cost intensity, which matters, and as such capital does not include land. This discussion is general and applies equally well to the case of human capital. When the application of the new technique requires a special skill whose total endowment is given, the extent of its implementation depends on the ability to mobilize workers with this skill from other occupations.

Returning to the illustration in Figure 6.6, the numbers in parentheses identify the implemented techniques. Panel II presents the corresponding price function. The function is monotone and continuous but not differentiable at $\tilde{p} = p(\tilde{\omega})$. The transformation curve is given in panel IV. As agriculture in this case is the labor-intensive sector, the increase in its output requires an increase in its capital-labor ratio. But by Property 6.2, such an increase leads to a shift toward the capital-intensive technique. Therefore, with high agricultural production, only technique 2 is used in agriculture. The middle segment represents the coexistence of the two techniques. Finally, when agricultural output is relatively low, only technique 1 is used in agriculture. Panel III portrays the corresponding agricultural supply relationship. It is important to note that when the two techniques coexist, the agricultural supply is infinitely elastic. This result is of great importance and we will discuss its ramifications at a later stage.

PROPERTY 6.7 (supply elasticity) When the two techniques coexist, the supply is perfectly elastic.

The discussion was conducted under the assumption that agriculture is labor intensive. When agriculture is capital intensive so that $k_a > k > k_n$, some of the results are modified. In this case, the only way to increase k_a is to initiate the changes within agriculture itself. This can be done by shifting labor to nonagriculture, but because the capital-labor ratio of nonagriculture is fixed within the area of coexistence, the shift of labor has to be accompanied by a shift of capital. The result is a decline of the share of agriculture in total resources. However, this does not mean a decline in total agricultural output. The new technique is more productive and therefore produces higher output with less resources. This is illustrated in Figure 6.6, where the movement along the line of technique-coexistence represents a higher production frontier than that given by the use of single techniques. The case where agriculture is capital intensive is more applicable to high-income countries, and indeed in these countries the share of agriculture in total resources is relatively small.

COROLLARY TO PROPERTY 6.6. When agriculture is capital intensive, the introduction of capital-intensive techniques is likely to reduce the share of agriculture in total resources even though output increases.

The reversal of the relationship between the use of the techniques and the relative importance of agricultural production is also reflected in the reversal of the relationship between the use of the techniques and p. However, what has not changed is the relationship between the choice of a technique and the wage-rental ratio or the capital-labor ratio in agriculture. This is the essence of the process.

PROPERTY 6.8 (technique choice and factor prices) An increase in the wage-rental ratio leads to the replacement of labor-intensive techniques by capital-intensive techniques.

The Effect of Capital Accumulation

Bringing in the demand functions, we can determine the short-run equilibrium. From the point of view of the present discussion it is desirable to distinguish between two cases: $p = \tilde{p}$ and $p \neq \tilde{p}$. The latter case is identical to that discussed in Chapter 4 and need not be repeated here. Thus we turn to the case where the two techniques coexist and prices are constant. In this case, an increase in k shifts the transformation curve and income increases. As p is fixed in the region of coexistence, the new equilibrium solution reflects only income effect on demand.

When the technology of each sector consists of a single technique, the supply effect of a change in k is signed by the Rybczynski proposition. When techniques coexist, however, this proposition cannot be applied because $y_i(\tilde{p})$ does not have a single value. We can still sign the supply effect of capital accumulation by modifying the Rybczynski proposition. What drives the proposition is the fact that constant prices fix the value of the sectoral factor ratios. We can state this result as the condition of the proposition and turn to the full employment condition in (6.15) to derive the proposition. Thus an increase in k, with k_a and k_n held constant, increases the proportion of the capital-intensive sector in total resources. Under the assumption of $k_n > k_a$, $\partial \ell_a / \partial k \,|_{k_a, k_n} < 0$. Since $y_i = \ell_i f_i(k_i)$, $i = a, n$, any output plan obtained under constant k_i is shifted by capital accumulation so that the output of the capital-intensive sector increases and that of the labor-intensive sector declines. This is illustrated in Figure 6.7 where point B^* is southeast of B and the two points are obtained for the same values of k_a and k_n.

Bringing the changes in demand and supply together, and maintaining $p = \tilde{p}$ an increase in k leads to a new equilibrium point, E. The equilibrium quantities of the two sectors increase at rates proportional to their income

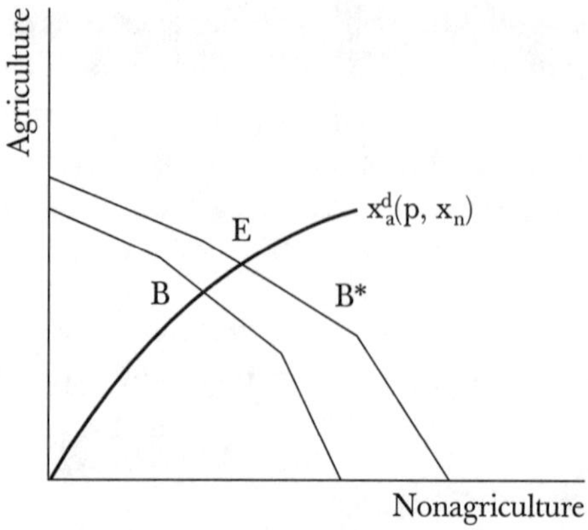

Figure 6.7 Equilibrium: Capital accumulation and a composite production function

elasticities. The movement from B to E is decomposed to an expansion effect, a movement from B to B^*, and to a movement along the new transformation curve, from B^* to E. Both effects take place at a constant ω, and therefore k_n is also constant. Hence, the total movement from B to E implies an increase of y_n at a constant k_n. This requires an increase of ℓ_n, which in turn implies a decrease in ℓ_a. Increasing ℓ_n while k_n is constant implies a shift of capital and labor to the n-sector. But at the same time y_a also goes up in spite of the decline in ℓ_a, and this can only be accomplished by increasing k_a. This in turn implies substituting the modern technique for the traditional technique and thereby supplying the labor to the n-sector. The discussion is now summarized:

PROPERTY 6.9 (technique choice and capital accumulation) An increase in the overall capital-labor ratio that maintains the state of coexistence of the two techniques generates only an income effect on demand. The change in demand is met by a shift of resources to the capital-intensive sector and by a rise of the relative importance of the capital-intensive technique.

The Rate of Implementation of New Techniques

The foregoing discussion highlighted the fact that the rate of adoption of new capital-intensive techniques is subject to a capital constraint, and therefore it depends on the rate of capital accumulation. For this reason, when dealing with an important sector of the economy, the introduction of a new technique may take time to accomplish. If we refer to Figures 6.1 and 6.3, this long-run problem can be described as movement of point N on the frontier of the composite production function.

In addition, there is the short-run problem of a movement to the new frontier with the existing capital stock. When a new technique is introduced, the initial point becomes inefficient in that it is not on the frontier of the new composite function as illustrated by point A in Figure 6.1. The question is whether the movement from A to N, which does not require more overall capital, is immediate. This is obviously an empirical question, but it is reasonable to assume that in many cases this movement is not instantaneous. The determinants of the pace of such a movement often given in the literature can be classified into two groups, those related to heterogeneity of capital and those related to uncertainty and imperfect knowledge.

Heterogeneous capital

In the foregoing discussion, it was implicitly assumed that capital goods are homogeneous, so that horses and tractors are the same thing. They both represent foregone consumption, and as such they are the "same." This sameness is historical, however, and at present, the two capital goods do not serve the same function. The recognition that capital goods are heterogeneous introduces another dimension into the discussion. If the two techniques in question require different forms of capital, then the pace of moving from A to N will be determined by the pace of changing the composition of the capital stock so as to relieve the bottleneck generated by the capital components in which the new techniques are intensive. In general, the disappearance of the capital good associated with the traditional technique is determined by obsolescence or discard, and the introduction of the capital good associated with the new technique is determined by gross investment. Consequently, the rate of implementation of the new technique will be determined by the rate of *gross investment,* whereas the decline in the traditional technique will depend on the rate of disappearance of the capital good associated with it. Thus, the movement from A to N would imply a gradual reduction of the capital-labor ratio in the traditional technique from k_a to $\tilde{k}_1$. In this process ω will gradually decline from its level at A, as determined by the traditional technique, to $\tilde{\omega}$.

The essence of the argument on heterogeneity of capital is that the two techniques may require different compositions of the various capital goods. If this is the case, then the change in the composition of the two techniques will depend on the necessary change in the composition of the various capital goods. This process may require time, and the pace of convergence of the economy to the new frontier will depend on the rate of *gross investment.*

PROPERTY 6.10 When capital is heterogeneous and the new technique requires a different composition of capital goods, the pace of the movement to the new efficiency frontier generated by the technique depends on the pace of *gross investment,* whereas the movement to a new equilibrium point on the new frontier depends on the pace of *net investment.*

So far we have treated the modern technique as a new entity completely unrelated to the traditional technique. However, from a strictly formal point of view, once the new technique is available, it can be expressed as if it were obtained by some parametric change of the existing production function. Of special interest is the case where the modern technique can be described as a Hicks-neutral technical change in the traditional technique. In this case, the $\omega(k)$ function is unaffected by the technical change, so that the threshold values of the two techniques are identical. The new technique completely dominates the old technique, and it is therefore inefficient to employ the two techniques simultaneously. One reason for the coexistence of techniques in this case is that the two techniques use different capital goods. This is the case of the embodiment hypothesis developed by Solow (1962). Under this hypothesis, the new technique is embodied in a new capital good, say a machine, and it cannot be applied with the old machine. Consequently the pace of introduction of the new technique will depend on the flow of new machines, which depends on the rate of *gross investment,* rather than *net investment.* In this case, the traditional technique will disappear eventually, even if there is no net investment.

The situation is different when the modern technique can be expressed as a factor-augmenting technical change of the traditional technique so that the $\omega(k)$ function changes. In contrast to the previous case, factor-augmenting technical change generates a difference in the threshold value so that $\tilde{k}_2 > \tilde{k}_1$. In this case, if the new threshold value exceeds the available capital-labor ratio, the rate of implementation will eventually depend on *net investment.* Thus, if the economy does not accumulate capital, it will not discard the traditional technique. This is the difference between this model and that of embodied technical change. It follows

PROPERTY 6.11 The pace of the implementation of embodied technical change that does not change the capital-labor ratio depends on the pace of *gross investment.* When the new techniques are more capital intensive, the pace of adoption depends on *net investment.*

Human capital

The foregoing discussion has dealt with physical capital, but it is equally applicable to human capital. Human capital has two aspects pertinent to the present discussion. First is the actual appearance of new techniques, which will be treated in a subsequent section. Second is the specific knowledge needed to take advantage of the new techniques. From the point of view of our presentation, this element can be considered as a component of k in the above illustration. Thus Property 6.10 also applies to the case of skill accumulation. It also follows that when a new technique requires a new skill for its operation, the pace of implementation will depend on the pace of investment in the needed skill. This suggests that a low level of human capital will be associated with low per capita output and that an increase in the rate of investment in human capital will increase the growth rate of per capita output. It sounds so simple; why then don't low-income countries speed up the accumulation of their human capital? The mere fact that we have to raise this question suggests that perhaps things are somewhat more complicated. To deal with this question, we draw an analogy between the two types of capital. Basically, human capital, like physical capital, is endogenously determined. The appearance of a new technique increases the rate of return to the specific knowledge or skill associated with this technique, and this in turn is expected to stimulate learning. For example, the appearance of computers generated demand for programmers, and this was reflected in their returns. However, the implementation of the new techniques may be constrained by other factors, such as physical capital. When the capital stock is too low for the implementation of the new technique, there is no point in investing in the knowledge needed for its implementation, because it will remain unutilized for a long time to come. It follows that low-income countries with a low level of physical capital will not invest in acquiring knowledge needed for the operation of techniques that they cannot afford to acquire. Low-income countries do not invest in space research, for example, because they do not have the resources needed to make use of such knowledge. This brings us back to the important role played by physical capital in the implementation of new techniques.

Information

The foregoing discussion dealt with the question of knowledge needed to operate the new technique. There is another kind of knowledge that affects the implementation, knowledge about the performance of the new technique. Farmers know how to grow wheat, but they may lack knowledge about the potential performance of a new variety. The new technique may be superior, but farmers do not know it and may require time to sample it. A flow of new techniques generates a process of search that requires resources. At the farm level, the amount of resources devoted to the search depends on their cost (Feder and Slade, 1984). Such cost depends on the time allocated to the search and the ability to digest it. The latter, as Schultz (1964) postulated, may depend on the level of education. Hence the speed of implementation that reflects imperfect knowledge is also positively related to capital in the form of human capital.

Another reason for uncertainty is related to the stochastic nature of the production process associated with the various techniques. Some techniques may have a higher variance in their performance than others. For instance, it has been debated whether or not the yields of the modern varieties have a higher variance than that of the traditional varieties. It is in this sense that the degree of implementation will depend on the stochastic performance of the techniques and the attitude of producers toward risk (Just and Zilberman, 1983). The importance of this source needs empirical quantification.

Sustainable Technology and Learning by Doing

The dependence of the implemented technology on resource endowment implies that if for any reason there is a decline in the capital-labor ratio, the economy will retreat to labor-intensive techniques, and with those there may be a loss in productivity. To dramatize the case, consider a major destruction of physical capital due to an earthquake or a war. The question is in what way would the reduction of capital affect the performance of the economy. The answer depends largely on what part of the technology is sustainable in the sense that it does not diminish with the reduction of the capital stock. This component represents cumulative experience, which is similar in nature to Arrow's "learning by doing." That may include knowledge that initially required capital to acquire but which, once acquired, does not depreciate and is not susceptible to destruction. In this we can also include changes in market organizations or economic policies that result in higher productivity, which might have been costly to implement, but once implemented, will continue without additional capital requirements. This also includes the introduction of new varieties or other elements of new knowledge. It is expected that these elements would be increasing with positive gross investment but would not be eliminated with negative investment.

In recent literature, learning by doing plays a more explicit role in the determination of technological progress. We return to this subject in the next chapter and also in Chapter 15.

Choice of Techniques and Land Expansion

The appearance of new techniques affects our analysis of land expansion. When a new technique is more capital intensive than the existing one, the response of agriculture depends on the availability of capital. The subject can be illustrated in terms of Figure 6.1, which we now assume to represent the production function for quality q land. When capital is not constrained and agriculture is a price taker, the capital-land ratio will change with the introduction of the new technique from k_0 to k_2. The rent on the marginal land increases due to the higher productivity of the new technique from OE to OH, and more land will come under production. The actual increment will depend on the thickness of the margin, as was discussed in Chapters 4 and 5. We also note that the appearance of the new technique increases the capital-land ratio.

PROPERTY 6.12 When agriculture is a price taker, the appearance of a more productive and more capital-intensive technique will result in an increase in total capital, land, and output in agriculture.

In the case of a capital constraint, the appearance of the new technique increases the demand for capital; therefore its shadow price increases, and the marginal productivity of land declines. In this case, the decline in the marginal productivity of land is from OE to OD in Figure 6.1. If the tax, c, is larger than OD, then the rent becomes negative, and this land will go out of production. If this land was initially marginal, then by definition c is equal to OE and the land will be set idle. The capital released by the exit of the marginal land will be distributed to higher-quality land, and this will make it possible to increase the capital intensity on this land, thereby increasing the share of the new technique on it. Recall from Figure 4.8 that $k(q)$ increases with q to conclude

PROPERTY 6.13 When agriculture is subject to a capital constraint, the appearance of a more productive and more capital-intensive technique will increase the quality of the marginal land, and land will go out of production. The degree of implementation of the new technique will increase with the land quality.

A comparison of Properties 6.12 and 6.13 shows that the *same* technical change can be classified as land expanding under unconstrained capital and land substituting under a capital constraint. The outcome under a capital constraint can be viewed as the short-run effect, whereas the long-term effect is achieved under no resource constraint. Thus if the introduction of a modern, capital-intensive technique causes land to go out of production, this can be viewed as a temporary outcome.

New Techniques and Income Distribution

New techniques are generated by firms, private or public, that spend resources on research and development. Given the state of science, there is generally a choice to be made in determining the research strategy. For the purpose of our discussion, the key variable is the capital intensity of the new techniques. The foregoing discussions indicated that capital accumulation causes a shift of resources to capital-intensive techniques and thus generates demand for them. It is no surprise then that new techniques are often capital intensive. However, overshooting is counterproductive. The demand for the new techniques depends on the expected rate of their implementation, which in turn depends on capital availability. For the new techniques to be implemented, therefore, their threshold level should not be too high.

This story can be told by looking at the firm level. In the absence of a new capital-intensive technique, capital accumulation increases capital-labor ratios, thereby causing a rise in wage and a decline in the rental rate. Consequently, the owners of capital will be interested in investing their capital in techniques that prevent the rate of return from falling. This generates the demand for the capital-intensive techniques.

By its very nature, this process leads to a decline in the labor share, S_L, and as such can be considered labor saving. This can be illustrated by observing changes in $\theta = \omega/k = S_L/(1 - S_L)$. Note that θ is monotonically increasing with S_L. If we refer to Figure 6.3, we see that the movement from T to N increases k with ω held constant. Consequently θ, and therefore S_L, decline. The transition from A to N implies a decline in ω under a constant k, which again results in a decline of the labor share.

With technology consisting of more than one technique, Hicks-neutral technical change (NTC) in one technique has the effect of factor-saving technical change for the sector as a whole. Of special interest is NTC of the capital-intensive technique that generates an overall effect of labor-saving technical change. An improvement in the productivity of the capital-intensive technique increases the shadow price of capital, or equivalently causes a decline in ω. The threshold values of the various techniques decline accordingly, from $\tilde{k}_j(0)$ to $\tilde{k}_j(t)$. Let ℓ be the share of the labor-intensive technique in employment and use (6.9) to write

$$\frac{1-\ell}{\ell} = \frac{k - \tilde{k}_1}{\tilde{k}_2 - k}. \tag{6.16}$$

This ratio rises as $\tilde{k}_j$ declines, implying a decline in the relative importance of the labor-intensive technique. Thus we have demonstrated that the net effect of a Hicks-neutral technical change in the capital-intensive technique is labor saving. The details of this argument are assigned as an exercise. Indeed, as we saw in Chapter 1, labor share in agriculture has declined.

In this illustration, the modern technique is the subject of the NTC for a purpose. If, as has been argued, the process of capital accumulation causes a shift in the direction toward capital-intensive techniques, then–other things being equal–the demand will call for development of the NTC to be implemented on the modern techniques. In a more detailed framework, the cost of producing and changing techniques, as well as the required research time, should be introduced. If the required time is significant, by the time the research is completed, the traditional technique may not be of any importance. Therefore, efforts will be directed at increasing the productivity of the modern technique. This consideration has a dynamic aspect. With time, the modern techniques become traditional. They have already been worked on so that the easy gains have already been made, and additional gains may be subject to increasing cost. Thus from both the demand side and the supply side, it is likely that the effort of improving an existing technique will be aimed at modern techniques.

Total Factor Productivity

What is the rate of technical change? This subject is an important one in empirical analysis, and in practice there is more than one answer, depending on the method of measurement. To begin with, there is the difference between partial and total factor productivity (TFP). Partial productivity measures are measures of average factor productivity, such as average labor productivity. Changes in this measure reflect changes in the amount of inputs used per worker in addition to changes in technology. The same holds true for average land productivity, or simply yields. To measure the net effect of changes in technology, it is necessary to allow for the effect of changes in all inputs. The outcome gives the total factor productivity. To illustrate, consider a differentiable production function $Y = F(X, t)$, where X is a vector of inputs and t is a measure of technology. Then the rate of growth of output is obtained by logarithmic differentiation:

$$\hat{Y} = \sum_j \beta_j \hat{X}_j + \widehat{\mathrm{TFP}},$$

where β_j is the production elasticity of factor j. The first term on the right-hand side is a measure of the aggregate input. This equation defines the relative change in TFP. Using discrete time measures, the TFP in year t is $\mathrm{TFP}_t = \mathrm{TFP}_{t-1}(1 + \widehat{\mathrm{TFP}}_t)$.

To estimate the changes in the TFP, it is necessary to obtain estimates of the production elasticities. Those are obtained by estimating the production function, or by replacing them with factor shares, assuming that the production function is linear homogeneous and that the competitive conditions are met. The various aspects of obtaining empirical production functions are discussed in Part III. Our present interest is conceptual in nature, and it is related to the question of what function to estimate.

To illustrate the question, refer to Figure 6.1. Initially, only the traditional technique is available, and output is at point A with input ratio k_0. As the discussion indicated, the response to the introduction of the modern technique may take various forms. Under a resource constraint, the movement is to point N, and this movement generates a relative change in TFP of Y_N/Y_A. As more resources become available, the movement will be along the tangent line from N to $\tilde{M}$ and thereafter along the function f_2 to M. This movement from point N on will show no TFP, because it is all explained by the input change. Alternatively, if the sector is a price taker, the movement is from point A to point M with an input ratio of k_2. Here the change in the TFP is obtained by first calculating the effect of the input change by extending the line tangent to the production function at point A to point B and then computing the ratio Y_M/Y_B. The result is different from that obtained in the first case above. The conclusion is that the outcome is path dependent. This discussion abstracts from the question of time needed to travel in each path. Actual calculations are made for data collected for calendar time, mostly annual data. The annual results will differ with the changes in the pace of the yearly movement. When the annual results are integrated, however, the final outcome will depend on the path followed by the economy. Obviously, the path taken under a resource constraint will give a smaller value to the TFP because the potential of the technical change is not fully utilized. We will see in Chapter 13 the empirical implication of this discussion.

Exercises

6.1 Assume a two-sector economy where the agricultural technology consists of two techniques; the modern technique (MV) is more capital intensive than the traditional technique (TV).

(i) The composite production function of agriculture derived in the chapter is

$$Y_a/L_a \equiv f_a(k_a) = \ell f_1(k_1) + (1-\ell) f_2(k_2).$$

Derive the marginal productivity of capital in the domain of coexistence of techniques.

(ii) Assume that total resources (k) are given and that agriculture is capital intensive. Answer the following questions with the aid of the four-panel diagram (Figure 6.6).

(a) What is the relationship between the level of agricultural output, the implemented techniques, the agricultural price, and the wage-rental ratio?

(b) What happens to sectoral outputs, prices (p and ω), and the use of techniques when k increases?

(c) In evaluating this process, which concept of agricultural capital is more adequate: with or without land included?

6.2 Write the optimization problem to show that when the technology consists of two techniques, Hicks-neutral technical change in the capital-intensive technique has the net effect of labor-saving technical change for the sector as a whole.

6.3 Can a technical change in one sector affect the measure of TFP in the other sector?

PART TWO

Factor Growth and Allocation

7

Growth Models: An Overview

Up to this point it has been assumed that the resources available to the closed economy are exogenously endowed. We now remove this assumption for capital. At any point in time, households and firms generate savings that are invested by the firms, thereby affecting the capital stock of firms and consequently the amount of capital in the economy. The response of the economy to changes in capital was explored in Chapter 4. In this chapter we examine the growth of the capital stock. The growth of the capital stock depends on, among other things, the state of the technology. However, the issues that result from technical change are different from those that exist under constant technology, and therefore it is convenient to separate the two and to start with the discussion of accumulation under constant technology.

The process of capital accumulation in the sectoral economy under investigation is similar in principle to that of a single-sector economy. Focusing on a single-sector economy simplifies the discussion considerably, and this will be a point of departure. The discussion of capital accumulation requires a multiperiod framework. Consumers live for more than one period and therefore plan their consumption over their expected life horizon under a budget constraint that includes present and future income. They are also concerned about their children, which leads them to transfer wealth to the next generation. Decisions based on more than one period generally result in a difference between current income and consumption.

Saving releases an output or, more generally, resources that are saved from producing that output, for future consumption. Firms, anticipating future consumption, prepare their production capacity accordingly. In so doing they acquire durable inputs, such as machines, that contribute to current and future production. The inputs acquired in the present for future production are produced by resources released by the decision of households to save. The stock of such inputs evaluated by the value of the foregone consumption and accumulated over time constitutes the capital stock.

There is a separation between the decision to invest and the decision to save. The first is made by firms; the second is made primarily by households. However, firms plan their future production capacity in anticipation of future consumption; this generates a link between the consumption and production paths. Some of the saving is generated by firms that belong to households. This is typical for agriculture, where most of the world production still comes from family farms. Another important component of saving, often negative, is generated by the government, which in this context has a life of its own, although this is not explicitly used in the present discussion.

To sum up, saving frees resources (output) produced in the current period for investment, and as such it augments the capital stock, thereby facilitating an increase in future output. The ultimate purpose of growth, as perceived in economic analysis, is to increase consumption or the utility thereof. Per capita consumption increases monotonically with per capita production; therefore, in examining capital accumulation the focus is placed on the change in the capital per capita, or the capital-labor ratio, rather than on the total capital stock. As the size of the labor force grows, additional capital is needed to supply the additional workers with capital in order to maintain the prevailing capital-labor ratio in the economy. Capital also depreciates and has to be replaced. Hence the evolution of the capital stock over time depends on the relative magnitude of the supply of new resources, namely savings, in relation to the resources needed to maintain the prevailing capital-labor ratio, which we refer to as the maintenance requirement. The relationship between saving on the one hand and the maintenance requirement on the other hand is an important determinant of the dynamics of the economy.

We begin with a review of growth theory for a single-sector economy under both constant technology and a constant savings rate, providing the background for the introduction of the Solow model. This model establishes the existence of a stable long-run equilibrium for the economy. Such a solution, with basically weak assumptions, resolved the problem of the stability, and hence sustainability, of growth that had been discussed in the literature (Domar, 1947; Harrod, 1948). This solution is stable in the sense that if for any reason the economy is not in equilibrium, it will converge to it. This opened up the question of the speed of convergence, which remains a subject of empirical work. The most important message that comes out of this model is that in the absence of technical change, the economy will be stagnant. To escape stagnation, technical change is introduced, and its compatibility with steady-state growth is examined.

The main thrust of the results is largely independent of savings behavior, and specifically of the assumption of a constant savings rate. However, the assumption on saving implies an assumption on consumption behavior, and it is not instructive to assume consumption behavior rather than to derive it. The extension of the analysis to cover the determination of savings behavior introduced dynamic models into the analysis. Such models have become the workhorse of the current literature and will be used here to deal with some of the approaches to discuss endogenous growth. Without a loss in generality, the discussion is carried out for the one-sector economy; the main results that are obtained for a single-sector economy apply to the sectoral economy.

Initial Specification

The total saving (S) in the economy is proportional to total output $(Y): S = sY$, where s is the savings rate. The saved resources are used for net capital formation and for the replacement of depreciated capital: $\dot{K} = sY - dK$, where d is the depreciation rate. The rate of growth of the capital stock, $\hat{K} \equiv \dot{K}/K$, is

$$\hat{K} = sY/K - d. \tag{7.1}$$

Without a loss in generality, we assume that the labor force is identical to the population, which grows at the constant rate n. The ratio Y/K is expressed in per capita terms, y/k, where $y = Y/L$ and $k = K/L$. Note that $\hat{K} = \hat{k} + n$ and apply equation (7.1) to the growth of the capital-labor ratio:

$$\hat{k} = sy/k - m. \tag{7.2}$$

The term $m = n + d$ represents the proportion of the capital stock that has to be invested in order to maintain the per capita capital stock at its current level. The rate of growth of the capital-labor ratio is thus expressed in terms of the difference between the supply of capital goods and the maintenance requirement. Clearly, when $s \neq mk/y$, $\hat{k}$ changes. The direction of the change is given by sign $\hat{k} = \text{sign}(sy/k - m)$.

In a comparative statics analysis, an economy is in equilibrium when changes in the endogenous variables occur only as a result of changes in the exogenous variables or in the parameters. This view of equilibrium is also applicable to the dynamic process under consideration. Accordingly, the equilibrium capital-labor ratio should remain constant as long as the exogenous variables do. This notion of equilibrium is referred to as the steady-state solution of (7.2). It is characterized by the fact that output, employment, and the capital stock all grow at the same constant proportionate rate, referred to as balanced growth.

For the capital-labor ratio to remain constant over time, K must grow at the same rate as L, which in turn requires the equality $s = mk/y$. For output to grow at the same rate as capital and labor, the production function has to be linear homogeneous in K and L.

The condition for the steady-state solution is sometimes referred to as the Harrod-Domar consistency condition (Solow, 1970). Domar (1947) and Harrod (1948), in somewhat different frameworks, raised the question of meeting this consistency condition. Basically their frameworks assume constant values for the three parameters in (7.2). Specifically, they assume: (a) a constant savings rate, s; (b) a constant rate of population growth, n; and (c) a constant capital-output ratio, $v = K/Y$. Such constancy can be obtained from a fixed-coefficient production function. When all three of these parameters are fixed and independent of the state of the economy, the economy will not reach a stable steady state. For instance, assume a fixed-coefficient production function, and when capital is the scarce factor, output will be $Y = K/v$. Use equation (7.1) to determine that the economy will grow at the rate $\hat{Y} = \hat{K} = s/v - d$ until the idle labor supply is exhausted, and at that point growth will come to a halt. This is an early version of the AK model that is discussed below.

In the absence of a steady state, the economy will diverge from the equilibrium and will not be sustainable. To achieve such a convergence to a stable steady state, one or more of these parameters has to be endogenized. A natural modification is to endogenize the capital-output ratio by allowing for input substitution in the production function. This approach, introduced by Solow (1956) and Swan (1956), constitutes the cornerstone of neoclassical growth theory.

The Solow Model

Technology is summarized by a production function having all the properties that we assumed in Chapter 2: $Y = F(K, L)$, $Y/L = y = f(k)$, $f(0) = 0$, $f'(k) > 0$, $f''(k) < 0$, $f'(0) = \infty$, and $f'(\infty) = 0$. The last two conditions are termed the Inada conditions. We now use equation (7.2) to write the time derivative of k,

$$\dot{k} = sf(k) - mk. \tag{7.3}$$

The existence of a steady-state solution where $\dot{k} = 0$ is demonstrated in Figure 7.1. The function $sf(k)$ is drawn for a constant s. The maintenance requirement is represented by the straight line mk. By the strong concavity of $f(k)$, $f'(\infty) = 0$. If $f'(0) > m/s$, the two functions intersect at some k, say k^*, so that $sf(k^*) = mk^*$. The requirement that $f'(0) > m/s$ is fulfilled under the

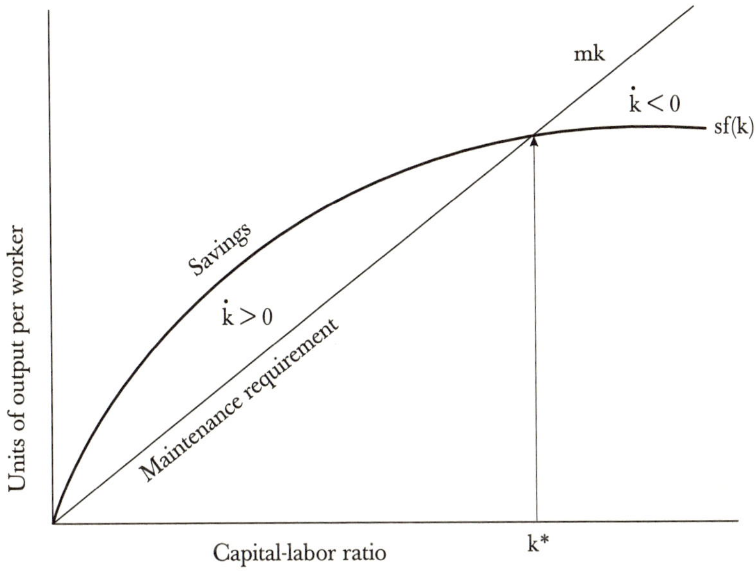

Figure 7.1 Capital accumulation: The Solow diagram

assumption that $f'(0) = \infty$. The solution establishes an equilibrium capital-labor ratio that remains constant as long as the state variables are constant. Because labor increases exogenously at rate n, capital must grow at the same rate in order for k to remain constant. Furthermore, because the production function is linear homogeneous, output increases at the same rate n as the inputs, and per capita output remains constant.

To sum up, allowing the factor proportion to vary leads to the existence of a stable dynamic equilibrium. This result has far-reaching implications. The equilibrium solution implies constant per capita production and consumption, or simply stagnation. The stagnation can be at an affluent consumption level, but it is still stagnation. To escape the stagnation it is necessary to obtain growth, and this requires technological change.

The dynamic stability is equally important in that it makes the equilibrium solution meaningful. However, while the stability is accepted as a theoretical finding, the importance of the convergence to equilibrium from any arbitrary point has been questioned on quantitative grounds. Numerical simulation (Sato, 1966) indicated that the convergence is very slow. A positive view of this finding, however, is possible. This result indicates that because the adjustment is slow, it is unlikely that the economy will be thrown off its equilibrium position. As such, it makes the whole analysis much more relevant.

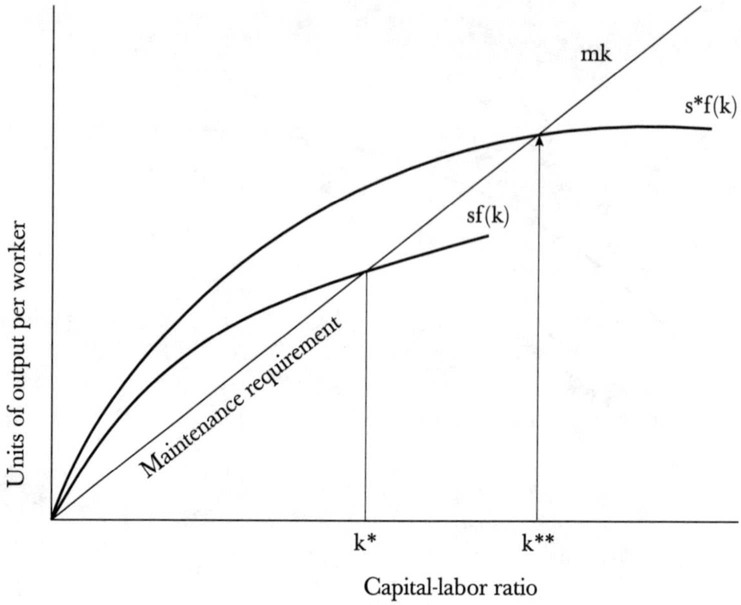

Figure 7.2 Capital accumulation: The role of the savings rate

This interpretation is related to empirical studies of convergence that will be discussed below.

Growth versus Level

The growth rates of output, capital, and consumption in this model are determined by the rate of population growth and thus are independent of the savings rate and of the distribution parameters of the production function, or simply the factor shares. The savings rate determines the *level* of output but not its *rate of growth.* This is illustrated in Figure 7.2, where the steady-state values of k and y are higher for the savings rate s^* than for s, $s^* > s$. Why then don't we increase the savings rate and obtain higher outputs? The answer is twofold. First, increasing the savings rate will increase the rate of growth only temporarily, during the transition to the new steady-state solution. Second, the ultimate objective of the economic activity is not to increase output per se but to increase welfare, which in the present case is equal to consumption. For instance, we can think of raising the savings rate to 1, in which case the steady-state output will be maximized. But then there would be no consumption, so this cannot be thought of as a desirable solution.

A natural choice criterion is to find a savings rate that maximizes the steady-state value of per capita consumption. This is referred to as the golden rule of capital accumulation. To find the solution, we note that per capita consumption is $c(k) = f(k) - mk$ and $c'(k) = f'(k) - m$. Hence the path of maximum sustainable consumption is achieved at the point of equality, $f'(k^*) = m$.

Endogenous Savings

The golden rule does not take into account the fact that consumers prefer present to future consumption. To do this, we outline the problem of intertemporal optimization due to Cass (1965) and Koopmans (1965) and rooted in the work of Ramsey (1928). This has become a standard framework in the discussion of optimal growth as well as many other topics.

Let c_t be the consumption (per capita) at time t, and $u(c)$ is the instantaneous utility function of an individual. The utility function is positive, increasing and strictly concave in c, and twice differentiable. The intertemporal utility is assumed to be additive. The individual is assumed to live forever. The infinite horizon is suitable to discuss the choices made by society or the choice made by an individual representing a family. Standardize the size of the population at the initial point in time to be one so that the size of the population at time t is $(1+n)^t$. The welfare function over the planning horizon is $U(0) = \sum_{t=0}^{\infty}(1+n)^t\beta^t u(c_t)$, where β is the discount factor and for $U(0)$ to be bounded, $(1+n)\beta < 1$. The objective is to choose a time path, c_t and k_t, that maximizes $U(0)$. The choice is subject to an intertemporal resource constraint. Thus the problem is stated as

$$\max_{c_t} \sum_{t=0}^{\infty}(1+n)^t\beta^t u(c_t), \tag{7.4}$$

subject to: (a) $f(k_t) \geq c_t + i_t + nk_t$; (b) $k_{t+1} = (1-d)k_t + i_t$, $t = 0, 1, 2, \ldots$, given initial k_0 and terminal conditions that are not written here. The Lagrangian equation is

$$L(k, c, p) = \sum_{t=0}^{\infty}(1+n)^t\beta^t u(c_t) + p_t[f(k_t) - c_t - k_{t+1} + (1-m)k_t]. \tag{7.5}$$

The nonnegativity constraints on k_t are not binding and are therefore ignored. Let $f_k(\cdot)$ be the partial derivative of $f(\cdot)$ with respect to k, and leaving the details to Appendix 7A.1, the optimal path has to maintain the following condition, to be referred to as the Euler equation:

$$\phi(\cdot)_{t+1}(1+n)\beta u'(c_{t+1}) = u'(c_t); \quad \phi(\cdot)_{t+1} \equiv [1 + f(\cdot)_{k_{t+1}} - m]. \quad (7.6)$$

To interpret this condition, consider reducing consumption at t by one unit, investing it, and consuming it at $t+1$. The loss of utility at t is $u'(c_t)$. The gain in consumption at $t+1$ consists of the initial investment plus the marginal productivity of capital net of the maintenance requirement. The condition in (7.6) states that the discounted utility of the additional consumption at $t+1$ is the same as that at t, which implies that on the optimal path it is impossible to gain by changing the consumption pattern. Note that when $\phi(\cdot)_{t+1}(1+n)\beta > 1$, $u'(c_{t+1}) < u'(c_t)$ and hence $c_{t+1} > c_t$. When $\phi(\cdot)_{t+1}(1+n)\beta = 1$, per capita consumption is constant over time. This condition is equivalent to $f_{k(t+1)} = m + (\rho - n)/(1+n)$, where $\rho = (1-\beta)/\beta$. If $(\rho - n) > 0$, this solution involves a smaller k than in the golden rule. This is the outcome of preferring present to future consumption, which leads to lower present investment and therefore to lower capital stock. The higher ρ is, the lower k is on the optimal path.[1] Let k^* be a steady-state value, then with a CRS production function, the corresponding per capita output and consumption are $f(k^*)$ and $c(k^*)$ respectively and the saving rate is $1 - c(k^*)/f(k^*)$. Note that k^* is a function of ρ, d, n, and the parameters of the production and the utility functions, $f(\cdot)$ and $u(\cdot)$, respectively.

To express the result in terms of per capita consumption, rather than utility, we will use the constant elasticity utility function, $u(c) = c^{1-\sigma}/1-\sigma$.[2] With this specification, the Euler equation (7.6) takes the form

$$(c_{t+1}/c_t)^{\sigma} = \beta(1+n)\phi(\cdot)_{t+1}. \quad (7.7)$$

Label $c_{t+1}/c_t \equiv 1+g$, note that for a small x, $\ln(1+x) \cong x$, and rewrite equation (7.7) as $\sigma g + \rho = f(\cdot)_k - d$, or $g = [f(\cdot)_k - (d+\rho)]/\sigma$. Under the Inada condition, the right side converges to zero at the steady-state value of k^*. This value is inversely related to ρ and σ. The lower ρ is, the smaller is the preference for present consumption, and the lower σ is, the less important it is for households to smooth consumption.

To sum up, all the three cases of savings behavior considered above yield a stable steady-state solution, including the case of endogenous savings. This is achieved by the decline in the marginal productivity of capital as k increases, which is the essence of the Solow model. The changes in the assumption on the consumption rule changed the capital-labor ratio at the steady state, and with it the level of activity. The common feature to all these alternatives, however, is that there is no growth in per capita output or capital. This is the power of the Solow model. The discussion of endogenous saving makes an explicit connection between the savings rate and the discount rate and the parameters of the utility function. If we believe that the discount rate and the utility function are fundamentally more stable than other economic variables, then the model is built on more solid foundations. Against this achievement loom two facts. First, if these determinants result in a unique savings rate, then the information embedded in them can be read off the savings rate. If the savings rates are affected by other variables as well, then those should also be considered in the model, at least at a preliminary stage that will allow a judgment on whether or not they should be retained. Second, in any case, the only thing we can observe is the savings (or consumption) behavior, and therefore whatever the virtues of the more fundamental model are, they are not manifested in positive economics because they are not utilized in empirical analysis.

To get sustainable growth, it is necessary to have technical change. Yet on the surface, it appears that the condition in (7.6) offers possibilities of sustainable growth without technical change. Basically, if the production function has the property that as $k \to \infty$, $\lim f_{kt} - m > 0$, then $c_{t+1} > c_t$.

Two questions come up: is this condition important and is it plausible? The answer to the first question is that it is extremely important because it escapes the strong concavity effect of the Solow model, and as such it allows sustainable growth. The answer to the second question is less satisfying. There are explicit algebraic forms for the production function that display this property, but this does not prove anything. The validity of the case does not depend on whether or not one can provide an explicit algebraic form for the production function. The real question is to determine the underlying process that is represented by such forms and whether it actually represents constant technology. To illustrate, we now consider two cases that fall within this category.

Linear Production Functions: The AK model

The importance of the strong concavity of the per capita production function is highlighted by considering the limiting case of a linear production function known as the AK model. The production function is $Y = AK$, or written in per capita terms:

$$y = Ak \tag{7.8}$$

so that $f_k = A$. When the coefficient A is sufficiently large, the condition of unbounded growth is achieved. Per capita output grows at the same rate as the capital-labor ratio. How realistic is this model? To answer this question, note that the factor share of capital is 1 and that of labor is 0. This attribute does not represent any existing economy. To overcome this shortcoming, it is sometimes suggested that k should be broadly interpreted to include human capital (Barro and Sala-i-Martin, 1995, p. 141). This is hardly a model of constant technology, and in any case does not resolve the problem of no returns to labor.

Heterogeneous Technology

We adopt here the framework of heterogeneous technology developed in Chapter 6, and examine a one-sector economy and two techniques of production, labeled 1 and 2. In the area of coexistence of techniques, where the capital-labor ratio is bounded by the threshold values, $k \in [\tilde{k}_1, \tilde{k}_2]$, the composite function (6.11) takes the form

$$f(k) = \tilde{w} + \tilde{r}k, \quad f_k = \tilde{r}. \tag{7.9}$$

For a sufficiently large $\tilde{r}$, the economy will continue to grow within the domain of coexistence. If the process does not converge within the domain of coexistence, it will do so outside this domain where only f_2 (technique 2) is employed, and in this case, the behavior of the economy is described by the Solow model.

How important is this case? It depends on the size of the domain of coexistence and on the implied marginal productivity of capital. Because the difference in capital intensity between developed and developing (or alternatively, affluent and poor) countries is large, it is applicable to developing economies. They can grow along the composite production function with constant marginal productivity of capital. The larger this marginal productivity, the larger the scope for sustainable growth achieved by the shift of capital to the capital-intensive technique. In this respect, it is similar to the AK model. However, the source for the heterogeneous technology is technical change, which generates new techniques. Therefore we cannot claim that we have growth without technical change. The difference of this model from the conventional discussion lies in the fact that we distinguish between the changes in the available technology and in its implementation.

Technical Change

A Single Episode

The role of technical change can be illustrated graphically in the Solow diagram. For this purpose, we rewrite the production function as $y = A_t f(k)$,

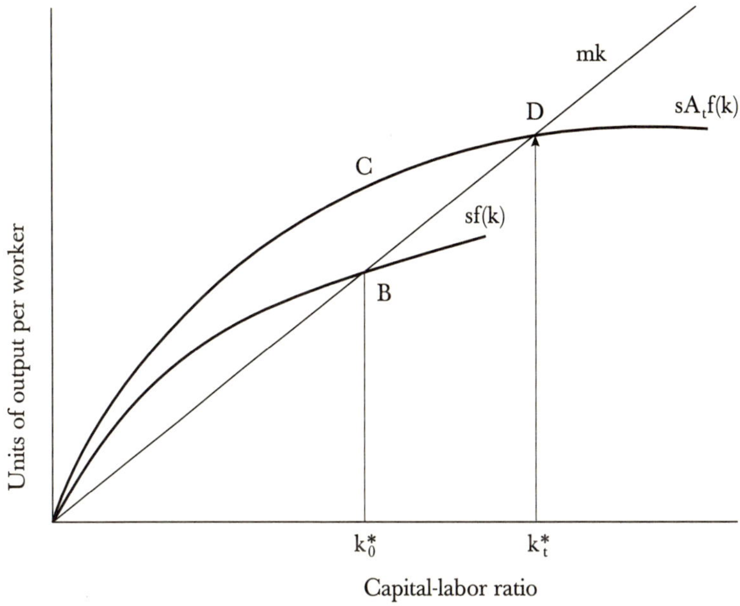

Figure 7.3 Capital accumulation: Technical change

where A_t is the technology index at time t, and at the base period, $A_0 = 1$. As A_t increases, the function is rotated upward (Figure 7.3). A rise in output increases the supply of resources for investment over and above the maintenance requirement, and this causes the capital stock to grow. The economy then converges to a new steady-state solution characterized by a capital-labor ratio k_t^* and output $A_t f(k_t^*)$. The growth in output is decomposed to two components: the productivity effect, indicated by a movement from point B to point C, and the expansion effect (similar to the allocation effect considered in Chapter 5), indicated by a movement from point C to point D. When the technical change is a one-shot episode, the steady-state solution will change to a new position, and once the economy has moved to this position, it will stop growing. However, technical change is not a single episode, but rather a sequence of episodes. For analytic simplification it is often taken to be a continuous process, but there is no empirical support for this assumption.

Factor Augmentation

How does technical change affect the steady-state solution? In general, not all types of technical change are consistent with balanced growth. To see this, consider the production function $Y_t = F[A_{Lt}L_t, A_{Kt}K_t]$. The rate of growth of output is given by

$$\hat{Y} = (1 - S_K)(\hat{A}_L + \hat{L}) + S_K(\hat{A}_K + \hat{K}). \tag{7.10}$$

Assume that $\hat{A}_L$ and $\hat{A}_K$ are constant. Under this assumption, the rate of change of Y is constant in two cases: Cobb-Douglas technology or/and no capital-augmenting technical change.[3] In fact, much of the discussion in the literature is carried out in terms of these two assumptions, which calls for care in generalizing the results to other cases.

In what follows, we consider the case of labor-augmenting technical change. The production function is $Y_t = F[L_t^e, K_t]$, where $L_t^e = A_t L_t$. The rate of growth of output is given by

$$\hat{Y} = S_L \hat{L}^e + (1 - S_L)\hat{K}. \tag{7.11}$$

This case is the Solow model, where labor is measured in quality units, and the production function, in per capita terms, is $y^e = f(k^e)$; $y_t^e = Y_t/L_t^e$, and $k_t^e = K_t/L_t^e$. The steady-state solution is k^{*e}, implying $0 = \hat{k}^{*e} = \hat{K} - (\hat{L} + \hat{A}_L)$. Hence the growth rate in physical terms is $\hat{y} = \hat{A}_L = \hat{k}$. To differentiate between the productivity growth and the expansion effect, use $\hat{A}_L = \hat{k}$ and rewrite the growth rate of output as

$$\hat{y} = (1 - S_L)\hat{k} + S_L \hat{A}_L, \tag{7.12}$$

where the first term on the right-hand side is the expansion effect and the last term is the productivity effect.

The graphical presentation of the steady-state solution is the same as in Figure 7.1 with $f(k^e)$ and k^e replacing $f(k)$ and k respectively. This is the Harrod-neutral technical change discussed in Chapter 5, where it is shown that factor shares remain constant along a growth path which maintains the constancy of Y/K. The steady-state per capita output in quality terms, $f(k^e) = y^{e^*}$, is constant, and therefore per capita output in physical terms increases at the rate of the technical change: $y_t^* = e^{gt} y^{e^*}$; $g \equiv \hat{A}_L$.

To sum up, in this model the growth rate is determined by the rate of the labor-augmenting technical change. The level of the optimal output at time t is summarized by the function $Y(A_{Lt}, s, n, d)$. The productivity function, A_{Lt}, captures the increase in the productivity of labor, but does not reveal the source of this improvement. It is common to relate this improvement to the change in the level of schooling of the labor force; the higher the level of education, the higher the productivity and the output. However, this association of technical change with education is not an explanation, just an interpretation.

The essence of the foregoing result is independent of the assumption of a constant savings rate. To illustrate, consider the case of endogenous savings. For this purpose, assume $u(c) = c^{1-\sigma}/(1-\sigma)$, constant population ($n = 0$), and a CRS production function with labor-augmenting technical change, $y_t = f(k_t, A_t)$ where A is the productivity function, and $A_{t+1} = (1+g)A_t$.[4] With this specification, the condition in equation (7.7) takes the form:

$$c_{t+1}/c_t = [\beta\phi(\cdot)_{t+1})]^{1/\sigma}. \tag{7.13}$$

For balanced growth, f_{kt} must be constant for all t, and with a CRS production function, k_t/A_t is also constant, hence $k_{t+1} = (1+g)k_t$. Also, $y_{t+1} = (1+g)y_t$. From the definition of the evolution of capital, $i_t = (g+d)k_t = (g+d)(1+g)k_{t-1} = (1+g)i_{t-1}$. Consequently, from the resource constraint, $c_t = y_t - i_t = (1+g)c_{t-1}$. Thus y, c, k, and i all grow at the same rate g.

Endogenous Technology

Technical change is the result of human effort, and the big question is what are the processes and the economic forces that generate it. Answering this question is the subject of current research, and there is no unique answer that has unambiguous empirical support. Models differ to the extent that the effort of changing the technology is made explicit. Models with externalities assume that as the economy grows, there is an accumulation of knowledge that improves the overall productivity. This accumulation can be related to the growth in the capital stock (Arrow, 1962; Romer, 1986), or to human capital (Lucas, 1988), or to research expenditures (Romer, 1986). The general idea, supported by heuristic arguments, is that there is a learning process induced by the variables that generate the externalities. The externalities affect the productivity of the private sector, but there is nothing that firms or households can do to affect this process; the scope is for actions by the social planner. As such, externalities may have policy implications for affecting growth. For the private sector to have an influence on growth, a connection must exist between the decisions taken by individuals and the growth rate. The presentation here is limited in terms of coverage. An overview of the field is provided by Jones and Manuelli (1997), on which the following discussion draws in part. These models, on the whole, do not explicitly accommodate the issue of implementation.

Externalities: Physical Capital

Arrow (1962) related the learning to new investment, which, with some assumptions, can be expressed in terms of the capital stock. Strictly speaking, the learning is relevant to the performance of a new task; this is also the message in the motivating empirical example that Arrow provides from the aircraft industry. Thus we deal here with changes in productivity that come about in response to a technical change (new task); the changes in productivity are more in line with the implementation of a new technique rather than with its invention. This model is interesting for analytic and empirical purposes. It raises the issue of the effect of externalities and its empirical counterpart, a convex production function in the observed inputs. In Chapter 13 we attribute this apparent increasing returns to scale to the fact that new techniques are capital intensive. This comes later, though, and we now turn to examine the following model.

There are I identical firms, each using the production function $Y_i = AK_i^b L_i^{1-b}$, or written on a per worker basis, $y_i = Ak_i^b$. Let L be the total labor force, $\ell_i = L_i/L$, and $k = \sum_i \ell_i k_i$ is the average capital-labor ratio. The assumption is that the technology index is related to the average capital-labor ratio, $A(k) = k^\gamma$. The firms operate in the same environment, and without a loss in generality, it is convenient to assume that they employ the same input level, so that $\ell_i = \ell$, $k_i = k$, and therefore $\sum \ell_i k_i^b = \ell \sum k^b = k^b$. The production function is $y_i = A(k)k_i^b$; $A(k) = k^\gamma$. To simplify the analysis, we keep the population (L) constant. The problem is to choose a consumption path c_t so that $\max \sum_{t=0}^{\infty} \beta^t L c_t^{1-\sigma}/1-\sigma$, subject to $Y_t \geq Lc_t + K_{t+1} - (1-d)K_t$. We can divide by L and write the Lagrangian equation in per capita terms:

$$L(k, c, p) = \sum_{t=0}^{\infty} \beta^t c_t^{1-\sigma}/(1-\sigma) + p_t[A(k_t)k_t^b - c_t - k_{t+1} + (1-d)k_t]. \quad (7.14)$$

The social planner is aware of the effect of changes in k on productivity and therefore takes this into account in the decision. The Euler equation reflecting the decision is

$$(1 + g_{ct})^\sigma = \beta[1 - d + (b+\gamma)k_{t+1}^{\gamma+b-1}], \quad (7.15)$$

where $c_{t+1}/c_t \equiv 1 + g_{ct}$. Consumption will grow as long as $\beta[1 - d + (b + \gamma)k_{t+1}^{\gamma+b-1}] \geq 1$, but the growth rate need not be constant. When $\gamma + b > 1$, the growth rate of consumption is increasing with k. When consumption grows but $\gamma + b < 1$, the marginal productivity of capital is decreasing with k, and eventually the bracketed term will reach zero and growth will stop. Constant consumption growth is achieved when $\gamma + b = 1$, in which case the model takes the form of the AK model.

To assess the growth rate of k, note that g_y is larger (smaller, equal) than g_k if and only if $\gamma + b$ is larger (smaller, equal) than 1. Write the time change of the resource constraint, $g_y y_t = g_c c_t + g_k(g_k k_t)$, or $g_y = (c_t/y_t)g_c + (g_k k_t/y_t)g_k$. This is a weighted average of the ratio of growth rates, and hence, when $\gamma + b$ is larger (smaller, equal) than 1, g_c is larger (smaller, equal) than g_y.

The case of equality is of special interest, because this is the case where the productivity index can be thought of as labor augmenting. To see this, write $Y_i = K_i^b(KL_i)^a$; or $y_i = K^a k_i^b L_i^{a+b-1}$, and set $a = \gamma$.

The foregoing analysis does not apply to a decentralized economy where the effect of the firms' decisions on the technology is negligible and therefore ignored. In this case, the Euler equation takes the form $(1 + g_{ct})^\sigma = \beta[1 - d + bk_{t+1}^{\gamma+b-1}]$. Obviously, the marginal productivity of capital is smaller than in the centralized case, and this results in a smaller growth rate of consumption. In this discussion we deal only with solutions based on the existence of the equality (7.15). Recall the interpretation of equation (7.6): for investment to take place, the marginal productivity of capital must be sufficiently large to compensate for the sacrifice in utility of postponing consumption. If this is not met, there will be no investment. Thus to have investment, the right-hand side of equation (7.15) should not be smaller than the left-hand side.

An important empirical implication of the model is that a production function derived from aggregate (industry or economy) data will show increasing returns to scale if $\gamma + b > 1$. Consequently empirical production functions with increasing returns to scale have been considered to be supportive of this model. We return to the issue of increasing returns to scale in Chapter 13.

Externalities: Human Capital

In the foregoing model, there is no explicit role for the economic agents to take in order to affect productivity growth. This is different in the model of Lucas (1988) where the externalities come from the accumulation of knowledge. As in Uzawa (1965), individuals allocate their time between work to produce consumption goods, on the one hand, and the accumulation of human capital needed to improve their productivity, on the other.[5] The meaning of human capital in the model is derived from the assertion that individuals can improve their productivity by spending time on learning. Individuals spend a fraction u of their time (net of leisure) working, and the remaining time is spent on accumulating human capital, h. The law of motion of this effort is given by

$$h_{t+1} - h_t = a(1 - u)h_t \tag{7.16}$$

where a is the productivity of time spent in learning, and the rate of accumulation of h is $g_h = a(1 - u)$. The human capital affects productivity through the labor input, measured in quality units, $hL = L^e$, and overall external effect, $A(h_{at})$, where h_a is the average level of human capital. The presentation is simplified by assuming that individuals are identical, so that $h_a = h$ and $A(h_{at}) = A(h_t)$. It is assumed that the rate of growth of A is equal to γg_h. All these assumptions are reflected in the production function: $Y_t = h_t^\gamma (K_t)^b (u_t h_t L_t)^{1-b}$.

The concavity of the neoclassical production function is broken here twice. First, the production function is CRS in quality labor and capital. However, because h is now a decision variable, the production function displays increasing returns to scale in K, L, and h. Second, the term $A(h)$ reflects the spillover effect of the growing h. These two additions are reflected in the growth rate of per capita output (assuming constant u),

$$\hat{y} = b\hat{k} + (1 - b + \gamma)a(1 - u). \tag{7.17}$$

The term $(1 - b + \gamma)a(1 - u)$ replaces $S_L \hat{A}_L$ in equation (7.12). Although this model determines the growth rate of human capital, rather than treat it as exogenously given, the impact of h on growth is the same in the two models. In each case, the economy can grow without limit as h grows. This is true even if there is no external effect, $\gamma = 0$; the externality only supplements this growth.

We present here the main results of this model, leaving the details of the analysis to Appendix 7A.2. The model calls for

$$\max_{c_t} \sum_{t=0}^{\infty} \beta^t c_t^{1-\sigma}/(1 - \sigma), \tag{7.18}$$

subject to

1. $y_t \equiv A(h_t) f(k_t, u_t h_t) \geq c_t + i_t + nk_t; \quad A(h_t) = h_t^\gamma$
2. $k_{t+1} = (1 - d)k_t + i_t, \quad t = 0, 1, 2, \ldots,$
3. $h_{t+1} = h_t[a(1 - u_t) + 1]$

given initial k_0 and h_0 and terminal conditions that are not written here.

The growth rate of c, k, and y is expressed in terms of g_h:

$$g = \left(\frac{1 - b + \gamma}{1 - b}\right) g_h. \tag{7.19}$$

This equation underscores the role of human capital in this model. Without growth in h, the economy is stagnant. The growth rate of human capital depends on whether the external effect is taken into account in the decision on the optimal level of h (the efficient path) or not (the competitive path). In the competitive economy individuals choose h by taking $A(h)$ as given, and this results in

$$g_h^c = \frac{(1-b)(a-\rho)}{\sigma(1-b+\gamma)-\gamma}. \tag{7.20}$$

The social planner takes the external effect into account, and the outcome is

$$g_h^e = \frac{1}{\sigma}[a - \frac{(1-b)}{(1-b+\gamma)}\rho]. \tag{7.21}$$

In the case of $\gamma = 0$, the efficient and the competitive solutions coincide, $g_h = (a-\rho)/\sigma$. The growth rate increases with the productivity of learning, a, and decreases with the degree of impatience, ρ, and with the elasticity of risk aversion, σ. In this case of lack of external effect, $g = g_h$, implying that the externality is not essential for a sustainable growth. The engine of growth here is human capital. The effect of the externality is to speed up the growth.

Knowing g_h, u is determined from $g_h = a(1-u)$. Because g_h is constant, so is u. The ratio of human to physical capital on the long-run path is determined from

$$\sigma g + \rho = -m + bA(h_t)\left(\frac{uh_t}{k_t}\right)^{1-b}. \tag{7.22}$$

The pivotal element in this model is the accumulation of human capital as formulated by equation (7.16). Human capital means different things to different people. Lucas is quite specific, and he places importance on exchanges among people as the source for the externality. It seems that the essence of the model is more general in that it suggests that there is a scope for human effort to enhance productivity and that this requires the input of time. The time can be spent by the whole population's going to school longer, by training on the job, by doing research, or by inventions. It is difficult to differentiate among the contributions of each of these components and the relationships among them. We return to this subject in Chapter 13.

As in the previous case, the empirical implication is an increasing returns production function in the physical inputs and a measure of human capital. Equation (7.22) also shows that, given a Cobb-Douglas function, there should be a rigid relationship between h and k, and that as $A(h)$ increases, the ratio h/k declines. That is, the larger the level of human capital, the smaller the demand for it.

One-Sector Growth: Summary

There is a close relationship between capital and growth. In the absence of the growth of per capita output, the capital-labor ratio is constant. Growth is induced by technical change. We examined models that treat the technical change as exogenous, and those that relate it to human capital. There is also an in-between case of learning by doing or externalities, where growth is generated in an atomistic economy unintentionally as a result of investment in physical or human capital. Other models, not discussed here, deal with the processes of innovations and the underlying industrial organization that are conducive to this process. It is worth noting that the work on "new growth" was motivated by the need to explain the wide cross-country differences in per capita output and growth rates. The empirical analysis has not been supportive of any particular version and has generated puzzles of its own. In part, we attribute this to the fact that the theoretical models do not distinguish between the available and the implemented technology. If indeed not all that is known is actually implemented, the observations are not the variables that are called for by the model in that they represent a heterogeneous technology. The reason is that the observations are dated and the implementation of the new technology takes time. We shall consider this in Chapters 13 and 15. In any case, when new technology is appearing, there is a need to change the resource allocation. This is not an immediate process. The next three chapters are devoted to this subject.

A Two-Sector Economy

The foregoing discussion has dealt with one sector, but the findings need not be limited to a single-sector economy. We now turn to extend the analysis to a two-sector economy. In specifying the economy, it is important to indicate where the capital goods are produced. Realistically, each sector produces some capital goods. Agriculture produces livestock and seeds, and nonagriculture produces machines. As an extreme case, we can think of each sector as producing its own capital goods. This case will resemble the one-sector case, and therefore it can be anticipated that a stable steady-state solution exists. Thus if there are some specific difficulties inherent in a two-sector economy, they are to be sought at the other extreme, where one sector specializes in the consumer goods and the other sector, referred to as the industrial sector, specializes in the production of capital goods. This is the case that was first analyzed by Uzawa (1961).

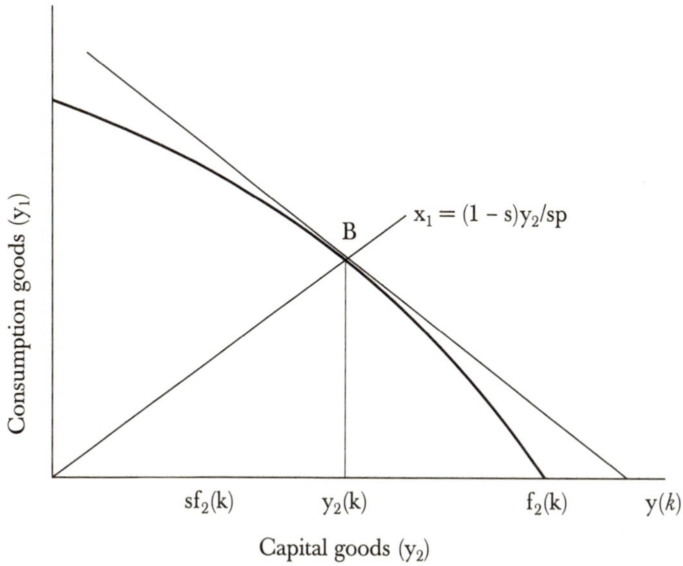

Figure 7.4 The short-run equilibrium with a fixed savings rate

As we have seen, the demand specification does not affect the main conclusions related to growth, and the analysis is simplified by applying the assumptions of the Solow model. In addition, it is assumed that nonagriculture specializes in the production of capital goods, whereas agriculture produces only consumer goods. Consequently the saving function is identical with the demand function. Under the constant saving rate, the demand function has a unit income elasticity and a unit price elasticity:

$$x_2 = sy = s(py_1 + y_2). \tag{7.23}$$

Imposing the equilibrium conditions of $x_i = y_i$:

$$x_1 = (1 - s)x_2/sp. \tag{7.24}$$

The short-run equilibrium position of the economy is shown by point B in Figure 7.4, where equilibrium production of y_2 is determined by sy. The effect of this production on the (net) capital-labor ratio is again given by

$$\dot{k} = sy - mk. \tag{7.25}$$

When the economy is not in equilibrium, k will change. Suppose that $\dot{k} > 0$, in this case the production possibilities of the economy expand. The

Rybczynski proposition tells us that, with p held constant, such an expansion leads to an expansion of the *equilibrium output* of the capital-intensive sector. Thus the equilibrium path depends on the factor intensity. If the consumption sector is capital intensive, an excess supply of consumption goods is generated, and the price p declines. Consequently the income and the price effects supplement each other, and the share of consumer goods in total production will increase. The production of capital goods either declines or increases, but at a lower rate than that of the consumer goods, until the equilibrium is reached where the output of y_2 is just equal to the maintenance requirements.

Alternatively, when the sector producing capital goods is capital intensive, its price will decline along the growth path as the output increases. The question is whether such an increase will eventually slow down to the point where it just meets the maintenance requirement. The answer depends on several factors:

1. The extent to which capital deepening affects the (supply) price. This depends on the difference in capital intensities between the two sectors and the elasticities of substitution.
2. The strength of the demand response. This is a general qualifier, because in this section the response is explicitly given by the savings equation.
3. The marginal productivity of capital in the industrial sector. If its marginal productivity diminishes rapidly, the process of accumulation will not go very far.

In view of these considerations, the existence of a steady-state solution is not immediately obvious. Note, however, that what emerges from the foregoing discussion is that in this case accumulation increases the relative importance of the industrial sector, and that the pace of such an expansion depends on the technology in that sector. This observation is used to give a general proof on the existence of a stable steady state.

PROPERTY 7.1 Under the specialization of industry in the production of capital goods and constant savings rate, there exists a stable steady state.

Proof: The proof is based on Mundlak and Mosenson (1970). Referring to Figure 7.4, we mark three outputs in terms of the industrial good: $y(k)$, the value of the equilibrium output, $f_2(k)$, the value of output under specialization in industry, and $y_2(k)$, the equilibrium value of the industrial output. It immediately follows that $sf_2(k) < sy(k) \equiv y_2(k)$, and consequently

$$sf_2(k) < sy(k) < f_2(k). \tag{7.26}$$

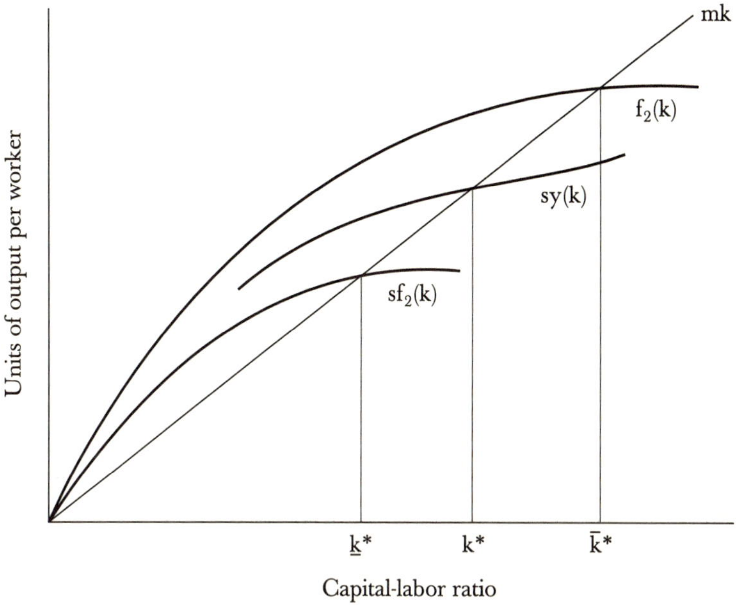

Figure 7.5 Determination of a steady state in a two-sector economy

The two bounds of the inequality are now expressed in terms of the industrial production function alone. By the concavity of that function, we know that there exist values of k, say $\underline{k}^* < \bar{k}^*$, such that,

$$sf_2(\underline{k}^*) - m\underline{k}^* = 0 \tag{7.27}$$

$$f_2(\bar{k}^*) - m\bar{k}^* = 0. \tag{7.28}$$

Combining (7.26), (7.27), and (7.28), we have

$$sy(\underline{k}^*) - m\underline{k}^* > sf_2(\underline{k}^*) - m\underline{k}^* = 0$$

$$sy(\bar{k}^*) - m\bar{k}^* < f_2(\bar{k}^*) - m\bar{k}^* = 0.$$

The two points $sy(\underline{k}^*)$ and $sy(\bar{k}^*)$ are shown in Figure 7.5. Since the function $sy(k)$ is continuous in k, there is a value k^*, $\underline{k}^* < k^* < \bar{k}^*$, such that $sy(k^*) - mk^* = 0$. By the same reasoning, it is clear that there exists a steady state that is locally stable, but not necessarily unique. ∎

The above proof can be generalized to other forms of saving behavior. This is inspired by noting that the essence of the proof of existence consists of: (1) $\bar{k}^*$ determined by (7.28), independently of the saving assumption; (2) continuity of $y(k)$; and (3) $\underline{k}^*$ is defined by (7.27). This last value depends on the saving behavior. However, note that this value was used in the proof in a specific way that can now be made part of the assumption of the proposition. The role of $\underline{k}^*$ was to establish a point with a positive accumulation. Consequently any saving behavior that results in a positive accumulation at some k and does not destroy the continuity of the function $y(k)$ leads to a stable steady state. It has just been argued that

PROPERTY 7.2 Under specialization in the production of capital goods and a saving behavior that maintains the continuity of $y_2(k)$, a necessary and sufficient condition for the existence of a stable steady state is that there is a value of k at which there is a nonnegative change in the capital-labor ratio.

This property was proved by Danin (1973). Local stability at k, in the neighborhood of k^*, is obtained if $\dot{k}(k^* - k) > 0$. When $y_2(k)$ is differentiable, this condition requires $\hat{y}_2(k^*)\hat{k} < 1$. The steady state is globally stable when the condition holds for all k.

Human capital

While the existence of a steady-state solution is robust to the demand specification, it depends heavily on the strong concavity of the production function. If, for instance, $f_2'(k)$ were constant for all k, then the proof would not hold. If k grows at some point, it will continue to grow forever, and if the industrial sector is capital intensive, then the economy will continue to grow. If we now think of k as representing human capital and of sector 2 as the educational sector, and assume it to be the intensive sector in terms of human capital, then we can describe the Uzawa-Lucas model in terms of the two-sector framework. For an outline of this approach, see Jones and Manuelli (1997).

Appendix 7A

1. Endogenous savings

   Given the Lagrangian equation (7.5)

$$L(k, c, p) = \sum_{t=0}^{\infty} (1+n)^t \beta^t u(c_t) + p_t[f(k_t) - c_t - k_{t+1} + (1-m)k_t],$$

derive the first-order conditions:

$$\frac{\partial L}{\partial c_t} = (1+n)^t \beta^t u'(c_t) - p_t = 0 \tag{7A.1}$$

$$\frac{\partial L}{\partial k_t} = p_t[1 + f_{k_t} - m] - p_{t-1} - 0. \tag{7A.2}$$

Using (7A.1) for two points in time,

$$\frac{u'(c_t)}{(1+n)\beta u'(c_{t+1})} = \frac{p_t}{p_{t+1}}. \tag{7A.3}$$

Using (7A.2) for time $t+1$,

$$f_{k_{t+1}} + (1-m) = p_t / p_{t+1}. \tag{7A.4}$$

Combining (7A.3) and (7A.4),

$$[1 + f_{k_{t+1}} - m](1+n)\beta u'(c_{t+1}) = u'(c_t). \tag{7A.5}$$

2. Human capital

Outlined here is the model presented in Lucas (1988, sec. 4). The notations are introduced in the chapter. The problem is

$$\max_{c_t} \sum_{t=0}^{\infty} \beta^t u(c_t), \tag{7A.6}$$

subject to

1. $y_t \equiv A(h_t) f(k_t, u_t h_t) \geq c_t + i_t + nk_t; \quad A(h_t) = h_t^{\gamma}.$ (7A.7)
2. $k_{t+1} = (1-d)k_t + i_t, \quad t = 0, 1, 2, \ldots,$ (7A.8)
3. $h_{t+1} = h_t[a(1-u_t) + 1]$ (7A.9)

given initial k_0 and h_0 and terminal conditions that are not written here. Let $L(\cdot) = L(k, c, h, u)$. Then the Lagrangian equation is

$$L(\cdot) = \sum_{t=0}^{\infty} \beta^t u(c_t) + p_t[y_t - c_t - k_{t+1} + (1-m)k_t]$$
$$+ w_t[h_t(a(1-u_t)+1) - h_{t+1}].$$

The nonnegativity constraints on k_t are not binding and are therefore ignored. Label the partial derivative of y with respect to $x (x = k, u, h)$

as y_x, and write the first-order conditions:

$$\frac{\partial L}{\partial c_t} = 0 \rightarrow \beta^t u'(c_t) = p_t \tag{7A.10}$$

$$\frac{\partial L}{\partial k_{t+1}} = 0 \rightarrow y_{k_{t+1}} + 1 - m = \frac{p_t}{p_{t+1}} \tag{7A.11}$$

$$\frac{\partial L}{\partial u_t} = 0 \rightarrow \frac{y_{u_t}}{ah_t} = \frac{w_t}{p_t} \tag{7A.12}$$

$$\frac{\partial L}{\partial h_{t+1}} = 0 \rightarrow \frac{p_{t+1}}{w_{t+1}} y_{h_{t+1}} + 1 + a(1 - u_{t+1}) = \frac{w_t}{w_{t+1}}. \tag{7A.13}$$

These equations, together with the constraints, solve for $\{c_t, k_t, h_t, u_t\}$ and thereby for their growth rate. The solution is outlined for the following utility and production functions:

$$u(c) = \frac{1}{1-\sigma} c^{1-\sigma} \tag{7A.14}$$

$$y_t = A(h_t)(k_t)^b (u_t h_t)^{1-b}. \tag{7A.15}$$

Using (7A.10) for two points in time,

$$\frac{1}{\beta}\left(\frac{c_{t+1}}{c_t}\right)^{\sigma} = \frac{p_t}{p_{t+1}}. \tag{7A.16}$$

Label $(c_{t+1}/c_t) \equiv (1+g)$, and combine equations (7A.11), (7A.15), and (7A.16):

$$\frac{1}{\beta}(1+g)^{\sigma} = 1 - m + bA(h_t)\left(\frac{u_t h_t}{k_t}\right)^{1-b}. \tag{7A.17}$$

For balanced growth, the left-hand side of (7A.17) is constant over time. Then this equation determines the ratio of two types of capital $u_t h_t / k_t$ as a function of h_t^{γ} and the other parameters in the equation. Label $g_h = \ln(h_{t+1}/h_t) = a(1 - u_t)$, and for balanced growth, $u_t = u$ for all t.

As in the model discussed in Appendix 7A.1, the growth rates of c and k are equal. This is determined in terms of the growth rate of human capital. To see this, use (7A.17) for two points in time, and simplify

$$g = \left(\frac{1 - b + \gamma}{1 - b}\right) g_h. \tag{7A.18}$$

The private decision on h takes the common level of technology as given so that $Y_{ht}/Y_{ut} = u/h_t$. Substitute (7A.12) in (7A.13) and simplify,

$$\frac{w_t}{w_{t+1}} = ah_{t+1}\frac{y_h(t+1)}{y_u(t+1)} + 1 + a(1-u) = 1 + a. \qquad (7A.19)$$

Finally, use (7A.12) for two points in time:

$$\frac{p_{t+1}}{p_t}\frac{h_t}{h_{t+1}}\frac{y_u(t+1)}{y_u(t)} = \frac{w_{t+1}}{w_t}. \qquad (7A.20)$$

Note that for a small x, $\ln(1+x) \cong x$. Thus, $\ln(c_{t+1}/c_t) \equiv \ln(1+g) = g$, and using (7A.16), $(\ln p_{t+1} - \ln p_t) = -(\sigma g + \rho)$. Simplifying (7A.20), using (7A.18)

$$-(\sigma g + \rho) + (\gamma - b)g_h + bg = -a \qquad (7A.21)$$

or

$$g_h = \frac{(1-b)(a-\rho)}{\sigma(1-b+\gamma) - \gamma}. \qquad (7A.22)$$

Equation (7A.22) determines the growth rate of human capital in terms of the parameters of the model. This completes the solution of the competitive economy generated by the atomistic decisions of individuals not taking into account the impact of their action on overall productivity.

Taking the external effect into account, equation (7A.19) is replaced by

$$\frac{w_t}{w_{t+1}} = 1 + a + \frac{au\gamma}{1-b}. \qquad (7A.19s)$$

Equation (7A.21) is replaced by

$$-(\sigma g + \rho) + (\gamma - b)g_h + bg = -a - au\gamma/(1-b). \qquad (7A.21s)$$

Simplifying

$$\frac{g_h}{1-b}[-\sigma(1-b+\gamma) + \gamma] = \rho - a + \frac{\gamma(g_h - a)}{1-b}$$

$$g_h = \frac{1}{\sigma}[a - \frac{(1-b)}{(1-b+\gamma)}\rho]. \qquad (7A.22s)$$

Exercises

7.1 Redraw Figure 7.1 and add to it the per capita output. Show in the figure for a given k, per capita output, consumption, the maintenance requirement, and the change in net capital.

7.2 Let the production function be $y = Ak^{\beta}$. Use equation (7.6) to solve for the steady-state values of k, y, and c (consumption) in terms of m, s, and the parameters of the production function.

7.3 (The golden age of capital accumulation)

(a) Write the steady-state per capita consumption as a function of the saving rate, s, and differentiate to show that the condition for the maximum consumption path is achieved at k which maintains the equality $f'(k) = m$.

(b) Show graphically, using a figure similar to that drawn in question 1, how this condition determines the golden age solution.

7.4 Explain why in the Solow model the growth rate is determined only by the rate of population growth.

7.5 What is the reason for the stability of the steady-state solution in the model?

7.6 (Heterogeneous technology)
Use equations (7.2) and (7.9) to compare the rate of convergence with the steady state in the Solow model with that of heterogeneous technology in the domain of coexistence.

8

Dynamics and Distortion in Factor Markets

The model developed in Chapters 2 to 7 makes some stringent assumptions that are difficult to find in any real situation. The main problem lies in the assumption that markets are sufficiently efficient so that the economy is always on its efficiency frontier. This assumption is a hard sell to observers of many countries that are in "special situations," such as the former communist countries, including China; countries with a history of strong government intervention, such as India; countries with high political instability plagued by wars (the list of which varies with time); countries that lack the social, political, or economic organization to secure a smooth operation of markets; and countries which, due to ill-conceived government policies, fall into a long period of volatility and stagnation, such as some countries in Latin America. Have we left any country off of this list for which we can apply the analysis without reservation? Yes, but not very many, and these have less than half of the world population.

With this gloomy view, what is the value of the framework, and how should it be amended to make it more realistic? Interestingly, the model produces strong predictions that are consistent with the general trends of the sectoral developments as indicated by the aggregate empirical observations referred to in the course of the discussion. In other cases, however, it fails. For instance, the model is inconsistent, with data showing a discrepancy in the two measures of factor intensity and as such calling into question its ability to predict changes in the supply function. This suggests that the fundamentals governing agriculture, namely the demand for its products and technical change, dictate some results in a less than adequate model. Why should we compromise on such a model, however, if we can do better? The task is then to consider a modified model, one that is more permissible in terms of its assumptions, that will provide a more relevant description of reality and serve as a useful framework for thinking about the dynamics of the economy.

One indication of an economy situated off its efficiency frontier is that factor returns are unequal across sectors. The phenomenon of unequal factor prices is sometimes discussed in the literature under the heading of distortion in the factor market. Indeed, unequal prices for homogeneous factors can arise from interference with the competitive process, and this can signify distortion. However, a price differential may also arise when resource mobility is subject to some cost. For instance, in most countries wages in agriculture have been lower than in nonagriculture for a long time, and it is conjectured here that the rates of return to capital differ in the opposite direction. These gaps are attributed to mobility restrictions of cost as well as other factors (Chapters 9 and 10).

The discrepancy in factor prices affects the operation of the economy in important respects, as the discussion here and in the next two chapters will show. In this chapter we examine this subject within a somewhat narrow framework where we impose a specific pattern of factor-price differentials. Such a differential, referred to as distortion in factor prices, can also arise from differential tax rates on factors in the various sectors. Whatever the reason, distortion affects the factor intensities as well as the cost of production in each sector. In turn, the intersectoral ranking of factor intensity and of factor-cost intensity is affected. The product supply functions change and may even become negatively sloped. Nevertheless, equilibrium exists, although it need not be unique. Characterizing the equilibrium solution facilitates tracing the effects of changes in the exogenous variables or of policy programs.

The reduction of distortion has an expansion effect, and as such it constitutes an important source of economic growth. The resource allocation associated with a change in distortion follows a different pattern from that observed in our previous discussion in that the sectoral capital-labor ratios move in opposite directions. In the long run the economy responds to capital accumulation in a way similar to that of the standard case, in that the wage-rental ratios increase with k. Local exceptions are possible, though unlikely because those require increasing the distortion in such a way that capital will concentrate in one sector and labor will concentrate in the other sector. Policies of concentrating capital in one sector of the economy, such as heavy industries, have been followed unsuccessfully by some countries. The present analysis helps to clarify the costs of such policies.

Finally, we examine the long-term consequences of the model and show that the economy is likely to converge eventually to the efficiency frontier.

Supply

It is assumed that competition prevails *within* sectors, whereas factor prices are allowed to vary across sectors. Thus, the competitive conditions are

$$p_i(\partial F_i/\partial K_i) = r_i, \quad p_i(\partial F_i/\partial L_i) = w_i. \tag{8.1}$$

The four conditions in equation (8.1) together with the full employment and the technology equations, (2.1)–(2.3), specify the supply side of the model. The demand specification is unchanged.

The analysis in this chapter is conducted in terms of the intersectoral factor price ratios, namely

$$\delta_r \equiv r_1/r_2, \quad \delta_w \equiv w_1/w_2, \quad \text{and} \quad \delta \equiv \delta_w/\delta_r = \omega_1/\omega_2, \tag{8.2}$$

where $\omega_i = w_i/r_i$. At this point, these ratios are given exogenously. They are endogenized in subsequent analyses in Chapters 9 and 10.

Resource Allocation

The sectoral wage-rental ratios determine the capital-labor ratios so that for any pair of feasible values (ω_1, ω_2), there is a corresponding pair $[k_1(\omega_1), k_2(\omega_2)]$. Under full employment conditions, the resource allocation is uniquely determined. Let $\ell = L_1/L$, then

$$\ell(\omega_1, \omega_2, k) = \frac{k_2(\omega_2) - k}{k_2(\omega_2) - k_1(\omega_1)}. \tag{8.3}$$

Once the resource allocation is determined, outputs are determined as well. Holding k constant, $\ell(\cdot)$ increases in ω_i, $i = 1, 2$, when sector 1 is labor intensive. This can be seen by writing

$$\frac{\ell}{1-\ell} = \frac{k_2(\omega_2) - k}{k - k_1(\omega_1)}.$$

An increase in ω_1 increases the value of k_1 and L_1 by equation (8.3); hence K_1 must increase, and therefore K_2 must decline. Similarly, an increase in ω_2 increases k_2, but by equation (8.3), L_2 declines and L_1 increases while k_1 remains constant; therefore K_1 must increase and K_2 decline. The consequences for output changes are straightforward. This is summarized by

PROPERTY 8.1 (resource allocation) Labor, capital, and output are monotonically increasing (declining) in the labor-intensive (capital-intensive) sector with the wage-rental ratio of *either* sector.

The Production Possibilities

The production possibilities for a given distortion rate, δ, are bounded by a transformation curve labeled $T(k, \delta)$ to emphasize the dependence on k

and δ. In a way, this is a generalization of the case of $\delta = 1$ associated with the competitive system. Let $[y_1, y_2(y_1)]$ describe the production plans on the transformation curve $T(k, \delta)$, then $y_2(y_1)$ is a declining function.

To generate $T(k, \delta)$, the factor-price ratios should change so as to keep δ constant, implying that $\hat{\omega}_1 = \hat{\omega}_2$. By Property 8.1, it is clear that in this case, the outputs of the two sectors move in opposite directions. Thus, under the full employment condition in equation (8.3) and the competitive conditions in equation (8.1), a feasible production set, bounded by $T(k, \delta)$, is defined. Varying δ changes the transformation curve and thereby the feasible set. However all such curves that are generated for a constant k have in common the two points of specialization, $[\bar{y}_1(k), 0]$ and $[0, \bar{y}_2(k)]$, because they are independent of δ. It then follows:

PROPERTY 8.2 (transformation curve) Under the assumptions of the model, the transformation curve is determined by k and δ. With k given, the end points obtained under specialization are common to all δ.

Supply Price and the Supply Function

Following the discussion in Chapter 2, we utilize the assumption that the competitive condition holds within each sector, and that the production function is CRS to write for the average cost in sector j, $p_j = c_j(w_j, r_j)$, where c_j is linear homogeneous in the factor prices. The supply price can be written as

$$p^s = p_1/p_2 = \delta_r p(\delta, \omega_2). \tag{8.4}$$

Under distortion there is a difference between the social cost and the private cost of changing the output composition. The social cost is given by the slope of the transformation curve, $dy_2/dy_1 |_\delta$, whereas the private cost is given by the supply price. The relationship between the two can be expressed as follows:[1] $dy_2/dy_1 = -h(\delta_r, \delta_w, \omega_2)p^s$, where h is a positive function that becomes unity when $\delta_r = \delta_w = 1$. The investigation of the concavity of the transformation curve can proceed by analyzing the behavior of dy_2/dy_1. In such an investigation, it is possible that distortion may destroy the concavity of the transformation curve and thereby affect the behavior of the social cost.[2] What matters in the study of the behavior of the economy, however, is the relationship between the output and the supply price.

To sharpen the difference between the supply price and the social cost, consider the special case of $\delta_w = \delta_r = \delta_0$, where δ_0 is an arbitrary number. In this case, $\delta = 1$ and therefore the feasible production set is bounded by the competitive transformation curve. However, in view of equation (8.4),

$p^s = \delta_0 p(\omega) = -\delta_0(dy_2/dy_1)\mid_\omega$. The difference between the social cost and the supply price is determined by the degree of the distortion. If the returns to capital and labor in agriculture are the same fraction of that in nonagriculture, the resource allocation *within* agriculture is unaffected by the distortion, but the income in agriculture is affected by it. Thus farmers can be efficient but poor, a theme developed by Schultz (1964). Their welfare can be improved by moving their resources out of agriculture. Of course, such mobility is not done by decree, and the essence of the discussion in this and the following two chapters deals with the determinants of the mobility and its consequences.

To examine the effect of distortion on changes in the supply price, differentiate the price equation, as in equation (2.16):

$$\hat{p}^s = (S_{1L}\hat{w}_1 + S_{1K}\hat{r}_1) - (S_{2L}\hat{w}_2 + S_{2K}\hat{r}_2). \tag{8.5}$$

Rearranging:

$$\hat{p}^s - I\hat{\omega}_2 = S_{1L}\hat{\delta}_w + S_{1K}\hat{\delta}_r, \tag{8.6}$$

where as before, $I = S_{1L} - S_{2L}$ measures the factor-cost intensity. To gain insight into the nature of the supply relationships, we examine some leading cases.

Constant Distortion

We begin by evaluating the changes associated with movements along a given transformation curve, similar to the changes examined in Chapter 2 for the undistorted economy. For this we need the assumption that δ_r and δ_w are constant, referred to as Strong Constant Distortion (SCD). Under this condition, equation (8.6) reduces to

$$\hat{p}^s = I\hat{\omega}_2 = I\hat{\omega}_1. \tag{8.7}$$

The analysis is conducted conditional on the distortion rate, δ, and as such reflects the allocation effect. Combining equation (8.7) and Property 8.1 makes it possible to sign the slope of the supply function. This is done by relating the directional changes of y_1/y_2 and p^s. Thus, with sector 1 being labor intensive, an increase in the wage-rental ratio in either sector increases (decreases) the output of the labor(capital)-intensive sector, $(\hat{y}_1 - \hat{y}_2)/\hat{\omega}_2\mid_\delta > 0$. With p^s being the price of the labor-intensive sector, sign $\hat{p}^s/\hat{\omega}_2\mid_\delta =$ sign I.

The question then is what is sign I? In the absence of distortion, the two measures of factor intensity are consistent so that the product $I(\ell_1 - \rho_1)$ is positive, and therefore $[(\hat{y}_1 - \hat{y}_2)/\hat{\omega}_2][\hat{p}^s/\hat{\omega}_2] > 0$. This, however, is no longer true in the present case. In general, distortion changes the factor shares, and as a result the simple relationship between factor shares and factor ratios disappears. For instance, the labor-intensive sector (in terms of factor ratios) may pay to capital a larger share of its output than the capital-intensive sector. Consequently, an increase in the wage-rental ratio increases the relative cost of production in the sector with the larger labor share, which, in this example, happens to be the capital-intensive sector. Qualitatively this is the main deviation from the standard model. Under such a case, an increase in ω increases y_1/y_2 but decreases p^s–in other words, there is a negative relationship between the supply of y_1 and its price.

PROPERTY 8.3 (product supply) Under Strong Constant Distortion, the slope of the supply function of a product is positive if the product is labor intensive by the two measures, factor ratios and cost intensity. It is negative if the two measures contradict in signs.

Factor Intensity

In view of Property 8.3, we want to examine the effect of distortion on factor intensities. For the purposes of our discussion, we consider the ratio of sectoral factor ratios. Recall that $\omega_1 = \delta\omega_2$. Define $R(\delta, \omega_2) \equiv k_1(\delta, \omega_2)/k_2(\omega_2)$, and note that this ratio is smaller (larger) than 1 when sector 1 is labor (capital) intensive. We can consider $R(\delta, \omega_2)$ as a function of δ for a given value of ω_2. If under no distortion sector 1 is labor intensive, designated as $R(1, \omega_2) < 1$, then $R(\delta, \omega_2)$ is an increasing function of δ; it reaches a value of 1 (equal factor intensities) at $\delta = \omega_1(k)/\omega_2(k) \equiv \Gamma(k) > 1$, and exceeds 1 (reversal of factor intensity) when $\delta > \Gamma(k)$.

Factor-Cost Intensity

A possible inconsistency between the cost and factor intensities exists because the former, unlike the latter, depends on the elasticities of substitution. This situation is illustrated in Figure 8.1 for a simple case where the $\omega_i(k_i)$ functions are identical. As before, we label the ratio of labor to capital shares as $\theta_i(\omega_i) \equiv \omega_i/k_i$, so that S_{iL} is monotonically increasing in θ_i and $d \ln \theta_i/d \ln \omega_i = 1 - \sigma_i$.[3] When $\delta < 1$, $\omega_A = \omega_1$ and $\omega_B = \omega_2$, and hence $R < 1$ independent of σ_i. However, the ratios of the factor shares in the two sectors differ in the two panels. When $\sigma > 1$, the labor share in sector 1 is larger than that in sector 2, and the factor-cost intensity is the same as the factor intensity. The opposite is true for $\sigma < 1$. We derive this result in the appendix to this chapter. Obviously, under $\delta = 1$ the two measures of factor intensities are equal for all ω_2.

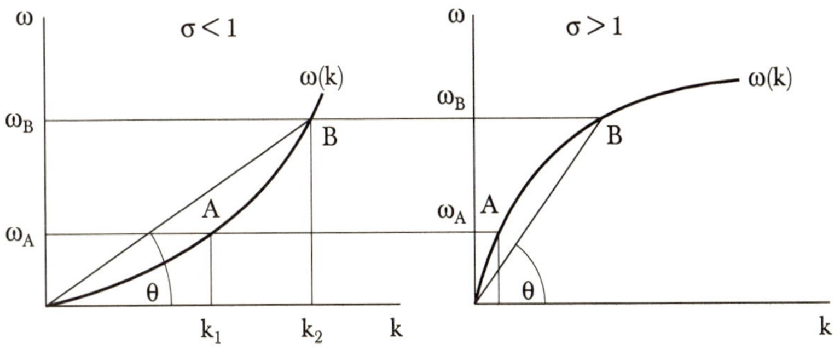

Figure 8.1 Factor and cost intensities

Cost Effect

To isolate the effect of changes in the distortion rates on the supply price, consider changes in δ_w and δ_r that keep δ intact, namely $\hat{\delta}_r = \hat{\delta}_w \neq 0$. We refer to this case as the Weak Constant Distortion (WCD). This change induces a change of the price function (equation 8.4). If initially factor prices are lower in agriculture, a closure of the gap would imply an increase in the supply price at any given allocation identified by (δ, ω_2). This change raises the boundaries of the feasible prices for (k, δ) and with it the equilibrium price in the economy. The difference of this case from the SCD is in that under WCD movements along the transformation curve reflect the cost effect in addition to the allocation effect.

Changes in Efficiency

Considering more general changes in distortion, we assert now the fact that output can be increased by reducing the rate of distortion. This is illustrated in Figure 8.2 with the aid of the Edgeworth box diagram. Points *A* and *B* represent feasible allocations with $\delta < 1$ and $\delta > 1$ respectively. A movement from *A* to *C* represents higher production in both sectors. The same is true for a movement from *B* to *D*. The improvement is caused by the decline in the distortion rate, that is, by δ moving toward 1. However, when the movement is from *A* to *C*, δ increases, whereas it decreases when moving from *B* to *D*. We can summarize the two cases by measuring an improvement by a decline in the absolute value of the difference of δ and 1, $|\delta - 1|$. Using this measure and noting that the sign of $\delta - 1$ matters, compare two situations: $|\delta - 1| > |\delta^* - 1|$, for $(\delta - 1)(\delta^* - 1) > 0$ so that we deal with uniform convergence to 1. Then for

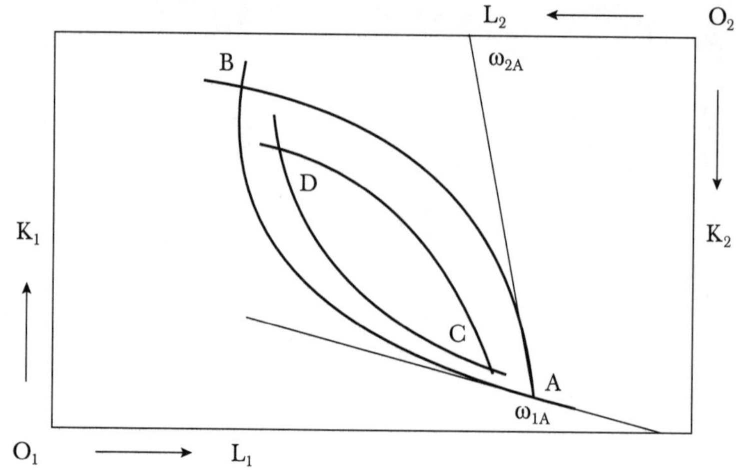

Figure 8.2 Welfare gain from distortion reduction

every output vector y such that $y \in T(k, \delta)$, there exists $y^* \in T(k, \delta^*)$ such that $y^* > y$.

PROPERTY 8.4 (efficiency) A decline in the distortion rate, $| \delta - 1 |$, increases the production possibilities of the economy.

The improvement in efficiency is achieved by changing the resource allocation to a different pattern from that encountered before. For instance, the movement from A to C in Figure 8.2 indicates an increase in both outputs, whereas the sectoral capital-labor ratios change in opposite directions. An increase in y_2 associated with a decline of k_2 can only occur if L_2 increases, which means a decline in L_1. Consequently, the only way for y_1 to rise is to increase K_1.

PROPERTY 8.5 (factor utilization and distortion) Let y^0 be an output point on $T(k, \delta^0)$. For a small change in δ that reduces the distortion rate, $\hat{\delta}(1 - \delta) > 0$, the directional changes in the economy are

$$\begin{gathered}\hat{\omega}_1/\hat{\delta} > 0, \quad \hat{k}_1/\hat{\delta} > 0, \quad \hat{\ell}_2/\hat{\delta} > 0, \quad \hat{\rho}_1/\hat{\delta} > 0 \\ \hat{\omega}_2/\hat{\delta} < 0, \quad \hat{k}_2/\hat{\delta} < 0, \quad \hat{\ell}_1/\hat{\delta} < 0, \quad \hat{\rho}_2/\hat{\delta} < 0\end{gathered} \tag{8.8}$$

In what follows, the expansion of the feasible production set due to a decline in $| 1 - \delta |$ is referred to as the expansion effect. A positive expansion effect means an expansion of the output of two products.

We have considered various kinds of distortions and their effect on the supply. The question is how they affect the equilibrium position of the economy. We begin with a discussion of the case of the SCD, which is a generalization of the short-run equilibrium discussed in Chapter 2. The importance of this discussion is in the existence of such stable equilibria. This raises the question of what dynamic would lead the economy out of this inefficient equilibrium. This discussion follows the discussion on the short-run equilibrium.

Equilibrium under Strong Constant Distortion

The production set of the economy is bounded from above by $T(k, \delta)$. Recall that δ is uniquely determined by the pair δ_w and δ_r. Under the SCD the supply price can be written as $p^s(y_1 \mid \delta_w, \delta_r)$, and it is a continuous function of y_1 for all $(y_1, y_2) \in T(k, \delta)$. As indicated above, for any (k, δ), ω_i is bounded, implying that $k_i(\omega_i)$ is bounded, and thus p^s is bounded. Let $\underline{p}$ and $\overline{p}$ be the extreme values of $p^s(y_1 \mid \delta_\omega, \delta_r)$ for $y_1 \in T(k, \delta)$. Hence if an equilibrium price exists, it must belong to the closed interval $[\underline{p}, \overline{p}]$.

We turn to Figure 8.3 to illustrate the determination of equilibrium.[4] To emphasize the difference from the standard case, consider a nonconvex production set. The demand functions $x_1 = D(p, x_2)$ are drawn for $\underline{p}$ and $\overline{p}$ in panel I. The intersection of these functions with $T(k, \delta)$ have the coordinates $\overline{x}_1$ and $\underline{x}_1$. The demand conditions imply that any feasible output plan with $0 < y_1 < \underline{x}_1$ would be purchased with $p^d > \overline{p} \geq p^s$, and hence in this interval $p^d > p^s$. Similarly for the interval $\overline{x}_1 < y_1 < \overline{y}_1$, $p^d < p^s$. Both p^d and p^s are continuous in y_1; therefore there exists $y \in T(k, \delta)$ at which $p^d = p^s$. Furthermore, the equilibrium output is characterized by $\underline{x}_1 < y_1 < \overline{x}_1$.

Panel II of Figure 8.3 illustrates the determination of the equilibrium in a closed economy using the supply and demand prices. The demand function drawn in panel II is the inverse demand function, expressing the demand price as a function of the outputs read from the transformation curve. Thus for any $y \in T(k, \delta)$, we have $dy_2/dy_1 \mid_\delta < 0$, and consequently $(\partial p^d/\partial y_1) \mid_\delta < 0$. When $p^s(y_1)$ is everywhere increasing with y_1, as in the standard case, equilibrium is determined uniquely at E. However, the supply price may decline with y_1, as indicated above. In this case there may be multiple equilibria, as shown in panel III of Figure 8.3. Furthermore, p^s need not be monotonic in y_1, as shown in panel IV of Figure 8.3, and this also leads to multiple equilibria.

The foregoing discussion illustrates the existence of equilibria. The convergence rule states that when the unit profit is positive, meaning that the cost of production is below the price that consumers are willing to pay, production

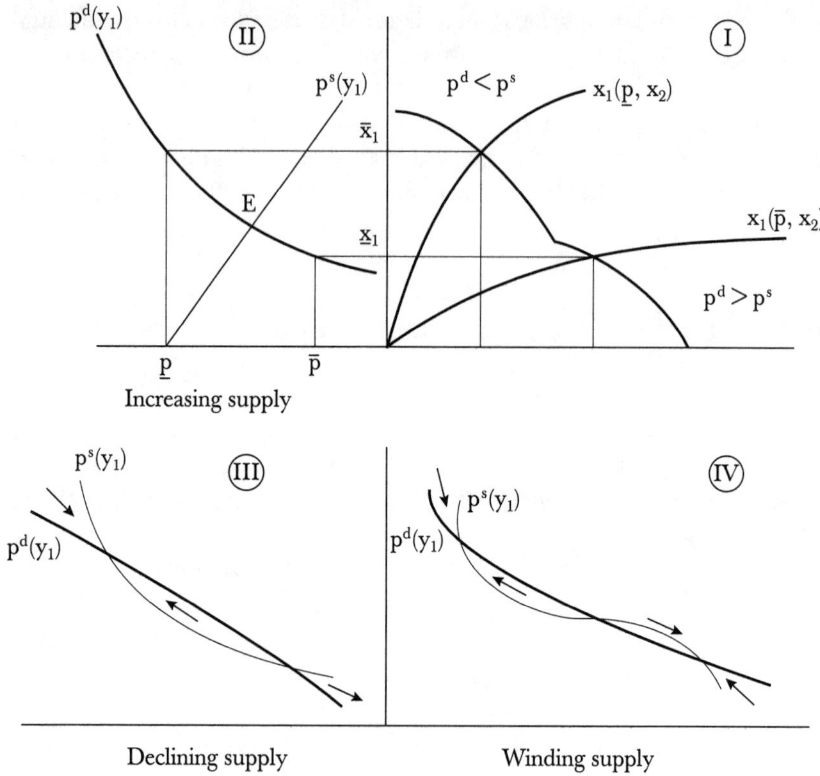

Figure 8.3 Short-run equilibrium in a distorted economy

will increase. Formally, let $\pi = p^d - p^s$, then $\pi(y_1)dy_1 > 0$. Said differently, production increases when profits exist and declines when losses are realized. This rule dictates the direction of the arrows in panels III and IV of Figure 8.3.

For a small open economy, the equilibrium position can be obtained by drawing a vertical line representing the world price in panels II–IV. Its intersection with the demand and supply functions will indicate the quantities demanded and supplied at this price and consequently the net import. In the case of multiple equilibria a monotone change in the world price does not necessarily cause a monotone change in the net import position; it may oscillate.

Changes in Distortion

It is now possible to summarize the discussion of the effect of a change in distortion on the equilibrium. Assume that the economy is in equilibrium with constant resources and technology. Factor intensity and factor shares are different in the two sectors. The distortion in the factor market is reduced so that $\hat{\delta}(1-\delta) > 0$. Then

PROPERTY 8.6 (expansion and cost effects) The *expansion effect* of a reduction in distortion is positive for the two products, whereas the *cost effect* is either of opposite sign for the two sectors, or does not exist at all. The equilibrium output of the sector whose relative cost of production is reduced will expand; the direction of the change in the other output depends on the relative strength of the income and substitution effect of demand.

Implications for the Long Run

There is a relationship between the stability of the equilibrium solution and the behavior of the economy in the process of capital accumulation. It can be shown that along the equilibrium path obtained under SCD, ω increases with k if and only if the short-run equilibrium at which it is evaluated is stable.[5] If the economy is not in a stable equilibrium, it can only be locally so, and eventually the wage-rental ratio must increase with capital accumulation. This result follows from the monotonicity of $\omega_i(k_i)$. With reference to Figure 8.4, the economy has an initial resource endowment k_A and wage-rental ratio $\omega_A \in [\underline{\omega}_A, \overline{\omega}_A]$. The capital-labor ratio increases to k_B. If ω_A increases, then $\omega'(k) > 0$ and the equilibrium is stable. Thus consider the case where ω declines locally with k, so that equilibrium now results in $\omega_B < \omega_A$. This is the meaning

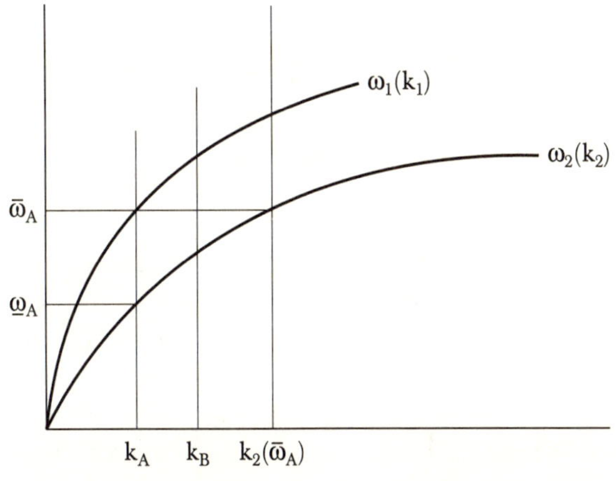

Figure 8.4 The wage-rental ratio increases with the capital-labor ratio

of $\sigma < 0$. Note, however, that this process is bounded from below because there is a capital-labor ratio beyond which $\overline{\omega}_A$ is not admissible, namely, for all $k > k_2(\overline{\omega}_A)$, $\omega(k) > \overline{\omega}_A$.

This result, which ensures global stability, is obtained under SCD. It is of course possible to change the distortion rate constantly in order to offset the effect of capital accumulation on factor prices by lowering the wage-rental ratio in one of the sectors, say sector 1, and increasing it in sector 2. This would require accumulating capital in one sector and labor in the other sector. This situation highlights the danger of development programs involving capital-intensive industrialization which extracts capital from agriculture and prevents off-farm labor migration. The description of the industrialization in India given by Mellor (1976) is an example of such a process. Obviously such programs increase the distortion and have negative efficiency effects. They are inconsistent with a flow of resources in response to differential remuneration, and as such they slow down rather than speed up development. As indicated earlier in this chapter, it is more reasonable to expect that in the long run capital accumulation will eventually result in a decline of distortion. Whether or not this is the case depends on how the distortions are formed.

Once we have established the existence of a short-run equilibrium, it is possible to examine the behavior of the economy in the long run in the face of capital accumulation and technical change. Fixing δ allows us to use some of the results obtained for the undistorted economy. For instance, the Rybzcynski proposition is maintained, and it is applicable given the actual factor intensities that exist under δ. This follows directly from the full employment condition in equation (8.3). In a similar way it is possible to repeat the analysis of Chapter 5 to trace the effects of technical change. The evaluation of a long-run growth path under the constraint of a constant δ, however, seems somewhat artificial. It is expected that as the economy develops, the factor price differentials will change as well.

Dynamics

We turn now to examine the longer-term behavior of the distorted economy. The fundamental assumption made is that resource allocation and technology at time t are determined in $t - 1$. They determine the output and the marginal productivity of labor and capital in the two sectors. Given the demand, the price is determined. Because competition prevails within each sector, equation (8.1) indicates that factor prices are determined so as to equate the value marginal productivity.

ASSUMPTION 8.1 (Economic Law of Gravity) When factor prices are unequal across sectors, resources will be allocated so as to satisfy

$$\dot{\ell} = a(\delta_w - 1); \quad a > 0$$
$$\dot{\rho} = b(\delta_r - 1); \quad b > 0. \tag{8.9}$$

Basically, if resources are free to move, other things being equal, they will move in the direction of higher returns. This is a form of the tatonnement. Label $\Delta x(t) = \int_t^{t+1} x(\tau)d\tau$, then the resource allocation in $(t+1)$ is

$$L_i(t+1) = L_i(t) + \Delta L_i(t)$$
$$K_i(t+1) = K_i(t) + \Delta K_i(t). \tag{8.10}$$

The dynamics of the system are determined by equations (8.9), (8.10), and the remaining equations of the model. The question is what can we say about the implied dynamics of such a system. We begin the discussion for an economy with constant resources and technology.

Constant Resources and Technology

Production at time t is predetermined by the allocation in the previous period and the technology, and the economic problem of a closed economy is to determine the relative product price, p. The solution is shown in Figure 8.5. Point A in the right panel indicates the supply of the two products at the beginning of the period. The price is determined from the inverse demand

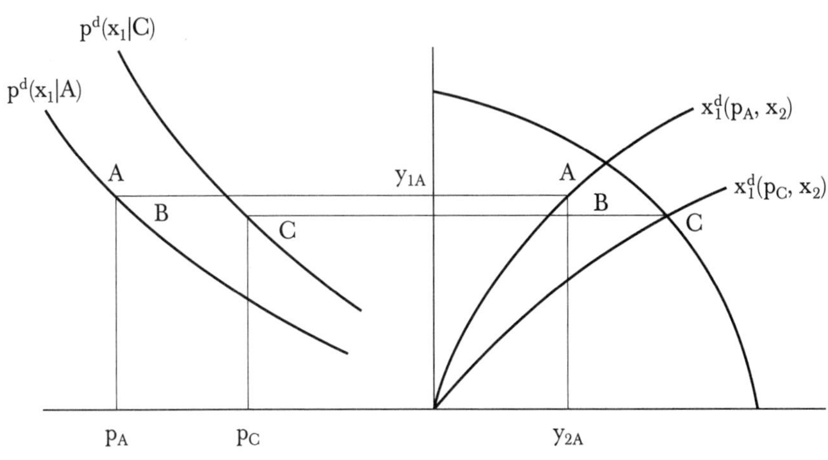

Figure 8.5 The determination of equilibrium price

function, $p^d(x_1, x_2)$, at the points where y_i is equal to x_i. This is the price that corresponds to the demand curve that goes through point A. The solution is also illustrated in the left panel where the inverse demand function, written as a function of y_1 alone, goes through y_{1A}.

As indicated by equation (8.1), the marginal productivity determines the real sectoral factor prices. The intersectoral differences in factor prices determine the changes in resource allocation as indicated by equation (8.9). This change in allocation determines, through equation (8.10), the resource allocation for the next period. This process converges to an equilibrium point where $w_2 = w_1$, $r_2 = r_1$, and consequently, $\dot{L}_1 = \dot{K}_1 = 0$, and hence $\dot{y}_1 = \dot{y}_2 = \dot{p} = 0$. Furthermore, this equilibrium is stable. To see this, assume that $w_2 > w_1$ and $r_2 > r_1$, a gap that generates an outflow of resources from agriculture. Consequently agricultural output will decline and that of nonagriculture will increase. As a result p will increase, and that will cause the factor price differentials to decline. The process is illustrated in Figure 8.5. The output in $t + 1$ is shown by point B. The limit of the process is given by point C, where factor prices are equal for both sectors, and thus the point is located on the competitive transformation curve. It is important to note that as the economy moves toward C, agricultural supply declines while its price increases. This relationship between price and output is of course in the opposite direction to that obtained for movements along a transformation curve, and in empirical analysis it will appear as if the supply function has a negative slope.

Consider alternatively that $w_2 > w_1$ and $r_2 < r_1$, implying that $\omega_2 > \omega_1$. This is the case examined in Figure 8.2. With these price differentials, the convergence rule calls for a decline in agricultural labor and an increase in its capital stock, with opposite changes in nonagriculture. As the rate of distortion declines, the output increases in both sectors as illustrated by the movement from A to C in Figure 8.2. This is in contrast to a decline in agricultural output observed in the first case considered above, where δ_w and δ_r are both smaller than 1. Therefore, there is no automatic increase in the agricultural price along the convergence path. To pursue the behavior of p on the convergence path, we note that the reduction of distortion generates a positive income effect on demand. But since agricultural demand is income inelastic, the tendency will be for p to decline so that the net resource flow will have to be in favor of larger expansion in nonagriculture. This is similar in nature to the effect on p of HNTC of equal rates in the two sectors examined in Chapter 5. We can now summarize this discussion:

PROPERTY 8.7 (dynamics of agricultural supply) A convergence path that requires a decline in agricultural output generates a negative relationship between output and price. When the convergence path generates expansion of output in both sectors, the direction of the price change is ambiguous.

The nature of the convergence is such that the immediate response to shocks is in prices. The price change is gradually transformed to changes in resource allocation, a time-consuming process. The foregoing discussion asserts the existence of a stable competitive equilibrium, a subject discussed in Chapter 2. If this assertion is true, why then is it that the system was in disequilibrium in the first place? The answer is given by the discussion of Chapters 4 and 5. Changes in resource accumulation and in technology lead to changes in the equilibrium position. The present discussion of dynamics assumes resources and technology to be constant, and thus there is no reason for the economy not to converge to equilibrium. We therefore extend the discussion to allow for resource variations.

Convergence under Resource Change

Let us assume, at this point, that the change in resources is determined exogenously. We begin with a change in capital, where new investment is allocated to the two sectors according to equation (8.10). When $\dot{K} \neq 0$, equation (8.9) can be transformed to:

$$(r_2 - r_1)(\hat{K}_1 - \hat{K}) < 0. \tag{8.11}$$

Most likely, the first term in this inequality is negative, and consequently $\hat{\rho}$ is expected to be positive. However, even when $\hat{\rho} < 0$ and the *relative* share of agriculture in the capital stock declines, the *stock* of agricultural capital can still grow. Therefore a decline in the *relative* importance of agriculture in factor employment is not inconsistent with an increase in agricultural output even when the technology is held constant.

When capital grows and technology improves, the production frontier of the economy expands, and consequently there is no a priori reason to assume that the economy will converge *uniformly* to the competitive equilibrium, as in the case of constant resources and technology discussed above. Scenarios of the possible dynamics are illustrated in Figure 8.6, where the initial point is A_0 and the competitive equilibrium for the economy, given the initial resources, is at C_0. In the next period, the economy moves to A_1, whereas the competitive equilibrium moves to C_1. Since capital and technology changes are assumed to be the cause for disequilibrium in the first place, it is not surprising that they may also increase the degree of distortion. Whether or not that actually

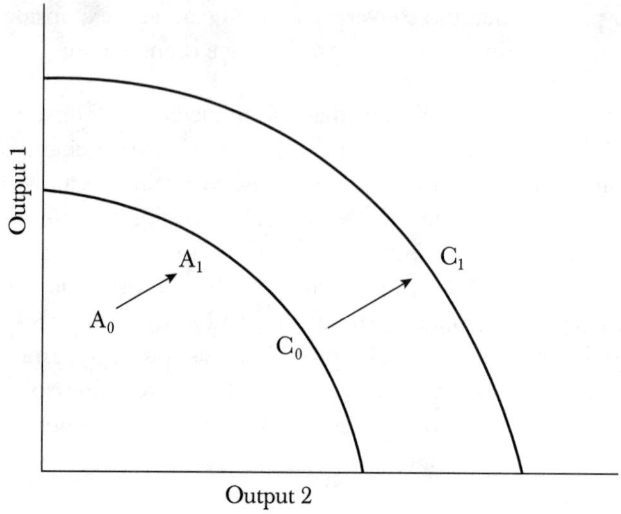

Figure 8.6 Dynamics with resource change

happens depends on the speed of factor adjustment and on the magnitude of the capital and technology changes.

Thus far it has been assumed that the labor force, or population, is held constant. In such a case the economy may accumulate capital forever. The purpose of holding the population constant was to emphasize the role of resource changes in generating disequilibrium. Having done this, we can now extend the discussion to include population growth, utilizing the discussion in Chapter 7. We know that with a *constant* population growth rate and *constant* technology there is a steady-state solution. That means that at some point the growth in the capital-labor ratio will slow down. At this point, the rate of intersectoral factor mobility may be large enough to yield a convergence to the competitive solution. Looking at the process from the point of view of factor price differentials, there may be a long time period during which factor price differentials will not decrease, or even increase, although factor mobility will be in line with equations (8.9).

The dynamics of the economy can be examined with reference to a Liapounov function of the state variables $\delta_w = w_1/w_2$ and $\delta_r = r_1/r_2$, where a and b are the coefficients of equation (8.9),

$$\begin{aligned}\Phi(\delta_w, \delta_r) &= a(\delta_w - 1)^2 + b(\delta_r - 1)^2 \\ &= (\delta_w - 1)\dot{\ell} + (\delta_r - 1)\dot{\rho}\end{aligned} \tag{8.12}$$

Clearly, $\Phi \geq 0$ with $\Phi = 0$ if and only if $\delta_w = \delta_r = 1$. At any other point we have

$$\dot{\Phi} = \dot{\delta}_w \dot{\ell} + \dot{\delta}_r \dot{\rho} + (\delta_w - 1)\ddot{\ell} + (\delta_r - 1)\ddot{\rho}, \tag{8.13}$$

where $\ddot{x}$ is the second time derivative. For the economy to converge to the equilibrium point we need $\dot{\Phi} < 0$ for all nonequilibrium points. A sufficient condition for such a convergence is given by:

ASSUMPTION 8.2 (factor-price convergence)

$$\dot{\delta}_w(\delta_w - 1) \leq 0, \quad \dot{\delta}_r(\delta_r - 1) \leq 0, \quad \dot{\delta}_\omega(\delta_\omega - 1) \leq 0 \tag{8.14}$$

with equality only when both terms are equal to zero.

The assumption states that when, for instance, the agricultural wage is lower than that of nonagriculture, the gap will decline. Recall that the Economic Law of Gravity assumption asserts that under such a wage gap the proportion of agriculture in the labor force will decline. However, now this is not the only change that takes place. Changes in technology and total resources affect the marginal productivity and hence the factor prices and as such may offset the impact of the resource allocation under the Economic Law of Gravity. Assumption 8.2 need not be maintained locally, but as the resource allocation continues, it will *eventually* lead to the closure of the wage gap. The reason is that as $k_i \to \infty$, $w_i \to \infty$; it is this condition that places bounds on the intersectoral migration. The outcome is consistent with the fact that agriculture is continuously losing its relative importance in the economy as well as with a casual observation of data on dynamics of intersectoral wage gaps and can serve as a formal hypothesis for empirical analysis. This is the basis for our discussion.

Combining Assumptions 8.1 and 8.2, the first-order terms in equation (8.13) are negative, $\dot{\delta}_w \dot{\ell} \leq 0$, $\dot{\delta}_r \dot{\rho} \leq 0$. To sign the second-order terms, we have to rely on the discussion in Chapter 9 of the off-farm migration equation. Let m be the ratio of off-farm migration to the agricultural labor force. At this point it is sufficient to indicate that $m = m(\delta_w, x)$ is a monotone function of the income differential between agriculture and nonagriculture, δ_w, and a vector of all the other variables that affect migration, x. The hypothesis $m_w(\cdot) \equiv \partial m(\delta_w;\, x)/\partial \delta_w < 0$ is tested and not rejected in the next chapter. Let n be the rate of population growth; then, by definition, $\ell(t)/\ell(t-1) = 1 - (m/(n+1))$ and $d \ln \ell/dt = -m/(n+1) < 0$. Hence $\dot{\ell} \cong -(m/(n+1))\ell(t-1)$, and $\ddot{\ell} = -[\ell(t-1)/(n+1)]m_w(\cdot)\dot{\delta}_w$. Then, sign $\ddot{\ell} = -$ sign $m_w(\cdot)\dot{\delta}_w =$ sign $\dot{\delta}_w =$ sign$(1 - \delta_w)$.

In Chapter 10 we shall see that the intersectoral allocation of investment follows a pattern similar to that of labor migration. Consequently, $\dot{\Phi} < 0$, and under this assumption the system converges uniformly to the competitive equilibrium. The essence of this discussion is that when capital and technology change, there is no reason to expect the condition in equation (8.14) to hold everywhere. Consequently, uniform convergence cannot be expected. However, the degree of divergence from equilibrium is bounded by the conditions on the production function, which eventually force convergence.

Equilibrium with Endogenous Investment

The various components of the system are now pulled together to examine its behavior when capital accumulation depends on the state of the economy. The discussion differs from that of Chapter 7 in that we now allow for factor prices to differ across sectors. It is assumed that there is only one capital good, produced in nonagriculture. The investment can be allocated between the sectors. However, once capital has been allocated to a given sector, the cost of changing the allocation is prohibitive so that existing capital is committed.

There are now two demand components in nonagriculture: x_2^d, demand by consumers, and x_2^i, demand by investors. Equation (2.17) is the demand for final consumption, whereas the demand for the capital good is given by the saving equation:

$$x_2^i = sy, \quad \text{where } y = py_1 + y_2. \tag{8.15}$$

The resource utilization identities are: $y_1 \equiv x_1^d$, $y_2 \equiv x_2^d + x_2^i$. The price is determined by $p^d = p^d(y_1, y_2 - x_2^i)$. Thus part of y_2 is now used for capital goods, and this affects the short-run equilibrium price. The analysis of this case is similar to that of government consumption conducted in Chapter 3, except that now the additional term, investment demand, depends on the state of the economy. Ignoring this fact for the moment, we can apply Figure 3.6 to analyze the present case. The conclusion is that the larger the investment demand, the larger the aggregate demand for nonagriculture, and the higher its price or, equivalently, the lower the value of p. The only new element in the present discussion is that it is assumed that in the "short run," resource allocation and technology are predetermined; hence there is no supply response and all the variations in demand due to variations in investment demand are adjusted for in the short run by price variations. This makes the necessary price adjustment stronger in the short run than in the long run, when supply responds to prices.

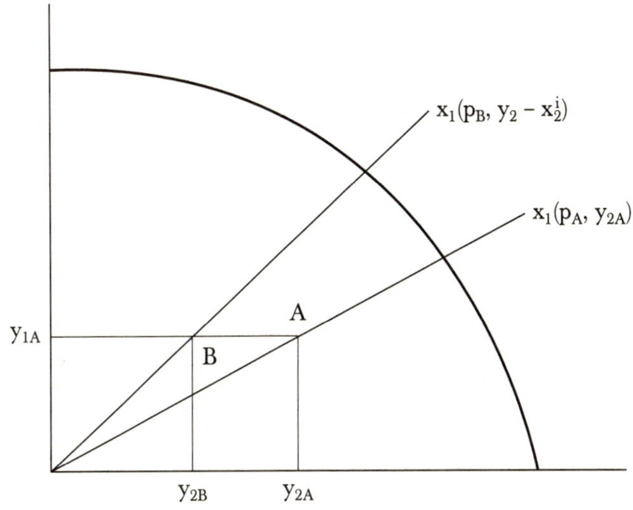

Figure 8.7 Short-run equilibrium with savings

In Figure 8.7, the predetermined resource allocation and technology led to production y_{iA}. In the absence of demand for capital goods, the price is p_A, as determined by the demand curve that passes through point A. When part of y_2 is used for investment, the quantity available for final consumption declines to $y_{2A} - x_2^i = y_{2B}$. This generates excess demand for y_2, and p declines to p_B, the price of the demand curve that goes through point B, $p^d(y_{1A}, y_{2B})$.

Next we remove the assumption that x_2^i is exogenous. To do so, differentiate equation (8.15) $\partial x_2^i/\partial p = sy_1 + y\partial s/\partial p$. Under the constant saving rate, $\partial x_2^i/\partial p > 0$. This implies that the aggregate demand for x_1 declines in p, and therefore the analysis goes through without any modification. For this to be negated it is necessary that $\partial s/\partial p$ will be negative and sufficiently large. This does not seem to be plausible or interesting.

In conclusion, the short-run equilibrium determines the level of investment that will be allocated to the two sectors depending on their relative profitability. Labor, which at this stage is still assumed to grow exogenously, is also allocated to the two sectors as described by the migration equation. Technology changes as well, and new output is obtained. A new short-run solution is obtained by determining a new price and the level of investment, and the process repeats itself.

Appendix 8A

1. The dependence of cost-factor intensity on the elasticities of substitution.

   The cost intensity is measured in terms of the ratios of the factor shares. Label $\theta_i(\omega_i) \equiv \omega_i/k_i$, so that S_{iL} is monotonically increasing in θ_i and $d \ln \theta_i / d \ln \omega_i = 1 - \sigma_i$. Then $\theta \equiv \theta_1/\theta_2$ is a measure of cost intensity in that $[\theta - 1][I(\delta, \omega_2)] \geq 0$, where the equality is achieved if and only if the two terms are equal to zero. We can then write $\theta(\delta, \omega_2) = (\omega_1/\omega_2)(k_2/k_1) = \delta/R(\delta, \omega_2)$ and examine the behavior of $\theta(\delta, \omega_2)$ in δ: $\partial\theta(\delta, \omega_2)/\partial\delta\,|_{\omega_2} = (1 - \sigma)/R(\delta, \omega_2)$. Thus, when $\sigma > 1$, an increase in δ is associated with a decrease in θ. R is increasing in δ (independently of σ). Therefore, when $\sigma > 1$, the two measures of factor intensity move in the same direction; when $\sigma < 1$, they move in opposite directions. The case where the elasticities of substitution differ across sectors is examined in Mundlak (1970).

9

The Dynamics of Resource Allocation: Labor

The discussion in Chapter 8 extends the results of the unconstrained competitive model to analyze the behavior of the economy under the assumption of constant distortion rates. It is still not general enough to guide empirical analysis, however, in that it assumes that the rate of distortion is given exogenously rather than being determined within the economic system itself. This requires that at any point in time intersectoral resource allocation is carried out to the extent needed to maintain the exogenously given distortion rate. If this assumption has empirical validity, what is the mechanism that stops the resource flow at the point of the constant distortion rate and thereby prevents resources from moving until price differentials disappear?

To overcome the limitations of exogenous distortions, the factor price differentials are now endogenized. This is done by recognizing that the process of resource allocation requires real time. The generation of intersectoral factor price differentials leads to a flow of resources from low to high returns, as summarized by the Economic Law of Gravity in Chapter 8. The adjustment, however, is not quick enough to close the gap in price differentials, or a substantial part of it, in one period. Consequently, at any given time the resource allocation is assumed to be predetermined. In such a model the rate of distortion is endogenous; it is determined by the changes in factor supply and demand that occur over time.

Several questions are raised with respect to this process: (1) What is the theoretical justification for such a formulation? (2) What is the empirical evidence to support it? (3) What are the consequences for the dynamics of the economy? and (4) How should it assist us in an empirical evaluation of sectoral growth? This chapter deals with the first two questions for labor, the next chapter does the same for capital, the previous chapter discussed the third question, and the last question is dealt with in subsequent chapters.

Agricultural Labor Supply

The most significant process concerning agricultural labor is the continuous off-farm labor migration which goes on for decades in every country and which reduces the labor force in agriculture to a small fraction of the total labor force. The universality and the strength of the process calls for an explanation that holds for a wide diversity of economic environments. In so doing, we pass over a variety of interesting subjects related to rural labor markets. Some of this work is surveyed by Rosenzweig (1988).

Sectoral labor demand has been analyzed in our foregoing discussion as part of the production side of the economy. We come back to it in the discussion of the empirical analysis of the production side of the economy in Part III. The present discussion deals mainly with the sectoral labor supply, which consists of changes in the total labor supply in agriculture and the choice of occupation. The principle of occupational choice is first introduced within the simpler framework of landless labor. The discussion of farm operators adds details that are pertinent for the understanding of the agricultural labor supply and as such are pertinent for empirical analysis. This discussion serves as a base for the formulation and estimation of the migration equations.

Landless Labor: A Single Occupation

The labor supply of an individual to a given occupation is determined by his overall labor supply and by competing alternatives. We therefore begin the discussion by briefly reviewing the principles of labor supply (Becker, 1965). The individual allocates his time (T) between productive activities (L) to generate or finance consumption (c) and leisure (T^c), subject to the time constraint:

$$T = T^c + L. \tag{9.1}$$

The individual is both a consumer and a seller of time. Consumption consists of goods and leisure. The price of leisure is the wage rate, w, and the value of leisure consumed is $w(T - L)$. Income comes from wages and from other sources, exogenously determined, denoted by a. The budget constraint is $c = a + wL$. The individual chooses c and T^c subject to the budget constraint. To express the problem in a form familiar from demand analysis, the concept of full income is used: $y = a + wT$, where wT is the value of total time available, evaluated at the market wage rate. This is a convenient analytic expression which overlooks the fact that working in the market 24 hours a day for 365 days a year, in addition to being not optimal, is not feasible because there is no market demand for such an option. The question does not arise in discussions because the optimal solution provides a much shorter working day, but this should be attributed to the structure of the utility function and not to the market demand. With this caveat, the budget constraint is

$$c + wT^c - y = 0. \tag{9.2}$$

We can think of c as an aggregate of all consumption goods, represented by a vector x_1, with a corresponding vector of prices p_1. When the utility function is weakly separable in leisure and the various consumption components, the composition of x_1 does not affect the demand for leisure.[1] Building on the standard analysis of consumer behavior summarized in Appendix 2A and maintaining the notations used there, we label $w = p_2$ and $T^c = x_2$, $p = (p_1, p_2)$, $x = (x_1, x_2)$ and derive the demand for leisure and consumption by solving the following problem:

$$\max_x [u(x) - \lambda(px - y)]. \tag{9.3}$$

We can now write the equivalence of the uncompensated (x) and compensated (h) demand functions as

$$x(p, y) \equiv h[p, v(p, y)] \tag{9.4}$$

$$h(p, u) \equiv x(p, e(p, u)], \tag{9.5}$$

where v and e are the indirect utility and expenditure functions respectively. The Slutsky equation is obtained by differentiating identity (9.5), $\partial x_2/\partial p_2 \mid_y = \partial x_2/\partial p_2 \mid_u + x_2\, \partial x_2/\partial y$, and substituting $L = T - x_2$ and $w = p_2$ to obtain

$$\frac{\partial L}{\partial w}\mid_y = \frac{\partial L}{\partial w}\mid_u + \frac{\partial L}{\partial y}\mid_u (T - L). \tag{9.6}$$

Assuming leisure to be a normal good, the effect of income on labor supply, $\partial L/\partial y$, is negative. An individual in the labor force is a net seller of time, and therefore the income effect of a change in the wage rate on labor supply is negative. The substitution effect is positive, and the higher the wage rate, the lower the demand for leisure–and hence the higher the compensated supply of labor. Thus when the substitution effect dominates the income effect, the supply of labor increases with wages. This is a standard result of labor supply theory.

An interesting issue is what is the decision-making unit and whose utility function is considered–individual, family, present unit, or dynasty of units–and what weights are assigned to the various participants. In order to focus on the main subject these hosts of issues are overlooked, although some aspects are referred to when needed. It suffices to say at this point that the utility function may depend on demographic and other factors, such as the size and composition of the family, age distribution, and education. Consequently the labor supply may depend on all these factors.

Next we turn to examine the choice among several employment opportunities, referred to as occupations. In this we distinguish between landless labor and farm operators.

Landless Labor: Occupational Choice

For landless labor, the main consideration in choosing occupation is the wage rate. Other things equal, an individual will choose the employment with the highest wage rate. If the individual is not currently employed in the highest-paying job, changing jobs may involve a cost. In the current discussion we are interested in the movement from agriculture and refer to such a cost as the cost of migration (cm). The individual will prefer a higher-paying job provided the income differential covers the cost of migration. With wage rates and migration costs being constants, the optimal solution will consist of only one job. This is illustrated in Figure 9.1, where market lines are drawn for wage rates w and w' respectively and no other sources of income exist. The market line AB', corresponding to the wage rate w', dominates the line AB that corresponds to the wage rate w. However, when the cost of migration is brought in, the income from the second occupation, $Lw' - cm$, is represented by the budget line $A'C$. This line intersects the market line of the first occupation at D. Thus the relevant income frontier for this individual is a combination of two lines given by the segments ADC. The actual choice depends on the utility function. A tangency of the indifference curve between leisure and consumption and the market line in the segment AD implies that the individual continues in the low-wage occupation, whereas a tangency solution to the left of D implies a change to the higher-paying job in spite of the cost of migration. These points can be found by drawing the demand curve for the two alternative wages and locating their intersection with the corresponding market lines.

The choice between the two alternative solutions requires a comparison of their utility levels. This, in turn, requires a computation of the values of the indirect utility function for the various alternatives, $v(p_j, cm_j)$, where p_j and cm_j represent the prices (including wages) and the cost of migration associated with occupation j. The optimal occupation, $j = o$, is that which generates the highest value for the indirect utility:

$$v(p_o, cm_o) > v(p_j, cm_j) \quad \text{for all } j. \tag{9.7}$$

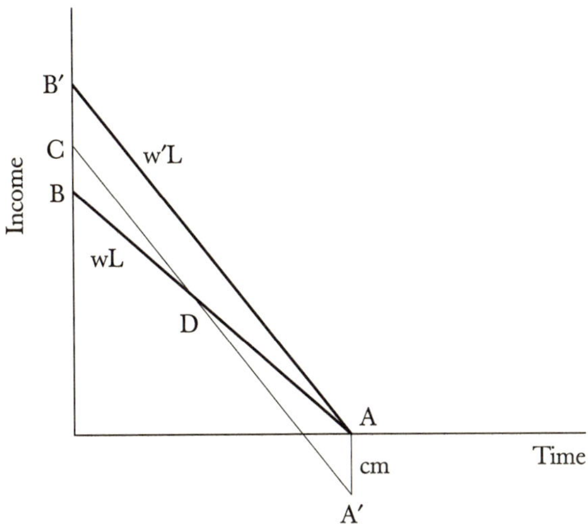

Figure 9.1 Choice of occupation: Landless labor

Note that v is nondecreasing in the wage rate and nonincreasing in the prices of the consumer goods. Consequently, lower consumer prices in rural areas may compensate for lower wage rates.

The essence of this discussion is the distinction made between the total labor supply of a worker and his supply to a particular occupation or market. This is analogous to the distinction between the aggregate supply function and a supply of a particular product. In the absence of institutional or other constraints on employment in the two markets, there will be no multiple occupations. Once the migration cost is covered, labor will specialize in the high-wage job. Multiple job holdings under constant wages have to be explained by external constraints such as lack of full-time employment, institutional arrangements, risk considerations, or nonlinear market functions. In the appendix to this chapter, the problem is formulated within the choice of technique framework.

Farm Operators: The Existence of Labor Markets

Farm operators draw their income, in part or in full, from their farm operation. As such, their income depends on their own performance, and it is not fully represented by the market wage. This is true for farm owners who work on their farms as well as for tenants whose income has a profit component. In principle, the demand for their labor input is a derived demand from their profit opportunities in farming, which in turn reflect the technology, the markets for their products and inputs, and the institutional arrangements under which they operate. All these lead to a different budget constraint from that of landless labor. The difference is in the source of income which now includes farm income (Singh, Squire, and Strauss, 1986).

There are several leading cases to be examined. We begin with the case of homogeneous labor in the sense that there is no difference between family and hired labor, and there exists a labor market with wage rate w. Also, to simplify the graphical presentation, it is assumed that production is a function of two inputs only. With capital and technology fixed, the farm income is given by $pF(L^f, K) - wL^f$, where L^f is the labor used on the farm. The optimization problem is

$$\max_x \left\{u(x) - \lambda[c - (a + pF(L^f, K) + w(L - L^f))]\right\}. \tag{9.8}$$

Without a loss of generality it is assumed here that the budget constraint is binding and that there is only one consumption good.

The solution of the optimization problem in (9.8) consists of two separate decisions: one involves the level of labor input on the farm, or simply the farm labor demand, and the other involves the labor supply. Accordingly, the maximization can be carried out in stages. First optimize the farm decision by selecting the level of the farm labor input. This calls for the derivation of the restricted profit function defined as

$$\pi(p, w, K) \equiv \max_{L^f} pF(L^f, K) - wL^f.$$

The second stage involves the choice of consumption and labor supply:

$$\max_x \{u(x) - \lambda[c - (a + \pi(p, w, K) + wL)]\}.$$

The results derived for landless labor apply here as well with one modification; income now includes the profit from the farm operation. Specifically, identity (9.4) becomes

$$x[p, y + \pi(\cdot)] = h[p, v(p, y + \pi(\cdot))].$$

Consequently

$$\frac{\partial L}{\partial w}\Big|_y = \underset{+}{\frac{\partial L}{\partial w}\Big|_u} + \underset{-}{\frac{\partial L}{\partial y}}\underset{?}{(L - L^f)}. \tag{9.9}$$

The last term of this equation is the difference between the farm labor supply and the farm labor demand. When the farmer hires labor, $L^f > L$, and

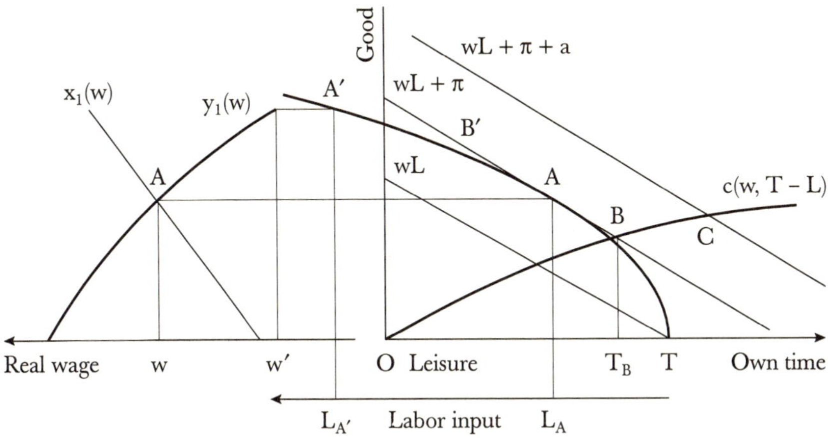

Figure 9.2 Time allocation: Farm operator

therefore the income effect of an increase in the wage rate on his labor supply is positive. The income effect is negative for landless labor and for farm operators who work off the farm, and it is zero for operators who do not hire labor and do not work off the farm.[2] Consequently the income effect on the aggregate agricultural labor supply of *farm operators* depends on the composition of the agricultural labor force. It is likely to be relatively unimportant where most of the farming is done by family labor with little access to the labor market, but it will be positive where hired labor is important.

The discussion is illustrated in Figure 9.2, where production is drawn as a function of labor with an origin at T. The farmer's leisure is measured from the origin to the right, whereas the labor input to the farm is measured from T (zero labor) to the left. Thus T is the origin for the production function, and point A indicates the output achieved with labor input L_A. The farm labor input can extend beyond the origin of the farmer's time. For instance, at point A' the input is $L_{A'}$. To simplify the notation of Figure 9.2, output is normalized so that its price is one and w is the real wage. The line wL shows the labor cost of the farm operation. Assuming that labor is the only cost, profit is measured by the vertical distance between the production function and the market line. Given w, π is maximized at point A. A decline in the labor cost due to a decline in w (a decline in the wage rate or a rise in the product price) would be represented as a rotation of the market line. The increase in output associated with a decline in w can be shown in the figure. The reader is invited to fill in the details needed to show that under $w > w^*$, the optimum output is at a point to the left of A, say A^*, a point to be inserted in the figure, with $L_{A^*} > L_A$ and profit $\pi_{A^*} > \pi_A$.

Without a loss in generality, where the explicit expression is not needed, we let w stand for the wage in terms of the consumption (or production) good. The production side can be summarized by the product supply function, $y_1(w)$, or the labor demand, $L^f(w)$. The two functions decline in w, and therefore are monotonically increasing in each other. They are represented by the same line in the left panel of Figure 9.2. It is also possible to show the profit function, $\pi(w)$, in the same diagram, and this is left as an exercise for the reader.

Regarding the consumption decision, there are three pertinent income lines: wL is the labor income, regardless of whether the farmer works on or off the farm. Consequently, the line wL represents two different concepts, labor cost to the farm and labor income to the individual with a labor supply L. The line $wL + \pi$ is the labor income plus farm profit, and the last line also includes exogenous income, a. Following the presentation introduced in Chapter 2, the demand for consumption and leisure can be presented by the demand curve $c(w, T - L)$ that expresses consumption as a function of the price ratio w (wage in terms of the consumption good).[3] This curve intersects the income line at B for the case of $a = 0$. In this case, leisure is T_B, and labor supply is $T - T_B$. The input demand by the farm is L_A, and the amount of hired farm labor is $L^f - L = L_A - (T - T_B)$. With exogenous income a, the optimal consumption changes from B to C, increasing the amount of leisure and hence of hired labor, but the production plan does not change. If the demand curve intersected the income line to the left of A, say at B', the farmer's labor supply would exceed the farm demand, and the farmer would spend some of his time working off the farm.

The problem has been reduced to the framework used in the discussion in Chapter 2 of equilibrium determination in a small open economy. Given the market wage w, the labor supply and demand are determined, and the traded quantities indicate whether the farmer is a net buyer or seller of labor. At high w, the farmer purchases some of the good (c) and is a net supplier of labor to the market. When w declines, the income of a farmer who hires labor will go up, whereas that of a farmer who works off the farm will decline. The various solutions can be shown in the left panel of Figure 9.2 using the restricted product demand or labor supply functions following the analysis of Chapter 2.

The criterion of occupational choice stated in (9.7) also applies to farm operators, with some natural modifications. First, the income attainable at given prices depends on the capital stock, landholding, and technology. These variables should therefore appear in the indirect utility function. Second, the decision to quit farming depends on the marginal productivity of labor for low labor inputs, or alternatively for high capital-labor ratios. Presumably, a farmer will quit farming if, at the margin, off-farm income will be higher than farm income, that is if as $L \to 0$, $[\lim \partial F(\cdot)/\partial L] < w$. This criterion is sufficient, but not necessary. A farmer may also quit farming even if, as $L \to 0$, $\lim \partial F(\cdot)/\partial L \to \infty$. The reason is the existence of other costs in addition to the labor cost, such as a land tax, in the operation of the farm. Also, there is an opportunity cost of the capital tied up in the farm operation. To account for such costs, π has to be properly defined. This is done in the formal presentation in the appendix. For the present discussion, it is sufficient to introduce a fixed cost, fc_a, for the farm operation. Consequently the indirect utility function for the farm operation can be written as $v(p_a, s_a)$, where s_a is the vector of state variables, $s_a = (K, T, fc_a)$, and T stands for technology. The individual will quit farming if for some $i \neq a$,

$$v(p_a, s_a) < v(p_i, fc_i). \tag{9.7'}$$

This is a general expression that applies to the case where the marginal labor productivity at $L^f = 0$ approaches a finite value or alternatively tends to infinity. It is a useful exercise to show these two cases in terms of Figure 9.2.

Farm Operators: Absence of Labor Markets

In the absence of a labor market, farm labor is all the individual's own labor, and there is no off-farm employment. This is analogous to the case of a closed economy, discussed in Chapter 2, where the equilibrium is determined by the intersection of the demand curve with the transformation curve. At that point the shadow wage, w, is determined as the slope of the transformation curve between time and output, or simply the production function of labor. This can be illustrated in terms of Figure 9.2. Let $a = 0$, then given w, production is at A with labor demand, L_A. To avoid additional notations, assume now that point B represents the intersection of $c(w, T - L)$ with the transformation curve (rather than with the market line), so that the labor supply is $T - T_B$. Obviously the supply is smaller than the demand; hence w is not an equilibrium wage. The equilibrium point is located somewhere between A and B.

The shadow price of labor is determined endogenously so as to generate zero excess demand for labor, z. In order to examine its dependence on exogenous variables, s, write for the equilibrium w

$$z(w, s) = L^f(w, s) - L(w, s) = 0.$$

Differentiating this identity with respect to s and rearranging:

$$\frac{\partial w}{\partial s} = -\frac{\partial z/\partial s}{\partial z/\partial w}. \tag{9.10}$$

By definition, the denominator is

$$\underset{-}{\partial z/\partial w} = \underset{-}{\partial L^f/\partial w} - \underset{+}{\partial L/\partial w}.$$

The first term on the right-hand side is the slope of the farm labor demand, and the last term is the slope of the labor supply which is signed locally using identity (9.5). Consequently, the denominator of (9.10) is negative, and we have

$$\text{sign } \partial w/\partial s = \text{sign}(\partial L^f/\partial s - \partial L/\partial s). \tag{9.11}$$

Hence, to sign the response of the shadow price to an exogenous change in the supply or demand functions, it is sufficient to sign the difference in the response of the labor demand and supply. If the state variables in s do not appear in the utility function, then their effect on labor supply is solely through the income effect. As such, the effect is not independent of the changes in labor demand. Taking this into account, we write,

$$\partial L/\partial s = \partial L/\partial y \; \partial y/\partial L^f \partial L^f/\partial s,$$

where y is income. Substituting this in (9.11) we obtain that

$$\text{sign } \partial w/\partial s = \text{sign } \partial L^f/\partial s.$$

This result is intuitively clear. Factors that increase farm labor demand increase the shadow wage rate. Meeting the increased demand requires diverting time from leisure, and this becomes increasingly more expensive. Thus changes in the product price, in the level of other (complementary) inputs such as capital, or in technology, or the opening of new markets due to improvements in infrastructure are all expected to affect the shadow price.

The most important of these determinants is of course technical change. The case of Hicks-neutral technical change is illustrated in Figure 9.3. This is analogous to the presentation of technical change in one sector considered in Chapter 5. Initially, the economy is in equilibrium at point E. As a result of the technical change, the production function rotates; the productivity effect is shown by point B, and the cost effect is given by the movement from B to C. Thus, at constant prices labor demand increases from L_E to L_C.

The increase in consumption opportunities, or simply in income, associated with the technical change increases the demand for leisure and goods as

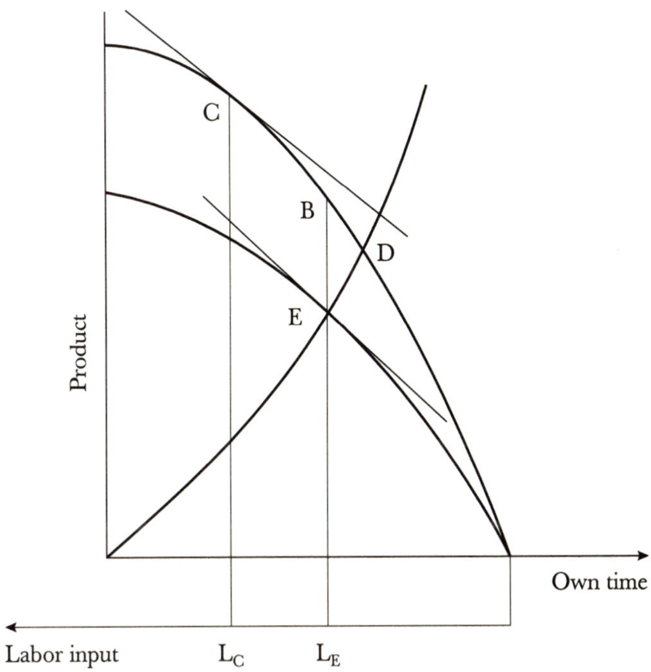

Figure 9.3 Time allocation: Technical change

indicated by a movement along the demand curve from E to D. As such, there is an excess demand for leisure, or an excess supply of goods. The new equilibrium will be located between D and C. It will be to the right of B when the demand elasticity for c is less than 1. In this case the outcome is a decline in labor input and an increase in the shadow wage.

In the decision on occupational choice, the indirect utility function for the farm operator will be like that in equation (9.7′), with one modification; the shadow wage rate will replace the market wage. As such it will depend on all the determinants of farm profitability. Although we deal here with a farm household, the discussion also applies to the economy at large where all goods are aggregated. Thus the long-term effect of technical change is an increase in leisure (a decrease in working hours) and in consumption.

Part-time Farming

The foregoing discussion indicates the scope for part-time farming. When the labor supply exceeds the farm demand, labor will seek off-farm employment.

Table 9.1 Percentage of farm operators reporting off-farm work

Country	Percentage	Year	Source
United States	53	1982	Census of Agriculture
Canada	34	1976	Bollman (1979)
Israel	47	1981	Census of Agriculture
Germany	43	1983	Robson, Gasson, and Hill (1987)
France	33	1983	Robson, Gasson, and Hill (1987)
Italy	29	1983	Robson, Gasson, and Hill (1987)
Netherlands	19	1983	Robson, Gasson, and Hill (1987)
Belgium	33	1983	Robson, Gasson, and Hill (1987)
U.K.	25	1983	Robson, Gasson, and Hill (1987)
Ireland	25	1983	Robson, Gasson, and Hill (1987)
Denmark	34	1983	Robson, Gasson, and Hill (1987)
Greece	40	1983	Robson, Gasson, and Hill (1987)
Australia	26	1978	Robinson, McMahon, and Quiggon (1982)
India	41	1971	Rosenzweig (1980)
Java	24	1980	Benjamin (1988)

Source: Kimhi (1991).

The extent to which this is done depends on the employment opportunities. In investigating part-time farming, we can think of the family, rather than the individual, as the decision-making unit. Some members of the family will work on the farm, and others will work off the farm. This requires us to define the utility function in such a way that it represents the preferences of all the members of the family. Such an extension raises some interesting problems, and there has been work done on issues related to the intrafamily distribution of benefits and contributions. These issues are not examined here because their solution does not affect the aggregate behavior in agriculture in any substantive way.

Part-time farming is rapidly developing with urbanization, improvement in transportation, capital accumulation, and technological change.[4] Urbanization brings labor markets closer to farm areas. The construction of roads and improvements in transportation reduce the cost of commuting. At the same time capital accumulation and technological change are largely labor saving, as discussed in Chapter 6. Thus less labor is needed on the farm, and more opportunities exist off the farm.

Table 9.1 presents evidence on the extent of part-time farming. In most of the countries covered in the table, one-fourth to one-half of the farm operators report off-farm employment. An interesting question is whether part-time farming serves as an intermediate stage between full-time farming and the entry to or exit from farming. What follows will provide the framework to deal with this question but will not answer it. There is no unambiguous analytic answer. It is likely that the empirical evidence will also be ambiguous. In any case, the answer will not affect the main course of our discussion.[5]

Differences in Ability

A more detailed examination of the behavior of farm operators should differentiate between the farmer's own labor and hired labor. The farmer's input is a combined input of his labor and his management ability or entrepreneurship. It is hard to characterize this variable, and in the literature it is referred to by different names. What is important for the present discussion is that this attribute is not adequately traded in the labor market. Basically, it is not traded because the entrepreneur has a more favorable evaluation of his qualities than the market does. This is an example of asymmetric information. We refer to this attribute as managerial ability or management in short. Bringing into the analysis the managerial input has several repercussions.

Labor Supply

Farm operators may spend part of their time in off-farm work if a labor market exists. To account for the managerial input in terms of Figure 9.2, we take the income opportunities of the farmer to be identical with the production function from its origin at T to the point of tangency with the market line, such as point A. In this case, the market line represents the choices to the left of point A. This extension is relevant only when the labor supply exceeds the farm demand for labor, in which case the farm does not provide sufficient employment with above-market returns. Such a situation of coexistence of occupations is illustrated by point B'. Such coexistence was not optimal for landless labor. This result is derived analytically in the appendix.

As long as the farmer is specializing in farming, the response of his time allocation to changes in the market wage reflects only the income effect due to the higher cost of the hired labor. If he does not hire labor, then his behavior is similar to that of a farmer who has no access to the market, as discussed previously.

The Distribution of Management

Differences in managerial ability account for the fact that some farmers remain in agriculture, some leave, and new ones enter, a subject to be discussed below. We can think of Figure 9.3 as describing two farmers. Obviously the difference in their productivity makes it possible for the more productive farmer to

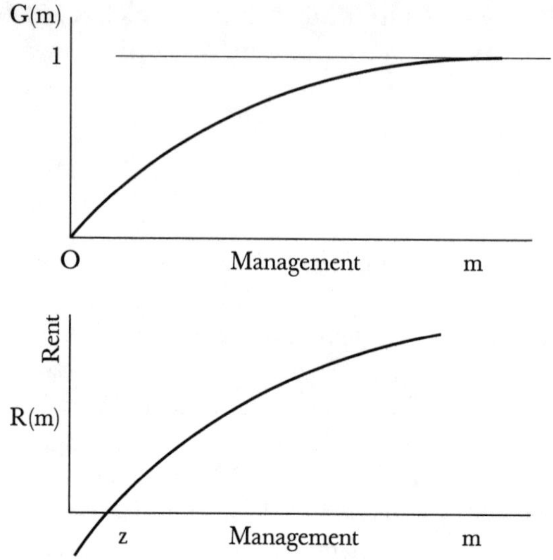

Figure 9.4 Hypothetical distribution of management

buy out the less productive one. We can now generalize this by considering the micro production function of the ith farmer: $Y_i = F_i(X_i, m_i, t)$, where Y is output, X is a vector of inputs, m is the managerial ability, and t is an index of technology. The function is CRS in X and m. This means that for a given farmer, the function displays decreasing returns to scale in the inputs X. Without a loss in generality for the present discussion, assume that all farmers are profit maximizers and price takers in the output and input markets. We can then write the profit function of the ith farmer: $\pi_i = \pi(p, w, m_i, t)$. Profit is increasing monotonically with managerial ability, and therefore managers are ranked according to the level of their profit in the same way that land quality was ranked in Chapter 4 according to rent. To deal with entry and exit, the relevant measure of profits is the long-term profit, referred to as *rent to management.* Similarly to Figure 4.7, the distribution of managers is illustrated in Figure 9.4, where the vertical axis in the lower panel measures the long-term returns to management. Farmers that incur negative profits are forced out of production. There is however an intrinsic difference between the distribution of managers and that of land. The distribution of managers portrays a current situation which changes with time. Every year, new cohorts enter the labor force, and the reservoir of potential farmers of all qualities increases. Thus we can think of the supply of managers as elastic in the long run. With this interpretation, we can go back to our specification of the aggregate production function for agriculture in Chapter 2. In the short run, differences in m imply that an increase in output will require the entry of less efficient farmers, and therefore the production function will display decreasing returns to scale. However, in the long run, we can think of the supply of managers as perfectly elastic, and this justifies the CRS property of the aggregate function. Empirical support for this is provided in our empirical discussion of entry and exit.

Measuring Management and Its Impact

How important is the management variable in understanding developments in agriculture? For an empirical answer, we need to have a measure of management. As with the case of technology, the measure of management is derived as a residual after taking into account the effect of other variables. Here we examine the conceptual problem, its implications, and the empirical evidence. The statistical topics are discussed in Chapter 12.

We differentiate between a measure of average performance of this variable in the aggregate and the performance of the individual farmer. When we consider management to be a factor of production, its relative importance in the contribution to output is given by its factor share. When we know the share of all other inputs, the factor share of management is obtained as a residual from one. The order of magnitude of the share of management in the sample underlying Figure 9.5 (to be discussed below) is 0.2. This means that on average

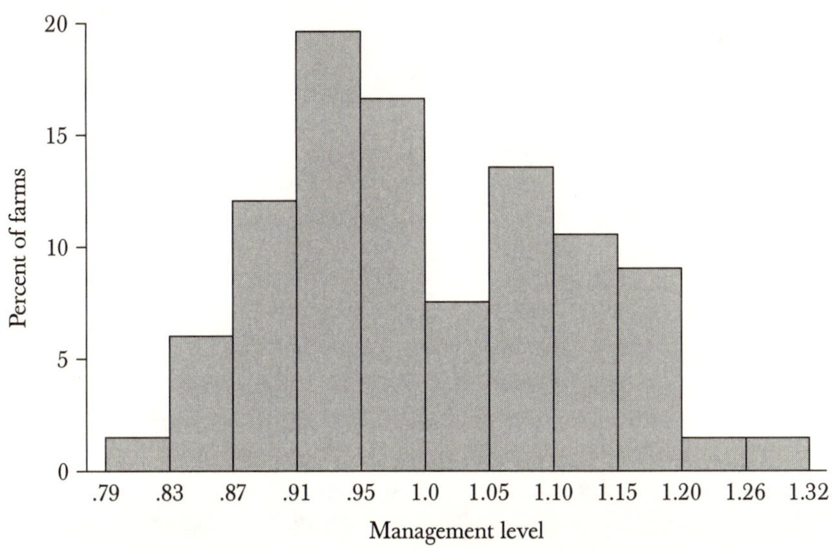

Figure 9.5 Empirical distribution of management. (From Mundlak 1964, p. 75.)

for the sample, 20 percent of the output was not attributed to the various inputs and as such was left as a residual for management, or simply gross profit. The average returns to management are reflective of the conditions in agriculture but are not indicative of the distribution of management and its effect on output and income in the population.

In examining the impact of the spread, we hold the technology constant. Assume a production function displaying CRS in X and m, $Y = mf(X/m)$, and, without a loss in generality, we assume X to be a single input. Differentiating, we obtain $\partial Y/\partial(X/m) = mf'(X/m)$ and $\partial Y/\partial X = f'(X/m)$. Let w be the real price of X, then assuming profit maximization, $f'(X/m) = w$ and $X/m = \phi(w)$ or $X = m\phi(w)$, where $f'(X/m) = \phi^{-1}$. Substituting in the production function, $Y = m\Phi(w)$, where $\Phi(w) = f[\phi(w)]$. The total effect of m on output is decomposed as $dY/dm = \partial Y/\partial m + \partial Y/\partial X\ dX/dm$. The first term on the right-hand side is the productivity effect of management, in that it shows the effect of a change in m on output with inputs held constant. The second term is analogous to the cost effect of technical change, in that it gives the indirect effect of m on output that comes through the change in the inputs needed to maintain the first-order conditions for profit maximization. The productivity effect can be measured in relative terms. From these, we see that the size of the firm measured either by output or input is increasing monotonically with m.

In practice, the measure of the productivity effect is based on the difference between the output of the firm and the value of its employed resources.[6] Therefore, a positive value implies that the firm is utilizing its input bundle more productively compared with the average performance in the sample, and a negative value indicates the opposite. Figure 9.5 presents results reported in Mundlak (1964) of a distribution of such a measure obtained for 66 family farms in Israel for the period 1954–1959. To have a reference point for the quantitative significance of the spread, we can evaluate its contribution to the spread of output in the sample used for the calculations. What follows summarizes the results and discussion of Mundlak (1964, pp. 75–79). The order of magnitude of the variance in management is the same as that of the disturbance in the production function. A 95% confidence interval is constructed, and the values of the interval are expressed relative to the average output to be taken as one. The interval due to management alone (assume no disturbance) is 0.816–1.226. The interval due to the disturbance alone is 0.804–1.243, and the interval due to the combined effects of management and disturbance is 0.742–1.347. The ratios of the high and low limits of the interval for the three cases respectively are 1.5, 1.55, and 1.82. This provides quantitative insight on the contribution of the spread in management to the spread in income in the population. As we shall see in Chapter 12, there are rational idiosyncratic differences in the first-order conditions due to differences in the attitude toward risk and to the processing of information that further increase the spread in the income distribution. These income differences affect the decision on entry to and exit from agriculture, as discussed below.

Heterogeneity and Equilibrium

Our discussion thus far has dealt with sectoral aggregates. To examine changes in the number of farms and the sectoral allocation of labor, we need to introduce heterogeneity, as we have just done by bringing in management. This raises the question of who will be in agriculture and who will be out. The equilibrium solution for the industry can be obtained under various assumptions with respect to factor supply, as we have done in the discussion on the quality of land. Lucas (1978) analyzes the size distribution of firms under a resource constraint. This leads to a joint determination of the marginal firm and the inputs used by the individual firms. On the other hand, we can consider the industry to be a price taker, in which case the input use is determined independently of the determination of the marginal firm. Marginal firms are those where the rent to management is zero. We can then rely on the discussion in Chapters 2–6 to assess the changes that take place over time in the industry and trace their consequences on the marginal firms as well as on the firms' size. With technical change, real product prices decline, and therefore marginal firms quit. With time, technical change increases the optimal size of operation of any farmer; consequently, small farms will not be profitable and will either sell out or expand. The discussion has concentrated on the role of m in the determination of the marginal farm. This is not the only factor that affects the decision whether or not to farm. To continue the discussion, we need to bring in other considerations and particularly to place the analysis within a multiperiod framework.

Off-farm Migration

Multiperiod Choice: Landless Labor

When it comes to agricultural labor, the choice of occupation requires for most people a change of residence, because the local employment opportunities are too limited to absorb all the labor that leaves agriculture. Such a move involves costs to be covered by the income in the new job. The cost of migration and income flows have different time paths. The cost of migration is incurred largely in the first period of migration, whereas the benefits last as long as the individual maintains the new occupation. The problem should therefore be considered within a multiperiod framework.

To simplify the formulation, it is assumed that the utility function is separable over time. The discounted stream of utility, evaluated from the indirect utility function for an individual of age g is

$$V(p, g) = \int_{g}^{T} e^{-rt} v(p(t))dt. \tag{9.12}$$

The indirect utility that enters equation (9.12) is derived for each of the possible occupations, and the choice is the occupation that produces the highest level of utility, taking into account the cost of migration. Label the level of utility achievable with a cost of migration cm and a time path of prices in nonagriculture p_n, including the wage rate, as $V(p_n, cm)$. Other variables that may affect the decision are suppressed in the notation unless the effect is discussed explicitly. Let p_a label the path of prices and the wage rate in agriculture, then a landless laborer is assumed to migrate from agriculture if

$$V(p_n, cm) > V(p_a). \tag{9.13}$$

The off-farm labor migration is a universal phenomenon that continues over a long time. Why does it take such a long time before it comes to an end? If nonagriculture is more attractive, then all farm labor should leave it at once. A long lag in response cannot be attributed to incorrect expectations or lack of knowledge, because the conditions that trigger the migration have been well known for a long time. To consider this question we have to extend the analysis and bring in another aspect of reality, the heterogeneity of individuals. In any given situation, some people find it to their advantage to move while others prefer to stay.

The most important factor that differentiates labor in the decision to migrate is age. Other things equal, the younger the person is, the larger the integral in equation (9.12). Age also affects the cost of migration. The cost is likely to increase with age, and similarly, the flexibility and the ease of learning skills needed in the new environment are likely to diminish with age. Other attributes specific to the individual include education, gender, and the amount of information available on costs and opportunities. Education may increase the probability of being employed and may also reduce the cost of migration. Another variable that affects the cost of migration is the distance (d), broadly defined, to the new employment opportunities (Ravenstein, 1889).

The act of traveling a physical distance generates migration costs. However, there are also other costs related to distance, including the cost of acquiring information about distant locations, changes in regional languages and culture, lack of extended family support in distant areas, and so on. We should think of distance, broadly defined, as inclusive of these additional factors. The importance of the distance may depend on the state of the development of the economy (y) reflected in the development of the infrastructure, such as roads, motorization, and communication, all of which bring the remote areas closer to labor markets. To summarize, the cost of migration is written as $cm(g, d, y, s)$, where s is the vector of the personal attributes; the signs of the partial derivatives of *cm* are $+$, $+$, $-$, and ambiguous respectively.

Migration takes place in spite of existing unemployment in nonagriculture. This phenomenon was explained by Todaro (1969), who suggested that the decision to migrate takes place according to the expected, rather than the actual, wage rate, where the expected wage is the product of the wage rate and the probability of getting a job (q_n). We should add that the use of expected income as the decision criterion is applicable only to risk-neutral agents. In this case, when the wage differential is high, it pays to migrate even when the probability of getting a job is less than one. The same consideration also applies in evaluating the prospects of staying in agriculture. To sum up, the criterion for off-farm migration of landless labor can be rewritten as

$$V(\underset{+}{w_n}\underset{+}{q_n}, \underset{-}{p_n}, \underset{-}{g}, \underset{-}{cm}(g, d, y, s)) > V(\underset{+}{w_a}\underset{+}{q_a}, \underset{-}{p_a}, \underset{-}{g}), \tag{9.14}$$

where the signs are those of the partial derivatives. Note that in order to write explicitly the expected wage, wq, we differentiate between the wage rate and the prices in equation (9.14). Risk-averse agents will also consider the stability of income. If income in agriculture is less stable than in nonagriculture, migration will take place even if income in both sectors is equal. Clearly the time path of the arguments, or state variables, of the indirect utility functions is unknown. For the purposes of the present discussion, it is assumed that the choice is based on expected values.

Multiperiod Choice: Farm Operators

A similar extension to multiperiod optimization applies also to the decision made by farm operators, where we also have to consider their on-farm opportunities. This calls for a two-stage optimization: the first derives the multiperiod profit function, and the second determines the time allocation to the various employment alternatives along the optimal path. The first stage is discussed briefly in the next chapter. For now, label the maximum present value of profits on the optimal path, derived for the state variables s, as $\pi(p_a, s)$. There is a difference in the role of age between the case of landless labor and that of farm operators. Farmers reaching old age have to quit, and the question of whether they continue to stay on the farm or leave may depend on personal considerations. Thus we may see farmers leaving agriculture at old age. On the other hand, new entrants to agriculture are likely to be young.

As in the case of landless labor, the time path of the state variables is replaced by their expected values. Thus, the criterion for the farm operator to stay in agriculture is

$$V(p_a, s, g) > V(wq, p, g, cm(g, s, d, y)). \tag{9.15}$$

When there is no labor market, w_a is not a component of p_a.

Wages or Income?

So far we have examined off-farm migration from the point of view of returns to labor. This has been the approach that evolved from the Lewis model (Ranis and Fei, 1961; Jorgenson, 1966). This is only a partial view, however, because it does not take into account the multiperiod consequences of the decision to migrate nor does it take into account other sources of income such as returns to capital.

Not only do migrants change their current job, but they change the profile of their stream of future income. It is possible to start at a low wage in a sector with prospects of acquiring skills that will eventually lead to higher income. As early as 1953, Johnson observed that migrant workers do not keep their first low-paying job in nonagriculture for very long and change when the opportunity arises (Johnson, 1953). Furthermore, workers who care about the income prospects of their children may choose to migrate to sectors that offer better education possibilities even if their own income will not change or will even decrease. This was brought up by Tcha (1992), who concluded that families frequently migrated in Korea to take advantage of better schooling and thereby enhance career opportunities for their children. To take this factor into account in the formulation, the welfare of children is introduced into the utility function of parents, and the integral in equation (9.12) should extend over the lifetime of the descendants.

As for nonwage income, it may seem strange to bring up this issue because most workers leaving agriculture are too poor to think in terms of capital income. Whether or not the conclusion accords with the facts is an empirical question, but what can we expect? In the first place, farm operators, as poor as they are, possess capital. More generally, we expect the decision to be based on a comparison of the standard of living in alternative sectors, which is a function of all incomes. As long as labor saves, the capital income is relevant. Moreover, capital income also includes returns to human capital, and as just indicated, the opportunities for such income and for the buildup of human capital may differ across sectors. As the human capital that a person builds up is embodied, it goes with the person, and therefore the return to it is a consideration in the migration decision. It thus appears that when migration involves a major change in the economic environment, such as a change in location rather than just a change of occupation, it is the income rather than wages that should matter. Therefore, in this case we interpret w in the indirect utility functions, such as equations (9.14) and (9.15), as income.

Finally, the use of income as the decision criterion takes into account the Todaro point that migration takes place even where there is unemployment in the urban sector. To conclude, the discussion suggests that the driving force in the migration decision is the income differential rather than wages. However, the choice can be treated as an empirical question.

The Migration Function

Label the indirect utility functions for an individual i evaluated for the conditions in nonagriculture and agriculture by $V_i(n)$ and $V_i(a)$ respectively and introduce an index function h that takes on values of either 0 or 1 to be determined by

$$\left[V_i(n) - V_i(a)\right] h_i(a, n) \geq 0. \tag{9.16}$$

When the bracketed term is positive, the individual benefits from migration, and the function $h(a, n)$ takes on a value of 1; otherwise its value is 0. Labor can also migrate into agriculture and to account for it, the sectoral notation is reversed:

$$\left[V_i(a) - V_i(n)\right] h_i(n, a) \geq 0. \tag{9.17}$$

Summing over the sectoral labor force gives the number of migrants:

$$M(a, n) = \sum_i^{L_a} h_i(a, n) - \sum_i^{L_n} h_i(n, a). \tag{9.18}$$

$M(a, n)$ is a function of the arguments of the indirect utility functions in the two sectors, labeled $\phi(a, n)$. By definition, it is also a function of the size of the labor force in the origin. The number of migrants generated by the same economic environment characterized by (a, n) will vary by the size of the labor force and its sectoral composition. The larger the labor force in agriculture, the larger the migration. The size of the labor force in the destination also matters. Other things equal, the larger the labor market at the destination, the easier it should be for the new migrant to find employment. We introduce the labor force into the equation in such a way as to maintain the constant-returns-to-scale property with respect to the sectoral labor:

$$M(t) = \phi(a, n) L_a(t)^{1-\beta} L_n(t)^{\beta}, \quad \text{for } 0 \leq \beta \leq 1, \tag{9.19}$$

where $L_a(t)$ and $L_n(t)$ are the labor force in agriculture and nonagriculture respectively.

To introduce the functional form used in the empirical analysis, we divide both sides of equation (9.19) by $L_a(t-1)$ and label the migration as a proportion of agricultural labor by $m = M/L_a$, the sectoral labor ratio by $r = L_n/L_a$, and the ratio of sectoral income by $\delta = w_n/w_a$. An interesting reference point for δ is the value at which there would be no migration. A natural value is $\delta = 1$, the point at which sectoral incomes are equal. As discussed below, however, there may be several reasons why this value can differ from 1. To evaluate this issue empirically, we introduce a parameter c to represent the cost of migration and other considerations and assume that migration ceases when $\delta = c$.

In the empirical analysis we use lagged values for the labor force and note that in the absence of migration, $L_a(t)^{(1-\beta)} L_n(t)^{\beta} \equiv L_a(t-1)^{(1-\beta)} L_n(t-1)^{\beta}(1+n)$, where n is the natural rate of growth of the labor force. Incorporating these modifications, we obtain the functional form used in the empirical analysis:

$$m(t) = \beta_0 \left[\delta(t-1) - c\right]^{\beta_1} r(t-1)^{\beta_2} s(t-1)^{\beta_s} (1+n) u, \tag{9.20}$$

where s represents an exogenous state variable. When s is a vector, the expression will be extended to include additional terms. The error term u is written in a multiplicative form, but it can also be thought of as being additive.

Empirical Considerations

In the empirical applications reviewed below, the sectoral income is measured by the average productivity of the labor force. It is computed by dividing sectoral output by the economically active population in that sector. The labor force includes the unemployed, and therefore the ratio of income to the labor force reflects the probability of obtaining employment. The hypothesis is that $\partial m/\partial \delta > 0$.

In the foregoing discussion, we have reviewed many considerations that may affect the decision to migrate which are not introduced explicitly in equation (9.20) and as such may affect the estimate of c. There is a difference in the sectoral cost of living that enters equation (9.14), but it is seldom measured and therefore cannot be assessed. Had the data been available, it would have been possible to deflate the income or wage figures by the respective sectoral cost of living. When this is not done, c is expected to be larger than 1 because the price of food is lower in agriculture, and this compensates for the lower income. There are nonpecuniary considerations, such as the "city lights" effect or the better quality of education in nonagriculture, calling for a lower value of c. On the other hand, it is possible that the quality of life effect should keep people with preferences for country life in agriculture, even if their income is lower than in nonagriculture.

Uncertainty of income in the source and in the destination is another consideration. Other things equal, risk-averse individuals will prefer the sector with the more stable income. To the extent that uncertainty is quantitatively important, its effect on the estimate of c depends on where the income is less stable.

The vector of exogenous variables, s, should include all the variables that are related to the individual's choice. When dealing with aggregates, however, the spread of these variables among individuals is of less significance because it is relatively stable over time, for instance age. Thus it is more difficult to detect their influence.

The dependent variable in the empirical analysis, m, is unobserved and has to be inferred. In all the studies reviewed below m is derived by comparing the rate of growth of agricultural labor with the rate of growth of the total labor force. To repeat the presentation in Chapter 8, with $L_1(t-1)$ denoting the agricultural labor in year $(t-1)$ and n as the rate of population growth, serving as a proxy for the rate of growth of the labor force, it is expected that in the absence of migration, the agricultural labor in year t will be $L_1(t-1)(1+n)$. The difference between this value and the actual labor force is attributed to migration:

$$m = (n+1) - (L_1(t)/L_1(t-1)). \qquad (9.21)$$

Other variables used are described with each of the studies summarized below.

Evidence

Our main interest is the effect of the income differential on the migration rate, because this is the driving force for the dynamics of labor allocation. It is therefore desirable to have a sample with a spread in migration rates and in the income differential. Such a spread is detected in cross-country data. Table 9.2, taken from Larson and Mundlak (1997, table 2), presents summary data for the period 1950–1990 for all countries for which observations on the variables needed to estimate the migration equation were available. There are 66 countries in the first decade and over 90 for the remaining decades. Those added after the first decade were on the whole lower-income countries. The average annual rate of off-farm migration for the whole sample in the period 1950–1990 was about 2.13 percent of the agricultural labor force, and the average rate of growth of the labor force was 2.12 percent. Thus, *on average,* the rate of growth of the labor force was roughly equal to the rate of off-farm migration, which is indicative of the relative stability of the overall labor force in agriculture. The average income differential was 3.80. As Larson and Mundlak (1997, fig. 4) show, there is considerable spread in this variable, particularly at the low-income level. However, the striking fact is the sharp decline of this ratio, as well as of its spread, as income grows. This is consistent with the assumption of factor-price convergence of Chapter 8, which serves as a sufficient condition for the convergence of the sectoral economy to its efficiency frontier.[7]

Cross-country Analysis

The empirical migration equation that was initially estimated from cross-country data was of the form (Mundlak, 1979)

$$\ln(m + c_0) = \beta_0 - \beta_1 \ln(\delta - c) + \beta_2 \ln(L_n/L_a) + \beta_3 s + u. \qquad (9.22)$$

The equation was estimated for a group of 70 countries for the decade 1960–1970. For 17 OECD countries data were available for 1950–1960 and 1960–1970, and this made it possible to check the robustness of the process over two decades for these countries.

Some countries had negative migration values, and therefore a parameter c_0 was introduced to facilitate the presentation of the process by a double-logarithmic function. The study iterated over a small number of values for c_0 and c. The results were not very sensitive to these variations.[8] The income differential (δ) was measured by the ratio of average product per person in the labor force (including the unemployed). In addition, the equation included L_n/L_a, $(1+n)$, and a measure of education. The results are summarized in the first row of Table 9.3. The elasticity of m with respect to δ is about 0.5 and so is also the elasticity with respect to L_n/L_a. The coefficient with respect to $(1+n)$ is large; we return to this below. Education is measured as the proportion of the secondary school enrollment in the relevant-age population. The coefficient is

Table 9.2 Off-farm migration and related data: Selected statistics

Decade	Number of obs.	Migration rate (%)	Growth rate for labor force	Ratio of income	Ratio of sectoral labor	Education of labor force	Share of workers under age 40
1950–1960	66	1.63	1.46	2.67	1.57	3.21	0.60
1960–1970	93	2.16	1.94	4.04	2.02	3.22	0.60
1970–1980	95	2.24	2.62	4.18	3.19	3.61	0.60
1980–1990	98	2.34	2.24	3.98	4.54	4.37	0.62
1950–1990	352	2.13	2.12	3.80	2.96	3.65	0.61
Standard deviation	352	1.78	1.22	4.08	5.80	2.59	0.04

Source: Larson and Mundlak (1997), table 2.

Table 9.3 Migration Equations, Cross-Country Data

Period	Countries	$\delta - c$	L_n/L_a	$(1+n)$	Ed	R^2
1960–1970	70	.511	.489	8.623	.197	.58
		(3.4)	(4.5)	(2.6)		
1950–1970	17	.370	.372	10.88		.431
		(2.0)	(3.8)	(1.4)		
1960–1980	65	.789	.555	−4.03		.572
		(2.9)	(3.6)	(.4)		
1950–1990	98	.36	.20	.32	.29	.53
		(5.8)	(4.0)	(.9)	(4.1)	

Source: Rows 1, 2–Mundlak (1979), chapter 2 and appendix.
Row 3–Kislev and Siegel (1987).
Row 4–Larson and Mundlak (1997).
Note: The reported R^2 is the "adjusted" R^2.
$c = .85$ in regression 2, otherwise $c_0 = 0$, $c = 0$.
Numbers in parentheses are t-ratios.
δ = the ratio of output per participant in the labor force, nonagriculture to agriculture.
L_n/L_a = the ratio of the labor force, nonagriculture to agriculture.
Ed = a measure of education.

positive, but its value is sensitive to the method of estimation.[9] Other measures of education resulted in nonsignificant coefficients.

The results for the OECD countries for the two decades (second row) show somewhat smaller elasticities, about 0.4 for δ and 0.372 for (L_n/L_a). Interestingly, there is no "decade effect," implying that the same regression fitted the data for the two decades equally well.

As indicated above, the computation of migration is based on an assumption regarding the rate of rural population growth. In this analysis, it was assumed to be equal to the overall rate of population growth for the country as a whole. Estimates were also obtained for an alternative measure of migration that allows for higher rates of growth for the rural population.[10] The empirical results were similar, with a somewhat lower value for $E_{m/\delta}$, about 0.32. However, when this method of calculating migration was applied to the OECD countries, the estimated value of $E_{m/\delta}$ increased somewhat.

Several variables that were tried did not prove to be statistically significant. The model assumes CRS in the sectoral labor, and this was tested empirically by adding the nonagricultural labor force as another variable; the assumption was not rejected. An attempt to add an age variable did not yield any significant change, perhaps because of the small spread of this variable in the data. Finally, the rate of expansion of the nonagricultural sector was introduced to measure the expansion in demand for migratory labor; it also was not significant. An explicit treatment of an unemployment variable was not tried for lack of data.

Kislev and Siegel (1987) fitted a similar regression to a group of 65 countries using data for two decades, 1960–1980. Their regression allows for different intercepts for developed and developing countries. They get similar results for the elasticities with respect to δ and L_n/L_a (third row). As in the OECD sample, there is no decade effect, indicating the stability of the process over time.

The study by Larson and Mundlak (1997) is most comprehensive in terms of the data coverage; it uses data for five decades, 1950–1990, for 98 countries for which data are available for at least one decade. The data are summarized in Table 9.2. The empirical equation is the same as equation (9.20), with one exception; the error term is additive, a change that calls for a nonlinear estimation of the parameters. The results appear in the last row of Table 9.3. The results are reported for the same set of variables that appeared in the other studies in order to facilitate a comparison. It also included an age variable that has a coefficient of 0.5 with a t-ratio of 1.2. Note that the coefficient of $\log(1+n)$ is very unstable. The reason is that n is a very small number, 0.02 on average; hence the log of the variable is nearly zero, and the measurement errors dominate the measured variable. Because this is not an important variable for our main interest, no attempt was made to refine the estimate.

In spite of the larger sample that includes more countries over a longer period and a different method of estimation (nonlinear), the results from Larson and Mundlak (1997) are quite similar to those in Mundlak (1979). Here again, a test does not reject the hypothesis of the absence of a decade effect. It thus appears that the results are robust and indicate a stable process.

Other versions of the regression were tried with the following modifications. A continent dummy was introduced, showing a negative effect (lower migration rates) for Africa and Asia. Migration rates were also obtained under different assumptions with respect to the fertility rates in agriculture and nonagriculture. The main conclusions of the analysis were not changed. The introduction of per capita income, as a measure of development, to represent changes in the cost of migration did not change the results. This variable is correlated with most of the explanatory variables, and its effect may be reflected in the coefficients of those variables. Following McMillan and Barkley (1992), variables representing political freedom and civil liberties were also tried, but the results were equivocal. The estimated values were insignificant and were of differing signs (positive for civil liberties and negative for political liberties). Also, unlike results given by McMillan and Barkley, including or excluding the variables had limited effect on the estimated coefficient of the income differential.

Country Studies

The country studies cited here differ somewhat from the cross-country studies. The rate of population growth does not vary much over the time series, and its importance is therefore undetectable empirically. In addition, the ratio of the labor force was sometimes not statistically significant, indicating that variations of the nonagricultural labor force were not affecting migration. Instead, what appears important is a measure of unemployment in nonagriculture. This is a more direct indicator of employment opportunities. This measure, unless indicated otherwise, was obtained by computing the relative decline of the current nonagricultural output from its historical peak. In some cases (Argentina, the United States), land prices were available. They are introduced to the equation to represent, in a summary form, the expected profitability of agriculture.

Argentina. Cavallo and Mundlak (1982) report results for the period 1940–1973. A nonlinear estimation of the equation yields $c_0 = 0.306$ and $c = 0.965$, but not significantly different from 1. The income ratio, δ, was measured as the ratio of the sectoral average labor productivity. The values for income-differential elasticity, $E_{m/\delta}$, varied in the range of 3.5 to 5.4, higher by far than that obtained in the cross-country analysis. Alternative treatments of the basic labor data resulted in somewhat different regressions, but the values for the elasticities were in that range. This is also the case when δ was measured by the wage differential. However, in the latter case, L_n/L_a became nonsignificant. Instead, unemployment in the urban sector became important. The analysis was repeated by Mundlak, Cavallo, and Domenech (1989) for a much longer period, 1913–1984, with similar results. The equation included a measure of unemployment in nonagriculture with a negative effect on migration. A negative effect was also obtained for the price of land. The elasticity with respect to δ was 5.6 and that with respect to land price was −2.5, indicating that an increase in the price of land reduces migration, as expected.

Chile. Coeymans and Mundlak (1993) report results for the period 1962–1982 using a semilogarithmic form of equation (9.20) where m is measured in natural units. The empirical results were better when the income differential, δ, was measured as the ratio of wages in nonagriculture to the average labor productivity in agriculture. An adjustment was made to allow for differences in the cost of living in the two sectors. This adjustment was not important.

Actual unemployment in nonagriculture had a negative effect on migration. Its coefficient was about twice that of δ. Under Todaro's formulation the coefficient should be the same. The result suggests that the migrants gave more weight to the probability of employment than to the income variable. The composition of the labor force was also significant. The elasticity with respect to δ at the median migration rate was 7.

Japan. Mundlak and Strauss (1978) analyzed the Japanese experience for the prewar period of 1911–1940 and the postwar period of 1951–1970. Strong multicollinearity forced a specification with a small number of coefficients. On the whole, the analysis indicates that the income differential variable was important in the postwar period, whereas in the prewar, the rate of growth of the economy was the main determinant of migration. This variable is related to the probability of finding employment in nonagriculture.

Strict restrictions exist on the transfer of land in Japan that are not conducive to migration. A person leaving agriculture is unlikely to recover the intrinsic value of his property. For this reason, it is of interest to obtain insight from micro studies. Arayama (1986, 1989) analyzed in detail the response of the agricultural labor force to market forces. He indicates that the occupational migration from agriculture took several forms:

1. A decline of the farm *household* population from 36 million in 1955 to 23 million in 1980. The corresponding share in the population changed from 41 to 18 percent.
2. A decline in the proportion of farm households that are classified as full-time farmers from 35 percent in 1955 to 13 percent in 1980.
3. A decline in the size of the family in farm households.

United States. Using the same framework as the studies reviewed above, Barkley (1988) presents results for the United States distinguishing between three kinds of farm labor: hired, operators, and family. Two measures of income differentials are examined: the ratio of the sectoral average labor productivity and alternatively the ratio of per capita income in nonagriculture to that in agriculture. The results are qualitatively similar.

The coefficient of the income differential is 0.30, which yields an average elasticity, $E_{m/w} = 2.65$. The values of this elasticity for the different labor types are 6.3 for hired labor, 3.3 for farm operators, and 1.5 for family labor. Thus hired labor is most responsive to changes in income differentials. The elasticity of migration of total labor with respect to land price is about −4, indicating a strong response to the conditions in agriculture. This coefficient is not significant for hired labor, whereas it is the same for farm operators and for family labor.

Unemployment has the correct sign. It is important for hired labor and family labor and unimportant for farm operators, suggesting that the decision to exit the sector is less sensitive to transitory changes. The equation also includes a measure of government payments to farmers, but this variable is not significant. It is likely that such payments are fully capitalized in land values.

Entry and Exit

The foregoing studies do not focus on the subject of the entry and exit of farm operators. This mobility reflects two basic processes. First, farming is largely a family operation, and biological attrition forces people to quit farming. The operation may be continued by their children, but this is a new decision to be taken by different individuals with different managerial qualities. Thus, in a static situation, a certain proportion of the operators will quit. Second, dynamic changes occur in agriculture and in the economy at large; there is a change in the optimal farm size for every level of management.

Table 9.4 presents data on the number of farms in the United States in the period 1850–1990. Although the underlying definitions changed somewhat over time, the trend is clear. The number of farms increased from nearly 1.5 million in 1850 to almost 7 million in 1935 and declined from then on to a level of slightly over 2 million in 1990, a level similar to that of 1860. The situation is similar in Canada. Bollman and Steeves (1982, table II) present data on the number of farm operators for the period 1911–1976. The number (in thousands) increased from 682 in 1911 to 733 in 1941 and declined thereafter, reaching a level of 338 in 1976. These numbers do not fully reflect the magnitude of the traffic. For Canada, "Census farm operators who were continuous farmers in the 1966 to 1976 period constituted only 31 per cent of all Canadian farm operators who had entered, exited from or stayed in agriculture during the period. Indeed, 56 per cent of the total number of Canadian census farm operators had departed by 1976 while 44 percent of the 1976 operators had entered since 1966" (ibid., p. 576). The authors' data also show that there is considerably more traffic in both directions (entry and exit) in low-capital farmers, and the proportion of entrants and exiters declines considerably as the capital value increases. This may be interpreted as indicating that the cost of entry or exit (like the cost of migration) affects the probability of change.

One way to decrease the capital requirement to enter farming is to rent land (and farms). Indeed, renting has become pervasive in many countries. For Canada, "As of 1981, 53.9% of Canada's total farm area . . . were utilized by farmers who were part-owners and part-renters" (Ehrensaft et al., 1984,

Table 9.4 Number of farms, United States, 1850–1990

Year	Number[a]
1850	1,449,073
1860	2,044,077
1870	2,659,985
1880	4,008,907
1890	4,564,641
1900	5,737,372
1910	6,361,502
1920	6,448,343
1925	6,371,640
1930	6,288,648
1935	6,812,350
1940	6,096,799
1945	5,859,169
1950	5,382,162
1954	4,782,416
1960	3,962,520
1965	3,356,170
1970	2,949,140
1975[b]	2,521,420
1980[b]	2,439,510
1985[b]	2,292,530
1990[b]	2,140,420

Source: USDA Agricultural Statistics, 1972, 1977, 1978, 1988, 1990.

Note: The number of farms for the years 1850–1954 excludes Alaska and Hawaii.

a. The definition of a farm prior to 1979 was a place of 10 or more acres having annual sales of agricultural products of $50 or more and places of less than 10 acres that had annual sales of $250 or more (applies to the data prior to 1975).

b. The definition of a farm since 1979 is an establishment that as of June 1 sold or would normally have sold $1000 or more in agricultural products during the year (applies to above data since 1975).

p. 827). There has been a big turnover in land, and thus "32% to 35% of all land 'owned by the operator' was released in a five year period" (ibid.). The data also show that some older farmers at the top end of the size scale continue to expand their operation rather than stabilizing or contracting it (ibid.). The implication is that good managers expand at the expense of inferior ones, at all ages.

Micro studies attempt to shed more light on the process by characterizing the attributes of the entrants and exiters. Probably due to lack of income data, success in farming does not appear as an explanatory variable, and as such, these studies are not comparable to the aggregate studies reviewed above. The lack of income data may also account for the very low predictive power of these studies.[11] Nevertheless, they highlight some points. The most important one is the role of age. Kimhi and Bollman compare the experience of Canada and Israel and state that "the effect of age is to decrease the exit tendency at younger ages and increase it at older ages. This is true in both countries" (Kimhi and Bollman, 1997, p. 13). Similar results are reported by Weiss (1996) for the upper-Austrian farm sector.

The discussion has concentrated on the role of heterogeneity among individuals; in addition there is a heterogeneity in situations. An important consideration is the quality of the farm balance sheet. Historical decisions taken in the face of uncertainty may result in high liabilities relative to income flow. Such farms are very vulnerable to adverse shocks in agriculture and may be forced to leave if they cannot meet their current obligations. Past decisions might have been completely rational, but *ex post* turned out to be unfortunate.

Summary of the Empirical Results

The foregoing results substantiate the empirical validity of the dynamic process outlined in Chapter 8. The income differential is the driving force of labor migration, and the rate of migration is determined by the magnitude of the gap. The income-differential elasticities are higher in the country than in the cross-country studies. This difference may reflect the larger measurement error expected to be present in the cross-country data. Measurement errors tend to bias the estimate downward. Sectoral labor is not measured with the same precision in the various countries. To the extent that some of this error is country specific, it does not affect the time-series study of a particular country as much as the cross-country study.

Migration tends to disappear when the average income differential vanishes. Thus all the arguments given in the literature, some of which are reviewed above, that suggest a permanent income differential are not supported by the empirical results. What does a vanishing income differential imply for the intersectoral wage differential? The answer depends on the sectoral factor share of labor. As a matter of definition we can write

$$\frac{w_n}{w_a} = \frac{S_{Ln}}{S_{La}} \frac{y_n/L_n}{y_a/L_a}, \tag{9.23}$$

where S_{Lj} is the labor share in the output of sector j. As shown by Larson and Mundlak (1997), the ratio of the sectoral average productivity declines drastically with a rise of income, and this implies a closure of the wage gap also. If that were not the case, the labor share in agriculture would have to tend to zero, and this is inconsistent with the data. As we shall see in the discussion on empirical production functions, the labor share in agriculture has declined somewhat in the process of growth, but the change is not anywhere near the decline in the income ratio. We can then conclude this discussion by noting that the assumption on factor-price convergence made in Chapter 8 is consistent with the data, and it is achieved by labor allocation through off-farm migration.

There is another issue; will the wage gap close completely? The answer is no, unless the labor shares are the same in the two sectors. This follows from the convergence to no sectoral income difference and equation (9.23). This is summarized by

PROPERTY 9.1 Intersectoral income equality will result in wage equality only when the two sectors have equal labor shares. When the labor share in agriculture is lower than in nonagriculture, wages in agriculture will tend to be lower than in nonagriculture.

This interesting result indicates that an economy reaches an equilibrium where factor costs are not equal across sectors. The reason for this inequality is that agricultural labor receives nonlabor income that compensates for the lower wages as well as the migration cost. This is an indication that the dynamic equilibrium may be different from the static equilibrium if shifting between occupations involves migration or, more generally, transaction costs.

There are several sources of income in agriculture that cannot be fully transferred with migration. One is returns to agriculture-specific human capital that cannot be adequately marketed in nonagriculture. A second is returns to land and the specific physical capital in agriculture. In the Larson-Mundlak study, a negative continent effect on migration was found for Africa and Asia. In Africa, the lack of land titles makes it difficult to sell land at a price that reflects its economic value to the operators. Asia may have a similar problem that makes it difficult to cash in the full value of land. Feder et al. (1988) state that the owners of 50 percent of the privately held land in Thailand have certificates that are not good as collateral nor can they be legally transferred. In some countries, such as Japan, there are institutional constraints on the sale of farm land.

The possibility of a permanent wage differential does not change the convergence process of the economy to the frontier, but rather modifies it. Of course, when the market correctly evaluates all the farm assets and there are no restrictions on the sale of land, and if the migration cost becomes relatively small, the reasons for the inequality will disappear. Investments made in infrastructure, transportation, and communication greatly reduce the cost of migration and thereby contribute to the disappearance of wage inequality.

"Unlimited Supplies of Labor"

In 1954 Arthur Lewis published his article "Economic Development with Unlimited Supplies of Labor," which had a considerable impact on the development literature (see Ranis and Fei, 1961, and Jorgenson, 1961). The article sought to provide a theory of growth for poor countries. The duality of these countries consists of a traditional and a capitalistic sector; the first produces only for consumption and thereby generates no surplus, whereas the second produces only for profits, which are the source of savings and therefore capital accumulation. As the latter sector grows, total savings and therefore capital stocks grow. The dynamics of the system draw labor from the traditional to the capitalistic sector. Lewis's postulate was that such a migration is conducted at a constant wage, determined by a social convention. This was interpreted as a perfectly elastic labor supply.

The discussion of the labor supply in the article left room for controversies. Sen (1966) and others examined forms of household behavior pertinent to the dualistic economy. This literature was reviewed and interpreted by Findlay (1982), whose analysis benefited from a perspective gained during the three decades that had elapsed, years that saw both the economic development of many less-developed countries and various developments in economics.

The dichotomy of the Lewis economy is somewhat different from the sectoral dichotomy followed here. The traditional sector is not identical with agriculture and consists of other occupations as well. Agriculture constitutes the major activity in the traditional sector in the early stage of development, however, and therefore the literature uses examples from agriculture. The essence of the thesis is that labor migrates from the traditional to the capitalistic sector. In this sense, our model is in the spirit of this hypothesis. However, we have said nothing about unlimited labor supply. It thus appears that the assumption of unlimited supply is not essential for generating a growth process in a dual economy. Still, the attempt to rationalize it and the discussion that it generated justifies a brief examination.

As indicated above, the labor supply under investigation is that faced by the modern sector. It is therefore equal to the excess supply of the traditional sector. The empirical evidence in the background is that of England in the period 1780–1840, where the industrial revolution took place at a virtually constant real wage. To place this observation within the right perspective, we note that in drawing evidence from time-series data on the labor force, it is important to take account of the increase in the labor force. Thus one can think of a completely stagnant traditional sector with a population growth rate n and migration rate m. When $m = n$, the labor force in the modern sector will increase constantly over time at a given wage rate as determined in the stagnant traditional sector. This does not imply that at any point in time one can draw any arbitrary quantity of labor at a constant wage. In fact, the strong empirical message obtained from the migration equation indicates that this is not the case.

Although the assumption of perfectly elastic labor supply is not necessary, the discussions to justify it actually have served to refute it. Lewis believed in surplus labor in the traditional sector in the sense that the number of people in the labor force can be reduced without affecting the output. On the surface this implies that the marginal productivity of labor is zero, but this is not what Lewis had in mind. The decision unit for labor supply is the family. When a member migrates to the other sector, the other members of the family "will be willing to work harder in these circumstances" (Lewis, 1954, p. 141). This very statement indicates, first, that the marginal productivity of labor is not zero, and second, that in order to work harder the individuals have to be compensated, which means an upward-sloping labor supply. This simple justification makes it clear that the problem can be discussed within the neoclassical framework of labor supply.

Is there any reason for the wage rate in the traditional sector to remain constant? Apparently the phenomenon was related to situations where the average productivity of labor in agriculture is at its maximum, that is, at the point of equality to the marginal labor productivity. Under those circumstances people can be drawn out of agriculture without affecting the wage rate by simply varying the quantity of land under cultivation. This approach has several difficulties. First, the traditional sector, in Lewis's view, is not identical with agriculture. Second, this kind of behavior, as Findlay indicates, lacks any empirical evidence. Perhaps the United States in the days of the moving western frontier could serve as an example. This, of course, does not make the argument sufficiently general as required by the assumed generality of the theory itself. Furthermore, it requires a great deal of imagination to think of U.S. agriculture in the days of the moving frontier as lacking the motive of profit maximization.

Finally, as Findlay indicates, development with constant wages is not in line with the data, which show increasing wages. He does suggest, however, that increasing wages may reflect returns to human capital and not to unskilled labor. This may be the case. It may also reflect an increase in nonhuman capital.

Recall, though, that the traditional sector produces for consumption and is not investing, and thus this cannot be good supporting evidence for the theory. Indeed, there is an increase in the capital-labor ratio, both physical and human, as well as in technology and infrastructure. To accommodate all this, the model has to be broadened, as indeed has been attempted here.

What then remains of the argument is its essential part, that given the opportunity, there will be intersectoral labor migration. This does not require a constant wage or horizontal labor supply. In fact, the evidence presented above indicates that the rate of flow depends on the intersectoral income differential–this refutes the hypothesis of horizontal labor supply.

Appendix 9A. The Labor Supply by Occupation: A Formal Analysis

The labor allocation among occupations can be formulated as a choice of technique problem. Following the discussion in the chapter, and without a loss of generality, we assume that there are two possible techniques, and that the problem is to allocate total time to them and to leisure. Let L_1 and L_2 be the labor supply to the two alternatives; then leisure is $x_2 = T - L_1 - L_2$. The optimization is performed in two stages. In the first stage, the income in each alternative is maximized conditional on the amount of labor allocated to this alternative; in the second stage, the allocation of labor to the various alternatives is determined. Denote the net income derived from the jth alternative as $\pi_j(L_j) - c_j I_j$, where c_j is the cost, independent of the level of employment, associated with the jth alternative, I_j is an index function that takes on a value of 1 if $L_j > 0$ and a value of 0 if $L_j = 0$. When the jth alternative is working for wages, $\pi_j(L_j) = w_j L_j$. In the case of a farm operator, $\pi_j(L_j)$ is the restricted profit function, concentrated on L_j. In the special, but unlikely, case of no difference between own and hired labor, $\pi_j(L_j)$ is the same as working for wages.

The optimization problem calls for a choice of c (consumption), L_1, and L_2 so as to maximize

$$\mathcal{L}(c, L_1, L_2, \mu_1, \ldots \mu_5) = u(c, T - L_1 - L_2) - \mu_1\{c - [\sum_j (\pi_j(L_j) - c_j I_j] + a\}$$

$$- \mu_2(-L_1) - \mu_3(-L_2) - \mu_4[c_1 I_1 - \pi_1(L_1)] - \mu_5[c_2 I_2 - \pi_2(L_2)].$$

The constraints are nonpositive, and the Lagrange multipliers are nonnegative. Let u_j be the partial derivatives with respect to the jth argument of u and write the first-order conditions

(a) $[u_1 - \mu_1]c = 0.$

(b) $[\mu_1\pi_1' + \mu_2 + \mu_4\pi_1' - u_2]L_1 = 0.$

(c) $[\mu_1\pi_2' + \mu_3 + \mu_5\pi_2' - u_2]L_2 = 0.$

(d) $\{c - [\sum(\pi_j(L_j) - c_j I_j) + a]\}\mu_1 = 0.$

(e) $L_1\mu_2 = 0.$

(f) $L_2\mu_3 = 0.$

(g) $[c_1 I_1 - \pi_1(L_1)]\mu_4 = 0.$

(h) $[c_2 I_2 - \pi_2(L_2)]\mu_5 = 0.$

Under the assumption that all goods, including leisure, are desirable, $c > 0$; therefore by (a), $u_1 = \mu_1$, implying that $\mu_1 > 0$, and thus by (d), the budget constraint is binding. This is assumed to be the case throughout the discussion.

There are two leading cases of employment alternatives: specialization in one occupation and diversification. Without a loss of generality, assume that in both cases, $L_1 > 0$. This implies that $\mu_2 = 0$ (by e) and $\mu_4 = 0$ (by g). Then from (b), $u_2 = \mu_1\pi_1'$, indicating the equality of the marginal productivity of labor and the marginal utility of leisure (reservation wage), both measured in terms of the units of the consumption good. If the first employment alternative is joining the labor market, $\pi_1 = w_1 L_1$ and $\pi_1' = w_1$. In this case, the reservation wage is equal to the market wage. Because $L_1 > 0$, $I_1 = 1$, and the budget is net of the fixed cost associated with this occupation. There are two possible reasons for specialization: first, the fixed cost is not covered in the second occupation. This case violates the constraint in (h), and it is ruled out. In the second case the marginal labor productivity in the two employment alternatives differs. As $L_2 = 0$, $\mu_3 > 0$ and because the fixed cost is covered, $\mu_5 = 0$. Then substitute $u_2 = \mu_1\pi_1'$ from (b) in the bracketed term in (c) to obtain

$$\pi_1' - \pi_2' > \mu_3/\mu_1 > 0$$

so that the marginal productivity of labor in occupation 2 is below that of occupation 1, and therefore labor is specializing in occupation 1.

Under diversification, or coexistence, of occupations, $L_2 > 0$, hence, $\mu_3 = \mu_5 = 0$ (f, h) and $\pi_1' = \pi_2'$. If the two alternatives are working for wages, then this equality does not hold, except for the special case of equal wages. Consequently, diversification requires that at least for one occupation, π will be nonlinear in the labor input. This is the case of part-time farming.

10

The Dynamics of Resource Allocation: Capital

Although capital is a key variable for understanding the dynamics of agriculture, there is very little information on its magnitude, composition, or growth. This information is not contained in any of the international data sets, nor is it reported in the national statistics of many countries. To overcome this shortcoming, Crego et al. (1998) took a first step by assembling in a systematic way all the readily available information to construct an agricultural capital series for 58 countries. It is expected that the recognition of the importance of this information will grow, and consequently the data coverage will be broadened and refined. What follows is a review of the available evidence as a background for subsequent discussion.

National accounts ordinarily contain information on total investment (capital formation). The information on the sectoral composition of investment is more scarce. Some countries report investment in agriculture as a component of "fixed investment." It seems to cover only investment based on purchases from other sectors, including imports, and therefore we refer to it as investment of nonagricultural origin. This investment is largely in structures and equipment (SE). The data are deflated to allow for changes in the general price level, but they reflect changes in the relative prices, unless indicated otherwise. The details of the data construction and the sources are presented in Crego et al. (1998) and supplemented in Larson et al. (1999).

The distribution of the fixed investment–output ratio in agriculture is presented in Figure 10.1. The medians of the distributions for 1970 and 1990 are 15.6 and 13.4 percent respectively (see Table 10.1).[1] The corresponding figures for the economy as a whole are in the range of 19–20 percent. The corresponding values for manufacturing are 18.7 and 16.5 percent respectively.

The spread of the distributions can be measured by the ratio of the ninth to the first decile. From the values of the deciles presented in Table 10.1, it may be seen that the spread is considerably larger in agriculture. In 1970, for instance, this ratio was 13.2 (39.5/3.0) for agriculture as compared with 2.0 (26.8/13.2) for the economy as a whole and for manufacturing. The values for 1990 show

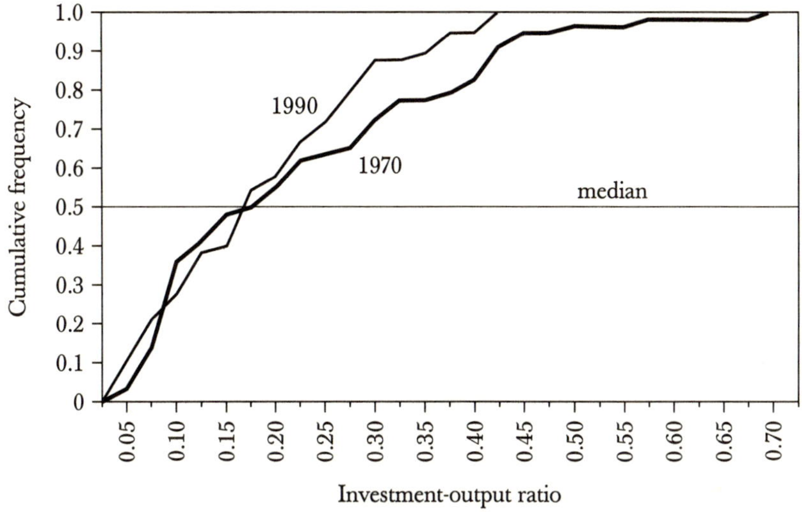

Figure 10.1 Agriculture: Fixed investment-output ratio (1990 US$), 58 countries, 1970–1990. (From Mundlak, 1999, fig. 7. Figures 10.1–10.5 are based on data in Crego, 1998.)

Table 10.1 Fixed investment: Summary data

Variable	Period	Decile: First	Decile: Median	Decile: Ninth
	Investment-output ratio (percent)			
Economy	1970	13.2	19.0	26.8
	1990	15.3	19.8	26.1
Agriculture	1970	3.0	15.6	39.5
	1990	2.5	13.4	31.6
Manufacturing	1970	12.7	18.7	25.4
	1990	10.9	16.5	27.2
	Share of sectoral investment in total investment (percent)			
Agriculture	1970	3.4	7.4	15.3
	1990	1.8	4.6	11.5
Manufacturing	1970	12.7	18.7	26.7
	1990	9.6	16.1	23.6
	Investment: Manufacturing-agriculture ratio			
	1970	1.2	2.5	5.5
	1990	1.6	3.0	9.3

Source: Based on data from Crego et al. 1998.

Table 10.2 Fixed-capital stock: Summary data

Variable		Decile First	Decile Median	Decile Ninth
	Share of total stock (percent)			
Agriculture	1970	3.4	9.1	17.3
	1990	2.4	5.6	12.8
Manufacturing	1970	10.7	15.7	23.4
	1990	8.4	13.3	22.6
	Capital-output ratio			
Economy	1970	1.4	1.8	2.6
	1990	1.9	2.4	3.1
Agriculture	1970	0.3	1.4	3.0
	1990	0.5	1.8	4.8
Manufacturing	1970	1.0	1.4	2.3
	1990	0.9	1.5	2.6
	Capital stock: Manufacturing-agriculture ratio			
	1970	0.9	1.7	3.8
	1990	1.2	2.3	4.8

Source: Based on data from Crego et al. 1998.
Note: 1970 and 1990 stand for the averages of the ratios for the periods 1967–1974 and 1985–1992 respectively.

a similar pattern, although the spread in agriculture is smaller. It is possible that the agricultural data are more contaminated with errors than the other data. However, the difference between the spread in the share of agriculture and manufacturing in the total capital stock, reported in Table 10.2, is by far smaller, so the data cannot be the only culprit responsible for the large spread in the fixed investment–output ratio. We may interpret this spread as evidence of large cross-country variability in the capital requirement of the techniques implemented in agriculture as compared with other sectors.

As shown in the second panel of Table 10.1, agriculture accounts for a much smaller share of total fixed investment than manufacturing, but the shares of both sectors declined over the two decades. The median share in agriculture declined from 7.4 to 4.6 percent, as compared with a decline from 18.7 to 16.1 percent in manufacturing. The decline is universal, as shown in Figure 10.2, where nearly the entire distribution of agricultural share in total fixed investment is shifted to the left. A similar shift took place in manufacturing. This is indicative of the rise in the relative importance of services, the income

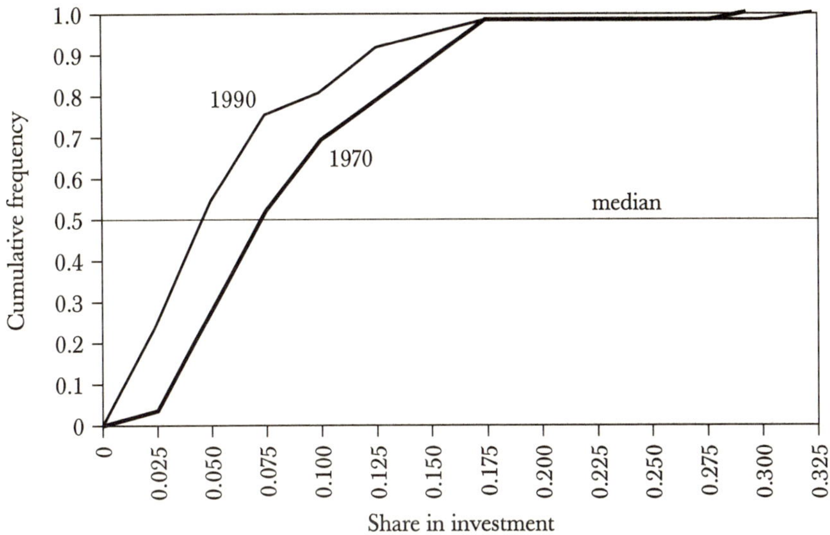

Figure 10.2 Share of agriculture in total fixed investment (1990 US$): 58 countries, 1970–1990. (From Mundlak, 1999, fig. 8.)

elastic sector. The decline is stronger in agriculture, the income inelastic sector, and as shown in the third section of Table 10.1, the median ratio of fixed investment in manufacturing to that in agriculture increased from 2.5 to 3.0 over the two decades.

The share of agriculture in investment determines its share in capital, and as shown in Figure 10.3, the entire distribution of agricultural share in fixed capital in 1990 is to the left of that in 1970. Table 10.2 shows that the median share of agriculture in the total fixed-capital stock declined from 9.1 percent in 1970 to 5.6 percent in 1990. At the same time the median share of manufacturing capital declined from 15.7 to 13.3 percent. These findings are consistent with the observation that the relative importance of agriculture and manufacturing, referred to more generally as goods–in contrast to services–is declining with time. However, as in the case of fixed investment, there is a larger spread in the distribution of the fixed-capital stock in agriculture, where the ratio of the ninth to the first percentile is on the order of magnitude of 5 as compared to 2–3 for manufacturing.

How are these trends reflected in technology? We will examine this question in detail in Chapter 13, but we can obtain some insight by observing capital-output ratios and changes in capital-labor ratios. First, the median share of agriculture in the labor force in 1990 (Figure 1.14) was 30 percent, whereas

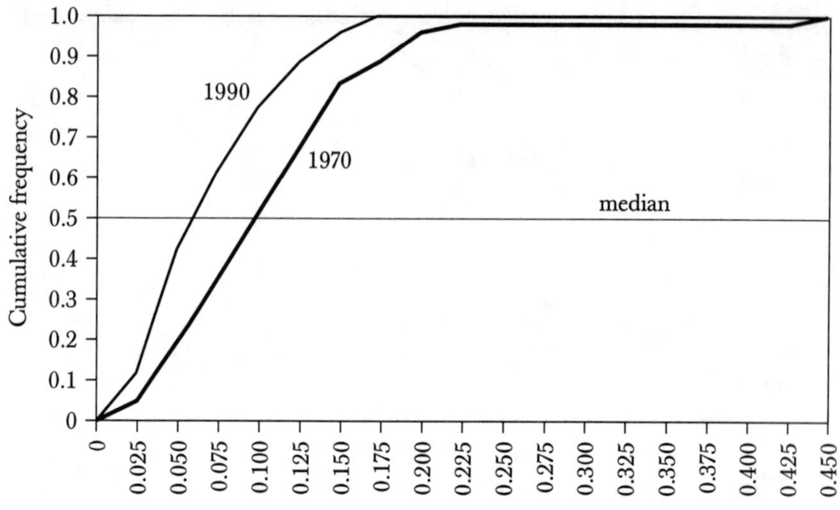

Figure 10.3 Share of agriculture in total fixed capital (1990 US$): 58 countries, 1970–1990.

its share in the fixed-capital stock was only 5.6 percent. This is a clear indication that agriculture is labor intensive by direct measure. Indeed, the capital figures refer to a smaller group of countries, and fixed capital is only one component of total capital, but these qualifications are not sufficiently important to change this conclusion. Second, the second section of Table 10.2 summarizes the distribution of sectoral fixed capital–output ratios. In a way of generalization, the lowest median values are observed in manufacturing, and the economy as a whole shows the highest values. Agriculture underwent capital deepening between 1970 and 1990, as indicated by the relative increase in the median of the capital-output ratios between these two periods. This is reflected clearly by the complete shift to the right of the distribution of the fixed capital–output ratio in agriculture, as seen in Figure 10.4. Again, there is a much larger spread in the fixed capital–output ratio in agriculture, where the ratio of the ninth to first percentile is around 10 as compared with under 2 for the economy and 3 for manufacturing.

The distributions of the growth rates for some of the variables are summarized in Table 10.3. Fixed-capital stock grew faster in the economy as a whole than in either manufacturing or agriculture. Consequently, as previously mentioned, the shares of these two sectors in the total fixed-capital stock declined between 1970 and 1990. Also, fixed capital grew at a higher rate than did the labor force. This is observed in the changes in the capital-labor ratio, as

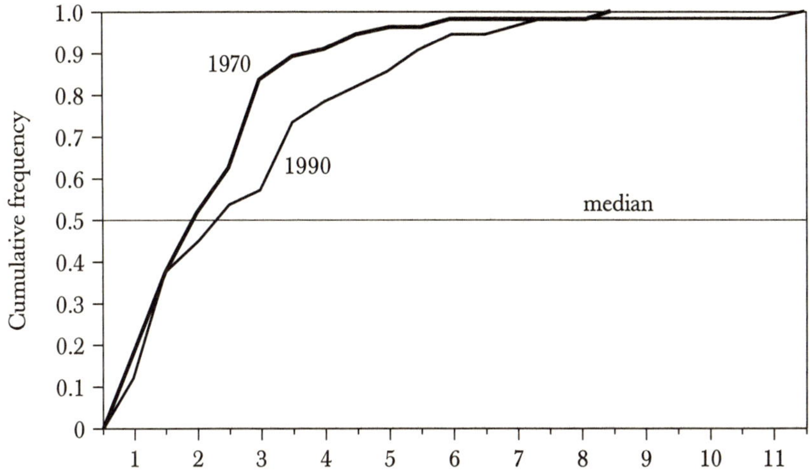

Figure 10.4 Agriculture: Fixed capital–output ratio (1990 US$): 56 countries, 1970–1990. (From Mundlak, 1999, fig. 9.)

can be seen in Figure 10.5. The median growth of the capital-labor ratio was 2.2 percent for the economy as a whole and 2.9 percent for agriculture. The growth was negative in only one-eighth and one-fourth of the sample countries for the economy and for agriculture respectively. This reflects the decline in agricultural labor. As shown in Figure 1.14, the median share of agriculture in the total labor force in 148 countries declined from 70 percent in 1950 to 30 percent in 1990.

The data on fixed investment does not cover investment of agricultural origin, such as in livestock and orchards. To fill this gap, Crego et al. (1998) used FAO data on orchards and livestock to build a capital series for these two major components of agricultural investment. The total value of this investment in some countries is close to that of fixed capital. Taking this into account, it appears that the capital deepening in agriculture considerably exceeded that in the economy as a whole.

Keeping in mind the preliminary nature of these data, we can summarize the evidence:

- The share of agriculture in total fixed investment is smaller than its shares in total output and in the labor force, as reported in Chapter 1.
- The same is true for the share of agriculture in the total fixed-capital stock. Thus the direct measure of factor intensity indicates that agriculture is labor intensive.

Table 10.3 Fixed capital and related variables–annual growth rates (percent), 1967–1992: Summary data

Variable	Decile		
	First	Median	Ninth
	Capital stock		
Economy	1.8	4.6	9.9
Agriculture	−0.6	2.1	8.7
Manufacturing	0.8	4.1	9.5
	Ratio of capital stocks		
Agric./Total	−4.9	−2.1	0.6
Mfg./Total	−2.9	−0.9	1.6
Mfg./Agric.	−2.2	1.8	4.8
	Capital-output ratio		
Economy	−0.3	1.3	3.0
Agriculture	−1.7	1.6	4.9
Manufacturing	−2.1	0.5	2.4
	Capital-labor ratio		
Economy	−0.6	2.2	7.9
Agriculture	−2.6	2.9	8.5

Source: Based on data from Crego et al. 1998.

Note: The growth rates were calculated from a semilogarithmic regression on time for the period 1967–1992, except for the capital-labor ratios where the period is 1967–1990 (due to lack of labor data).

- This is also consistent with the fact that the fixed capital–output ratio in agriculture is smaller than that for the economy as a whole.
- The share of agriculture in total fixed investment has been declining since 1970, the first year reviewed here.
- As in agriculture, there is a decline in the share of manufacturing in total investment and the capital stock. This decline indicates that other sectors, probably services, have attracted increasing shares of investment.
- In the study period, the capital-output ratio increased in agriculture and in the economy as a whole, indicating capital deepening.
- In most countries the capital-labor ratio has grown over time in the economy as a whole and in agriculture.

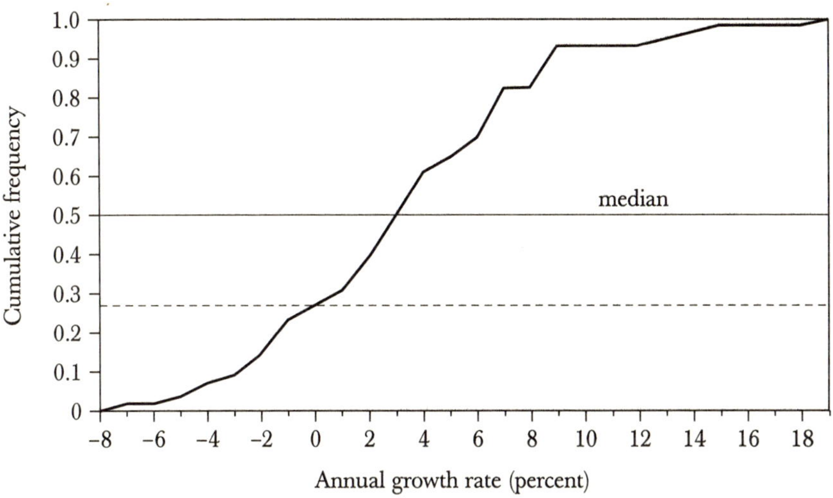

Figure 10.5 Agriculture: Rate of growth of fixed capital–labor ratio, 56 countries, 1967–1990. (From Mundlak, 1999, fig. 10.)

- In general, the distributions of the various measures of investment and capital show a much larger spread in agriculture than in manufacturing or in the rest of the economy.

How can we account for the evidence summarized above? These developments have taken place in response to changes in the economic environment, and it is the purpose of the empirical analysis to unveil the connection between the various elements of the economic environment and investment. The discussion in Chapters 4–6 provides a framework for thinking about the response of input demand to changes in the economic environment. Such changes generate expansion and substitution effects. The tendency toward decline in the share of agriculture in total fixed investment indicates that the expansion effect is dominating, because agriculture is the income inelastic sector. On the other hand, nonagriculture net of manufacturing, to be referred to as services, is the income elastic sector, and the growth of its share in investment is the other side of the expansion effect. Similarly, an examination of the components of investment that are not shown here indicates a growth in components such as livestock and orchards, which also reflects demand expansion. The growth of other components of investment, such as machines, reflects changes in technology and factor supply. The growth of the capital-labor ratio in agriculture to a large extent reflects off-farm migration. The rise in the capital-output ratio indicates a shift to more capital-intensive techniques. The larger spread in the measures of agricultural investment, as compared with the economy as a whole, suggests that there is a much larger spread in the implemented techniques in agriculture than in the rest of the economy.

All these hypotheses are consistent with our discussion but nevertheless should be supported and quantified empirically to shed light on the relative importance of the various determinants. With this background, it is surprising that there is very little published work on investment behavior in agriculture. What follows therefore reviews the work in nonagriculture with an emphasis on general aspects of the empirical analysis of investment. This will provide the framework for evaluating the few results to be presented here as well as for future work. The implications of the evidence on investment are discussed in subsequent chapters.

Initially, the empirical analysis of investment was inspired by comparative statics analysis of capital demand, which highlighted the long-term effects of the economic environment on such demand. This framework served for a long time as the workhorse for deriving empirical investment functions. However, investment is a key variable in the study of the variability of output, and in this context, it is the timing of investment that matters. Thus, to confront these functions with the data, a dynamic behavior had to be specified. Initially this was done by superimposing a distributive lag structure on the model to account for the gradual closure of the gap between the actual and the desired capital stock. However it has not been insightful to impose an arbitrary adjustment process, and models with an endogenous adjustment process have been developed. The driving force in these models is the adjustment cost.

Capital Demand

The discussion in Chapter 7 provides the framework for thinking about capital demand at the economy level. In a closed economy, the optimal path of capital is determined jointly with the path of consumption. Capital formation is equal to foregone consumption, namely savings. This connection between the decision on consumption and investment takes a different form in an open economy, where domestic investment can be financed by foreign savings and domestic savings can be invested abroad. The decision on where to invest is affected by the relative profitability of the investment, various forms of risk, and similar considerations. The implication for empirical analysis is that we can study investment behavior separately from savings decisions. Nevertheless, we still maintain the primary feature of the analysis–that investment demand is derived from the demand for capital (Haavelmo, 1960).

Investment involves a transfer of resources from the present to the future. How far ahead is the future? It can be a few months, as in stored grains or working capital (the cost of inputs in production). However, the main economic questions related to growth, as well as measurement problems, are concerned with investment in durable goods. A building lasts for many years, and it is indivisible in time so that it is impossible to obtain the building at a prorated cost for a shorter period. A firm can sometimes rent, rather than acquire, a capital good for a period of time, but this option is not available to the economy as a whole because someone must possess the good. For this reason, the possibility of rental is ignored here.

Firms invest because they expect discounted future returns on the investment to be higher than its cost. As such, a decision to invest requires an evaluation of the profitability of the investment over its lifetime. Since future values of prices and technology are unknown, they are replaced with expectations. The treatment of expectation is a prominent subject in the econometrics of investment, but its importance should be placed in perspective. The foregoing empirical review indicates that when output expands so does the capital stock. The instant at which firms anticipate the growth is an important component of their investment decision. When demand is growing, however, firms will realize it sooner or later. Of course, firms may overreact and invest more than is justified by the demand expansion–and in this case they will correct for it in future decisions.

To sharpen this point, it is useful to distinguish between two aspects of the empirical analysis of investment, growth and variability. Growth concerns the dependence of investment on the fundamentals, such as technology, factor supply, and product demand, whereas variability refers to the timing of investment. This is a difficult distinction to make in empirical analysis, but it is a useful one to make in our attempt to interpret the data. Our discussion begins with the growth aspects, and for this purpose it abstracts from uncertainty and examines the simpler case of a deterministic world. In this world we get a solution for the desired capital stock as a function of the economic environment. The model provides a framework to review discussions in the literature pertinent to our purpose with an emphasis on the role of prices, technology, output, and scale economy. The underlying theory is micro in nature, but the empirical work is applied mostly to aggregate data at the industry or economy level. The shift to an aggregate level requires us to consider constraints faced by the industry, such as positively sloped factor supply. Such an extension is of specific interest for the analysis of the intersectoral allocation of investment.

The analysis generates the investment demand, and dynamic adjustment is superimposed on the model. We then consider examples of empirical work from agriculture.

It is a matter of fact that it usually takes time to close the gap between desired and actual capital stock, and models differ in the way that they account for this pattern of adjustment. Chirinko (1993) classifies the approaches according to whether the dynamics are exogenous or endogenous. Models with exogenous dynamics impose a gradual closure of the gap. This approach, initiated by Koyck (1954), dominated work in the 1950s and 1960s. On the other hand, models with endogenous dynamics derive the dynamics endogenously from the optimization problem of the firm. The trigger for the dynamics in these models is the cost of adjustment, developed by Eisner and Strotz (1963), Lucas (1967), Gould (1968), and Treadway (1969), to be discussed below. This approach is attractive because the dynamics are derived rather than imposed arbitrarily. The derivation is based on a single element, however, and ignores the various considerations discussed in earlier work which may be prominent in the decision of timing.

There is a more fundamental dichotomy related to the dependent variable of the empirical analysis. The choice is between the explanation of the difference in the *actual* or the *optimal* capital stock. The first is intended to explain the changes in the data, and the second focuses on the changes in our perception of the capital stock on the optimal path. The problem with the second approach is that the optimal values are unobservable, so regardless of the good intentions, at the end of the day the analysis is geared to explain the variability in the data.

The Firm Problem

It is postulated that the competitive firm chooses inputs that affect the flow of present and future profits with the objective of maximizing its present value. We consider here a simple case where a single output, Y, is produced with capital, K, and a nondurable input, say labor, L, that can be hired at the ongoing wage rate, $w(t)$, using a concave and twice differentiable production function, $Y = F(K, L, \tau)$, where τ represents technology. The various variables are functions of time, and the income flow at time t is

$$R_t = F(K_t, L_t, \tau_t) - c(I_t) - w_t L_t - q_t I_t. \tag{10.1}$$

Income (R) and factor prices are measured in units of output, q and w are the real price of the investment good (I) and the wage rate, respectively, and $c(I)$

is the real cost of adjustment. The underlying idea behind the adjustment cost is that the marginal cost of investment increases as a function of the investment rate, and hence if the firm acts too fast this cost will be excessively high. Various aspects of this concept are discussed in what follows. The logic of the concept calls for expressing the adjustment cost as a function of gross investment and to normalize the investment by a measure of the firm size, say by K. The function is presumably increasing in the ratio I/K, and the cost is measured in terms of output.

Let r be the interest rate, $\beta = (1+r)^{-1}$ is the discount factor, and the investment in period j is $I_j = K_{j+1} - (1-d)K_j$, where K_j is the capital stock at the beginning of period j and d is the depreciation rate of capital. The optimization problem is to select the time path of inputs $\{L_j, K_j\}$ so as to maximize the expected value of the firm at the base period, 0,

$$V_0 \equiv \max_{K_{j+1}, L_j} E_0 \sum_{j=0}^{\infty} \beta^j \{R_j - \lambda[I_j - (K_{j+1} - (1-d)K_j)]\}, \qquad (10.2)$$

subject to the initial value K_0. The expectation, E_0, is taken over the future values of prices and technology whose distribution is unknown.

To obtain the first-order conditions we first differentiate (10.2) with respect to L_j:

$$E\{\frac{\partial F(\cdot)}{\partial L_j} - w_j\} = 0 \qquad (10.3)$$

By assumption, the employment at any time j has no effect on the revenue in subsequent periods, and therefore its level is determined by equating the expected value of the marginal productivity to that of the real wage in each period, as shown by equation (10.3). Consequently, the optimization problem can be solved in steps. First, determine for each period the optimal level L_j as a function of prices and K_j, substitute the result in the production function to obtain the function, $F(K_j, s_j)$, where $s_j \equiv (\tau_j, w_j, q_j, r, d, c)$ is the vector of the state variables. The second stage consists of solving

$$\begin{aligned} \max_{K_{j+1}} E_0 \sum_{j=0}^{\infty} \beta^j \{F(K_j, s_j) - q_j I_j - c(I_j, K_j) \\ - \lambda[I_j - (K_{j+1} - (1-d)K_j)]\} \end{aligned} \qquad (10.4)$$

Differentiate (10.4) with respect to K_{j+1} and rearrange the result to obtain

$$E_0\{\beta[F_K(j+1) - c_K(j+1)] - [c_I(j) - hc_I(j+1)] - [q_j - hq_{j+1}]\} = 0, \tag{10.5}$$

where we use the notation $F(K_j, s_j) \equiv F(j)$ and similarly for other functions, $h \equiv (1-d)\beta < 1$, and the subscripts K and I indicate the direction of the partial derivatives of the functions in question. The optimal path is obtained by solving (10.5) subject to the initial capital stock, K_0, and the transversality condition

$$\lim_{j\to\infty} E_0\{\beta^j[(F_K(j) - c_K(j)) - c_I(j) - q_j]K_j\} = 0 \tag{10.6}$$

Let $\hat{q} \equiv \dot{q}/q$ and note that $q_j - hq_{j+1} = q_j[1 - h(1+\hat{q}_j)] = q_j\beta[r + d - (1-d)\hat{q}_j] \cong \tilde{q}_j$ is the rental cost of capital, or briefly the rental rate, evaluated at time j. It is the product of the initial price of the capital good, q, and the annual "charges" consisting of the discount and depreciation rates, adjusted for the expected capital gain, $\hat{q}$.

To interpret the Euler equation in (10.5), label $m(j) \equiv [F_K(j) - c_K(j)]$, and note that $m(j)$ is the marginal productivity of capital net of the change in the adjustment cost caused by a change in the capital stock. Also, label $\Delta c(j) \equiv c_I(j) - hc_I(j+1)$, and note that this term indicates the change in the adjustment cost caused by increasing the investment by one unit in j rather than in $j+1$. Then rewrite (10.5)

$$E_0\{\beta m(j+1) - [\Delta c_I(j) + \tilde{q}_j]\} = 0 \tag{10.7}$$

On the optimal path, the expected discounted value of the marginal productivity of capital in every period is equal to the expected value of the rental rate, adjusted for changes in the adjustment cost. Given (10.7), it is impossible to gain by changing the timing of investment. The message is that a higher adjustment cost implies a higher cost on investment, and as such it affects not only its pace but also the optimal level of capital. In the absence of adjustment cost, the condition in (10.7) reduces to the equality of the marginal productivity of capital and the rental rate (Jorgenson, 1967). This solution is quite sensitive to changes in the state variables, as will be shown in the next section.

The solution characterizes the condition along the optimal path. Alternatively, this condition can be expressed in terms of the shadow price of capital defined as the present value of the marginal productivity of capital, net of the adjustment cost, in present and future production: $M_t \equiv \sum_{j=0}^{\infty} h^j m(t+j)$. As shown in the appendix to this chapter, the system can be solved to yield

$$E_t\{M_t - [q_t + c_I(t)]\} = 0 \tag{10.8}$$

This condition states that investment is carried out to the point where the shadow price of capital, generated by the investment, is equal to the cost of investment including the cost of adjustment. The marginal productivity depends on the technology and the inputs at the various points in time, and therefore its evaluation requires an assumption that the investment under consideration is the only investment to be made. If other investments are contemplated, the marginal productivity would have to be evaluated conditional on such investments.

The State Variables

To gain some insight into the meaning of the solution, we use a Cobb-Douglas production function, $Y = AL^a K^b$. The first-order condition in (10.3) provides a solution for L, the nondurable input, $L = (a/w)Y$. This solution is substituted into the production function to yield, with some simplification,

$$Y = (Aa^a)^{1/(1-a)} w^{-a/(1-a)} K^{b/(1-a)} \tag{10.9}$$

The marginal productivity of capital conditional on w is[2]

$$\frac{\partial Y}{\partial K}\Big|_w = \frac{b}{1-a}(Aa^a)^{1/(1-a)} w^{-a/(1-a)} K^{(b+a-1)/(1-a)} \tag{10.10}$$

This derivative is equated to the rental price of capital to provide a solution for K, when such a solution exists.

Incentives: No Adjustment Cost

Equation (10.9) is the short-run supply function conditional on K. Output declines with w, but as w is the ratio of nominal wage to output price, p, output increases with p. To obtain the long-run solution without the adjustment cost, the condition in equation (10.7) simplifies to

$$E_0\{\beta F_{Kj} - \tilde{q}_j]\} = 0 \tag{10.11}$$

The long-run values (starred) are obtained by using equations (10.9) and (10.11) to yield

$$K^* = (b/\tilde{q})Y^*, \quad Y^* = (Aa^a b^b)^{\epsilon} w^{-a\epsilon} \tilde{q}^{-b\epsilon}, \quad \epsilon = 1/(1-a-b) \tag{10.12}$$

Accordingly, K^* is determined in terms of Y^*, the elasticity of output with respect to capital, and the real rental rate. Prices affect the desired capital directly through the rental rate and indirectly through the effect on the optimal output. It is important to differentiate between the direct and the indirect price effect. A change in the wage rate has only an indirect effect on capital with an elasticity $E_{K/w} = -a\epsilon$. The elasticities of the real rental rate, $E_{K/\tilde{q}}$, are -1, $-b\epsilon$, and $(a-1)\epsilon$ for the direct, indirect, and total effect respectively. Similarly, the elasticities of capital with respect to a change in the product price are 1, $(a+b)\epsilon$, and ϵ for the direct, indirect, and total effect respectively. Note that the indirect effect $(a+b)\epsilon$ can be considerably stronger than the direct effect. It is useful to illustrate the order of magnitude of the elasticities in question for arbitrary values of the parameters: $a = 0.3$, $b = 0.6$, and $\epsilon = 10$:

	Capital elasticities		
Variable	Direct	Indirect	Total
w	0	−3	3
$\tilde{q}$	−1	−6	−7
p	1	9	10

The discussion has several implications for empirical analysis. The difference between the short- and the long-run response is often overlooked, and equation (10.9) is used erroneously in investment analysis to express the relationship between K and Y along the expansion path (Jorgenson, 1963). The elasticities for long-run response express the response with respect to lasting price changes. Transitory changes are likely to affect output along the short-term supply but as such should not have an important effect on K.

To simplify the discussion, we have abstracted from taxes. To add taxes, they have to be inserted in the income expression in (10.1). Consequently, the prices in the foregoing results have to be adjusted for taxes (Jorgenson, 1963). The empirical evaluation of the effect of taxes is done in two steps: first, evaluate the effect of the tax on the time path of the rental rate, and second, determine the response of investment to price. It is the latter that is the focus of the empirical analysis.

Technology

Neutral technical change is perceived as a change in the multiplicative coefficient of the production function, A. It affects output and thereby the desired capital level without affecting the capital-output ratio. Following the numerical example above, a 1 percent technical change causes a 10 percent increase in the desired capital stock. Capital using technical change, captured here as an increase in b, generates an increase in output as well as an increase in the capital-output ratio. The overall effect on output depends on what happens to the degree of the function. When the degree is held constant, an increase in b implies a decline of a, and therefore the net effect on output is ambiguous. However, the effect on the capital-output ratio is unambiguously signed.[3]

Returns to Scale and the Cost of Adjustment

Under decreasing returns to scale, $a + b < 1$, the marginal productivity of capital is declining in K, and the firm size is determined, as seen in equation (10.12). If for any reason a gap is generated between the marginal productivity of capital and the rental rate, investment will lead to convergence of the capital stock to its optimal level.

When constant returns to scale are imposed, the size of the firm is indeterminate because the marginal productivity of capital is independent of the level of capital already accumulated. The introduction of the cost of adjustment cannot resolve this indeterminacy.[4] In general, the adjustment cost is generating a continuous change in the capital stock because without it, the adjustment to a changing environment is instantaneous. Such changes result in a sequence of *short-run* equilibria conditional on the existing capital stock. In this case the firm can grow forever because there is no built-in mechanism to stop this growth, and the ultimate size of the firm remains indeterminate. Perhaps the fact that some firms grow steadily is taken as evidence of constant returns to scale. This is misleading, though, because the question of size determinacy should be evaluated conditional on the assumption of constant technology and demand. Time-series data reflect changes in demand or technology which in turn affect optimal firm size and thereby investment decisions.

Aside from the fact that the adjustment cost does not solve the problem of size indeterminacy, there is a more subtle problem of inconsistency to the economies of scale. "Installation competes with production of marketable output for the internal resources of the firm, including capital and labor services. The opportunity cost of a higher level of investment is a lower level of output for given levels of capital and labor input" (Jorgenson, 1972, p. 220). The question is what are the "internal resources of the firm." If they are labor and capital, those are endogenous in a competitive industry and can be changed according to demand. However, there are other resources, such as management, that are intrinsic to the firm and do not change easily. In this case, such resources should enter as arguments of the production function. Then if the production function is constant returns to scale in all the inputs, it displays decreasing returns to scale for labor and capital alone. Alternatively, if the function is constant returns to scale in labor and capital, it displays increasing returns to scale in *all* inputs. In this case, paying labor and capital their market rates leaves nothing to pay the internal resources. This cannot be accepted as a reasonable description of reality.

The concept of internal adjustment cost has served the purpose of explaining why investment is stretched out over time and has become an important element in investment studies, largely of theoretical nature. However, there is little empirical evidence to support it. When it comes to agriculture, it is hard to think of examples that justify the inclusion of such internal adjustment cost. What seems to be more relevant for agriculture is the scarcity of investment goods. An example from the green revolution was discussed in Chapter 6. This scarcity simply reflects the fact that at any time, resources are finite, and if more of them are demanded in one industry they have to be bidden away from another industry–a process that requires a price adjustment to equate supply with demand. This price adjustment represents the external cost of adjustment. In this case, each firm maintains $F_K = \tilde{q}$, but the rental rate is determined so as to allocate the available investment goods among all firms. The essence of this view is that there is a difference between the supply of investment goods perceived by a price-taking firm and that faced by the industry. In addition, other constraints, such as credit, may prevail. In this case, the determination of the rental rate will take place through the adjustment in the interest rate paid by farmers. We return to this below.

Investment: Industry Level

The analytic model determines the optimal path for the capital stock. The numerical example gives the order of magnitude of the changes in the desired capital in response to changes in the economic environment, and it is clear that this calculated response is enormous. Because we do not see such wide variations in the capital stocks of firms, it is reasonable to assume that something is still missing from the analysis. The model, by its very nature, does not capture all the information that affects firms' decisions. Specifically, the economic environment is not constant as was assumed above, and new information relevant to the investment decision is flowing in all the time. The firm then has to base its decision on long-range forecasting. Since reality may differ from expectations, firms have to make occasional adjustments to their investment decisions. We return to this subject below, but at this stage it is important to note that in general the data consist of observations taken away from the optimal path.

As indicated above, two concepts of investment demand are used in the literature. The first views investment demand at time t to be the difference between the optimal capital stock, $K^*(t)$, and the available capital stock, $K(t)$. The second views investment demand as the change in $K^*(t)$. According to the first approach, the investment demand of firm f is

$$I_f^d(\tilde{q}, s, t) = K_f^*(\tilde{q}, s, t) - K_f(t), \tag{10.13}$$

where s represents all the state variables other than $\tilde{q}$. Note that the state variables appear as levels. In the second approach, investment is a function of the change in $K^*(t)$, which in turn, by linearizing (10.12), becomes a function of the *change,* rather than the *level,* of the state variables. In principle, this distinction can be translated to an empirical hypothesis that can help to sort out the relevance of the two concepts.

In what follows, we take the first approach. Summing over all firms in the industry, we obtain the industry demand, $I^d(\tilde{q}, s, t) = \Sigma_f I_f^d(\tilde{q}, s, t)$, and $\partial I^d(\tilde{q}, s, t)/\partial\tilde{q} < 0$.

The actual investment is determined by the demand and supply of investment goods. Much of the empirical work views firms as price takers. This may be an adequate assumption at the micro level, but it does not automatically apply to aggregate data. In general, the supply of capital goods can be written as $I^s(q^s, s, \tau)$, $\partial I^s/\partial q^s > 0$, where s represents state variables that affect supply. In what follows, the vector s contains all the state variables that are pertinent to the particular equation which are not introduced explicitly. Then $\tilde{q}$ is determined by equating

$$I^d(\tilde{q}, s, t) = I^s(\tilde{q}, s, t). \tag{10.14}$$

The essence of this formulation is that the rental rate is not exogenous, and it cannot be assumed that the industry can invest any amount without affecting this rate. An increase in investment demand causes an increase in the rental rate and therefore a decline in the investment rate as compared with the case where the industry is a price taker. This type of external adjustment cost reflects the fact that resources are finite, but it shifts the scarcity from the firm to the industry level.

In general, empirical analysis treats positive and negative accumulation symmetrically even though the costs involved are completely different. The cost of acquisition of a new capital good is different from the cost of selling a used capital good. This point and its implications were discussed by Johnson (1958), Edwards (1959), Johnson and Quance (1972, pp. 185–195), and more recently by Chavas (1994), and Hamermesh and Pfann (1996). To place this detail in perspective, we note that on the whole agricultural investment is positive for most of the time; therefore the subject of disinvestment is of secondary importance and does not affect our views on the development of agriculture. Its empirical importance is largely limited to the behavioral analysis based on micro data.

There are three important reasons for the difference between the acquisition and the selling price. First, the service life of the new capital good is longer than that of the used one, and therefore it is more valuable. This aspect could be handled by detailing the capital goods by age and vintage and pricing the different goods accordingly. On this score, the need to differentiate between selling and acquisition prices is not structural, but is the outcome of the aggregation of the capital goods over age and vintage. If an old machine is sold, someone is buying it because it meets his needs. This indicates that there is a market for all types of machines that are actually traded. The extension of the analysis to include this heterogeneity should give a different result from that obtained from the standard formulation that does not include the option of purchasing the used equipment (who will then buy it?).

Second, part of the gap between the price of new and used equipment can be attributed to marketing charges and asymmetric information. Third, there is the cyclical element. There is a tendency to sell unutilized capacity in bad times when the excess demand for capital goods is declining and with it the price of used equipment. The price behavior is likely to differ according to the origin of the capital goods. Used machines are supplied by farmers, and for our purposes they should be considered to be capital goods of agricultural origin, the same as cows. Their price is determined endogenously within agriculture and reflects the expected stream of the marginal productivity of capital over its remaining lifetime. To trace the consequences of this extension, it is necessary to work out the market equilibrium for used equipment. This will result in a market clearing price, and used equipment will be employed accordingly. New machines are of nonagricultural origin. Thus their supply price reflects the conditions in nonagriculture, and therefore the price may be less sensitive to the cyclical conditions in agriculture as compared with used machines. To sum up, the introduction of a secondhand market adds details to the analysis that are not essential for our discussion.

The asymmetry between investment and disinvestment is more pronounced in models with internal adjustment costs. Obviously the demolition of a building or the slaughter of a cow does not stretch out over time. The symmetry assumption simplifies the formulation, but it is unrealistic. Its restrictive nature goes undetected because much of the empirical work is based on aggregate data.

Sectoral Allocation

In the case of a two-sector economy, the solution for the rental rate, $\tilde{q}$, equates the total sectoral demand with supply, and the allocation of investment to the sectors satisfies

$$I^s(\tilde{q}, s, t) = I_1^d(\tilde{q}, s_1, t) + I_2^d(\tilde{q}, s_2, t). \tag{10.15}$$

An increase in the relative profitability of one of the sectors increases its demand for investment, and it will thus increase its share in total investment.

The overall resource constraint is the source of the sectoral competition for existing resources, and as such it is the main force that drives the intersectoral allocation of investment. As a consequence, similar to the analysis of the intersectoral allocation of labor, the allocation of investment will depend on the differential profitability of the various sectors. The empirical formulation is based on (10.15). The supply price of the capital good is postulated to increase with the rate of investment. In empirical analysis, when the observations are taken from economies which differ greatly in size, it is desirable to normalize investment for the size of the economy. This can be done by taking the ratio of investment to the capital stock:

$$\tilde{q}^s(I/K, s, t), \quad \partial\tilde{q}^s/\partial(I/K) > 0. \tag{10.16}$$

Write the inverse function, $I^s/K = I(q, t)$, then $\tilde{q}$ is determined by equating

$$I^d(\tilde{q}, s, t) = I^s(\tilde{q}, s, t, I/K). \tag{10.17}$$

Substituting the price which solves this equation back in (10.16), we can write the investment function for sector i:

$$I_i(I/K, s, t). \tag{10.18}$$

Let θ_i be the share of sector i in total investment and use (10.18) to write

$$\theta_i = I_i/\Sigma I_i \cong \theta_i(I/K, s, t). \tag{10.19}$$

To sum up, the reason for the gradual response of investment to the changing market environment is shifted from resource scarcity at the firm level, as assumed by the internal cost of adjustment, to resource scarcity at the industry or economy levels.

Empirical Specification

In general, time series of aggregate investment show a positive serial correlation. The determination of the source for this dynamic relation is a key question in investment research. For a variety of reasons, there is a time difference between the date of a firm's decision on a new investment and its completion. There are two aspects to the delayed response. The first is the response of the *desired* capital stock to changes in the market signals. This response is related to the way firms perceive the signals and their need for additional information before reaching a decision on changes in the capital stock. We refer to this response as endogenous dynamics, and it is discussed below. In any case, strictly speaking, these dynamics deal with variables on the optimal path which are unobserved. The second is the adjustment of the *actual* stock to changes in the desired stock. There is little that the theory has to say about this process, and therefore for a lack of a better term we refer to it as the exogenous dynamics. An obvious reason for the delayed response of the capital stock to the desired value is the time needed to complete the project. Take, for example, investment in beef cattle. If there is a change in the economic environment that generates a demand for larger herds, the industry cannot expand to the desired level if there are not enough breeding cows. It thus often takes several years to get to the new level. This is the reason behind the long cattle cycles (of about ten years). This period of gestation cannot be reduced by increasing the cost of adjustment. Other reasons include time needed for delivery, financial constraints, and the indivisibility of assets.

Exogenous Dynamics

The implication of dynamics is that a decision taken by the firm in a given year may affect investment in future years, or alternatively, the investment in a given year reflects past decisions and more so, past signals. Such a time distribution of the response was a major justification for the distributed lags analysis, referred to as the flexible accelerator models, originated by Chenery (1952) and Koyck (1954). In such models, the actual capital stock differs from the desired stock. Koyck's formulation uses geometric weights to express the current capital stock as a weighted average of past values of desired capital:

$$K_t = \mu \sum_{j=0}^{\infty} (1-\mu)^j K^*_{t-j}; \quad 0 < \mu < 1. \tag{10.20}$$

The expression can be transformed to

$$K_t - K_{t-1} = \mu(K_t^* - K_{t-1}).^5 \tag{10.21}$$

Let I_t and δK_t be gross investment and the depreciation in year t respectively. The empirical equation is

$$I_t = \mu\gamma_0 + \mu\gamma Y_t^* - (\mu - d)K_{t-1} + \text{ error.} \tag{10.22}$$

When the dependent variable is *net* investment, d is eliminated from the equation. The product $\mu\gamma$ is referred to as the short-run coefficient, μ is the coefficient of adjustment, and γ is the long-run coefficient. There are various forms for the relation between the actual and the past values of the desired capital stocks; see, for instance, Jorgenson (1963).

The main subjects of interest in empirical analysis are: (1) the determination of the desired capital stock and (2) the effect of a change in the desired capital stock on investment. The relevance of the first subject is not immediately obvious, but it is implicit in the analysis. In the case of the Cobb-Douglas illustration, the desired capital stock is proportional to the long-run output, Y^*. However, Y^* is both unobserved and different from the actual output, which replaces Y^* in empirical analysis. Thus the variable used in the analysis measures with error the relevant variable and thereby introduces a downward bias in the estimation (Mundlak, 1966). Apparently, there is no consensus on this claim: "Mundlak assumes decreasing returns to scale; his analysis of Koyck's model presumes that long-run equilibrium is characterized by a supply function for output and demand functions for labor and capital input. Under constant returns to scale these supply and demand functions do not exist, so Mundlak's analysis of Koyck's model is completely erroneous. . . . While such a model would be appropriate under decreasing returns, the empirical evidence we have reviewed supports the assumption of constant returns. For this description of technology Mundlak's distributed lags investment model is inappropriate" (Jorgenson, 1974, p. 362). Essentially, the argument consists of two parts: first, the production function is constant returns, and second, actual output can therefore be viewed as desired output. This argument seems to assume that constant returns precludes a difference between short-run and long-run outputs. This is of course unfounded; short-run variations in output reflect shocks not taken into account in the long run. Indeed, this is the essence of the difference between the first-order conditions for the variable and the durable input given by (10.3) and (10.5) respectively. Therefore, the original claim that replacing the long-run desired output with actual output may lead to erroneous results is not invalidated by this argument. In this connection, see Eisner (1963), who shows that between-industry regressions, where the data are aggregated over time, give a coefficient of investment on sales (sum of lagged sales) near unity, whereas within-industry regressions, where the data are subject to annual variations, give a much lower coefficient, 0.4 to 0.5. This is in line with the idea that output variations are in part transitory and should not trigger an investment response.

The second subject is related to the pattern and stability of the weights (μ in equation 10.21). The underlying assumption is that the adjustment is gradual, but this is not always the case. Often there are distinct scale economies in the size of the investment, where the unit cost declines with the size of the project, and the optimal size of the investment unit exceeds the demand or requires more resources than are currently available. Consequently, the firm may delay the investment until it is justifiable to construct a larger project at a lower unit cost. Such a situation can be detected from firm data but may not show up in aggregate data. This was observed in Mundlak (1964, chap. 6), where an analysis of 66 family farms in six moshavim (cooperative villages) in Israel in the period 1954–1958 concluded that "[a]n examination of the data shows that not every farm invested annually. This may be the result of a decision and thus is explained by the model but it is also partly related to the lack of continuity in investment. Presumably it is possible to expand poultry capacity little by little according to needs, especially in the case of batteries. Actually investment is usually carried out in relatively large units. A situation is possible where for a certain year a gap exists between desired and actual capacity and yet no investment will be made. Instead of closing the gap at a fixed annual rate the farmers may prefer investments in large units at time intervals exceeding a year" (ibid., pp. 105–106).

This situation was supported empirically by estimating equations similar to (10.22) to explain variations in the capital stock of two types of structures, poultry and dairy cows. The equations were estimated for the pooled annual data and for the data aggregated over a five-year period for each farm to yield the between-farm regression. For instance, in the case of poultry structures, the results for the annual data gave a poor fit and low values for the short-run response and the coefficient of adjustment. On the other hand, the results for the between-farm regression, where the data are summed over the sample period, were by far better and more consistent with the distributed lag interpretation.

To conclude, the phenomenon of lumpy investment at intervals longer than a year is inconsistent with the internal adjustment cost assumption. This is not easily detected, however, because macro data are obtained as aggregates over firms and as such conceal it. For instance, if one-fourth of the firms make a lumpy investment in any given year, the analysis of the aggregate data can be erroneously interpreted as showing gradual adjustment at the firm level. Similarly, aggregation of the data over time for an individual farm creates an identification problem. This is related to the more general problem of identifying the dynamics from data aggregated over time, introduced in Mundlak (1961a).

Endogenous Dynamics

There has been a great deal of empirical work based on equation (10.5) or (10.8), mainly with the use of nonagricultural data. These equations involve unobservable variables, and to overcome this limitation, alternative approaches have been taken; these are reviewed by Chirinko (1993) and Galeotti (1996). Work with agricultural data has been based on the dual approach. Without any loss in substance, the discussion of this work is postponed to Chapter 14.

Euler Equations

To present an empirical version of equation (10.5), we assume $c(\cdot) = (c/2)I^2$ for the cost of adjustment so that $c(\cdot)$ does not depend on the capital stock and $c_I(\cdot) = cI$. Let z be the expected gap between the marginal productivity of capital and the rental rate. To deal with time series, we allow the base period to vary so that the terms are evaluated for time t, $z_{t+j} \equiv E_t\{\beta F_K(t+j+1) - \tilde{q}_{t+j}\}$. Rearranging, it follows from equation (10.5) that

$$E_t(I_{t+j}) - hE_t(I_{t+j+1}) = \frac{1}{c} z_{t+j}. \tag{10.23}$$

An expected decline in the rental rate or an expected increase in the productivity of capital causes an increase in z, and hence the difference between current investment and expected next-year investment increases. This means that at the margin, current investment increases in order to take advantage of the current opportunities. For the purpose of estimation, F_K is spelled out explicitly in terms of its arguments, and thus the parameters of the production function enter the equation. Similarly, in some applications, the cost of adjustment is formulated so as to depend on some variables, including output. When this is done, the empirical equation contains output and prices. Thus this equation is used in empirical analysis to estimate the parameters of the production function, of the cost of adjustment function, and of h. Unlike in the exogenous dynamics models, it is assumed here that the observed capital stock is always equal to the optimal one.

There are several problems in using this equation for empirical analysis. First, in this formulation the adjustment-cost parameters are, by assumption, the only source for the dynamics. When in reality the time pattern of investment is affected by other causes, their influence will be captured by the cost of adjustment parameters, and the empirical analysis will give a distorted picture of the dynamics. Second, the Euler equation, (10.23), provides arbitrage conditions between adjacent periods that have to be met on the *optimal path.* When the observations are located off the path, this condition is inconsistent with the data. If the model is stable, deviations from the optimal path generate a correction toward the path. This correction is not described by the model, but it is empirically important and as such it affects the estimates. This may be the reason for the fact that empirical estimates obtained from the Euler equations do not produce robust results. Third, the Euler equation is not an efficient way to estimate the parameters of the production function. As argued in Chapter 12, it is more efficient to estimate the production function directly. Fourth, recall that $h = (1-d)/(1+r)$, so that h is not a stable parameter and should be treated as a variable. When h is treated as a constant, variations in h are captured by the equation error, and as such the error is not independent of the investment term on the right-hand side of the equation. This causes a bias in the estimate. These problems may be the reason for the observation made by Chirinko (1993) that empirical estimates obtained from the Euler equations do not produce robust results.

Deviations from the optimal values should have a relatively smaller effect on the capital stock than on investment, and therefore it may be better to estimate the Euler equation expressed in terms of capital. For this purpose, we rewrite equation (10.23) and ignore the expectation operator,

$$z_{t+j} = c\{K_{t+j} - (1-d)K_{t+j-1} - h[K_{t+j+1} - (1-d)K_{t+j}]\}. \tag{10.24}$$

Using the lag operator and rearranging, leaving the details to the appendix, we get

$$K_{t+j+1} = (1-d)K_{t+j} + \frac{1}{c(1-hL^{-1})} z_{t+j+1}, \tag{10.25}$$

where

$$\frac{1}{1-hL^{-1}} z_{t+j+1} = \sum_{i=0}^{\infty} h^i z_{t+j+1+i}.$$

Equations (10.23) and (10.25) involve unknown future values, and their use in empirical analysis requires the use of expectations. Estimates of price and output elasticities obtained from those equations for U.S. manufacturing are subject to wide fluctuations (Chirinko, 1993, p. 1894), and this limits their value.

If the main purpose of the analysis is to study the dynamics, it is possible to eliminate the need to estimate the parameters of the production function by imposing a simple technology such as a fixed-coefficient technology (Hansen and Sargent, 1981; Sargent, 1987, chap. 14). The assumption of fixed coefficients goes too far, however, because it does not stand on its own but requires the assumption of the cost of adjustment. Otherwise, by setting $c(\cdot) \equiv 0$, the condition (10.5) reduces to $\beta F_K(\cdot) = E_t\{\tilde{q}_{t+j}\}$ similar to (10.6) with $c = 0$. Under fixed-coefficient technology, $F_K = f$, where f is the output-input coefficient, and the condition becomes $\beta f = \tilde{q}_{t+j}$. This condition is meaningless because it involves neither capital nor investment. This difficulty is eliminated when the cost of adjustment is a function of investment. The fact that the fixed-coefficient assumption simplifies the analysis, however, should not be confused as a reading on the technology. In general, the productivity of capital should be allowed to depend on technology and prices.

Direct Forecasting

This approach attempts to overcome the fact that M_t in equation (10.8) is unknown by assuming a simple structure on $m(t)$, the net marginal productivity of capital, and thereby replacing M_t with $m(t-1)$. The procedure raises some substantive questions, but we can omit a discussion on the subject because, in any case, "Closed-Form Forecasting models have generally yielded rather small price elasticities" (Chirinko, 1993, p. 1897).

q-models

These models are based on utilizing the market value of the firm as an indicator for the investment demand, an idea that goes back to Keynes, used by Grunfeld (1960) and developed by Brainard and Tobin (1968). Firms are assumed to compare their capital stock to their market value. A high ratio of the market value of the firm relative to its capital stock is attractive for investment because this is interpreted to mean that the valuation by the market of a new investment more than offsets its cost. Note that this ratio is a measure of the *average* productivity of capital, evaluated over its lifetime, and in this respect it differs from the marginal value that appears in equation (10.8). Conditions for the equality of the two measures developed in the literature form the framework for using the observed average productivity in place of the unobserved marginal productivity in empirical analysis. These conditions are restrictive, and as such they highlight the limitation of the model.

The *q*-model approach is not directly applicable to agriculture, because there is no stock market for farms that allows one to relate investment to the market value of the farms. But even where applicable, as in manufacturing, the empirical performance of this approach is generally disappointing (Abel and Blanchard, 1986, p. 249; Chirinko, 1993, p. 1889). In part, the source of the difficulty is not the theory but the assumption about the expectation of the value of the firm by the market. "Differentials between market values and fundamentals are generally attributed to 'investor sentiment', that is excess volatility, mean aversion, fads or speculative bubbles in financial markets. Sentiment creates a problem for the q-model insofar as investment decisions are based on fundamentals" (Chirinko, 1993, p. 1889). Such doubts have more general implications for the formation of rational expectations. Perhaps there is another difficulty, common to other models as well, stemming from the fact that the theory does not cover some of the reasons for investment such as investment triggered by new products or, more generally, by technical change.

Summary

In summarizing the record, Chirinko writes of the models using explicit (endogenous in our terminology) dynamics: "In practice, however, Explicit Models offer a mixed performance, as the q and Direct Forecasting models are generally less successful empirically than Euler Equation models. The more favorable results may be due to output variables appearing in the Euler Equation models or to the reduction of the unobservable expectation problems to one-period-ahead projections, which may be easier to estimate than the long leads appearing in the q and Direct Forecasting models." (ibid., p. 1899).

This summary of the empirical experience is interesting and can be related to our discussion. The lack of robustness probably reflects the fact that the theoretical restrictions refer to the optimal path or steady state but, because of factors not taken into account, may not be a good description of the data. The discrepancy between a model and reality is the rule rather than exception in empirical analysis, but the consequences may be more severe in dynamic models. The fact that output performs better than prices in explaining investment can be interpreted in light of equation (10.12): output depends on prices, the existing stock of capital, and, most important, on technology, and therefore there is little scope left for the direct effect of prices on investment.

Uncertainty

Investment behavior is affected by uncertainty about the future values of the state variables, largely prices and technology. There is a similarity in that the two variables appear in the profit or short-run supply functions. Yet the two differ in nature and in their predictability. Investment studies are generally more oriented toward price variability. For instance, Lucas (1966, p. 55) deals with the question of "[h]ow should a firm with given production possibilities and initial assets respond to an anticipated pattern of future prices and interest rates." The response of investment to price variability is closely related to the interest in business cycles. From a long-run perspective, however, technology is the engine of growth, and probably of business cycles as well, and as such should play a prominent role in efforts to understand the investment behavior of the industry.

A key issue, both conceptual and practical, is how to deal with expectation formation. Rational expectations, as the name indicates, introduce rationality in processing the available information for expectation formation. This does not, however, produce a unique procedure. One approach to construct rational expectations is to take an industry or macro view of the economic environment rather than a mechanical micro view. Lucas and Prescott (1971) solved an investment model with rational expectations for an industry with a finite number of identical firms. A linear form of their model is presented by Sargent (1987, pp. 399–402). Each firm determines the optimal capital path and with it the output path. Aggregation over firms provides the industry supply conditional on the assumed sequence of product prices. This sequence of supply is matched with a sequence of future industry demand. The two sequences are solved to provide the sequence of prices and output and the corresponding sequence of optimal capital. The prices generated by the system are the rational expectations prices that are used by the firms to determine their capital stocks.

This procedure is not unique, because it depends upon the assumptions made and the degree of aggregation. A more pragmatic approach often used in empirical analysis is to allow the data to determine the form of the empirical distribution of the variables to be forecasted within a predetermined class of autoregressive, or other, distributions.

The situation is completely different when it comes to forecasting technology, a major determinant of investment. Conceptually, there is no way to form a rational expectations prediction of the basic changes of the components of technology that follow a random walk process. We return to this subject in Chapter 13.

Empirical Results

The discussion here is limited to the estimation of investment functions and skips over the important conceptual and practical issues involved in measurements of capital (see, for instance, Griliches 1963c, Hulten 1990, Ball et al. 1993, Larson et al. 1999). Unlike production or supply functions, about which there are many studies, there are only a few empirical studies of investment in agriculture based on the primal approach, and those are mainly of the exogenous dynamic type. Griliches (1960a) studied the demand for tractors in the United States in 1921–1957 using a distributed lags framework, where the desired stock is determined by the ratio of the price of tractors to the product price and by the interest rate. The results show stock price elasticities of about −0.25 in the short run and about −1.5 in the long run, and interest elasticities of about −1.0 and −5.8 in the short and long run respectively. The ratio of the long- and short-run elasticities is about 6. Heady and Tweeten (1963, chap. 11) analyzed the purchases of all farm machinery in the United States in the period 1926–1959, excluding 1942–1947. They report a garden variety of regressions. The core explanatory variables are machines-to-commodity price ratio, a ratio of equity to liabilities of the farm sector, or alternatively a measure of farm income, a time trend, and in some cases, the lagged value of the dependent variable. They conclude that "a 1 percent increase in the price of either trucks, tractors or equipment aggregate . . . is predicted to increase respective annual purchases 1 percent; stock .2 percent in one or two years. In four years the elasticity of machinery purchases Q_i with respect to P_i remains about unity, but with respect to P_R [commodity price–YM] is 2 or more. A sustained 1 percent rise in prices received by farmers is expected to increase stock for these same items .2 percent in one or two years, .5 percent in four years and more than 2 percent in the long run" (pp. 327–328). The trend variable was robust, and the equity/liability ratio had the right sign and was significant. This can be interpreted as a sign of cyclical behavior, with higher investment in good times.

As in many empirical applications, their equations contain fewer variables than what is called for by the theory. Presumably, the equation should include all prices and a measure of technology. In general, with a short time series the empirical equation does not sustain all the pertinent variables. For instance, in the study of Heady and Tweeten, the inclusion of more prices was not supported by the data. One way to deal with this problem is to collapse the prices and other exogenous variables into one measure, the rate of return. The higher the expected rate of return, the higher the investment demand. The rate of return is related to the gap between the expected marginal productivity of capital and the rental rate, labeled z in equation (10.23): the higher the gap, the higher the rate of return. The rate of return was used in the studies of the sectoral investment allocation reviewed below.

Mundlak (1964, chap. 6) used a panel of farm micro data to study investment in farm structures using the accelerator formulation and demonstrated the importance of aggregating the data over time in order to eliminate the noise that exists in annual micro data. This finding is consistent with lumpy investment and is not supportive of the idea of a convex cost of adjustment function that results in a gradual adjustment. As indicated earlier, this may be typical for many investments in agriculture.

The application of firm theory to the estimation of the aggregate industry investment function overlooks the fact that the supply of capital goods is not perfectly elastic. One way to incorporate this element is to estimate the allocation of total investment to the various sectors. The sectoral investment allocation equation was estimated for Argentina in Cavallo and Mundlak (1982) for the period 1942–1972 and in Mundlak, Cavallo, and Domenech (1989) for the period 1913–1984 with similar results with respect to the main variables, although there are some differences in the specification, estimation, and the sample period. In Argentina, the share of agriculture in the capital stock reached its peak of more than 30 percent in the 1920s and has declined since then to a level of 10 percent, reflecting a decline in the share of agriculture in total investment. The empirical equation is a modification of equation (10.19). The dependent variable is the share of agriculture in total investment, θ^I. The explanatory variables are the share of agriculture in the capital stock, θ^k, and the ratio of the rate of return in agriculture to that in nonagriculture, decomposed into "anticipated" and transitory components, δ_r^e and δ_r^u respectively. The anticipated part was obtained from a regression of the current values on two lagged values and some exogenous variables, and the transitory part is the residual from this regression. In such a formulation, the effect of technical change is reflected in the rate of return, but it is diluted by the fact that the variable is the intersectoral differential rate of return. Thus it captures the *difference* in sectoral rates of technical change, which is not as potent as the sectoral *level*. The equation was estimated within a system of simultaneous equations:

$$\begin{aligned}\ln \theta^I = \underset{(0.6)}{-0.058} + \underset{(1.9)}{0.255} \ln \theta^k + \underset{(1.9)}{0.14} \ln \delta_r^e + \underset{(1.7)}{0.17} \ln \delta_r^u \\ + \underset{(7.6)}{0.732} \ln \theta_{t-1}^I; \quad \overline{R}^2 = 0.90,\end{aligned} \tag{10.26}$$

where the numbers in parentheses are t-ratios for the null hypothesis. The two components of the differential rate of return have a positive effect on the share of agriculture in total investment. As the profitability of agriculture declined over the years, it caused a decline in its share in total investment as well as in the total capital stock.

When the rates of returns are equal in the two sectors, the logarithms of their ratio is zero, which leaves θ^I to depend on θ^k alone. The steady-state value of the elasticity of θ^I with respect to θ^k is $0.255/(1 - 0.732) = 0.95$. This means that under equal sectoral profitability, the share of agriculture in total investment will tend to equal its share in the capital stock. The implication is that the observed decline in θ^I can be attributed to the differences in sectoral profitability.

Coeymans and Mundlak (1993) applied a similar approach to Chile for the period 1962–1982. Total investment was allocated to four sectors: agriculture, mining, manufacturing, and services. The equation is similar to that estimated for Argentina in that it contains expected and transitory measures for the sectoral rates of returns. It concludes: "Sectoral investment is responsive to the own rates of return as well as to the other sectors. The cross effects reveal the existence of competitive relationships among sectors" (ibid., p. 74).

Conclusions

What is the relevance of our discussion to the explanation of the trend in agricultural capital reviewed at the beginning of the chapter? "Good" investment studies show the price response of investment or the capital stock. The relevant price is the cost of capital, which has several components, some of which are not subject to long-term trends. The depreciation rate is fairly stable. The interest rate is subject to cyclical fluctuations but not to a trend. The price of capital goods used in agriculture, properly measured, might have declined somewhat. On the other hand, as indicated in Chapter 1, the real price of agricultural output has been declining for a long time. Such a decline is consistent with a decline in the agricultural share in investment and the capital stock. The increase in the capital-labor ratio is explained, in part, by off-farm migration, which represents a movement toward the efficiency frontier discussed in Chapter 8. The increase in the capital-output ratio is to be explained by capital using technical change. The large spread in the distribution is postulated to reflect large cross-country variability in the implemented techniques, which vary widely in their capital intensity.

These results are related to the growth aspects of investment. They can be obtained with the more traditional exogenous dynamics studies. The endogenous dynamics models should be in a better position to explain the *timing* of investment. This does not occur, however, because the theory deals with the unobservable changes along the optimal path. There is also no reason to believe that the internal cost of adjustment is the only factor, or the dominant one, in causing the investment to be stretched over time. As to the timing, the formulation contains a key term, the expected capital gains. Given the fundamentals, the actual timing may depend on the real price of the investment good. Thus it is more profitable to invest when the cost of the investment good is low and the product price is high. However, by its very nature it is difficult to include such a variable in empirical analysis. Rational expectations intend to present the fundamentals and not transitory deviations. In the Argentine studies quoted above the rate of returns was decomposed into predictable and transitory components, and it was found that both components are relevant in explaining investment allocation. In Chapter 14 we review investment studies based on duality.

Appendix 10A

1. The Euler equation in terms of K.

   Insert the assumption $c(\cdot) = \frac{1}{2}cI^2$ into (10.5):

$$c[I(t+j) - hI(t+j+1)] = E_t\{\beta F_K(t+j+1) - (q_{t+j} - hq_{t+j+1})\} \equiv z_{t+j}.$$

   Use $I_t = K_t - (1-d)K_{t-1}$,

$$\frac{1}{c}z_{t+j} = K(t+j) - (1-d)K(t+j-1) - h[K(t+j+1) - (1-d)K(t+j)],$$

   use lag operator

$$= -h\{1 - [\frac{1}{h} + (1-d)]L + \frac{(1-d)}{h}L^2\}K(t+j+1),$$

   factor out

$$= -h(1 - \frac{1}{h}L)[1 - (1-d)L]K(t+j+1).$$

   The stable and unstable roots are $(1-d)$ and $1/h$ respectively. Use the latter to solve in the forward direction

$$[1-(1-d)L]K(t+j+1)=\frac{-1}{ch}\frac{1}{(1-\frac{1}{h}L)}z_{t+j}$$

$$K(t+j+1)=(1-d)K(t+j)-\frac{1}{ch}\frac{1}{(1-\frac{1}{h}L)}z_{t+j}.$$

Note that

$$-\frac{1}{h}\frac{1}{(1-\frac{1}{h}L)}z_{t+j}=-\frac{1}{h}\frac{-(\frac{L}{h})^{-1}}{1-(\frac{L}{h})^{-1}}z_{t+j}=\frac{L^{-1}}{1-hL^{-1}}z_{t+j}$$

$$=\frac{1}{1-hL^{-1}}z_{t+j+1}.$$

Hence, we obtain (10.25).

2. The condition in terms of the shadow price of capital.
Let $F_K - c_K = m$ and $c_I + q = x$ and rewrite (10.5)

$$E_t\{m(t+j)-[L-h]x(t+j)\}=0$$

$$E_t\{\frac{1}{[L-h]}m(t+j)-x(t+j)\}=0$$

$$\frac{1}{[L-h]}m(t+j)=-\frac{1}{h}\frac{1}{(1-L/h)}m(t+j)=-\frac{1}{h}\frac{-(L/h)^{-1}}{[1-(L/h)^{-1}]}m(t+j)$$

$$=-\frac{1}{h}\frac{-h/L}{(1-h/L)}m(t+j)=\frac{1}{L}\frac{1}{(1-h/L)}m(t+j)$$

$$=L^{-1}(1+hL^{-1}+h^2L^{-2}+\ldots)m(t-1)$$

$$=m(t)+hm(t+1)+h^2m(t+2)+\ldots$$

$$=\sum_{j=0}^{\infty}h^j m(t+j)\equiv M_t$$

$$E_t\{M_t-(q_t+c_I(t))\}=0,$$

where $M_t \equiv \sum_{j=0}^{\infty} h^j m(t+j)$ is the shadow price of capital determined as the present value of the net (of adjustment cost) marginal productivity of capital in present and future production.

PART THREE

Technology

11

Agricultural Production Functions: An Overview

Technology, along with the competitive conditions, constitutes the core of the supply side of the economy. There is hardly a subject in economics that can be discussed with production sitting in the balcony rather than taking center stage. Among the core subjects in agricultural economics research are product supply, factor demand, technical change, income distribution, the relationships between factor prices and product prices, the competitive position of agriculture, returns to scale, the size distribution of firms, and capital accumulation. The nature of the relationships and the conclusions derived in any particular analysis depend on the order of magnitude of the parameters in question. Hence the empirical analysis of technology and its changes is of cardinal importance, and measurement problems are pertinent even if on the surface it seems that the subject matter is "not technical."

This and the following three chapters deal with the various aspects of the analysis. As will become clear, much of the discussion in the literature is methodology driven, often unaccompanied by substantive applications. In as much as methodological innovations are desirable, the question is how do they help us to think of, or deal with, specific issues of interest. This is a question that readers should try to answer for themselves, depending on their particular interest. To assist in this endeavor, this chapter provides an overview of the empirical analyses that bear on the main parameters of interest and highlights important methodological issues pertinent to the interpretation of empirical studies and to future research. The empirical findings themselves have been reviewed in Mundlak (2000). In many cases, the empirical results display a wide range of subjects and as such highlight the need for an appropriate framework for their evaluation. The choice of subjects and the discussion are carried out with the purpose of constructing a uniform framework to meet the purpose. This is built on the cumulative experience and contributions provided by numerous studies and on the evolution of thought that is so valuable in the reading and interpretation of the data.

There have been two fundamental approaches to estimating production functions: direct and indirect, using duality. Chapter 12 will argue that indirect estimation of the production structure is inferior to direct estimation and will propose an estimator that uses all the available information most efficiently. The discussion brings up the role played by various error components in the identification of the production function. This is done for the case of a Cobb-Douglas function, but the message is general. Most of the literature is based on the assumption that there exists a unique production function to be estimated, but many of the empirical results are inconsistent with this naive assumption. Chapter 13 extends the analysis by following the discussion in Chapter 6 and allowing the technology to consist of more than one technique. The choice of the implemented techniques is an economic decision, and consequently the analysis is modified. A key question is the role of prices in production decisions. Chapter 14 examines this question in depth. The issues discussed in these chapters are also relevant to the empirical discussions in Chapters 9 and 10.

Introduction

Empirical work on agricultural production functions seems to have originated in a methodological paper by Tintner (1944) and an application by Tintner and Brownlee (1944), which appeared as a short paper in the Notes section of the *Journal of Farm Economics* and was followed by a full paper by Heady (1944). This work was influenced by the work of Cobb and Douglas (1928). It thus took about fifteen years to adopt the work of Douglas in an agricultural economics application. Since then, the applications have grown and expanded in various directions. The evolution of the empirical analysis of agricultural production functions has been surveyed elsewhere (Mundlak, 2000). This chapter considers some of the main conclusions of this survey as an introduction to the discussions in the remainder of this volume.

There are two fairly distinct periods in the study of agricultural production functions, as well as for other sectors: before and after duality. The changing of the guard occurred in the early 1970s, although a few studies employing direct estimation continued to appear after 1970. The introduction of duality changed not only the method of estimation but also the questions asked to such an extent that there is little continuity in the subjects of interest. This can be accounted for by the fact that much of the work is driven by methodology rather than by the conviction that the old questions have been adequately answered or by any explicit agenda.

Primal Estimates, or the Cobb-Douglas Culture

The centerpiece in the primal estimation is the Cobb-Douglas function. The approach does not impose the competitive conditions but instead submits them to empirical testing. Such testing often shows a difference between the factor shares and the estimated production elasticities. This is not an absolute rejection of the prevalence of the competitive conditions but rather a conditional result, based on the model used and the statistical procedure. Still, such results are indicative of wide gaps. Several points of interest are related to the earlier studies:

- They were prompted by a methodological innovation introduced by Douglas. Nevertheless, their orientation is applicative in nature, and they address substantive issues related to the efficiency of production.
- Sampling from the same data source yields different elasticities. This difference suggests sensitivity of the estimates to output composition and perhaps to differences in the physical environment.
- The sum of the elasticities is less than one.

A major methodological issue was introduced at a very early stage by Marschak and Andrews (1944), who pointed out that the inputs are endogenous and therefore OLS estimates of the production function are biased. Their paper extended the scope of the analysis by introducing issues related to the statistical properties of the estimates. Their work and that of Haavelmo (1947) on the consumption function were early examples of the problems of simultaneity in economic analysis and thus revived the question that had been asked by Working in 1927 about the meaning of statistical demand equations. This subject is discussed in Chapter 12.

The approach formulated by the early studies served as a framework for the production function estimation for more than two decades, with data varying from observations on individual farms to cross-country comparisons. The attention was focused on the following issues:

- The contribution of various factors to the explanation of output variations in cross-section and over time
- Production elasticities and their significance
- The robustness of the estimates
- The role and magnitude of economies of scale
- The importance of input quality

- The treatment of management and its relation to the properties of the estimates
- The functional forms
- Technical change

The empirical results show that the elasticity of labor in agriculture never exceeds 0.5, and in most cases it varies in the range of 0.25 to 0.45. This value is well below the elasticity of labor in nonagriculture. If one considers all nonlabor income as capital income, the result supports the position that agriculture is capital-cost intensive and therefore is less susceptible to increases in the wage rate than nonagriculture. In addition, the labor elasticity declines with time, indicating that the technical change has been labor saving. The elasticity of land varies between zero in some cases to about one-third. It seems that the higher value is obtained when technology is controlled for in the analysis (Chapter 13).

The sum of elasticities of farm inputs (that is, inputs decided on by the farmer, in contrast to public inputs) is used as a measure of economies of scale. In most, but not all, studies it is not significantly different from one indicating constant returns to scale. In some of the studies based on a cross-section of aggregate data this sum is greater than one, and this was taken by the authors as evidence of increasing returns to scale. The result, however, can be attributed to statistical bias, which arises from the fact that the regressions do not represent a production function (Chapter 13).

One justification for estimating production functions is to provide weights for the computation of technical change. However, this approach has not provided any substantive advantage as compared with the use of factor shares, even though factor shares may differ from production elasticities, because mistakes in specification and interpretation made by statistical studies are often greater than the discrepancies between the factor shares and the true production elasticities. The most damaging error has been the one involved in the finding of increasing returns to scale and its incorporation in the computation of total factor productivity, which has led to the elimination of the residual in a comparison of growth over time or productivity differences across countries.

An important feature common to many of the studies is the lack of robustness of the estimates and their dependence on the variables used and the sample coverage. This result is interpreted here as evidence of the sensitivity of the results to the techniques of production that are aggregated. This subject is taken up in Chapter 13.

The Cobb-Douglas functional form is somewhat restrictive, and one direction of the work has been to explore less restrictive functional forms. Arrow et al. (1961) introduced the constant elasticity of substitution (CES) function, which was widely used by economists but had only a negligible impact on agricultural production functions. Heady introduced quadratic functions (Heady and Dillon, 1961), but this did not have much of a following until Christensen, Jorgenson, and Lau (1973) introduced a quadratic function in logarithms (translog). Other forms of quadratic functions were also tried.[1]

Quadratic production functions, by their nature, contain many variables that are intercorrelated, and therefore the estimated parameters suffer from low precision to the extent that they often do not make sense. To overcome this problem, it has become a common procedure to estimate the production function parameters by fitting the factor shares, with or without the binding constraint on the estimates of the production function itself. The implicit idea is that the factor share variations observed in the sample can be attributed to differences in input ratios or, said differently, to different locations on the production function. Judging by the trend in the literature, the estimates of such functions, the most popular being the translog function, were not satisfying, and therefore a rescue was sought in the form of profit or cost functions. By this shift, the factor shares become functions of prices rather than of quantities. This shift is somewhat arbitrary in that it is not backed by any explicit justification.

The Duality Culture

The basic idea of duality is that a point on the production function corresponds uniquely to a vector of price ratios and vice versa. Consequently, variations in prices cause, and as such reflect, variations in quantities. But this equivalence raises the question: if regressing shares on quantities was not satisfactory, why should the use of prices as regressors do a better job? To answer this and related questions, we now turn to summarize the empirical evidence on duality.

Under duality, the technology is summarized by profit, cost, or revenue functions, referred to as dual functions. The profit function is expressed in terms of factor and product prices, the cost function is expressed in terms of factor prices and output, and the revenue function is expressed in terms of product prices and inputs (McFadden, 1978). In empirical analysis of time-series data, these functions generally include a measure of technology, usually a time trend. In addition, the profit or cost functions are allowed to include some fixed inputs and as such are qualified as restricted or short run. Similarly, the revenue or profit functions can be restricted by the inclusion of a constraint on output (that is, a production quota).

Duality theory became a standard subject in economic analysis in the late 1960s.[2] It was adopted for empirical applications with great hopes, but as with many innovations, the test of time has been less generous. There were several reasons for such optimism. For competitive firms, prices, unlike quantities, are exogenous, and therefore when used as explanatory variables they do not cause the simultaneous equations bias that is part of life in the primal estimation. This property is indeed valid but with a limited liability. First, it is not automatically applicable to aggregate data at the market or industry level. Second, as we will see in the next chapter, it is unnecessary to estimate a dual function in order to utilize the exogeneity of prices, when this is indeed the case.

More profoundly, the econometric literature was initially motivated by the ease that duality offers in characterizing the production structure. Heuristically speaking, duality means that the conditions derived from the optimization are used to move from a production function to dual functions (or behavioral functions, namely product supply and factor demand) and vice versa. This is a simple journey under self-duality when both the technology and the dual functions have closed-form expressions. Examples are the Cobb-Douglas or the CES functions. The problem arises when self-duality does not exist, as is the case with the more complicated functional forms such as the quadratic functions. The move to duality in this case shifts the weight from one foot to the other in that it makes the derivation of the behavioral functions direct, but it ignores the fact that questions asked about the production function itself require the exact indirect computations that were to be avoided by moving to dual functions.

For instance, given the profit, or cost, function, what is the marginal productivity of an input and how is it affected by the input ratios? The answer to the first question is simple, because by construction the competitive conditions are imposed, and therefore the marginal productivity is equal to the observed real factor price. The determination of the dependence of the marginal productivity of a given input on the level of other inputs is a question that has only a complicated answer, except when the function is self-dual. The truth of the matter is that the empirical (econometric) literature on duality does not ask these questions. Thus it appears that in practice duality is just a name, and the property is not fully exploited in the sense that the estimated behavioral functions are not used to answer questions related to relationships between inputs and outputs. In part this may be explained in terms of the computational difficulties in moving from one system to the other. This obstacle should be alleviated with the progress made in the ease of obtaining numerical solutions. But by the same token, such progress should also make it possible to estimate the production function directly and then derive the dual functions from it. As such, the potency of duality paves the way to avoid its use in estimation. The choice of whether to estimate a primal or a dual function should then be made on the basis of other criteria. These are discussed in Chapters 12 and 13. This chapter summarizes applications related to agriculture.[3]

The combination of duality and the use of quadratic functions has shifted the analysis to cover topics related to the properties of the production structure and comparative statics that, with some exceptions, had not been part of the agenda of most studies in the pre-duality era. Of particular interest is the attempt to fit production systems that are consistent with the assumptions of comparative statics. To fully describe all the properties of comparative statics, the single-output function with m inputs, or the corresponding dual function, should have at least $(m+1)(m+2)/2$ parameters (Hanoch, 1975). A quadratic function that maintains the symmetry conditions has exactly this many parameters, and as such it is considered flexible, in the sense that it can provide a second-order approximation to the unknown true production function. But there is a cost to this approximation because the empirical equation contains many variables. Since inputs tend to move together, it is statistically difficult to estimate the function directly with precision. Therefore the procedure has been to fit the factor shares to the data. It is in this respect that such procedures are basically an extension of the factor share estimator, originally suggested by Klein (1953).

For the dual functions to describe a production system consistent with comparative statics, they have to maintain some properties that can be tested empirically; the less trivial ones are monotonicity and convexity (or concavity, as the case may be). Monotonicity imposes signs on the first partial derivatives of the dual functions, whereas convexity imposes conditions on the second partial derivatives of the dual functions or, more to the point, on the sign of the Hessian matrix. If these conditions are not met, the system is inconsistent with profit maximization. Besides these regularity properties, the dual form is used to test various hypotheses about the production structure such as separability, homotheticity, and the form of technical change. The studies vary in the initial functional forms, in the type of function used in the estimation, and in the questions asked. The summary here is oriented to our needs. The details are given in Mundlak (2000).

Studies Based on Cost Functions

The cost function is defined as: $C(w, k, Y, t) = \min_v[w'v; Y = F(v, k, t)]$, where v is a vector of unconstrained inputs whose prices are denoted by w, k is a vector of constrained inputs, Y is a vector of outputs, prime indicates transpose, and t is a technology index.[4] Let $S_j(\cdot)$ be the factor share of the jth factor in total cost, then by the envelope theorem (Shephard's lemma):

$\partial \ln C(w, k, Y, t)/\partial \ln w_j \equiv S_j(w, k, Y, t)$. Various restrictions are imposed in empirical analysis on the function and most of the studies assume that all inputs are variable or unrestricted, in which case k is not part of the argument. In what follows, to simplify the notation we will use this assumption, unless indicated otherwise.

Homotheticity: $C(w, Y, t) = \phi(Y)C(w, t)$; hence, $S_j(w, Y, t) = S_J(w, t)$.

Neutral technical change: $C(w, Y, t) = A(t)C(w, Y)$; hence, $S_j(w, Y, t) = S_j(w, Y)$.

Homotheticity and neutrality: $S_j(w, Y, t) = S_j(w)$.

The cost function is often expressed as a quadratic function in the variables or as a monotonic transformation of the variables, most commonly logarithmic (translog function), so that the implied share equations are linear in the same variables. Unless indicated otherwise, the technology is represented by a time trend. The empirical analysis deals with the estimation of the factor share equation under one or more of the above restrictions, often not tested empirically. There is no single central issue in these studies; different studies emphasize different topics. The most frequent ones are related to the behavior of factor shares with respect to changes in factor prices, the trend in the shares (time as an index of technology), and the effect of output when homotheticity is not assumed. Some studies emphasize methodological aspects by testing the properties of the function needed to describe a production system consistent with comparative statics.

What Is the Message?

Factor shares have undergone changes over time; particularly, the share of labor declined, while that of machinery and purchased inputs increased. How much of these can be attributed to economic factors? On the whole, some of the changes in factor shares were associated with changes in factor prices, but the major part of the change is attributed to changes in output or reflects a time trend. There is a trade-off in the empirical analysis between the role of homotheticity and the neutrality of the technical change. When output was included in the equation, it tended to replace the role of the time variable. This result is consistent with the choice of technique framework; higher output was achieved with the implementation of new techniques that became available with time. The new techniques use factor ratios different from those used by old techniques.

Two conceptual limitations to the empirical analysis of cost functions may distort the results. First, the cost function is derived for a price-taker agent and as such does not apply to macro data where prices are determined by market supply and demand. The factor demand is derived from the cost function, and therefore it is affected by shocks affecting the cost function. These shocks are thereby translated to the factor prices. In short, factor prices need not be exogenous. This limitation applies to all studies that use market data–rather than firm data–including studies based on profit functions. This is not a trivial point, because agriculture cannot be assumed to be a price taker in the rural labor and capital markets and definitely not in the land market.

Second, a cost function is derived conditional on output, and this is interpreted erroneously in empirical analysis to mean that output is exogenous. In general, there is no reason to believe that the marginal cost, and therefore output, is independent of shocks to the cost function. This problem is not shared by profit functions.

Studies Based on Profit Functions

In addition to endogenizing output, the profit function provides a compact form to summarize a multiproduct technology and an efficient way to introduce the properties imposed by theory on this system. There is no real discussion in the literature on the choice of whether to estimate a profit or cost function, and the choice is not empirically tested. The comparison between the two empirical models is not immediate, particularly when the cost function is not homothetic and output appears as a variable in the share equations.

Many of the empirical studies fail to confirm the conditions for the convexity of the profit function and as such eliminate the justification for their use. In fact, those studies where convexity is not confirmed should go no further because the remaining results have no theoretical support. To enable the derivation of certain results, some authors impose convexity as well as other conditions, a procedure that limits the value of such results. The product-supply and factor-demand elasticities are often low, a subject discussed at length in Chapter 14. The main variable that accounts for the changes over time in output and inputs, or in their shares, is the trend, and this simply reflects what can be seen by looking at the data without any sophisticated analysis. The analysis is sensitive to the level of aggregation. Finally, no dominant functional form emerges from all these studies, which suggests that the functional form is of secondary importance. This finding is related to the importance of the heterogeneous technology discussed in Chapter 13.

Duality: Summary and Conclusions

In summarizing the empirical findings, it has to be kept in mind that the published studies are mostly for the United States, Canada, and Japan, so the numerical values may not be fully representative. The main developments in these countries, however, are shared by other countries. The postwar period is characterized by a strong technical change in agriculture, both in level and in the direction of factor use. Yields increased together with improved varieties and the use of chemicals, while labor was replaced by machines. As such, the results have broad implications, and they facilitate the drawing of important methodological conclusions.

What distinguishes the dual approach from the primal is the appearance of prices in the empirical equation. Hence, in evaluating the performance of this approach we address the following questions:

- What has been the contribution of prices to the empirical equation?
- What additional information is obtained from the dual equations and how can they be interpreted?
- Are the underlying assumptions of duality met?
- What are the statistical benefits of this approach?
- Where do we go from here?

The Role of Prices

The dual estimates are generally obtained by regressing factor shares on prices, time trend, and sometimes output. When the change in the use of inputs is decomposed to price, time (usually referred to as technology), and output effects, it is found that trend and output capture most of the changes, whereas the role of prices is the least important. Thus the direct contribution of prices to the explanation of inputs or output variations is rather limited.

The price elasticities of factor demand and product supply are usually obtained under the assumption that their supply is perfectly elastic. On the whole, the own-price elasticities are less than 1. There is no uniformity in the signs of the cross elasticities, but in general, most inputs appear to be substitutes. The strength of the own and cross elasticities partly reflects the fact that factor supplies are not perfectly elastic as the models assume, and therefore the results need not represent the demand-driven substitution as it is thought. This is the case with respect to elasticities related to labor, land, and capital, whose sum is between 0.8 to 0.9; therefore the supply elasticity is expected to be low (Chapter 14).

Additional Information

On the whole, the studies based on duality do not show increasing returns to scale. Technical change, obtained by including a time trend in regressions of factor shares, is largely labor saving, capital using, and fertilizer using, while the results on land are somewhat ambiguous. This is reflective of the data, which means that whatever the effect of prices was, it was not sufficient to change conclusions that could be drawn from the raw data. This does not give a strong mark to the analysis in that the results are obvious without it.

Assumptions of Duality

Duality between technology and prices hold under well-defined conditions that can be tested empirically. In most studies these underlying conditions are not fully met; in particular, the concavity of the cost function or the convexity of the profit function is frequently violated. The estimated technology is therefore inconsistent with the basic premises of the model. In a way, this is the most disappointing result because duality is a very powerful theory, and the question is why it does not come through in the empirical analysis. There is probably more than one reason, some of which have been mentioned above; one is that duality is a micro theory but most of the studies use macro data. As such, the implemented technology is endogenous, and the production function is not properly identified. What seem to be the more important reasons are examined in depth over the next three chapters.

Statistical Benefits

One of the expected virtues of duality has been related to its solution of the simultaneous equation bias realized in some primal estimators. However, a closer examination of this issue in Chapter 12 indicates that in general dual estimators are inferior to primal estimators.

Heterogeneous Technology

As indicated above, some of the empirical results do not make economic sense under the assumption of homogeneous technology. Consequently the analysis is extended to take account of the fact that the technology consists of more than one technique. Chapter 13 continues the discussion in Chapter 6 and examines the implications of heterogeneous technology for our view of production and the related empirical analysis.

Under heterogeneous technology producers choose the employed or implemented technology in response to the economic environment. As a result, the coefficients of the implemented production function become functions of variables representing the economic environment. Thus policies affect outputs and inputs through their impact on the implemented technology in addition to their direct effect on resource allocation. This constitutes a major difference from traditional analysis, where the impact of the economic environment on production is limited to the direct effect on resource allocation. The various aspects of this approach and its impact on the estimation of the production function are discussed in Chapter 13.

Agricultural supply has drawn special attention, and work on the subject had started long before the work on agricultural production functions. Analytically, the two topics are strongly related through duality, but as the discussion in Chapter 14 indicates, the analysis of supply has expanded in various directions. Of particular importance is the analysis of the role and behavior of quasi-fixed factors. The discussion of dynamics in Chapter 10 is further extended to cover dynamic-dual models. Such models provide powerful analytic techniques but, as in the case of the static-dual models, the empirical results are not convincing. Finally, the integration of the production model in an economywide model of sectoral growth is the subject of Chapter 15.

12

Empirical Production Functions: Statistical Aspects

As early as 1944, Marschak and Andrews showed that inputs may be correlated with the shocks of the production function, and therefore OLS estimates of the production function are subject to simultaneous equations bias, or simply are inconsistent. This chapter deals mainly with the problem of simultaneity. We begin the discussion with the analysis of the consequences of simultaneity and of methods to overcome it in empirical analysis. Duality uses the fact that prices are exogenous and can therefore be utilized to produce consistent estimates. Using prices is one possibility, but there are others; the most important one is using the deviations from the first-order conditions for maximization. Do such deviations constitute errors of optimization made by firms, as commonly assumed in the literature, or do they reflect incomplete knowledge on the part of the econometrician? To gain insight on this subject we consider a simple model of firm behavior under uncertainty to show that such deviations can be the outcome of rational decisions. Finally, we examine some aspects of measurement errors that are related to the proposed estimators.

The Root of the Simultaneity Problem

The problem of simultaneity stems from the fact that the econometrician has less information than the firms about the production process. The firms determine the level of inputs and outputs on the basis of their information, whereas econometricians have to infer the underlying technology on the basis of incomplete data and their own knowledge of the process. As a consequence, the inference is potentially erroneous.

The problem can be presented in terms of Figure 12.1, where production functions of two firms are drawn. It is assumed that the two firms meet the first-order conditions for profit maximization and face the same prices. Firm 1 is located at point A and firm 2 is located at point A'. Fitting a production function to a sample consisting of points A and A' will not reproduce the function of

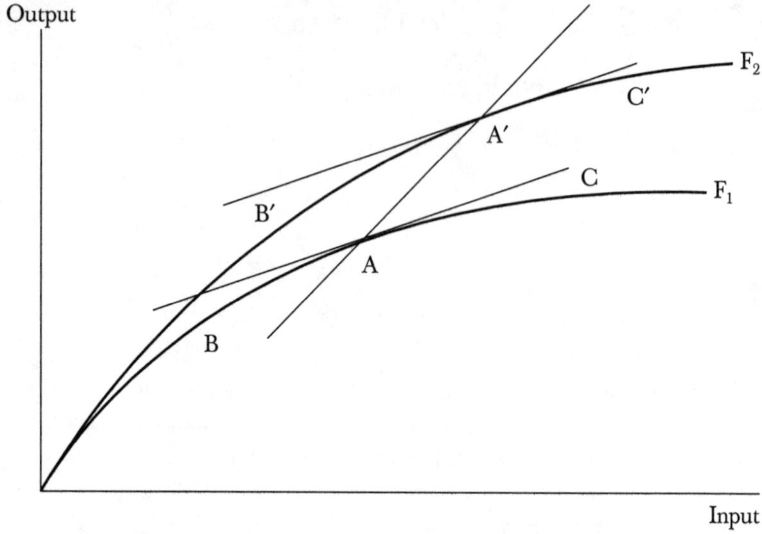

Figure 12.1 Observations on production functions

either firm, for the reason that there is a missing variable known to the firms and taken into account in their optimization, making the inputs endogenous. As this variable is unobserved, it is omitted from the analysis, and the empirical function is a biased estimator of the underlying function.

In order to trace the production function empirically, it is necessary to have a spread in observations on the *same* function. For instance, such a spread is given by points A, B, and C on F_1 in Figure 12.1. The utilization of this spread in inputs for the purpose of estimation depends on the causes of the spread. Two major reasons are apparent:

1. Differences in prices faced by firms. This is the easy case for the econometrician. In this case, if the firms meet the competitive condition, then the prices reveal the slope of the production function (marginal productivity). Knowing the slope of the function makes it possible to obtain a numerical solution for the function if the algebraic specification is manageable. This approach leads to either the factor share estimator, which utilizes the first-order condition directly, or to estimates based on duality. With two types of firms, a similar spread is also obtained for firms of type F_2.

If the missing variable that differentiates between the two types is independent of prices, the data can be pooled and the same procedure followed. This is the case when the variability in the production function reflects the variability in managerial ability or in entrepreneurship in the population. Because prices are exogenous to the firms in a competitive industry, they are not correlated with managerial ability. This is probably the reason that estimates of the production function based on duality have been widely used. This approach fails, however, if the choice of the implemented production function depends on prices, a subject examined in the next chapter.

2. Errors in optimization. Firms operate in a stochastic environment, and as such their behavior depends on their attitude toward risk and on their method of processing the flow of information for expectation formation. These two elements generate a gap between the information available to the firm and that available to the econometrician. The term "error" in optimization refers to the difference between the first-order condition as viewed by the econometrician, based on his information set, and that perceived by the firms in making their decisions. As such the error is that of the econometrician and not of the firm.

Although all firms in a competitive industry face the same prices, they differ considerably in their inputs and outputs. Prices are generally unknown, and therefore production decisions are based on forecasts of future prices. Such forecasts require processing of the available information, a costly operation with its own cost-benefit considerations, leading to interfirm, as well as intrafirm, variations. Furthermore, acting on the basis of a forecast generates uncertainty, and firms differ in their attitude toward risk. Hence in general the maximization of expected profit is not a sufficient criterion for explaining firm behavior. This is not a trivial point. It is possible that a small sacrifice in expected profit in order to reduce risk will lead to a considerable difference in the endogenous variables of the firm (Mundlak, 1971; Mundlak and Volcani, 1973).

While unobserved firm-specific variables in the production function cause inputs to be endogenous, such variables in the first-order conditions help in the estimation of the function. To summarize, unobserved differences in production functions known to the firms and taken into account in the optimization make the inputs endogenous. However, inputs vary in the sample also as a result of variations in prices and of errors in optimization. Such variations in inputs are exogenous if the prices or the deviations from optimization are uncorrelated with the disturbances in the production function. These considerations and their consequences are now discussed in more detail.[1]

A Simple Model

Duality theory is basically a micro theory, and as such its empirical implications are related to firm, rather than market, data. Initially, the discussion is conducted within this framework, and as such we ignore further complications that arise from the use of aggregate market data. The conceptual problems in the choice of estimators can be presented in terms of a well-known simple model. Whatever other virtues more complex models possess, the problems discussed here are not resolved by the added complexity.

Let the production function be

$$Y = AX^{\gamma} e^{m_0 + u_0}, \tag{12.1}$$

where m_0 is the firm effect, a firm-specific factor known to the firm but not to the econometrician (incomplete information), and u_0 is a random term whose value is not known at the time the production decisions are made. The conditional expectation of the output, given the input, of firm i is:

$$Y_i^e \equiv E(Y\,|_{X_i}) = AX_i^{\gamma} e^{m_{0i}+\eta_i}, \tag{12.2}$$

where $e^{\eta_i} = E(e^{u_0}\,|_i)$. Indexing this term with i allows for possible differences among firms in the evaluation of the distribution of u_0. At this stage we assume that the price is known and that the firm chooses the input so as to maximize the expected profit:

$$\max_{X_i} = PY_i^e - X_i, \tag{12.3}$$

where P is the real product price measured in input units. It is assumed that the first-order condition is met up to a stochastic term:

$$dY^e/dX = (1/P)e^{m_1+u_1}, \tag{12.4}$$

where m_1 is a term known to the firm, but not to the econometrician, and u_1 is a transitory component. To avoid sidetracking, we postpone the discussion of m_1 to a later stage, where it will be shown that it reflects the firm's expectation formation and its utility function.

To obtain the production system, differentiate (12.2) and substitute in (12.4). Label Z_{it} the *it*-th observation on a variable Z for firm i in year t, $i = 1, \ldots, N; t = 1, \ldots, T; T \geq 1; Z = X, Y, P; j = 0, 1$. We write the system in logarithms, where lowercase letters denote here deviations, in log forms, from the sample means, $z_{it} = \ln Z_{it} - \frac{1}{n}\Sigma_i \Sigma_t \ln Z_{it}$, $n = NT$. There is no need to differentiate here between m_{1i} and η_i, and we therefore combine them and redefine $m_{1i} = m_{1i} - \eta_i$. We can write the system as

$$y_{it} - x_{it}\gamma = m_{0i} + u_{0it} \tag{12.5}$$

$$y_{it} - x_{it} = -p_{it} + m_{1i} + u_{1it} + u_{0it}. \tag{12.6}$$

When prices are exogenous, the reduced form for x is

$$x_{it} = (p_{it} - u_{1it} - m_{1i} + m_{0i})(1 - \gamma)^{-1}. \tag{12.7}$$

The four error components are assumed to be identically and independently distributed (IID) with the following first two moments:

$$u_{jit} \sim (0, \sigma_{jj}); \quad m_{j}, \sim (\mu_j, \tau_{jj}); \quad j = 0, 1. \tag{12.8}$$

The assumption of independence of u over time implies no serial correlation. We can think of u as a disturbance that reflects variables, such as weather, that firms cannot predict. There may be shocks that affect all firms in a given year, such as a flood, and thereby generate correlation in u among firms. Such shocks generate a time effect that can be treated in the same way as the firm effect. The extension to include a time effect is straightforward and need not be reviewed here (see Mundlak, 1963).

Equation (12.7) shows that the input is a function of the firm effect, m_{0i}, which is also part of the production function shock, and therefore the input is not exogenous. The mean of the firm effect in production is set at zero, $\mu_0 = 0$. This is an arbitrary decision that does not affect the analysis. On the other hand, the mean of the firm effect in the first-order condition, μ_1, is determined by the distribution of u_1, and therefore cannot be set a priori arbitrarily at zero. The expected value of all cross products of the error components are zero. There is nothing in the model that suggests correlation between m_0 and m_1. Any deviation from the optimal value of m_1 implies a loss in expected profits for the desired level of risk. Consequently, there is no efficient deviation from optimal m_1 that could correspond to production efficiency. It simplifies the exposition, without a sacrifice in substance, to assume zero correlation between the two components.

Estimators

The discussion deals with the estimation of γ. Before examining the various estimators, we take up two special cases. First is the case where CRS is imposed on the function, a practice often followed. In this case, $\gamma = 1$ and there is no need for estimation. This may seem to be a trivial comment at this stage, but its relevance will become apparent later when the problem is extended to more than one input. This is now generalized:

PROPERTY 12.1 (degree of the function) A numerical assumption about the degree of the function is an identifying restriction.

The second case is that of exogenous output, an assumption made in the estimation of the cost function. Under this assumption, the production function can be estimated directly using the output as an instrumental variable to produce a consistent estimator.

The various estimators are presented here within a uniform framework based on instrumental variables. The efficiency of the estimator increases with the correlation of the instrumental variables and the input, x. The neat property of this model is that equation (12.7) indicates explicitly all the sources of input variations. Hence we have an explicit framework for evaluating the consequences of the various estimators. It is apparent that the most efficient instrumental variable would be the sum of p, u_1, and m_1. But u_1 and m_1 are unobserved and to extract efficiently the pertinent information that they contain, it is necessary to rely on observed variables. This is the essence of the estimation problem. In order to gain an insight into the common estimators we begin with special cases, interesting by themselves, that are subsequently generalized.

The statistical properties of the various estimators are evaluated within the framework of large samples. Throughout, the probability limits are evaluated for $N \to \infty$ and finite T. The criterion used here to evaluate the performance of the consistent estimators is the variance of the limiting distribution. We label $V(\hat{\gamma})$ to indicate plim $n(\hat{\gamma} - \gamma)^2$, where $\hat{\gamma}$ is a consistent estimator. In what follows, we use matrix notations: let $z_t \equiv (z_{1t}, \ldots, z_{Nt})'$ be the vector of observations on all firms for year t and $z \equiv (z_1', \ldots, z_T')'$, $m_j(i) \equiv (m_{j1}, \ldots, m_{jN})'$ is the vector of the firm effects in equation j. Because $m_j(i)$ is the same for all t, we form a vector m_j with T components: $m_j \equiv [m_j(i), \ldots, m_j(i)]'$. With these notations we rewrite the system:

$$y - x\gamma = m_0 + u_0 \tag{12.5'}$$

$$y - x = -p + m_1 + u_1 + u_0 \tag{12.6'}$$

$$x = (p - u_1 - m_1 + m_0)(1 - \gamma)^{-1}. \tag{12.7'}$$

In what follows it is efficient to use matrix notations. We will use repeatedly projection (symmetric and idempotent) matrices that generate residuals. We label W, $W(i)$, and $B(i)$ for the matrices that generate residuals from the overall mean (pooled residuals), within-firm residuals, and between-firm residuals. They can be defined in terms of their operation on an arbitrary vector $z = \{z_{it}\}$ of order NT : $Wz = (z_{it} - z_{..})$, $W(i)z = (z_{it} - z_{i.})$, $B(i)z = (z_{i.} - z_{..})$, where $z_{i.} = \sum_t z_{it}/T$, and $z_{..} = \sum_{it} z_{it}/NT$. Because we have already defined our transformed variables as deviations from the overall mean, we have for those variables $Wz = z$.

Dual Estimator

The dual estimator uses the information in p. As we have seen, estimates based on duality are often obtained by estimating factor demand or product supply, which are the first-order derivatives of cost or profit functions. In the present model the estimator can be described by[2]

$$\hat{\gamma}_p = \frac{p'y}{p'x}. \tag{12.9}$$

Using equation (12.5),

$$\hat{\gamma}_p = \gamma + \frac{p'(m_0 + u_0)}{p'x};$$

hence, plim $\hat{\gamma}_p = \gamma$.

In passing we note that the original problem of identifying the production function as posed by Marschak and Andrews (1944) assumed no price variations across competitive firms. In that case, it is impossible to estimate the supply and factor demand functions, and the dual estimator cannot be computed. Thus a major claimed virtue of empirical dual functions–that prices are more exogenous than quantities–cannot be attained.

PROPERTY 12.2 As the dual estimator requires a spread in prices, the sample should contain observations on agents operating in different markets.

The markets can be separated geographically, in time, or in other attributes.

As to the measure of precision, let $\mathrm{Var}(p) \equiv \sigma_{pp}$, then

$$V(\hat{\gamma}_p) = (1-\gamma)^2 \frac{\sigma_{00} + \tau_{00}}{\sigma_{pp}}. \tag{12.10}$$

Ordinary Least Squares (OLS)

The OLS estimator uses input as an instrumental variable. Inspecting equation (12.7), we see that x is a sum of four terms, of which p and u_1 are uncorrelated with the errors in the production function and thus maintain a requirement of instrumental variables for estimating γ. When m_1 is uncorrelated with m_0, as assumed here, it also serves as an instrument. However, when x is a function of m_0, it is not qualified to be an instrumental variable because it is correlated with the error term in (12.5). We therefore differentiate the cases according to the availability of information.[3] The estimator is

$$\hat{\gamma}_o = \frac{x'y}{x'x}. \tag{12.11}$$

Incomplete Information ($\tau_{00} > 0$)

In this case, the firm knows m_0, but the econometrician does not; therefore it is part of his error.[4] Referring to equation (12.7), we see that x contains all the relevant information for the estimation and, unfortunately, more than that because it is also a function of m_0. As such, it is generally correlated with the error term in (12.5). It then follows:

$$\hat{\gamma}_o = \gamma + \frac{x'(m_0 + u_0)}{x'x}.$$

Using (12.7),

$$\text{plim } \hat{\gamma}_o - \gamma = (1-\gamma)^{-1}\frac{\tau_{00}}{V_x}, \tag{12.12}$$

where V_x is the variance of x.

Complete Information ($\tau_{00} = 0$)

The firm does not have more information than the econometrician; hence x is independent of the production function disturbance.[5] It follows from (12.12) that the estimator is consistent, and it is most efficient because it utilizes all the available information.

$$V(\hat{\gamma}_o) = (1-\gamma)^2\frac{\sigma_{00}}{V}, \tag{12.13}$$

where $V = \sigma_{11} + \sigma_{pp} + \tau_{11}$. Comparing the dual and the OLS estimators using (12.13) and (12.10):

$$\frac{V(\hat{\gamma}_o)}{V(\hat{\gamma}_p)} = \frac{\sigma_{pp}}{V} \leq 1. \tag{12.14}$$

Under complete information, the conditions of the Gauss-Markov theorem apply, hence:

PROPERTY 12.3 With complete information, the OLS primal estimator is superior to the dual estimator.

Incomplete Information: Panel Data

When panel data are available, we take advantage of the fact that m_0 and m_1 are time invariant and that u_0 and u_1 are serially uncorrelated and use the *within* estimator:

$$\hat{\gamma}_w = \frac{x'W(i)y}{x'W(i)x}. \tag{12.15}$$

Using this transformation, we rewrite equation (12.5) for the it-th observation:

$$y_{it} - y_{i.} = \gamma(x_{it} - x_{i.}) + (u_{0it} - u_{0i.}).$$

This transformed production function expresses time variations of the variables in question for a *given* firm, and as such it is free of the firm-specific effect, m_0. The estimator in (12.15) is unbiased and consistent. To see this, use equation (12.7) to express the reduced form in matrix notation: $W(i)x = [W(i)p - W(i)u_1](1-\gamma)^{-1}$; hence, $W(i)x$ contains the two instruments, p and u_1, in a time deviation form, and it ignores the interfirm variations in the variables. Label $\mathrm{Var}(W(i)p) \equiv \sigma^w_{pp} I_{NT}$, then the variance of this estimator is:

$$V(\hat{\gamma}_w) = (I-\gamma)^2 \frac{\sigma_{00}}{\sigma^w_{pp} + \sigma_{11}}. \tag{12.16}$$

To compare the dual and the *within* estimators, decompose the total variance of w to the *within* and *between* components, $\sigma_{pp} = \sigma^w_{pp} + \sigma^b_{pp}$:

$$\frac{V(\hat{\gamma}_w)}{V(\hat{\gamma}_p)} = (1-\rho_0)\frac{\sigma^w_{pp} + \sigma^b_{pp}}{\sigma^w_{pp} + \sigma_{11}}, \tag{12.17}$$

where the intraclass correlation coefficient, $\rho_0 = \tau_{00}/(\sigma_{00} + \tau_{00})$, is bounded by 0 and 1. For the ratio in (12.17) to be smaller than 1 it is sufficient that the variance of the optimization error exceeds that of the between price variations. More generally, it is unlikely that this ratio will be larger than 1 because for this to happen, it is necessary that $(1-\rho_0)\sigma^b_{pp} > \rho_0\sigma^w_{pp} + \sigma_{11}$. To summarize:

PROPERTY 12.4 In general, the *within* primal estimator is superior to the dual estimator.

A Generalization

The relative efficiency of the *within* estimator, as compared with the dual estimator, originates from two sources: first, from the smaller variance of the dependent variable, and second, from the additional information provided by the optimization error, u_1. The latter is the reason that deviations from the first-order conditions contribute to the identification of the production function. However, by construction, the *within* estimator does not utilize the between-firm variations in the price. This shortcoming can be amended by combining several instrumental variables. Define an $(nx2)$ matrix $Z \equiv [p, W(i)x]$, and a projection matrix, $K \equiv Z(Z'Z)^{-1}Z'$. The proposed estimator is

$$\hat{\gamma}_g = \frac{y'Kx}{x'Kx}. \tag{12.18}$$

The estimator is consistent and cannot be less efficient than either the *within* or the *dual* estimators.[6] In principle, it improves on the *within* estimator by utilizing the between price variations. The price can be decomposed to two orthogonal components, within $[W(i)p]$ and between $[B(i)p]$. The information of the within component is already contained in $W(i)x$, and hence the contribution of p to the estimator is due to the between component. The question is whether in practice this improvement is actually noticeable. To answer this question, we can regress x on Z and test whether one of the two instruments can be omitted.

Another extension along this line can be considered. Following Amemiya and MaCurdy (1986), we might consider the various lags and leads of p : $Z \equiv [p_1, \ldots, p_T, W(i)x]$. The contribution of the additional instruments is an empirical question and will probably vary among applications.

This approach can now be extended further in order to utilize the information in m_1 as well. Such information can be extracted from the average productivity. Label $q \equiv y - x$ and note from equation (12.6) that q contains all the information related to the variability of x, but unfortunately, it also depends on u_0. As such, it serves as a good instrument in the original Marschak and Andrews model, where the information is complete, so that $\sigma_{00} = 0$ (Mundlak, 1963). When this is not the case, using q as an instrumental variable leads to an inconsistent estimator. However, when u_0 are serially uncorrelated, we can use lagged or lead values of q as instruments (Mundlak, 1983, 1996; Conlon, 1988). There is no empirical experience on the basis of which we can evaluate the potential of this estimator in empirical analysis.

Finally, the efficiency of the various estimators can be enhanced by noticing that the variance of the error in the production function is heteroskedastic. Let $\Sigma_0 = \text{Var}(u_0 + m_0)$, $\otimes$ is the Kronecker product, $\Sigma_0 = [\sigma_{00} I_{NT} + \tau_{00}(\iota_T \iota_T' \otimes I_N)]$, and ι_T is a T-vector of ones. Label a consistent estimator of Σ_0 as $\hat{\Sigma}_0$, and define H such that $H'H = \hat{\Sigma}_0$, then

$$\hat{\gamma}_{gg} = \frac{y'HKH'x}{x'HKH'x} \tag{12.19}$$

This is a feasible 3SLS (three-stage least squares). The estimate of Σ_0 is obtained by first computing $\hat{\gamma}_g$, using the estimator in (12.18) to obtain the residuals, which can then be used to estimate the variance components σ_{00}, τ_{00}, which in turn are used to compute H.

More than One Input

When the function has $k > 1$ inputs, the model consists of equation (12.5) and k equations of the form of (12.6). As observed by Cavallo (1976), discussed by Fuss, McFadden, and Mundlak (1978, p. 261), and also used by Schmidt (1988, p. 368), the difference between the first-order conditions of any two inputs, say 1 and 2, written in logs as deviations from the means, is free of m_0 and of u_0:

$$x_2 - x_1 = p_2 - p_1 + u_2 - u_1 + m_2 - m_1. \tag{12.20}$$

Therefore $x_2 - x_1$ can serve as an instrumental variable. The right-hand side of (12.20) contains *all* the information related to the two inputs.

There are $k - 1$ such independent instruments, and there is a need for one more instrumental variable to estimate all the parameters in question. Thus the problem of multiple inputs collapses to that of a single input. This is a strong result in two respects. First, there are no further complications in moving from one to more inputs. Second, imposing one more restriction provides a complete identification of the production function. Assuming CRS does this. It thus appears that the main problem of simultaneity is in the estimation of the degree of the function. Given CRS, a Cobb-Douglas function of average labor productivity as a function of the inputs-labor ratio is free of simultaneous equation bias. In many of the applications using dual functions, CRS is indeed assumed. It appears that in these cases a direct OLS is preferable.

PROPERTY 12.5 (consistency of OLS) Under CRS, OLS estimates of a k-input Cobb-Douglas production function in average productivity form are consistent.

Studies based on cost functions assume output to be exogenous (see Schmidt, 1988). In this case output provides the needed instrument, and CRS need not be imposed.

If none of these conditions is met, it is suggested that the estimator in equation (12.18) be used with Z redefined to include $k - 1$ independent conditions of the form of equation (12.20), all the prices, and the *within* deviations of the inputs. This will probably have numerous overidentifying restrictions that could be eliminated in the first stage of the estimation, which consists of the construction of the instrumental variables.

The whole discussion is based on the assumption of no correlation between the errors in the production function and those in the first-order conditions. The reason is related to the different natures of these two error types. This assumption can be tested empirically, and if rejected, the estimator can be further generalized by applying the 3SLS to the system as a whole. The framework is well known and need not be reproduced here.

Factor Shares

The factor share estimator proposed by Klein (1953) is a very simple estimator that provides useful information with little effort in calculation. The estimator is obtained from

$$\ln \hat{\gamma}_s = \frac{1}{n} \sum_t \sum_i \ln \frac{X_{it}}{(PY)_{it}}; \quad \hat{\gamma}_s = e^{\ln \hat{\gamma}_s}.$$

Substituting the reduced-form values:

$$\ln \hat{\gamma}_s = \ln \gamma - \frac{1}{n} \sum_t \sum_i (u_{1it} + m_{1i} + u_{0it}),$$

$$\text{plim}(\ln \hat{\gamma}_s) = \ln \gamma - \mu_1.$$

The estimator is inconsistent when there are systematic deviations from the first-order condition for profit maximization so that $\mu_1 \neq 0$. The existence of systematic deviations implies that the profit maximization as *perceived by the econometrician* is an inaccurate description of reality. This discrepancy is different in nature from that which accounts for the correlation between the inputs and the error in the production function. The limitation of the factor share estimator has to be placed in perspective by comparing it with the alternatives:

1. The inconsistency of the factor share estimator is a direct outcome of the assumption that the first-order condition for profit maximization is maintained. The same assumption is shared by other estimators, and specifically the dual estimator. However, the failure of the assumption has a different effect in both cases: While the mere *existence* of m_1 causes the dual estimator to lose efficiency, it causes the factor share estimator to be inconsistent *only if* the *mean* of m_1 is different from zero.

2. The factor share is constant only when the production function is Cobb-Douglas. In other functional forms the factor share varies with the input combinations. The algebraic presentation of the factor share in these cases is

more parsimonious in parameters than the production function itself. For this reason the parameters of the production functions are often estimated from an equation that "explains" the variations in the factor share.

3. The factor share estimator cannot be used to test discrepancies from the first-order conditions. This qualification is important, because we have no way to test parametrically whether the first-order conditions are maintained independently of the model actually used. However, the situation is different in the choice of techniques model discussed in Chapter 13. In this case, systematic differences between the marginal productivity and the corresponding factor price are expected to be absorbed by state variables, and thus the inconsistency is accounted for.

In spite of its limitations, there is a very important reason for using the factor share estimate, and that is its feasibility. Often it is the only estimator that can be obtained with the available information. It can be obtained from sparse national accounts data as well as from various surveys that exist for many countries for which the data needed to estimate a more refined production structure are simply unavailable. How much do we lose by using such a "second-best estimator"? It depends on the specific question asked, but often we lose very little. The computation of total factor productivity is often not very sensitive to small changes in the weights. Chapter 14 presents a simple estimator for supply elasticity that is based on factor shares. The price equation used repeatedly in the discussion of this volume can also be approximated by factor shares.

Allocation "Inefficiency"

Why are there deviations from the first-order conditions or, as they are often referred to, allocation errors? As a factual matter, a casual inspection of any sample of farms, or for that matter, firms in other competitive industries, will reveal a large spread in output and input composition relative to the spread in prices. If this spread were due to allocation errors, we would have to rethink the limited power of economic theory that is able to explain only a small part of the spread and generously attributes the rest to inefficiency. This has not only philosophical but also empirical implications. For instance, the literature on efficiency-frontier production functions considers deviations from the first-order conditions to be errors and develops estimators of the function accordingly.

We tend to think that such discrepancies are in part, even largely, due to incomplete information available to the econometrician about the behavior of firms. The gap in information may arise from a variety of reasons: differences in the quality of resources employed by the firms unaccounted for in the analysis, incorrect evaluation of the planning horizon, and the stochastic nature of production and market outcomes. In principal, the quality issue can be overcome, at least in part, by more detailed data collection. However, the situation is different with the evaluation of the effect of uncertainty, which depends on attitudes toward risk and expectation formation. It is important to note that when dealing with micro data what matters is the expectation formed by each individual. This depends on the resources needed to digest all the available information and the benefit from doing it. These elements vary across firms and are unobservable; therefore the econometrician does not take them into consideration in the analysis.

To illustrate the relevance of this discussion, we turn now to broaden the framework of the analysis by introducing uncertainty and assuming that the only adjustment that the firm can make to uncertainty is in its production plan. As such, we concentrate on the effect of uncertainty on production and ignore other possible adjustments to it. The qualitative results survive a generalization of the analysis. Such a simple extension will provide insight into the nature of this process. To make the analysis tractable, we use the mean-variance framework, which is consistent with the expected utility hypothesis when the error has a normal distribution or when the utility function is quadratic. Thus utility is a function of expected profit (π^e) and the standard deviation (σ_π) of profit. We also assume that the price is unknown at the time the production decision is made. By assumption, the level of input is determined conditional on expected price, P^e. The observed price is the product of the expected price and a shock,

$$P = P^e e^{\Delta P}; \quad \Delta P \sim (0, \sigma_{pp}). \tag{12.21}$$

These two components are independent, and the error term is uncorrelated with the other errors in the model. For the competitive firm, the market price distribution is independent of the output of the firm, hence the expected revenue is $R^e = P^e Y^e$. The actual revenue is $R = R^e e^\epsilon$, where $\epsilon = u_0 + \Delta P$ and as such is affected by the output and the price shocks.

We now examine the profit as a function of X, $\pi(X) = R^e(X)e^\epsilon - X$. To obtain the expected profit, expand e^ϵ around $\epsilon = 0$, ignore higher than second-degree terms, $\pi^e(X\,|_i) = R^e(1 + \frac{\sigma^2}{2}) - X\,|_i$, where $\sigma^2 = E(\epsilon^2)$. The variance of profits serves as a measure of risk. It is approximated by (see the appendix to this chapter for details)

$$\sigma_\pi^2(X) = E[\pi(X) - \pi^e(X\,|_i)]^2 \cong (R^e(X))^2\sigma^2(1 + \frac{1}{2}\sigma^2).$$

Note that the risk is taken to be proportional to the expected revenue in order to allow for the impact of a given shock to depend on the scale of operation.

The optimization problem is

$$\max_{X} U = U[\pi^e(X),\ \sigma_\pi(X)]. \tag{12.22}$$

Designate the first partial derivatives of U as U_π and U_σ and note that they are positive and nonpositive respectively (0 for risk neutrality). Label the marginal rate of substitution of σ_π and π^e at utility level U^0 as $\omega(U^0)$, then

$$\omega(U^0) \equiv -\frac{d\pi(U^0)}{d\sigma(U^0)} = \frac{U_\sigma^0}{U_\pi^0},$$

In what follows, we omit the explicit designation of the dependence on the level U^0. With this notation, the first-order condition for (12.22) is now written as:

$$\omega = \frac{d\pi^e(X)/dX}{d\sigma_\pi(X)/dX}. \tag{12.23}$$

Differentiate and simplify:

$$P^e \frac{dY^e}{dX} = [1 + \frac{\sigma^2}{2} - \sigma\omega(1 + \frac{\sigma^2}{2})^{\frac{1}{2}}]^{-1} \equiv m_1^*. \tag{12.24}$$

The expression in equation (12.24) provides a meaning to the firm effect in equation (12.4). There are three cases of interest:

1. Deterministic ($\sigma = 0$). Here $m_1^* = 1$ and the marginal productivity is equal to the real wage. This assumption is implicit in the empirical studies which utilize the first-order conditions for profit maximization. It is explicit in the literature on efficiency-frontier production functions, where the effect of allocation errors is considered.

2. Risk neutrality ($\omega = 0$). Here $m_1^* < 1$, the input and output are larger than in the deterministic case. This outcome results from the fact that expected profit is increasing in σ^2. Consequently, the larger the variance of prices, or of production shocks, the larger the expected profit.

3. Risk aversion ($\omega > 0$). The effect of risk aversion is to decrease input and output, as can be seen by inspecting equation (12.24). The comparison of this case with the deterministic one depends on the relative strength of the effect of σ and ω. For low values of ω, $m_1^* < 1$, implying larger input and output. As more weight is given to risk, that is, as ω increases, m_1^* increases and eventually becomes larger than 1. At this point, the level of input declines relative to the deterministic case. Thus it is the relative strength of the variance and the degree

of risk aversion that determine whether the input will be smaller or larger than in the deterministic case.

PROPERTY 12.6 The effect of risk on the level of input depends on the degree of risk aversion and cannot be signed a priori.

The foregoing discussion indicates that m_1^* is likely to vary among firms for two reasons. First, firms vary in their attitude toward risk, and second, they vary in their subjective evaluation of σ or, more generally, of the nature of the stochastic process. All producers have access to the same public information, but they may differ in the effort they apply to process this information and in the conclusions that they draw from it. The quantitative importance of these two factors in the context of the present discussion depends on the time horizon of the input.

By definition, m_1^* depends on ω, which may be a function of the income and risk and therefore need not be a constant. In this case, m_1^* represents the systematic part; the annual deviations are absorbed in u_1. As such m_1^* also reflects rational decisions. Similarly, there is no need to assume that σ is constant for the firm. Basically, it represents the spread of the production and market shocks related to the present decision and thus depends on the information set, which may vary from one year to the next as well as with the time horizon of the decision. With this view, the discussion can be extended to include durable inputs. The main point that comes out of such an extension is that the relevant price for durable inputs is the expectation of the price path for the duration of the service period. The longer the period, the larger the uncertainty with respect to such a price and the error of forecasting it. The argument is summarized:

PROPERTY 12.7 The longer the service period of an input, the less important the contribution of current prices will be to the spread in that input.

The main message of this discussion is that deviations from the first-order conditions need not be identified with allocation errors. How important are the variations in inputs due to discrepancies in the first-order conditions as compared with variations in prices? This is an empirical question, to be answered by estimating the variance components. However, it is important to note that small deviations from the point of maximum profit can produce big deviations in the optimum production plan (Mundlak, 1971). If the utility function of the firm is known, it can be incorporated into the analysis and lead to modified conditions for optimality as well as to a modification of the dual functions (Mundlak and Volcani, 1973).

Errors in Variables

The foregoing discussion has ignored errors in the variables. It appears that the damage caused by such errors to the *within* estimators draws special attention (Griliches, 1986). The essence of this concern is that by adding firm effects, we reduce the spread in the explanatory variables in the regression while the measurement errors are unaffected, and thereby we reduce the signal to noise ratio. This is indeed a possibility that is shared by any empirical analysis.[7] The problem is more conspicuous in the case of covariance analysis, because when a firm effect is introduced, the increase in the number of explanatory variables is equal to the number of firms, so the margin is rather thick. The issue of whether or not to add an effect can be viewed as a standard pretesting problem where a decision is taken on the variables to be included in the regression. However, instead of dealing with an all or none choice for the parameters representing the firm effect, it is possible to select a subset of nonredundant parameters (see Mundlak, 1981).

The treatment of errors in micro data depends on the nature of the error. The error can be generated by the agent who reports the data. There is a "Rashomon" phenomenon in that different people interpret differently, and consistently so, a question related to the same fact. Whether or not this is done consciously is irrelevant. What is important is that the error itself is likely to be subject to an "agent effect." If this is the case, then the *within* estimator may perform better than the other estimators considered above because it eliminates that part of the error which has an individual effect. In addition, methods of analysis such as those considered by Griliches and Hausman (1986), which assume that the measurement errors are serially uncorrelated, will fail because the individual effect produces serial correlation.

Firm-specific measurement errors is one interpretation that McElroy (1987) gives to her suggested specification for the production function, $Y = q(X - \epsilon; \theta)$, where X is the vector of observed inputs, θ is the vector of parameters common to all firms, and ϵ is the vector of firm effects known to the firm but not to the econometrician. As such, the specification is a generalization of the firm effect, but "additional interpretations . . . are available. The ϵ's may be regarded as the classic errors in measurement of the inputs" (p. 746).

The problem with this specification is that the error is additive, so that its relative importance is a function of X. Indeed, the distribution of ϵ must be truncated to ensure that $X - \epsilon > 0$. The dependence on X, if taken seriously, complicates the estimation. To avoid this problem, it is possible to reformulate McElroy's model so as to make the error unitless; $Y = q(X\epsilon; \theta)$. As such, the function is expressed in terms of inputs measured in efficiency units. This modification introduces a multiplicative error to the first-order conditions and provides another interpretation to m_1 in equation (12.4).[8]

Estimating the Dual

The foregoing discussion concentrated on the estimation of the production function, and the question is what are its implications for the estimation of a dual function as an end by itself. The essence of duality is that the knowledge of the parameters of the production function makes it possible to solve for the profit function or its derivatives.[9] The parameters in question can be estimated efficiently by the methods discussed above. The idea is to use the most efficient estimator for the parameters in question and apply the results to the various functions of interest. This implies that the most efficient way of estimating product supply or factor demand is to derive those from the empirical production function, rather than the reverse.

The foregoing discussion was conducted within the framework of micro analysis, but duality is usually used with macro data. It is therefore instructive to review the empirical scope of the dual estimator. The attraction of this estimator is that it uses prices, which are exogenous for competitive firms, as instrumental variables, and thereby the problem of simultaneity is overcome. Also it should be added that duality offers a very neat and powerful analytic framework. On the other hand, there are several serious limitations in its empirical application:

1. In a competitive industry the price variations among firms are expected to be relatively small.
2. When macro data are used, the exogeneity of the prices can usually be questioned and needs to be tested empirically.
3. By and large, the theory on which the empirical work is based is that of comparative statics without intertemporal considerations. Taking into account that quasi-fixed inputs are determined on the basis of expectations with respect to future prices, there is a built-in difference in the pertinent prices to be used. If the restricted profit functions are used, then the quasi-fixed inputs are included as variables, and the duality is applied only to the variable inputs.
4. Duality is based on the assumption that firms are profit maximizers and ignores other elements that enter the objective function, such as risk. To the extent that these additional elements are pertinent, the dual estimator loses its efficiency and may even be biased.

5. Any variability among firms in the allocation rule are informative but are not utilized by the dual estimator, whereas they are fully utilized in the primal estimators.
6. When panel data are available, the *within* estimators are unbiased and efficient.
7. Conditional on the assumption of the degree of the function, the OLS estimates of a Cobb-Douglas function are unbiased.
8. Under heterogeneous technology, the dual function loses the meaning attributed to it.

Although the discussion dealt with a Cobb-Douglas function, most of the conclusions carry over to more general functions. However, the discussion in the next chapter indicates that the Cobb-Douglas, properly constructed, is a good approximation to the more realistic situation of heterogeneous technology.

Summary and Conclusions

The one-input Cobb-Douglas production function model was used to examine the consequences of a fundamental problem in the estimation of production functions. This problem emerges from the fact that the econometrician has less information than the firms with respect to the two determinants of the production process: technology and optimization. The first leads to a correlation between the inputs and the error term of the production function (firm effect), and as a result OLS estimates of the production function are inconsistent.

This shortcoming is presumably overcome by estimating a dual function and using the estimate to infer about the production function itself. Such a procedure is based on the assumption that prices are exogenous and that they account for the variations in inputs. The duality, at least in the form that has been used in the econometrics of production functions, is obtained under the assumption that the first-order conditions for profit maximization are met. If this is not the case, then part of the variability in inputs is independent of prices.

Such variability is referred to as error in optimization. This term is used for convenience, but it is somewhat misleading because it may in fact result from rational behavior by the firms. This is demonstrated here by using a mean-variance utility function for firms facing price and production uncertainty. The outcome of the analysis is a discrepancy between the marginal productivity and the real factor price. This discrepancy depends on the utility function as well as on the variance of the stochastic element. Part of this discrepancy is firm specific and as such remains fairly constant for repeated observations. The other part is transitory, but even so, it reflects a decision by the firm. The econometrician does not have direct observations on either of these two components. However, because they both affect input levels, inputs contain all the pertinent information with respect to the errors of optimization. This implies that a direct estimation of the production function is based on more information than the dual, but at the same time it may be subject to simultaneous equation bias.

Although the analysis is conducted within a single-period framework, it is easily generalized to more than one period. The longer the life of the input, the larger the error of price forecasting is likely to be. This weakens the relationship between the price and the level of input and sometimes results in the consideration of such inputs as fixed, or exogenous. This is somewhat misleading, because the level of such an input is still being affected by the firm effect in the production function.

Several estimators were examined. They differ in the degree of information regarding the source of input variation and the error that is attached to this information. At the one end, the dual estimator utilizes only prices. At the other end, OLS utilizes all the information but is subject to the error due to the firm effect in the production function.

Many of the properties of the dual estimators are derived for competitive firms and are not automatically applicable to aggregates that do not meet the underlying assumptions. Specifically, it is likely that in such cases prices are not exogenous, and consequently, the dual estimator loses its main virtue.

To conclude, it seems that in most cases duality should be applied in reverse. When the ultimate objective is an empirical dual function, estimate the production function and use the estimates to derive the dual function or its derivatives, such as product supply or factor demand.

Appendix 12A

1. To outline the derivations of the variances, write the system

$$y - x\gamma = m_0 + u_0 \tag{12A.5$'$}$$

$$y - x = -p + m_1 + u_1 + u_0 \tag{12A.6$'$}$$

or

$$[y, x]\begin{bmatrix} 1 & 1 \\ -\gamma & -1 \end{bmatrix} = p[0, -1] + [m_0, m_1]\begin{bmatrix} 1 & 0 \\ 0 & 1 \end{bmatrix} + [u_0, u_1]\begin{bmatrix} 1 & 1 \\ 0 & 1 \end{bmatrix}$$

or

$$Y\Gamma = pB + m + uA$$

where

$$\Gamma^{-1} = -(1-\gamma)^{-1}\begin{bmatrix} -1 & -1 \\ \gamma & 1 \end{bmatrix}; \quad B\Gamma^{-1} = [\gamma, 1](1-\gamma)^{-1};$$

$$A\Gamma^{-1} = -(1-\gamma)^{-1}\begin{bmatrix} \gamma - 1 & 0 \\ \gamma & 1 \end{bmatrix};$$

Hence

$$y = (1-\gamma)^{-1}[p\gamma - \gamma m_1 + m_0 + (1-\gamma)u_0 - \gamma u_1];$$
$$x = (1-\gamma)^{-1}(p - u_1 - m_1 + m_0);$$

Precision: Dual

$$\begin{aligned} V(\gamma_p) &= \text{plim}\, n \frac{p'(m_0+u_0)(m_0+u_0)'p}{(p'x)^2} \\ &= \text{plim}\, \frac{(p'(m_0+u_0)(m_0+u_0)'p)/n}{(p'x/n)^2} \\ &= (1-\gamma)^2(\sigma_{00}+\tau_{00})/\sigma_{pp}. \end{aligned}$$

Precision: OLS–complete information

$$\begin{aligned} V(\gamma_0) &= \text{plim}\, n \frac{(x'u_0)(u_0'x)}{(x'x)^2} \\ &= \text{plim}\, \frac{1}{n}\frac{(x'u_0)(u_0'x)}{(\frac{x'x}{n})^2}. \end{aligned}$$

Substitute (12.7) for x to obtain (12.13).

2. Development of (12.24)

$$R^e = P^eY^e; \quad R = R^e e^{\epsilon}; \quad \epsilon = u_0 + \Delta P; \quad \pi = R^e e^{\epsilon} - X.$$

To obtain the expected profit expand e^{ϵ} around $\epsilon = 0$, ignore terms higher than second degree and label $\sigma^2 = E(\epsilon^2)$:

$$E(e^{\epsilon}) = E(1 + \epsilon + \epsilon^2/2 + \cdots) \cong 1 + \sigma^2/2$$

$R = (1 + \sigma^2/2)R^e$, and $\pi^e(X\,|_i) = (1 + \sigma^2/2)R^e - X_i$.

Assume normal distribution for ϵ so that $E(\epsilon^3) = 0$ and $E(\epsilon^4) = 3\sigma^4$,

$$\frac{\sigma_\pi^2}{R^{e2}} = \frac{E[\pi - \pi^e(X\,|_i)]^2}{R^{e2}} = E[e^{\epsilon} - (1 + \sigma^2/2)^2]$$

$$= E[1 + \epsilon + \frac{\epsilon^2}{2} + \cdots + (1 + \sigma^2/2)^2].$$

Squaring and applying the expectation operator

$$\frac{\sigma_\pi^2}{R^{e2}} = \sigma^2(1 + \frac{\sigma^2}{2}).$$

Differentiate

$$\frac{d\pi^e}{dX} = \frac{dR^e}{dX}(1 + \frac{\sigma^2}{2}) - 1; \quad \frac{d\sigma_\pi}{dX} = \frac{dR^e}{dX}\sigma(1 + \frac{1}{2}\sigma^2)^{\frac{1}{2}}.$$

Simplify and substitute in (12.23) to obtain (12.24).

13

Agricultural Productivity

As indicated in Chapter 11, many of the findings of the empirical analysis are inconsistent with the assumption of a constant production function over the sample points. In this chapter we extend the analysis and examine the implications of heterogeneous technology as discussed in Chapter 6.

Agricultural productivity is a short name for the productivity of resources in agricultural production. The concept of productivity, regardless of the actual method used in its computation, calls for a comparison of variations in outputs and inputs. In that, it is implicitly assumed that regularity in the relationship between inputs and outputs prevails over time or across producers so that the results of one comparison are valuable in predicting the response of output to input changes in another comparison. It is useful to define this property explicitly.

DEFINITION (repetitious property) Aside from random variations, the relationship between input and output obtained in one sample can be reproduced in another sample.

It is this repetitious property that justifies the study of input/output relationships, usefully summarized in terms of the production function. A particular writer or analyst may prefer to avoid the use of the concept of a production function or even object to it. However, the assumption of regularity in production gives rise to such a concept, so we can use it as a reference point without apologies.

When the output obtained from a given bundle of inputs increases, we say that there is an improvement in productivity or, more commonly, technical change. Such a comparison of two points with inputs held constant represents a conceptual exercise, because in practice we do not hold inputs constant and observe output growth; both outputs and inputs vary over time or among producers. Thus, in order to evaluate empirically changes in productivity, it is necessary to determine the change in inputs and outputs. Because the various inputs do not ordinarily change at the same rate over the sample, they have to be aggregated in order to yield a measure of total input change. Such an aggregation requires assigning weights to the contribution of the various inputs to output. The weights can be obtained by assuming that the observed factor shares provide an appropriate measure of the importance of the inputs in production. This procedure is based on assumptions with respect to the factor market behavior that should not be taken at face value in empirical analysis. Alternatively, it is possible to obtain the weights from empirical analysis by estimating the production function. Issues related to this approach are discussed in detail below. Similar considerations apply to the aggregation of outputs.

Much of the discussion of productivity in the literature deals with technology and its change over time. However, technology is an abstract concept and not an observable quantity; therefore it is not easily measured. We can identify and speak of specific techniques, such as a crop variety in a given region or a given type of computer, but once we want to generalize the concept to cover a technology that consists of more than one technique, the task becomes more complex. The inference about the technology is indirect and is made by comparing changes in output and inputs. As such, the inference is made on the implemented rather than on the *available* technology. But the implementation reflects the underlying economic conditions, as will be explained below.

The invention of new methods of production, or techniques, such as varieties, insecticides, and methods of irrigation, makes it possible to increase food production from a given cultivated area and thereby to increase the food supply. This is the only way to increase the *capacity* of food production (leaving the concept of capacity vague for the time being). However, actual production, being less than capacity production, as well as productivity in general, can be increased considerably without a change in capacity. The distinction between actual and capacity production helps to turn our attention to important sources of growth, aside from changes in the available technology.

First, not all outputs are produced by the most productive techniques. As reviewed in Chapter 6, this gap between the availability and the implementation of technology is often attributed to uncertainty, lack of information, and inability to comprehend new techniques, or simply inadequate human capital. Most important, it should be related to economic considerations.

Second, there are considerable differences in the efficiency of production among farmers. A regime that allows for free entry and exit is likely to lead to the redistribution of scarce resources, particularly land and water, in such a way that the more productive farmers will operate the available resources. This point is particularly important in light of two factors. (a) As seen in Chapters 1 and 9, the number of farmers and farms declines in the process of economic growth. This implies a redistribution of land. (b) Farming is largely a family operation and is therefore subject to life cycles. In the process of intergenerational transfer, the decision of members of the incoming generation on whether or not to stay in agriculture depends on their opportunities. This element exists even if the farm population remains constant. Such a shift of resources requires the appropriate economic environment that will provide a correct evaluation of the various opportunities. (c) A similar consideration is applied to the global distribution of agricultural production. This possibility is related to economic policies that countries follow. In a free-trade environment, more production will be forthcoming from areas where food production requires fewer resources or simply from countries with a comparative advantage in agriculture.

Although much of the research on technical change in agriculture is focused on the development of new technology, we concentrate here on the issues related to the implementation of this technology and its relation to economic policy.

The chapter begins by generalizing the discussion of the green revolution in Chapter 6 to provide a general framework for the analysis of the production structure (Mundlak, 1988). The choice of production techniques is endogenized, and the composition of techniques and their level of intensity, as measured by the inputs allocated to the various techniques, are determined simultaneously. This formulation allows for the evaluation of the direct effect of policies on productivity.

The empirical aspects of the analysis consist of algebraic presentation of the implemented technology, the scope for and role of dual estimation, and the implications of the fact that inputs are endogenous.

The supply of inputs to agriculture and their effect on productivity offers an indirect channel through which policies affect productivity. The last section summarizes some of the findings in order to evaluate the possible effects of various major policy measures.

The Production Structure

Formulation

Continuing the discussion in Chapter 6, we note that the production of a given commodity or service can be decomposed into a set of elementary activities or techniques. A technique is described by a production function. The degree of disaggregation, or refinement of the definition of a technique, depends on the purpose of the analysis. To simplify the analysis, we begin with a single-period optimization and single-output production functions. Let x be the vector of inputs and $F_j(x)$ be the production function associated with the jth technique, where F_j is concave and twice differentiable, and define:

DEFINITION The *available technology, T*, is the collection of all possible techniques:

$$T = \{F_j(x); \quad j = 1, \ldots, J\}. \tag{13.1}$$

Firms choose the implemented techniques subject to their constraints and the economic environment. To formalize this choice, we distinguish between restricted, or as commonly referred to, fixed (k) and unrestricted, or variable (v), inputs, $x = (v, k)$, and assume for simplicity that the fixed inputs have no alternative cost. The optimization problem calls for a choice of the variable (v_j) and the fixed (k_j) inputs to be assigned to technique j so as to maximize profits. The Lagrangian equation for this problem is

$$L(v_j, k_j, \lambda) = \Sigma_j p_j F_j(v_j, k_j) - \Sigma_j w v_j - \lambda(\Sigma_j k_j - k) \tag{13.2}$$
$$\text{subject to} \quad F_j(\cdot) \in T; \quad v_j \geq 0; \quad k_j \geq 0,$$

where p_j is the price of the product of technique j, w is the price vector of the variable inputs, and k is the available stock of fixed inputs. The Kuhn-Tucker necessary conditions for a solution are

$$(p_j F_{vj} - w)v_j = 0; \qquad p_j F_{vj} - w \leq 0 \tag{13.3}$$

$$(p_j F_{kj} - \lambda)k_j = 0; \qquad p_j F_{kj} - \lambda \leq 0 \tag{13.4}$$

$$(\sum k_j - k)\lambda = 0; \qquad \sum k_j - k \leq 0 \tag{13.5}$$

$$v_j \geq 0; \quad k_j \geq 0; \qquad \lambda \geq 0. \tag{13.6}$$

Let $s = (k, p, w, T)$ be the vector of state variables, and write the solution as $v_j^*(s)$, $k_j^*(s)$, $\lambda^*(s)$, to emphasize the dependence of the solution on the state variables. The optimal allocation of inputs v_j^*, k_j^* determines the intensity of implementing the jth technique, including the decision not to use the technique. When the terms in parentheses in equation (13.3) or (13.4) are negative, the corresponding inputs, v_j^* or k_j^* respectively, are equal to zero. To the extent that the implementation of a technique requires positive levels of some inputs, when the optimal levels of these inputs are zero, the technique is not implemented. We can then characterize the implemented technology.

DEFINITION The *implemented technology (IT)*:

$$IT(s) = \{F_j(v_j, k_j);\ F_j(v_j^*, k_j^*) \neq 0,\ F_j \in T\}$$

The optimal output of technique j is $y_j^* = F_j(v_j^*, k_j^*)$. To avoid ambiguities, we generalize the definition of factor intensity to the case of more than two factors:

DEFINITION (intensity) The input-output ratio associated with technique j is a measure of the input intensity of technique j.

PROPERTY 13.1 (endogeneity) The implemented technology is endogenous.

PROPERTY 13.2 (jointness) The implemented technology is determined jointly with the level of intensity at which the inputs are used.

The importance of these two related propositions cannot be exaggerated, because it is the implemented technology that is the subject of the empirical analysis. Property 13.2 implies that the locus of inputs and outputs does not, in general, trace a production function. As a result, the empirical production function need not possess the properties attributed to a production function. To illustrate, Figure 13.1 shows three production functions, f_1, f_2, and f_3, with the clusters of observations, Cj. The observations in $C1$ were obtained prior to the introduction of f_2. A function fitted to the observations in $C1$, $C2$, and $C3$ does not represent any of the underlying functions and in fact may be convex, as the figure shows. This can be summarized:

PROPERTY 13.3 (concavity) When the sample represents more than one technique, empirical production functions are not subject to a concavity constraint.

It is important to emphasize the difference between Property 13.3 and Property 6.4. The composite production function is constructed from techniques that are currently available. The empirical production function describes a situation in which we trace points chosen under different technologies. Hence, in terms of Figure 13.1, when f_1 was chosen, f_j, $j > 1$, were not available so the producers could not employ the corresponding techniques in part or in full.

Recall that the composite function was constructed in Chapter 6 from techniques that produce the same homogeneous product. When this is not the case, the product is defined in terms of value output, thereby making the composition depend on the prices. When prices change, the production functions of value product change as well. A graphical presentation of the

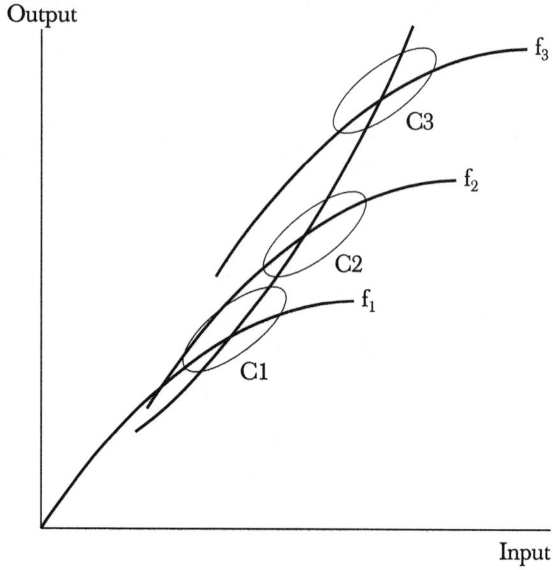

Figure 13.1 Intertechnique production function

outcome is similar to that portrayed in Figure 13.1, where in this case each of the functions can be associated with a different price set.

The implementation of the new technique requires an increase in inputs in which the technique is more intensive. A constraint on the supply of such an input will constrain the implementation of the new technique. If the input has to be bid away from other uses, the mere appearance of the new technique will increase the value marginal productivity of this input and will encourage its flow to the enterprise in question. For the same reason, higher product prices may be conducive to the introduction of the new technique f_2 through the encouragement of the investment necessary for the introduction of the new technique.

Duality

The analysis can be phrased in terms of the behavioral equations. Given the usual regularity conditions for F_j, a restricted profit function can be derived:

$$\pi(s) = \sum p_j F_j(v_J^*, k_J^*) - \sum w_j v_j^*. \tag{13.7}$$

The various theorems dealing with the duality between the profit and production functions hold true conditional on s. Specifically, the frontier of

$IT(s)$ is dual to $\pi(s)$ and vice versa. However, the exploitation of this property in empirical analysis is restricted by the fact that s varies over the sample. Thus, strictly speaking, each point in the sample may come from a different profit function, which in turn describes a different implemented technology. Using Hotelling's lemma, one can obtain the factors' demand aggregated over techniques, $\sum v_j^* = -\partial\pi(s)/\partial w$. Similarly, the supply of output from technique j is given by $y_j^* = \partial\pi(s)/\partial p_j$. If there is more than one technique for producing a given crop, then $\partial\pi(s)/\partial p_i = \sum_j y_{ji}^* = y_i^*$, where y_{ji}^* is the output of the ith crop produced by the jth technique and y_i^* is the total (optimal) output of crop i. It immediately follows:

PROPERTY 13.4 (duality) Prices are insufficient statistics for identifying the implemented technology.

As indicated in Chapter 11, it is often found in empirical analyses based on duality that the second-order derivatives of the profit function have the wrong sign. This is the analog of the situation described in Figure 13.1 in that it implies convex, rather than concave, production functions.

PROPERTY 13.5 (convexity of profit function) When the sample represents more than one technique, empirical profit functions are not subject to a convexity constraint.

We can now relax the assumption of fixed inputs and incorporate the discussion in Chapters 9 and 10 on the dependence of the time path of quasi-fixed inputs on state variables. Combining the two, we summarize the discussion:

PROPERTY 13.6 (production path) The output path is determined by the evolution of the state variables.

Efficiency-Frontier Production Functions

The concept of efficiency in production is often used in discussions as well as in empirical work. Efficiency-frontier production functions are estimated empirically by fitting a function so as to connect the points with the largest output for given inputs. A point located off the frontier is treated as inefficient.

Property 13.6 and the discussion in Chapter 6 highlight the difficulty with this concept. This can be also illustrated in terms of Figure 13.2, based on Figure 6.4. For instance, point A is efficient when the available technology consists only of the traditional technique. Once the modern variety is introduced, point

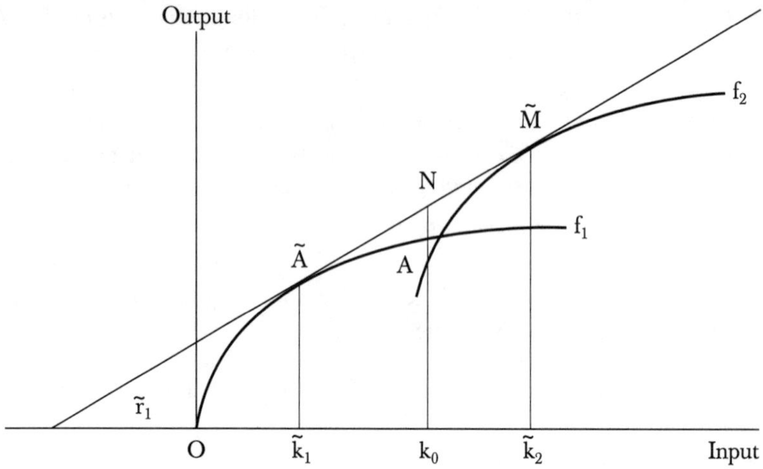

Figure 13.2 Efficiency under heterogeneous technology

A becomes inefficient because it is dominated by point N, which requires the same inputs but represents a higher output. What is changing here is the frontier, so that the efficiency of point A depends on whether or not the new technique is available. In other words, a correct evaluation of efficiency requires the identification of the available technology; otherwise the results are meaningless.

The same problem can arise from a change in other state variables. For instance, to illustrate the effect of product prices, we view the two production functions in Figure 13.2 as representing two different products, the outputs of which are measured in value terms, say dollars. The change in a product price causes a movement of the curve representing the production function of this product, and the optimal points change accordingly. This of course changes the envelope or the efficiency frontier.

Another example is a change in factor prices. To illustrate, consider the curves in Figure 13.2 as representing the value added, revenue net of the cost of variable inputs. The prices of the quasi-fixed inputs, or shadow prices, are endogenous and therefore do not affect the decision on the optimal production. A change in input prices changes the value added according to the intensity of the technique in the use of that input, and the curve, and with it the frontier, will change accordingly. For instance, a change in fertilizer price will affect the value added of the modern variety, which is intensive in fertilizer, more than that of the traditional variety. Thus any application of the concept of frontiers should recognize the role of prices.

Metaproduction Functions

A related concept that has been discussed in relation to agricultural production is that of the metaproduction function introduced by Hayami and Ruttan (1985):

> The metaproduction function can be regarded as the envelope of commonly conceived neoclassical production functions. In the *short run,* in which substitution among inputs is circumscribed by the rigidity of existing capital and equipment, production relationships can best be described with an activity with fixed factor-factor and factor-product ratios. In the *long run,* in which the constraints exercised by existing capital disappear and are replaced by the fund of available knowledge, including all feasible factor-factor and factor-product combinations, production relationships can be adequately described by the neoclassical production function. In the *secular* period of production, in which the constraints given by the available fund of technical knowledge are further relaxed to admit all potentially discoverable possibilities, production relationships can be described by a metaproduction function which describes all conceivable technical alternatives that might be discovered. (pp. 134–135)

This definition has two components. First, it distinguishes between the short- and long-run production functions, similar to Viner's short- and long-run cost curves, perhaps with the exception that they impose the unnecessary restriction of fixed factor-factor and factor-product ratios. Issues related to the dependence of the frontier on fixed inputs has been discussed in the literature on interfirm and intrafirm production functions (Reder, 1943; Bronfenbrenner, 1944; Smith, 1945) and recognized in the agricultural economics literature by Heady (1944). Second, there is the secular component that describes all conceivable technical knowledge. The implication of this component for empirical analysis is somewhat different from the first one. In principle, we can infer empirically only about techniques that are implemented and not about techniques that have not yet been developed. It appears that Hayami and Ruttan's interest in the last component is related to decisions with respect to new innovations:

> Thus defined, the metaproduction may appear to be the same as the innovation possibility curve advanced in Figure 4-2 in the previous chapter. In fact, we consider the metaproduction function an operational definition of the innovation possibility curve–operational in the sense that it can be measured empirically from observable production data. The metaproduction surface drawn in Figure 5-6 is the envelope

> of the most efficient production points available in the world. It is our basic assumption that such an envelope approximates the innovation possibility curve for the LDCs. (Hayami and Ruttan, 1985, p. 135)

It is not sufficiently clear from this description what is known and what is to be innovated. One way to avoid this difficulty is to say that techniques known in the advanced countries can be adopted in the LDC with some cost of research. It is in this sense that the metaproduction function can be thought of as a representation of what is known and an innovation surface at the same time. This interpretation appears to be consistent with their notion of induced innovation.

> Our more general hypothesis is that the relatively low production efficiency of LDC agriculture is explained mainly by the limited capacity of LDC agriculture research systems to develop a new technology in response to changes in relative factor prices and of farmers' capacity to adopt it. (ibid.)

There is, however, a fundamental problem that is also common to earlier writings on induced innovations, such as Fellner (1961), Kennedy (1964), Weisäcker (see Samuelson, 1965), and others as well as more recent studies of growth. These studies take the innovation frontier as given, and its use suggests the existence of a production function of knowledge. However, by its very nature, the production of knowledge is not repetitious. To emphasize this, it is stated as a proposition:

PROPERTY 13.7 (knowledge) The production function of knowledge is not repetitious.

Therefore, contrary to the common practice, the production of knowledge cannot be summarized *meaningfully* by a production function; the innovation frontier thus becomes a vague concept, and a successful meaningful empirical application of it still remains to be illustrated. In addition, it is clear that the "most efficient production point" is also a vague concept that requires more structure to be made operational. This is particularly the case when it is stated that it can be measured empirically from observable production data. This is the next subject.

Aggregation of Techniques

In general, data on individual techniques are not readily available, and it is therefore impossible to estimate the production functions associated with individual techniques. Most empirical analyses use data that are aggregates over techniques. We therefore turn now to examine the properties of the aggregate production function.

The aggregate production function, as commonly used, is perceived as an aggregation of outputs produced by a *given* set of micro production functions. In the present framework such an aggregate is not uniquely defined, because the set of functions actually implemented, and over which the aggregation is performed, is endogenous. The dependence of implemented technology on the state variables implies that changing either the constraints or the available technology, while holding prices constant, may cause a change in the product mix. The results of an empirical analysis that does not take this endogenous aggregation into account will depend on the combination of prices, constraints, and available technology that existed at each sample point. To explore the implication of this framework for the estimation of a production function using data aggregated over techniques, we write the aggregate production function:

$$\sum_j p_j y_j^*(s) \equiv F(x^*, s) \equiv \phi(s), \tag{13.8}$$

where x is the vector of inputs and $x^* = x(s)$ is its optimum level. The production function in (13.8) is defined conditional on s, but changes in s imply changes in x^* as well as in $F(x^*, s)$. It is therefore meaningless in this framework to think of changes in x, except by error, which are not instigated by changes in s. This means that it is impossible to reveal a stable production function from a sample of observations taken over points with changing available technology. We have thus argued:

PROPERTY 13.8 (identification) In general, the aggregate production function is not identifiable.

The empirical aggregate production function can be thought of as an approximation to (13.8) in a specific way. For (13.8) to be a production function in the usual sense, x should be disjoint from s. Such a separation requires a discrepancy between x and x^* that will allow us to write for the observed output:

$$\sum_j p_j y_j \cong F(x, s). \tag{13.9}$$

Strictly speaking, $F(x, s)$ is not necessarily a function, since x can be allocated to the various techniques in an arbitrary way. Different allocations will result in different outputs. It is only when we have an allocation rule leading to x^* that uniqueness can be achieved. With this caveat, we view $F(x, s)$ as a function of s, since s determines the techniques to which the inputs are allocated. Then, a discrepancy $x - x^*$ produces information on a given implemented technology. Note that as was shown in Chapter 12, such a discrepancy is also the source of information for identifying a given production function.

To make this concept operational, $F(x, s)$ is approximated by a set of functions of x^*, and as such of s. Under a weak assumption, $F(x, s)$ can be approximated by a set of functions:

$$F(x, s) \cong \sum a_i h_i(x, s) \equiv g(x, s), \tag{13.10}$$

where $g(x, s)$ is the approximating function, a_i are parameters, and h_i are known functions. $F(x, s)$ is expanded around x^*, and terms higher than second degree are omitted. Ignoring technical details (Mundlak, 1988), the result is:

$$\ln y = \Gamma(\cdot) + \mathrm{B}_1(\cdot) \ln x + (1/2)\mathrm{B}_2(\ln x)^2 \tag{13.11}$$

$$\mathrm{B}_1 = \alpha_{01} + \alpha_{11}s + u_x \tag{13.12}$$

$$\Gamma(\cdot) = \alpha_{00} + \alpha_{10}s + s\alpha_{20}s + u_0, \tag{13.13}$$

where y is the value added per worker, s is the vector of state variables, αs and B_2 are the coefficients to be estimated, and u_x, u_0 are the stochastic terms. The dependent variable in (13.12) is unobservable. In principle, the production function can be estimated directly by substituting (13.12) for $\mathrm{B}_1(\cdot)$. In general, direct estimation of quadratic functions yields imprecise results because of multicollinearity. Therefore, the estimation is done by using the first-order conditions, which implies the equality of the factor share and the production elasticity, $S = E_{y/x}$. In our case, the production elasticity is $E_{y/x} = \mathrm{B}_1(\cdot) + \mathrm{B}_2 \ln x$, and its empirical presentation is written as

$$S = \alpha_{01} + \alpha_{11}s + \alpha_{x1} \ln x + u_x. \tag{13.14}$$

In the absence of factor market distortion, the coefficient α_{x1} is the same as B_2. The estimated B's are substituted in (13.11), and the coefficients of Γ are estimated directly from (13.11). It is possible to estimate equations (13.11) and (13.14) jointly and thereby improve the precision of the estimates. The use of the factor share in the estimation is, strictly speaking, appropriate for competitive industries where the zero profit condition is maintained through entry and exit. The system can be adjusted to account for situations where this condition is not met.

Because we restrict ourselves to a second-degree approximation, B_2 is a constant, whereas B_1 is allowed to vary with the state variables. Variations in the state variables affect the production function coefficients directly as well as indirectly, through their effect on inputs. This, to be sure, is a description of reality under the present framework. If this reality is described and estimated by a constant coefficient function, the outcome will be unexplained variations in productivity, measured by any conventional method. Those variations are considered to be random to the researcher who takes no account of the state variables that determine the implemented technology.

Equations (13.11)–(13.13) indicate that the coefficients can vary either due to variations in the state variables, or in inputs. If the available technology consists of more than one technique, a change in the state variables may cause a change in the composition of techniques in addition to a change of input used on a given technique. In this case, the empirical function is a mixture of functions and as such may violate the concavity property of a production function. This is suggested as the explanation for the occasional failure in empirical analysis to obtain concavity at some sample points. Such a failure is rather serious, because the first-order conditions are imposed in the estimation procedure.

PROPERTY 13.9 (concavity of the aggregate function) The aggregate production function is not subject to a concavity constraint.

One direction of research aimed to correct the situation has been to introduce higher-degree polynomials to approximate the production function (Gallant, 1982). It is true that sufficiently high degree polynomials will approximate any function to a desired degree of accuracy. The question raised here is what is the meaning of the estimated function. The function that this method intends to estimate does not exist. In principle, there may be as many functions as there are sample points. Thus Property 13.9 is a generalization of the case covered by Property 13.3, which dealt with a sample of points, each generated by one technique.[1]

Turning to the factor shares, note that on the surface, there is similarity between equation (13.13) and the factor shares derived from translog functions (Christensen, Jorgenson, and Lau, 1973). When s is eliminated from equation (13.13), the factor shares will depend on inputs alone, the same as in the translog production function. Under the present framework, the use of the translog is appropriate only when the production elasticity is independent of the state variables. On the other hand, when the state variables consist of factor prices alone, equation (13.14) can be thought of as a generalization of the factor shares derived from a profit function. Again, if the available technology consists of more than one technique, a change in price may cause a change in the composition of techniques and as such does not represent, or trace, a movement on a given dual function.

To summarize, in the translog model the variations in the factor shares are caused only by variations in the input combinations, whereas in our case the factor shares can vary as a result of variations in the state variables that lead to changes in the composition of techniques. This difference has important consequences for the empirical estimates and their interpretation.

We have formulated the system to allow in the empirical analysis for a discrepancy between the factor share and the production elasticity that will occur when the α_{x1} is not equal to B_2. Given the model, when the two are equal, the production elasticity is equal to the factor share. A discrepancy between the two is an indication of a distortion in the factor market in the sense that factors are not paid their value marginal productivity. In the present formulation, such a distortion is attached to the inputs, and its relevance can be tested empirically by restricting the values of the coefficients to be the same. Other forms of a discrepancy between the factor shares and the production elasticities can be introduced. The form of the discrepancy, however, is a substantive question, but further elaboration of this point is beyond the scope of our discussion.

Evidence

A comparison of the studies by Tintner and Brownlee (1944) and Heady (1944), the studies that mark the beginning of the empirical analysis of agricultural production functions, indicates that the results are sensitive to output composition and perhaps the physical environment of the farms in the sample. This lack of robustness has surfaced in many of the studies that report more than one result, and it was recognized explicitly at an early stage of the empirical work (Hildebrand, 1960). The variability in the coefficients and several of the arguments given in the studies support the idea that much of the pattern of the observed technology reflects variability in the implementation of the available technology.[2] The foregoing discussion provides a framework for the interpretation of those results. In general, at each sample point, the data consist of the aggregation of techniques, and the collections of the aggregated technique changes over the sample points. As such, by Property 13.6, the production path is determined by the evolution of the state variables. By Property 13.8, the aggregate production function is not identifiable. In several studies, the subsistence conditions of monotonicity and convexity were not met. This is expected by Properties 13.3, 13.5, and 13.9.

If we turn to technical change, for most countries, the data show a decline in the share of labor and an increase in the shares of chemicals, machines, and capital in general. Thus, compared with the old techniques, the new ones are labor saving and capital using. The studies based on duality deal with the bias of technical change and less so with its rate. No explicit justification is given for this shift of interest, and perhaps the best interpretation is that this simply reflects the procedure that allows the inclusion of a time trend in the share equations in addition to prices and output. As these studies do not deal with the production function itself, the question of the rate of technical change does not come up. When the coefficient of time in a share equation is significantly different from zero, it is concluded that the technical change is not neutral. If the equation also contains output with a nonzero coefficient, it is concluded that the production function is not homothetic. However, in most cases only one of the two coefficients, of time and output, is significantly different from zero, and this indicates an empirical trade-off between the role of time trend and outputs. Thus some studies characterize the process as nonneutral technical change, whereas others characterize it as nonhomothetic production function. Neither one is fully informative. This trade-off disappears when homotheticity is imposed so that output is not included in the equation.[3]

This interpretation can be seen in terms of Figure 13.1, where the movement of observations from cluster to cluster reflects changes in time, technology, inputs, output, prices, and perhaps in other state variables such as constraints. Because each sample point uses a different technology, it is impossible to infer from such an analysis about the homotheticity of the given production function.[4]

The foregoing evaluation can be used to examine implications for the discussion of duality in Chapter 12.

Functional Stability and Implications for Duality

What interpretation can be given to a production function estimated in an environment of heterogeneous technology under the assumption of homogeneous technology? To answer this question, we return to the discussion in Chapter 12 that was based on the working hypothesis that all firms in the sample use the same production function up to the efficiency factor, m_0. We now assume that at any one time there are differences in techniques employed by firms and also that each firm may be operating with more than one technique. Changing techniques involves costs of acquisition, installation, and learning. These costs may depend on the technique that is currently used. A new technique may require only upgrading of the present one or alternatively may necessitate a complete replacement. The value of the experience with the previous technique and the existing physical setup, which is suppressed in the present formulation, also affects this cost. Let $c_i(jr)$ be the cost of installing technique j by firm i currently operating with technique r. For an entering firm $r = 0$, for a firm leaving the industry $j = 0$, whereas $j = r$ implies no change. At any time t the firm decides on the choice of a technique and the level of its implementation so as to maximize the value of its objective function. To avoid unnecessary complications, the analysis is maintained at the simplest level, where we also suppress the intertemporal optimization. Thus let the production function in (12.1) describe a specific technique and let $\pi^*[A_j, \gamma_j, P^e, m_{0i}, m_{1i}, c_i(jr)]$ be the profit function of firm i that switches from technique r to j, given (expected) real factor price P^e. Let J be the set of all the indices j representing the available techniques from which the firm can choose, and as such it represents the available technology. The optimal technique is obtained from

$$\max_j \pi^*[A_j, \gamma_j, P^e, m_{0i}, m_{1i}, c_i(jr), J]. \tag{13.15}$$

It is important to note that in view of Property 13.2, equation (13.15) involves a simultaneous choice of technology and the level of its implementation. The technology is characterized by two parameters, A and γ. Let $T = (A, \gamma)$; then the technology chosen by (13.15) is

$$T_i^* = T[P^e, m_{0i}, m_{1i}, c_i(jr), J]. \tag{13.16}$$

Equation (13.16) is the law of motion for the implementation of technology in this model where there are no constraints. In this world there are interfirm differences in inputs, outputs, implemented technologies, and productivity, regardless of the method one uses to measure productivity. The sources of variations appear in the argument of (13.16). The firm effects, m_{0i} and m_{1i}, generate a spread among firms even if they have the same price expectation. Their strategy of "modernization" will depend on their existing setup, as represented by $c_i(jr)$, and therefore on their history, on changes in the available technology, J, and on changes in the market conditions as represented by P^e. Therefore, changes in prices affect different firms differently. A more general formulation will also add constraints, such as capital or institutional limits, to the determinants of the implemented technology.

Under this framework there is no single production function that can be estimated from a cross-section of firms. This was experienced by Mairesse and Griliches (1990). It is possible, however, to estimate some average input-output relationships which may be very informative when the distribution of the state variables shows reasonable stability.

There is another important implication of this result for our discussion of dual estimates. Differences among individual production functions are part of the productivity shocks, and those may now be correlated with prices. When systematic price variations between firms exist, such a correlation will result in inconsistency of the dual estimator as an estimator of a given, or the average, function. Thus consistency, which is the main virtue of the dual estimator, vanishes in this case. Recall that between-firm price variations is the only information utilized by the dual and not by the *within* estimator. Under this framework, this advantage may turn out to be a limitation.

State Variables

The empirical application of the choice of technique framework requires a selection of the state variables. As a way of organizing one's thinking about them, they may be classified into four groups: constraints, incentives, environment, and available technology. We turn to a brief discussion of the variables in each.

Constraints

Constraints to the implementation of the available technology are represented by the vector k in (13.2). The main constraints are the level and composition of the capital stock. To summarize the discussion in Chapter 6, the overall level of the capital stock matters when new techniques are more capital intensive than the existing ones. Other things equal, an increase in the capital-labor ratio is expected to result in the adoption of more capital-intensive techniques. In this sense, the pace of implementation of new techniques is affected by *net* investment.

However, capital is not homogeneous and its *composition* matters when the new techniques require a different mixture of capital items than the existing ones. In a once-and-for-all change in technology, the composition of the current capital stock is important only in the short run, and with time it converges to the desired one through *gross* investment. In situations of continuing change, the composition may have to change accordingly and as such may remain a continuous constraint. Because investment influences changes in the implemented technology, it is expected to affect the *rate of change,* rather than the *level,* of output.

The foregoing considerations pertain to all forms of capital, including human capital. Thus the pace of the transition may depend on the availability of some specific skills and on the pace of their acquisition. The acquisition of skills is the analog of investment in the discussion of physical capital.

In theory, the role of investment in *empirical* analysis is somewhat ambiguous, because it includes additional aspects to those discussed above. In particular, the cost of adjustment argument (Chapter 10) implies a negative effect of investment on output and hence on productivity. Thus the theory does not predict the sign of the effect of investment on productivity. It is an empirical question. A positive effect will be taken as an indication that the cost of adjustment is dominated by the other effects. Another consideration is related to the information about the market conditions embedded in investment. Other things equal, the better the market prospects, the higher the investment. Thus investment can be viewed as a measure, subject to error, of incentives. As we have no direct measure of future market conditions, the information content of investment cannot be introduced explicitly into the empirical analysis.

Incentives

Incentives affect the relative profitability, as well as the risk, of the various techniques and thereby the degree of their implementation.[5] In an empirical analysis of micro data, or more generally of price-taker units, the natural variables to measure incentives, under constant technology, are prices. When prices are the only state variables, and the quadratic input terms are omitted from the production function, the empirical equations (13.11)–(13.14) are similar to those derived from a production model based on the profit function. However, as we have seen above, when the implemented technology is endogenous, a profit function depends on all the state variables that affect this choice, including prices. As such, different prices may yield different combinations of functions depending on the available technology and other constraints. This is the essence of Property 13.4, and it may lead to the violation of the convexity of the profit function.

With aggregate models and with small samples, it is not feasible to include all the relevant prices in the empirical equation so the less pertinent prices are omitted. Alternatively, it is possible to represent the incentives by a summary measure such as the rate of return, measured roughly as the ratio of nonwage income to the value of the capital stock. This measure embeds in it not only the wage rate but also the effect of taxes and subsidies and other outcomes of policies. This rate has a permanent and a transitory component. The permanent component is more relevant to the choice of techniques that require investment; the transitory component, to the extent that it can be forecasted by the producers, affects largely the current variable inputs.

When an important sector of the economy is the focus, the prices are replaced with product demand and factor supply. This requires a detailed structure that it is often convenient to avoid. A shortcut would be to use, in addition to the rate of return, a measure of shocks that affect such demand and supply. To illustrate, open economies are affected by external shocks, such as in the prices of their main traded products or in external interest rates. An improvement in the foreign terms of trade causes an expansion in the aggregate demand, which in turn affects sectoral demand. Indirectly, a similar effect in the case of a borrowing country is generated by a decline in the international rate of interest in that it reduces the burden of servicing the debt.

The response of sectoral demand to external shocks depends on the sector's degree of tradability and on its income, or absorption, elasticity. An expansion in sectoral demand causes an increase in the *net* import of tradable goods, whereas the augmented demand for nontradable goods can be met only by an increase in domestic production and therefore in their prices. The degree of the price change is inversely related to the degree of tradability of the particular sector. The degree of tradability of agriculture is relatively high, and it is therefore sensitive to variations in the terms of trade. This subject is discussed in Mundlak, Cavallo, and Domenech (1989, 1990a), where the effect of changes in the trade and macro environment on sectoral incentives is also examined.

The foregoing discussion dealt only with the level of the incentives and not with their variability. Following the thread of the discussion in Chapter 12, it is suggested that variability in the incentives is likely to have a negative effect on productivity, and by the same reasoning, the larger the variability in the performance of a technique, other things equal, the less likely it is to be employed.

Environment: Physical

Agricultural productivity is affected by the physical environment. Variables such as average rainfall, temperatures, length of growing seasons, and type of soils are of a permanent nature and as such affect the decisions with respect to the crops to be grown and the methods of production and should be included in analyses based on cross-section data. The effect of the permanent component of the environment can be evaluated by allowing for a "unit effect." For instance, in cross-country analysis, we can introduce a country effect (country dummies) to allow for the permanent component of the environment. The problem is that a country effect represents other variables as well. Thus, as a general principle, it is desirable to include the more important variables explicitly. In a cross-country analysis of agricultural productivity, Mundlak and Hellinghausen (1982) used measures of the potential production of a region based on agrotechnical evaluation; Binswanger et al. (1987) used a similar measure. Deviations from the average values of these variables affect the transitory variations of output and inputs and should be included in time-series analysis.

Environment: Institutional

Less tangible, but sometimes more important, is the political and institutional environment. With the collapse of the economies of Eastern Europe it does not require much imagination today to realize the importance of this element. An illustration of the importance of institutions on productivity is provided by the shift to the household responsibility system in China beginning in 1979 (Lin, 1986; Wen, 1989; John McMillan, Whally, and Zhu, 1989).[6]

Another example, land reform, was analyzed by Coeymans and Mundlak (1993) in a study of the Chilean experience when land reform was implemented during the 1960s and early 1970s. There are various studies that incorporate the effects of the political and institutional environment on the economic performance using different methodologies and approaches (Adelman and Morris, 1967; J. McMillan, Rausser, and Johnson, 1991).

Technology

Conceptually, technology is the most difficult variable to measure because it is an abstract concept rather than an observable quantity. We can speak of consequences of major inventions such as high-yielding crop varieties, electricity, radio, transistors, and so on. However, all this talk does not give us a direct measure of the technology. Empirical analysis therefore resorts to indirect measures. Such measures provide valuable information on the rate of technological change and its factor bias. A measure of technology can also be used as a variable in the production function and thereby allow a better estimate of the contribution of the inputs and state variables to output. An example of a frequent representation of changes in technology is the use of a time trend. Time trend is an associative variable that summarizes quantitatively changes over time, but otherwise contains little information and is of no help in the analysis of technology differences in the cross-section.

Another medium for representing technology is a measure of human capital such as schooling or expenditures on research and development. The term human capital refers to knowledge embodied in people as well as disembodied knowledge generated by people. Conceptually, we can measure directly the inputs of variables, such as schooling, which reflect the embodied component. What we cannot measure directly is the disembodied component, which includes the accumulated knowledge found in libraries and which, most significantly, determines the path of new research. This knowledge component is internationally available and countries have access to it, in one form or another, perhaps with some delay, even without investing in its development. This is particularly the case with respect to agriculture, where much of the new technology and the information for its use is a public good. Because we do not have a direct measure of the disembodied human capital, its contribution to production in any particular setting has to be derived indirectly from the production function after allowing for the contribution of the various inputs that can be measured, including measures of education. This is similar in spirit, but not in details, to the Solow residual, and as such it is subject to similar limitations. We return to this below.

As an empirical proposition it can be said that investing in research and development increases knowledge and improves the available technology. Property 13.7, however, limits the scope of economics to say fundamentally much about the productivity of this process beyond reporting past experience. It can then be assumed that the monotone relationship between investment in the production of knowledge and output of knowledge will continue and will improve the available technology as they did in the past. Whether in retrospect the "production function of knowledge" would be revealed to be concave or convex we do not know, although this type of information would be very valuable to have. We do not have it, however, because the relationship between investment in research and its output lacks the property of regularity and therefore is not repetitious.

New knowledge is translated to new techniques that appear, as argued in Chapter 6, to be more capital intensive. A similar argument can be applied to embodied human capital. New techniques generate demand for new skills; the development of the computer, for instance, created new subjects such as programming. Those who acquired the skill early realized good returns to their investment, and this in turn attracted more workers and talent to this field. At the same time, new techniques may decrease the demand for other skills. Skills, like machines, may become obsolete. Unlike machines, people with obsolete skills are retained; they remain part of the labor force, but their relative earnings may decline. The upshot of this is that the demand for skills, as well as for all inputs, is determined jointly with the implemented technology, and as such it depends on the same state variables.

With this background we turn to examine a way of incorporating a measure of technology into the analysis. The essence of the foregoing discussion is that the technology at the aggregate level is an unobservable quantity and the evidence on it is strictly circumstantial, in that we observe output to increase faster than inputs. We do not have the convenience that we have at the micro level, as in our example of the green revolution, of explicitly identifying techniques. Therefore, the key is to use indirect methods of measurement that follow the footsteps of our discussion of technical change. This suggests the introduction of an indirect measure of technology into the empirical equation. Mundlak and Hellinghausen (1982) relate the technology to an aggregate measure of comprehensive, physical and human, capital. Following and extending this approach, the aggregate production function is assumed to maintain CRS and is written as $y_t = F(k_t, h_t, s_t, u_t)$, where y is the average labor productivity, k is the vector of ratios of observed capital goods to labor, h is a similar vector for the unobserved components of capital, such as human capital, to be referred to here as technology, s is a vector of other state variables, and u is a random disturbance.

It is assumed that given (k, s, u), y is monotone increasing in h, and therefore we can write $h = H(k, y, s, u)$, $\partial h/\partial y > 0$. Because knowledge does not fluctuate much over short time periods, we can use past values to substitute for its current value. The past values of h can be extracted from the past values of output, after allowing for the effects of the other variables in the production function. Let $x \equiv (k, y, s, u)$ be the argument of H, and x_τ be some function of lagged values of x to be defined below, then $h_\tau = H(x_\tau)$. The idea is to substitute h_τ for h_t in the production function to get $y_t = F(k_t, h_\tau, s_t, u_t)$.

The measure of h_τ depends on u_τ, s_τ, and k_τ and as such is subject to error, which has to be eliminated. The fluctuations in u are by far larger than those in the capital stock, and they can be reduced by taking a moving average of y and assuming away the effect of this term. The effect of k_τ and s_τ on y_τ can be eliminated by introducing these variables explicitly into the analysis. In this, we build on the fact that a regression coefficient represents the effect of a variable, *net* of the (linear) effects of the other explanatory variables in the equation. We can then write, in a generic form, an empirical version that replaces equation (13.10):

$$y_t = F(y_\tau, k_\tau, s_\tau, k_t, s_t, u_t) \tag{13.17}$$

Because of the high correlation between k_τ and k_t, the former may have little to contribute and therefore may be omitted in empirical analysis. A similar argument follows for s_τ, but here the correlation with s_t is not as strong. Incentives are subject to transitory and cyclical variations; in times of low profitability output may decline, but this is not reflective of a decline in h. To take this into account, we use the historical peak of y, defined as

$$y_\tau = \max(y_{t-i}; 0 < i < t), \tag{13.18}$$

and label it as peak. The peak coefficient represents the net effects of the unobserved variables, such as the various forms of human capital, institutions, and organization that are referred to as technology and cannot be measured directly. Indeed, the captured technology effect is lagged, rather than current, but this is inevitable in this approach and it constitutes a small price to pay. This is particularly so in the case of cross-country analysis.

The general form of the estimated function is

$$y_t = F(y_\tau, k_t, s_t, u_t). \tag{13.19}$$

The effect of s_τ on y_τ is asymmetric in that it can only cause the peak to increase. Therefore, a decline in y_t is attributed to state variables other than the peak, which are random in nature with possible cyclical components. In order to reduce the effects of such variations on the peak in empirical analysis, it is suggested to use per capita output instead of average labor productivity.

To sum up, we use an indirect measure to clean the effect of technology on the coefficients of the remaining variables in the production function. This measure affects not only the intercept but also the slope of the function, and as such it allows for a shift in factor intensity.

The Impact of the State Variables

There is no easy way to summarize empirically the impact of the state variables, because the variables appear in two equations, one for the slope and one for the intercept. Also, and more important, the state variables may not be independent. A change in one state variable may affect the values of the others as well as the value of the capital-labor ratio. All this should be taken into account in evaluating the impact of the state variables on output. This is illustrated by evaluating the elasticity of average labor productivity with respect to a given state variable (say s_i):

$$\begin{aligned}\partial \ln y/\partial s_i = \sum_h \{&[\partial \Gamma/\partial s_h + \ln x \partial \mathrm{B}_1(\cdot)/\partial s_h] \\ &+ [(\mathrm{B}_1(\cdot) + \mathrm{B}_2(\cdot) \ln x)(\partial \ln x/\partial s_h)]\}\partial s_h/\partial s_i.\end{aligned} \tag{13.20}$$

The terms in the first set of square brackets show the response of the implemented technology to a change in the state variables, whereas the terms in the second set of square brackets show the output response to a change in inputs, under constant technology. The elasticities in (13.20) have a time index, which is suppressed here, indicating that they vary over the sample points. The innovation in the present formulation lies in the response of the implemented technology. To isolate this effect, we rewrite (13.20) under the assumption that $\partial s_h/\partial s_i$ is equal to zero for $h \neq i$, and holding x constant to yield the elasticities

$$E_i = \partial\Gamma(s)/\partial s_i + \ln x[\partial \mathrm{B}_1(s)/\partial s_i]. \tag{13.21}$$

The effect captured by (13.21) is part of the unexplained productivity residual in the standard productivity analysis under the assumption of constant technology.

Note that E_i depends on the level of x. When x is the capital-labor ratio, it is subject to cyclical variations. It is likely to be high in recessions and low in boom periods, capturing the cyclical variations of factor shares.

The effect of s on factor bias is indicated by the sign of $\partial \mathrm{B}_1(s)/\partial s_i$. It is capital (labor) saving when this derivative is negative (positive).

Empirical Evidence

The test of the choice of technique approach is not in how much it complicates the production model but rather in whether it helps us to understand facts that do not make sense under competing approaches. This can be illustrated by applications of this approach using time-series data (Cavallo and Mundlak, 1982; Mundlak, Cavallo, and Domenech, 1989; Coeymans and Mundlak, 1993). A related application is McGuirk and Mundlak (1991). These studies differ in the state variables used but, on the whole, support the importance of the constraints, incentives, technology, and environment on productivity. Some of these results will be presented in Chapter 15. What follows here illustrates an application of the approach to the study of the cross-country agricultural production function.

Cross-country estimates of production functions utilize national data, and their potential contribution comes from the large spread in inputs and other important variables that help to increase the precision of estimates. The practice in empirical studies has been to assume that technology is homogeneous and is represented by a production function applicable to all the observations in the sample. However, the essence of the system of equations (13.11)–(13.14) is that the production function coefficients depend on the state variables. It is therefore of interest to examine empirically what difference this extension makes. We do this by summarizing results reported by Mundlak, Larson, and Butzer (1999).

As a background, Table 13.1 provides results obtained in a series of cross-country studies.[7] Studies using data for a single period provide estimates for the between-country regression for that particular year. This is also the case for studies that use panel data and introduce time dummies (within-time regressions) but not country dummies. Studies with panel data that contain country dummies (with or without time dummies) provide estimates for the within-country (or within-country and time) regression. This point is elaborated below.

Except for Bhattacharjee, the studies in the table have shifters such as schooling, research and extension, and infrastructure. In general, the table shows that the between-country estimates of land elasticity are low in absolute terms and relative to estimates obtained from the *within* regression (compare the two versions of the Evenson and Kislev study). Two measures of capital have been used in most studies, machinery and livestock. The elasticity of machinery varies around 0.1 (a little higher for the between-country regression) and that of livestock concentrates in the range of 0.2–0.3. The estimates for the labor elasticity are less stable.

The estimation of the system of equations (13.11)–(13.14) requires factor shares. However, this information is not available for most countries. The strategy has therefore been to extract the pertinent information from panel data on inputs, outputs, and state variables. The statistical aspects of analysis are discussed in the appendix to this chapter. Briefly, data generated by using country and time dummies are cleaned from the systematic between-time and between-country variations in the data and as such should best represent a measure of the more stable technology, referred to as the core implemented technology. Data generated by using country dummies alone are cleaned of the systematic between-country variations but contain the variability over time. Similarly, data generated by using time dummies alone are cleaned of the systematic time variability but contain the cross-country variability. Most important, the system of regressions using various dummies can be expressed in terms of three canonical regressions: between-country, $b(i)$, between-time, $b(t)$, and within-country-time variations, $w(it)$. These regressions are block orthogonal.[8]

Data

The sample contains data for 37 countries for the period 1970–1991 and is described in Mundlak, Larson, and Butzer (1999). The variables are: ***Output and Input***–*Output*–agricultural GDP in 1990 U.S. dollars; *Land*–hectares of arable and permanent cropland, along with permanent pastures; *Labor*–economically

Table 13.1 Cross-country production functions: Comparison of results

	Bhattacharjee	Hayami & Ruttan	Evenson & Kislev	Yamada & Ruttan	Antle	Hayami & Ruttan	Nguyen	Evenson & Kislev	Mundlak & Hellinghausen
Date of study	1955	1970	1975	1980	1983	1970	1979	1975	1982
Sample:									
Number of countries	22	37	36	41	43	36	40*	36	58
Time period	1949	1960	1955, 1960, 1965, 1968	1970	1965	1955, 1960	1955, 1960, 1970, 1975	1955, 1960, 1965, 1968	1960, 1965 1970, 1975
Estimation method	OLS	OLS	OLS	OLS	PCR	OLS	OLS	OLS	PCR
Data specification	S; N	M; N	M; N	M; N	S; N	M; PW	M; N	M; N	M; N
Fixed effects included						year	year	country	country#
Elasticities									
Structures and equipment/machinery/tractors		0.12	0.10	0.11		0.11	0.14	0.06	0.07
Livestock and orchards/livestock		0.23	0.30	0.23	0.14**	0.28	0.33	0.35	0.19

Land	0.42	0.08**	0.04**	0.02**	0.16	0.07	0.02**	0.14	0.16
Labor	0.28	0.41	0.23	0.33	0.38	0.40	0.39	0.03**	0.46
Fertilizer	0.29	0.12	0.10	0.24	0.07**	0.14	0.10	0.09	0.11
Irrigation									0.01
Schooling/general education		0.32**		0.08**	0.25**	0.24	0.10**		
Technical education		0.14	0.04	0.14		0.12	0.17	0.00**	
Research and extension			0.14		0.17			0.07	
Infrastructure					0.21				
Sum of input elasticities	0.99	0.96	0.77	0.93	0.75	1.00***	0.98	0.67	1.00***

* Sample is not balanced, $n = 183$ for Nguyen study.
** Not significant at $P = .05$ for one-tailed test.
*** Linear homogeneity imposed.
# Country effects on slopes and intercept.
OLS and PCR are ordinary least squares and principal components regressions.
S and M represent single-year observations and multi-year averages.
PW represents per-worker averages of national aggregated data, N represents national aggregates.

active population in agriculture (a stock, rather than a flow, concept); *Fertilizer*–total fertilizer consumption in metric tons; *Capital*–fixed capital stock used in agriculture, plus capital in livestock and orchards. ***Environment***–two variables are used, *potential dry matter (PDM)* and a *factor of water deficit (FWD)*. The first variable intends to measure theoretical potential production calculated on the basis of the physical environment; the second variable measures the relative water availability as the ratio of actual transpiration to potential transpiration. ***Technology***–the technology block consists of several variables: *Schooling*–the mean school years of the total labor force serves as a proxy for the embedded human capital; *Peak yield*–country-specific Paasche indices (1990 = 1) of the historical peak commodity yields, weighted by land area, used to measure the level of technology in agriculture, and intended to capture country-specific changes in technology over time (as measured, the variable is inadequate to represent cross-country differences in technology; therefore, in the cross-country analysis the level of the peak yields are replaced by their average growth rates for the period); *Yield gap*–deviations from the peak yield (the deviations may affect the productivity of the various inputs); and *Development*–the state of development of the economy, measured by the per capita output in the country relative to that in the United States (this is a summary measure of the various variables that affect productivity and as such are likely to affect agricultural productivity). ***Incentives***–two measures are used to capture the direct effect of incentives on productivity over and above their indirect effect that comes through resource allocation and accumulation: *relative price,* or the terms of trade between agriculture and manufacturing obtained as the ratio of the sectoral prices, and *price variability,* calculated as a moving standard deviation from the three previous periods of the relative price.

For the between-country analysis, the measures are modified; the average rate of growth in the relative price over the period replaces the level of such price. In addition, the standard deviation of the relative price over the entire period is used in place of the moving standard deviation. The variability of agricultural prices reflects the market risk faced by agricultural producers. In addition to the sector-specific risk, there is an economywide market risk, that of price volatility for the economy as a whole as measured by the rate of inflation. This is calculated as the rate of change in the total GDP deflator.

Expected improvement of future profitability encourages investment and thereby augments the capital stock, which appears as a variable in the analysis. The regression coefficients of the incentive variables represent only the direct effect of prices that is not captured in input changes. To obtain the full impact of the incentives on productivity, it is necessary to add their indirect effect through investment, but this is not done here.

The average annual growth rate of output was 3.82 percent. The growth rates for the inputs appear in the first column of Table 13.2.

Empirical Results

The estimates for a base model are given in Table 13.2 and consist of three blocks. The first block presents the within-country-time estimates, which summarize the changes that took place over time and over countries after allowing for country and time effects. The elimination of these effects considerably reduces the effect of the state variables. As such, these estimates are based on observations taken from the more stable, or core, technology. The second block presents the between-time estimates, obtained from a short time series of the sample means for each year. This represents the time-series component, common to all countries, and as such it captures the impact of changes in the available technology. The last block presents the between-country estimates, based on the between-country variations which constitute the major component of the total sum of squares. It summarizes the locus of points that go across the different techniques implemented by the countries, all operating under the same available technology. All the regressions display CRS, which is not rejected empirically. This is in contrast to the results of those cross-country studies which show increasing returns to scale (for instance, Kawagoe, Hayami, and Ruttan, 1985, p. 120). This indicates that our specification succeeds in capturing the impact of cross-country differences in technology and thus eliminates the spurious result of increasing returns to scale.[9] The null hypotheses that blocks can be omitted are rejected, and therefore we should interpret the information embedded in all three blocks. The coefficients of the variables common to the various equations are quite different, confirming the basic initial hypothesis that the regressions summarize the combined effect of changes in inputs and technology, and therefore the *within* and *between* regressions summarize different processes. We now turn to interpret the results.

Inputs. The results are striking in several respects. Perhaps the most interesting result is the magnitude of the elasticity of capital, 0.37 in the *within* regression, 0.34 in the between-country, and 1.03 in the between-time regression. The latter represents the response common to all countries in the sample. It indicates that, on average for the sample, an increase in capital was accompanied with a proportional increase in output. This strong response is consistent with the view that physical capital has been a constraint to agricultural growth. This empirical proposition is well illustrated by McGuirk and Mundlak (1991) in the context of the green revolution. The strong response indicates that the

Table 13.2 Cross-country estimates of the production function

Variable	Average annual growth rate (%)	Within time and country		Between time		Between country	
		Estimate	t-score	Estimate	t-score	Estimate	t-score
Inputs							
Capital	4.25	0.37	6.90	1.03	6.01	0.34	13.13
Land	0.12	0.47	3.78			−0.03	−2.82
Labor	−0.04	0.08		−0.16	−0.16	0.26	13.67
Fertilizer	3.04	0.08	1.53	0.14	0.33	0.43	21.91
Technology							
Schooling	1.80	0.09	0.55	−0.28	−0.06	0.02	0.52
Peak yield	1.90	0.83	3.80	−0.32	−0.07	0.06	4.19
Development	−0.29	0.52	3.36	−0.21	−0.33	0.31	2.97
Prices							
Relative prices	−0.30	0.04	1.78	0.02	0.09	0.01	1.95
Price variability		−0.03	−0.97	−0.07	−0.26	−0.08	−2.82
Inflation		−0.00	−0.75	0.04	0.71	0.07	4.25
Environmental							
Potential dry matter						0.16	2.68
Water availability						0.44	7.96

Source: Mundlak, Larson, and Butzer 1999.
Note: R^2 for 777 obs. = .9696.

implementation of changes in the unobserved available technology was strongly affected by investment in agriculture.

The between-time regression shows that the shift to more productive techniques is associated with a decline in labor. The labor coefficient in the core technology is also relatively low, whereas that of the between-country regression is more in line with the other cross-country studies. The low labor elasticity obtained for the core technology and the between-time regressions is an indication of the labor-saving technical change in agriculture, which is consistent with the slight decline of labor over time. This is not news, but it is emphasized here because it comes out of an integral view of the production structure and the variability over time and between countries. These results highlight the importance of capital in agricultural production, and indicate that agricultural technology is capital-cost intensive compared with nonagriculture.

This last conclusion is further reinforced by the magnitude of the land elasticity in the core technology and is at variance with the view that land is not an important factor of production in modern agriculture (Kawagoe and Hayami, 1985, p. 91). This view is based on an incorrect reading of the data, where no distinction is made between changes in the technology and the movement along a given production function. The sum of capital and land elasticities is around 0.8 in various formulations, making it clear that agriculture should be more sensitive than nonagriculture to changes in the cost of capital and less to that of labor (Mundlak, Cavallo, and Domenech, 1989). The value of the sum is a bit high compared with the literature. It is possible that a different choice of countries and time periods would lead to somewhat different results. However, a sum of 0.8 for land and capital elasticities leaves room for the conclusion on the importance of capital to remain intact.

There is also a big difference in the elasticity of fertilizers. Recall that the dependent variable is the log of value added, which is net of fertilizers. Using the envelope theorem, under the competitive conditions, the coefficient of fertilizers should be close to zero. The difference from zero should reflect only interest charges for working capital, reflecting the time lapse between the purchase of the inputs and the time of the sale of the output. A value of 0.08 obtained in the within-country-time regression may seem to be low, but this is not the case. It indicates that about 8 percent of the changes in agricultural output are to be attributed to fertilizers over and above their cost. Moreover, this result is obtained for the aggregate agricultural output, whereas fertilizers are used only on plant products. It is likely that a production function for plant products alone would show a larger elasticity for fertilizers. Thus a value of 0.08 for aggregate output may even be biased upward. One possibility is that fertilizers capture the impact of other chemicals and, more generally, the modern inputs, as indicated above. Still, the coefficient of this "extended" input should be near zero. A possible explanation for this deviation from zero is that the elasticity reflects a high shadow price of fertilizers, signaling a supply constraint, and as such also captures some intertechnology effects. This explanation is consistent with the high value of the fertilizer elasticity obtained from the between-country regressions. This suggests that the locus of country means represents a changing technology package where the improvement in the implemented technology is fertilizer using. At the same time it is also capital using but land saving.

Technology. The technology variables play a dual role in the analysis. First, they serve as technology shifters and as such reduce, or eliminate completely, the bias of the estimated input coefficients that is caused by the correlation of inputs and technology. Second, we can examine empirically how well they describe the data and thereby guide us in the search for appropriate technology indicators.

The peak yield serves well as a shifter of the agricultural productivity, as measured by the core technology, with an elasticity of about 0.83. The level of development of the country relative to the United States is also an important explanatory variable of agricultural productivity. Note that the contribution of this variable is over and above that of the peak yield, which shows that the yield level is not exhaustive as a technology indicator; first, the yield variable does not represent the productivity in livestock production, which accounts for about one-third of output, and second, there is a scope for improving efficiency under a given technology by coming closer to the frontier, as represented by the performance of the United States.

The between-time regression shows that, for the sample as a whole, none of the technology variables was important in accounting for the changes in agricultural productivity over time. The explanation is made by physical capital. The implication is that even though schooling and peak yields increased with time (column 1), we get no evidence that they contributed to the benefits harvested from improvements in the available technology. It is the changes in the available technology that caused the increase in these variables, at least in peak yield and perhaps in schooling. But it was capital availability that was crucial for the countries to take full advantage of the available technology. This sheds light on the importance of physical capital in accounting for the changes in agricultural productivity in the study period.

The results are different for individual countries, as seen from the between-country regression, where the level of development is important in accounting for the productivity variations. This is a statement of the importance of the various attributes of the overall level of development of a country in determining the level of agricultural productivity. This may also be the reason that schooling appears to be irrelevant. To the extent that schooling matters, it may have an indirect effect through the development variable. However, to what extent schooling matters and how it can be measured using aggregate data is still an open question, highlighted by Pritchett (1996).

Prices. The test of the null hypothesis that the price block can be omitted from the analysis is rejected. It appears, however, that the allocation of the price effect to the individual price components is problematic. On the whole, the signs of the coefficients are in line with expectations, but the precision is low. Note that the small quantitative effect on agricultural productivity is obtained conditional on given inputs and on technology. Thus there is little scope for additional price effects. The fact that this effect is detected at all is of prime importance. The channels for the price effect are the level of inputs and the choice of technology, and these are represented by explanatory variables.

Comparing with Conventional Analysis

In general, regressions obtained from panel data are presented with either time or country dummies, which amounts to running a within-time or within-country regression respectively. The relationships between such regressions and those presented in Table 13.2 are established in the appendix, where it is shown that allowing for only one effect results in regression coefficients that reflect some between effects. The importance of the between component is determined by its relative weight in the total sum of squares. Thus the regression coefficients obtained with time dummies largely reflect the between-country regression because the relative weight of the between-country sum of squares is dominant. Similarly, the regression coefficients obtained with country dummies reflect the between-time regression, but not to the extent of the previous case because the variations in the variables over time are much smaller than those across countries. In any case, the mere fact that a regression is conducted with some dummies does not guarantee that it identifies a stable function.

Most of the studies presented in Table 13.1 are strictly cross-country and as such are comparable with the between-country results in Table 13.2. The similarity lies in the low land elasticity, and in addition the sum of the elasticities of machines and livestock is close to the elasticity of capital in the between-country regression. This similarity is consistent with the interpretation that these studies describe only between-country changes; hence they provide a limited and incomplete picture of the production process. In any case, they do not provide coefficients of a stable production function and as such, do not provide the appropriate weights for growth accounting, as they were intended to do.

Total Factor Productivity

In Chapter 6 we saw that the measure of changes in total factor productivity (TFP) is path dependent. The measure is always of the change in the implemented, rather than the available, technology. Because the implementation depends on the factor supply, so does the measure. We can now demonstrate this point in calculations based on the regressions in Table 13.2. Using the *within* elasticities and the median growth rates from Table 13.2, we find that aggregate input and total factor productivity residual technical change accounts for about one-half each of the annual growth in output of 3.82 percent. This evaluation of the contribution of aggregate input is substantially smaller than the rate reported in the cross-country studies of Table 13.1. These studies use between-country estimates where the weight of fertilizers is high and that of land is low. The median growth rate of land in the sample was 0.12 percent and that of fertilizers was 3.04 percent. The difference in the elasticities of these two variables accounts for much of the difference in the growth accounting. In addition, studies that report increasing returns to scale overstate the role of inputs and understate the role of technical change.

How well do we capture the residual technical change in terms of the state variables included in the *within* regression? To answer this question, we multiply the median values of the rate of change of the state variables by their elasticities to obtain that the contribution to growth was schooling, 0.16 percent and peak yield, 1.58 percent, whereas the relative price and development had small negative effects. Obviously, the peak yield appears to be the main carrier of the technology.

Recall that the purpose of introducing the state variables, including the technology block, was to capture the changes in the implemented technology so that we could measure the factor productivity net of the technical change. The results indicate that we have been quite successful. Thus the peak yield captures about 83 percent of the residual, and only 0.37 percentage points of the total growth of 3.82 percent (or 10 percent) is not represented by variables in the regression.

A completely different picture is obtained by using the weights from the between-time regression. The elasticity of capital is 1.03, and therefore, using the median growth rates, capital more than exhausts the growth in output, and the overexhaustion is compensated by a decline in the other variables. Thus the global picture is that the changes in the available technology did not constitute a constraint to growth in output. The pace of the implementation of the changes in the available technology was determined by the pace of capital accumulation. How do we account for the difference in the results between the two calculations? The exercise using the *within* estimates evaluated the contribution of the inputs along a "stable" production function, whereas the exercise using the between-time estimates gave a mixed effect of changes on the production function and across production functions, and the latter was dominating. In terms of Figure 13.2, the movement is along the path $AN\tilde{M}$.

This discussion highlights the importance of the weights used in the computation of the changes in the TFP. Studies that attribute large weights to inputs with higher growth rates reduce the importance of the changes in the TFP. The discussion in Chapter 6 indicates that the relationship between the weights and the growth rate is not coincidental. When inputs needed for the implementation of the new productive technique are in short supply, the changes in the available technology will induce a growth in their availability, which in turn generates a positive correlation between those inputs and the technology shock in the empirical production function. Consequently weights obtained from regressions that cut across techniques are biased.

We have dealt with measures derived from cross-country data. We now list other results to provide an order of magnitude. More information is available for the United States. The studies vary by periods and methods of calculation. Ball (1985) reports total factor productivity growth for the period 1948–1979 of 1.75 percent as compared with 1.7 percent obtained from USDA data. Capalbo and Vo (1988) review the evidence on agricultural productivity, and their result for 1950–1982 is TFP of 1.57 as compared with 1.95 as obtained by the USDA for the same period.[10] Ball et al. (1997) present the production accounts for U.S. agriculture for the period 1948–1994 and report growth rates for the period and subperiods, based on Fisher indexes. The average growth rates for the period as a whole are 1.88, −0.07, and 1.94 percent for production (including intermediate products), aggregate input, and TFP. A derived figure from this study for the change in the TFP during 1948–1979 is approximately 1.47 percent, which is lower than the figure reported in Ball (1985). It is important to note that the latter study reports a decline in the aggregate input, so that the change in the TFP is larger than the change in production. This is an extreme difference from the studies based on cross-state data for the United States which attribute most of the change in output to inputs rather than to productivity (Griliches, 1963a).

Rosegrant and Evenson (1992) examine total factor productivity growth and its sources in the crops sector in India, using district panel data for the period 1956–1987. The TFP in the Indian crops sector grew during 1957–1985 at an approximate average annual rate of 1 percent and accounted for about one-third of total output growth in that sector. The growth rate for the same period was 0.78 in Bangladesh and 1.07 in Pakistan.

This information gives an order of magnitude, but it should be noted that there is considerable variability across countries and time. This is no surprise if we go back to the review in Chapter 1, which shows a considerable cross-country spread in growth rates of output and partial land and labor productivity. The whole argument concerning the endogeneity of the heterogeneous technology suggests that we can expect variability in performance.

The terms of trade of agriculture depend on the productivity growth in agriculture relative to nonagriculture. Jorgenson and Gollop (1992) compare the postwar productivity performance of U.S. agriculture with sectors in the private nonfarm economy using the total price function. Productivity growth explains 82 percent of economic growth in agriculture, but only 13 percent in the private nonfarm economy. The average annual growth rate of TFP in agriculture during 1947–1985 was 1.58 percent, nearly four times larger than that of the rest of the economy. The figure for agriculture is in line with the other estimates reported above, but the gap between agriculture and the rest of the economy seems to be too wide. Martin and Mitra (1998) compare the growth in TFP in a large number of countries and find the rate of productivity growth in agriculture to be higher than in manufacturing both on average and for the group of countries at different stages of development. However, these differences are considerably smaller than those reported by Jorgenson and Gollop.

Appendix 13A: Estimation with Panel Data

We now broaden our discussion of the *within* estimator in Chapter 12 in order to place the various forms of analyses within a uniform framework. We label W, $B(i)$, $W(i)$, $B(t)$, $W(t)$, and $W(it)$ projection (symmetric and idempotent) matrices that generate residuals. They are defined in terms of their operation on an arbitrary vector $x = \{x_{it}\}$ of order NT. Let $x_{i.}$ and $x_{.t}$ denote the averages of x_{it} over t and i respectively, and the terms in parentheses contain the typical elements of the vectors in question:

$$Wx = (x_{it} - x_{..}), \quad W(i)x = (x_{it} - x_{i.}), \quad W(t)x = (x_{it} - x_{.t}),$$
$$W(it)x = (x_{it} - x_{i.} - x_{.t} + x_{..}), \quad B(i)x = (x_{i.} - x_{..}), \quad B(t)x = (x_{.t} - x_{..}),$$
$$i = 1, \ldots, N, \quad t = 1, \ldots, T.$$

The following identities can be derived where the matrices on the right-hand side of each line are orthogonal:

$$W = W(i) + B(i) \tag{13A.1}$$

$$W = W(t) + B(t) \tag{13A.2}$$

$$W = W(i) + W(t) + W(it) \tag{13A.3}$$

$$W = B(i) + B(t) + W(it). \tag{13A.4}$$

Let y be the vector of observations of the dependent variable and X be the matrix of observations of the explanatory variables. The regression coefficients of interest can be written in a generic form for a projection matrix P as

$$b = (X'PX)^{-1}X'Py, \tag{13A.5}$$

where P can be any one of the projection matrices of interest listed above with rank not smaller than rank X. To introduce the notation for the regression coefficients, we present in brackets the projection matrix and the corresponding vector of coefficients: Pooled: $[W, b]$; within-time-country: $[W(it), w(it)]$; within-country: $[W(i), w(i)]$; within-time: $[W(t), w(t)]$; between-time: $[B(t), b(t)]$; between-country: $[B(i), b(i)]$. The pooled regression can be presented as a matrix-weighted average of *within* and between regressions (Maddala, 1971). For instance, use (13A.1) and simplify:

$$b = (X'WX)^{-1}X'Wy = Gw(i) + (I - G)b(i)$$

$$\text{where} \quad G = (X'WX)^{-1}X'W(i)X.$$

When G, the share of the within component of the variance of X, is relatively small, the coefficients of the pooled regression will largely reflect the between-regression coefficients.

With reference to the identities presented above, it is seen that data generated by $W(it)$ (using country and time dummies) is cleaned from the between-time and between-country variations in the data and as such should best represent a measure of the more stable technology, referred to as the core implemented technology. Data generated by $W(i)$ (using country dummies) are cleaned of the between-country variations but contain the variability over time. Similarly, data generated by $W(t)$ (using time dummies) are cleaned of the time variability but contain the cross-country variability. This can be seen by rearranging the identities in (13A.1)–(13A.4):

$$W(i) = W(it) + B(t) \tag{13A.6}$$

$$W(t) = W(it) + B(i). \tag{13A.7}$$

The system of regressions using various dummies can thus be described in terms of three canonical regressions: $b(i)$, $b(t)$, and $w(it)$.

PART FOUR

Static and Dynamic Behavior

14

The Agricultural Supply

The underlying assumption in our discussion is that farmers respond to price changes in their production decisions. Is this empirically valid? In other words, do farmers really respond to prices? Strange as it seems, this question, which is almost like asking if farmers are immune to income, has been repeatedly raised in the literature. This appears to be a naive question because it is well demonstrated that farmers prefer higher prices, an improved technology, and improvements in the infrastructure, all of which increase their income. The same principle is also applicable to changes in the economic environment that create opportunities to be seized by changing production. This has certainly been the case with respect to new technologies. Thus to say that there is no response to price variations is to say either that there is nothing that farmers can do in response to prices or that they do not believe that the change in prices will last and therefore do not respond to it. The reason that the question has been raised at all is that the strength of the supply response has important policy implications, but at the same time it is not an easy quantity to measure. The source of the difficulties is discussed by Schultz (1956), who, in fact, anticipated areas of future research.

From its very beginning, supply response analysis has been very much concerned with policy issues rather than with the application or development of a formal econometric analysis. This is well revealed by titles such as "The Farmers' Response to Price" (Bean, 1929), "The Nature of Statistical Supply Curves" (Cassels, 1933), "The Maintenance of Agricultural Production during Depression: The Explanations Reviewed" (Galbraith and Black, 1938), and "Can Prices Allocate Resources in American Agriculture?" (Brewster and Parsons, 1946). Some of this discussion was motivated by the fact that agricultural production did not contract during the Great Depression of the thirties, when prices of agricultural products declined substantially. The explanation for this was provided by Johnson (1950), indicating that not only product prices decreased in the depression, but factor prices decreased as well. The decline of factor prices reduced the severity of the decline of product prices and thus facilitated the maintenance of agricultural output with declining product prices. The central theme, the role of prices in determining output, has not changed much since. The literature on supply and the empirical results was reviewed in Mundlak (1985), where the findings are summarized:[1]

1. The short-run supply elasticity, when estimated directly, falls in the range of 0.1 to 0.3.
2. The estimated elasticities decrease with the level of aggregation. Higher values are obtained for the elasticities of individual products than for the aggregate output.
3. Indirect estimation of the supply elasticity, obtained through the estimation of factor demand, resulted in larger values than those obtained by direct estimation.
4. It was observed that adding a lagged output to an empirical supply equation improves the fit and often eliminates the existing serial correlation. However, when measures of capital, or of fixed inputs, are added to the equation, the statistical relevance of the lagged dependent variable is reduced or vanishes. A similar result is obtained when a trend variable is added.
5. When the sample was divided into subperiods according to the direction of the price changes, it was found that
   (a) The supply elasticity was higher for a period of increasing prices.
   (b) When capital was included in the supply function, its coefficient was positive for periods of increasing prices and zero for periods of decreasing prices.
   (c) When a distributed lag was used, the rate of adjustment was higher for a period of increasing prices.
6. The dependence of the supply elasticity on the length of run reflects a constrained optimization. The severity of the constraints vanishes with time. This view leads to a formulation of a well-defined structure.

The concept of an agricultural supply function is too general to expect uniformity in empirical results. This generality can be illustrated by the foregoing discussion, where we have developed different supply functions depending on what has been assumed to be given in the derivation of the function. In Chapter 2 we developed the supply conditional on resources and technology, in Chapter 4 we allowed resources to change in response to prices, in Chapter

5 we introduced changes in output due to variations in technology holding prices constant, in Chapters 6 and 13 we introduced the choice of the production function. Further extensions that allow for deviations from the competitive conditions in the comparative statics sense were introduced in Chapters 8, 9, and 10.

The following discussion intends to provide a uniform framework for explaining the empirical results, as summarized above, and their meaning. We begin the discussion with the comparative static framework where inputs are classified as variables, with perfectly elastic supply, or fixed. The analysis deals with a more detailed specification than the one considered above in that we allow for more inputs that can vary according to their supply conditions. The application to the aggregate model is immediate. The discussion is then extended to cover varying factor supply. This is followed by extending the discussion in Chapter 10 on dynamic factor demand and by examining the implications of dynamic factor supply. This allows us to explain the apparent disequilibrium in the factor markets. Finally, the analysis is extended to incorporate the choice of techniques.

Comparative Statics

The Framework

Some inputs used in production are fully consumed within the period of production, say a year, whereas others are durable and serve for more than one period. Consequently, the two input groups respond differently to changes in the economic environment in a given year. The optimization problem that takes the future into account results in a recursive structure which differentiates between the decisions for the two groups, as shown in Chapter 10. However, some important issues can be discussed without an explicit statement of the intertemporal optimization. It is therefore convenient to postpone the discussion of this topic to a later stage.

The starting point for the analysis is the restricted profit function of an individual producer:

$$\pi(p, w, k, T) = \max_{y,v}(py - wv : y, x \in T), \tag{14.1}$$

where y is a vector of I outputs, x is a vector of J inputs decomposed to variable, v, and fixed, k, components: $x = (v, k)$ with dimensions (J_v, J_k), $J_v + J_k = J$, T is the available technology, p is the vector of product prices, and

w is the vector of factor prices decomposed to conform to the decomposition of x. Where ambiguity does not exist, such a decomposition is not made explicit.

By Hotelling's lemma, the product demand and factor supply functions are

$$y_i(p, w, k, T) = \frac{\partial \pi}{\partial p_i}, \qquad v_j(p, w, k, T) = -\frac{\partial \pi}{\partial w_j}. \tag{14.2}$$

The strength of the response of y and v to price changes depends on the decomposition of x. The unrestricted case when all inputs are variables ($J_v = J$) is referred to as the long run and is represented by the following behavioral functions:

$$y^*(p, w, T), \qquad v^*(p, w, T), \qquad k^*(p, w, T). \tag{14.3}$$

Empirical analyses are based on dated data. The decomposition of x to v and k is done according to the "ease" of changing the inputs within the period of analysis, usually a year. Consequently, the empirical analysis of (14.2) produces a restricted or short-run response. The relationships between the restricted supply as given in (14.2) and the unrestricted supply as given in (14.3) is given by the identity

$$y(p, w, k^*, T) \equiv y^*(p, w, T). \tag{14.4}$$

Hence

$$\frac{\partial y_i^*}{\partial p_i} \equiv \frac{\partial y_i}{\partial p_i} + \sum_j \frac{\partial y_i}{\partial k_j^*} \frac{\partial k_j^*}{\partial p_i}. \tag{14.5}$$

Thus the long-run response to a price change is the sum of the short-run response and the indirect price effect through its effect on investment in the quasi-fixed factors. Using logarithmic differentiation, the result can be expressed in terms of elasticities.

$$\epsilon_{ii}^u = \epsilon_{ii}^r + \sum_{j=1}^{J_k} \beta_{ij}^* \epsilon_{ji}, \tag{14.6}$$

where ϵ_{ii}^u and ϵ_{ii}^r are the unrestricted (long-run) and restricted (short-run) elasticities, respectively, $\beta_{ij}^* = \partial \ln y_i / \partial \ln k_j^*$ is the production elasticity of k_j, the jth component of k, in the production of the ith product, and $\epsilon_{ji} = \partial \ln k_j^* / \partial \ln p_i$ is the demand elasticity of k_j with respect to p_i. Note that the relationship in (14.6) is obtained under the identity in (14.4), and as such it is restricted to the long-run equilibrium. The discussion of disequilibrium is taken up below.

Supply and Scale Elasticities

There is a useful relationship between the supply and scale elasticity that yields a simple expression, requiring no elaborate computations, for evaluating the supply elasticity. This expression is also very useful in evaluating the importance of the length of run. To avoid unnecessary details, we concentrate here on a single output production function, and begin with a homogeneous function of degree $\mu < 1$ in the variable inputs. The corresponding cost function is a function of the prices of the variable inputs, the level of the fixed inputs, and output:

$$c = \phi(w, k)y^{1/\mu} \tag{14.7}$$

with marginal cost

$$\frac{dc}{dy} = \frac{\phi(w, k)}{\mu}y^{(1/\mu)-1}. \tag{14.8}$$

Unless otherwise indicated, we assume perfectly elastic demand so that the competitive conditions imply $dc/dy = p$. To derive the supply elasticity, we use (14.7)–(14.8):

$$\epsilon = \frac{d \ln y}{d \ln p} = \frac{\mu}{1 - \mu}. \tag{14.9}$$

This result highlights the sensitivity of the supply elasticity to the degree of homogeneity of the production function. With $\mu = 0.1$, $\epsilon = 0.11$, whereas when $\mu = 0.9$, $\epsilon = 9$.

To relate this to our discussion, we write the underlying production function as $y = F(v, k)$, let $\beta_j \equiv \partial \ln y/\partial \ln v_j$, and by the optimization condition, $\beta_j = w_j v_j/py \equiv S_j$, where S_j is the share of factor j in total output. As the production function is homogeneous in v, the degree of homogeneity is equal to $\Sigma\beta_j$, and therefore

$$\epsilon = \frac{\Sigma_j S_j}{1 - \Sigma_j S_j}, \quad j = 1, \ldots, J_v. \tag{14.10}$$

PROPERTY 14.1 (scale elasticity) Under the competitive assumption, the scale elasticity is equal to the sum of the factor shares of the variable inputs.

When the production function is not homogeneous, it can be approximated locally by a homogeneous function of degree e, where e is the scale elasticity (Carlson, 1956). Using obvious notations:

$$e(v, k) \equiv \frac{\lambda}{F(v, k)} \frac{dF(\lambda v, k)}{d\lambda} |_{\lambda=1} = \sum_j \frac{F_j d(v_j \lambda)/d\lambda}{F(v, k)} \tag{14.11}$$

$$= \sum_j F_j v_j / F(v, k) = \sum_j S_j, \quad j = 1, \ldots, J_v.$$

PROPERTY 14.2 (supply elasticity) Under the dichotomy of variable and fixed inputs the supply elasticity is equal to the ratio of the scale elasticity to its difference from one:

$$\epsilon = \frac{d \ln y}{d \ln p} = \frac{e(v, k)}{1 - e(v, k)}. \tag{14.12}$$

The scale elasticity need not be constant everywhere, as this approximation is defined locally and as such depends on the classification of inputs to v and k. What is important for the present discussion is that it can be evaluated in general from the sum of the factor shares of the variable inputs.

It is instructive also to derive the result through the use of the restricted profit function. When the variable inputs are at their optimal values, we can rewrite (14.1):

$$\pi = y - \sum_j w_j v_j$$

$$= y(1 - \mu); \quad \mu = \sum_j \beta_j.$$

Hence, when μ is locally constant, $\partial \ln \pi / \partial \ln w_j = \partial \ln y / \partial \ln w_j$, by Hotelling's lemma, $\partial \ln \pi / \partial \ln w_j = -w_j v_j / \pi$, which can be written in terms of the production elasticity, $\partial \ln \pi / \partial \ln w_j = -\beta_j / (1 - \mu)$. Finally, using $\sum_j \partial \ln w_j / \partial \ln p = -1$

$$\frac{\partial \ln y}{\partial \ln p} = \sum_j \frac{\partial \ln \pi}{\partial \ln w_j} \frac{\partial \ln w_j}{\partial \ln p} = \frac{\mu}{1 - \mu}.$$

This framework makes it possible to derive orders of magnitude of the short-run supply elasticity by using empirical evidence on the factor shares. This derivation can be done at various levels of aggregation. Here we concentrate on the aggregate supply, and thus we move from a firm to an industry response under the simplifying assumption that locally, factor supply functions facing the industry are perfectly elastic. Also, it is assumed that there is no redistribution of k among firms in response to price variations in the short run. In evaluating the aggregate supply function we assume that land, capital, and often labor are fixed in the short run. These inputs account for approximately 0.8 to 0.9 of total output, implying that the supply elasticity is between 0.11 and 0.25. These values are in line with the empirical results as summarized above.

Varying Factor Supply

The classification into variable and fixed inputs is to some extent arbitrary. Such a dichotomy implies a zero supply elasticity for the fixed inputs and infinite elasticity for the variable inputs. As seen in Chapter 11, the latter assumption is made, generally implicitly, in many of the production analyses using derivatives of the profit function. It holds true for the individual firm but not for the industry as a whole. For instance, the recognition of the importance of fertilizers that accompanied the green revolution could not be matched with unlimited supplies at the going price. Hence, fertilizer is to some extent fixed. On the other hand, the supply of the fixed inputs can be changed over time if prices justify it.

With these considerations taken into account, the analysis is generalized by introducing factor supply functions:

$$x_j = G_j(w_j, T_j), \tag{14.13}$$

where T_j represents the technology (or tastes when dealing with labor supply) in the sector producing input j, and let s_j be the factor supply elasticity, $s_j = \partial \ln x_j / \partial \ln w_j$.

We now show that the smaller the factor supply elasticities, the smaller the product supply elasticity.[2] This can be seen by incorporating (14.13) in the analysis. First, use (14.8) and the competitive condition to obtain

$$\ln p = \ln \phi - \ln \mu + (1/\mu - 1) \ln y.$$

Assuming for simplicity that μ is constant, total differentiation gives

$$\epsilon = \frac{d \ln y}{d \ln p} = [\frac{d \ln \phi(w)}{d \ln y} + (\frac{1}{\mu} - 1)]^{-1}. \tag{14.14}$$

Leaving the technical details to the appendix to this chapter, we obtain

$$\epsilon = \mu[(1 - \mu) + \Sigma_j(\alpha_j / s_j)]^{-1}, \quad s_j \neq 0, J_v = J, \tag{14.15}$$

where α_j is the share of factor j in total (variable) cost, $x_j w_j / c \equiv \alpha_j$. Equation (14.15) generalizes (14.10) in that when the factor supply functions are perfectly elastic for all factors, that is, $s_j = \infty$, the two equations become identical. A value of zero for s_j is ruled out in (14.15) because it is assumed that all inputs are allowed to vary. However, s_j can be small for some j, thereby making the supply elasticity small.

For a linear homogeneous production function, $\mu = 1$, and

$$\epsilon = (\Sigma_j \alpha_j / s_j)^{-1}, \quad \mu = 1, J_v = J. \tag{14.16}$$

Under CRS and the simplistic case of $s_j = s$ for all j, $\epsilon = s$, so that the aggregate supply elasticity is equal to the elasticity of factor supply. This result underscores the role of finite factor-supply elasticities in determining the size of the firm or sector under CRS.

When some inputs are fixed, that is, $s_j = 0$ for some j, equation (14.15) is still applicable if the production function is homogeneous in the variable inputs. In this case, the sum is taken over the variable inputs only; μ is defined accordingly, and the result is modified in a straightforward manner. To illustrate, group all inputs into two factors, $x_1 = v$, $x_2 = k$, and $\mu = \beta_1$, $1 - \mu = \beta_2$. In this case, $\partial \ln x_1 / \partial \ln y = 1/\beta_1$, $\partial \ln x_2 / \partial \ln y = 0$, and $\alpha_1 = 1$. Then

$$\epsilon = \beta_1 [(1 - \beta_1) + 1/s_1]^{-1}. \tag{14.17}$$

This expression shows clearly how the supply elasticity is affected by the factor supply elasticity of the variable factor. For instance, for $\beta_1 = 0.2$ and $s_1 = 1$, the product supply elasticity is 0.11 instead of 0.25 as derived above under the assumption of $s_1 = \infty$. This is in line with the empirical results summarized above.

Unfortunately, the results for nonhomogeneous functions are not as neat in detail but are similar in substance. We let z stand for the vector of exogenous variables, and sketch the derivation with reference to the following system:

$$y = F(x, z), \quad \text{production function,} \tag{14.18}$$

$$x = X(w, p, z), \quad \text{factor demand,} \tag{14.19}$$

$$w = W(x, z), \quad \text{factor supply.} \tag{14.20}$$

Differentiate the system logarithmically, holding z constant and noting that x is homogeneous of degree 0 in w, p:

$$\hat{y} = \beta'\hat{x} \tag{14.21}$$

$$\hat{x} = E(\hat{w}/p) = E[\hat{w} - \iota\hat{p}] \tag{14.22}$$

$$\hat{w} = S^{-1}\hat{x}, \tag{14.23}$$

where $\hat{x} = d \ln x$, β is the vector of production elasticities, $E = \{\epsilon_{jh}\}$ is the matrix of factor demand elasticities, ι is a vector of ones, and S is a diagonal matrix of factor supply elasticities. Solve the system to obtain

$$\hat{x} = -[I - ES^{-1}]^{-1}[E\iota\hat{p}] \tag{14.24}$$

$$\hat{y} = \beta'[ES^{-1} - I]^{-1}[E\iota\hat{p}]. \tag{14.25}$$

The supply elasticity is $\epsilon = \hat{y}/\hat{p} = \beta'[ES^{-1} - I]^{-1}E\iota$; simplifying,

$$\epsilon = \beta' S[E - S]^{-1}E\iota. \tag{14.26}$$

This finding makes it clear that the mere fact that empirical supply elasticities are low is insufficient to conclude that farmers behave differently from other producers. Most likely, the low supply elasticities reflect inelastic factor supply.

This analysis can now be applied to examine the effect of the level of aggregation. The elasticity of factor supply depends on the level of product aggregation. The lower the level of product aggregation, the more elastic the factor supply is likely to be. This in turn should generate a relationship between the level of aggregation and the value of the supply elasticity. We discuss this result for some leading cases of interest.

Aggregation over Firms

A firm competes for resources with other firms, thus even if aggregate factor supply is inelastic, the individual firm can respond to prices by bidding away resources from other firms. This raises the interesting question of why some firms expand more than others. The answer is given in Chapters 10 and 12. In short, it is related to differences among firms in productivity, in the opportunity costs of specific factors of production, and in risk assessment and the attitude toward risk.

The scope for expanding resources is narrowed down when it comes to a sector, rather than a firm. A positive supply response of a sector requires drawing resources from other sectors. The rate of intersectoral flow of resources depends on the differential rates of returns, which is positively related to the product price. This subject is discussed in Chapters 9 and 10 for labor and capital respectively. Raw materials presumably have more elastic supply, but this is not always the case. As already indicated, the sudden increase in the demand for fertilizers sparked by the green revolution could not be met by the available supply. The increase in the supply of fertilizers required investment in production capacity, and as such fertilizer use was subject to the overall capital constraint.

Product Aggregation

While intersectoral factor flow determines mainly the level of agricultural output, the intrasectoral flow determines the composition of agricultural output. Naturally there is more substitution within agriculture than between agriculture and other sectors. Consequently the supply response of individual crops is likely to be more elastic than the response of the aggregate supply. This is in line with the empirical findings summarized above. This result can be expressed in terms of the transformation curve for the agricultural sector. The transformation curve itself is determined by total resources and as such represents aggregate output. Movements along the curve are generated by changes in product price ratios. Thus, holding the level of aggregate output fixed, the composition of output varies in response to prices. The degree of intrasector substitution depends on factor specificity, including the physical environment. The less specific the factors, the higher the substitution and the more price responsive the supply is likely to be. In considering such intrasector substitution it should be noted that knowledge may be crop specific and as such may limit the rate of substitution.

Product Supply and Factor Demand

Griliches (1959) and subsequent work derived the supply elasticity indirectly by first estimating the elasticities of factor demand and then aggregating them. The empirical supply elasticities obtained by using this indirect approach are significantly larger than those obtained by direct estimation. No adequate explanation was provided for this discrepancy. However, the discrepancy is not a coincidence, and it can be accounted for in terms of the foregoing analysis. These studies implicitly assumed perfectly elastic factor supply. Under this assumption, the system of equations (14.21) and (14.22) and (14.26) yields $\epsilon = -\beta' E \iota$. The homogeneity of degree 0 of the factor demand functions implies, $-E\iota = E_p$, where $E_p = \{\epsilon_{jp}; \epsilon_{jp} = \partial \ln x_j/\partial \ln p\}$ is the vector of factor demand elasticities of x_j with respect to p. Hence the supply elasticity is a linear combination of the factor demand elasticities,

$$\epsilon = \beta' E_p. \tag{14.27}$$

Thus, knowing ϵ_{jp} and β_j, it is possible to calculate ϵ.

Three possible reasons can be offered for the difference between the direct and indirect estimates of supply elasticities. First, beginning with theory, the aggregate supply function should represent only the expansion effect of changes in factor prices, whereas due to misspecification the empirical functions also capture the substitution effect and thereby exaggerate the results. To prove this assertion, we follow Mundlak (1968, p. 228) and express the relationships between the elasticities of the two demand functions:

$$x^*(p, w, T) \equiv x[y^*(p, w, T), w, T]. \tag{14.28}$$

The left-hand side of (14.28) is derived from the profit function (Hotelling's lemma), whereas the right-hand side is derived from the cost function corresponding to the optimal output $y^*(p, w, T)$. Then, by differentiating (14.28), we obtain

$$\frac{\partial x_j}{\partial w_h} = \frac{\partial x_j}{\partial w_h}\Big|_{y^*} + \frac{\partial x_j}{\partial y}\frac{\partial y^*}{\partial w_h} \tag{14.29}$$

or, using obvious notation,

$$\epsilon_{jh} = E_{jh} + e_{jy}E_{yh}, \tag{14.30}$$

where $E_{jh} = \partial \ln x_j/\partial \ln w_h|_{y^*}$ is an elasticity of substitution.[3] Thus ϵ_{jh} is decomposed into substitution and expansion components. By the singularity of the substitution (Slutsky) matrix, we have

$$\sum_h \beta_h E_{jh} = 0. \tag{14.31}$$

Consequently, when the production elasticities are used as weights in the aggregation, the substitution components disappear, and the outcome of the aggregation is the expansion effect, as it should be. This can be seen by combining (14.27), (14.30), and (14.31) to obtain

$$\epsilon = -\sum_h E_{yh}. \tag{14.32}$$

Background details appear in the appendix. To sum up,

PROPERTY 14.3 (factor demand and product supply) The correct indirect evaluation of supply elasticity from factor demand should have all factor and product prices in each of the factor demand equations, and the system should be estimated under the constraint of the homogeneity and symmetry conditions.

When such a system is properly estimated, the substitution term in the coefficient of the own price is offset by the substitution terms in the coefficients of the other prices. But when each factor demand equation does not contain the prices of all the other factors, their substitution effect is not captured, and consequently under aggregation the results exaggerate the elasticity of derived demand. Thus, at best, the empirical results can serve as upper limits. In principle, such a system is estimated by Antle (1984).

Second, when computing the aggregate supply function it is unrealistic to assume perfectly elastic factor supply for all factors. The system of equations (14.21)–(14.23) represents a more complex system to which we return when discussing the dynamics of supply. Third, the input demands were estimated using distributed lags. The empirical equations showed a slow adjustment that led to considerable augmentation of the short-run elasticities to yield the long-run elasticities. This effect is discussed below.

Dynamic Aspects

The system of equations in (14.2) and (14.3) constitutes a recursive structure that determines the time paths of outputs and inputs. The long-run values of k are determined by (14.3), whereas the short-run values of v and y are determined by (14.2) conditional on k and prices. This analysis is now extended to take account of the fact that k affects output and cost in more than one period. The underlying optimization problem was discussed in Chapter 10, where a solution for the optimal time path of $k(t)$ was obtained. It is written schematically as

$$k^*(q, \hat{q}, w, r, c, p, T), \tag{14.3'}$$

where q is the price of the quasi-fixed input, and r is the discount rate. All the variables in (14.3′) are functions of time. Obviously, the decision on the time path of k requires knowledge of the time path of all the state variables. This information is seldom available, and therefore it has to be replaced by expectations. To sum up, the introduction of intertemporal optimization results in replacing (14.3) with (14.3′), thereby adding state variables as well as uncertainty with respect to the future time path of the exogenous variables.

The response to changes in the state variables is not immediate, and this needs to be taken into account. As discussed in Chapter 10, the dynamics is introduced either exogenously or endogenously. In either case, we note that the system has a recursive structure that should be taken into account in the analysis (Mundlak, 1967). This provides a different approach to the dynamics of supply than that of distributed lags (Nerlove, 1956, 1958, 1979). Therefore, before continuing with the discussion, we examine the meaning of estimates obtained from distributed lag analysis of the supply function.

The Time Path of Output and Distributed Lag Analysis

In evaluating distributed lag estimates of supply response it is important to note that the time paths of outputs and inputs are determined jointly by the time paths of the exogenous variables and of the random shocks (Mundlak, 1966). Consequently, the functional relationship between output and its lagged values is endogenous within the economic system and cannot be summarized by one parameter. Thus the results derived from distributed lag analysis lack any structural information. Nevertheless, distributed lag estimates appear "reasonable" and have been widely used.

The question is what information is revealed by distributed lag analysis of supply. We examine this question within the simplest possible model, which contains two explanatory variables, price and unobserved capital. The capital variable is broadly defined to represent physical capital, human capital, available technology, infrastructure, and similar variables that affect output. The equation, written in terms of deviations from the mean, is

$$y_t = \beta p_t + \gamma k_t + u_t. \tag{14.33}$$

The basic idea of the following analysis is to view lagged output as a measure, subject to error, of the unobserved capital stock and to evaluate the meaning of the coefficients in the empirical equation. The quality of this relationship depends on the time pattern of the various variables in equation (14.33). The evaluation requires some technical developments. Label $x_\tau \equiv x_{t-1}$; $x = y, k, p$; and assume: $u_t \sim IID(0, \sigma^2)$, $E(u_t p_{t'}) = E(u_t k_{t'}) = 0$, for all t and t'. In what follows, it is assumed that there is no uncertainty with respect to p_t, or alternatively, that p_t in (14.33) is the expected price. The regression equation obtained by OLS is

$$y_t = bp_t + cy_\tau + \hat{u}_t. \tag{14.34}$$

The common interpretation is that b represents the short-run supply response, $1 - c$ is the coefficient of adjustment, and $b/(1 - c)$ is the long-run response.

To evaluate the meaning of c, define $\tilde{y}_t$ and $\tilde{k}_t$ as the residuals from the regressions of y_t and k_t on p_t respectively. Assuming that p_τ is a poor predictor of k_t, it is shown in the appendix that

$$c \cong \tilde{c} \equiv \frac{y'\tilde{k}_t'\tilde{k}_\tau \gamma}{\tilde{y}_\tau'\tilde{y}_\tau}. \tag{14.35}$$

Thus $\tilde{c}$ represents the proportion of the total variations in lagged output, net of the price effect, generated by variations in k, net of the price effect, $0 \leq \tilde{c} \leq 1$. When the sequences $\{\tilde{k}_t\}$, $\{p_t\}$ are independent, plim $c =$ plim $\tilde{c}$. The variations in output due to k are of longer-run duration and can be viewed as systematic, whereas those that occur due to p or the disturbances can be viewed as transitory. When firms grow, k changes constantly and the systematic component is likely to dominate the transitory one, leading $\tilde{c}$ to be closer to 1. On the other hand, in a stagnant situation k is fairly stable, and $\tilde{c}$ is likely to be closer to zero; it is equal to zero in the extreme case when k is constant.

The quality of p_t as a predictor for k_t, k_{t-1}, and p_{t-1} is an empirical question. However, for the main carriers of the implemented technology, such as public inputs or available technology, the sequence $\{k_t\}$ is likely to be orthogonal to the sequence $\{p_t\}$.

Clearly, this analysis provides no basis for attributing to $1 - c$ the meaning of a coefficient of adjustment in the sense common to distributed lag analysis. Consequently, the ratio $b/(1 - c)$ calculated from the coefficients in (14.34) has nothing to do with a long-run price response.

This conclusion is based on a simple model, and the question is to what extent it is consistent with the data. The answer is readily obtained by reviewing published results of distributed lag analysis. As already indicated in our summary of the empirical results, the introduction of lagged output to an equation containing price improved the fit of the equation. It is important to note that most of the empirical evidence comes from aggregate time-series data. Because the industry has been expanding, output serves as a proxy for k_t, and the fact that lagged output is empirically relevant reflects the relevance of k. Indeed, in those studies that included a capital variable in the equation, the lagged dependent variable disappeared (Tweeten and Quance, 1969; Pandey, Piggott, and MacAuley, 1982). Griliches (1960b) reported a substitution between trend and the lagged dependent variable. Again, in this case trend can be considered as a proxy for the time path of capital. Regressions of output on price alone resulted in serial correlations. Such correlations were eliminated by the introduction of lagged output. But they were also eliminated by introducing capital into the equation, which is consistent with the interpretation that the serial correlation was caused by the omission of k_t. In addition, Tweeten and Quance (1969) suggest stronger response in periods of increasing prices than in periods of decreasing prices. Clearly, when prices decline, they decline all over; hence the salvage value of the capital stock is very low, and thus it is kept in production (Johnson, 1950). On the other hand, when prices increase, it is possible to adjust the capital stocks through new investments.

The foregoing discussion also applies to distributed lag estimates of factor demand. Quantitatively, demand studies, particularly those dealing with variable inputs, might be more distorted than supply studies, because capital deepening is a trend in agriculture. Thus when the fixed inputs play a prominent role in factor demand equations, the outcome is a low coefficient of adjustment and therefore a considerable augmentation of the short-run elasticities. All this is in line with the empirical evidence summarized above.

Endogenous Dynamics: The Dual Approach

The dual approach, as developed by McLaren and Cooper (1980) and Epstein (1981), has provided an elegant framework to deal simultaneously with several issues of dynamic adjustment in a practical fashion. It has been applied in agricultural economics research by Taylor and Monson (1985), Vasavada and Chambers (1986), Howard and Shumway (1988), Chang and Stefanou (1988), Luh and Stefanou (1991), Thijssen (1996), and Lansink and Stefanou (1997), among others. Some of these studies are influenced by Epstein and Denny (1983), which used manufacturing data. The literature is reviewed in Mundlak (2000); the approach and the main results pertaining to our discussion are summarized here.

As in the literature, the model is presented in continuous time, and the cost of adjustment appears as an argument in the production function. A crucial element in this framework is the assumption of static price expectation, whereby the present prices and technology are assumed to remain constant indefinitely. Modifications of this assumption are discussed below.

The production function, $F(k, I)$, is expressed in terms of the quasi-fixed factors, k, and the investment, I.[4] The variables are vectors of comparable dimensions. A partial list of the regularity conditions on the production function includes: $F_k(\cdot) > 0$, $F_I(\cdot) < 0$, and $F(\cdot)$ is strongly concave in I. The optimization calls for:

$$J(s) = \max_I \int_0^\infty e^{-rt}[F(k, I) - \tilde{q}'k + J_k'(I - dk)]dt, \qquad (14.36)$$

subject to $k(0) = k_0$, and the terminal conditions. $J(s)$ is the value function, $\tilde{q}$ is the vector of rental rates, $s = (k, \tilde{q}, r, d)$ is the vector of exogenous variables, and J_k is the vector of multipliers of the constraint $\dot{k} = I - dk$, and as such it represents the shadow price of capital. Note that (14.36) is expressed in terms of the rental rate, rather than in terms of the price of the capital good. Also, under static expectations, $\tilde{q}$ does not contain the capital-appreciation term. In what follows, unless indicated otherwise, r and d are assumed to be constant. All the variables are functions of time and, unless needed, the time notation is avoided. Because the prices and the technology are assumed constant, only their current values matter. This is the major analytic payoff of the assumption of static expectation. Consequently, the problem becomes similar to that of the duality used in the static analysis. The difference between the two models is in the nature of the solution. In the dynamic case, it consists of the time path of the control variables.

Under the regularity conditions on F, the value function J satisfies the Hamilton-Jacobi-Bellman equation (Kamien and Schwartz, 1991, p. 261):

$$rJ(s) = \max_I\{F(k, I) - \tilde{q}'k + J_k(s)'(I - dk)\} \qquad (14.37)$$

A partial list of the regularity conditions on the value function includes: $(d + r)J_k + \tilde{q} - J_{kk}\dot{k} > 0$ (equivalent to $F_k > 0$), $J_k > 0$ (positive shadow price of capital; follows from the adjustment cost assumption of $F_I < 0$), and a necessary condition that J is convex in prices (because J is a maximum problem).

The behavioral functions are derived by differentiating $J(\cdot)$ with respect to the exogenous variables to yield a generalized Hotelling's lemma. Specifically, a differentiation with respect to $\tilde{q}$ and rearrangement yields

$$\dot{k}^* = J_{\tilde{q}k}^{-1}[rJ_{\tilde{q}}(k, s) + k], \qquad (14.38)$$

where we write $J(k, s)$ to remind us that k is an argument of J. Thus the following holds on the optimal path:

$$rJ(s) \equiv F(k, \dot{k}^* + dk) - \tilde{q}'k + J_k(s)'\dot{k}^*. \qquad (14.39)$$

The steady-state value of k is obtained by setting $\dot{k}^* = 0$ and solving

$$k^* + rJ_{\tilde{q}}(k^*, s) = 0. \tag{14.40}$$

Given the regularity conditions on $J(\cdot)$, a duality between $F(\cdot)$ and $J(\cdot)$ can be established. As in the static case, this relation is seldom exploited in empirical work. Yet there is a revealed difference in aspiration between the static and dynamic analyses. In the static case, the empirical duality analysis sprang up as an alternative to the primal approach for estimating production functions. The dynamic analysis is focused on the derivation of the demand for the quasi-fixed factors of production. As such, the interest is in the empirical performance of (14.37) and (14.40) and the conditions underlying their derivation.

The empirical implementation requires algebraic formulation of the value function. The quadratic function, in the pertinent variables (or a monotone transformation thereof, such as logarithms or power functions), has been widely used because of its convenience:

$$J(s) = a_0 + \begin{pmatrix} a_k' & a_{\tilde{q}}' \end{pmatrix} \begin{pmatrix} k \\ \tilde{q} \end{pmatrix} + \frac{1}{2} \begin{pmatrix} k' & \tilde{q}' \end{pmatrix} \begin{pmatrix} A_{kk} & A_{k\tilde{q}} \\ A_{\tilde{q}k} & A_{\tilde{q}\tilde{q}} \end{pmatrix} \begin{pmatrix} k \\ \tilde{q} \end{pmatrix} \tag{14.41}$$

where a_k, $a_{\tilde{q}}$, k, and $\tilde{q}$ are column vectors, and the A_{ij} are matrices of conforming dimensions. Differentiate J with respect to $\tilde{q}$, substitute in (14.40) and in (14.38) and impose $k = k^*$:

$$k^* = -r(I^d + rA_{\tilde{q}k})^{-1}(a_{\tilde{q}} + A_{\tilde{q}\tilde{q}}\tilde{q}) \tag{14.42}$$

$$\dot{k}^* = M(k - k^*); \quad M \equiv (I^d + rA_{\tilde{q}k})^{-1}, \tag{14.43}$$

where here I^d is the identity matrix, and M is the adjustment matrix. This is a differential equation and thus it differs from equation (10.21). Other than that, equation (14.43) can be viewed as a multivariate generalization of equation (10.21). The empirical versions of the two equations is similar in form, and the foregoing discussion provides a foundation for the distributed lag formulation. Using a discrete time approximation, the empirical equation can be written as

$$k_t = (I^d - M)k_{t-1} - Mk_t^*. \tag{14.44}$$

The adjustment matrix, M, is constant, and is expressed in terms of coefficients of the value function. Under a different specification of the value function it can become a function of some exogenous variables.

We can now repeat the questions, pertaining to the performance of the model in empirical analysis, asked in the summary discussion of the static dual approach in Chapter11. These should be answered at two levels: methodological and substantive. On the methodological level, the answer is simple: the approach provides an efficient and powerful way to discuss and formulate dynamic factor demand. Similar to the static duality framework, this assertion is true regardless of the outcome of the empirical analysis. In this respect, the claim made by some of the authors that the empirical analysis tests the validity of competitive conditions is not accurate. The most that can be claimed for the empirical analysis is that the conducted tests are of the particular specification. A rejection of a particular specification is not a rejection of the competitive conditions.

The substantive message is more complex. As in the static case, the essence of the duality framework is the ability to identify the technology by means of prices. It is therefore only natural that we concentrate our attention on the role of prices. The results with the dual dynamic framework are similar, and perhaps more pronounced, to those obtained in the static case in that the convexity in prices of the value function is generally violated. Moreover, the price effect is relatively weak, and the elasticities, including the long-run elasticities, of the factor demands are relatively low. In some cases the whole price matrix is not significantly different from zero. All this suggests that the raison d'être of the duality model is called into question.

The work with the dynamic dual approach concentrates on the behavioral equations and grossly neglects the inference on the production function itself. The dynamic behavior indicates a gradual adjustment to the ever-changing gaps between the desired long-run values of the quasi-fixed factors and their current values. This result is obtained by the inclusion of lagged values of the dependent stock variable in the empirical equation, as has been the case with exogenous dynamics. The difference between the two approaches is that the dual dynamic model connects the adjustment coefficients to those of the value function. This can be considered the strength of the approach, but at the same time it also represents its weakness. In essence, this approach attributes the whole dynamics to the internal cost of adjustment. The empirical results show that in most cases the adjustment is sluggish, and in this respect it is also not different from those obtained under (the presumably naive approach of) exogenous dynamics.

The decision to invest in any given year has two aspects, growth and timing. The growth aspect reflects the long-term view about the prospects of the contemplated investment. The question is when to act. The timing aspect is related to the prevailing price variability that generates opportunities for cost reduction, or capital gains. This possibility is ruled out in a world of static expectations where the current prices are assumed to remain constant indefinitely. This is the reason that the value function can be formulated in terms of the annual capital charges (rental rates) rather than in terms of the total expenditures on capital goods. It is only under the latter formulation that the expected capital gains constitute a component of the rental rate. The prospects for capital gains introduce cyclical considerations into the model. This also holds true for the interest rate, which varies over time and also across individuals, reflecting their financial position. However, the interest rate is taken to be constant, as in the empirical investment studies reviewed in Chapter 10.

Furthermore, there is the problem of price expectations. There are no clear-cut systematic differences in the estimates associated with different assumptions about the nature of the price expectations. It is difficult to conceive that the expectations do not matter, so it must follow that the tried alternatives have something in common, probably an error component. When the price variables are subject to measurement error, their estimated coefficients are likely to be biased downward. This problem is more serious for the capital goods than for the variable inputs because they require price forecasts for the entire lifetime of the project. If this argument is true, the own-price elasticities of the variable inputs should have a lower downward bias and also be more precise (have higher t-ratios) than those of the durable inputs. A superficial inspection of the studies cited above indicates that this might be the case.

Duality is a micro theory, and therefore the applications with macro data add additional problems. The question of whether the macro function can be considered as that of the representative firm has already been mentioned above. But the test of the conditions for the ideal aggregation that will allow this interpretation deals only with the consequences of aggregation. There is still the problem that the factor supply and product demand are not perfectly elastic as the model assumes. Consequently there is an identification problem, and the estimated coefficients reflect both supply and demand. This problem is also shared with the static estimates, but the dynamic model has an additional problem in that the pace of the closure of the gap is likely to reflect the pace of the changes in the factor supply or product demand. For instance, in interpreting studies of U.S. agriculture it is important to note that labor and capital have moved in opposite directions. The decision of labor to leave agriculture is a decision made by households on their employment conditional on the opportunities outside agriculture. As for capital, its supply is not perfectly elastic, and agriculture has to compete with other industries for resources. This is consistent with the study by Lee and Chambers (1986), which tests for the credit constraint in U.S. agriculture in 1947–1980 and concludes that farmers do not face a perfectly elastic supply of funds or credit (p. 865). As such, it is also supportive of the discussion on the choice of technique.

The Dynamics of Intersectoral Resource Allocation

The next step is to bring in the factor supply.

Labor

Following the discussion in Chapter 9, the labor supply to agriculture (L_a) and nonagriculture (L_n) is described by

$$L_a(t) = L_a(t-1)(1+n-m) \tag{14.45}$$

$$L_n(t) = L_n(t-1)(1+n+m\frac{L_a(t-1)}{L_n(t-1)}), \tag{14.46}$$

where m is the rate of off-farm migration. The response of agricultural labor to a change in the agricultural price is

$$\partial L_a/\partial p = L_a(t-1)\partial m/\partial \delta \; \partial \delta/\partial p.$$

The response of the labor supply to a change in the agricultural price depends on the migration elasticity of the intersectoral income differential, δ, and the sensitivity of this differential to a change in price, $\partial \delta/\partial p$, where p is the price of agriculture in terms of the price of nonagriculture, or simply the agricultural terms of trade. The evaluation of $\partial \delta/\partial p$, taking into account the economywide changes, requires a more elaborate specification, to be discussed in the next chapter.

Capital

The intersectoral allocation of investment was discussed in Chapter 10, leading to the allocation equation:

$$\theta = \theta(\Delta_r, \rho, s), \tag{14.47}$$

where θ is the share of agriculture in total investment, Δ_r is the ratio of the rate of return to capital in agriculture to that in nonagriculture, ρ is the share of agriculture in the total capital stock, and s represents other variables that are not important for our current discussion.

The time path of the agricultural capital stock is obtained from

$$k_a(t) = k_a(t-1)(1-d) + \theta(t)I(t), \tag{14.48}$$

where d is the depreciation rate, $\theta(t)$ is determined empirically as a function of Δ_r and other variables as well, and total investment, $I(t)$, is determined either as a behavioral equation, with foreign saving being a residual, or alternatively is determined by the total saving in the economy. Thus the response of $k_a(t)$ to a change in the agricultural terms of trade is obtained from

$$\partial k_a(t)/\partial p = I(t)\frac{\partial \theta(t)}{\partial p} + \theta(t)\frac{\partial I(t)}{\partial p}. \tag{14.49}$$

Public inputs are thought to be of great importance in agriculture. This view is supported by empirical studies based on a sample with a wide spread in the variables representing public inputs such as cross-country data (Antle 1983, Binswanger et al. 1985, and the discussion in Chapter 13). The analysis indicates substantial positive effects on output of research, extension, irrigation, life expectancy, literacy, roads, and a measure of comprehensive capital.

The public inputs take on various forms, serving different purposes, some of which fall into the category of human capital while others are physical capital. What emerges clearly is that physical capital is at least as important as human capital. That is, technical change is enhanced by physical capital. For instance, roads and communications integrate remote areas with the markets. Roads were found to be important in affecting crop supply during the transition period to the modern varieties in the Punjab (McGuirk and Mundlak, 1991). The integrated areas change from a closed to an open economy, and this generates gains from trade. The integration with the market increases the proportion of aggregate output that is price responsive and as such, causes an increase in the price elasticity according to (14.10). Thus the integration affects both the level and the slope of the supply function.

The decisions on public inputs are influenced not only by economic considerations but also, and sometimes to a large extent, by political considerations. It is interesting to note that the relationships between the level of public inputs and the agricultural terms of trade can be negative rather than positive, as in the case for the private inputs (Schiff and Valdès, 1992). Many developing countries discriminate substantially against agriculture, using instruments such as export taxes, protection to nonagriculture, or overvalued exchange rates. These all deteriorate the terms of trade of agriculture. At the same time these countries provide the infrastructure in terms of physical and human capital that facilitates the growth of output even though prices are suppressed. This policy may make political sense, but it lacks any economic sense. Once investment is made, it would be more productive if it were fully utilized. However, deteriorating the terms of trade reduces the level of activity and therefore reduces the advantage of the public investment.

Varying Technology

So far in this chapter we have assumed that technology consists of a single technique, characterized by a production function. In this framework, when the technology changes, producers replace the old technique with the new one, but still implement only one technique. This assumption is inconsistent with the data, which show that at any time, several techniques coexist. This subject was discussed in Chapters 6 and 13. It was seen that an increase in the capital-labor ratio leads to the implementation of capital-intensive techniques at the expense of labor-intensive techniques. An increase in price perceived to be of long duration increases the expected rate of return in agriculture and thereby attracts investment to agriculture. This is conducive to an increase both in the implementation of capital-intensive techniques that still have not been fully implemented and in output. This is an indirect effect. We talk about capital as a single variable, but the discussion is equally applicable to a vector of capital goods where only some components constitute a constraint.

Uncertainty

So far, the subject of price uncertainty has been neglected in our discussion, but when dealing with empirical analysis, it has to be considered. Without going into details, it is clear that producers have to act on the basis of expectations generated conditionally on the available information set. To the extent that the expectation variable used in the analysis differs from that used by producers, an error of measurement appears. Such an error causes a downward bias in the estimated price coefficient. The larger the variance of the error, the larger the bias.

Evaluating Supply Response

We can now integrate the various components of the discussion in order to evaluate the dynamics of supply response. Basically, the system under fixed technology is presented in equations (14.21)–(14.23). The quantities of inputs with perfectly elastic supply are demand determined, and thus they are represented in the production function by their factor prices, deflated by the product price. This results in the restricted supply function as given in equation (14.2), where the inputs with less than perfectly elastic supply are represented in the equation by their quantities, k. The rest of the analysis depends on the supply conditions of k and on the response of technology to the state variables. The supply of labor and capital is given by equations (14.45), (14.46), and (14.48). It is also possible to bring in the supply function for land. As for raw materials such as fertilizers, insecticides, fuels, and so on, when their supply is perfectly elastic, they will be represented by their prices, w, or if this is not the case, they will be represented by their quantities, which will be estimated from their supply functions. These functions may have a dynamic structure, such as the supply of labor and capital, or may have a simpler form.

The statistical aspects of the estimation were discussed in Chapter 12, where it was argued that it is preferable to estimate the production functions and utilize the results to estimate the supply. Can such systems be estimated? The answer is positive, as a number of studies have demonstrated. Mundlak, Cavallo, and Domenech (1989) estimated such a system for Argentina for the period 1913–1984. A dynamic simulation of the system for the period 1930–1984 resulted in a long-run supply elasticity of 1. The elasticity increases gradually, and it converges to 1 in twenty years. A similar analysis for Chile by Coeymans and Mundlak (1992) also yields an elasticity of 1, but the convergence to this value takes ten years. Using a similar approach, Lachaal and Womack (1998) estimated a production system for Canadian agriculture for the period 1960–1992 and obtained by simulation a supply elasticity of 1.7. Their system does not contain equations for factor supply, and as such all the agricultural inputs are taken to be demand determined, unlike the systems estimated for Argentina and Chile. This exaggerates the estimated elasticity.

At a lower level of aggregation, McGuirk and Mundlak (1991) analyzed the role of prices in the transformation of Punjab agriculture under the green revolution, using district data for the period 1960–1979. The short-run elasticity for all crop output is low, but the long-run value, averaged for the period as a whole, is 0.77. This value is strongly dependent on the implemented technology; it increases with the proportion of the modern varieties in total output and reaches a value of 1.55 in 1975. This dependence is related to equation (14.12) in that the modern varieties have a larger component of variable inputs.

The foregoing studies give a time dimension to the elasticities. The delayed response is required because the necessary changes in factor supply and in the implemented technology require time, for the reasons discussed above. It is also important to note that under disequilibrium in the static sense, which generates lower returns to labor in agriculture, off-farm migration takes place even if there is an improvement in agricultural prices. A change in the income differential, which preserves its direction, affects the rate but not the direction of the resource flow. Thus the flow continues when the pertinent price remains constant or even when it declines. This yields a lower supply elasticity than what would have been obtained if producers were always operating on the efficiency frontier. In fact, this may sometimes result in an empirical supply function with a negative slope. This is related to the more general discussion in Chapter 10 on the behavior of inputs along the convergence path.

The essence of this analysis is that we cannot view the aggregate agricultural supply by the simple relationship $y(p)$, and any empirical analysis of such a relation is subject to errors of omission that invalidate its meaning. Different scenarios can be drawn depending on the level of aggregation and on the underlying market conditions, and therefore there is no unique value for the supply elasticity. Any measure of elasticity is to be interpreted against the underlying assumptions, and as such different values obtained under different assumptions may be consistent with one another. Coming up with an answer that takes into account all the effects in the factor markets and the choice of technique requires data and work that may not be feasible in many circumstances. It is therefore convenient to have a simple approximation, and this is provided by equation (14.12). The length of run will be reflected by the dichotomy to variable and fixed factors. A further refinement would call for incorporating factor supply, as for instance in (14.15), but this requires a knowledge of such elasticities. As indicated in the discussion, such elasticities are not fixed numbers and also depend on the state of the economy.

To sum up, it is clear that aggregate agricultural output responds to prices. This assertion is derived from economic analysis, and it has been verified empirically.

Appendix 14A

1. Derivation of the supply elasticity under varying factor supply: homogeneous production function.

   Using equations (14.7), (14.8), and $dc/dy = p$, we can write $\ln p = \ln \phi - \ln \mu + (1/\mu - 1) \ln y$. Assuming for simplicity that μ is constant, differentiate:

$$\epsilon = \frac{d \ln y}{d \ln p} = [\frac{d \ln \phi(w)}{d \ln y} + (\frac{1}{\mu} - 1)]^{-1}. \tag{14A.1}$$

An increase in output requires an increase in inputs. This increase causes a rise in input prices, thereby increasing costs. The first term on the right-hand side represents this effect:

$$\frac{d \ln \phi(w)}{d \ln y} = \sum_j \frac{\partial \ln \phi(w)}{\partial \ln w_j} \frac{d \ln w_j}{d \ln x_j} \frac{\partial \ln x_j}{\partial \ln y}. \tag{14A.2}$$

Evaluate term by term. From (14.7)

$$\frac{\partial \ln c}{\partial \ln w_j} = \frac{\partial[\ln \phi(w) + \frac{1}{\mu} \ln y]}{\partial \ln w_j} = \frac{\partial \ln \phi(w)}{\partial \ln w_j}$$

and using Shephard's lemma,

$$\frac{\partial \ln c}{\partial \ln w_j} = x_j w_j / c \equiv \alpha_j.$$

Next, $d \ln w_j / d \ln x_j = 1/s_j$. Finally, $\partial \ln x_j / \partial \ln y$ is the elasticity of x_j with respect to output, obtained under constant w, along the expansion path. For a homogeneous function it is equal to $1/\mu$. Then,

$$\epsilon = \mu[(1-\mu) + \Sigma(\alpha_j / s_j)]^{-1} \quad s_j \neq 0,\ J_v = J. \tag{14A.3}$$

2. Derivation of equation (14.32)

$$\begin{aligned}\epsilon &= \sum_j \beta_j \epsilon_{jp} = -\sum_j \beta_j \sum_h \epsilon_{jh} \\ &= -\sum_h E_{yh} \sum_j e_{jy} \beta_j = -\sum_h E_{yh}\end{aligned}$$

In this we use

$$\begin{aligned}\Sigma \beta_j e_{jy} &= \Sigma(\partial \ln y / \partial \ln x_j)(\partial \ln x_j / \partial \ln y)\,|_w = \Sigma(\partial y / \partial x_j)(\partial x_j / \partial y)\,|_w \\ &= \frac{1}{p} \Sigma w_j (\partial x_j / \partial y)\,|_w = \frac{1}{p} \frac{\partial c}{\partial y} = 1.\end{aligned}$$

3. Distributed lag analysis of supply.

Using matrix notation, let y, y_τ, p, k, and u be vectors of order n and $M = I - p(p'p)^{-1}p'$ is the projecting matrix of rank $n-1$ that generates residuals from regressions on p. We use M to define the following residuals:

$\tilde{y}_t \equiv My_t$, $\tilde{k}_t \equiv Mk_t$, $\tilde{p}_\tau \equiv Mp_\tau$. The regression coefficient c, in equation (14.34), can be written as $c = \tilde{y}_t'\tilde{y}_\tau / \tilde{y}_\tau'\tilde{y}_\tau$. Utilize (14.33) to write:

$$\tilde{y}_t'\tilde{y}_\tau = \gamma'\tilde{k}_t\tilde{k}_\tau\gamma + \gamma'\tilde{k}_t\tilde{p}_\tau\beta + e_{t\tau}$$

$$\tilde{y}_\tau'\tilde{y}_\tau = \gamma'\tilde{k}_\tau'\tilde{k}_\tau\gamma + \beta'\tilde{p}_\tau'\tilde{p}_\tau\beta + 2\beta'\tilde{p}_\tau'\tilde{k}_\tau\gamma + u_\tau'u_\tau + e_{\tau\tau},$$

where the error terms $(e_{t\tau}, e_{\tau\tau})$ involve cross-products of the residuals and the u's. The residuals can be considered as prediction errors of y_t and y_τ from regressions of these variables on p_t. A priori, p_t is likely to be a poor predictor of k_t or k_τ, and consequently $\tilde{k}_t$ is nearly equal to k_t and $\tilde{p}_\tau$ is likely to be uncorrelated with $\tilde{k}_t$. Then c is given by equation (14.35).

15

Growth and the Economic Environment

Our discussion of economic growth, as reviewed in Chapter 7, has attempted to understand the main forces that generate growth. It has been largely motivated by the desire to explain the large differences in growth rates across countries as well as within countries. If this were accomplished, we would have a better idea of what policies are conducive to growth. One thing is clear: there can be no long-term growth without technical change. Technical change is a human creation and results from human effort. The question is how much of the progress can be attributed to economic incentives–that is, how much of the progress can be thought of as endogenous within the economic system. Models differ in the emphasis they place on various aspects of human effort. Those that emphasize human capital accumulation concentrate on the choice made by individuals, and more generally by society, regarding how much time to divert from current production in order to improve the technology of future production. The benefit of the time allocated to human capital accumulation depends on the productivity of this input. Taking this productivity as given, as is often done, weakens the usefulness of the analysis. As suggested by the reservations expressed in Chapter 13, probably not much of future relevance can be said about this aspect of productivity, except for interesting historical summaries or anecdotes. Models that emphasize externalities and learning by doing concentrate on the accumulation of knowledge through experience. Broadly speaking, we can think of learning by doing as a process of evolution, but such a view has a passive tone, and therefore it is not satisfying when we are interested in finding means of speeding up the evolution. In any case, learning by doing suggests that there is something new to learn, and thus we still have to determine where new technology comes from.[1] This is the key question, and it is therefore important to be clear on whether we have any new insight to offer beyond saying that the more we research the more we invent.

The theoretical work draws its support from empirical evidence. By definition, however, the evidence is drawn from the technology that is actually implemented, and as such it is not informative about technology that is not in use. Thus data analysis cannot be used to test or support models that do not distinguish between available and implemented technology. The implementation itself involves considerations that do not play explicit roles in most of the discussions of growth, but which, nevertheless, are essential for understanding how progress is achieved. What is missing from the discussion is the recognition that the actual performance of the economy, on which the data are collected, depends on the economic environment, which, in turn, is affected by policies. This omission may be costly, because it diverts attention away from important factors that affect the evolution of the economy. The purpose of this chapter is to examine empirically the important role that the economic environment plays in influencing economic growth.

Policies and Growth

As a way of introduction, we will consider the cases of Chile and Argentina, both of which historically had good economic performances that were seriously interrupted by erroneous policies.[2] Figure 15.1 presents the per capita output in Chile over the period 1909–1990. Two aspects are striking. First, there was steady growth over the relatively long period of 1932–1970, reflecting an annual compounded growth rate of approximately 1.6 percent. Second, we can observe the consequences of the shocks to the economy introduced by the Allende government (1970–1973) and the difficulties of returning to normality (using whatever definition of normality one wishes). Basically, there were two periods of catching up: 1974–1981, which was followed by a deep recession in 1982, and the subsequent period of continuous growth. Both the fall and the rise of the growth rates are the result of policies, some of course with negative effects.

The second example is given in Figure 15.2, which shows the output path of Argentina in the period 1929–1984 in comparison with that of Canada and Australia, two countries which, like Argentina, are well endowed in land and were open to immigration in these years. These countries lagged behind Argentina in their economic growth from 1880 to 1920, but their fortunes turned around in the postwar period. The shocks that caused the deterioration in the performance of Argentina came initially from the Great Depression of the 1930s, but such decline was common to other countries with more successful performances. Argentina's postwar policies, even when they were

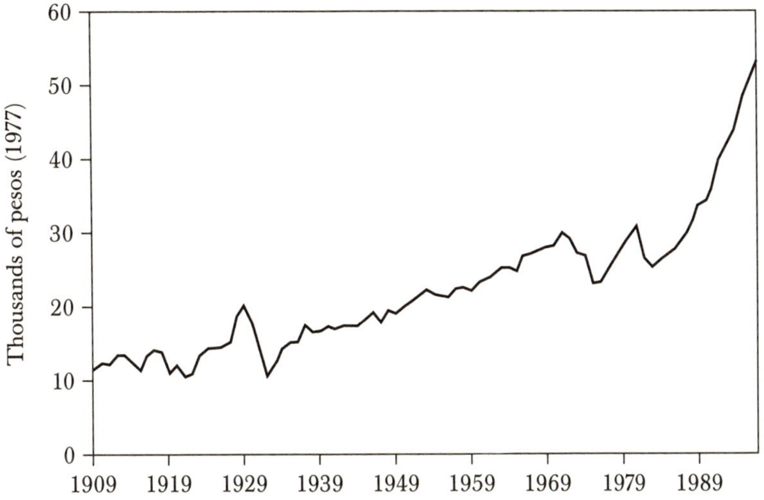

Figure 15.1 Per capita gross domestic product in Chile, 1909–1997. (From Coeymans and Mundlak, 1993, p. 6; data extended by Coeymans.)

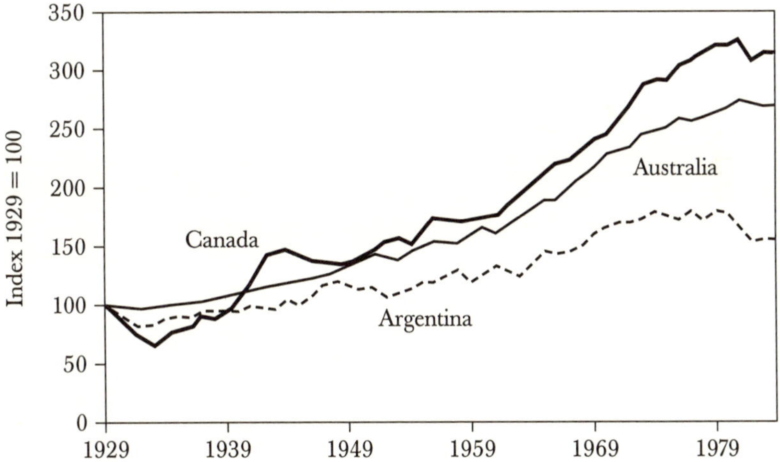

Figure 15.2 Growth trends in Argentina, Australia, and Canada, 1929–1984. (From Mundlak, Cavallo, and Domenech, 1989, p. 119.)

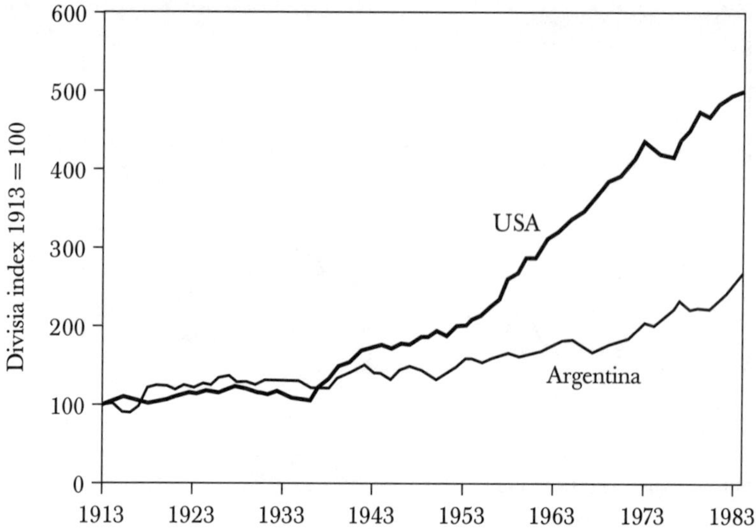

Figure 15.3 Crop yields, Argentina and the United States, 1913–1984. (From Mundlak, Cavallo, and Domenech, 1989, p. 13.)

well meaning, were notorious for their time inconsistency as well as their internal inconsistency. Perhaps more important, they not only damaged the natural comparative advantage of the country but also ruined the competitive structure of the economy by generating monopolies in key industries. Striking evidence of the consequences of the policies is shown in Figure 15.3, which compares the yield of the leading crops grown in Argentina with those of the same crops in the United States. The two countries had the same level of yields, with a slight edge to Argentina, until the mid-1930s. After that, Argentina started to lag behind the United States, and the gap increased with time. For the periods 1913–1930 and 1975–1984, U.S. average agricultural yields tripled, whereas Argentine yields did not even double. Argentina had not benefited from changes in technology, which in the case of agriculture are publicly available.

If growth depends only on human capital, then perhaps the effects of the policies should not have been as strong as they were. After all, the level of education, if anything, did not decline in Chile or in Argentina. (Nor, for that matter, is it low in Russia, which has suffered from negative growth.) If growth is induced solely by knowledge that accumulates with time or experience, then the low performance in Chile and Argentina should have been observed in the earlier years rather than later. It thus appears that human capital is not the only factor determining growth, and most countries could make further progress if it were only conditional on their prevailing level of human capital. It is for this reason that it is necessary to broaden the framework of the analysis and to examine the effect of the economic environment on the growth process. We will see that policies have a direct effect on productivity as well as an indirect one that works through the resource accumulation of physical and human capital. This is particularly important for the discussion of convergence of a country to some feasible superior path. The efforts to push the frontier are mainly the concern of developed countries, whereas most developing countries can grow within the potentials of the available technology.

Growth is thought of as a long-term process, and therefore our examination of variations over an intermediate run can be questioned. A mechanical justification is that most of the cross-country comparisons of growth cover periods of only two to four decades, so if this is how we draw our knowledge then we should be able to account for loss of growth over a decade or two. More fundamentally, if growth rates were written in the stars and a country would eventually achieve its starred rate, short-term variations of a decade or two can be termed "shocks" and be ignored. In this case we would conclude that growth is path independent. Is this approach valid? Most likely it is not. This is not an esoteric theoretical question, and its implications are important. A ten- or twenty-year period of growth loss can have a dramatic effect, particularly for those who spend their productive life in a period of lost opportunities. Their loss per se is not a reason to change the theory but helps to focus it. Ignoring essential "details" may lead to negative results; consider the attempt to move Russia and other former communist countries to a new steady state by following an agenda that is not well founded in realistic details. We thus take a modest posture and think of a foreseeable future, say a decade or two. This leads us to think of dynamic phenomena such as the determinants of the pace of the implementation of new technology and the pace of resource allocation. Perhaps a striking example to emphasize this point is the distinction made in Chapter 14 and repeated below between the strength of the supply response and its pace. The strength is easy to compute on the basis of common knowledge of the magnitude of certain parameters. The calculation may be fairly accurate for all practical purposes, but totally irrelevant if the time needed for its realization is ignored. Policies that ignore this aspect may never succeed, because along the way they generate efforts to annihilate them by groups in society that are not willing to pay the price needed in order to produce a better life for the next generation.

The Economic Environment and Growth: Argentine Agriculture

To examine the effect of the economic environment on growth the various topics in this volume may be pulled together to construct a model that describes the evolution of the sectoral economy in Argentina. The discussion draws heavily on Mundlak, Cavallo, and Domenech (1989). The model, empirical in nature, intends to trace the time path of the economy and to show how the path is influenced by the economic environment. We begin with a brief description of the development of the Argentine economy.

Historical Background

Until the Great Depression of the 1930s, agriculture was the backbone of the Argentine economy. Between 1860 and 1930, exploitation of land of the Pampas fostered economic growth, and Argentina grew more rapidly than the United States, Canada, Australia, and Brazil, which were similarly endowed with rich land and received large inflows of capital and of European immigrants. As Table 15.1 shows, during the first three decades of this century Argentina outgrew the other four countries in population, total income, and per capita income. In the 1930s, however, Argentina's economic vitality began to deteriorate, particularly in agriculture. The comparison of crop yields in Argentina and in the United States (Figure 15.3) tells much of the story.

Table 15.1 Comparative growth in income and population, 1900–1904 to 1980–1984

	Argentina	Australia	Brazil	Canada	United States
1900–1904 to 1925–1929					
Population	2.8	1.8	2.1	2.2	1.1
Income	4.6	2.6	3.3	3.4	2.9
Per capita income	1.8	0.8	1.2	1.2	1.3
1925–1929 to 1980–1984					
Population	1.8	1.7	2.5	1.5	1.3
Income	2.8	3.9	5.5	3.9	3.1
Per capita income	1.0	2.2	3.0	2.4	1.8

Source: Cavallo (1988).

Economic Policies

Agriculture has been largely affected by economic policies that on the surface appear to have been sector neutral, mainly macroeconomic and trade policies. Macroeconomic policies include decisions concerning the size of government expenditures, the way they are financed, and the rate of growth of the money supply. The size of government consumption measures the size of government. The percentage of government consumption in total income grew from a level of 5 percent in 1913 to a level of almost 30 percent in some years in the 1970s and 1980s. This rise is in line with the trend observed in other countries, which gained impetus after World War II, of increasing government involvement in the economy. However, the variability of this ratio around the trend was of considerable magnitude, and at times was associated with the formation of fiscal deficits of serious magnitudes. The ratio of the fiscal deficit to income was relatively low, mostly fluctuating between 0 and 5 percent, until 1940. It jumped to about 13 percent around 1947–1948, and from then on fluctuated greatly and passed the 15 percent mark in the early 1980s. The deficit was financed by borrowing and by expanding the money supply. The monetary policy after 1930 was very unstable, with large expansions in some years, followed by large contractions.

The trade policy included taxes on exports and tariffs on imports and quantitative restrictions on both. The terms of trade are measured by the ratio of the price of exportables to that of importables. The domestic terms of trade are calculated with domestic prices and are not the same as the terms of trade calculated with world prices. The difference is due to domestic taxes on imports and exports. The difference between the taxes on imports and that on exports is referred to as the wedge. The wedge was in the neighborhood of 10 percent between 1913 and 1930. It then jumped during the Great Depression to a level of 30 percent or more, where it stayed during the war years. Thereafter it fluctuated greatly, but in most years it remained quite high.

The wedge measures the direct taxation but not the effect of trade restrictions, which were imposed particularly on imports, where they were the dominant policy after the 1940s. Although there is no direct measurement of quantitative restrictions, they usually became more stringent whenever the black market exchange rate departed from the official rate. Like the other macro indicators, the black market premium fluctuated greatly over the period. It did not exist prior to 1930. Thereafter it fluctuated around 15 percent until the end of World War II, rose to 126 percent during 1946–1950, and then reached a peak of 314 percent in 1951. After that, it declined gradually. It vanished in 1960, but not for very long, and the fluctuation continued thereafter.

Macro policies are nominally sector-neutral, but this is only true in terms of the applied policy instruments and not in terms of their implications. The differential impact of such policies on the sectors reflects structural differences. The sectors differ in important attributes pertinent to their susceptibility to policies. As we shall see below, two such attributes are outstanding. First, agriculture is more capital-cost intensive than nonagriculture. In Argentina, the factor shares in the two sectors varied over the years, but on average, the capital share was 60 percent in agriculture and only 42 percent in nonagriculture. The difference was much greater in the earlier years than in the later ones. Second, agriculture is more internationally tradable than nonagriculture. Agriculture had on average a tradable component of 67 percent of sectoral output as compared with 47 percent of nonagriculture. Therefore, changes in the price of tradables, relative to that of the home good, or simply the real exchange rate, affect the two sectors differently according to their degree of tradability.

What does all of it have to do with growth? To answer this we have to go through an elaborate exercise that, unlike most of the discussions of growth, is not characterized by a search for a simple handle that can reveal the trick. In this sense, the following exercise is less exciting, but nevertheless it raises important issues that cannot be ignored in the explanation of economies' actual performance.

The Model

Even though our ultimate interest is agriculture, we consider the economy as a whole. The theme of this volume is that agriculture does not operate in isolation and its fortunes are related to what happens in the rest of the economy–and conversely, unless agriculture is of negligible importance. The analysis takes an explicit account of the dependence of agriculture on the economic environment, namely the available technology, world prices, domestic policies, political instability, and the like. It does this by analyzing the competition among sectors in the factor market, tracing the impact of shocks that affect resource accumulation in the economy and the real exchange rate, and examining the impact of political instability on the main sectors of the economy.

In the model, the sectoral economy consists of three sectors: agriculture, nonagriculture (private), and government. Most of the analysis is concerned with the two private sectors. However, the government sector plays an important role through its market and trade policies. Empirical results that can be reported by sector are presented here only for agriculture. The model consists of several blocks. We begin with the price block.

Price Block

Following the discussion in Chapter 3, here a complete system is presented to describe the evolution of the sectoral prices. The sectoral prices reflect the composition of outputs and inputs in terms of their degree of tradability, and to take this into account, they are expressed as a geometric average of the price of exportables and importables, as in equation (3.24). The foreign prices of exportables and importables are determined in the world market (small economy framework), but their domestic price depends also on the exchange rate, taxes on trade, and the cost of trade. The price of the home good is determined domestically. The government constitutes an important component of the demand for the home good, and by varying its expenditures, affects its price. This affects the real exchange rate, as indicated by equation (3.23), disaggregated for importables and exportables.

The relevance of the world prices and the response of the domestic price to the various shocks depend on the restrictions on trade and capital mobility. To allow for such effects we construct measures of the degree of commercial and financial openness of the economy (DO_c and DO_f). We use the ratio of trade to total income as a measure of openness to trade. Financial openness is measured as E/E_b, where E and E_b are the nominal and black market exchange rates respectively; thus a value of one indicates complete openness, and the ratio declines with the decline in openness. Substantive reductions in trade took place in the late 1920s, when DO_c declined from a level of 0.75 and more to less than 0.25 shortly after the Great Depression and thereafter. This was accomplished by imposing taxes on foreign trade, quantitative restrictions on imports, controls on foreign exchange, and a rise in government expenditures and fiscal deficits. Restrictions in commercial and financial markets are interconnected; import restrictions encourage the development of a black market to meet the excess demand for imports and for the foreign currency they require. The coefficients of the various price equations are expressed as linear functions of the measures of the degree of openness.

The estimates of the price block are presented in Table 15.2. The first equation expresses the degree of commercial openness in terms of predetermined variables of the system: the tax on trade, government expenditures, changes in the money supply, and the degree of financial openness. The second equation determines the real exchange rate for exportables. The elasticity of the real exchange rate with respect to the terms of trade, ω, was 0.6 to 0.7 before 1925, when the economy was very open to the rest of the world and the behavior of the prices of the home good followed closely the price of importables. This reflected a high degree of substitution in production and demand between the

Table 15.2 The price block: Empirical results

Degree of openness

$$\ln DO_c = \underset{(4.2)}{-0.516} + \underset{(4.0)}{0.648}\ln(T_x/T_m) - \underset{(4.2)}{0.170}\ln g - \underset{(8.3)}{0.590}\hat{\mu} + \underset{(4.0)}{0.146}\ln DO_f + \underset{(18.1)}{0.770}(\ln DO_c)_{-1}$$

$R^2 = 0.97$; D.W. $= 1.93$.

Real exchange rate: Exportable

$$D[\ln(p_x/p_h)] = \underset{(1.9)}{0.026} + \underset{(5.0)}{0.744}D[\ln(p_x/p_m)] + \underset{(2.7)}{0.349}D[\ln(p_x/p_m)\ln DO_c] + \underset{(1.6)}{0.194}\hat{Y} + \underset{(6.7)}{0.428}D[\ln g \ln DO_c] - \underset{(2.5)}{1.12}f - \underset{(1.4)}{1.31}f\ln DO_f - \underset{(1.2)}{0.130}\hat{\mu} + \underset{(2.1)}{0.022}D[\ln\mu\ln DO_f] + \underset{(9.5)}{1.88}D[\ln DO_c]$$

$R^2 = 0.89$; D.W. $= 1.59$.

Price of agriculture

$$D[\ln(p_1/p_3)] = \underset{(2.5)}{0.029} + \underset{(6.0)}{0.596}D[\ln(p_x/p_3)] + \underset{(2.6)}{0.219}D[\ln(p_x/p_3)[\ln DO_c + \ln(PY/P_1Y_1)]] - \underset{(5.5)}{0.756}\hat{g} - \underset{(1.2)}{0.360}f - \underset{(1.8)}{0.174}\hat{\mu}$$

$R^2 = 0.88$; D.W. $= 1.97$.

Price of nonagriculture: Private

$$D[\ln(p_2/p_3)] = \underset{(2.7)}{0.023} + \underset{(3.9)}{0.355}D[\ln(p_x/p_3) + \ln(p_m/p_x)] + \underset{(1.9)}{0.052}D[\ln(p_x/p_3) + \ln(p_m/p_3)][\ln DO_c + \ln(PY/P_2Y_2)] - \underset{(7.2)}{0.630}\hat{g} - \underset{(2.2)}{0.499}f - \underset{(1.2)}{0.080}\hat{\mu}$$

$R^2 = 0.85$; D.W. $= 2.13$.

Note: The four equations are estimated by nonlinear 3SLS. The predetermined variables are g, μ, DO_f, p_x^*/p_m^*, f, and $\hat{Y}$. The system has a recursive structure. The absolute values of the t-statistics are in parentheses.

Variables

x_{-1}	x lagged one year.
Dx	The first difference of x.
DO_c	Degree of commercial openness, measured as a ratio of trade to output (total or sectoral).
DO_f	Degree of financial openness, measured as the ratio of the exchange rate to the black market rate.
Y	Total income (represents expansion in demand as well as in supply due to changes in technology and resource accumulation).
g	Share of government consumption in total income.
f	Share in total income of government deficit financed by borrowing.
μ	Money supply (proportion of money in nominal income).
hat(ˆ)	Rate of change.
$(T_x = 1 - t_x)$	The proportion of the price of exportable net of tax.
$(T_m = 1 + t_m)$	The augmenting factor of the price of importable due to tariff.

importables and the home good. Later on, as the economy was closing up, this value declined, and it reached the lowest level of 0.07 in the early 1950s, when the economy was very closed. At that time the importables had little effect on the domestic price level. After the 1950s, the value of ω oscillated around 0.25. At such low values, the price of the home good was largely determined by the price of exportables.[3]

The government expenditures, g, had a negative effect on the real exchange rate.[4] This reflects the effect of government on the composition of total demand. The inflationary pressure generated by the expansion of g without a corresponding reduction in private demand is captured by the negative effect of the fiscal deficit, f, measured as the fiscal deficit financed by borrowing as a proportion of total income. This effect is more pronounced when the economy is more open financially. When the financial markets are closed, the increase in the deficit has a strong crowding-out effect on private expenditures, which leads to a decline in the aggregate demand.

The effect of money supply also depends on the openness of the economy. The elasticity is larger in absolute value when the economy is more closed to financial transactions with the rest of the world.[5] This is because financial openness dampens the real effect of nominal shocks in the money supply flows or in the exchange rate, given that capital inflows or outflows respond quickly to such shocks. This dampening effect does not operate when flows are obstructed, and a large black market premium is created.

The last two equations of the price block express sectoral prices as a function of the real exchange rate, as given by equations (3.21) and (3.22), with the addition of the macro variables as in equation (3.23). In the case of Argentina, we can ignore the importables from the price equation for agriculture and exportables from the price equation for nonagriculture. There is no variable that measures purely the price of the home good. It was approximated by the price index of government services, p_3, with the assumption that $\log(p_h/p_3)$ is a linear function of the macro variables, z. The estimated sectoral degree of tradability depends on the degree of commercial openness:

$$\frac{\partial(p_1/p_3)}{\partial(p_x/p_3)} = 0.596 + 0.219[\ln DO_c + \ln(PY/P_1Y_1)], \quad \text{for agriculture,}$$

$$\frac{\partial(p_2/p_3)}{\partial(p_m/p_3)} = 0.355 + 0.052 \ln[DO_c + \ln(PY/P_2Y_2)], \quad \text{for nonagriculture.}$$

The degree of sectoral tradability fluctuated with the openness of the economy. Before 1930 the degree of tradability of agriculture was around

0.75, while that of nonagriculture was about 55 percent. These were the highest values, and from then on they declined owing to the gradual closure of the economy. Agriculture was always more tradable than nonagriculture. The average for the period 1916–1984 was 0.67 and 0.48 for agriculture and nonagriculture respectively. The average elasticities with respect to the macro variables are g: -0.77 (-0.60); f: -0.33 (-0.42); $\hat{\mu}$: 0.17 (0.27) for agriculture (nonagriculture). The signs for g and f are as expected. The expected sign for $\hat{\mu}$ is ambiguous.[6]

To what extent did the policies affect the sectoral prices? To answer this question, the estimated price block was used to simulate the response to a change of policies that would have kept Argentina more integrated with the world economy. The assumed policy reform consisted of the elimination of taxes on exports and keeping a uniform tariff of 10 percent. The fluctuations of public expenditures were eliminated by maintaining smooth public expenditure growth during 1946–1953 and a constant level of expenditures from 1973 on. The deficit was reduced to match the reduction in expenditures. The relative change of the measure of the real money supply was kept constant at the average value for the period, $\hat{\mu} = -0.008$, and the wide short-term fluctuations were thereby eliminated. Finally, complete financial openness was imposed, which eliminated the premium on foreign exchange. A dynamic simulation of the system was carried out under these assumptions and was compared with the base run, which had been obtained under the historical conditions.

The results imply that if Argentina had been more integrated with the world economy after 1929, the relative volume of trade would have been almost 70 percent higher than its actual level. Moreover, domestic relative prices would have been more in line with international prices, implying much greater price incentives for both agriculture and nonagriculture. Compared with the base run for the period 1930–1984, the price of agriculture would have been, on average, 40 percent higher, and the price of private nonagriculture would have been 18 percent higher relative to the measure of the home prices.

Lachaal and Womack (1998) used this framework in estimating a similar, but less detailed, price block for Canada for the period 1960–1992. On the whole, the results are consistent with those reported for Argentina, and in particular, the macro variables all have the right sign and are of substantive magnitude. The elasticity of the domestic terms of trade on the real exchange rate for exportables is 0.61, obtained from an equation with a measure of government expenditures, money supply, and income, all with negative coefficients.

Inputs

Population growth is taken as exogenous, but employment and investment are determined endogenously. The equation for employment (L) is

$$L/N = \underset{(8.7)}{0.278} + \underset{(2.3)}{0.165}w^{p}_{-1} - \underset{(2.1)}{0.031}w^{g}_{-1} + \underset{(10.0)}{0.104}DC,$$

$$R^2 = 0.97$$

where N is the population, w is the wage rate, superscripts p and g stand for the private and government sectors, subscript -1 stands for a one-year lag, and DC is a dummy variable that takes a value of 1 for census data and 0 otherwise; the absolute value of the t-statistic is given in the parentheses. The government wage on total employment is determined exogenously and acts as a floor on wages in the rest of the economy. Consequently, a higher value for government wage tended to reduce total employment.

Total Investment

The treatment of total investment in an open economy has similarities to the decision on the intersectoral allocation of investment. Argentina has been an open economy and historically has drawn a considerable amount of foreign capital. In the same way that intersectoral differences in returns determine the allocation of investment among sectors, we can think of the inflow of capital as a function of the profitability of capital in domestic production relative to returns abroad. Naturally, high domestic returns to capital would be conducive to capital inflow. Owing to the lack of time-series data for the rate of interest for the entire period or a large part of it, the measure of per capita fiscal deficit, f^b, was used to measure the pressure in the capital market, where f^b is the fiscal deficit financed by borrowing reported in 1960 prices. As f^b increases, the rate of interest tends to increase and to crowd out private investment. The mechanism in an open economy for this effect is less direct than in a closed economy, but it works in both. The following equation describes the investment in the private sector:[7]

$$I_{1,2}/N = -\underset{(2.2)}{1.06} + \underset{(3.7)}{17.8}r^{e}_{1,2} + \underset{(7.8)}{0.372}D(Y_{1,2}/N) + \underset{(3.0)}{0.591}(I_3/N)_{-1}$$
$$- \underset{(2.0)}{0.110}(f^b/N) + \underset{(12.8)}{0.693}(I_{1,2}/N)_{-1},$$

$$R^2 = 0.95$$

where $I_{1,2}$ is private investment (in sectors 1 and 2), N is the population, $r^e_{1,2}$ is the rate of return on the private investment obtained from the fitted values of an AR(3) process of nonwage income divided by the capital stock in sectors 1 and 2, $D(x)$ is the first difference in x, $Y_{1,2}$ is the gross domestic income in sectors 1 and 2, and I_3 is the government investment, lagged one year; the absolute value of the asymptotic t-statistic is given in the parentheses.

The empirical results show that the expected rate of return and the accelerator variable $D(Y_{1,2}/N)$ have positive and significant effects, as does government investment, which suggests that government investment encourages capital accumulation in the private sector. This is consistent with a view that expansion of infrastructure increases productivity. However, there is a counterpart to this positive effect of government investment. The fiscal deficit financed by borrowing exerts a negative effect on private investment and gives empirical support to the assertion of the existence of a crowding-out effect. To conclude, a favorable economic environment has a positive effect on investment.

Resource Allocation

The production function determines the factor productivity in each sector, conditional on the state variables. The returns to factors in each sector are determined by their productivity and prices. In line with the "Economic Law of Gravity" (Chapter 8), the sectoral differences in factor returns determine the intersectoral allocation of labor (migration equation) and capital. Equation (9.20) is estimated for intersectoral labor migration, and equation (10.26), which is an empirical version of equation (10.19), is used for the allocation of capital.

Production Block

Following the discussion in Chapter 13, the production block is described by an aggregate production function for each sector of the Cobb-Douglas type, where the parameters are functions of the state variables, which affect the choice of techniques as well as the choice of inputs. This calls for the estimation of the system of equations (13.11)–(13.13). To illustrate the relevance of the approach, Figure 15.4 presents the capital share in agriculture for the period 1913–1984. It also includes simulated values to give an idea of the fit of the model. The series is volatile, and the spread ranges from roughly 0.31 in 1952 to nearly 0.8 at the beginning and the end of the period. One approach to the specification of empirical production functions is to attribute the variations in factor share to changes in factor proportions, as is done with the translog function. This

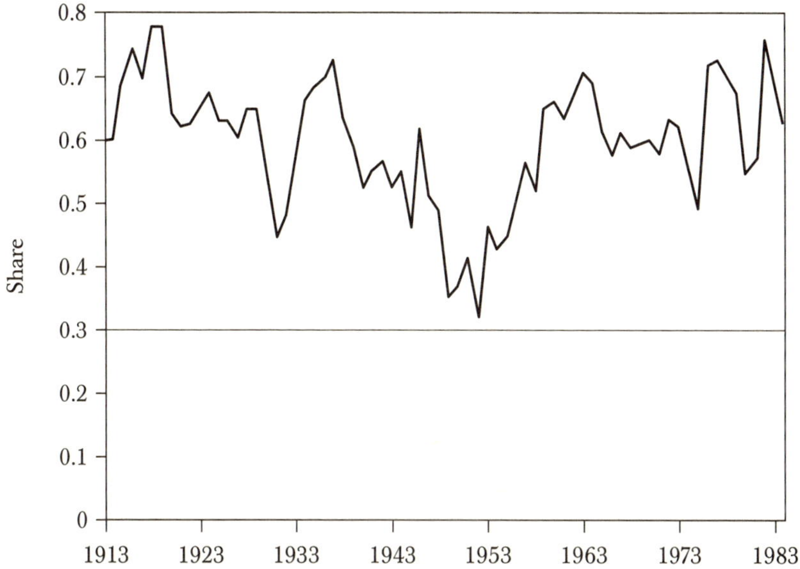

Figure 15.4 Capital share in agriculture, Argentina, 1913–1984. (From Mundlak, Cavallo, and Domenech, 1989, p. 67.)

approach was not helpful in this case. Such volatility can only be explained by changes in the composition of technologies caused by variations in the state variables.

The dependent variable in equation (13.11) is the value added per worker, or simply the average labor productivity. A good way to summarize the empirical results is to report the elasticities with respect to the state variables, conditional on the inputs, as in equation (13.21). Table 15.3 reports the elasticities for two alternative sets of state variables for each of the two sectors.[8] In regression A we use the peak variable, discussed in Chapter 13, as the carrier of technology. In addition there is a sectoral spillover effect: the output in one sector is favorably affected by the improved productivity in the other sector. An increase in the agricultural output by 1 percent results in a 0.23 percent increase in the output of nonagriculture. Similarly, the expenditures of government have a sizable impact on the production of nonagriculture. These cross-effects may represent the impact of common shocks, including demand shocks, which are pertinent for the impact of government on nonagriculture. The incentives are represented by a measure of the real exchange rate, p/p_3, which is positive and noticeable. Finally, the sectoral price variability has a negative effect for both sectors. The degree of openness has a positive effect on

Table 15.3 Production elasticities: Argentina, 1916–1984

	Regression A		Regression B	
	Elasticity of		Elasticity of	
	Agriculture	Nonagric.	Agriculture	Nonagric.
Peak	0.25	0.23		
Per capita capital			0.17	−0.54
Output of other sector	0.02	0.19	0.19	0.33
p_1/p_3			0.02	
p_2/p_3				0.03
p/p_3	0.10	0.33		
Government consumption		0.34		0.51
Standard deviation of sectoral prices	−0.03	−0.02	−0.05	−0.003
Openness	0.02	0.015	0.11	0.06
High inflation			−0.002	−0.01
Deflation				0.002
Bank failures				−0.006

Source: Based on Mundlak, Cavallo, and Domenech (1993).

Note: p_1, p_2, and p_3 stand for the prices of agriculture, nonagriculture private, and government respectively. p stands for the overall price.

productivity in both sectors. This result and that for government expenditure are robust under various specifications.

The dynamic solution of the model with the endogenous peak variable was somewhat complex and for this reason it was replaced with the overall capital availability (per capita capital stock). The elasticity of this variable is positive for agriculture but negative for nonagriculture, indicating a sectoral bias of total capital in favor of agriculture. This version (regression B) contains some macro variables representing extreme values of the prices and the economic activity. Their effects were important for specific subperiods but not strong enough to affect the average for the period as a whole.

The sign of the coefficients in the share equations (not presented here) indicates the partial effect of the state variable on the capital share. The following variables caused technology shifts that are capital using (or labor saving): capital deepening, the peak variable, lagged output, real sectoral prices, and the real exchange rate. This result is consistent with the hypothesis that capital accumulation, technical change, and favorable prices are all conducive to a shift in the direction of capital-intensive techniques. The impact of government

Table 15.4 Production elasticities: Chile, 1962–1982

Variables	Agriculture	Manufacturing	Services
Capital	0.666	0.59	0.582
Peak	1.144	0.175	0.584
Rate of return	1.264		0.573
Investment/capital		1.34	
Foreign terms of trade		0.826	0.811
Land reform	0		
Labor quality			−0.126

Source: Coeymans and Mundlak (1992).

expenditures is ambiguous, because it represents two contradictory effects: the expansion effect is likely to be capital intensive, as with the other expansionary variables; on the other hand, government demand is biased toward labor-intensive techniques.

The essence of the approach is that the environment dictates the implemented technology, but the end result depends on the environment and the way that it is represented in the analysis. Only cumulative experience with this approach will reveal the regularities that are common to a variety of environments. Thus, before continuing, it may be useful to mention two other studies using the same approach. Coeymans and Mundlak (1992) present estimates for three sectors in Chile for the period 1962–1982: agriculture, manufacturing, and services. The results are presented in Table 15.4. The specification includes the peak variable, and as such it is similar to regression A in Table 15.3. The peak variable is particularly strong in agriculture, weak in manufacturing, and in between for services. The rate of return is strong in agriculture and services, and the investment is in manufacturing. A measure of the external terms of trade has a strong impact on manufacturing and services. All this is in line with the results obtained for Argentina. The results differ in the sign of the state variables in the capital share equation. The effects are largely in the direction of labor-using techniques. This can be explained by the nature of the environment during the relatively short period covered by the study. The first part was characterized by restrictions on imports and on foreign exchange. This was followed by a number of years of very high unemployment rates. Neither regime in the period was favorable for the introduction of capital-intensive techniques.

Lachaal and Womack (1998) applied this framework to Canadian agriculture for the period 1960–1992. The state variables–per capita capital, the price ratio of agriculture to that of the home good (undefined), and the rate of return–are similar to those in regression B of Table 15.3. The authors do not present elasticities, and therefore it is difficult to compare the results with the other studies. The sign of all these variables in the capital share equation is positive, as in the case of Argentina, indicating that they are all associated with the implementation of capital-intensive techniques.

Policy Reforms

The core of the empirical model that describes the sectoral growth in Argentina has now been presented. The full system is spelled out in Mundlak, Cavallo, and Domenech (1989, chap. 9). The model was used to evaluate the consequences of possible policy reforms on the trajectory of the economy by running dynamic simulations. The impact was measured with respect to a dynamic simulation of the model conditional on the historical state variables (base run).

The first experiment was the evaluation of a supply response to a hypothetical 10 percent increase in agricultural prices starting in 1950. The price of private nonagriculture was kept constant and the price of the third sector, government services, was decreased by 9 percent, on average, in order to keep the overall price at its historical level. All agricultural inputs and the output responded positively to this price change, and the response gained strength with time. The implicit elasticity of supply response in agriculture was 0.38 after four years, and with time it converged to 1. The price change also had a positive effect on nonagricultural output. Because the price of government services is closely related to the price of the home good, its decline implies an increase in the real exchange rate to the two private sectors. Consequently the rates of return, and with it total investment, rose.

Once the price response property of the system was established, the full impact of the contemplated reform in macro and trade policies was examined. The reform is outlined above in connection with the policy-reform simulation of the price block.

The final outcome of this exercise is a simulated trajectory, which is more in line with the experience of other land-abundant countries (Mundlak, Cavallo, and Domenech, 1989, p. 119). The changes in the economy that are associated with this response are summarized in Table 15.5. They are reported separately for macro policies and for all policies (macro and trade). Had Argentina been more integrated into the world economy after 1929, the real exchange rate would have been 70 percent higher, on average, than its actual level, and relative prices would have been more in line with international prices so that incentives to the private sector would have been enhanced. For the period

Table 15.5 Effects of alternative economic policies (percentage of base-run values): Argentina, 1930–1984

	Average annual response		Response in 1984	
	Monetary, exchange, and fiscal policy changes	All policy changes	Monetary, exchange, and fiscal policy changes	All policy changes
Relative prices				
Price of land	9	29	32	46
Openness	4	77	1	57
RER	12	70	72	59
Agriculture (p_1/p_3)	12	45	72	81
Nonagriculture (p_2/p_3)	11	20	56	53
Agriculture				
Labor	5	31	0	64
Capital	5	26	20	59
Land	7	22	2	37
Output	12	42	41	115
Wages	3	18	18	26
Rate of return	15	47	104	140
Private nonagriculture				
Labor	2	−1	7	−8
Capital	5	20	33	50
Output	8	23	47	65
Wages	2	5	6	6
Rate of return	10	23	74	106
Government sector				
Labor	−4	−15	−24	−35
Wages	−5	−2	−11	6
Aggregate economy				
Labor	2	2	1	−3
Total capital	5	19	23	41
Output	8	24	40	63
Private				
consumption	10	27	46	70
investment	12	32	92	112
Exports	12	124	53	187
Imports	13	118	24	114
Wages	0	3	4	3

Source: Mundlak, Cavallo, and Domenech (1993), p. 176.

Note: Results reported in this table assume a tax-subsidy mechanism to transfer income from nonwage to wage earners. RER–real exchange rate.

1930–1984, the price of agriculture would have been, on average, 45 percent higher, and the price of private nonagriculture would have been 20 percent higher. The volume of trade would have increased drastically, and the impact on the economy as a whole would have been dramatic. Agriculture would have generated in 1984 an output 115 percent higher than its actual level. This increase in production would have resulted from both the accumulation of capital and an increase in employment. Moreover, nonagriculture would also have performed better.

One can ask what message is to be drawn from this exercise. The answer is that the economic environment, and specifically policies, matter substantively. It is possible to generate a considerable amount of growth in the intermediate run by maintaining an environment that encourages the full expression of the potentials embedded in society. Purposely, this is a very general statement with which it is hard to disagree. It is not directly connected with the mechanics of the policy reforms or with the construction of the model or with the statistical details involved in the generation of the data or the estimation. The details can be found in the references, whereas the economic logic underlying this approach has been discussed throughout this volume. Indeed this analysis includes some crucial details, such as the role assigned to the macro variables, the formulation of the price block and the production block, the dynamics of resource allocation, and most important, the treatment of technology. Still, the essence of the message is that when this structure is placed in a quantitative framework, it shows that distortions hurt. These distortions are sometimes hidden (as in macro policies), but they hurt just the same.

These findings are not custom-made for Argentina. Laachal and Womack (1998) report similar results for Canada. Their supply response exercise results in an elasticity of 1.76, higher than for Argentina. The two need not be the same. However, in making the comparison it is important to note that unlike the Argentina study, the Canada study implicitly assumes perfectly elastic factor supply to agriculture, and as the discussion in Chapter 14 indicated, this causes an upward bias in the result. The model was also "used to simulate the effects of a trade liberalization program implemented together with consistent macroeconomic policies" (p. 538). Results indicate that "had Canada been more integrated with the world economy, its volume of trade would have been almost 3% higher than its actual level, and the price incentives for agriculture would have been, on average, 8% higher" (p. 539).

The model used by Coeymans and Mundlak to study the Chilean economy is somewhat more complex than the one used for Argentina, in that it contains more sectors and includes input-output tables, and as such it is not easily described in a brief paragraph. Nevertheless, it also showed that policies had an important influence on the economy. The main channel there was the effect of the deterioration of the economy on the decline in the investment rates. Policies that alleviated this problem had a drastic effect on growth. The study period ended in 1982. Indeed, a year later, Chile began a process of growth that has lasted almost to date.

Suppose that everything is done right, then will the economy be exploiting all the potential for improvements and will this exhaust its growth potential? The answer is yes if there is no change in technology, but with technological change the answer is somewhat different, as discussed above. Here, the relevant question is how soon will the frontier of the available technology be reached? The answer is probably not soon, because the needed adjustment to the changing technology takes time.

What other evidence do we have that the stipulated effects will work in the future rather than simply be an impressive statistical exercise of past performance? This is a challenging question, one that is faced by much of the work in this area that has empirical aspirations. Thus, instead of speculating, let us return to Argentina in the post-study period. In 1991 Argentina implemented a convertibility plan that stabilized the economy. "Inflation dropped from 30 percent a month in March 1991 to an average of 0.4 percent a month during 1994" (Cavallo and Mondino, 1996, p. 19). In addition, "Argentina drastically reduced trade barriers, eliminating all quotas, taxes, and non-tariff barriers and reducing tariffs and the spreads between them. On the export side Argentina eliminated all export taxes and most regulatory institutions" (ibid., pp. 16–17). An aggressive privatization program was also instituted, as well as other reform measures. As a result, the total factor productivity grew at an annual average rate of 6.5 percent in the period 1990–1994, unprecedented for Argentina (ibid., p. 13). This performance continued beyond 1995, and when growth slowed down in 1997–1998, it was due to changes in the global economic environment and not because Argentina had reached its limit.

One consequence of the reform has been a sharp rise in trade and a flow of capital from abroad, much of it in the form of direct investment. Cavallo and Mondino emphasize the importance of stability in the success of the program. This is certainly the case when it comes to the flow of capital. Investment in physical capital has played an important role in the work reviewed above, as well as in the country-panel analysis of agricultural productivity discussed in Chapter 13. Investment also played an important role in the economywide growth (see Levine and Renelt, 1992). All this gives credence to the emphasis placed here on the importance of the economic environment. The discussion of the macro environment has not covered all the aspects of the subject, and specifically the dynamic aspects have been suppressed.[9] Nevertheless, it is clear that the economic environment can have a dramatic effect on the performance of the economy.

As has been demonstrated, the connection between the economic environment and growth is rather elaborate, and therefore no simple model will suffice. But the question is how to determine the gallery of alternatives that can help us sort out the performance across countries and over time, as was demonstrated in Chapter 13 with respect to agricultural productivity. In general, perhaps wisely so, most models that currently take center stage in the literature do not pretend to go that far. However, the point of departure in our discussion, the differentiation between available and implemented technology, is shared by some of them. Romer (1993), for example, talks about "using ideas and producing ideas." There can be no objection to changing the language by replacing "ideas" with "technology." But that by itself does not resolve anything, and the big questions remain the same.

Another model that basically emphasizes the implementation of available techniques is the Big Push model (Murphy, Shleifer, and Vishny, 1989; Krugman, 1993). It examines the allocation of labor to various techniques using labor as the only input. The marginal productivity of labor is constant, and modern techniques are subject to a fixed set-up cost. The set-up cost generates increasing returns and therefore calls for a noncompetitive industrial structure in the nonagricultural (industrial or modern) sector.

We also have the learning by doing approach discussed earlier. All these models share the desire to explain the growth of economies, but they differ in their structures and emphasis. Remember, though, "that we can write down a model of a phenomenon proves almost nothing. It does not make the idea right or wrong, important or unimportant. It is–at most–a test of certain logical relations of consistency of certain ideas. Formalizing ideas is extremely important for quite another set of reasons: it leads to better and more concise debate and to precise and more useful questions!" (Stiglitz, 1993, p. 41). It would certainly help if the models would also prove their empirical relevance. Under such a requirement, one could not start with the hypothesis that agriculture is the stagnant, or least productive, sector. As we have seen above, the growth of agricultural productivity has exceeded that of nonagriculture or, if we want to be conservative and universal, at least did not lag behind. We can now return to the background discussion in Chapter 1 and ask ourselves what of the analysis we can ignore and what we want to add in order to explain the evolution of agriculture and the lessons that can be drawn from it for the development of nonagriculture. Struggling with such issues is fundamental to research and to the extension of theory.

Notes

Preface

1. My own translation from a Hebrew edition (Gorki 1989), p. 74.

2. Quote from George Will, *Washington Post,* June 10, 1996.

1. Issues, Evidence, and Attributes

1. The empirical part of this chapter is based on Mundlak, Larson, and Crego (1998).

2. This research was conducted at the World Bank. The data were assembled from the known international sources, such as the Food and Agriculture Organization (FAO), International Labour Organization (ILO), the World Bank, and the International Monetary Fund (IMF), as well as from country publications. The results are presented in terms of empirical distributions. The number of countries and the period covered in the figures vary according to data availability.

3. Unless indicated otherwise, all growth rates are computed from a semi-logarithmic regression of the variable in question on time.

4. The number of countries varies across figures because of incomplete data sets.

5. In making such a statement, we note that the vertical axis in the two figures is the same and that the units of the horizontal axis are also the same.

6. Based on national accounts data, converted to dollars and deflated by the US GDP deflator.

7. The variance of the average land productivity is lower than that of the average labor productivity. This is due to a larger variance in the rates of change of the labor force than of land. The pattern of changes in land and labor productivity is discussed by Hayami and Ruttan (1985).

8. The data were assembled together with Rita Butzer but have not yet been published.

9. Part of the rent (residual income) may also be shared by tenants, depending on the nature of the contract.

10. The assumption of equal fertility rates is made here for purposes of illustration. The migration rates could be estimated under the assumption of different fertility rates.

11. The median in 1990 for a larger set of 110 countries is 9 percent. Figure 1.15 contains fewer countries for which we have data also for 1950.

12. As Williams and Wright (1991) show, the arbitrage condition and the nonnegativity of storage cause positive serial correlation in prices.

13. This is also the source of variations in the data which, ironically, is helpful in empirical analysis.

2. *The Economy under Constant Resources and Technology*

1. A function $f(x)$ is strongly concave if for any admissible values x_1 and x_2, and $0 \leq \lambda \leq 1$, $\lambda f(x_1) + (1-\lambda) f(x_2) < f[\lambda x_1 + (1-\lambda)x_2]$. The function is concave if the inequality is replaced by weak inequality ($\leq$). The function $f(x)$ is convex if $-f(x)$ is concave.

2. The derivatives of y and ℓ are not defined at the boundaries of $\omega(k)$.

3. This assumption was used by Mundlak and Mosenson (1970). The assumption of asymptoticity is equivalent to the assumption that the two products are desirable and the preferences display nonsatiation.

4. Much of the trade literature assumes homothetic preferences, resulting in unitary income elasticities for all products (see Jones, 1965). This assumption is unnecessarily restrictive and misleading in its implications when dealing with growth.

5. In the figure and throughout the text, when ambiguity does not arise, θ is used to label both the angle and its tangent, that is, $\theta = \text{tang}^{-1}(\omega/k)$ and ω/k.

6. As we know, $p^*(\underline{\omega}) \neq 0$. However, in view of (2.24), $p \to 0$ as $y_1 \to 0$ and $y_1 \to 0$ as $\omega \to (k)$. At this limit $k_1(\underline{\omega}) \neq 0$, hence $\ell(\underline{\omega}) = 0$ and $y_1^* = 0$. These details determine the behavior of the price and supply for small outputs. It is mentioned here for completeness, but it has no important consequences.

7. There is another aspect of food quality that is related to the composition of food. As income increases, consumers shift from cereals and starch to livestock products as well as fruits and vegetables. The latter are more expensive because they require more agricultural resources per unit of food. For instance, a kg of beef requires about 8 kg of cereals to produce, and therefore it costs more than a kg of cereals. This aspect of quality is captured in our framework by A, the measure of quantity.

3. *An Evaluation of Policy Measures*

1. The subsidy can be financed by a lump-sum tax or a proportionate tax on all outputs. This will still be a tax on the nonsubsidized sector. We leave the proof as an exercise.

2. Technically, for tt_1 to be positive, it is required that $t_2 > -1$. Using the budget constraint, this amounts to $p_2x_2 - t_1p_1x_1 > 0$. That is, the tax (subsidy) on one product should not exceed the consumption of the other product.
3. Differentiate

$$d \log x_1(pT) = \epsilon_{1d}(\hat{p} + \hat{T}), \quad d \log y_1(p) = \epsilon_{1s}\hat{p},$$

equate the two terms and simplify to obtain (3.6).

4. This presents a problem which countries that subsidize staple food face in policy reforms. In this case, when they eliminate the subsidy, low-income consumers pay a higher share of the immediate cost of the policy reform.
5. This assertion contradicts Abbott and McCarthy (1982), who state that the domestic price will rise if the income effect of aid exceeds the substitution effect.
6. See Appendix 3A for details.

4. *The Consequences of Resource Changes*

1. The assumption simplifies the discussion.
2. For instance, Frenkel and Razin (1975) incorrectly identify the price with the slope of the tangent line.
3. Let $dY_i = F_{iK}dK_i + F_{iL}dL_i = (rdK_i + wdL_i)/p_i$. Under fixed factor supply, $dK_1 = -dK_2$, $dL_1 = -dL_2$, and therefore $-dY_2/dY_1 = p_1/p_2 = p$. Under varying capital supply, $dK_1 \neq -dK_2$, and this result is invalid.
4. The distribution is given by $G(q) = \int_0^q A(x)dx / \int_0^\infty A(x)dx$.
5. The production function can be viewed as a restricted profit function concentrated on land and capital.
6. Under the assumption of $f'(0) = \infty$, if $c = 0$ all the land will be cultivated, or equivalently $z = 0$, and for every $q > z$ there is $k(q) > 0$ that maintains $r = f'(q)$. Thus to account for uncultivated land, it is necessary to have either $c > 0$ or to change the assumption with respect to the production function. We take the first route.
7. Note that

$$\sigma = -\frac{f'(q)/f''(q)}{k(q)/q}.$$

8. The total differentiation gives

$$f(\cdot)dz + f'(\cdot)[dk(z) - \frac{k(z)}{z}dz] = \frac{r}{p}dk(z) + k(z)d\frac{r}{p} + d\frac{c}{p}.$$

Collect terms, set $p = 1$ and use the FOC to obtain (4.17).

9. The slope of the demand for capital is $dK/dr = \partial K/\partial r + (\partial K/\partial z)(\partial z/\partial r)$, where the first term on the RHS is a substitution effect and the second term is the expansion effect; both are negative. The sign of the substitution effect follows from

$$\frac{\partial K}{\partial r} = \int_z^\infty \frac{\partial k(q)}{\partial r} A(q)dq = \Phi'(r)Q < 0.$$

10. Solving (4.25) using (4.26), we obtain

$$\frac{\partial z}{\partial K} = \frac{\partial r}{\partial K}\frac{zk(z)}{c},$$

or written as an elasticity:

$$E(z, K) = E(z, r)E(r, K) = E(r, K)\frac{S(k; z)}{S(c; z)} < 0. \tag{4N.1}$$

$$E(A, K) = E(A, z)E(z, r)E(r, K) > 0. \tag{4N.2}$$

The response of the capital intensity to a change in K is

$$E(k(q), K) = E(k(q), r)E(r, K) > 0. \tag{4N.3}$$

To compare the response of the two margins with a change in K we divide equation (4N.3) by equation (4N.2), and the result is the same as that obtained for the first model.

11. $pf(\cdot)dz + zf(\cdot)dp + pf'(\cdot)[dk(z) - \frac{k(z)}{z}dz] = rdk(z) + k(z)dr + dc.$

12. Note that by (4.14),

$$\frac{dk(q)}{d(r/p)} = q\Phi'(r/p),$$

and hence,

$$dY = \int_z^\infty f'(q)\frac{\partial k(q)}{\partial (r/p)} d\left(\frac{r}{p}\right) A(q)dq - Y(z)dz$$

$$= \frac{r}{p}\Phi'(\frac{r}{p})d(\frac{r}{p}) \int_z^\infty qA(q)dq - Y(z)dz.$$

5. *The Consequences of Technical Change*

1. A similar interpretation would hold if A_{iL} were some monotone function of schooling.
2. For a proof that Harrod neutrality implies labor augmenting technical change, see Burmeister and Dobell (1969).
3. The same result can also be obtained from the constancy of the capital share.

4. $d \ln r = d \ln \tau + d \ln f'(\cdot)$, where

$$d \ln f'(\cdot) = -\frac{1}{\sigma}\left[\frac{d\tau}{\tau} + \frac{dk(q)}{k(q)}\right] \quad \text{and}$$

$$\frac{1}{\sigma} = -\frac{f''(\cdot)}{f'(\cdot)}\frac{\tau k(q)}{q} > 0.$$

Combine the equations and set $dr = 0$ to obtain (5.38).

5. By differentiation,

$$dr = f''(\cdot)\left[\frac{dk(\tau q)}{\tau q} - \frac{k(\tau q)}{\tau^2 q}d\tau\right]. \tag{N5.1}$$

We want to express $d \ln k(\cdot)/d \ln \tau$ in terms of $d \ln r(\cdot)/d \ln \tau$. Let $(\cdot) = (\tau q)$ and recall that $k(\tau, q) = \tau q \phi(r)$. Differentiate $k(\tau q)$:

$$\frac{1}{\tau q}\frac{dk(\cdot)}{dr} = \phi'(r) = \frac{1}{f''(\cdot)} < 0, \quad \text{rearrange (N5.1)}$$

$$r\phi'(r)\frac{d \ln r}{d \ln \tau} + \frac{k(\cdot)}{\tau q} = \frac{dk(\cdot)}{d \ln \tau}\frac{1}{\tau q} \tag{N5.2}$$

$$\phi(r)\left[\frac{r\phi'(r)}{\phi(r)}\frac{d \ln r}{d \ln \tau} + 1\right] = \frac{dk(\cdot)}{d \ln \tau}\frac{1}{\tau q}.$$

Simplifying yields (5.43).

6. Differentiate, $\tau\phi(r)dQ + \tau\phi'(r)Qdr + \phi(r)Qd\tau = dK$.
Impose $dK = 0$, use (4.6) to write $dQ = -zA(z)dz$, and rewrite (5.45)

$$\tau\phi(r)zA(z)dz - \tau\phi'(r)Qdr = \phi(r)Qd\tau.$$

Rearrange, using $\phi'(r)/\phi(r) = -\sigma/r$, to yield equation (5.46).

6. Heterogeneous Technology

1. Pertinent results are reported by Papanek and Mujahid (1983). Although they did not deal with the choice of technique, they explored the effects of irrigation and various forms of water control on the rate of growth of output. They conclude that a more rapid expansion of cropped area in the Punjab was due in part to extensive government surface irrigation and the greater effectiveness of tubewells rather than canals in increasing cropped area and output.

2. The discussion on the production structure draws on Danin (1973), and Danin and Mundlak (1979). See also Melvin (1968) and Samuelson (1953).

3. The relationships between $V(Y)$ and the production function are dual in the sense that it is possible to use the production function derived from $V(Y)$ to derive the input requirement set. Alternatively, any production function defines an input requirement

set. In turn, the derived input requirement set can be used to derive a production function. This derived function is identical with the original function. For details, see Diewert (1976).

7. Growth Models: An Overview

1. Except for very low values of n, the same is true for n. The change in the marginal productivity due to a change in n (recall that $m = n + d$) is

$$\frac{\partial f_k}{\partial n} = 1 - \frac{(\rho - n)}{(1+n)^2} - \frac{1}{(1+n)} = \frac{-(\rho+1)}{(1+n)^2} + 1.$$

Rearrange, $\partial f_k / \partial n > 0$ iff $(2+n)n/\rho > 1$.

2. Let $u(c)$ be an increasing concave utility function. The degree of the concavity of the function is measured by the elasticity of the marginal utility, $d \ln u'(c)/d \ln c$, referred to as the coefficient of relative risk aversion. For $u(c) = c^{1-\sigma}/1 - \sigma$, $d \ln u'(c)/d \ln c = -\sigma < 0$. When σ is large, there is a strong preference for smooth consumption over time. The reciprocal of σ is the intertemporal elasticity of substitution.

3. Using equation (7.10) with $b = S_K$, the rate of growth of output is given by

$$\hat{Y} = (1-b)(\hat{A}_L + \hat{L}) + b(\hat{A}_K + \hat{K}). \tag{7N.1}$$

The Harrod-Domar consistency condition is now expressed in terms of capital-quality labor. By differentiation of the condition, we obtain: $\hat{s} + \hat{Y} - \hat{K} = 0$. Since s is bounded, changes in s are not good candidates for explaining long-term growth. Hence we can conveniently ignore such changes by setting $\hat{s} = 0$ to yield $\hat{Y} = \hat{K}$. Substituting this condition in (7N.1) and simplifying:

$$\hat{Y} = \hat{A}_L + \hat{L} + \frac{b}{1-b}\hat{A}_K. \tag{7N.2}$$

Equation (7N.2) presents the rate of growth of output conditional on the maintenance requirement with a constant saving rate. The question is under what conditions equation (7N.2) leads to constant growth of output. Obviously, the answer depends on the rates of change of A_K and A_L and on the ratio of the factor shares. In order to observe regular patterns, we take $\hat{A}_L$ and $\hat{A}_K$ to be constant, implying $A_j(t) = e^{\hat{A}_j t}$, $j = K, L$. Under this assumption, the rate of change of Y is constant in two cases, Cobb-Douglas technology and no capital-augmenting technical change.

In the case of the Cobb-Douglas production function, the factor shares are constant, and it is impossible to distinguish empirically between A_K and A_L. It is therefore possible to redefine $\hat{A}_L$, $\hat{A}_L^* = \hat{A}_L + (b/(1-b))\hat{A}_K$. This reduces the problem to the second case, in which the technical change is exclusively labor augmenting so that $\hat{A}_K = 0$. Consequently equation (7N.2) reduces to $\hat{Y} = \hat{A}_L + \hat{L}$, which indicates that the rate of growth of output is equal to that of labor measured in quality units, $L^e = A_L(t)L_t$. The asymmetry between A_L and A_K is due to the imposition of the consistency requirement.

4. We change here to discrete time notation.
5. For a broad perspective of growth models, see McKenzie (1998).

8. Dynamics and Distortion in Factor Markets

1. For details, see Mundlak (1970).
2. See Bhagwati and Srinivasan (1971).
3. To avoid confusion, note that both the angle and its tangent are labeled θ_i. In the figure, only θ_B is presented. The reader is invited to draw θ_A and compare the two to complete the graphical presentation of the discussion.
4. This discussion is based on Mundlak and Tropp (1979).
5. The derivative along the equilibrium path, $\hat{\omega}/\hat{k}\mid_{\text{eq}}$, is referred to as the overall elasticity of substitution. For a discussion of the stability, see Mundlak and Tropp (1979).

9. The Dynamics of Resource Allocation: Labor

1. Weak separability implies that the marginal rates of substitution of the various components of x_1 are independent of the level of leisure.
2. The differences in the income effect on labor supply to the market was used by Rosenzweig (1980) as a test criterion for the relevance of the neoclassical competitive framework of labor supply.
3. This is done under the assumption that it is not necessary to be explicit about the composition of c in terms of the components of x_1.
4. Taking a broad historical perspective, Boserup (1981, p. 120) observes that agriculture was a part-time occupation. Farmers had to produce tools and household commodities on the farm (Schmitt, 1989, p. 1271). This is a somewhat different concept from the one used here, where we deal with off-farm rather than nonagricultural work. But this distinction is not of considerable importance in what follows.
5. See Bollman and Steeves (1982) for evidence on Canada.
6. The evaluation is based on the average productivity of the inputs in the sample. Statistically, this is the firm effect in the estimation of a production function from panel data. The measure presented in Figure 9.5 is based on a Cobb-Douglas function.
7. Schmitt (1989) attributes the sectoral differences in average labor productivity to an incorrect measure of the labor force in agriculture, ignoring nonagricultural output produced by what is recorded as agricultural labor. This indeed may be a source

of error, but because no empirical evidence is provided on its magnitude, here it is considered of second-degree importance and is ignored.

8. A distinction has to be made between the effect of c_0 on the coefficients of the particular regression and its effect on the elasticity. For instance let $\ln(m + c_0) = b\ln(\delta - c) +$ residual, then the elasticity of migration with respect to δ is

$$E_{m/\delta} = \frac{\partial \ln m}{\partial \ln \delta} = b\frac{m + c_0}{(\delta - c)}\frac{\delta}{m}.$$

As c and c_0 change, so does the regression coefficient b. It is $E_{m/\delta}$, which was quite robust over the iterations.

9. An instrumental variables version of this equation gave similar results for all coefficients except for education; its coefficient was practically zero.

10. See Mundlak (1979, chapter 2).

11. "Only 2.6% of all exits that actually occurred between 1986 and 1990 have been correctly predicted which indicates that a number of important explanatory variables are missing in the above shown specification" (Weiss, 1996, p. 5).

10. The Dynamics of Resource Allocation: Capital

1. For lack of space, we present here only a selected set of distributions and summarize some additional information in the tables. Unless indicated otherwise, the values for 1970 and 1990 are averages for 1967–1974 and 1985–1992 respectively.

2. This derivative is evaluated for L kept at its short-run optimal level, which is different from the derivative conditional on L derived from the production function:

$$\frac{\partial Y}{\partial K}\,|_{L} = b\frac{Y}{K}.$$

3. This statement excludes the neutral component of technical change (Chapter 5).

4. This statement is inconsistent with the assertion that "[t]he introduction of installation costs results in a determinate level of investment and in a determinate scale of output for any set of prices. The optimal level of investment and output at any point of time depend on the amount of capital already accumulated" (Jorgenson, 1972, p. 221).

5. Nadiri and Rosen (1969) extended this model to more than one quasi-factor.

11. Agricultural Production Functions: An Overview

1. For a discussion of functional forms, see the survey by Fuss, McFadden, and Mundlak (1978).

2. See McFadden (1978, p. 5) and Jorgenson (1986) for a brief review of the history of duality and its aspiration.

3. The survey by Jorgenson (1986) covers applications in other sectors.
4. The usual dichotomy is between variable and fixed inputs. Fixity reflects supply or institutional settings.

12. Empirical Production Functions: Statistical Aspects

1. The discussion of the estimation problem overlaps in part with Mundlak (1996).
2. This estimator is identical with indirect least squares:

$$\hat{\gamma}_p = \frac{y'p/p'p}{x'p/p'p},$$

where the numerator and the denominator are the OLS estimates of the product supply and factor demand elasticities respectively. We refer to this estimator as the dual estimator because it is obtained from derivatives of the profit function. Since the production function is identified and it is self-dual, it is possible to move from the parameters of the reduced form to those of the production function.

3. The two cases, incomplete and complete information, are the transmitted and non-transmitted error, respectively, considered by Mundlak and Hoch (1965).
4. The use of covariance analysis as a solution to the simultaneity problem is due to Mundlak (1961b) and Hoch (1962).
5. This is the case studied by Zellner, Kmenta, and Dreze (1966).
6. Technically, the instrument is obtained by projecting x onto the space spanned by $W(i)x$ and p.
7. Let $y = x_1\beta_1 + x_2\beta_2 + u$, where x_j is nxk_j matrix, $j = 1, 2$, and the other dimensions conform. Let b_1 be the OLS estimate of β_1. It is well known that its variance can be written as $\sigma^2/x_1'M(2)x_1$, where $M(2) = [I - x_2(x_2'x_2)^{-1}x_2']$. Let x_1^* and e_1 be the true and error orthogonal components of x_1 respectively, then $x_1'M(2)x_1 = x_1^{*\prime}M(2)x_1^* + e_1'(M(2)e_1$. As the number of columns (variables) in x_2 increases, the sum of squares of the true component declines and with it the precision of the estimate.
8. McElroy also emphasizes the consistency between the errors in the production function and the behavioral functions. This is similar in spirit to self-duality, which is a neat concept but often unattainable.
9. "It is for this reason that it is useful to concentrate on the production and behavioral function at the same time. Whatever is said about one is reflected in the other" (Mundlak, 1963, p. 140).

13. Agricultural Productivity

1. Chalfant (1984, p. 219) reports that estimates resulting from the use of the Fourier flexible form failed to satisfy the negative own elasticities.

2. As indicated in Mundlak (2000), this is the key to explaining some of the findings in Antle (1984, p. 420), Lee and Chambers (1986), Shumway and Alexander (1988, p. 160), and Shumway, Saez, and Gottret (1988). The lack of identification is also related to the effort to determine the source of jointness in multiproduct production functions, such as in Shumway, Pope, and Nash (1984) and Chambers and Just (1989).

3. See, for instance, Lopez (1980).

4. Kako (1978) finds that the decline in labor in Japanese rice farming was mainly due to technical change and not due to a substitution under a given technology. Antle (1984) finds that changes in factor use in U.S. agriculture were more a function of technical change and less price responsive in the postwar period.

5. The role of incentives is consistent with the view of Cochrane (1958): "when do farmers typically adopt new practices . . . ? They do so when prices are good, when price and income expectations are good (i.e., risk is minimized) and when the asset position of farmers is good" (p. 97). Why is that? Because "the adoption of new practices . . . requires the acquisition of additional capital inputs involving cash outlays or financial commitments" (ibid.).

   Antle (1984) comments: "Cochrane's historical analysis suggests that although agricultural research made important advances during the 1930s, farmers were not provided strong economic incentives to adopt new technology until after the war. In addition, basic scientific research during the war provided an impetus to agricultural research" (p. 414).

6. There is, however, an interesting question of how much of the growth in agricultural output that followed the shift to the household responsibility system can be attributed to this change and how much is simply a supply response to an increase in the real price of grains (Mundlak, 1992).

7. We review only studies where the quantities (outputs and inputs) are expressed either as country totals or in per worker terms. Studies where the quantities are average per farm raise issues not essential to our discussion and are therefore not covered here.

8. By block orthogonal we mean that the variables in one of the three blocks are orthogonal (linearly independent) to the variables in the other blocks.

9. The finding of increasing returns to scale in cross-country analysis found justification in similar results by Griliches (1963b) in cross-regions analysis for the United States. For more evidence, see Kislev and Peterson (1996).

10. The cost shares used by Capalbo and Vo (1988) were:

Year	Labor	Equipment and livestock	Land and structures	Chemicals	Energy	Other
1960	0.24	0.25	0.16	0.04	0.04	0.26
1980	0.11	0.21	0.41	0.06	0.04	0.17

The average annual growth rates were output 1.76, labor −1.32, family labor −3.09, equipment 2.04, animal capital 0.38, structures and land 0.1, fertilizer 5.01, pesticides 6.07, energy 1.58, other materials 1.2, and all inputs 0.17.

14. *The Agricultural Supply*

1. Some of these observations are also made in the surveys by Binswanger (1989) and Chhibber (1988, 1989).
2. This is a form of external diseconomies and has been discussed in relation to the difference between the industry supply function and the horizontal sum over firms of their marginal cost functions (Friedman, 1962). See also Brandow (1962) and Floyd (1965).
3. It is related to the Allen elasticity of substitution, A_{jh}, by $E_{jh} = A_{jh}\alpha_j$, where α_j is the factor share of the jth factor in total cost.
4. Initially, all inputs can be considered to be quasi-fixed, and it is up to the analysis to determine if a particular input is variable. Alternatively, the production function can be the concentrated function in the quasi-fixed variables.

15. *Growth and the Economic Environment*

1. To gain perspective for the scope of learning by doing, it is insightful to sample views of some of its advocates:

   "Perhaps learning by doing can be conceived as an exploration and actualization of the productive potential of new technologies; if you will, a series of minor technical innovations that are learned from major technical breakthrough. . . . In the absence of the introduction of technical processes, it is likely that learning by doing cannot be sustained" (Young, 1991, p. 372). See also foonote 9 from the same page: "It is interesting to note that in his seminal paper Arrow [1962] used cumulative investment, as opposed to cumulative output, as an index of experience precisely because he believed that, in the absence of substantial changes in the productive environment, learning by doing is bounded." This statement assigns a crucial role to physical capital as a carrier of technology. Lucas's (1993) treatment of learning by doing is based on the assumption of an exogenous flow of new technologies.
2. I lean heavily on illustrations from Chile and Argentina because of my research experience.
3. Note that when the domestic prices behaved like the price of exportables, a change in the export tax had only a small effect on the real exchange rate.
4. Note that $\log(DO_c)$ is negative.
5. The elasticity is $-0.13 + 0.022D[\log DO_f]$. A single equation estimate of this equation gave an elasticity −0.44 when the economy is financially open.

6. $\hat{\mu}$ measures real changes in the money supply and thereby generates a real balance effect because prices lag behind monetary shocks. The positive value for the elasticity indicates that the propensity to spend on tradable goods is higher than on goods represented by p_3.
7. The regression was estimated as a part of a larger system by nonlinear 3SLS.
8. The fit of each of the regressions reported in this section is very good, and the asymptotic t-ratios are quite high. As a group, the state variables account for a large proportion of the variability in output. The background material and the details of the analysis can be found in the references.
9. For a discussion of macro variables and growth based on cross-country comparisons, see Fischer (1993).

References

Abbott, Philip C., and F. Desmond McCarthy. 1982. "Welfare Effects of Tied Food Aid." *Journal of Development Economics,* 11(1): 63–79.

Abel, Andrew B., and Olivier J. Blanchard. 1986. "The Present Value of Profits and Cyclical Movements in Investment." *Econometrica,* 54(2): 249–273.

Adelman, Irma, and Cynthia Taft Morris. 1967. *Society, Politics, and Economic Development: A Quantitative Approach.* Baltimore: Johns Hopkins Press.

Amemiya, Takeshi, and Thomas E. MaCurdy. 1986. "Instrumental-Variable Estimation of an Error-Components Model." *Econometrica,* 54(4): 869–880.

Antle, John M. 1983. "Infrastructure and Aggregate Agricultural Productivity: International Evidence." *Economic Development and Cultural Change,* 31(3): 609–619.

—— 1984. "The Structure of U.S. Agricultural Technology, 1910–78." *American Journal of Agricultural Economics,* 66(4): 414–421.

Arayama, Yuko. 1986. "Time Allocation of Japanese Farm Households." Ph.D. dissertation, Department of Economics, University of Chicago.

—— 1989. "Out-migration from Agriculture and Time Allocation within Farm Households," pp. 63–74 in *Agriculture and Governments in an Interdependent World: Proceedings of the 20th International Conference of Agricultural Economists,* ed. Allen Maunder and Alberto Valdès. Brookfield, Vt.: Gower Publishing Co.

Arrow, Kenneth J. 1962. "The Economic Implications of Learning by Doing." *Review of Economic Studies,* 29: 155–173.

Arrow, Kenneth J., Hollis B. Chenery, Bagicha S. Minhas, and Robert M. Solow. 1961. "Capital-labor Substitution and Economic Efficiency." *Review of Economics and Statistics,* 43(3): 225–250.

Balassa, Bela. 1964. "The Purchasing-Power Parity Doctrine: A Reappraisal." *Journal of Political Economy,* 72(6): 584–596.

Ball, V. Eldon. 1985. "Output, Input, and Productivity Measurement in U.S. Agriculture: 1948–79." *American Journal of Agricultural Economics,* 67(3): 475–486.

Ball, V. Eldon, J.-C. Bureau, J. Butault, and H. P. Witzke. 1993. "The Stock of Capital in European Community Agriculture." *European Review of Agricultural Economics,* 20:437–450.

Ball, V. Eldon, J.-C. Bureau, R. Nehring, and A. Somwaru. 1997. "Agricultural Productivity Revisited." *American Journal of Agricultural Economics,* 79(4): 1045–1063.

Barkley, Andrew. 1988. "The Determinants of Off-Farm Migration and Agricultural Investment in the United States: 1940 to 1985." Ph.D. dissertation, Department of Economics, University of Chicago.

Barro, Robert J., and Xavier Sala-i-Martin. 1995. *Economic Growth.* New York: McGraw-Hill, chap. 4.

Bautista, Romeo M., and Alberto Valdès. 1993. *The Bias against Agriculture: Trade and Macroeconomic Policies in Developing Countries.* San Francisco: ICS Press.

Bean, L. H. 1929. "The Farmers' Response to Price." *Journal of Farm Economics,* 11: 368–385.

Becker, Gary S. 1965. "A Theory of the Allocation of Time." *Economic Journal,* 75(September): 493–517.

Benjamin, Dwayne. 1988. "Household Composition and Labor Demand: A Test of Rural Labor Market Efficiency." Working Paper 244. Princeton Industrial Relations Section, Princeton, N.J.

Bhagwati, Jagdish N., and T. N. Srinivasan. 1971. "The Theory of Wage Differentials: Production Response and Factor Price Equalisation." *Journal of International Economics,* 1(1): 19–35.

Bhalla, G. S., and Dilawar Ali Khan. 1979. *New Technology and Agricultural Transformation: A Comparative Study of the Punjab, India and the Punjab, Pakistan.* Nagoya: United Nations Center for Regional Development Country Monograph.

Bhattacharjee, Jyoti P. 1955. "Resource Use and Productivity in World Agriculture." *Journal of Farm Economics,* 37(1): 57–71.

Binswanger, Hans P. 1978. "Induced Technical Change: Evolution of Thought," pp. 13–43 in *Induced Innovation: Technology, Institutions, and Development,* ed. Hans P. Binswanger and Vernon W. Ruttan. Baltimore and London: Johns Hopkins University Press.

—— 1989. "The Policy Response of Agriculture," pp. 231–258 in *Proceedings of the World Bank Annual Conference on Development Economics.* Washington, D.C.: World Bank.

Binswanger, Hans P., and Pasquale I. Scandizzo. 1983. "Patterns of Agricultural Protection." Discussion Paper no. ARU 15. Agriculture and Rural Development Department, World Bank, Washington, D.C.

Binswanger, Hans, Yair Mundlak, Maw-Cheng Yang, and Alan Bowers. 1985. "Estimation of Aggregate Agricultural Supply Response." Discussion Paper no. ARU 48. Agriculture and Rural Development Department, World Bank, Washington, D.C.

—— 1987. "On the Determinants of Cross-Country Aggregate Agricultural Supply." *Journal of Econometrics,* 36: 111–131.

Bollman, Ray D. 1979. "Off-Farm Work by Farmers: An Application of the Kinked Demand Curve for Labour." *Canadian Journal of Agricultural Economics,* 27(3): 37–60.

Bollman, Ray D., and Allan D. Steeves. 1982. "The Stocks and Flows of Canadian Census Farm Operators, 1966–7." *Canadian Review of Sociology and Anthropology,* 19(4): 576–590.

Boserup, Ester. 1981. *Population and Technological Change: A Study of Long-Term Trends.* Chicago: University of Chicago Press.

Brainard, William C., and James Tobin. 1968. "Pitfalls in Financial Model Building." *American Economic Review,* 58(2): 99–122.

Brandow, G. E. 1962. "Demand for Factors and Supply of Output in a Perfectly Competitive Industry." *Journal of Farm Economics,* 44(3): 895–899.

Brewster, John M., and Howard L. Parsons. 1946. "Can Prices Allocate Resources in American Agriculture?" *Journal of Farm Economics,* 28(4): 938–960.

Bronfenbrenner, M. 1944. "Production Functions: Cobb-Douglas, Interfirm, Intrafirm." *Econometrica,* 12(1): 35–44.

Burmeister, Edwin, and A. Rodney Dobell. 1969. "Disembodied Technological Change with Several Factors." *Journal of Economic Theory,* 1(1): 1–8.

Capalbo, Susan M., and Trang T. Vo. 1988. "A Review of the Evidence on Agricultural Productivity and Aggregate Technology," pp. 96–137 in *Agricultural Productivity: Measurement and Explanation,* ed. Susan M. Capalbo and John M. Antle. Washington, D.C.: Resources for the Future.

Carlson, Sune. 1956. *A Study on the Pure Theory of Production.* New York: Kelley and Millman.

Cass, David. 1965. "Optimum Growth in an Aggregative Model of Capital Accumulation." *Review of Economic Studies,* 32(July): 233–240.

Cassels, John M. 1933. "The Nature of Statistical Supply Curves." *Journal of Farm Economics,* 15(2): 378–387.

Cavallo, Domingo F. 1976. "A Note on a Consistent Estimation of a Production Function with Partially Transmitted Errors." Department of Economics, Harvard University. Mimeograph.

—— 1988. "Argentina," pp. 267–284 in *The Open Economy: Tools for Policymakers in Developing Countries,* ed. Rudiger Dornbusch and F. Leslie C.H. Helmers. New York: Oxford University Press for the World Bank.

Cavallo, Domingo F., and Guillermo Mondino. 1996. "Argentina's Miracle? From Hyperinflation to Sustained Growth," pp. 11–22 in *Annual World Bank Conference on Development Economics, 1995,* ed. Michael Bruno and Boris Pleskovic. Washington, D.C.: World Bank.

Cavallo, Domingo F., and Yair Mundlak. 1982. *Agriculture and Economic Growth in an Open Economy: The Case of Argentina.* Research Report no. 36. Washington, D.C.: International Food Policy Research Institute.

Chalfant, James A. 1984. "Comparison of Alternative Functional Forms with Application to Agricultural Input Data." *American Journal of Agricultural Economics,* 66(2): 216–220.

Chambers, Robert G., and Richard E. Just. 1981. "Effects of Exchange Rate Changes in U.S. Agriculture: A Dynamic Analysis." *American Journal of Agricultural Economics,* 63(1): 32–46.

—— 1989. "Estimating Multioutput Technologies." *American Journal of Agricultural Economics,* 71(4): 980–995.

Chang, Ching Cheng, and Spiro E. Stefanou. 1988. "Specification and Estimation of Asymmetric Adjustment Rates for Quasi-Fixed Factors of Production." *Journal of Economic Dynamics and Control,* 12(1): 145–151.

Chavas, Jean Paul. 1994. "Production and Investment Decisions under Sunk Cost and Temporal Uncertainty." *American Journal of Agricultural Economics,* 76(1): 114–127.

Chenery, Hollis B. 1949. "Engineering Production Functions." *Quarterly Journal of Economics,* 63(4): 507–531.

—— 1952. "Overcapacity and the Acceleration Principle." *Econometrica,* 20(1): 1–28.

Chhibber, Ajay. 1988. "Raising Agricultural Output: Price and Nonprice Factors." *Finance and Development,* 25(2): 44–47.

—— 1989. "The Aggregate Supply Response: A Survey," pp. 55–68 in *Structural Adjustment and Agriculture: Theory and Practice in Africa and Latin America,* ed. Simon Commander. London: Overseas Development Institute in collaboration with James Curry Publishers.

Chirinko, Robert S. 1993. "Business Fixed Investment Spending: A Critical Survey of Modeling Strategies, Empirical Results, and Policy Implications." *Journal of Economic Literature,* 31(4): 1875–1911.

Christensen, Laurits R., Dale W. Jorgenson, and Lawrence J. Lau. 1973. "Transcendental Logarithmic Production Frontiers." *Review of Economics and Statistics,* 55(1): 28–45.

Cobb, C. W., and P. H. Douglas. 1928. "A Theory of Production." *American Economic Review,* 18(1): 139–165.

Cochrane, Willard W. 1958. "Some Additional Views on Demand and Supply," pp. 94–106 in *Agricultural Adjustment Problems in a Growing Economy,* ed. Earl O. Heady, Howard G. Diesslin, Harald R. Jensen, and Glenn L. Johnson. Ames: Iowa State College Press.

Coeymans, Juan Eduardo, and Yair Mundlak. 1992. "Endogenous Technology and Sectoral Productivity: Chile, 1962–82." *Journal of Productivity Analysis,* 3(3): 257–275.

—— 1993. *Sectoral Growth in Chile: 1962–82.* Research Report no. 95. Washington, D.C.: International Food Policy Research Institute.

Conlon, John R. 1988. "Inputs, Environment, and Production Function Estimation." Ph.D. dissertation, Department of Economics, University of Chicago.

Crego, Al, Donald Larson, Rita Butzer, and Yair Mundlak. 1998. "A New Database on Investment and Capital for Agriculture and Manufacturing." World Bank Working Paper no. 2013. World Bank, Washington, D.C.

Danin, Y. 1973. "Patterns of Sectorial Development in the Course of Economic Growth." Ph.D. dissertation, Hebrew University of Jerusalem.

Danin, Y., and Y. Mundlak. 1979. "The Introduction of New Techniques and Capital Accumulation." Working Paper 7907. Center for Agricultural Economic Research, Rehovot.

Diewert, W. E. 1976. "Exact and Superlative Index Numbers." *Journal of Econometrics,* 4(2): 115–145.

Domar, Evsey D. 1947. "Expansion and Employment." *American Economic Review,* 37(1): 34–55.

Dunham, Denis. 1984. *Food Cost Review 1983.* Agricultural Economic Report no. 514. Washington, D.C.: U.S. Department of Agriculture, Economic Research Service.

Edwards, Clark. 1959. "Resource Fixity and Farm Organization." *Journal of Farm Economics,* 41(4): 747–759.

Ehrensaft, Philip, Pierre LaRamée, Ray D. Bollman, and Frederick H. Buttel. 1984. "The Microdynamics of Farm Structural Change in North America: The Canadian Experience and Canada-U.S.A. Comparisons." *American Journal of Agricultural Economics,* 66(5): 823–828.

Eisner, Robert. 1963. "Investment: Fact and Fancy." *American Economic Review,* 53(2): 237–246.

Eisner, Robert, and Robert H. Strotz. 1963. "Determinants of Business Investment," pp. 60–233 in *Impacts of Monetary Policy,* prepared for the Commission on Money and Credit. Englewood Cliffs, N.J.: Prentice Hall.

Epstein, Larry G. 1981. "Duality Theory and Functional Forms for Dynamic Factor Demands." *Review of Economic Studies,* 48(1): 81–95.

Epstein, Larry G., and Michael G. S. Denny. 1983. "The Multivariate Flexible Accelerator Model: Its Empirical Restrictions and an Application to U.S. Manufacturing." *Econometrica,* 51(3): 647–674.

Evenson, Robert E., and Yoav Kislev. 1975. *Agricultural Research and Productivity.* New Haven: Yale University Press.

Feder, Gershon, and Roger Slade. 1984. "The Acquisition of Information and the Adoption of New Technology." *American Journal of Agricultural Economics,* 66(3): 312–320.

Feder, Gershon, Tongroj Onchan, Yongyuth Chalamwong, and Chira Hongladarom. 1988. *Land Policies and Farm Productivity in Thailand.* Baltimore: Johns Hopkins University Press for the World Bank.

Fellner, William. 1961. "Two Propositions in the Theory of Induced Innovations." *Economic Journal,* 71(282): 305–308.

Findlay, Ronald. 1982. "On W. Arthur Lewis's Contributions to Economics," pp. 1–14 in *The Theory and Experience of Economic Development–Essays in Honor of Sir W. Arthur Lewis,* ed. Mark Gersovitz, Carlos F. Diaz-Alejandro, Gustav Ranis, and Mark Rosenzweig. London: George Allen & Unwin.

Fischer, Stanley. 1993. "The Role of Macroeconomic Factors in Growth." Working Paper 4725. National Bureau of Economic Research, Cambridge, Mass.

Floyd, John E. 1965. "The Effects of Farm Price Supports on the Returns to Land and Labor in Agriculture." *Journal of Political Economy,* 73(2): 148–158.

Frenkel, Jacob A., and Assaf Razin. 1975. "Variable Factor Supplies and the Production Possibility Frontier." *Southern Economic Journal,* 41(3): 410–419.

Friedman, Milton. 1962. *Price Theory.* Chicago: Aldine Publishing Co.

Fuss, Melvyn, Daniel McFadden, and Yair Mundlak. 1978. "A Survey of Functional Forms in the Economic Analysis of Production," pp. 219–268 in *Production Economics: A Dual Approach to Theory and Applications,* ed. Melvyn Fuss and Daniel McFadden. Amsterdam: North-Holland Publishing Co.

Galbraith, John K., and John D. Black. 1938. "The Maintenance of Agricultural Production during Depression: The Explanations Reviewed." *Journal of Political Economy,* 46(3): 305–323.

Galeotti, Marzio. 1996. "The Intertemporal Dimension of Neoclassical Production Theory." *Journal of Economic Surveys,* 10(4): 421–460.

Gallant, A. Ronald. 1982. "Unbiased Determination of Production Technologies." *Journal of Econometrics,* 20(2): 285–323.

Gorki, M. 1989. *My Universities.* Hebrew translation. Tel Aviv: Am Oved.

Gould, J. P. 1968. "Adjustment Costs in the Theory of Investment of the Firm." *Review of Economic Studies,* 35(1): 47–55.

Griliches, Zvi. 1959. "The Demand for Inputs in Agriculture and a Derived Supply Elasticity." *Journal of Farm Economics,* 41(2): 309–322.

—— 1960a. "The Demand for a Durable Input: Farm Tractors in the United States, 1921–57," pp. 181–207 in *The Demand for Durable Goods,* ed. Arnold C. Harberger. Chicago: University of Chicago Press.

—— 1960b. "Estimates of Aggregate U.S. Farm Supply Function." *Journal of Farm Economics,* 42: 47–55.

—— 1963a. "The Sources of Measured Productivity Growth: United States Agriculture, 1940–1960." *Journal of Political Economy,* 71(4): 331–346.

—— 1963b. "Estimates of the Aggregate Agricultural Production Function from Cross-Sectional Data." *Journal of Farm Economics,* 45(2): 419–428.

——- 1963c. "Capital Stock in Investment Functions: Some Problems of Concept and Measurement," in *Measurement in Economics: Studies in Mathematical Economics and Econometrics, in Memory of Yehuda Grunfeld,* ed. Carl F. Christ et al. Stanford, Calif.: Stanford University Press.

—— 1986. "Data Problems in Econometrics," pp. 1466–1514 in *Handbook of Econometrics,* vol. 3, ed. Zvi Griliches and Michael D. Intriligator. Amsterdam: North-Holland Publishing Company.

Griliches, Zvi, and Jerry A. Hausman. 1986. "Errors in Variables in Panel Data." *Journal of Econometrics,* 31(1): 93–118.

Grunfeld, Yehuda. 1960. "The Determinants of Corporate Investment," pp. 211–266 in *The Demand for Durable Goods,* ed. Arnold C. Harberger. Chicago: University of Chicago Press.

Haavelmo, Trygve. 1947. "Methods of Measuring the Marginal Propensity to Consume." *Journal of the American Statistical Association,* 42: 105–122.

—— 1960. *A Study in the Theory of Investment.* Chicago: University of Chicago Press.

Hag Elamin, N. A., and E. M. El Mak. 1995. "Adjustment Programs and Agricultural Incentives in Sudan: A Comparative Study." Presented at the workshop of the African Economic Research Consortium.

Hamermesh, Daniel S., and Gerard A. Pfann. 1996. "Adjustment Costs in Factor Demand." *Journal of Economic Literature,* 34(3): 1264–1292.

Hanoch, Giora. 1975. "Production and Demand Models with Direct or Indirect Implicit Additivity." *Econometrica,* 43(3): 395–419.

Hansen, Lars Peter, and Thomas J. Sargent. 1981. "Linear Rational Expectations Models for Dynamically Interrelated Variables," pp. 127–156 in *Rational Expectations and Econometric Practice,* ed. Robert E. Lucas, Jr., and Thomas J. Sargent. Minneapolis: University of Minnesota Press.

Harberger, Arnold C. 1971. "Three Basic Postulates for Applied Welfare Economics: An Interpretive Essay." *Journal of Economic Literature,* 9(3): 785–797.

Harrod, R. F. 1948. *Towards a Dynamic Economics.* London: Macmillan.

Hayami, Yujiro, and Vernon W. Ruttan. 1970. "Agricultural Productivity Differences among Countries." *American Economic Review,* 60(5): 895–911.

—— 1985. *Agricultural Development: An International Perspective.* Baltimore: Johns Hopkins University Press.

Heady, Earl O. 1944. "Production Functions from a Random Sample of Farms." *Journal of Farm Economics,* 28(4): 989–1004.

Heady, Earl O., and John L. Dillon. 1961. *Agricultural Production Functions.* Ames: Iowa State University Press.

Heady, Earl O., and Luther G. Tweeten. 1963. *Resource Demand and the Structure of the Agricultural Industry.* Ames: Iowa State University Press.

Hecksher, E. 1919. "The Effect of Foreign Trade on the Distribution of Income." *Ekonomisk Tidskrift,* 497–512; reprinted in *Readings in the Theory of International Trade.* Cambridge, Mass.: Harvard University Press.

Hildebrand, John R. 1960. "Some Difficulties with Empirical Results from Whole-Farm Cobb-Douglas-Type Production Functions." *Journal of Farm Economics,* 42(4): 897–904.

Hoch, Irving. 1962. "Estimation of Production Function Parameters Combining Time-Series and Cross-Section Data." *Econometrica,* 30(1): 34–53.

Houthakker, Hendrik S. 1957. "An International Comparison of Household Expenditure Patterns, Commemorating the Centenary of Engel's Law." *Econometrica,* 25(4): 532–551.

Howard, Wayne H., and C. Richard Shumway. 1988. "Dynamic Adjustment in the U.S. Dairy Industry." *American Journal of Agricultural Economics,* 70(4): 837–847.

Hulten, R. C. 1990. "The Measurement of Capital," pp. 119–152 in E. R. Berndt and J. E. Triplett , eds., *Fifty Years of Economic Measurement,* Studies in Income and Wealth, vol. 54. Chicago: University of Chicago Press for the National Bureau of Economic Research.

Johnson, D. Gale. 1950. "The Nature of Supply Function for Agricultural Products," *American Economic Review,* 40(4): 539–564.

—— 1953. "Comparability of Labor Capacities of Farm and Nonfarm Labor." *American Economic Review,* 43(3): 296–313.

—— 1973, 1991. *World Agriculture in Disarray.* London: Macmillan.

Johnson, Glenn L. 1958. "Supply Function–Some Facts and Notions," pp. 74–93 in *Agricultural Adjustment Problems in a Growing Economy,* ed. Earl O. Heady, Howard G. Diesslin, Harald R. Jensen, and Glenn L. Johnson. Ames: Iowa State College Press.

Johnson, Glenn L., and C. Leroy Quance. 1972. *The Overproduction Trap in U.S. Agriculture.* Baltimore: John Hopkins University Press for Resources for the Future.

Jones, Larry E., and Rodolfo E. Manuelli. 1997. "The Sources of Growth." *Journal of Economic Dynamics and Control,* 21(1): 75–114.

Jones, Ronald W. 1965. "The Structure of Simple General Equilibrium Models." *Journal of Political Economy,* 73(6): 557–572.

Jorgenson, Dale W. 1961. "The Development of a Dual Economy." *Economic Journal,* 71(June): 309–334.

—— 1963. "Capital Theory and Investment Behavior." *American Economic Review,* 53(2): 247–259.

—— 1966. "Testing Alternative Theories of the Development of a Dual Economy," pp. 45–60 in *The Theory and Design of Economic Development,* ed. Irma Adelman and Erik Thorbecke. Baltimore: Johns Hopkins Press.

—— 1967. "The Theory of Investment Behavior," pp. 129–155 in *Determinants of Investment Behavior,* ed. Robert Ferber. New York: Columbia University Press, National Bureau of Economic Research.

—— 1972. "Investment Behavior and the Production Function." *Bell Journal of Economics and Management Science,* 3(1): 220–251.

—— 1974. "Investment and Production: A Review," pp. 341–366 in *Frontiers of Quantitative Economics,* vol. 2, ed. Michael D. Intriligator and David A. Kendrick. Amsterdam: North-Holland Publishing Co.

—— 1986. "Econometric Methods for Modeling Producer Behavior," pp. 1841–1915 in *Handbook of Econometrics,* vol. 3, ed. Zvi Griliches and Michael D. Intriligator. Amsterdam: North-Holland Publishing Co.

Jorgenson, Dale W., and Frank M. Gollop. 1992. "Productivity Growth in U.S. Agriculture: A Postwar Perspective." *American Journal of Agricultural Economics,* 74(3): 745–750.

Just, Richard E., and David Zilberman. 1983. "Stochastic Structure, Farm Size and Technology Adoption in Developing Agriculture." *Oxford Economic Papers,* 35(2): 307–328.

Kako, Toshiyuki. 1978. "Decomposition Analysis of Derived Demand for Factor Inputs: The Case of Rice Production in Japan." *American Journal of Agricultural Economics,* 60(4): 628–635.

Kamien, Morton I., and Nancy L. Schwartz. 1991. *Dynamic Optimization.* 2d ed. Amsterdam: North-Holland Publishing Co.

Kawagoe, Toshihiko, and Yujiro Hayami. 1983. "The Production Structure of World Agriculture: An Intercountry Cross-Section Analysis." *Developing Economies,* 21:189–206.

—— 1985. "An Intercountry Comparison of Agricultural Production Efficiency." *American Journal of Agricultural Economics,* 67: 87–92.

Kawagoe, Toshihiko, Yujiro Hayami, and Vernon W. Ruttan. 1985. "The Intercountry Agricultural Production Function and Productivity Differences among Countries." *Journal of Development Economics,* 19: 113–132.

Kennedy, Charles. 1964. "Induced Bias in Innovation and the Theory of Distribution." *Economic Journal,* 74(295): 541–547.

Kimhi, Ayal. 1991. "Occupational Choice in Israeli Cooperative Villages." Ph.D. dissertation, Department of Economics, University of Chicago.

Kimhi, Ayal, and Ray Bollman. 1997. "Family Farm Dynamics in Canada and Israel: The Case of Farm Exits." Halbert Centre for Canadian Studies, Occasional Paper no. 20. Jerusalem: Hebrew University.

Kislev, Yoav, and W. Peterson. 1996. "Economies of Scale in Agriculture: A Reexamination of Evidence," pp. 156–170 in *The Economics of Agriculture, Papers in honor of D. Gale Johnson,* vol. 2, ed. John M. Antle and D. Sumner. Chicago: University of Chicago Press.

Kislev, Yoav, and Paul B. Siegel. 1987. "An Intercountry Analysis of Employment and Returns to Labor in Agriculture." Development Research Department, Discussion Paper no. 230, World Bank, Washington, D.C.

Klein, Lawrence R. 1953. *A Textbook of Econometrics.* Evanston, Ill: Row, Peterson and Co.

Koopmans, Tjalling C. 1965. "On the Concept of Optimal Economic Growth," pp. 225–300 in *The Econometric Approach to Development Planning.* Amsterdam: North-Holland Publishing Co.

Koyck, L. 1954. *Distributed Lags and Investment Analysis.* Amsterdam: North-Holland Publishing Co.

Krueger, Anne O. 1992. *A Synthesis of the Political Economy in Developing Countries,* vol. 5 of *The Political Economy of Agricultural Pricing Policy,* ed. Anne O. Krueger, Maurice Schiff, and Alberto Valdès. Baltimore and London: Johns Hopkins University Press for the World Bank.

Krugman, Paul. 1993. "Toward a Counter-Counterrevolution in Development Theory," pp. 15–38 in *Proceedings of the World Bank Annual Conference on Development Economics, 1992,* ed. Lawrence H. Summers and Shekhar Shah. Washington, D.C.: World Bank.

Lachaal, Lassaad, and Abner W. Womack. 1998. "Impacts of Trade and Macroeconomic Linkages on Canadian Agriculture." *American Journal of Agricultural Economics,* 80(3): 534–542.

Lansink, Alfons Oude, and Spiro E. Stefanou. 1997. "Asymmetric Adjustment of Dynamic Factors at the Firm Level." *American Journal of Agricultural Economics,* 79(4): 1340–1351.

Larson, Donald, and Yair Mundlak. 1997. "On the Intersectoral Migration of Agricultural Labor." *Economic Development and Cultural Change,* 45(2): 295–319. Copyright 1997 by The University of Chicago.

Larson, Donald, Rita Butzer, Yair Mundlak, and Al Crego. 1999. "A Cross-Country Database for Sector Investment and Capital." Center for Agricultural Economic Research Working Paper no. 9903. Rehovot.

Lee, Hyunok, and Robert G. Chambers. 1986. "Expenditure Constraints and Profit Maximization in U.S. Agriculture." *American Journal of Agricultural Economics,* 68(4): 857–865.

Levine, Ross, and David Renelt. 1992. "A Sensitivity Analysis of Cross-Country Growth Regressions." *American Economic Review,* 82(4): 942–963.

Lewis, W. A. 1954. "Economic Development with Unlimited Supplies of Labour." *Manchester School of Economic and Social Studies1,* 22(2): 139–191.

Lin, Justin Yifu. 1986. "The Household Responsibility System in China's Agricultural Reform: A Theoretical and Empirical Study." Ph.D. dissertation, University of Chicago.

Longmire, J., and A. Morey. 1983. *Strong Dollar Dampens Demand for U.S. Farm Exports.* FAER no. 193. Washington, D.C.: Economic Research Service, United States Department of Agriculture.

Lopez, Ramon E. 1980. "The Structure of Production and the Derived Demand for Inputs in Canadian Agriculture." *American Journal of Agricultural Economics,* 62(1): 38–45.

—— 1985. "Supply Response and Investment in the Canadian Food Processing Industry." *American Journal of Agricultural Economics,* 67(1): 40–48.

Lucas, Robert E., Jr. 1966. "Optimal Investment with Rational Expectations," pp. 55–66 in *Rational Expectations and Econometric Practice,* vol. 1, by Robert E. Lucas and Thomas J. Sargent. Minneapolis: University of Minnesota Press. 1981.

—— 1967. "Optimal Investment Policy and the Flexible Accelerator." *International Economic Review,* 8(1): 78–85.

—— 1978. "On the Size Distribution of Business Firms." *Bell Journal of Economics,* 9(2): 508–523.

—— 1988. "On the Mechanics of Economic Development." *Journal of Monetary Economics,* 22(1): 3–42.

—— 1993. "Making a Miracle." *Econometrica,* 61(2): 251–272.

Lucas, Robert E., Jr., and Edward C. Prescott. 1971. "Investment under Uncertainty." *Econometrica,* 39(5): 659–681.

Luh, Yir Hueih, and Spiro E. Stefanou. 1991. "Productivity Growth in U.S. Agriculture under Dynamic Adjustment." *American Journal of Agricultural Economics,* 73(4): 1116–1125.

Maddala, G. S. 1971. "The Use of Variance Components Models in Pooling Cross-Section and Time Series Data." *Econometrica,* 39(2): 341–358.

Mairesse, Jacques, and Zvi Griliches. 1990. "Heterogeneity in Panel Data: Are There Stable Production Functions?" pp. 192–231 in *Essays in Honor of Edmond Malinvaud,* vol. 3: *Empirical Economics,* ed. Paul Champsaur et al. Cambridge, Mass.: MIT Press.

Marschak, Jacob, and William H. Andrews, Jr. 1944. "Random Simultaneous Equations and the Theory of Production." *Econometrica,* 12(3–4): 143–205.

Martin, Will, and Devashish Mitra. 1998. "Productivity Growth and Convergence in Agriculture and Manufacturing." Development Research Group, World Bank. Mimeograph.

McElroy, Marjorie B. 1987. "Additive General Error Models for Production, Cost, and Derived Demands or Share Systems." *Journal of Political Economy,* 95(4): 737–757.

McFadden, Daniel. 1978. "Cost, Revenue, and Profit Functions," pp. 3–109 in *Production Economics: A Dual Approach to Theory and Applications,* ed. Melvyn Fuss and Daniel McFadden. Amsterdam: North-Holland Publishing Co.

McGuirk, Anya, and Yair Mundlak. 1991. *Incentives and Constraints in the Transformation of Punjab Agriculture.* Research Report no. 87. Washington, D.C.: International Food Policy Research Institute.

McKenzie, Lionel W. 1998. "Turnpikes." *American Economic Review,* 88(2): 1–14.

McLaren, Keith R., and Russell J. Cooper. 1980. "Intertemporal Duality: Application to the Theory of the Firm." *Econometrica,* 48(7): 1755–1762.

McMillan, John, and Andrew Barkley. 1992. "Political Freedom and the Response to Economic Incentives: Labor Migration in Africa, 1972–1987." Working Paper Series no. IPR 32. Institute for Policy Reform, Washington, D.C.

McMillan, John, Gordon Rausser, and Stan Johnson. 1991. "Freedoms and Economic Growth." Working Paper Series, no. IPR 27. Institute for Policy Reform, Washington, D.C.

McMillan, John, John Whally, and Lijing Zhu. 1989. "The Impact of China's Economic Reforms on Agricultural Productivity Growth." *Journal of Political Economy,* 97(4): 781–807.

Mellor, John W. 1976. *The New Economics of Growth: A Strategy for India and the Developing World.* Ithaca, N.Y.: Cornell University Press.

Melvin, James R. 1968. "Production and Trade with Two Factors and Three Goods." *American Economic Review,* 58(5): 1248–1268.

Mundlak, Yair. 1961a. "Aggregation over Time in Distributed Lag Models." *International Economic Review,* 2(2): 154–163.

—— 1961b. "Empirical Production Function Free of Management Bias." *Journal of Farm Economics,* 43(1): 44–56.

—— 1963. "Estimation of Production and Behavioral Functions from a Combination of Cross-Section and Time-Series Data," pp. 138–166 in *Measurement in Economics: Studies in Mathematical Economics and Econometrics, in Memory of Yehuda Grunfeld,* ed. Carl F. Christ et al. Stanford, Calif.: Stanford University Press.

—— 1964. *An Economic Analysis of Established Family Farms in Israel, 1953–1958.* Jerusalem: Falk Project for Economic Research in Israel.

—— 1965. "The Terms of Trade of Agriculture in Context of Economic Growth." Paper presented at a conference held by the International Economic Association, Rome.

—— 1966. "On the Microeconomic Theory of Distributed Lags." *Review of Economics and Statistics,* 48(1): 51–60.

—— 1967. "Long-run Coefficients and Distributed Lag Analysis: A Reformulation." *Econometrica,* 35(2): 278–293.

—— 1968. "Elasticities of Substitution and the Theory of Derived Demand." *Review of Economic Studies,* 35: 225–236.

—— 1969. "The Terms of Trade of Agriculture in Context of Economic Growth," pp. 630–657 in *Economic Problems of Agriculture in Industrial Societies,* ed. Ugo Pap and Charles Nunn. New York: Macmillan.

—— 1970. "Further Implications of Distortion in the Factor Market." *Econometrica,* 38(3): 517–532.

—— 1971. "Maximization with Several Objective Functions," pp. 441–451 in *Policies, Planning, and Measurement for Agricultural Development,* proceedings of the International Association of Agricultural Economists, ed. N. Westermarck. Oxford Institute for Agrarian Affairs.

—— 1979. *Intersectoral Factor Mobility and Agricultural Growth.* Research Report no. 6. Washington, D.C.: International Food Policy Research Institute.

—— 1981. "On the Concept of Non-Significant Functions and Its Implications for Regression Analysis." *Journal of Econometrics,* 16(1): 139–149.

—— 1983. "Lecture Notes in Econometrics." Rehovot: Faculty of Agriculture, Hebrew University of Jerusalem.

—— 1985. "The Aggregate Agricultural Supply." Working Paper no. 8511. Rehovot: Center for Agricultural Economic Research. An earlier draft was circulated as a background paper for the World Development Report, 1985.

—— 1986. "Agricultural Growth and the Price of Food," pp. 611–623 in *Agriculture in a Turbulent World Economy: Proceedings of the 19th International Conference of Agricultural Economists,* ed. Allen Maunder and Ulf Renborg. Brookfield, Vt.: Gower Publishing Co.

—— 1988. "Endogenous Technology and the Measurement of Productivity," pp. 316–331 in *Agricultural Productivity: Measurement and Explanation,* ed. Susan M. Capalbo and John M. Antle. Washington, D.C.: Resources for the Future.

—— 1992. "Agricultural Productivity and Economic Policies: Concepts and Measurements." Development Centre, Technical Paper no. 75. Paris: Organisation for Economic Co-operation and Development.

—— 1993. "Land Expansion and Land Augmentation with Application to Thailand." Mimeograph.

—— 1996. "Production Function Estimation: Reviving the Primal." *Econometrica,* 64(2): 431–438.

—— 1999. "The Dynamics of Agriculture," in *Food Security, Diversification, and Resource Management: Refocusing the Role of Agriculture?* ed. G. H. Peterson and J. Von Braun. ©Ashgate Publishing Co., Brookfield, Vt. (The Elmhirst Lecture, delivered at the 12th International Conference of Agricultural Economists, Sacramento, Calif., August 1997.)

—— 2000. "Production and Supply," *Handbook of Agricultural Economics,* ed. B. R. Gardner and G. C. Rausser. Amsterdam: Elsevier Science.

Mundlak, Yair, and Rene Hellinghausen. 1982. "The Intercountry Agricultural Production Function: Another View." *American Journal of Agricultural Economics,* 64(4): 664–672.

Mundlak, Yair, and Irving Hoch. 1965. "Consequences of Alternative Specifications in Estimation of Cobb-Douglas Production Functions." *Econometrica,* 33(4): 814–828.

Mundlak, Yair, and Donald F. Larson. 1992. "On the Transmission of World Agricultural Prices." *World Bank Economic Review,* 6(3): 399–422.

Mundlak, Yair, and Ran Mosenson. 1967. "Differential Growth in an Extended Two Sector Model." Report no. 6718, Center for Mathematical Studies in Business and Economics, University of Chicago, February.

—— 1970. "Two-Sector Model with Generalized Demand." *Metroeconomica,* 22(3): 227–258.

Mundlak, Yair, and John Strauss. 1978. "Occupational Migration out of Agriculture in Japan." *Journal of Development Economics,* 5(1): 55–71.

Mundlak, Yair, and Zvi Tropp. 1979. "Distortion in the Factor Markets and the Short-Run Equilibrium," pp. 136–156 in *On the Stability of Contemporary Economic Systems: Proceedings of the Third Reisensberg Symposium,* ed. Oldrich Kyn and Wolfram Schrettl. Gottingen: Vandenhoeck and Ruprecht.

Mundlak, Yair, and Zvi Volcani. 1973. "The Correspondence of Efficiency Frontier as a Generalization of the Cost Function." *International Economic Review,* 14(1): 223–233.

Mundlak, Yair, Domingo Cavallo, and Roberto Domenech. 1989. *Agriculture and Economic Growth in Argentina, 1913–84.* Research Report no. 76. Washington, D.C.: International Food Policy Research Institute.

—— 1990a. "Economic Policies and Sectoral Growth: Argentina, 1913–1984." Development Centre, Technical Paper no. 18. Paris: Organisation for Economic Co-operation and Development.

—— 1990b. "Effects of Macroeconomic Policies on Sectoral Prices." *World Bank Economic Review,* 4(1): 55–79.

—— 1993. "Agriculture and Growth: The Experience of Argentina," pp. 159–176 in *The Bias against Agriculture: Trade and Macroeconomic Policies in Developing Countries,* ed. Romeo Bautista and Alberto Valdés. Washington, D.C.: International Center for Economic Growth.

Mundlak, Yair, Donald Larson, and Rita Butzer. 1999. "The Determinants of Agricultural Production: A Cross-Country Analysis." Policy Research Working Paper 1827, World Bank, Washington, D.C. Also forthcoming (1999) in *Annales de l'insee.*

Mundlak, Yair, Donald Larson, and Al Crego. 1998. "Agricultural Development: Evidence, Issues, and Consequences," in *Contemporary Economic Issues,* vol. 2: *Labour, Food, and Poverty,* ed. Yair Mundlak. London: Macmillan; New York: St. Martin's Press.

Murphy, Kevin M., Andrei Shleifer, and Robert W. Vishny. 1989. "Industrialization and the Big Push." *Journal of Political Economy,* 97(5): 1003–1026.

Nadiri, M. Ishag, and Sherwin Rosen. 1969. "Interrelated Factor Demand Functions." *American Economic Review,* 59(4): 457–471.

Nerlove, Marc. 1956. "Estimates of the Elasticities of Supply of Selected Agricultural Commodities." *Journal of Farm Economics,* 38(2): 496–509.

—— 1958. "Distributed Lags and Estimation of Long-Run Supply and Demand Elasticities: Theoretical Considerations." *Journal of Farm Economics,* 40(2): 301–313.

—— 1979. "The Dynamics of Supply: Retrospect and Prospect." *American Journal of Agricultural Economics,* 61(5): 874–888.

Nguyen, Dung. 1979. "On Agricultural Productivity Differences among Countries." *American Journal of Agricultural Economics,* 61(3): 565–570.

Obstfeld, Maurice, and Kenneth Rogoff. 1996. *Foundations of International Macroeconomics.* Cambridge, Mass.: MIT Press.

Ohlin, B. 1933. *Interregional and International Trade.* Cambridge, Mass.: Harvard University Press.

Pandey, S., R. R. Piggott, and T. G. MacAulay. 1982. "The Elasticity of Aggregate Australian Agricultural Supply: Estimates and Policy Implications." *Australian Journal of Agricultural Economics,* 26(3): 202–219.

Papanek, Gustav F., and Eshya Mujahid. 1983. "Effect of Policies on Agricultural Development: A Comparison of the Bengals and the Punjabs." *American Journal of Agricultural Economics,* 65(2): 426–437.

Parks, Richard W. 1967. "Efficient Estimation of a System of Regression Equations When Disturbances Are Both Serially and Contemporaneously Correlated." *Journal of the American Statistical Association,* 62(June): 500–509.

Prais, S. J., and H. S. Houthakker. 1955, 1971. *The Analysis of Family Budgets.* Cambridge: Cambridge University Press.

Pritchett, Lant. 1996. "Where Has All the Education Gone?" Policy and Human Resources Division, Policy Research Working Paper 1581. Washington, D.C.: World Bank.

Ramsey, Frank P. 1928. "A Mathematical Theory of Saving." *Economic Journal,* 38(December): 543–559.

Ranis, Gustav, and J. C. H. Fei. 1961. "A Theory of Economic Development." *American Economic Review,* 51(4): 533–565.

Rausser, Gordon C., James A. Chalfant, H. Alan Love, and Kostas G. Stamoulis. 1986. "Macroeconomic Linkages, Taxes, and Subsidies in the U.S. Agricultural Sector." *American Journal of Agricultural Economics,* 68(2): 399–412.

Ravenstein, E. G. 1889. "The Laws of Migration." *Journal of the Statistical Society,* 52(2): 284–301.

Reder, M. W. 1943. "An Alternative Interpretation of the Cobb-Douglas Function." *Econometrica,* 11(3–4): 259–264.

Robinson, Chris, Pat McMahon, and John Quiggon. 1982. "Labour Supply and Off-Farm Work by Farmers: Theory and Estimation." *Australian Journal of Agricultural Economics,* 26(1): 23–38.

Robson, Nigel, Ruth Gasson, and Berkeley Hill. 1987. "Part-time Farming–Implications for Farm Family Income." *Journal of Agricultural Economics,* 38(2): 167–191.

Romer, Paul M. 1986. "Increasing Returns and Long-Run Growth." *Journal of Political Economy,* 94(5): 1002–1037.

—— 1993. "Two Strategies for Economic Development: Using Ideas and Producing Ideas," pp. 63–91 in *Proceedings of the World Bank Annual Conference on Development Economics, 1992,* ed. Lawrence H. Summers and Shekhar Shah. Washington, D.C.: World Bank.

Rosegrant, Mark W., and Robert E. Evenson. 1992. "Agricultural Productivity and Sources of Growth in South Asia." *American Journal of Agricultural Economics,* 74(3): 757–761.

Rosenzweig, Mark R. 1980. "Neoclassical Theory and the Optimizing Peasant: An Econometric Analysis of Market Family Labor Supply in a Developing Country." *Quarterly Journal of Economics,* 94(1): 31–55.

—— 1988. "Labor Markets in Low-Income Countries," pp. 714–762 in *Handbook of Development Economics,* vol. 1, ed. Hollis Chenery and T. N. Srinivasan. Amsterdam: Elsevier Science Publishers.

Rybczynski, T. M. 1955. "Factor Endowment and Relative Commodity Prices." *Economica,* 22: 336–341.

Samuelson, Paul A. 1948. "International Trade and the Equalisation of Factor Prices." *Economic Journal,* 58: 163–184.

—— 1949. "International Factor-Price Equalisation Once Again." *Economic Journal,* 59: 181–197.

—— 1953. "Prices of Factors and Goods in General Equilibrium." *Review of Economic Studies,* 21: 1–20.

—— 1964. "Theoretical Notes on Trade Problems." *Review of Economics and Statistics,* 46(2): 145–154.

—— 1965. "A Theory of Induced Innovation along Kennedy-Weisäcker Lines." *Review of Economics and Statistics,* 47(4): 343–356.

Sargent, Thomas J. 1987. *Macroeconomic Theory,* 2nd ed. Boston: Academic Press.

Sato, K. 1966. "On the Adjustment Time in Neo-Classical Growth Models." *Review of Economic Studies,* 33(95): 263–268.

Schiff, Maurice, and Alberto Valdès. 1992. *A Synthesis of the Economics in Developing Countries,* vol. 4 of *The Political Economy of Agricultural Pricing Policy,* ed. Anne O. Krueger, Maurice Schiff, and Alberto Valdès. Baltimore and London: Johns Hopkins University Press for the World Bank.

Schmidt, Peter. 1988. "Estimation of Fixed-Effect Cobb-Douglas System Using Panel Data." *Journal of Econometrics,* 37: 361–380.

Schmitt, Gunther. 1989. "Simon Kuznets' 'Sectoral Shares in the Labor Force': A Different Explanation of His (I+S)/A Ratio." *American Economic Review,* 79(5): 1262–1276.

Schuh, G. Edward. 1974. "The Exchange Rate and U.S. Agriculture." *American Journal of Agricultural Economics,* 56(1): 1–13.

Schultz, Theodore W. 1956. "Reflections on Agricultural Production, Output, and Supply." *Journal of Farm Economics,* 38(3): 748–762.

—— 1960. "Value of U.S. Farm Surpluses to Underdeveloped Countries." *Journal of Farm Economics,* 42(5): 1019–1030.

—— 1964. *Transforming Traditional Agriculture.* New Haven: Yale University Press.

Sen, Amartya K. 1966. "Peasants and Dualism with or without Surplus Labor." *Journal of Political Economy,* 74(5): 425–450.

Shumway, C. Richard, and William P. Alexander. 1988. "Agricultural Product Supplies and Input Demands: Regional Comparisons." *American Journal of Agricultural Economics,* 70(1): 153–161.

Shumway, C. Richard, Rulon D. Pope, and Elizabeth K. Nash. 1984. "Allocatable Fixed Inputs and Jointness in Agricultural Production: Implications for Economic Modeling." *American Journal of Agricultural Economics,* 66(1): 72–78.

Shumway, C. Richard, Roberto R. Saez, and Pablo E. Gottret. 1988. "Multiproduct Supply and Input Demand in U.S. Agriculture." *American Journal of Agricultural Economics,* 70(2): 330–337.

Siamwalla, Ammar, Suthad Setboonsarng, and Direk Patamasiriwat. 1993. "The Thai Economy in Transition: Agriculture," pp. 81–117 in *The Thai Economy in Transition,* ed. Peter G. Warr. New York: Cambridge University Press.

Singh, Inderjit, Lyn Squire, and John Strauss, eds. 1986. *Agricultural Household Models: Extensions, Applications, and Policy.* Baltimore and London: Johns Hopkins University Press for the World Bank.

Smith, Victor E. 1945. "The Statistical Production Function." *Quarterly Journal of Economics,* 59(4): 543–562.

Snape, Richard H. 1989. "Real Exchange Rates, Real Interest Rates, and Agriculture," pp. 519–532 in *Agriculture and Governments in an Interdependent World: Proceedings of the 20th International Conference of Agricultural Economists,* ed. Allen Maunder and Alberto Valdès. Brookfield, Vt.: Gower Publishing Co.

Solow, Robert M. 1956. "A Contribution to the Theory of Economic Growth." *Quarterly Journal of Economics,* 70(1): 65–94.

—— 1962. "Technical Progress, Capital Formation, and Economic Growth." *American Economic Review,* 52(2): 76–86.

—— 1967. "Some Recent Developments in the Theory of Production," in *The Theory and Empirical Analysis of Production,* ed. Murray Brown. New York: National Bureau of Economic Research, distributed by Columbia University Press.

—— 1970. *Growth Theory: An Exposition.* New York: Oxford University Press.

Stiglitz, Joseph E. 1993. Comment on "Toward a Counter-Counterrevolution in Development Theory," pp. 39–49 in *Proceedings of the World Bank Annual Conference on Development Economics, 1992,* ed. Lawrence H. Summers and Shekhar Shah. Washington, D.C.: World Bank.

Stolper, Wolfgang F., and Paul A. Samuelson. 1941. "Protection and Real Wages." *Review of Economic Studies,* 9(1): 58–73.

Strauss, John, and Duncan Thomas. 1998. "Health, Nutrition, and Economic Development." *Journal of Economic Literature,* 36(2): 766–817.

Swan, Trevor W. 1956. "Economic Growth and Capital Accumulation." *Economic Record,* 66: 334–361.

Taylor, Timothy G., and Michael J. Monson. 1985. "Dynamic Factor Demands for Aggregate Southeastern United States Agriculture." *Southern Journal of Agricultural Economics,* 17(2): 1–9.

Tcha, Moonjoong. 1992. "Altruism and Migration–Evidence from Korea and the U.S." Ph.D. dissertation, Department of Economics, University of Chicago.

Thijssen, Geert. 1996. "Farmers' Investment Behavior: An Empirical Assessment of Two Specifications of Expectations." *American Journal of Agricultural Economics,* 78(1): 166–174.

Tintner, Gerhard. 1944. "A Note on the Derivation of Production Functions from Farm Records." *Econometrica,* 12: 26–34.

Tintner, Gerhard, and O. H. Brownlee. 1944. "Production Functions Derived from Farm Records." *Journal of Farm Economics,* 26(3): 566–571 (correction in *JFE,* Feb. 1953, 35: 123).

Todaro, Michael P. 1969. "A Model for Labor Migration and Urban Unemployment in Less Developed Countries." *American Economic Review,* 59(1): 138–148.

Tolley, G. S., and S. Smidt. 1964. "Agriculture and the Secular Position of the U.S. Economy." *Econometrica,* 32(4): 554–575.

Treadway, A. B. 1969. "On Rational Entrepreneurial Behaviour and the Demand for Investment." *Review of Economic Studies,* 36(2): 227–239.

Tweeten, Luther G., and C. Leroy Quance. 1969. "Positivistic Measures of Aggregate Supply Elasticities: Some New Approaches." *American Economic Review,* 59(2): 175–183.

Tyers, Rod, and Kym Anderson. 1992. *Disarray in World Food Markets: A Quantitative Assessment.* New York: Cambridge University Press.

Uzawa, Hirofumi. 1961. "On a Two-Sector Model of Economic Growth." *Review of Economic Studies,* 29(1): 40–47.

—— 1963. "On a Two-Sector Model of Economic Growth II." *Review of Economic Studies,* 30(2): 105–118.

—— 1965. "Optimum Technical Change in an Aggregative Model of Economic Growth." *International Econonomic Review,* 6(1): 18–31.

Vasavada, Utpal, and Robert G. Chambers. 1986. "Investment in U.S. Agriculture." *American Journal of Agricultural Economics,* 68(4): 950–960.

Weiss, Christopher R. 1996. "Exits from a Declining Sector: Econometric Evidence from a Panel of Upper-Austrian Farms." Institut für Volkwirtschaftlehre, Arbeitspapier Nr. 9601 (February), Johannes Kepler Universität, Linz-Auhof.

Wen, James Guanzhong. 1989. "The Current Land Tenure System and Its Impact on Long Term Performance of Farming Sector: The Case of Modern China." Ph.D. dissertation, Department of Economics, University of Chicago.

Williams, Jeffrey C., and Brian D. Wright. 1991. *Storage and Commodity Markets.* New York: Cambridge University Press.

Working, E. J. 1927. "What Do Statistical Demand Curves Show?" *Quarterly Journal of Economics,* 41: 212–235.

Yamada, Saburo, and Vernon W. Ruttan. 1980. "International Comparisons of Productivity in Agriculture," pp. 509–594 in *New Developments in Productivity Measurement and Analysis,* ed. John W. Kendrick and Beatrice N. Vaccara. Chicago: University of Chicago Press.

Young, Alwyn. 1991. "Learning by Doing and the Dynamic Effects of International Trade." *Quarterly Journal of Economics,* 106(2): 369–405.

Zellner, A., J. Kmenta, and J. Dreze. 1966. "Specification and Estimation of Cobb-Douglas Production Function Models." *Econometrica,* 34(4): 784–795.

Author Index

Abbot, P. C., 443
Abel, A. B., 310
Adelman, I., 372
Alexander, W. P., 450
Amemiya, T., 340
Anderson, K., 57
Andrews, W. H., 321, 331, 337, 340
Antle, J. M., 378, 404, 413, 450
Arayama, Y., 275
Arrow, K. J., 213, 322, 451

Balassa, B., 153
Ball, E. V., 312, 387
Barkley, A., 273, 274, 275
Barro, R. J., 210
Bautista, R., 57
Bean, L. H., 393
Becker, G. S., 248
Benjamin, D., 258
Bhagwati, J. N., 447
Bhalla, G. S., 167
Bhattacharjee, J. P., 377, 378
Binswanger, H. P., 57, 147, 372, 413, 451
Black, J. D., 393
Blanchard, O. J., 310
Bollman, R. D., 258, 276, 278, 447
Boserup, E., 447
Bowers, A., 372, 413
Brainard, W. C., 309
Brandow, G. E., 451
Brewster, J. L., 393
Bronfenbrenner, M., 361
Brownlee, O. H., 320, 366
Bureau, J. C., 312, 387
Burmeister, E., 444
Butault, J., 312
Buttel, F. H., 276
Butzer, R., 11, 284, 289, 312, 376, 377

Capalbo, S., 387, 450
Carlson, S., 398
Cass, D., 207
Cassels, J. M., 393
Cavallo, D., 57, 67, 75, 274, 313, 341, 371, 376, 383, 415, 424, 436, 439
Chalamwong, Y., 279
Chalfant, J. A., 75, 449
Chambers, R. G., 75, 407, 411, 450
Chang, C. C., 407
Chavas, J. P., 301
Chenery, H. B., 130, 304, 322
Chhibber, A., 451
Chirinko, R. S., 294, 307, 308, 309, 310
Christensen, L. R., 323, 365
Cobb, C. W., 320
Cochrane, W. W., 450
Coeymans, J. E., 274, 314, 372, 376, 415, 435, 438
Conlon, J. R., 340
Cooper, R. J., 407
Crego, A., 11, 284, 289, 312, 441

Danin, Y., 222, 445
Denny, M. G. S., 407
Diewert, E., 446
Dillon, J. L., 130, 323
Dobell, A. R., 444
Domar, E. D., 202, 204
Domenech, R., 67, 75, 274, 313, 371, 376, 383, 415, 424, 436
Douglas, P. H., 320
Dreze, J., 449
Dunham, D., 48

Edwards, C., 301
Ehrensaft, P., 276
Eisner, R., 294, 306
El Mak, E. M., 57
Epstein, L., 407
Evenson, R. E., 377, 378, 387

Feder, G., 191, 279
Fei, J. C. H., 266, 280
Fellner, W., 362
Findlay, R., 280, 281
Fischer, S., 452
Floyd, J. E., 451
Frenkel, J., 104, 109, 443
Friedman, M., 451
Fuss, M., 341, 448

Galant, R. A., 365
Galbraith, J. K., 393
Galeotti, M., 307
Gasson, R., 258
Gollop, F. M., 388
Gorki, M., 441
Gottret, P. E., 450
Gould, J. P., 294
Griliches, Z., 312, 347, 368, 387, 402, 406, 450
Grunfeld, Y., 309

Haavelmo, T., 293, 321
Hag Elamin, N. A., 57
Hamermesh, D. S., 301
Hanoch, G., 325
Hansen, L. P., 309
Harberger, A. C., 61
Harrod, R. F., 202, 204
Hausman, J. A., 347
Hayami, Y., 361, 362, 378, 381, 383, 441
Heady, E. O., 130, 312, 320, 323, 361, 366, 420
Hecksher, E., 95
Hellinghausen, R., 371, 374, 378
Hildebrand, J. R., 366
Hill, B., 258
Hoch, I., 449
Hongladarom, C., 279
Houthakker, H. S., 48
Howard, W. H., 407
Hulten, R. C., 312

Johnson, D. G., 57, 86, 266, 393, 407
Johnson, G. L., 301
Johnson, S., 372
Jones, L. E., 213, 222
Jones, R. W., 32, 50, 442
Jorgenson, D., 266, 280, 296, 298, 299, 305, 323, 365, 388, 448, 449
Just, R. E., 75, 192, 450

Kako, T., 450
Kamien, M. I., 408
Kawagoe, T., 381, 383
Kennedy, C., 362
Khan, D. A., 167
Kimhi, A., 278
Kislev, Y., 273, 377, 378, 450
Klein, L. R., 325, 342
Kmenta, J., 449
Koopmans, T. C., 207
Koyck, L., 294, 304
Krueger, A., 57
Krugman, P., 440

Lachaal, L., 415, 430, 435, 438
Lansink, A. O., 407
LaRamée, P., 276
Larson, D., 11, 86, 270, 273, 278, 284, 289, 312, 376, 377, 441
Lau, L. J., 323, 365
Lee, H., 411, 450
Levine, R., 439
Lewis, A. W., 280, 281
Lin, J. Y., 372
Longmire, J., 75
Lopez, R. E., 450
Love, A., 75
Lucas, R. E., 115, 213, 215, 223, 263, 294, 311, 451
Luh, Y. H., 407

MacAulay, T. G., 406
MaCurdy, T. E., 340
Maddala, G. S., 389
Mairesse, J., 368
Manuelli, R. E., 213, 222
Marshack, J., 321, 331, 337, 340
Martin, W., 388
McCarthy, F. D., 443
McElroy, M. A., 347, 449

McFadden, D., 323, 341, 448
McGuirk, A., 170, 376, 381, 413, 415
McKenzie, L. W., 447
McLaren, K. R., 407
McMahon, P., 258
McMillan, J., 372
McMillan, John, 273, 274, 372
Mellor, J. W., 238
Melvin, J. R., 445
Michael, J. M., 569
Minhas, B. S., 322
Mitra, D., 388
Mondino, G., 439
Monson, M. J., 407
Morey, A., 75
Morris, C. T., 372
Mosenson, R., 50, 220, 442
Mujahid, E., 445
Mundlak, Y., 11, 46, 47, 48, 50, 57, 67, 75, 86, 114, 162, 170, 220, 246, 262, 270, 273, 274, 275, 278, 284, 289, 305, 306, 307, 312, 313, 314, 319, 320, 325, 333, 335, 340, 341, 346, 347, 355, 364, 371, 372, 374, 376, 377, 378, 381, 383, 394, 403, 405, 407, 413, 415, 424, 435, 436, 438, 441, 442, 445, 447, 448, 449, 450
Murphy, K. M., 440

Nadiri, M. I., 448
Nash, E., 450
Nehring, R., 387
Nerlove, M., 405
Nguyen, D., 378

Obstfeld, M., 110
Ohlin, B., 95
Onchan, T., 279

Pandey, S. R., 406
Papanek, G. F., 445
Parsons, H. L., 393
Patamasiriwat, D., 162
Peterson, W., 450
Pfann, G. A., 301
Piggott, R., 406
Pope, R. D., 450
Prais, S. J., 48
Prescott, E. C., 311
Pritchett, L., 385

Quance, C. L., 301, 406, 407
Quiggon, J., 258

Ramsey, F. P., 207
Ranis, G., 266, 280
Rausser, G. C., 75, 372
Ravenstein, E. G., 264
Razin, A., 104, 109, 443
Reder, M. W., 361
Renelt, D., 439
Robinson, C., 258
Robson, N., 258
Rogoff, K., 110
Romer, P. M., 213, 440
Rosegrant, M. W., 387
Rosen, S., 448
Rosenzweig, M. R., 248, 258, 447
Ruttan, V., 361, 362, 378, 381, 441
Rybczynski, T. M., 94

Saez, R. R., 450
Sal-i-Martin, X., 210
Samuelson, P. A., 31, 50, 153, 362, 445
Sargent, T. J., 309, 311
Sato, K., 205
Scandizzo, P. I., 57
Schiff, M., 57, 413
Schmidt, P., 341
Schmitt, G., 447
Schuh, G. E., 75
Schulz, T. W., 75, 191, 231, 393
Schwartz, N. L., 408
Sen, A. K., 280
Setboonsarng, S., 162
Shleifer, A., 440
Shumway, C. R., 407, 450
Siamwalla, A., 162
Siegel, P. B., 273
Singh, I., 252
Slade, R., 191
Smidt, S., 50
Smith, V. E., 361
Snape, R. H., 75
Solow, R. M., 130, 190, 204, 322
Somwaru, A., 387
Squire, L., 252
Srinivasan, T. N., 447
Stamoulis, K. G., 75
Steeves, A. D., 276, 447

Stefanou, S. E., 407
Stiglitz, J., 440
Stolper, W. F., 50
Strauss, J., 48, 252, 275
Strotz, R. H., 294
Swan, T. W., 204

Taylor, T. G., 407
Tcha, M., 266
Thijssen, G., 407
Thomas, D., 48
Tintner, G., 320, 366
Tobin, J., 309
Todaro, P. M., 265
Tolley, G. S., 50
Treadway, A. B., 294
Tropp, Z., 447
Tweeten, L. G., 312, 406, 407
Tyers, R., 57

Uzawa, H., 50, 215, 218

Valdès, A., 57, 413
Vasavada, U., 407
Vishny, R. W., 440
Vo, T. T., 387, 450
Volcani, Z., 333, 346

Weiss, C. R., 278, 448
Wen, J. G., 372
Whally, J., 372
Williams, J. C., 442
Witzke, H. P., 312
Womack, A. W., 415, 430, 435, 438
Working, E. J., 321
Wright, B. D., 442

Yamada, S., 378
Yang, M. C., 372, 413
Young, A., 451

Zellner, A., 449
Zhu, L., 372
Zilberman, D., 192

Subject Index

Agriculture: attributes, 18–20; contribution to growth, 16–18, 143; development of, 16–18; farmers and, 12–16, 20; global experience of, 1–16; growth experience of, 1-5; labor and, 8–11; political power of, 20; trade in, 6

Capital: demand, 292–294; Euler equation, 315-316; evidence on, 284–292; firm demand and, 294–298; intersectoral allocation and, 412–413; technology and, 298–299. *See also* Investment
Capital accumulation, 201–202; golden rule and, 207, 208, 226
Capital constraint and land, 123–125, 160–161, 168–169
Comparative advantage, 95–96
Competitive conditions, 26, 27; free entry, exit, 31; zero profits, 31
Competitive position, 127–128
Constant returns to scale, 31
Cost function, 31

Demand, 35–36; agricultural, 19; compensated, 54; duality, 53–54; elasticity, 62, 101; and Engel's law, 47, 101; evidence on, 47–48; excess, 39; expenditure function, 54; income elasticity, 135–136; restricted, 38–40, 67, 79–80; Slutsky equation, 54
Duality, 52–55

Economic Law of Gravity, 239, 247
Envelope theorem, 31
Equilibrium, 36–41; in closed economy, 36, 38; convergence, 39; distortion: factor-market, 235–237; duality, 54–55; with endogenous investment, 244–245; endowment, 98–101; endowment and aid, 113; endowment and tax, 112–113; factor price responsive, 110–113; heterogeneity, 263; in open economy, 37; stability, 237–238; and technical change-biased, 150; and technical change-neutral, 137, 140
Euler equation, 208
Exchange rate: nominal, 76, 89–91; real, 75–83, 89–91, 153–154
Exit and entry, 276–278

Factor intensity, 28, 31, 357; agriculture and, 48–50; distortion, 232; equal intensities, 40–41
Factor-cost intensity, 31, 232, 246
Factor market distortion, 227–238, 247
Factor market dynamics, 238–244
Factor price equalization, 32
Factor shares, 31
Factor supply, 104–112
Firm size, 26
Food, 46–47
Food aid, 71–75, 113; closed economy, 71–72; open economy, 73–74; mixed economy, 74
Full employment condition, 27

Government expenditures, 77–81
Green revolution, 167–177
Growth: agriculture-based, 141; AK model, 209–210; Argentine experience, 424–426; Argentine model, 426–440; balanced, 211–213, 224; Domar-Harrod, 203–204; and economic environment, 420–440; and externalities, 213–217; and heterogeneous technology, 210, 226; learning by doing,

Growth *(continued)*
213–215; nonagriculture-based, 141; overview of, 201–203, 419–420, 436–440; policies, 420–423, 436–440; sectoral, 156–157; Solow, 204–206; sources, 354–355; stable, 222; steady-state, 204, 211; in two-sector economy, 218–222

Hamilton-Jacobi-Bellman equation, 408
Heckshler-Ohlin theorem, 95–97
Hicks composite good, 53
Hotelling's lemma, 53
Human capital, 190–191, 215–217, 222–225

Income differentials, 278–279
Income distribution, 42–43, 152, 194–195
Investment: adjustment cost, 294–295, 299–300; empirical results regarding, 312–314, 431–432; Euler equation, 307–309, 315–316; evidence on, 284–292; endogenous dynamics of, 307–311; exogenous dynamics of, 304–307; industry demand for, 300–302; intersectoral allocation, 303, 313–314; specification, 304; uncertainty, 311. *See also* Capital

Labor: intersectoral allocation, 412
Labor supply, 248–257, 259, 280–283, 431; farm operators, 251–255; landless labor, 248–251; no labor market, 255–257; and technical change, 256–257
Land, 43–46; evidence on, 7-8, 161–165; margins, 119–121, 124–127; output quota, 125–127; prices, 13–14; price responsive supply, 114–128; quality, 114–117; resource constraint, 123–125; tax, 117–121, 124–125, 127; and technical change, 157–165
Learning by doing, 192, 213–215
Long run, 93

Management, 259–263
Migration: evidence on, 269–276; function, 267–269; off-farm, 263–266

Occupational choice, 282–283; farm operators, 251–255; landless labor, 250–251
Openness, 85–86

Part-time farming, 257–259
Policies: macro, 77–83; reform, 67, 436–440; sector-neutral, 75–85; trade, 81–82. *See also* Subsidies; Tax(es)
Price equation (function), 31, 32, 97, 230–232
Price(s): admissible, 32, 96–97; agricultural, 3, 154–156; competitive conditions, 29; demand, 36, 61; endowment, 100–101; factor, 27, 62, 86, 105, 180; factor price equalization, 31–32, 88; law of one, 86–88; price block, 427–430; product, 29; sectoral, 83–85; solution, 28–29; supply, 61, 150, 230–232; technique coexistence, 184; transmission elasticity, 87
Production block, 432–436
Production functions: allocation efficiency, 343–346, 351–352; composite function, 179–183, 210, 357; concavity (convexity), 209, 216, 221, 222, 357, 365; cost functions, 325–327; cross-country, 376–385; duality, 323–329, 358–359; efficiency frontier, 359–360; empirical studies, 319–330, 366–367; errors in the variables, 347; functional stability, 367–369; heterogeneous technology, 329–330; identification, 335–337, 363; Inada conditions, 204; knowledge, 362; meta functions, 361–362; primal estimates, 321–323; production structure, 177–183, 354–359; profit functions, 327, 450–453, 501; repetitious property, 353; returns to scale, 381, 397–398, 450; simultaneity, 331–335; specification, 363–366; translog, 365–366. *See also* Production functions, estimators
Production functions, estimators, 335–343; dual, 336–337, 348–349; factor shares, 342–343; general, 339–341; OLS, 337–338, 341–342; panel, 339, 388–389; precision, 350–351
Production path, 359
Productivity: agricultural experience, 9–12; Solow residual, 373; total factor, 195–196, 386–388
Profit: function, 327, 352, 359; unit, 52; zero, 31
Punjab agriculture, 170–177

Rent, 45–46, 62–63, 117, 122–123, 260

Resource allocation, 29, 30, 50–51; admissible, 50–51; allocation effect, 148; dynamics, 238–244; endowment, 102–104; and technique coexistence, 185; threshold values, 180, 182; under distortion, 229
Revenue function, 52–53
Rybczynski proposition, 94, 100, 106, 148, 180, 187

Savings, 201–203, 207–209, 213, 222–223
Sectoral inputs. *See* Capital; Labor; Resource allocation
Shephard's lemma, 31
Stolper-Samuelson proposition, 69
Subsidies, 58–64; food-closed economy, 58–63; food-open economy, 63–64; welfare gain (loss), 61–64, 88, 233–235
Supply, product: aggregation, 401–402; comparative statics, 395–396; distributed lags of, 405–407, 417–418; duality and, 52–53, 407–412; dynamics-endogenous, 407–411; dynamics-exogenous, 404–407; elasticity, 62, 397–399, 416–417; factor demand, 402–404, 417; factor-market distortion, 232; factor supply, 94, 101, 107–112, 399–401, 416–417; function, 44; graphical presentation, 32–33; overview, 393–395; price, 44, 230–232; response, 30, 414–416; small open economy, 33–34; specialization, 33; structure, 26–34; and technique coexistence, 186; uncertainty, 414

Tariff, 64–67; openness, 66; welfare gain (loss), 61, 65–66, 88
Tax(es): factors of production, 68–71; factor-product equivalence, 69; indirect, 65; land, 117. *See also* Subsidies
Technical change, 130–165, 179; and allocation effect, 147–149, 151; capital-augmenting, 158–160; cost effect, 138, 149, 151; embodied, 190; empirical implications of, 154–157; factor-augmenting, 132, 143–151, 211–213; factor-saving (-using), 147; general, 130–133; global effect, 141–143; growth, 210–217; Harrod-neutral, 132, 152, 212; Hicks-neutral, 132–143, 190, 194–195, 256–257; induced innovations, 362; labor-augmenting, 212; land-augmenting, 158, 160–161; land-expanding, 193; land-substituting, 193; productivity effect, 134, 151; Solow neutral, 132, 153
Technique choice, 166–197; aggregation, 362–366; and capital accumulation, 187–188; and capital heterogeneity, 189–190; and coexistence of techniques, 168; constraints, 356–358, 369–370; and the economy, 183–187; empirical specification, 363–366; evidence on, 366–367, 376–385; environment-institutional, 372; environment-physical, 371–372; factor prices, 187, 360; and human capital, 190–191; incentives, 370–371; information, 191–192; investment-gross, 189–190; investment-net, 190; and land expansion, 192–193; and learning by doing, 192; and resource allocation, 184–186; and state variables, 369–375; and state variables' impact, 375–376
Technology: available, 178, 218, 354, 356; endogenous, 167–197, 213–217; heterogeneous, 177–197; implemented, 179, 182–183, 188–192, 218, 354, 356–358; representation, 372–375, 384–385
Terms of trade: external, 83; internal, 82–83
Tradability, 83–85
Trade: account, 77; and endowment, 99–100; liberalization, 67; restrictions, 67; and technical change, 135–136, 139–140
Transformation curve, 30; concavity, 51; under distortion, 229–230

Wage differentials, 278–279
Wage-rental ratio: admissible, 28; competitive condition, 27; distortion, 229, 234, 237–238